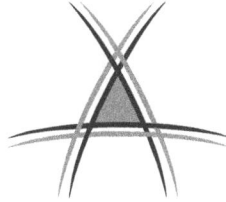

ASCENT®
CENTER FOR TECHNICAL KNOWLEDGE

Autodesk® Inventor® 2021
Advanced Assembly Modeling

Learning Guide
Mixed Units - 1ˢᵗ Edition

AUTODESK.
Authorized Publisher

ASCENT - Center for Technical Knowledge®
Autodesk® Inventor® 2021
Advanced Assembly Modeling
Mixed Units - 1st Edition

Prepared and produced by:

ASCENT Center for Technical Knowledge
630 Peter Jefferson Parkway, Suite 175
Charlottesville, VA 22911

866-527-2368
www.ASCENTed.com

Lead Contributor: Jennifer MacMillan

ASCENT - Center for Technical Knowledge (a division of Rand Worldwide Inc.) is a leading developer of professional learning materials and knowledge products for engineering software applications. ASCENT specializes in designing targeted content that facilitates application-based learning with hands-on software experience. For over 25 years, ASCENT has helped users become more productive through tailored custom learning solutions.

We welcome any comments you may have regarding this guide, or any of our products. To contact us please email: feedback@ASCENTed.com.

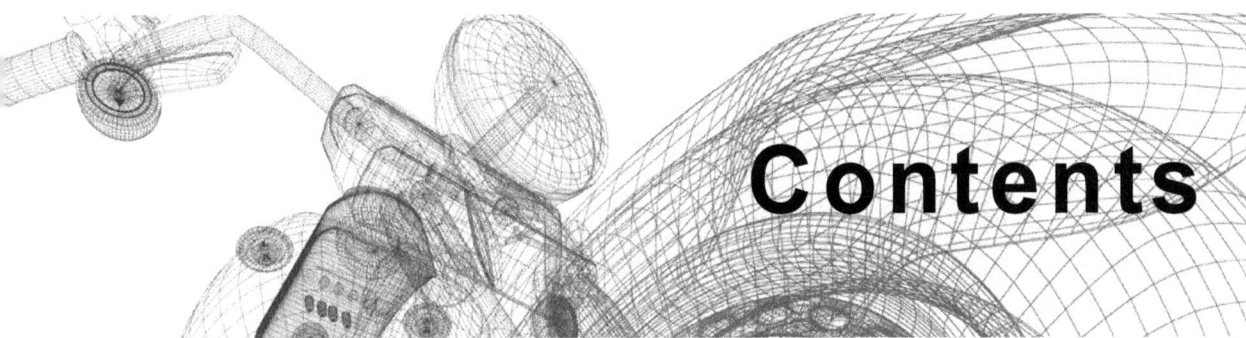

Contents

© 2020, ASCENT - Center for Technical Knowledge®

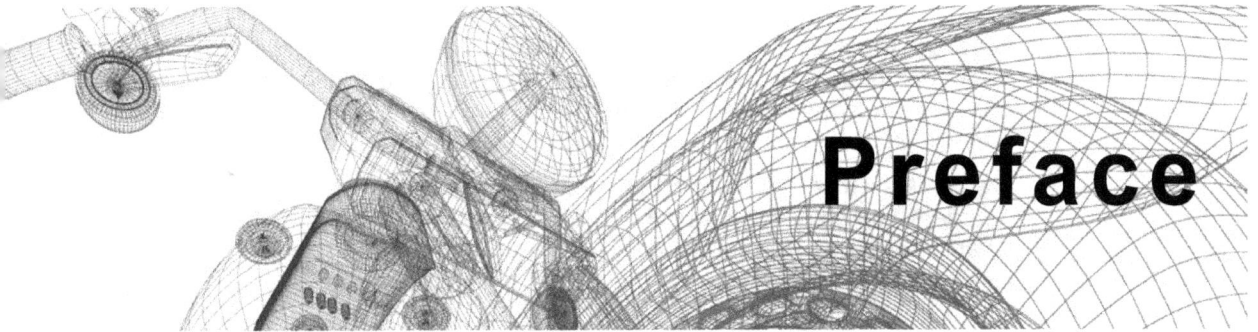

Preface

The *Autodesk® Inventor® 2021: Advanced Assembly Modeling* guide builds on the skills acquired in the *Autodesk Inventor 2021: Introduction to Solid Modeling* and *Autodesk Inventor 2021: Advanced Part Modeling* guides to take you to a higher level of productivity when creating and working with assemblies.

You begin by focusing on the Top-Down Design workflow. You learn how tools are used to achieve this workflow using Derive, Multi-Body Design, and Layouts. Other topics include model simplification tools, Positional and Level of Detail Representations, iMates and iAssemblies, Frame Generator, Design Accelerator, and file management and duplication techniques. A chapter has also been included about the Autodesk® Inventor® Studio to teach you how to render, produce, and animate realistic images.

Topics Covered

- Applying motion to existing assembly constraints using Motion and Transitional Constraints.

- Introduction of the Top-Down Design technique for creating assemblies and its components.

- Tools for Top-Down Design, such as associative links, adaptive parts, multi-body and layout design, derived components, and skeleton models.

- Creating Positional Representations to review motion, evaluate the position of assembly components, or document an assembly in a drawing.

- Using Shrinkwrap and other model simplification tools to create a part model that represents an overall assembly.

- Creating Level of Detail Representations to reduce the clutter of large assemblies, reduce retrieval times, and substituting models.

- Using the Design Accelerator to easily insert standard and customizable components and features into your model.

- Creating rendered realistic images and animations of parts and assemblies using Autodesk Inventor Studio and the Video Producer.

Prerequisites

- Access to the 2021.0 version of the software, to ensure compatibility with this guide. Future software updates that are released by Autodesk may include changes that are not reflected in this guide. The practices and files included with this guide are not compatible with prior versions (e.g., 2020).

- The class assumes mastery of Autodesk Inventor basics as taught in *Autodesk® Inventor®: Introduction to Solid Modeling*. In addition, *Autodesk® Inventor®: Advanced Part Modeling* knowledge is recommended.

- The use of Microsoft® Excel is required for this training course.

Note on Software Setup

This guide was written for the 2021.0 release of the Autodesk Inventor software. Future software updates that may be released by Autodesk may incorporate changes to workflows that will not be reflected in this guide. This guide assumes a standard installation of the software using the default preferences during installation. Lectures and practices use the standard software templates and default options for the Content Libraries.

Students and Educators Can Access Free Autodesk Software and Resources

Autodesk challenges you to get started with free educational licenses for professional software and creativity apps used by millions of architects, engineers, designers, and hobbyists today. Bring Autodesk software into your classroom, studio, or workshop to learn, teach, and explore real-world design challenges the way professionals do.

Get started today - register at the Autodesk Education Community and download one of the many Autodesk software applications available.

Visit www.autodesk.com/education/home/

Note: Free products are subject to the terms and conditions of the end-user license and services agreement that accompanies the software. The software is for personal use for education purposes and is not intended for classroom or lab use.

Lead Contributor: Jennifer MacMillan

With a dedication for engineering and education, Jennifer has spent over 20 years at ASCENT managing courseware development for various CAD products. Trained in Instructional Design, Jennifer uses her skills to develop instructor-led and web-based training products as well as knowledge profiling tools.

Jennifer has achieved the Autodesk Certified Professional certification for Inventor and is also recognized as an Autodesk Certified Instructor (ACI). She enjoys teaching the training courses that she authors and is also very skilled in providing technical support to end-users.

Jennifer holds a Bachelor of Engineering Degree as well as a Bachelor of Science in Mathematics from Dalhousie University, Nova Scotia, Canada.

Jennifer MacMillan has been the Lead Contributor for *Autodesk Inventor Advanced Assembly Modeling* since 2007.

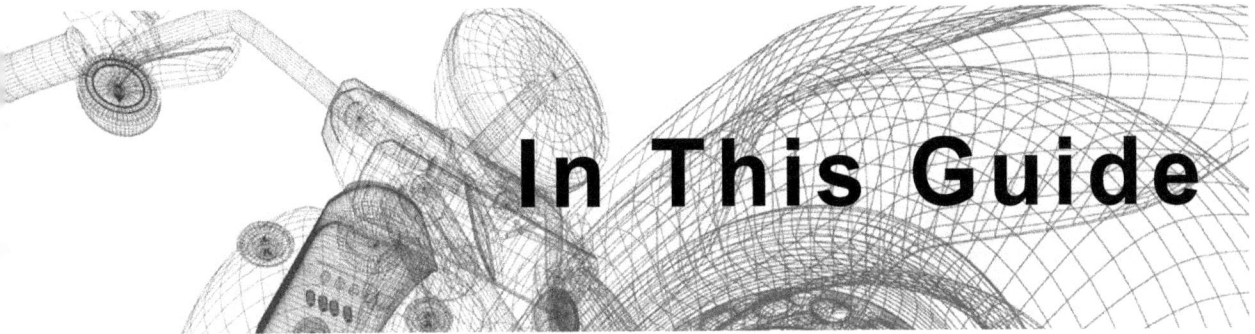

In This Guide

The following highlights the key features of this guide.

Feature	Description
Practice Files	The Practice Files page includes a link to the practice files and instructions on how to download and install them. The practice files are required to complete the practices in this guide.
Chapters	A chapter consists of the following - Learning Objectives, Instructional Content, Practices, Chapter Review Questions, and Command Summary. • **Learning Objectives** define the skills you can acquire by learning the content provided in the chapter. • **Instructional Content**, which begins right after Learning Objectives, refers to the descriptive and procedural information related to various topics. Each main topic introduces a product feature, discusses various aspects of that feature, and provides step-by-step procedures on how to use that feature. Where relevant, examples, figures, helpful hints, and notes are provided. • **Practice** for a topic follows the instructional content. Practices enable you to use the software to perform a hands-on review of a topic. It is required that you download the practice files (using the link found on the Practice Files page) prior to starting the first practice. • **Chapter Review Questions**, located close to the end of a chapter, enable you to test your knowledge of the key concepts discussed in the chapter. • **Command Summary** concludes a chapter. It contains a list of the software commands that are used throughout the chapter and provides information on where the command can be found in the software.
Appendices	Appendices provide additional information to the main course content. It could be in the form of instructional content, practices, tables, projects, or skills assessment.

Practice Files

To download the practice files for this guide, use the following steps:

1. Type the URL **exactly as shown below** into the address bar of your Internet browser, to access the Course File Download page.

    Note: If you are using the ebook, you do not have to type the URL. Instead, you can access the page simply by clicking the URL below.

    ## https://www.ascented.com/getfile/id/anthocharis

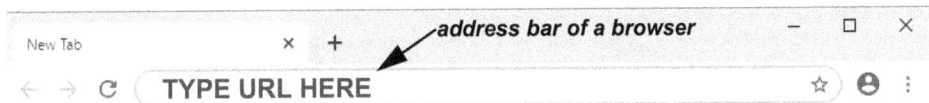

2. On the Course File Download page, click the **DOWNLOAD NOW** button, as shown below, to download the .ZIP file that contains the practice files.

3. Once the download is complete, unzip the file and extract its contents.

    The recommended practice files folder location is:
    C:\Autodesk Inventor 2021 Advanced Assembly Modeling Practice Files

    Note: It is recommended that you do not change the location of the practice files folder. Doing so may cause errors when completing the practices.

    Stay Informed!
    To receive information about upcoming events, promotional offers, and complimentary webcasts, visit:
    www.ASCENTed.com/updates

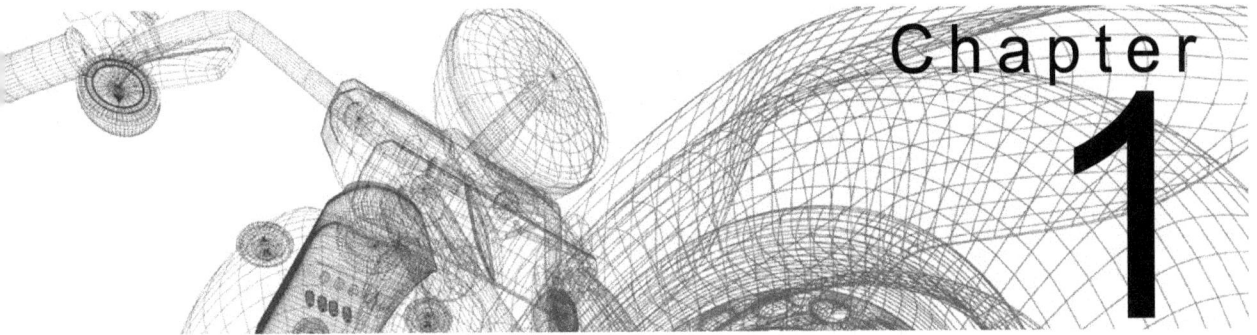

Advanced Assembly Tools

The use of Motion and Transitional constraints provides added flexibility in constraining components and allowing motion between them. This chapter discusses the motion constraint, as well as a number of additional miscellaneous assembly tools available in the Autodesk® Inventor® software. Knowing how to access and use these tools will help you be more productive when working in an assembly.

Learning Objectives in This Chapter

- Add a constraint that permits movement of one surface relative to another.
- Add a constraint that permits movement of one surface relative to a continuous set of surfaces.
- Use various methods to assemble multiple components in an assembly.
- Clarify and organize an assembly by sorting and changing the display names and folder structure in the Model Browser.
- Replace a selected component in an assembly with a copy of itself.
- Access additional constraint options, including assigning specific constraint names and limits.
- Identify assembly components that have degrees of freedom.
- Constrain components in reference to a user coordinate system (UCS), another component's origin, or the assembly's origin.

1.1 Motion Constraints

In addition to the five assembly constraints (mate, angle, tangent, insert, and symmetry), a motion constraint can also be used to describe the movement of one surface relative to another. You cannot apply a Drive to a motion constraint.

How To: Create a Motion Constraint

1. Create and place components into an assembly.

2. In the *Assemble* tab>Position panel, click ⬚ (Constrain) to create a constraint relationship. Select the *Motion* tab in the Place Constraint dialog box, as shown in Figure 1–1.

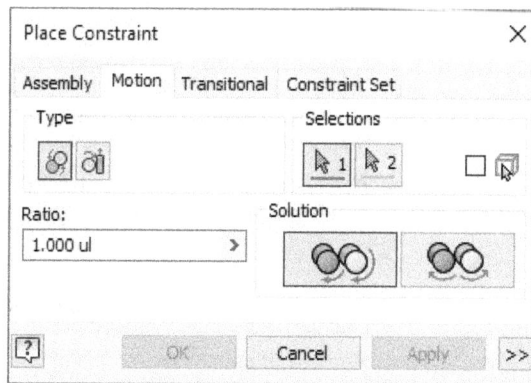

Figure 1–1

3. Select the motion type and references. References can be applied between linear, planar, cylindrical, and conical elements on two components. You can create two types of motion constraints:

   • Use ⚙ (Rotation) to constrain one component relative to another, so that one component rotates when the other rotates (e.g., pulleys or gears), as shown in Figure 1–2. To assign the constraint, select the component surfaces.

Two rotating components

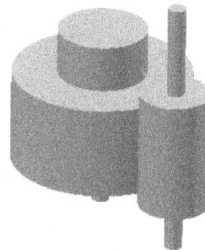

Figure 1–2

▷ *(Pick part first) limits the geometry that is available for selection to a single component. It is useful when components are in close proximity or partially obscured by one another.*

- Use ◌ (Rotation-Translation) to move (translate) one component when the other one rotates (e.g., a rack and pinion), as shown in Figure 1–3. To assign the constraint, select a surface on the rotating component and an edge on the moving component.

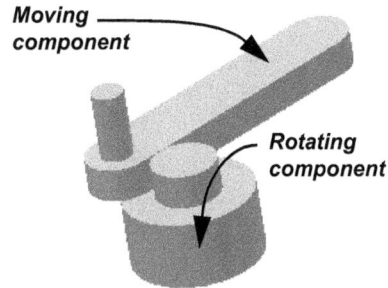

Figure 1–3

4. Select the motion type solution.

- For a rotation motion constraint, the two solutions shown in Figure 1–4 enable you to define the direction the components rotate relative to one another (forward or reverse).

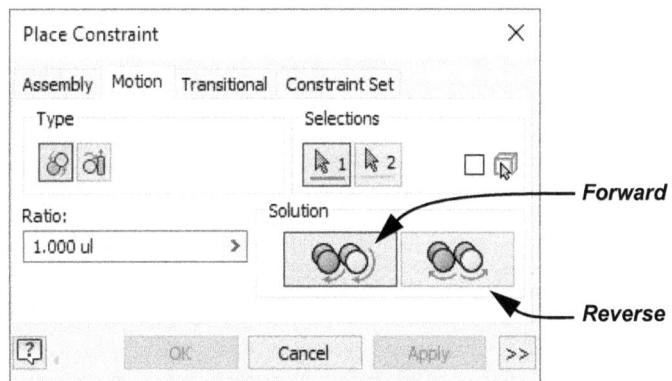

Figure 1–4

- For a rotation-translation motion constraint, the solutions shown in Figure 1–5 enable you to define the direction the components rotate and move relative to one another (forward or reverse).

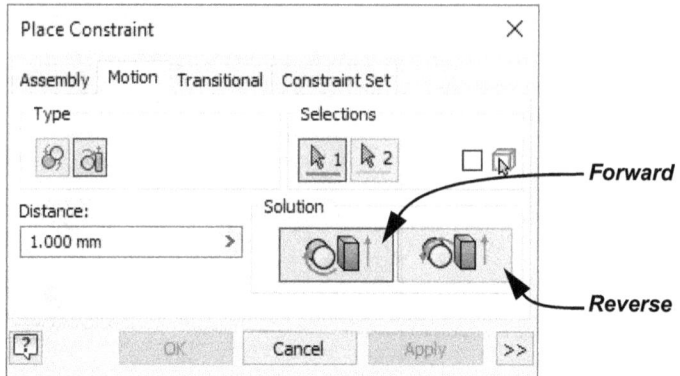

Figure 1–5

5. Enter the *Ratio* and *Distance* values.

- For rotation constraints, enter a ratio in the *Ratio* field to determine how many revolutions the second component makes per revolution of the first. By default, the ratio relative to the circumferences is automatically calculated and therefore the order of selection is important.

- For rotation-translation constraints, enter a distance in the *Distance* field. The distance determines how far the second component moves per revolution of the first. If the first component selected is a cylindrical surface, the software sets the distance to the circumference of the cylinder.

6. Click **Apply** to complete constraint placement and continue adding constraints. Once the component is fully constrained, click **OK** to close the Place Constraint dialog box.

1.2 Transitional Constraints

In addition to the five assembly constraints (mate, angle, tangent, insert, and symmetry), a transitional constraint can also be used to describe the movement of one surface relative to a continuous set of surfaces, such as a cam in a slot of an assembly, as shown in Figure 1–6. You cannot use the drive constraint tool for transitional constraints.

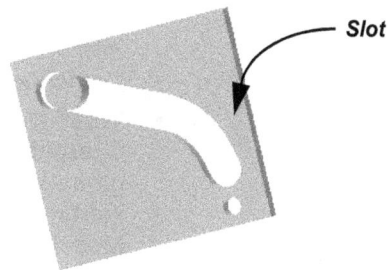

Slot

Figure 1–6

How To: Create a Transitional Constraint

1. Create and place components into an assembly.

2. In the *Assemble* tab>Position panel, click ⬜ (Constrain) to create a constraint relationship. Select the *Transitional* tab in the Place Constraint dialog box, as shown in Figure 1–7.

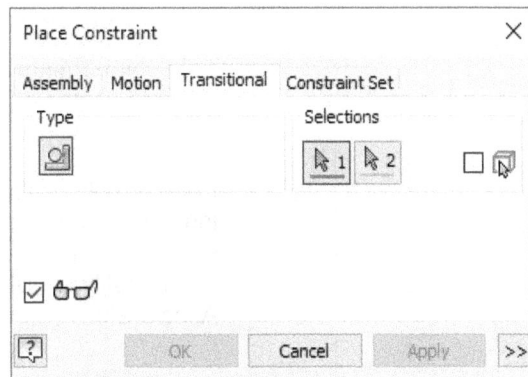

Figure 1–7

Use 🔲 (Pick part first) to limit the geometry that is available for selection to a single component.

3. Select the surfaces on both components that are in contact. To display a preview of the constraint, ensure that

   ☑ 👓 (Preview) is enabled.

4. Click **Apply** to complete constraint placement and continue adding constraints. Once the component is fully constrained, click **OK** to close the Place Constraint dialog box.

1.3 General Assembly Tips

Multiple Component Placement

Consider the following when assembling multiple components in an assembly:

- Multiple components can be placed in an assembly at the same time.

  - Hold <Ctrl> to select individual components or <Shift> to select a range of components.
  - Components are assembled and sorted alphabetically.
  - When placing, if you right-click and select **Place Grounded at Origin**, all of the components placed are grounded. Alternatively, once placed, you can ground an individual component by right-clicking its name in the Model Browser and selecting **Grounded**.

- To place multiple instances of a single component, place the first instance and then drag and drop additional instances from the Model Browser.

  - Any constraints assigned to the initial instance relationships are lost and must be reassigned.
  - To help maintain the orientation of the last assembled instance, you can select **Use last occurrence orientation for component placement** in the *Assembly* tab, in the Application Options dialog box.

- If using the AutoDrop functionality with the Content Center, multiple components can be retrieved into the assembly, provided the selected reference has other similar references on the same placement face.

  - For example, with AutoDrop you can place eight instances of the same fastener on eight holes on the same face, if they are all the same size. The AutoDrop functionality is discussed more in depth with the Design Accelerator.

Assembly Folders

Assembly folders help organize an assembly by grouping components and simplifying the Model Browser. Unlike subassemblies, folders do not create a component. Folders have no impact on relationships or degrees of freedom and do not become a rigid body.

To create a folder, use either of the following:

- Right-click on the component(s) you want to add to the folder and select **Add to New Folder**, as shown in Figure 1–8.

- Right-click on the model name at the top of the Model Browser and select **Create New Folder**. Once a folder is created, you can drag-and-drop components into or out of the folder.

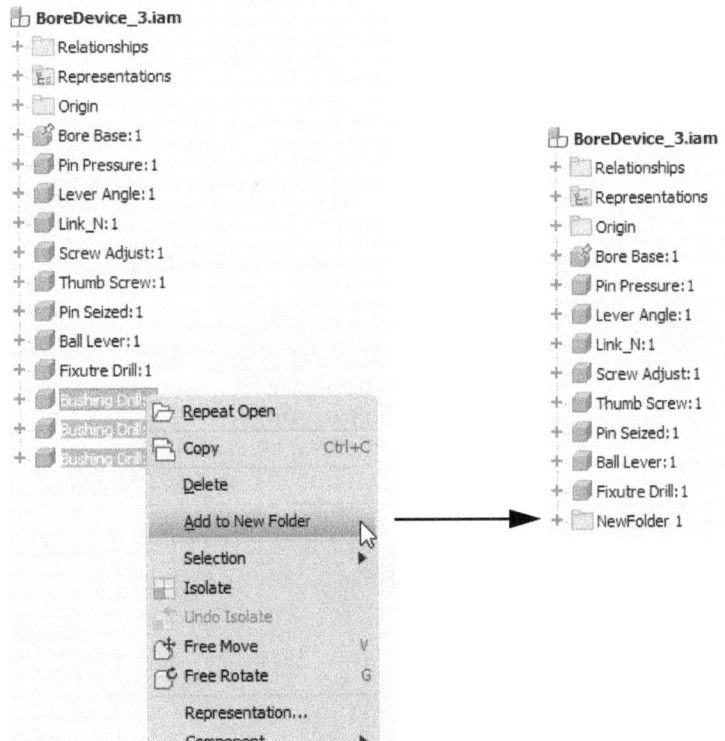

Figure 1–8

To rename the folder, select the folder in the Model Browser (do not double-click), then click on the folder again and enter a new name.

Save and Replace Components

The **Save and Replace** option enables you to replace a selected component in an assembly with a copy of itself. The newly created copy maintains all the same relationships as the original component. This tool can be used to test design scenarios in assemblies.

How To: Replace a Component with a Saved Copy

1. In the *Assemble* tab>expanded Productivity panel, click

    (Save and Replace).
2. Select the component to be replaced.
3. In the Create Part dialog box, enter a name for the newly copied component and click **Save**. The selected component is replaced with the copy.

Alpha Sort Component

The **Alpha Sort Component** option (*Assemble* tab>expanded Productivity panel> $\frac{A}{Z}\downarrow$ (Alpha Sort Component)) enables you to sort assembly components alphabetically in the Model Browser. This option does not sort items in subassemblies.

Rename Browser Nodes

The **Rename Browser Nodes** option (*Assemble* tab>expanded Productivity panel> (Rename Browser Nodes)) changes the way browser nodes display. Components can be displayed in the browser by filename, part number, or in the default configuration. This option enables you to quickly change the long names that often display from content center items, as well as switch from filenames to your company part numbering schemes. Using this option with $\frac{A}{Z}\downarrow$ (Alpha Sort Component), you can quickly sort Browser nodes as required.

1.4 Relationship Tips

Expanded Constraint Options

When assigning a constraint using the Place Constraint dialog box, you can click to access additional options. Consider the following:

- You can assign a custom name to the constraint to help identify it.

- Set limit values for a translational or rotational constraint, as shown in Figure 1–9. This assigns a maximum and minimum allowable range for the *Offset* or *Angle* values used when assigning a constraint. A constraint with limits has **+/-** appended to its name.

- The **Use Offset As Resting Position** option uses the specified *Offset* value as the resting position. If not set, you can drag and move the component within the range of values and the component rests where it is dropped.

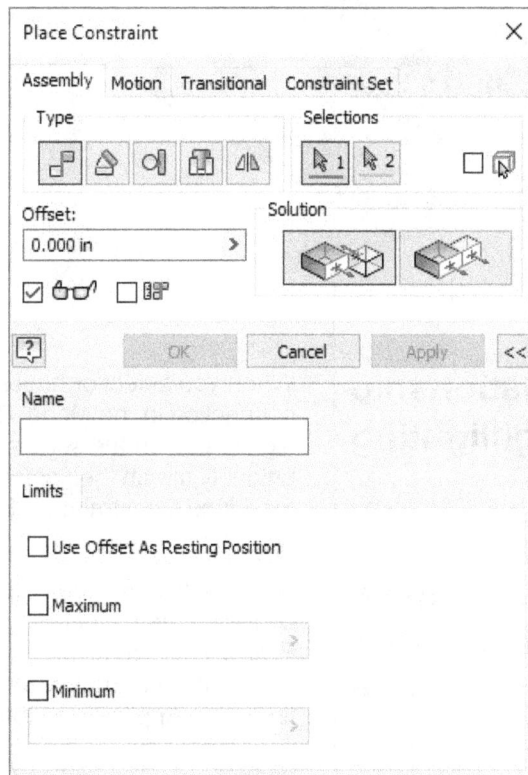

Figure 1–9

Degree of Freedom Analysis

In the *Assemble* tab>Productivity panel, click 🔧 (Degree of Freedom Analysis) to open the Degree of Freedom Analysis dialog box. This tool provides a summary of the degrees of freedom remaining in all assembly components.

- Information on the remaining translational and rotational degrees of freedom for each component is presented.

- Select a component in the dialog box to graphically view the remaining degrees of freedom, as shown in Figure 1–10.

- Select the **Animate Freedom** option to visually animate the degrees of freedom remaining on the selected component.

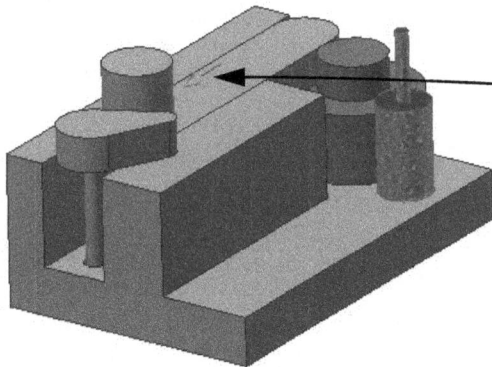

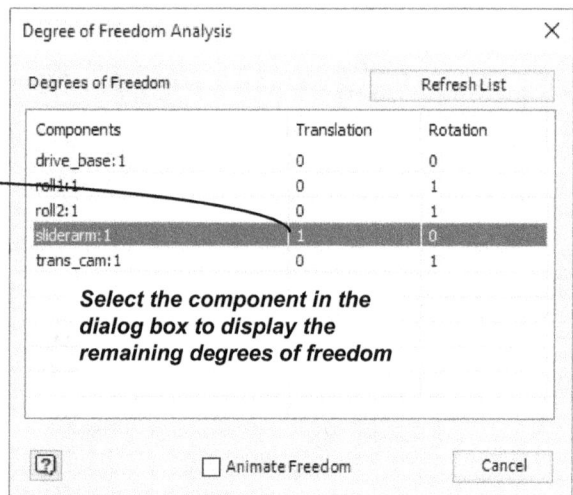

Figure 1–10

Relationship Highlighting

When you select or hover the cursor over a constraint or joint connection in the Model Browser, the assembly references are highlighted on the screen. The first and second references uniquely match their color indicator under the respective arrow in the Place Constraint and the Place Joint dialog boxes.

Show Relationship Name

You can display the names of components next to the applicable constraint and joint listings in the Model Browser, as shown in Figure 1–11. To display the component names, select **Display component names after relationship names** in the *Assembly* tab in the Application Options dialog box (*Tools* tab>Options panel> 📋 (Application Options)).

This command is especially useful when the Assembly browser is in Modeling View because you can see the component names listed in the **Relationships** *folder.*

BoreDevice_3.iam
+ Relationships
+ Representations
+ Origin
− Bore Base: 1
  + Origin
    Mate: 2 (Lever Angle: 1, Bore Base: 1)
    Mate: 3 (Lever Angle: 1, Bore Base: 1)
    Insert: 5 (Fixutre Drill: 1, Bore Base: 1)
    Insert: 6 (Bore Base: 1, Fixutre Drill: 1)
    Mate: 5 (Pin Pressure: 1, Bore Base: 1)
− Pin Pressure: 1
  + Origin
    Mate: 5 (Pin Pressure: 1, Bore Base: 1)
    Mate: 6 (Pin Pressure: 1, Link_N: 1)
    Mate: 7 (Thumb Screw: 1, Pin Pressure: 1)
    Mate: 8 (Pin Pressure: 1, Thumb Screw: 1)
  + Lever Angle: 1

Figure 1–11

Assembling Using a UCS and Constraint Sets

A user coordinate system (UCS) consists of three planes, three axes, and a center point. The only difference between a UCS and the Origin is that you can have multiple UCSs in a model, which can all be oriented differently. Once created, a UCS is listed in the Model Browser at the point it was created. It is identified by a special triad icon, as well as a sequential number associated with its feature name.

A UCS can be used as a reference in constraining components using the *Constraint Set* tab in the Place Constraint dialog box, as shown in Figure 1–12. UCS Constraint Sets match Plane to Plane, Axis to Axis, and Origin to Origin to locate two components relative to one another. To constrain the components, select the UCS in each component.

This tab only enables you to constrain one UCS to another UCS. UCS references cannot be used as references for Joint connections.

Figure 1–12

Place at Component Origin

The **Place at Component Origin** option enables you to quickly constrain a newly added component to an existing assembly component. The system automatically creates three mate flush constraints to align the YZ, XZ, and XY planes from each component.

How To: Place a Newly Added Component at an Existing Component's Origin

1. In the *Assemble* tab>Productivity panel, click 🔲 (Place at Component Origin).
2. In the graphic window or Model Browser, select the existing component to which the newly placed component is going be constrained.
3. In the Open dialog box, select a component or multiple components to be added to the assembly and click **Open**.

Ground and Root Component

If existing relationships are in conflict, the ⚠ icon displays and must be manually resolved.

The **Ground and Root Component** option (*Assemble* tab> expanded Productivity panel> 🔲) enables you to do all of the following in a single operation:

*   Ground a selected component (**Ground at Origin**).

*   Align the origin of a selected component with the origin of the assembly (**Create origin flush constraints**). Three flush constraints are added to mate flush the YZ, XZ, and XY planes in the selected component and the assembly.

*   Reposition a selected component as the first component in the Model Browser (**Reposition to the top of the browser**).

Assembly Restructure

You can promote and demote components in an assembly structure without losing their relationships. To promote or demote, right-click on a component and select **Component> Promote** or **Component>Demote**.

When demoting you are prompted to create a new subassembly. If a subassembly already exists, select and drag the component into the subassembly to demote it. Dragging and dropping can also be used to promote a component.

Practice 1a

Motion and Transitional Constraints

Practice Objectives

- Relate the motion of one component to another component by adding motion and transitional constraint relationships.
- Simulate motion in an assembly by driving a newly added angle constraint relationship.

In this practice, you will use motion and transitional constraints to relate the motion of one part to another part in an assembly. You will apply an Angle constraint to two assembly components and simulate motion in the assembly by driving the angle constraint. The assembly is shown in Figure 1–13.

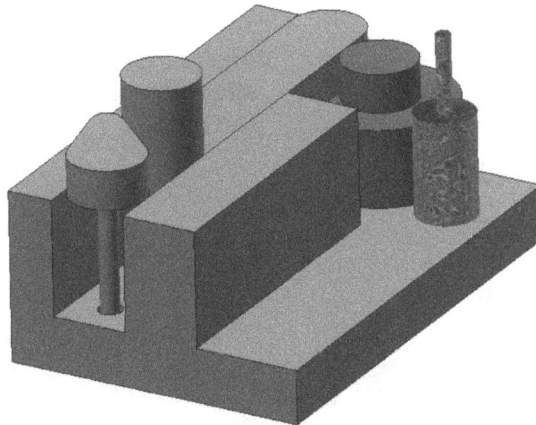

Figure 1–13

Task 1 - Open an assembly file.

1. In the *Get Started* tab>Launch panel, click (Projects) to open the Projects dialog box. Project files identify folders that contain the required Autodesk Inventor models.

This project file is used for the entire training material.

2. Click **Browse**, browse to the *Autodesk Inventor 2021 Advanced Assembly Modeling Practice Files* folder, and select **Advanced Assembly.ipj**. Click **Open**. The Projects dialog box updates and a checkmark displays next to the new project name, indicating that it is the active project. The project file tells the Autodesk Inventor software where your files are stored.

3. Click **Done**.

4. Open **drive.iam** from the top-level practice files folder. Textures have been added to the two **Roll** components so that you can easily see them when they are rotated.

5. Examine the existing relationships in the assembly and display the components' degrees of freedom. To display the degrees of freedom, switch to the *View* tab>Visibility panel and click ✏ (Degrees of Freedom). The base component is grounded. The **roll1** and **roll2** components are free to rotate about their central axes, and the **sliderarm** is free to slide in one direction only.

6. As an alternative to simply displaying the degrees of freedom for the components, you can run an analysis. In the *Assemble* tab>expanded Productivity panel, click ✏ (Degree of Freedom Analysis). The Degree of Freedom Analysis dialog box opens, as shown in Figure 1–14. The **sliderarm** can translate, and the **roll1** and **roll2** components can rotate.

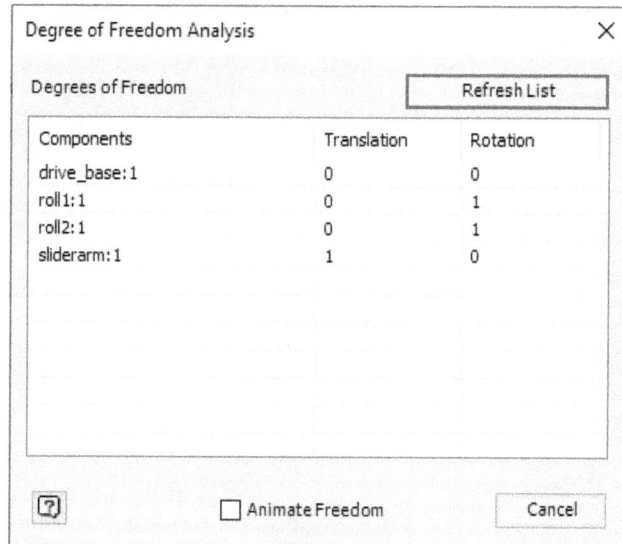

Degree of Freedom Analysis			✕
Degrees of Freedom		Refresh List	
Components	**Translation**	**Rotation**	
drive_base:1	0	0	
roll1:1	0	1	
roll2:1	0	1	
sliderarm:1	1	0	
⑦	☐ Animate Freedom	Cancel	

Figure 1–14

7. Select **Animate Freedom** at the bottom of the dialog box.

8. Select the **sliderarm** component in the dialog box and note the translational movement of the component.

9. Select the **roll1** and **roll2** components in the dialog box to see their rotational freedom. Using the **Degree of Freedom Analysis** command enables you to visualize more easily the available degrees of freedom in an assembly.

10. Click **Cancel** to close the dialog box.

Task 2 - Place and constrain trans_cam.ipt.

1. Place one instance of **trans_cam.ipt** in the assembly.

2. Apply a Mate constraint between the center line of the **trans_cam** rod and the center line of the round hole in **drive_base.ipt**, as shown in Figure 1–15.

The ⌾ (Axial Mate) symbol displays when a mate constraint is used to align the axes of cylindrical or conical features.

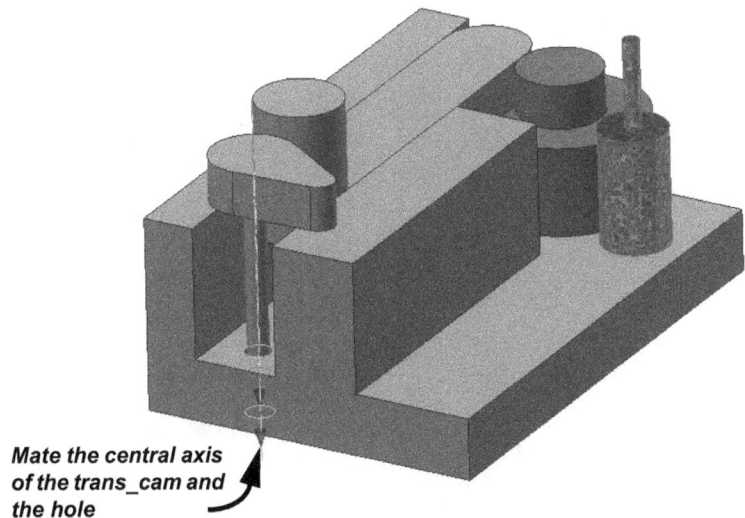

Mate the central axis of the trans_cam and the hole

Figure 1–15

3. Apply a Mate constraint between the surfaces shown in Figure 1–16. One rotational degree of freedom remains.

Mate these surfaces

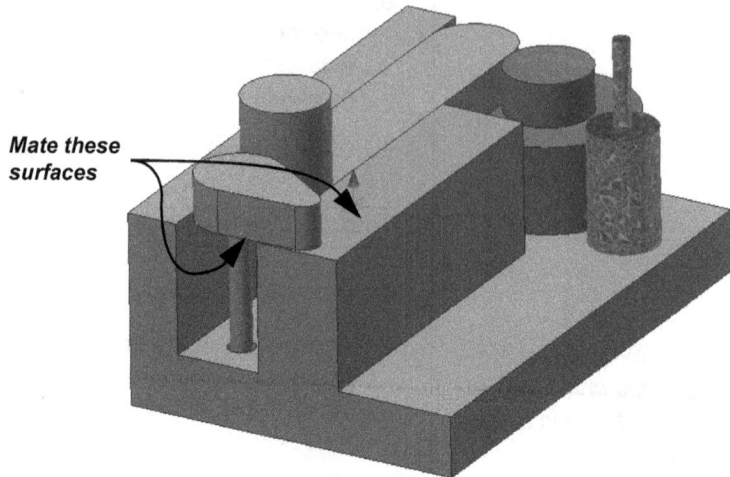

Figure 1–16

4. Open the Place Constraint dialog box, if not already open, and select the *Motion* tab.

5. Apply a 🔗 (Rotation) motion constraint between the outside cylindrical faces of **Roll1** and **Roll2**. Select **Roll1** first (the smaller cylinder) and **Roll 2** second (the larger cylinder). Based on the order that you selected, the default ratio is .40. The ratio determines how many revolutions the second component makes per revolution of the first.

6. Set the parts to rotate in the reverse direction, as shown in Figure 1–17, by clicking [∞]. Click **OK**.

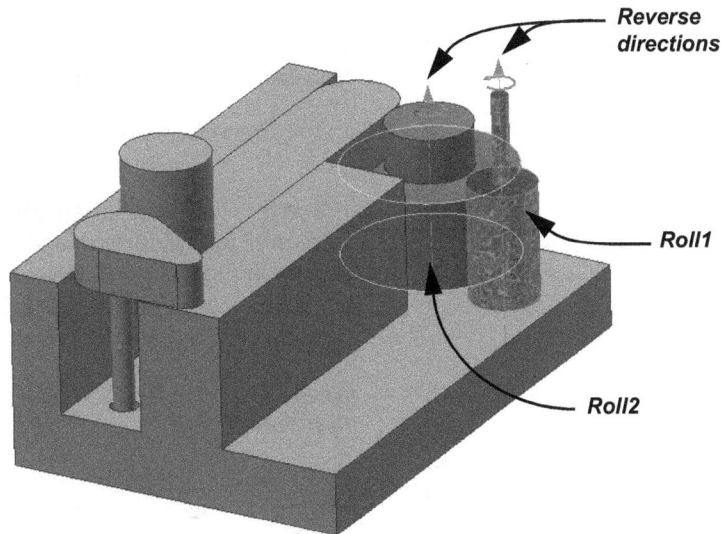

Figure 1–17

7. Select the **Roll1** component and drag it to simulate motion.

8. Apply a ⬛ (Rotation-Translation) motion constraint between **Roll2** and **Sliderarm**. Select **Roll2** first and the **Sliderarm** edge second, as shown in Figure 1–18. Set the motion to rotate in the Forward direction by clicking ⬛. Click **OK**.

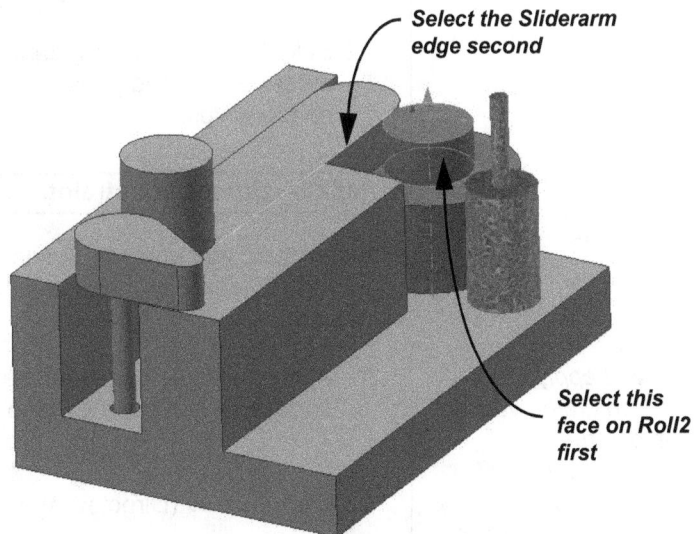

Figure 1–18

9. Select the **Roll2** component and drag it to simulate motion. When **Roll2** rotates, **Sliderarm** translates and **Roll1** rotates. You can also select and drag **Sliderarm** or **Roll1**.

10. In the Place Constraint dialog box, select the *Transitional* tab.

11. Place a ![icon] (Transitional) constraint between the cylindrical portion of the Slider arm and the round face of **trans_cam**, as shown in Figure 1–19. Select the cylinder first and a surface on **trans_cam** second. Click **OK**.

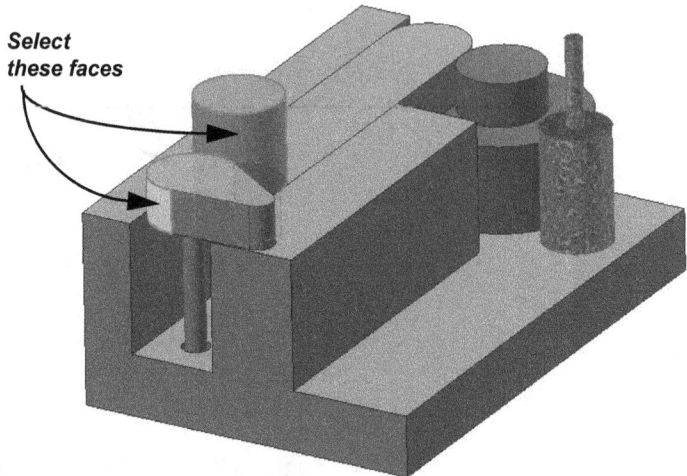

Select these faces

Figure 1–19

12. Select and drag **trans_cam** back and forth to rotate it. The other constrained parts should move according to their relationships.

Task 3 - Drive a constraint.

In this task, you apply an Angle constraint between **sliderarm** and **trans_cam**, and then use this relationship to simulate motion.

1. Apply an Angle constraint between the XZ Plane of **sliderarm** and the YZ Plane of **trans_cam**.

2. Click ![icon] (Directed Angle).

3. Type **0.00** as the angle between the two planes, and click **OK** to apply the constraint relationship.

When you apply the Angle constraint, you might lose the transitional constraint references. Edit it and re-apply the references in the Edit Constraint dialog box.

4. In the Model Browser, right-click on the Angle constraint relationship and select **Drive**. The Drive dialog box opens.

5. Type **-60.00** in the *Start* field and **60.00** in the *End* field.

6. Expand the Drive dialog box, select **Start/End/Start**, and type **10** in the *Repetitions* field.

7. Click ▶ to start the simulation.

8. Close the dialog box once the simulation has finished.

9. Save the file and close the window.

Practice 1b

Assembly Tools

Practice Objectives

- Investigate the remaining degrees of freedom of components in a constrained assembly.
- Vary the display and organization of the Model Browser by adding an Assembly folder, and renaming and sorting nodes in the Model Browser.

In this practice, you will use some assembly tools to perform a variety of tasks on the mechanical pencil assembly shown in Figure 1–20.

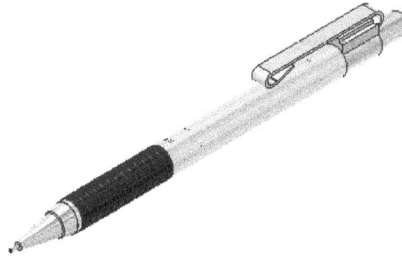

Figure 1–20

Task 1 - Open an assembly and view the model.

1. Open **Mechanical Pencil.iam** from the *Mechanical_Pencil_ Assembly Tools* folder.

2. Select the *View* tab.

3. In the Visibility panel, click ⊞ (Half Section View), as shown in Figure 1–21.

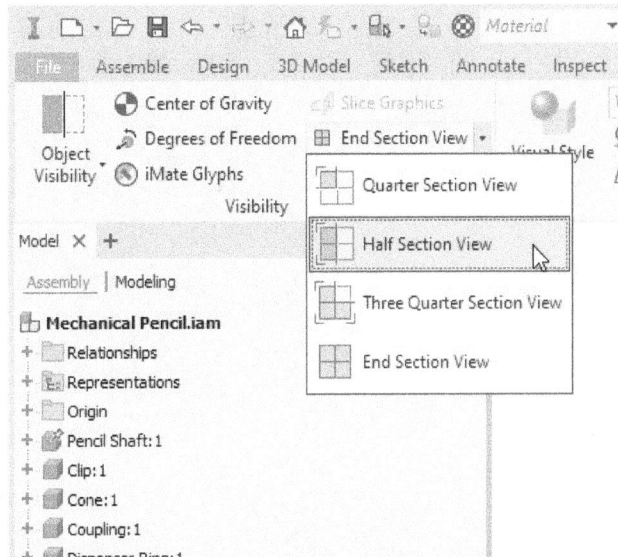

Figure 1–21

4. In the Model Browser, expand the **Origin** node, select the **YZ Plane**, and click ✓. The model displays as shown in Figure 1–22. Review the model, noting the internal detail.

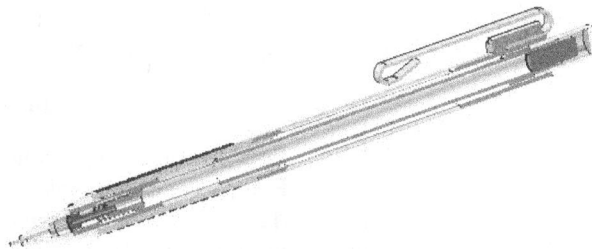

Figure 1–22

Task 2 - Investigate the degrees of freedom of the components.

In this task, you will investigate the degrees of freedom remaining in the assembly, using the Degree of Freedom Analysis dialog box. This productivity tool provides an overview of all remaining degrees of freedom for the entire assembly.

1. In the *Assemble* tab>expanded Productivity panel, click

   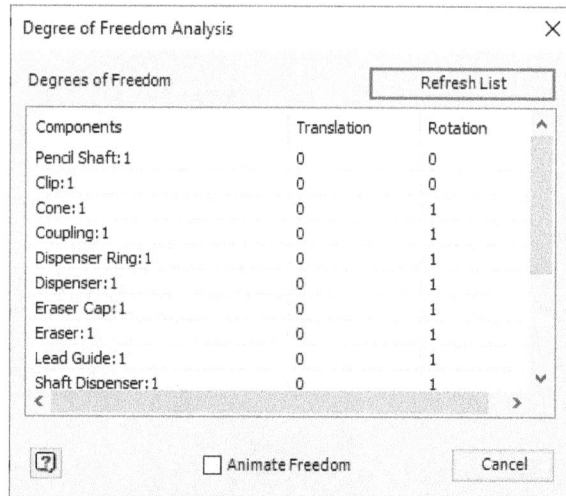 (Degree of Freedom Analysis). The Degree of Freedom Analysis dialog box opens, as shown in Figure 1–23.

Degree of Freedom Analysis		
Degrees of Freedom		Refresh List
Components	Translation	Rotation
Pencil Shaft: 1	0	0
Clip: 1	0	0
Cone: 1	0	1
Coupling: 1	0	1
Dispenser Ring: 1	0	1
Dispenser: 1	0	1
Eraser Cap: 1	0	1
Eraser: 1	0	1
Lead Guide: 1	0	1
Shaft Dispenser: 1	0	1

☐ Animate Freedom   Cancel

Figure 1–23

The Degree of Freedom Analysis dialog box lists all of the components in the assembly and their degrees of freedom. The components are fully constrained translationally, while some still have a rotational degree of freedom remaining.

2. In the Degree of Freedom Analysis dialog box, select the **Cone:1** component. The rotational degree of freedom highlights on the model.

3. Select **Animate Freedom**.

4. Zoom in on the tip section of the pencil, as shown in Figure 1–24, and select the **Spring:1** component in the dialog box. The degree of freedom remaining for the spring is animated on the screen.

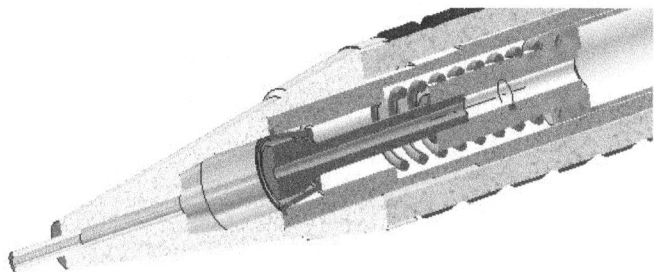

Figure 1–24

5. Select other components to observe their remaining degrees of freedom. Maintaining a rotational degree of freedom in the components is acceptable for this assembly.

6. Click **Cancel** to close the dialog box.

Task 3 - Create an assembly folder.

In this task, you will create an assembly folder. Assembly folders help organize the Model Browser and quickly manipulate features inside the folder.

1. In the Model Browser, right-click on **Mechanical Pencil.iam** and select **Create New Folder**.

2. Type **External** as the folder name and press <Enter>.

You can drag all of the components into the Assembly folder in a single operation by pressing <Ctrl> while selecting the components.

3. Drag the **Clip**, **Cone**, **Eraser Cap**, **Eraser**, **Lead Guide**, **Upper Shaft**, **Sleeve**, **Grip**, and **Ring** components into the *External* assembly folder, as shown in Figure 1–25.

The order of the components might be different for you

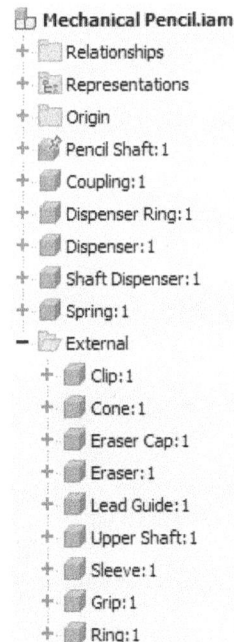

Mechanical Pencil.iam
+ Relationships
+ Representations
+ Origin
+ Pencil Shaft: 1
+ Coupling: 1
+ Dispenser Ring: 1
+ Dispenser: 1
+ Shaft Dispenser: 1
+ Spring: 1
− External
  + Clip: 1
  + Cone: 1
  + Eraser Cap: 1
  + Eraser: 1
  + Lead Guide: 1
  + Upper Shaft: 1
  + Sleeve: 1
  + Grip: 1
  + Ring: 1

Figure 1–25

4. In the Model Browser, right-click on the *External* folder and clear the **Visibility** option. The model displays as shown in Figure 1–26. All components were cleared at once.

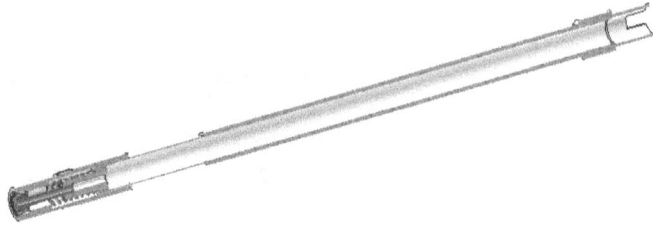

Figure 1–26

5. Toggle the **Visibility** of the *External* folder back on.

Task 4 - Reorganize the Model Browser.

In this task, you will use two productivity tools to reorganize the Model Browser: **Rename Browser Nodes** and **Alpha Sort Components**.

1. In the expanded Productivity panel, click [icon] (Rename Browser Nodes).

2. In the New Name drop-down list, select **Filename**, as shown in Figure 1–27, and click **Apply**. The Model Browser updates to display the full filename of each component.

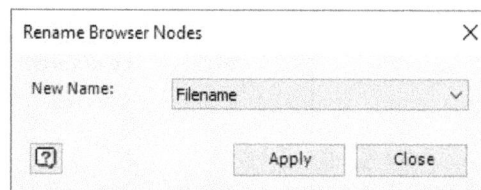

Figure 1–27

3. In the New Name drop-down list, select **Part Number** and click **Apply**. The Model Browser updates to display the part number for each component.

4. Click **Close**.

5. In the expanded Productivity panel, click [icon] (Alpha Sort Component). The Model Browser is reordered by part number.

6. Expand the *External* assembly folder. The components inside the folder were also sorted. A limitation of this command is that it will not sort subassemblies. For subassemblies, you must activate a subassembly first and then sort it.

7. Right-click on the *External* assembly folder and select **Delete Folder**. The folder is removed from the Model Browser and the components in it are placed back into the top level of the browser.

8. Run the **Alpha Sort Component** command again.

9. The grounded part is now buried in the Model Browser. To correct this, drag **PP-09** back to the top of the browser, as shown in Figure 1–28.

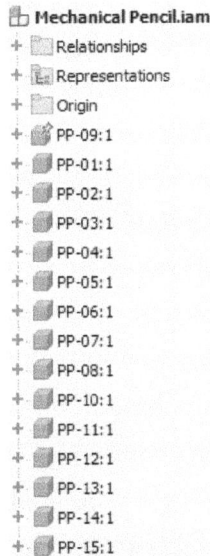

```
⊞ Mechanical Pencil.iam
  + ▢ Relationships
  + ▢ Representations
  + ▢ Origin
  + ▢ PP-09:1
  + ▢ PP-01:1
  + ▢ PP-02:1
  + ▢ PP-03:1
  + ▢ PP-04:1
  + ▢ PP-05:1
  + ▢ PP-06:1
  + ▢ PP-07:1
  + ▢ PP-08:1
  + ▢ PP-10:1
  + ▢ PP-11:1
  + ▢ PP-12:1
  + ▢ PP-13:1
  + ▢ PP-14:1
  + ▢ PP-15:1
```

Figure 1–28

10. Save the file and close the window.

Chapter Review Questions

1. What is the purpose of using an assembly folder?

   a. To store component files.

   b. To promote components.

   c. To help organize an assembly.

   d. To demote components.

2. Assembly folders have an impact on the relationships/ degrees of freedom of the components in the folder.

   a. True

   b. False

3. What is the purpose of the *Constraint Set* tab shown in Figure 1–29?

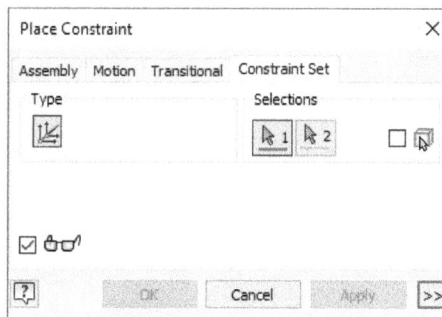

Figure 1–29

   a. Adds multiple constraints at the same time.

   b. Enables you to constrain components using a user coordinate system (UCS).

   c. Enables constraints to be grouped together.

   d. None of the above.

4. $\frac{A}{Z}\downarrow$ (Alpha Sort Component) sorts all of the components that exist at the top-level assembly and in subassemblies and assembly folders.

   a. True

   b. False

5. What do Motion constraints enable you to do?

   a. Describe the movement of one surface relative to another.

   b. Describe the constraints that keep components from moving.

   c. Restrict the motion of components.

6. If a Rotation motion constraint enables one component to rotate when another rotates, what does the Rotation-Translation motion constraint do?

   a. Enables two components to rotate when another rotates.

   b. They are the same.

   c. Enables one component to move translationally when another rotates.

   d. Enables one component to move translationally when another moves translationally.

7. What do Transitional constraints enable you to do?

   a. Describe the movement of one surface relative to a continuous set of surfaces.

   b. Describe the movement of one surface relative to another.

   c. Change constraint options depending on a component's other constraints.

   d. Transition from one type of constraint to another.

Command Summary

Button	Command	Location
NA	Add to New Folder	• (context menu in the Model Browser)
A↓Z↓	Alpha Sort Component	• **Ribbon:** *Assemble* tab>Productivity panel
	Application Options	• **Ribbon:** *Tools* tab>Options panel
	Constrain	• **Ribbon:** *Assemble* tab>Position panel
NA	Create New Folder	• (context menu in the Model Browser)
	Degree of Freedom Analysis	• **Ribbon:** *Assemble* tab>Productivity panel
	Ground and Root Component	• **Ribbon:** *Assemble* tab>Productivity panel
	Place	• **Ribbon:** *Assemble* tab>Component panel
	Place at Component Origin	• **Ribbon:** *Assemble* tab>Productivity panel
	Rename Browser Nodes	• **Ribbon:** *Assemble* tab>Productivity panel
	Save and Replace Component	• **Ribbon:** *Assemble* tab>Productivity panel

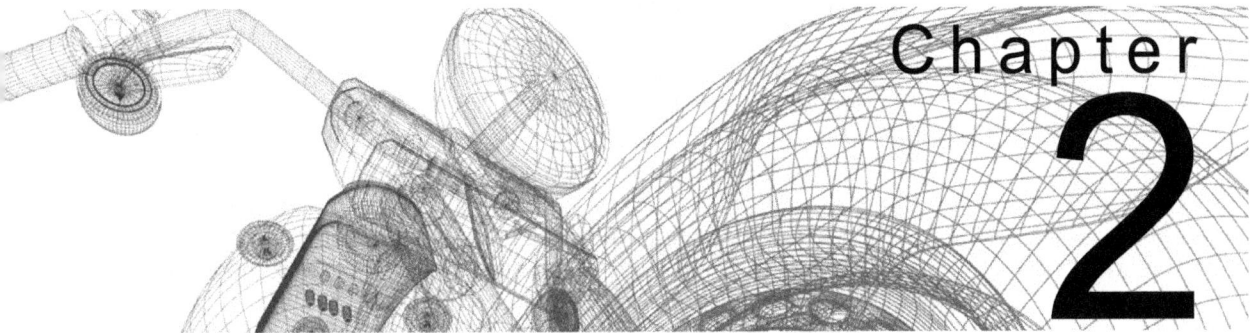

Introduction to Top-Down Design

The top-down design approach places critical information in a top-level assembly, then communicates that information to lower levels of the product structure. Planning the assembly using the top-down design approach helps create clean, reusable geometry that interacts as expected with the rest of the assembly.

Learning Objectives in This Chapter

- Define and compare the differences between bottom-up and top-down design.
- Describe how to enforce design intent using three major top-down design techniques.
- Describe the tools you would use to create 3D models from either sketch blocks generated in a layout sketch, multiple bodies in a single part, or a reference file.

2.1 Top-Down Design Process

Two different design methodologies can be used to build the top-level assembly: bottom-up and top-down.

Bottom-Up vs. Top-Down Design

In a traditional bottom-up design approach, part geometry is created independently of the assembly and other components. Any design criteria established before modeling the part is not shared between models. Once all part models are completed, they are brought together for the first time in the assembly. At this point in the design, problems often result with the assembly because engineering information is not correctly communicated. Problems might include interference, misalignment, or incomplete design. Additionally, any modifications must be manually propagated throughout the assembly. The concept of bottom-up design is shown in Figure 2–1.

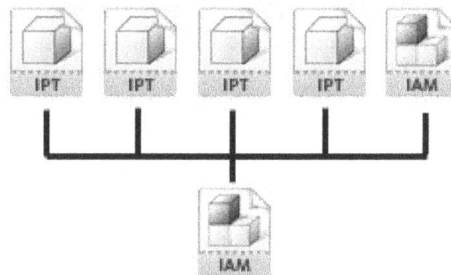

Figure 2–1

The top-down design approach places critical information in a top-level assembly, then communicates that information to lower levels of the product structure. The first step in creating a top-down design model is to create an initial assembly structure in the form of a reference part model. Design information is placed in a reference model using parametric design intent, solid bodies, sketch blocks, or other standard modeling tools. Lower level components and the assembly itself is then created manually or automatically depending on the design method.

Using the various Autodesk® Inventor® software techniques, you can create geometry referencing the initial reference model or other components in the assembly. Any changes made to the initial design intent is automatically propagated to all affected components.

The three main methods of top-down design, Layout, Adaptive, and Multi-Body Design, are shown in Figure 2–2.

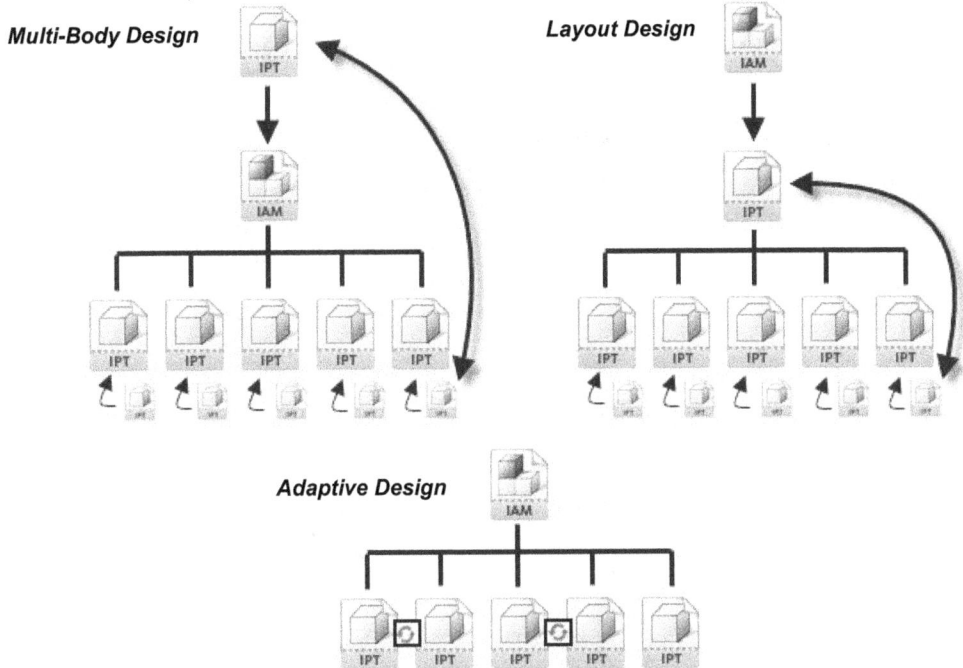

Multi-Body Design

Layout Design

Adaptive Design

Figure 2–2

Top-Down Design Process

Top-down design has been an engineering CAD methodology used in the Autodesk Inventor software for some time, where you create single part files (skeletons) in the context of an assembly model and use the part file to derive components for the assembly. Top-down design has been made easier with the use of tools that enable multi-body part files and layout designs. You can also use Adaptive reference modeling to implement a top-down design strategy in your assemblies.

As with any technique, using top-down design in your assemblies should involve a process. This process should be followed regardless of the technique (Multi-Body Modeling, Layout Design, or Adaptive Modeling) that you are using. Consider the following stages in the process:

1. **PLANNING** the assembly using top-down design helps create clean, reusable geometry that reacts as expected.
2. **ENFORCING** design intent ensures interactions and dependencies between components.
3. **CHANGING** top-level information propagates to all referenced components.

Planning

The top-down design technique organizes and helps enforce the interactions and dependencies between components. Many interactions and dependencies exist in an actual assembly and it is desirable to capture these dependencies when modeling. With appropriate planning during the initial design stage, you can consider all areas of a final model before creating any geometry.

Consider the following questions during the planning stage:

- What does the assembly do?

- How does a specific model interface with other components?

- What are the inputs and outputs of the assembly?

The answers to these questions help you to plan and correctly execute your design intent. Spending time planning the assembly helps you create a final model that reacts as expected.

Enforcing

Many commands and tools in the software can be used to enforce top-down design. The following are the three major top-down design techniques used to enforce design intent:

- Multi-Body Modeling

- Layout Design

- Adaptive Modeling

Multi-Body Modeling

Multi-Body part files enable you to create your entire assembly design in the Part environment using part modeling feature commands. The design is arranged into separate bodies in the single part file. Figure 2–3 shows a model that has two solid bodies. **Solid2** is selected and highlighted on the model. These separate bodies can then be extracted to derive individual parts for a new assembly.

Features can be shared between different bodies.

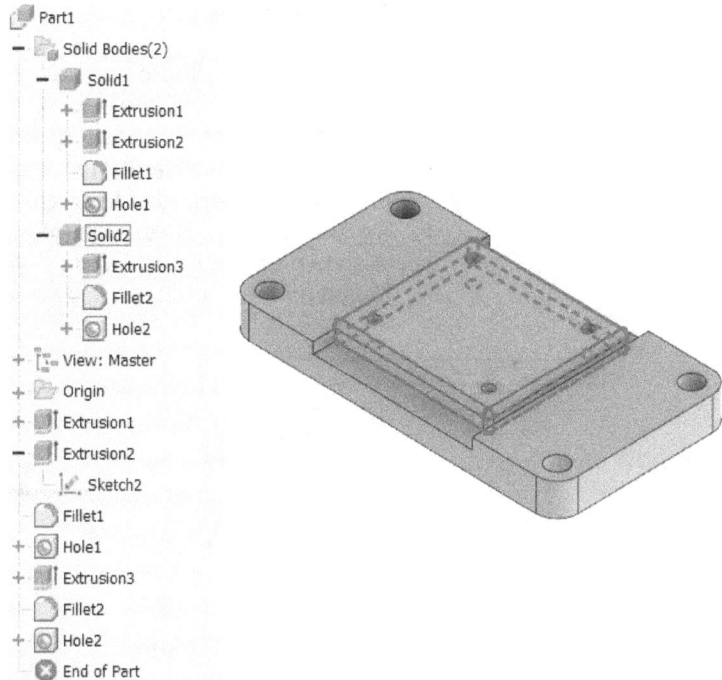

Part1
- Solid Bodies(2)
    - Solid1
        + Extrusion1
        + Extrusion2
            Fillet1
        + Hole1
    - Solid2
        + Extrusion3
            Fillet2
        + Hole2
+ View: Master
+ Origin
+ Extrusion1
- Extrusion2
        Sketch2
    Fillet1
+ Hole1
+ Extrusion3
    Fillet2
+ Hole2
    End of Part

Figure 2–3

The advantages of using Multi-Body design include the following:

- Top-down design is more streamlined. You do not need to set up an initial complex file and directory structure to design parts in the context of a top-level assembly. The entire design resides in a single file. Bodies are later extracted to create parts.

- A complex part file can be better organized using separate bodies with respect to their function or position in the model.

- Relationships between bodies can be easily set up and broken.

- You can control the visibility of bodies as a group rather than at the individual feature level.

- This method is useful for plastic part design, where interior components for a predefined shape can be designed in context and then extracted.

Layout Design

To accomplish a top-down design environment using Layout Design, you convey the design intent of a model by using a 2D sketch as a central repository for overall dimensions, spatial locations, and the general shape of components. The design information is stored in the form of Sketch Blocks in the layout. An example of a 2D sketch (made up of multiple Sketch Blocks) is shown on the left in Figure 2–4. 3D models are generated based on the sketch, as shown on the right in Figure 2–4.

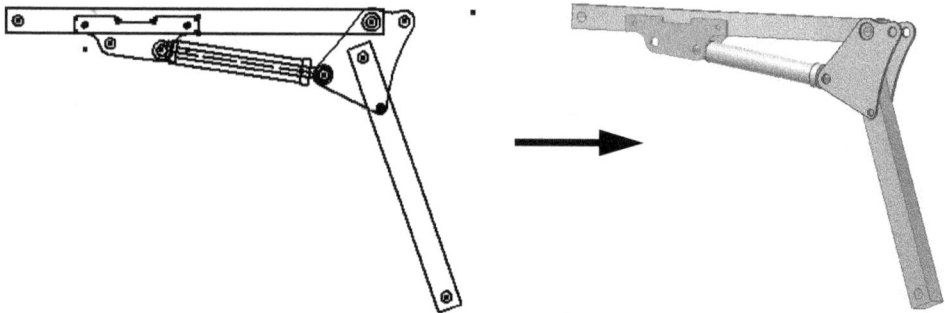

Figure 2–4

Layout Design is used for the following reasons:

- **3D Geometry Creation:** The entities that are created in a layout sketch are used in a target model to derive the solid geometry, as shown in Figure 2–5. By doing this, you maintain a link to the layout sketch and any changes to the layout are propagated to the components.

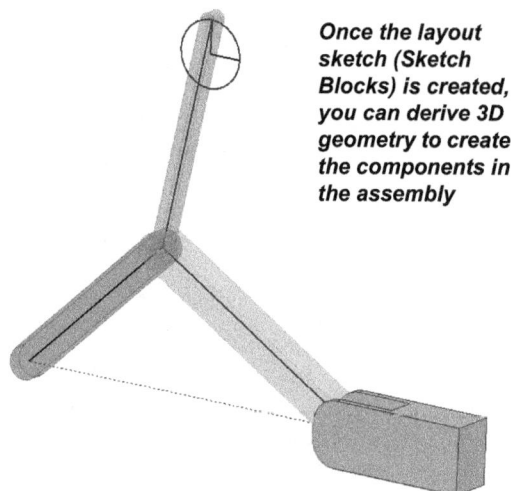

Once the layout sketch (Sketch Blocks) is created, you can derive 3D geometry to create the components in the assembly

Figure 2–5

- **Testing Assembly Motion:** When creating a layout sketch, the ability to test the motion of the assembly before spending time creating 3D geometry is a valuable asset. By modifying the sketch dimensions, as shown in Figure 2–6, you can ensure that you capture the required design intent before moving on with the design.

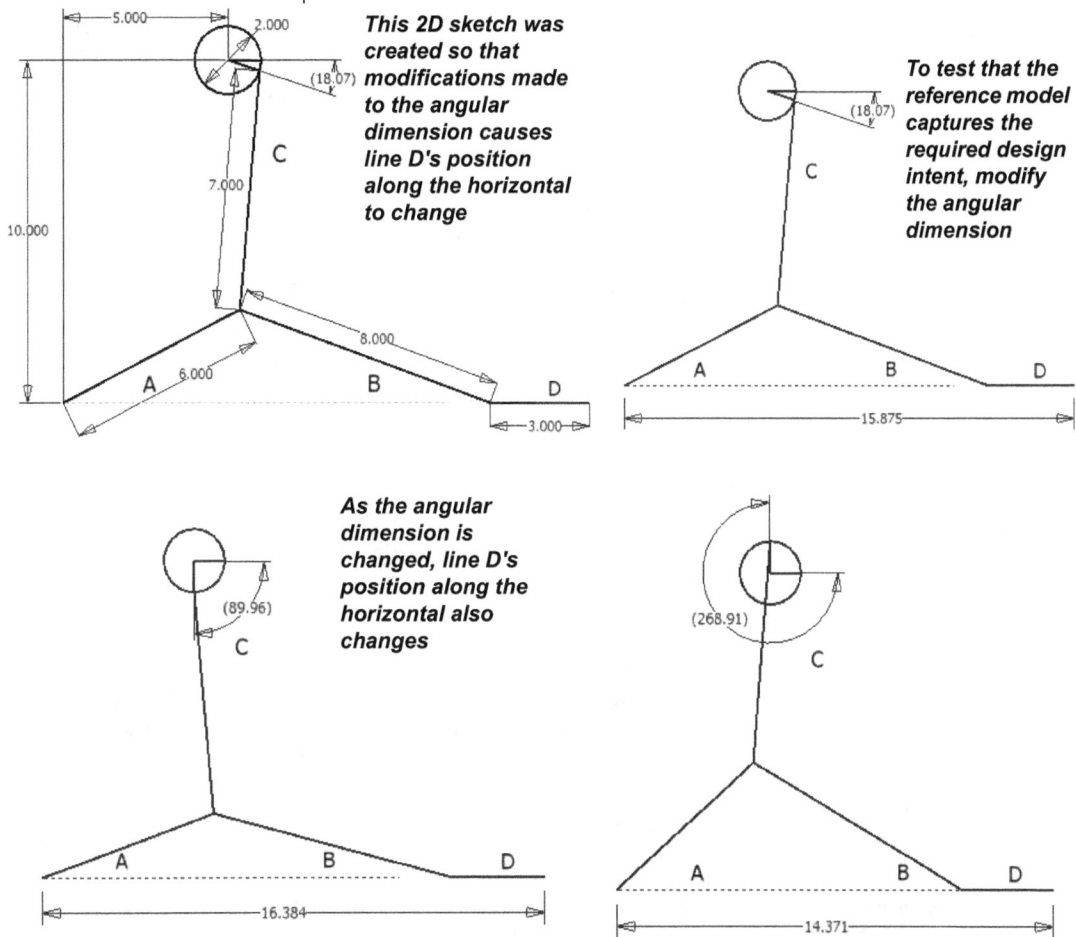

This 2D sketch was created so that modifications made to the angular dimension causes line D's position along the horizontal to change

To test that the reference model captures the required design intent, modify the angular dimension

As the angular dimension is changed, line D's position along the horizontal also changes

Figure 2–6

- **Controlling Parent/Child Relationships:** Deriving portions of geometry from a layout instead of referencing other components directly in an assembly reduces the chance of creating unwanted parent/child relationships between components. Using this technique makes operations (such as suppressing, deleting, and interchanging components) in the assembly easier, since fewer dependency relationships exist.

Adaptive Modeling

Adaptive Modeling, sometimes referred to as cross-part projection, uses references already inside the assembly for geometry creation by projecting references from one part to another. Typically, new parts are created directly inside the assembly to accomplish this, but can also be made to adapt even after assembly creation. Adaptive modeling has certain restrictions because of the nature of file associations and multiple occurrences of the same part inside an assembly.

Adaptive models are used for numerous reasons, including the following:

- **Creating Mating Parts:** You can adapt outlines of the geometry of parts to create a matching insert or outline, thus recreating the original geometry in a mating fashion. Updates to originating geometry update the references used on the new part. This is similar to using Project Geometry in a part file, but in this case, it is used to project geometry from other sources.

- **Determining Tolerances:** Use projected geometry to determine a reference of component placement or sizing inside a component that has to maintain a specific tolerance to the mating component. You can adjust the size of the original part and use parametric control in the new component to maintain the correct tolerance sizing.

- **Location of Geometry:** Use adaptive models with unconstrained sketches and features to enable the geometry to flex inside the assembly based on what is constrained. This permits for open design decisions during conceptual modeling or fit iterations.

Changing

By effectively planning for the required design intent and enforcing it using top-down design techniques, you can create an assembly model that reacts as expected when changes are made. You can make changes to the assembly by editing the reference model and then updating all components that reference it. By this stage in the design, all 3D models should be completed, enabling you to check fits, clearances, or interferences in the assembly. This enables you to quickly vary the design and functionality of the assembly.

2.2 Top-Down Design Tools

The following top-down design tools are discussed in more detail throughout this guide.

Multi-Body Design Tools

Much like modeling a single body model, multi-bodies are modeled using the same feature commands to define different components in the assembly. The only difference is that each new feature is assigned to a body. Once multiple solid bodies exist in the model, you can further manipulate them. You can redefine them as part of another solid body, move them, split them, combine them, insert additional bodies from other models, or use them to create separate parts and assemblies.

Make Layout

Layouts are created and added as a grounded component in an assembly using the **Make Layout** command. A new standard part file is generated to hold the layout sketch that holds all of the design data. Once the sketch layout is created, you group the entities into sketch blocks to represent the components or subassemblies of the assembly.

Make Components and Make Part

Using the **Make Components** and **Make Part** commands, you can quickly create 3D models from the Layout design's sketch blocks or the bodies in a Multi-body Design. These components remain associative to their source, so that when changes are made to 2D sketch blocks or multi-bodied design, the generated 3D models also update.

Derive

Without the Layout Design and Multi-Body workflows, the manual methodology of using the **Derive** command with a reference model was tedious, but effective. This was commonly called Skeletal Modeling.

As a basis, deriving geometry is accomplished by accessing a reference model for data in order to create geometry in a new model. You can make changes to the assembly by editing the reference model and then updating all components that reference it.

Parts in Assembly

The Autodesk Inventor software enables you to create parts within the context of an assembly. As with assembly features, you need to be careful about creating feature relationships when creating a part in the assembly environment.

Assembly Features

Features can also be created in the top-level assembly or at the subassembly level. This process is often used to add secondary machining operations for weldments, but it can also be used to create alignment holes and other features. The important rules to remember with this tool are:

- It occurs at the assembly level and does not propagate geometry to the part level.

- Reference selection creates feature relationships.

Associative Links and Adaptive Parts

*Using **Copy Object** at the part level inside an assembly also can create associative links.*

Each time you reference geometry (i.e., projecting geometry, dimensioning to edges or faces on other components) to create a section of the sketched feature, the software applies an associative link between the reference geometry and the sketched feature. Associative links make the geometry *adaptive*.

Associative links are a powerful tool in design projects. Many dimensions can change frequently and having to manually modify any and all dimensions associated with them can be overwhelming and inefficient. In addition, some dimensional changes might impact more than one part model. By ensuring that all features and parts are built with the required design intent, you can save time and create more robust models.

The size and shape of a part might evolve as you put an assembly together. Rather than switch frequently between several files to edit the parts, you can enable adaptivity. This enables you to specify geometric entities of part features to change, while controlling the size or location of other entities in an assembly. When you edit an adaptive part in the assembly, the adaptive components update accordingly.

Assembly Equations

Equations are user-defined mathematical relationships between parameters, that capture and control design intent in components. Equations can be between dimensions in a part or between assembly components. Assembly-level equations can drive dimensions and parameters in one component and equate them to dimensions and parameters in other components. This can be accomplished using derived components, linked spreadsheets, adaptivity, or a combination of these tools.

Component Generators

Component Generators enable you to create common components and perform calculations for them based on mechanical attributes. Component Generators rely on the Content Center for their geometric designs while using references inside the assembly.

Frame Generator

Frame Generator enables you to create the parts in a structural framework. The frame components use predefined cross-sections in the software and are generated based on geometry in a reference model.

Chapter Review Questions

1. What problems are associated with the bottom-up design approach? (Select all that apply.)

   a. Interference or misalignment between components.

   b. Incomplete design.

   c. Modifications to components must be manually propagated throughout the assembly.

2. Which is not an advantage of the top-down design approach?

   a. Organizes and helps enforce interactions and dependencies between components in an assembly.

   b. Creates part geometry independent of the assembly or any other component.

   c. Forces you to consider all areas of a final model before creating any geometry.

   d. Helps create clean, reusable geometry that interacts as expected with the rest of the assembly.

3. Which is not a top-down design technique that is available as a specific tool in the Autodesk Inventor software?

   a. Adaptive Modeling

   b. Layout Design

   c. Skeletal Modeling

   d. Multi-Body Design

4. You can create 3D models from sketch blocks that were created in the Layout Design.

   a. True

   b. False

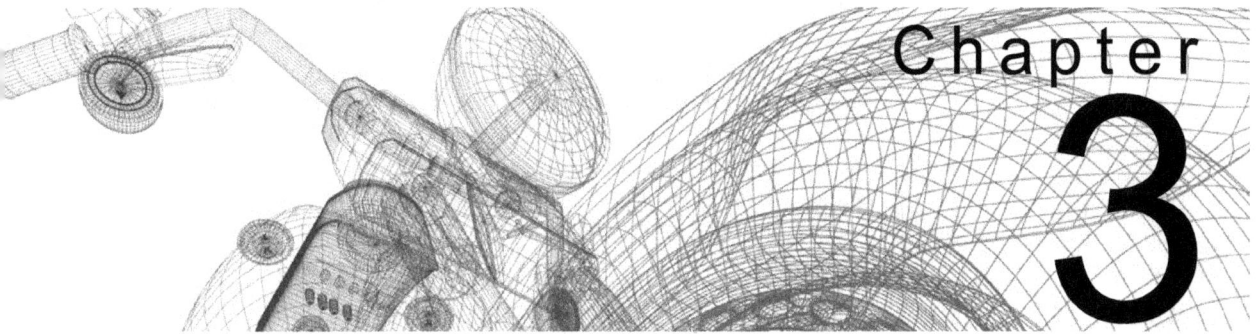

Chapter

3

Derived Components

Derived components use an existing model as their base component. Features
are copied from the base component into the new one to communicate design
information. This information is then used to create the geometry in the new
derived component.

Learning Objectives in This Chapter

- Derive new geometry in a part by importing and referencing objects from a source part.
- Describe the steps required to modify a derived component when updating it from its
  referenced model, adjusting the derived options, or breaking the associative link.

3.1 Derived Components

The **Derive Component** command enables you to create new geometry in a part by importing and referencing objects from a source model (i.e., a part or assembly). Based on the source geometry type, the newly created derived component is called either a derived part or derived assembly. When the source model changes, the derived part or assembly also changes.

General Steps

Use the following general steps to create a derived component:

1. Select a component to derive.
2. Select the derive style.
3. Select options for parts and assemblies.
4. Complete the operation.

Step 1 - Select a component to derive.

To create a derived part, create a new or open an existing part file. In the *Manage* tab>Insert panel, click (Derive) and open the part or assembly file from which to derive. The Derived Part or Derived Assembly dialog box opens, as shown in Figure 3–1.

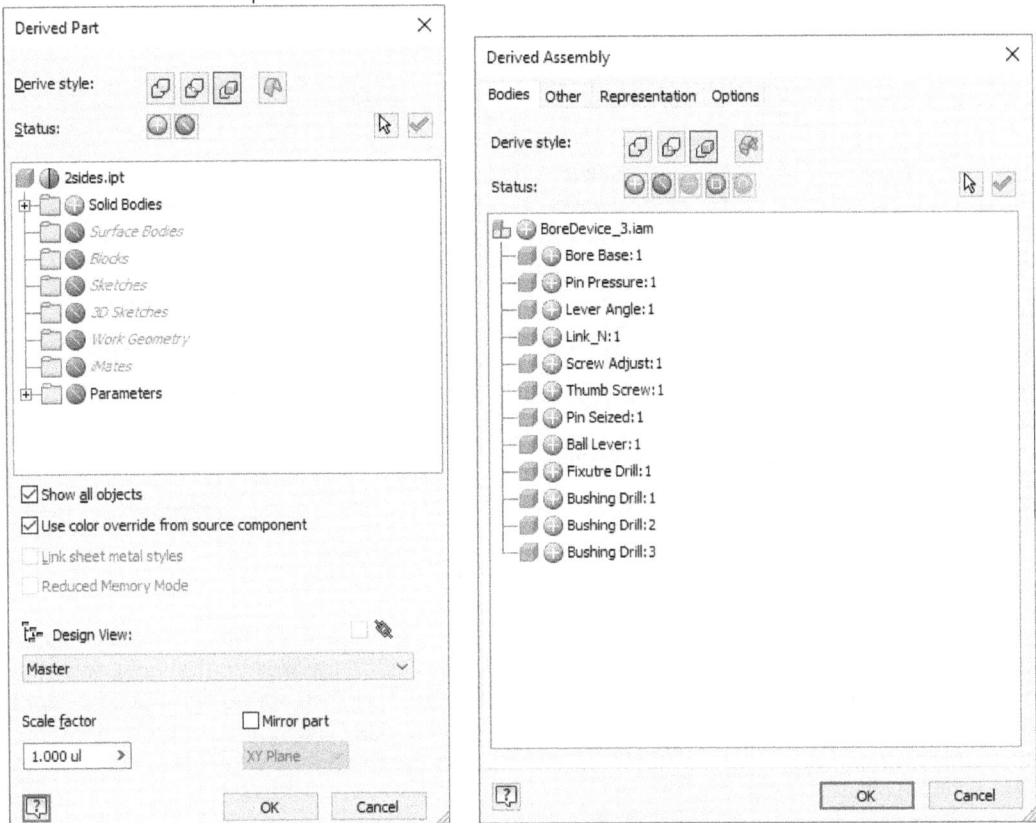

Figure 3–1

Step 2 - Select the derive style.

Select a *Derive style* icon from the top of the dialog box to define how to derive the component. The icons are as follows.

	Create a single solid body where seams between planar faces are removed.
	Create a single solid body between seams of planar faces are kept.
	Keep each solid as an individual solid body.
	Create the body as a work surface.
	Create a single composite feature. This option is only available if you are deriving a body from an assembly model.

Step 3 - Select options for parts and assemblies.

The available items that can be imported from the referenced part or assembly are listed in the tree structure in the dialog box (e.g., Sketches, 3D Sketches, Parameters, and iMates). For assemblies, it is listed on the *Other* tab. The items that you can import include the following:

The Composite Features option is only available when the source file already contains a derived assembly or composite feature.

- Solid Bodies
- Surface Bodies
- Blocks
- Sketches
- 3D Sketches

- Work Geometry
- iMates
- Parameters
- Composite Features

*To reduce the amount of clicks used to select all parts of a Derive, you can right-click on the assembly and select **Select All Parts**.*

To change the status of an item in the part or assembly dialog box (i.e., to include or exclude it), click on the symbol next to that item until it toggles to the required status symbol or select the item and click the Status icon. The options vary depending whether you are using the Derived Part or Assembly dialog box.

The Status symbols are described as follows:

- A yellow circle with a plus symbol ( ) indicates that the geometry is included in the derived part or assembly.

- A gray circle with a slash symbol ( ) indicates that the geometry is not included in the derived part or assembly.

- A red circle with a minus symbol ( ) indicates that the volume of that part is to be subtracted.

Use this option to reduce memory consumption while maintaining a place holder for the component in the derived assembly.

- A green circle with a square symbol ( ) indicates that the component is represented by a bounding box of the models size.

- A blue circle with an upside down U shape ( ) indicates that the selected component intersects with the derived part.

- A circle that is half yellow and half gray ( ) indicates that some geometry within the object type are included, while some are not.

Consider using the following options to further customize a derived part:

- Use **Show all objects** to refine the tree to show all objects that can be included/excluded. Clear the option to only see items previously set up in the originating component using the **Export Objects** command.

- By default, color overrides from the original part copy to the derived part. Clear the **Use color override from source component** option to remove this default behavior.

- Use **Link sheet metal styles** to include the sheet metal thickness and other parameters in the derived part

- Use **Reduced Memory Mode** to create a part using less memory. This option excludes source bodies from the cache to that no source bodies display in the Model Browser. If you break or suppress the link, the memory savings are lost.

- Use the Design View drop-down list to select the required representation to use. The Associative link checkbox enables you to control whether associativity is maintained with the source model's design view. The setting of this checkbox persists between Inventor sessions. When deriving part geometry, ensure that this is set appropriately.

- Adjust the size of the derived component using a scale factor.

- Use **Mirror Part** to mirror the component about a selected origin work plane (XY, YZ, or XZ).

The remaining tabs in the Derived Assembly dialog box are shown in Figure 3–2.

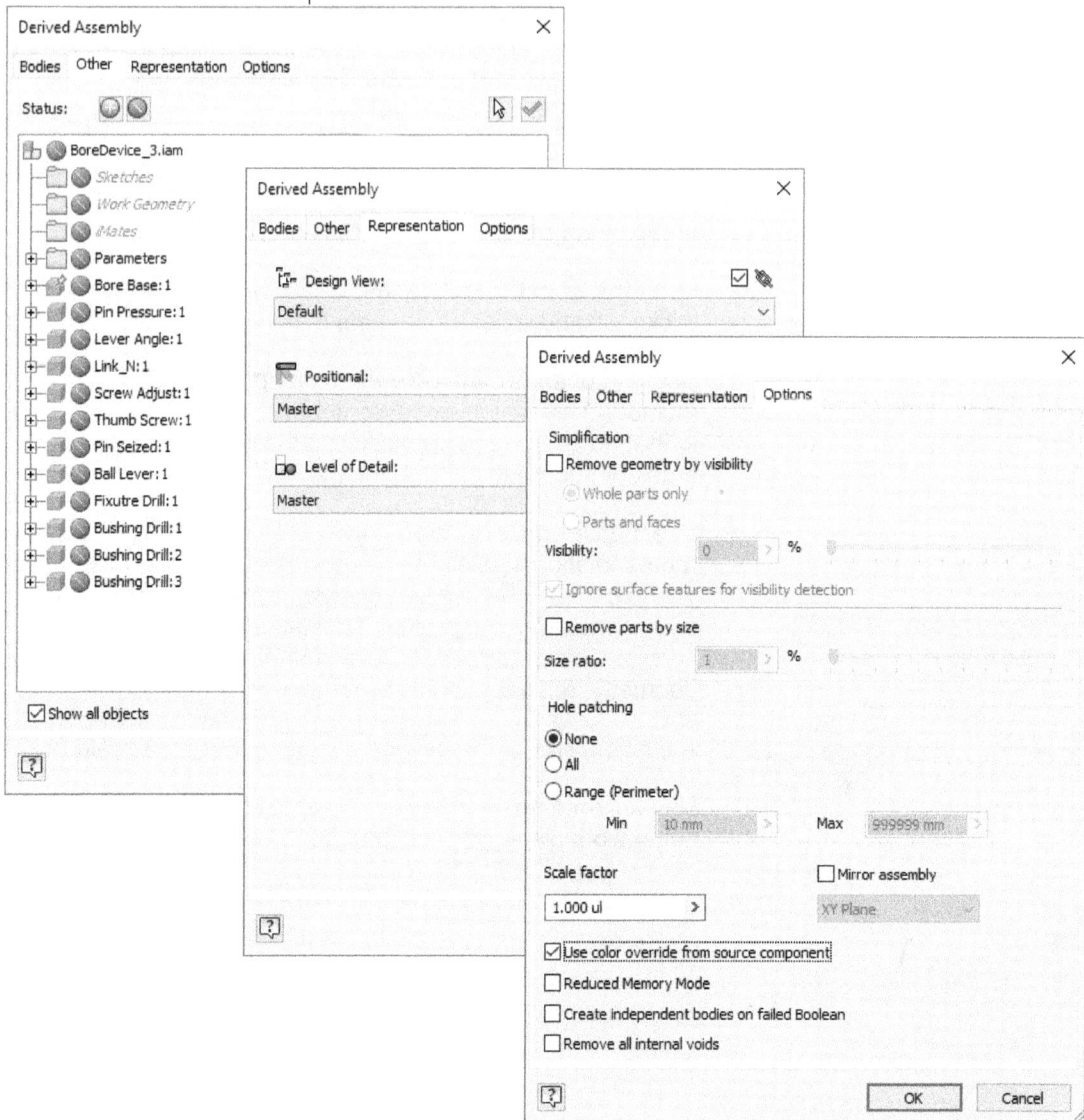

Figure 3–2

- Use the *Other* tab to include the items of the components in the derived assembly in the same manner as that for derived parts.

- Use the *Representation* tab to select the required representation to use. The Associative link checkbox enables you to control whether associativity is maintained with the source assembly's representations. The setting of this checkbox persists between Inventor sessions. When deriving assembly components, ensure that this is set appropriately.

- Use the *Options* tab to simplify model geometry, control hole patching, and scale or mirror an assembly. The following options are only found in the Derived Assembly dialog box:

Simplification	Use the options in this area to define what geometry is kept, based on its visibility status in the original component.
	By default, the Parts and faces of the original assembly are kept with a Visibility of 0%. Using this option, all faces that are not exposed in any view orientation are removed. Increase the Visibility percentage to remove parts or faces that have a specified percentage visible in any view orientation removed from the shrinkwrap part.
Remove parts by size	Use this option to remove geometry based on size. Any component smaller then the specified percentage of the overall assembly is removed.
Hole patching	Use this option to keep or remove holes. You can also remove holes of a specified size.
Create independent bodies on failed Boolean	Use this option to create a multi-body part when a single solid body cannot be generated.
Remove all internal voids	Use this option to fill all of the internal void shells in the derived solid body part.

Step 4 - Complete the operation.

Click **OK** to create the derived part and close the dialog box.

A derived component uses an existing part or assembly as its base feature and features can be added to it.

The original part is listed in the Model Browser as the base component. For a derived assembly, the components of the assembly that were included are combined into one part, but the individual components are listed, as shown in Figure 3–3, depending on the Derive Style used. Individual components can still be suppressed.

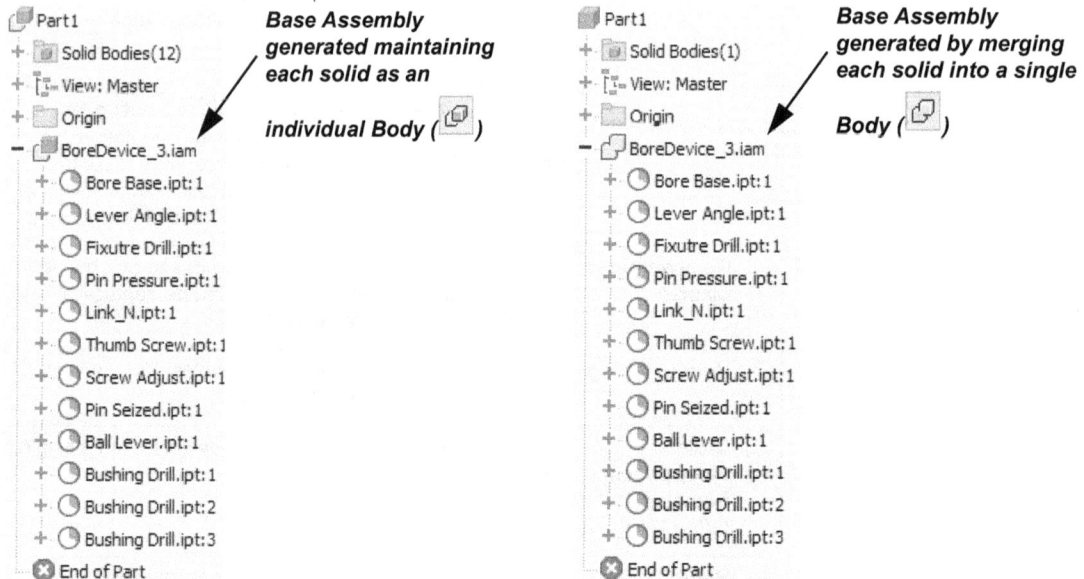

Part1
+ Solid Bodies(12)
+ View: Master
+ Origin
− BoreDevice_3.iam
  + Bore Base.ipt: 1
  + Lever Angle.ipt: 1
  + Fixutre Drill.ipt: 1
  + Pin Pressure.ipt: 1
  + Link_N.ipt: 1
  + Thumb Screw.ipt: 1
  + Screw Adjust.ipt: 1
  + Pin Seized.ipt: 1
  + Ball Lever.ipt: 1
  + Bushing Drill.ipt: 1
  + Bushing Drill.ipt: 2
  + Bushing Drill.ipt: 3
  End of Part

Base Assembly generated maintaining each solid as an

individual Body ( )

Part1
+ Solid Bodies(1)
+ View: Master
+ Origin
− BoreDevice_3.iam
  + Bore Base.ipt: 1
  + Lever Angle.ipt: 1
  + Fixutre Drill.ipt: 1
  + Pin Pressure.ipt: 1
  + Link_N.ipt: 1
  + Thumb Screw.ipt: 1
  + Screw Adjust.ipt: 1
  + Pin Seized.ipt: 1
  + Ball Lever.ipt: 1
  + Bushing Drill.ipt: 1
  + Bushing Drill.ipt: 2
  + Bushing Drill.ipt: 3
  End of Part

Base Assembly generated by merging each solid into a single

Body ( )

Figure 3–3

If you have the derived component open and you want to open the part or assembly that the derived component is referencing, right-click on it and select **Open Base Component**, or double-click on the base part or assembly in the Model Browser.

Once created, additional features can be added to a derived part or assembly (such as additional cuts and holes).

3.2 Modify Derived Components

Once a derived component is created, you can modify it in any of the following ways:

Update Derived Components

If changes are made to the referenced model, the symbol next to the base feature in the derived component changes to ⚡ . This indicates that a change was made and an update is required. In the Quick Access Toolbar, click 🗂 (Update) to update the derived component to match the referenced model.

Edit Derived Components

You can edit derived components once you finish creating them, if required. Editing derived components enables you to modify all of your selections made during the creation process.

How To: Edit a Derived Component

1. Right-click on the base part or assembly in the Model Browser and select **Edit Derived Part** or **Edit Derived Assembly**. The original dialog box opens.
2. Redefine the options, as required.
3. Click **OK**.

Break the Associative Link

You can break or suppress the associative link between the referenced model and the derived component so that changes to the referenced model no longer or temporarily affect the derived component. Right-click on the base part or assembly in the Model Browser and select either **Break Link with Base Component** or **Suppress Link with Base Component**. The icon for the base part or assembly displays in the Model Browser with a broken link icon or a suppressed link icon, as shown in Figure 3–4.

A suppressed link can be unsuppressed at any time, but a broken link cannot be re-established.

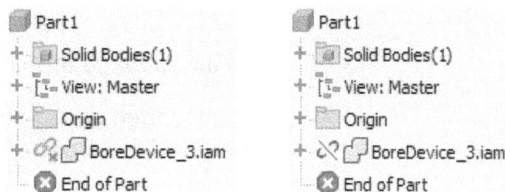

Figure 3–4

Practice 3a

Derived Components

Practice Objectives

- Create a new component derived from an assembly and then modify the base assembly file and update the derived component.
- Redefine the options for a derived component.
- Break the link between a base assembly and its derived component.

In this practice, you will create a derived part from an assembly. The derived part is edited, and changes are made to investigate how it affects the other components. The assembly and derived parts are shown in Figure 3–5.

Figure 3–5

Task 1 - Create a new component derived from an assembly.

1. Open **Derive Assem.iam**. The model displays in Isometric view. The assembly consists of four parts. This assembly will act as the reference for the derived part.

2. Create a new part using the **Standard(mm).ipt** template.

3. In the *Manage* tab>Insert panel, click (Derive).

4. In the Open dialog box, select the **Derive Assem.iam** file to derive. Click **Open**.

5. Ensure that the Derive style is set to ⬚ (Single solid body merging out seams between planar faces). Keep the remaining default selections in the Derived Assembly dialog box to verify that all four components are included. Click **OK**. The model displays as shown in Figure 3–6.

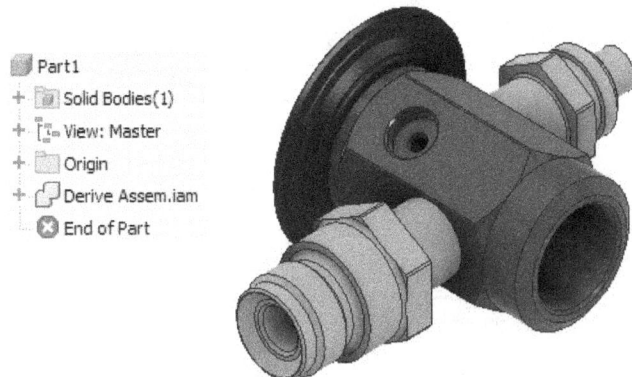

Part1
+ Solid Bodies(1)
+ View: Master
+ Origin
+ Derive Assem.iam
  End of Part

Figure 3–6

6. Save the derived part as **Derived Part.ipt**. The derived part generated looks identical to the assembly, except it is only one file (a single part), compared to four individual part files placed in an assembly file. Right-click on the name of the file in the Model Browser and select **iProperties**. In the *General* tab, note the size of the file.

Task 2 - Modify the derived component settings.

1. Double-click on **Derive Assem.iam** in the derived part's Model Browser to open the base assembly file, or select its tab at the bottom of the main window if it is still open.

2. In the Model Browser, double-click on the part **102650** to open it in the context of the main assembly. In the Quick Access Toolbar, use the Color Override drop-down list to change its color from *Orange* to **Red**, as shown in Figure 3–7.

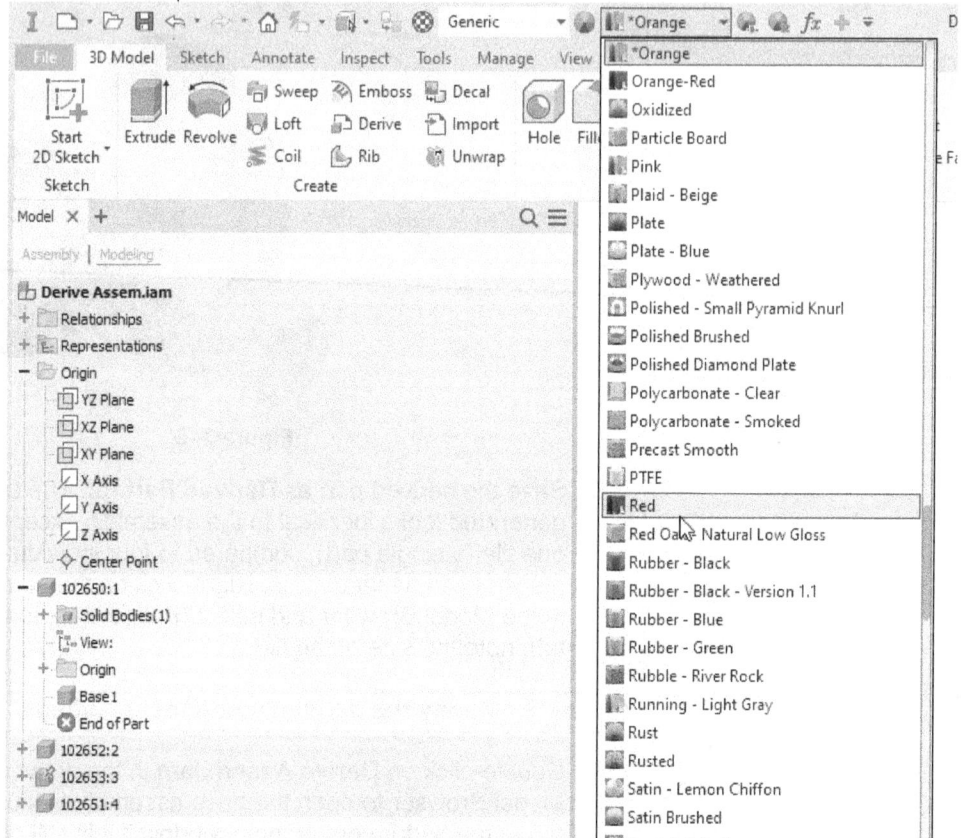

Figure 3–7

3. In the *3D Model* tab>Return panel, click (Return) to return to the main assembly.

4. Save the assembly and click **OK** in the Save dialog box.

5. Switch to the **Derived Part.ipt** file by selecting its tab at the bottom of the main window.

6. The lightning bolt icon (⚡) in front of **Derive Assem.iam** in the Model Browser, as shown in Figure 3–8, indicates a change was made to the original deriving component.

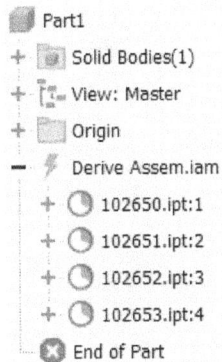

> Part1
> + Solid Bodies(1)
> + View: Master
> + Origin
> − ⚡ Derive Assem.iam
>   + 102650.ipt:1
>   + 102651.ipt:2
>   + 102652.ipt:3
>   + 102653.ipt:4
>   ❌ End of Part

Figure 3–8

7. In the Quick Access Toolbar, click ⬚ (Update) to update the derived part. The lightning bolt is removed and **102650.ipt** displays in red.

8. Right-click on **Derive Assem.iam** in the Model Browser and select **Edit Derived Assembly**. The original Derived Assembly dialog box opens.

9. In the *Bodies* tab, click 🗗 (Maintain each solid as a solid body) as the Derive style.

10. Select the *Representation* tab, clear 🔗 (Associative) for the Design View.

11. Switch to the *Options* tab, select **Remove parts by size** in the *Simplification* area, and set the *Size ratio* to **40%**. Set the *Hole patching* option to **All**. Click **OK**. The model displays as shown in Figure 3–9.

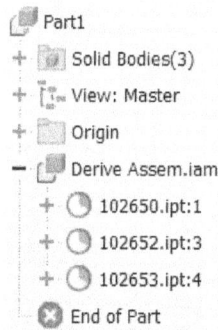

Figure 3–9

12. Note that the Solid Bodies node is now populated with additional bodies because (Maintain each solid as a solid body) was selected. One component has also been removed from the assembly because of the size ratio setting, and the holes (or cavities) are now patched in the derived part. In addition, by removing associativity () to the Design Views, changes to color and visibilities will not update if they are modified in the original files.

13. Save the file and check its size in the iProperties. Note that the size of the file is now smaller.

14. Right-click on **Derive Assemb.iam** in the Model Browser and select **Edit Derived Assembly**. In the *Bodies* tab, select any one of the components currently included and click (Includes bounding boxes of the selected components) to toggle the icons. Change the other two components to display as bounding boxes as well. Click **OK**. The model displays as shown in Figure 3–10.

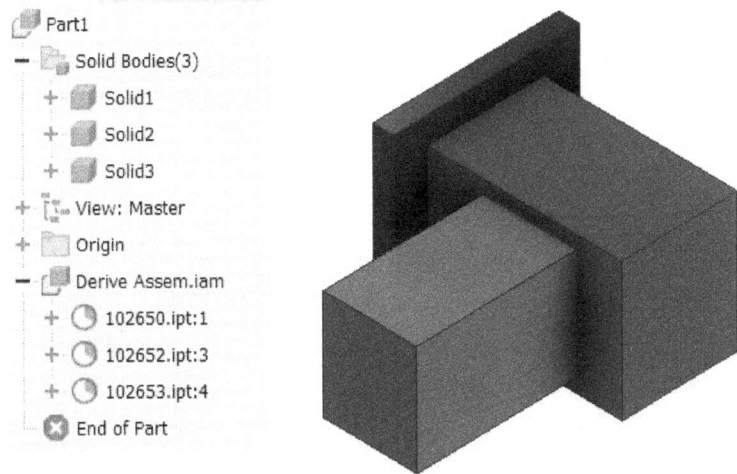

Figure 3–10

15. Note that the parts are replaced with bounding boxes that represent their size extents in a simplified manner. Save the file again and check its size in the iProperties. Note that the size of the file is considerably smaller.

16. Right-click on **Derived Assem.iam** in the Model Browser and select **Suppress Link With Base Component**.

    (Suppressed Link) displays in front of the assembly in the Model Browser.

17. Attempt to open the base assembly by double-clicking on **Derived Assem.iam** in the Model Browser. Note that it will not initiate because the link has been suppressed. The **Edit Derived Assembly** is also no longer available in the shortcut menu, as shown in Figure 3–11.

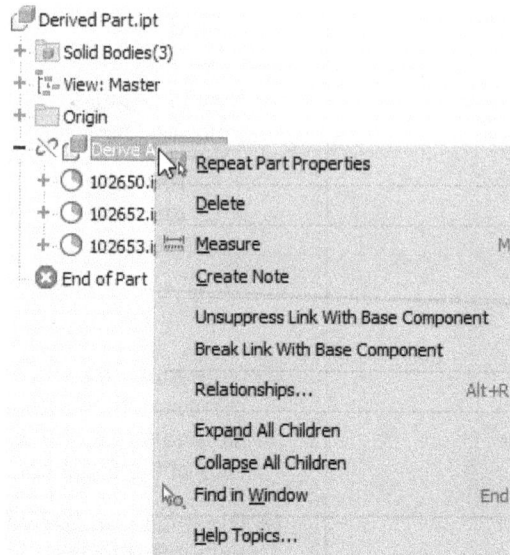

Figure 3–11

18. In the Model Browse, right-click on **Derived Assem.iam** and select **Break Link With Base Component**. (Broken Link) displays in front of the assembly in the Model Browser.

19. In the Model Browse, right-click on **Derived Assem.iam** and note that an option is not available to redefine the link to the original file. Only executing the **Undo** command at this point will resolve the link to the original file. Performing a save and exiting will permanently disassociate the geometry. Breaking a link is beneficial if the original files do not need to be referenced again, but it is important to ensure this before breaking the link.

20. Save and close the files.

Chapter Review Questions

1. Additional feature geometry can be added to a model that has been created based on derived geometry from another model.

   a. True

   b. False

2. Which of the following items cannot be imported from the referenced part or assembly?

   a. Parameters

   b. Solid Bodies

   c. Composite Features

   d. Drawings

3. Match the symbols used to create a derived part (in the right column) with their definition shown in the left column.

   Answer

   a. The geometry is included in the derived part.

   b. Some geometry is included while some is not included in the derived part.

   c. The geometry is not included in the derived part.

4. Match the symbols used to create a derived assembly (in the right column) with their definition shown in the left column.

Answer

a. The component is represented by a bounding box. _____

b. The volume is to be subtracted from the derived assembly. _____

c. The selected component intersects with the derived assembly. _____

d. The geometry is not included in the derived assembly. _____

e. The geometry is included in the derived assembly. _____

f. Some geometry is included while some is not included in the derived assembly. _____

5. When deriving a part model into a new part file, which of the following can you use to customize the derived geometry? (Select all that apply.)

a. Select a specific Design View to derive from.

b. Select parameters to include in the new file.

c. Patch holes in the derived geometry.

d. Specify a scale factor to set a size for the derived geometry.

6. A link that is broken with the base component can be unbroken; however, a suppressed link cannot be unsuppressed.

a. True

b. False

Command Summary

Button	Command	Location
	Derive	• **Ribbon:** *Manage* tab>Insert panel
	Update	• **Quick Access Toolbar**

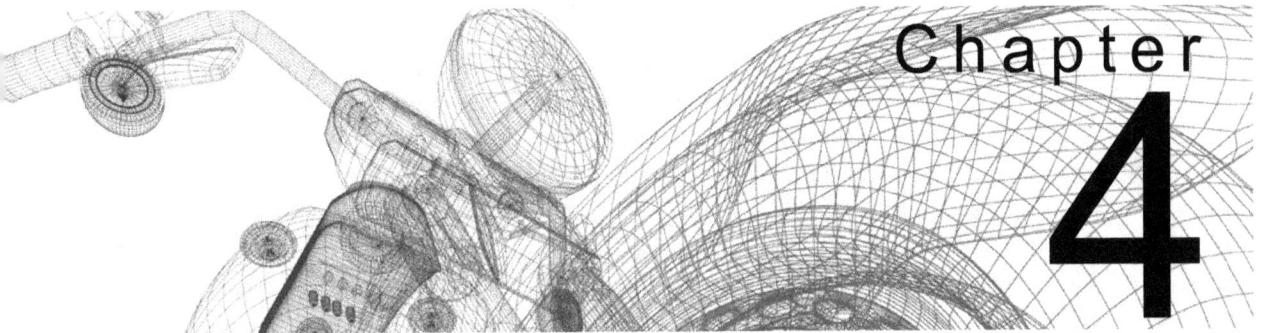

Multi-Body Part Modeling

Multi-body modeling is a top-down design technique where you create a single part file in the context of an assembly model. Multi-body part files enable you to create your entire assembly design in the part environment using part modeling feature commands.

Learning Objectives in This Chapter

- Describe the advantages of building a part file using multiple solid bodies.
- Create solid bodies and correctly assign features to specific solid bodies.
- Modify the various solid bodies in a model by moving, removing, splitting, combining, or redefining them.
- Create new parts and assemblies from the multi-bodies in a single part.
- Individually control the visibility of and access to the properties for various solid bodies.

4.1 Multi-Body Part Modeling

Multi-body part files enable you to create your entire assembly design in the part environment using part modeling feature commands. This technique is commonly used when creating complex plastic or cast parts that require very intricate geometry. The design is arranged into separate bodies in the single part file. Figure 4–1 shows a model that has two solid bodies. **Solid2** is highlighted on the model. These separate bodies can then be extracted into individual parts for a new assembly.

Features can be shared between different bodies.

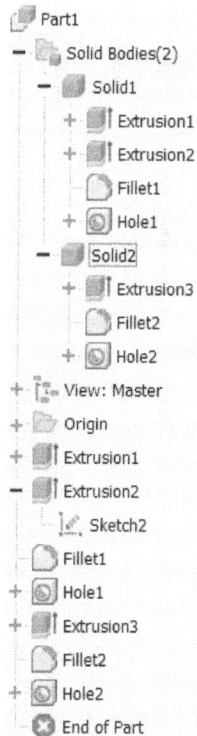

Figure 4–1

The advantages of using multi-bodies include the following:

• You do not need to create an initial complex file and directory structure to design parts in the context of a top-level assembly. The entire design resides in a single file and bodies are later extracted to create parts.

• A complex part file can be better organized using separate bodies with respect to their function or position in the model.

• Relationships between bodies can be set up and broken.

- You can control the visibility of bodies as a group rather than at the individual feature level.

- This method is useful for plastic part design, where interior components for a predefined shape can be designed in context and then extracted.

Creating the First Solid Body

With the creation of the first solid feature in any part file, the first solid body is automatically created and the *Solid Bodies* folder is added to the Model Browser. Figure 4–2 shows that Extrusion1 was the first solid features and it was included in the Model Browser as a feature and as geometry in Solid1.

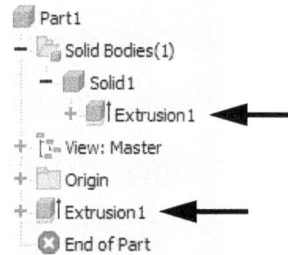

Figure 4–2

Creating Additional Solid Bodies

Once the first solid body is added to the model, each additional feature is automatically applied to it, unless a new feature is explicitly set to be created as a new solid body. To create a new solid body, create its feature as you normally would, and click

(New Solid) as the Boolean operation in the feature creation dialog box or palette. Once selected, a second body is added.

Assigning Features to Solid Bodies

Once two or more solid bodies are in a model, the selection of the placement/sketch planes are important to correctly locate the new feature in the required solid body. Consider the following:

- When creating a sketched feature, it is by default added to the same solid body as that of the sketch plane. For features to be added to a different solid body, activate the *Solids* field of the feature dialog box or palette and select the required solid body.

- When creating a pick-and-place feature, it is by default added to the same solid body as the placement references. In the case of a fillet, for example, it is added to the same solid body as the parent feature of the placement edge. If multiple edges are selected that belong to multiple solid bodies, the feature is added to each solid body.

- When creating a sketch-based or pick-and-place feature, it is only extended through its parent solid body, even if the **Through All** depth is selected. For features to interact with another solid body, activate the *Solids* field of the feature dialog box or palette and select additional solid bodies to be included.

Manipulating Solid Bodies

Once multiple solid bodies exist in the model, you can further manipulate them. You can redefine them as part of another solid body, move them, split them, and combine them.

Redefining/Removing Features in Solid Bodies

Once a feature is created and assigned to a solid body, you can re-assign it to another solid body or remove a solid body from interacting with the feature. To do so, redefine the original feature and activate the *Solids* field in the Output area of the feature dialog box. You can select the new solid to apply it to or, if you want to remove a solid body from the initial selection set, press and hold <Ctrl> and select the solid body to remove.

Moving Bodies

You might need to move the various bodies in a multi-body part.

How To: Move a Solid Body

*The **Move** command is only available when working with solid bodies.*

1. In the *3D Model* tab>expanded Modify panel, click ⬚ (Move Bodies). The Move Bodies dialog box opens.
2. Select the solid bodies to move. If you need to select multiple bodies, you must click ⬚ (Bodies) again after selecting the first body to select additional bodies.

3. Select a move operation using the drop-down list in the Move Bodies dialog box, as shown in Figure 4–3.

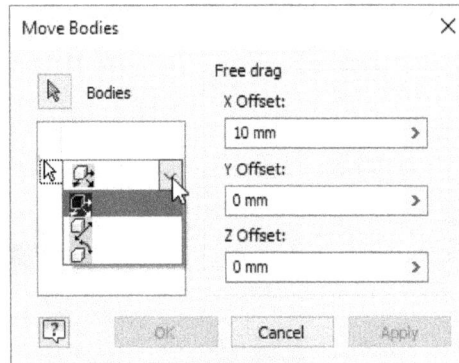

Figure 4–3

Each icon in the list enables you to move the body, as follows:

- (Free drag): Enables you to enter a precise X, Y, or Z offset value, or drag the preview in any direction.

- (Move along ray): Enables you to enter a precise offset value, or drag the preview offset from a selected reference.

- (Rotate about line): Enables you to enter a precise rotational angle value, or drag the preview around a selected axis.

4. Depending on the move operation selected, enter values and select references using the right side of the dialog box to define the movement.

5. To define a second move operation, if required, select **Click to add** and select a new move operation, as shown in Figure 4–4.

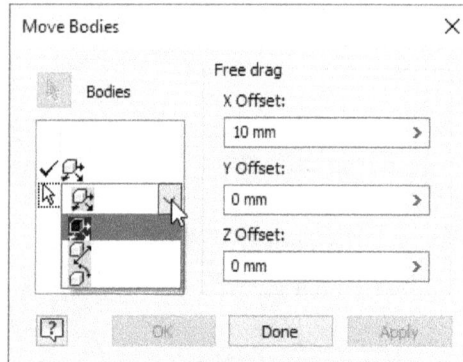

Figure 4–4

6. Continue to add move operations as required for the selected body.
7. Click **OK** to complete the feature. A Move Body feature is added to the bottom of the Model Browser, as well as into each of the Solid Bodies selected to be moved.

*To edit the Move Body feature, right-click on it and select **Edit feature**.*

Splitting Bodies

You can split a single body so that you can manipulate the resulting bodies independently.

How To: Split a Solid Body

1. In the *3D Model* tab>Modify panel, click 🗐 (Split). The Split palette opens as shown in Figure 4–5.

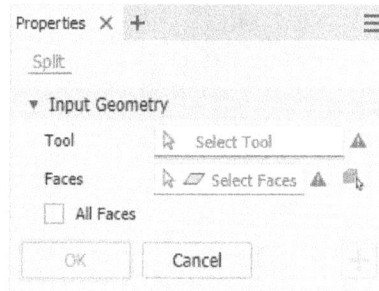

Figure 4–5

The split's Tool reference must completely intersect the entire body being split.

2. Ensure that the *Tool* field is active and select the reference geometry that is to define where the split is to occur. This reference can be a work plane, surface, or sketch geometry.

3. Toggle the ⬛ button to enable solid selection, as shown in Figure 4–6. The faces/solid setting will persist in the palette the next time the Split command is started.

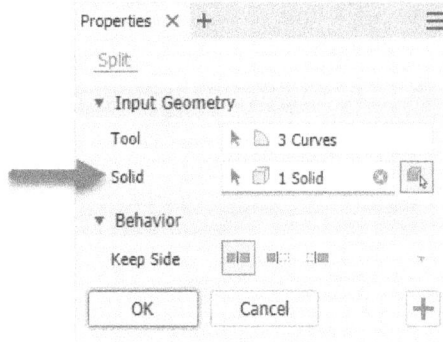

Figure 4–6

4. Ensure that the Solid field is active and select the solid to be split.

   - If there are multiple solids in the model, you must explicitly select the solid(s) to be split; otherwise, the solid is automatically selected.

5. When splitting a solid, the palette provides additional settings in the *Behavior* area. This enables you to use the split to remove geometry from the model. By default, both sides of the split are kept (⬛); however, you can select ⬛ or ⬛ to remove one side of the split or the other. When one of these side options is selected, a red arrow appears on the model indicating the side that will be removed. Toggle these options as needed to remove the required side.

6. Click **OK** or ✓ to complete the split. Alternatively, right-click and select **OK (Enter)** or press <Enter>.

Combining Bodies

If you created two solid bodies separately during an initial design, you might decide later that they should be combined. Using the **Combine** command, you can add or remove material based on selected bodies.

How To: Combine Features

*The **Combine** command is only available when working with solid bodies.*

1. In the *3D Model* tab>Modify panel, click ◢ (Combine). The Combine palette opens as shown in Figure 4–7.

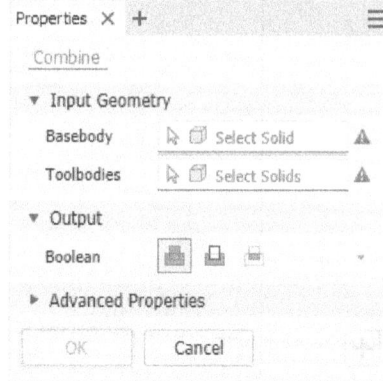

Properties ✕ ＋   ≡

  Combine

  ▼ Input Geometry

    Basebody   ▷ ⬚ Select Solid   ⚠

    Toolbodies   ▷ ⬚ Select Solids   ⚠

  ▼ Output

    Boolean   ▣ 🗗 ⬜   ▾

  ▶ Advanced Properties

     OK   Cancel

Figure 4–7

2. The Basebody field should be active by default. If not, select it to activate it and select the solid body to use as the basebody reference. The basebody is the solid body that will be kept after the operation.

You can only select one basebody, but you can select multiple toolbodies, if required.

3. Select in the Toolbodies field to activate it. Select the solid body to use as the toolbody reference. The toolbody is the solid body or bodies that will be combined with the basebody.

4. (Optional) To maintain the toolbody as a solid body after the operation, select **Keep Toolbodies** in the *Advanced Properties* area. If you select this option, the toolbody becomes invisible. Its visibility can be enabled to manipulate or use it, as required.

5. In the *Output* area, select an operation to perform on the basebody. The available operations include joining (▣), cutting (🗗), and intersecting (⬜) the toolbody from the base.

6. Click **OK** to complete the feature. The Combine feature is listed at the bottom of the Model Browser and in the solid body used as the basebody reference.

Inserting Components into Parts

Refer to the Derived Components chapter for more information on this command.

Using the **Derive** option, you can selectively include/exclude solid bodies (or other objects) from a source model to import it into a new or existing part file.

Creating Parts from Part Bodies

The steps for creating a part is similar to that for deriving a part.

You can extract individual bodies from a multi-body part into separate parts.

How To: Extract a Body to Create a New Part

1. In the *Manage* tab>Layout panel, click ![icon] (Make Part). The Make Part dialog box opens as shown in Figure 4–8. Alternatively, you can select the bodies to be used in the Model Browser, right-click, and select **Make Part**.

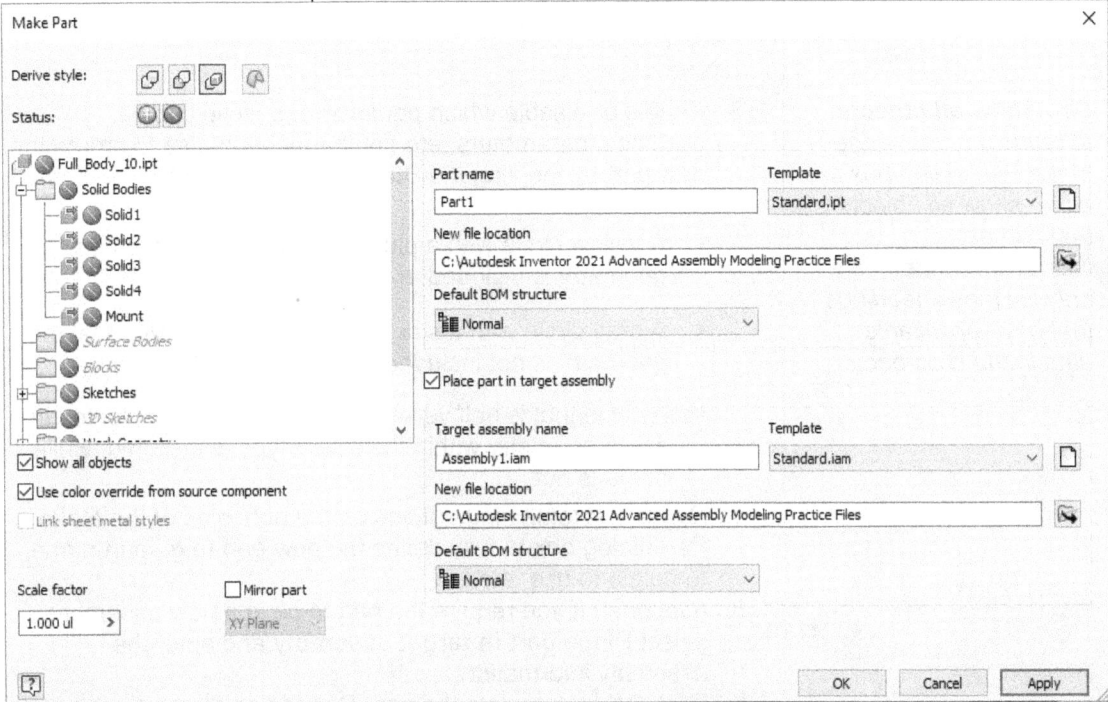

Figure 4–8

2. Select a Derive style icon from the top of the dialog box to define how to create the component. The icons are described as follows:

Icon	Description
	Create single solid body where seams between planar faces as removed.
	Create single solid body where seams between planar faces are kept.
	Keep each solid as an individual solid body.
	Create the body as a work surface.

*Use **Show all objects** to refine the tree in the Make Part dialog box to either show all objects that can be included/excluded, or to only list those headings that have applicable data in the solid body.*

3. Enable or disable which portions (e.g., solid bodies, sketches, parameters, etc.) of the model to use to create the new part by toggling the **Status** icons adjacent to the item name.
   - A yellow circle with a plus symbol ( ) indicates that the geometry is included in the new part.
   - A gray circle with a slash symbol ( ) indicates that the geometry is not included in the new part.
   - A circle that is half yellow and half gray ( ) indicates that some geometry within the object type is included, while some is not.

4. Define the remaining options on the right side of the Make Part dialog box to fully define the new part (e.g., part name, template to use, etc.).

5. (Optional) If you require the part to be in a new assembly, select **Place part in target assembly** and enter the assembly information.

6. Click **OK** to complete the part. Depending on the *Derive style* selected, the new part might combine the selected bodies into a single body, or keep each body separate.

The newly created part remains associative to the multi-body part, unless you explicitly break the link. In the newly created part, right-click on the source part name that has been imported and select **Break Link With Base Component**. The link can be suppressed (instead of broken) by selecting **Suppress Link With Base Component**.

Creating Components from Part Bodies

Selected bodies in a multi-body part can be extracted into separate components that are combined in a new top-level assembly.

How To: Extract Solid Bodies and Create a New Assembly from Them

Consider using the
Make Component
command and disabling
*the **Insert components***
in target assembly
option instead of using
*the **Make Part***
command multiple times
when creating more
than one component.

1. In the *Manage* tab>Layout panel, click ![icon] (Make Components). The Make Components: Selection dialog box opens. Alternatively, you can select the bodies to be used in the Model Browser, right-click, and select **Make Components**.
2. Select the solid bodies to extract in the Model Browser. All selected solid bodies are listed in the dialog box.
3. Ensure that the **Insert components in target assembly** option is selected.
4. Specify the remaining options on the right side of the Make Components: Selection dialog box to fully define the new component (e.g., target assembly name, template to use, etc.). The dialog box displays similar to that shown in Figure 4–9 once components have been selected.

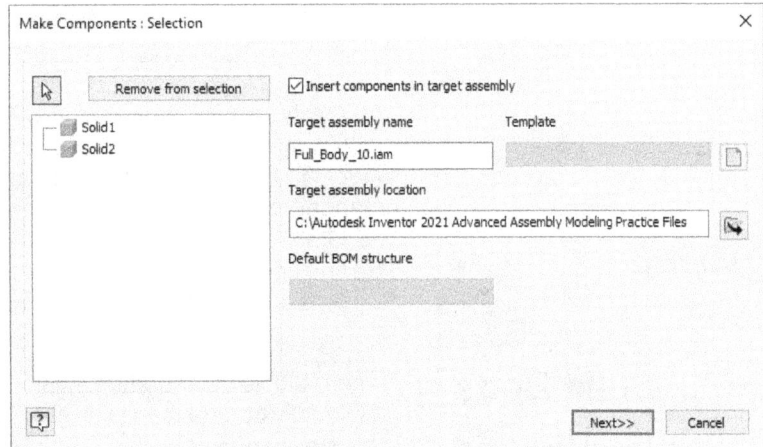

Figure 4–9

5. Click **Next**. The Make Components: Bodies dialog box opens.

The solid body name in the source model is used as the default name for the component.

6. Using the Make Components: Bodies dialog box, you can make changes to individual components that are being created as part of the assembly. You can click in each column to rename the resulting component, or change its template or BOM Structure. The dialog box opens similar to that shown in Figure 4–10.

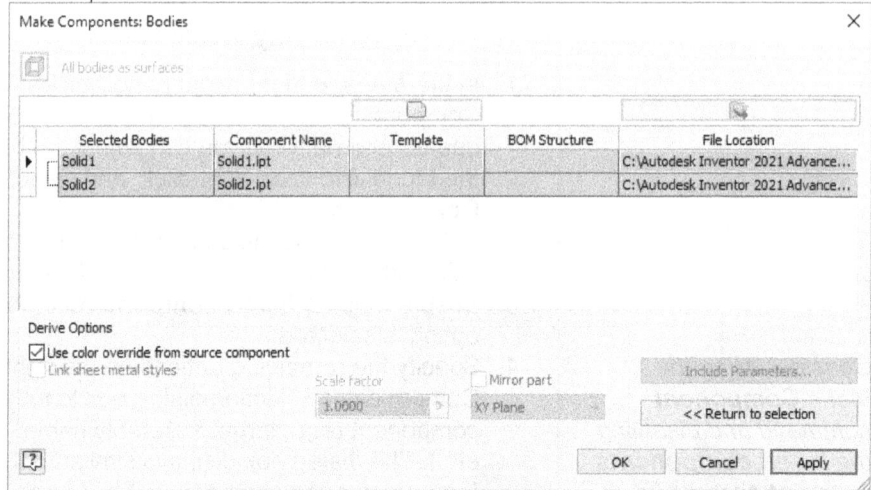

Make Components: Bodies

All bodies as surfaces				
Selected Bodies	Component Name	Template	BOM Structure	File Location
Solid1	Solid1.ipt			C:\Autodesk Inventor 2021 Advance...
Solid2	Solid2.ipt			C:\Autodesk Inventor 2021 Advance...

Derive Options
☑ Use color override from source component
☐ Link sheet metal styles

Scale factor 1.0000   >   ☐ Mirror part   XY Plane

Include Parameters...

<< Return to selection

OK   Cancel   Apply

Figure 4–10

7. Set the options in the *Derive Options* area, as required.
8. Click **OK** to complete the operation.

The newly created parts and assembly remain associative to the multi-body part unless you explicitly break the link to the parent model. To break the link, you must open each created component, then right-click on the source part name that has been imported and select **Break Link With Base Component**. The link can be suppressed instead of broken by selecting **Suppress Link With Base Component**.

Solid Body Display

Once multiple solid bodies exist in a model, you may want to individually control the visibility of various solid bodies. To control the visibility of a solid body, right-click on the solid body and enable or disable the **Visibility** option.

A representation of the model can be saved using a design view. This enables you to capture the visibility settings of the solid bodies for reuse at a later time without having to enable and disable visibility.

How To: Save a Solid Body Display Configuration

1. Right-click on the *View* folder and select **New**. By default, the model exists as a Master view. When a new view is created, it is automatically set to be active.
2. Configure the view display.
3. Select the new view, click again (do not double-click) and enter a descriptive name for the view.
4. To lock the design view, right-click on the view name in the Model Browser and select **Lock**. Locking restricts you or others from making changes to the design view representation.

A design view can also store other display options, such as section view settings and colors.

To display an alternate design view, right-click on its name in the Model Browser and select **Activate**. Alternatively, you can double-click on its name.

Design views can be used when creating drawing views.

Solid Body Properties

To access the properties for a solid body, right-click on the solid body name and select **Properties**. The Body Properties dialog box opens as shown in Figure 4–11.

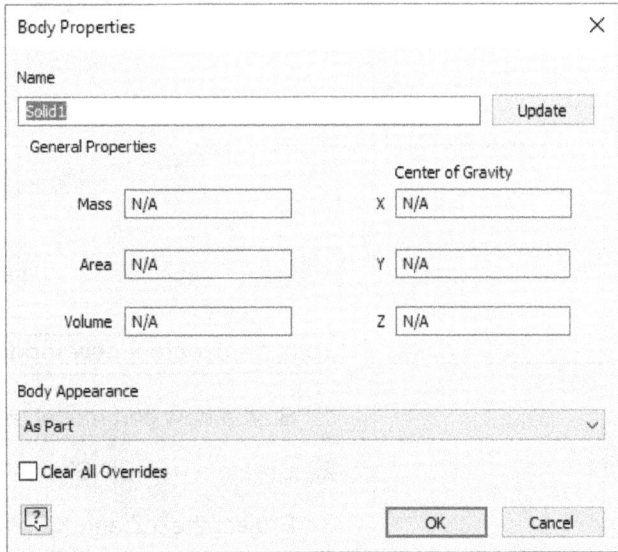

Figure 4–11

Using the Body Properties dialog box, you can do the following:

- Rename the solid body. You can also rename a solid body directly in the Model Browser.

- Update and provide the general properties for the solid body.

- Set a color style for the solid body.

*The **Clear All Overrides** option removes color overrides from individual faces contained in the solid body.*

Practice 4a

Multi-Body Part Design

Practice Objectives

- Create multiple solid bodies in a single part, and modify and add features to specific bodies.
- Create new part files by extracting solid bodies from a single part.

In this practice, you will create a single part file containing two solid bodies. In creating these solid bodies, you will learn to create multiple bodies in a model, add features to the bodies, and make changes to the bodies. To complete the practice, you will extract the solid bodies from the part file to create two individual part files. The completed model is shown in Figure 4–12.

Figure 4–12

Task 1 - Create a new model.

1. Start a new part model using the **Standard (in).ipt** template.

2. Create a new 2D Sketch on the XY Plane.

3. Project the YZ and XZ planes.

4. Sketch a rectangular entity centered on the projected origin planes, as shown in Figure 4–13.

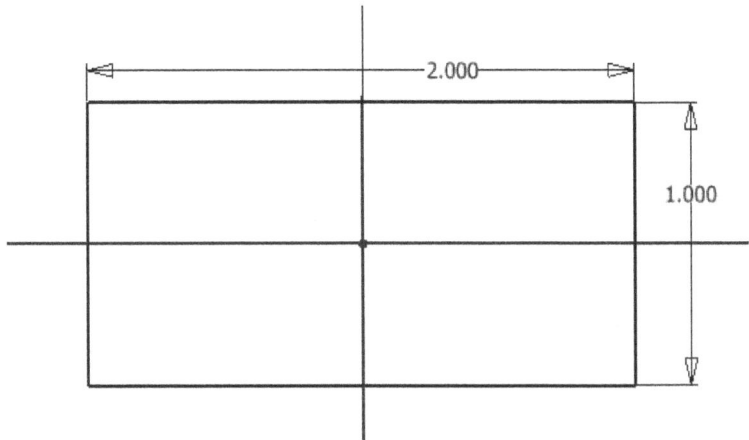

Figure 4–13

Assigning a parameter name to a dimension directly in the Edit Dimension dialog box prevents having to do so in the Parameters dialog box.

5. With the sketch still active, double-click on the 2.000 dimension and type **width = 2 in**, as shown in Figure 4–14.

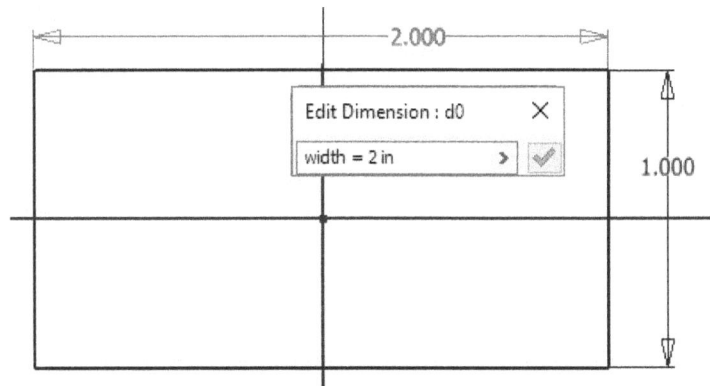

Figure 4–14

6. Double-click on the 1.000 dimension and type **depth = 1 in**.

7. Finish the sketch.

8. Extrude the rectangular sketch a distance of 0.5 inches by typing **Height = 0.5 in** as the *Distance A* value in the Extrude palette. The Extrude palette displays as shown in Figure 4–15.

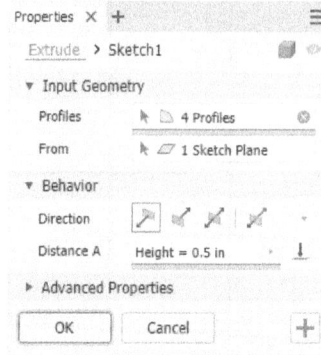

Figure 4–15

9. Complete the extrude.

10. Review the Model Browser. **Extrusion1** displays below the Origin, as it is a feature of the part. Expand the **Solid Bodies** node and note that, currently, only one Solid Body is in the model, called **Solid1**. Expand **Solid1** and **Extrusion1** displays there as well, as shown in Figure 4–16.

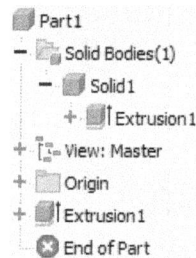

Figure 4–16

Task 2 - Create additional features in the model.

1. Create a new sketch on the surface shown in Figure 4–17.

2. Project the YZ plane.

3. Sketch the linear entity shown in Figure 4–17. Align it to the YZ work plane through the center of the model. Project any additional edges to create an enclosed section on the left-hand side of the sketch plane.

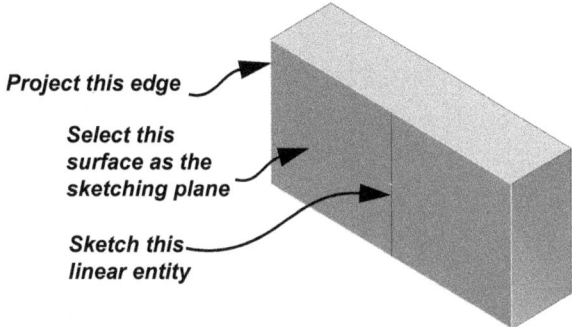

Project this edge

Select this surface as the sketching plane

Sketch this linear entity

Figure 4–17

4. Finish the sketch.

5. Create an Extrude. In the Extrude palette, click (Cut) and select the left profile to remove.

6. Set the *Distance A* value to **cutdepth=height/2**. Note that (New Solid) is not selected in the palette because this is the second feature in the model and it defaults to being a feature in the first solid body.

7. Complete the extrude.

8. Add two **.125 in** fillets to the geometry, as shown in Figure 4–18.

9. Review the Model Browser. **Extrusion2** and **Fillet1** have been added after **Extrusion1**. Expand the **Solid Bodies** node. Note that only one Solid Body, **Solid1**, is currently still in the model, and that **Extrusion2** and **Fillet1** have been added there as well. **Extrusion1**, **Extrusion2**, and **Fillet1** are all features in **Solid1**. The model and the Model Browser display as shown in Figure 4–18.

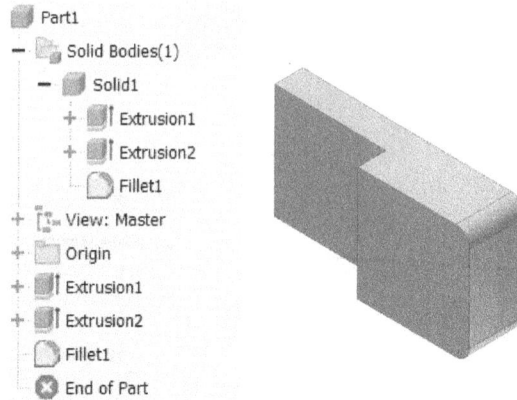

Figure 4–18

Task 3 - Review the modified parameter names.

1. Open the Parameters dialog box. The parameter names and equations that were entered during model creation are assigned in the dialog box, as shown in Figure 4–19.

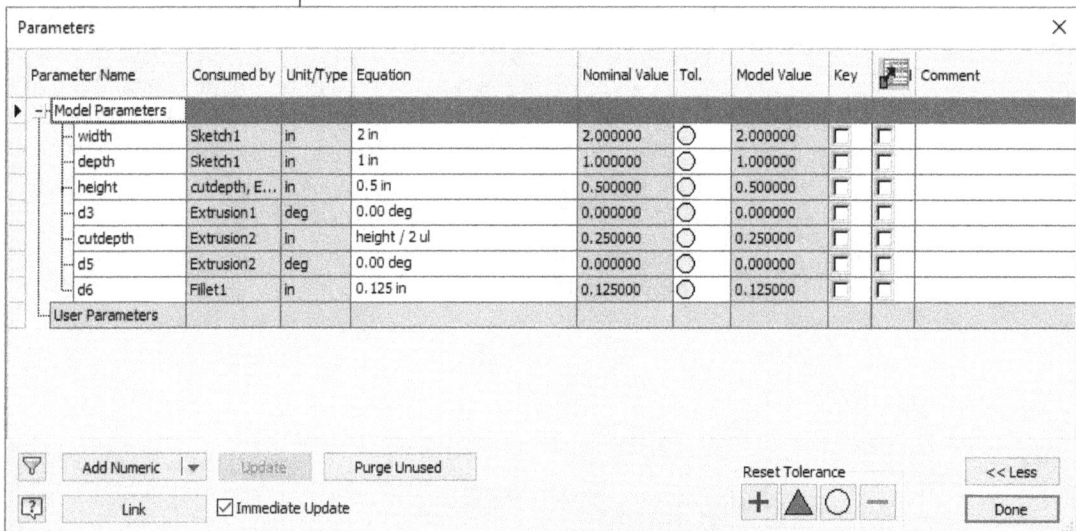

Parameter Name	Consumed by	Unit/Type	Equation	Nominal Value	Tol.	Model Value	Key		Comment
Model Parameters									
width	Sketch1	in	2 in	2.000000	○	2.000000	☐	☐	
depth	Sketch1	in	1 in	1.000000	○	1.000000	☐	☐	
height	cutdepth, E...	in	0.5 in	0.500000	○	0.500000	☐	☐	
d3	Extrusion1	deg	0.00 deg	0.000000	○	0.000000	☐	☐	
cutdepth	Extrusion2	in	height / 2 ul	0.250000	○	0.250000	☐	☐	
d5	Extrusion2	deg	0.00 deg	0.000000	○	0.000000	☐	☐	
d6	Fillet1	in	0.125 in	0.125000	○	0.125000	☐	☐	
User Parameters									

Add Numeric | ▼   Update   Purge Unused   Reset Tolerance   << Less

Link   ☑ Immediate Update   + ▲ ○ —   Done

Figure 4–19

2. Close the Parameters dialog box.

Task 4 - Create a second solid body in the model.

1. Create a 2D sketch on the lower surface of the model that was just cut away.

2. Sketch a spline similar to that shown in Figure 4–20. Project the required edges to create a closed sketch above the spline. Ensure that the spline and projected edges are constrained as **Coincident**.

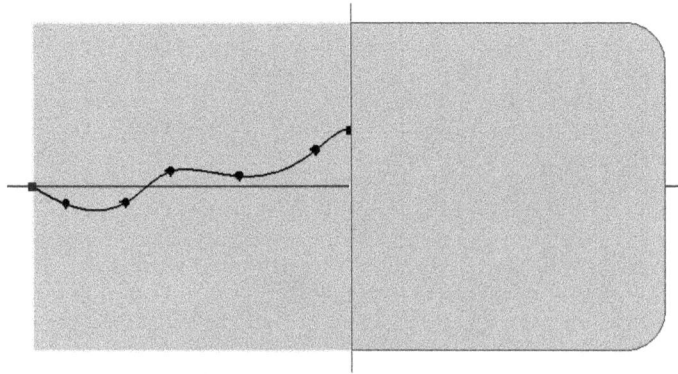

Figure 4–20

3. Once complete, click ✓. Once the spline is complete, points display on each spline point to enable you to edit the spline in the sketch.

4. Select the points and manipulate the shape of the spline. Do not worry about dimensioning the sketch.

5. Finish the sketch.

6. Create an Extrude. Select the upper section of the sketch as the section to extrude.

7. In the Extrude palette, click ▣⁺ (New Solid) to create the extrude feature as a separate solid body.

8. Set the *Distance A* value to **height**. This creates a relationship between the two features.

9. Complete the feature.

10. Review the Model Browser. **Extrusion3** has been added after **Fillet1**. Expand the **Solid Bodies** node and note that two Solid Bodies are now in the model. **Extrusion1**, **Extrusion2**, and **Fillet1** are all features in **Solid1**, and **Extrusion3** is in **Solid2**. A re-oriented version of the model and the Model Browser display as shown in Figure 4–21.

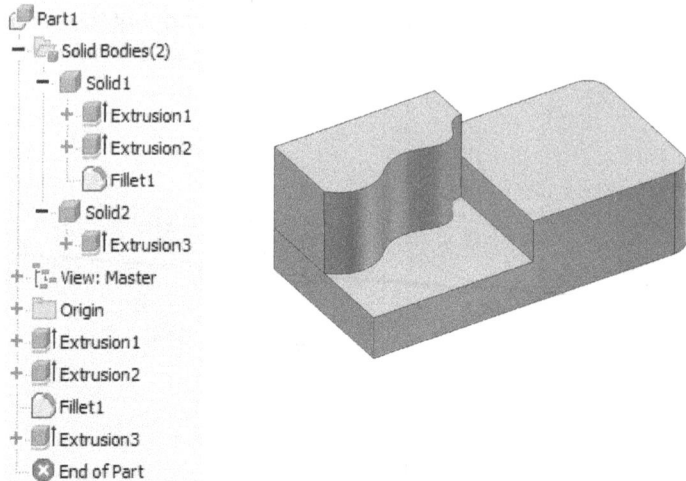

Figure 4–21

Task 5 - Modify the properties of a solid body.

---

1. In the Model Browser, right-click on **Solid2** (under the **Solid Bodies** node) and select **Properties**.

You can assign a new name to the solid body in the Body Properties dialog box.

2. In the Body Appearance drop-down list, select **Blue - Wall Paint - Glossy** to change the color of **Solid2**.

3. Click **Update** to update the mass, area, and volume of this single body.

4. Click **OK** to close the Body Properties dialog box.

Task 6 - Add features to the solid bodies.

1. Create a Fillet on the edges shown in Figure 4–22. The two edges are from different solid bodies. Keep the default **.125 in** value as the radius for the fillets.

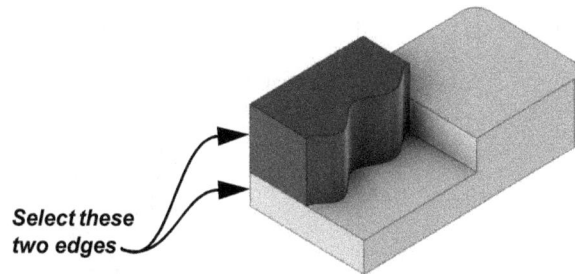

Select these
two edges

Figure 4–22

2. Complete the feature.

3. Review the Model Browser. **Fillet2** has been added after **Extrusion3**, as well as to both of the solid bodies. A re-oriented version of the model and the Model Browser display as shown in Figure 4–23. The benefit of having them created together is that if the value changes, both update. If you want them separated, you must create them as separate features.

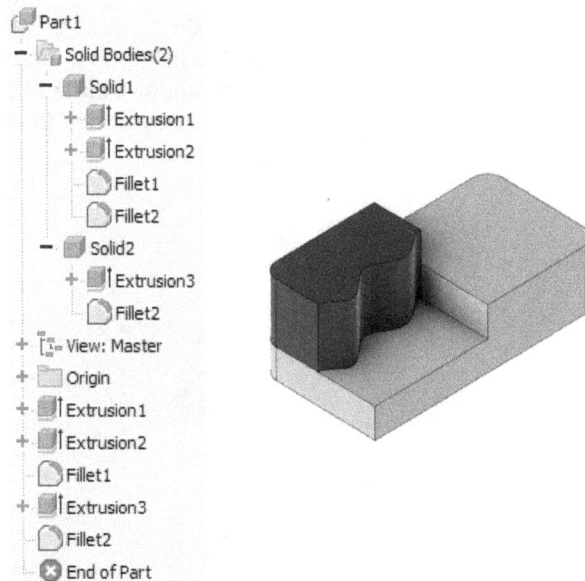

Figure 4–23

4. Re-orient the model to display the bottom of the model, as shown in Figure 4–24.

5. Create a sketch on the bottom surface and create three points at the centers of the fillets, as shown in Figure 4–24.

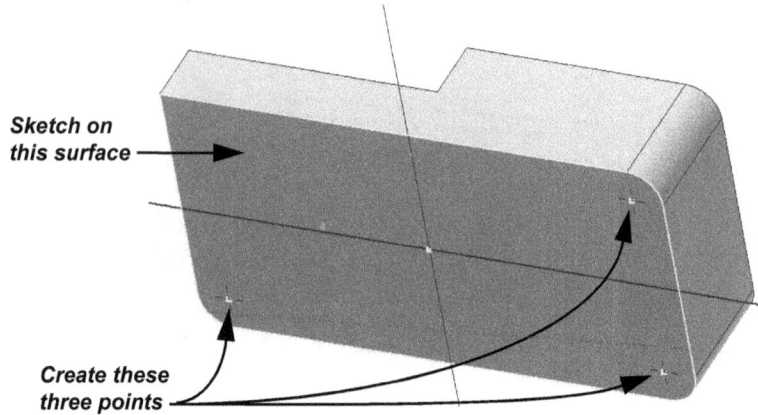

Sketch on this surface

Create these three points

Figure 4–24

6. Complete the sketch.

7. Create holes at all three points. Set the *Termination* to **Through All** and type **.125 in** for the *Diameter*.

8. Complete the feature.

9. Rotate the model, as shown in Figure 4–25, and note that the holes extrude through all of **Solid1** but not through **Solid2**. **Hole1** is listed as a feature in the Model Browser and a feature under **Solid1** in the **Solid Bodies** node. A feature is automatically added to the body from which the sketch plane is selected.

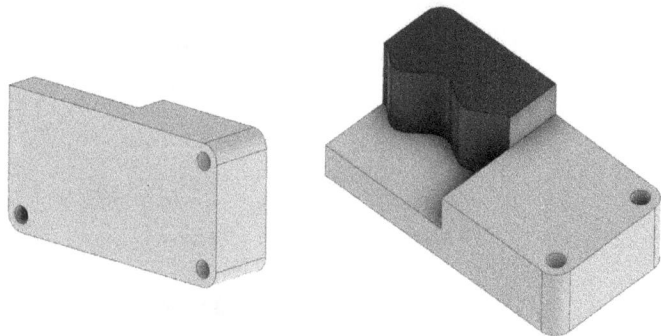

Figure 4–25

10. Double-click on **Hole1** in either location in the Model Browser to edit the hole.

11. In the Hole palette, click in the *Solids* field to activate it, and then select **Solid2** to include the holes as part of this solid body. All sketched features enable you to assign the feature to multiple bodies.

12. Complete the feature. The holes now extrude through both solid bodies, as shown in Figure 4–26.

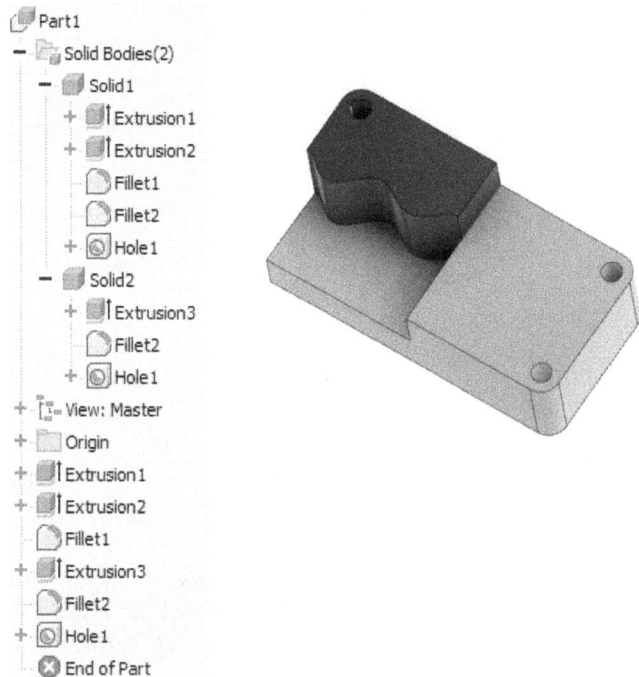

Figure 4–26

13. Save the model as **solid body practice.ipt**.

Task 7 - Extract the solid bodies to create two new part files.

1. In the *Manage* tab>Layout panel, click (Make Components).

   • When creating more than one component from a multi-body, the **Make Components** command, with the **Insert components in target assembly** option cleared, can be more efficient than using the **Make Part** command multiple times.

*Alternatively, you can select both **Solid1** and **Solid2** in the Model Browser, right-click, and select **Make Components**.*

2. In the Model Browser, in the **Solid Bodies** node, select **Solid1** and **Solid2**.

3. Clear the **Insert components in target assembly** option. The Make Components: Selection dialog box displays as shown in Figure 4–27.

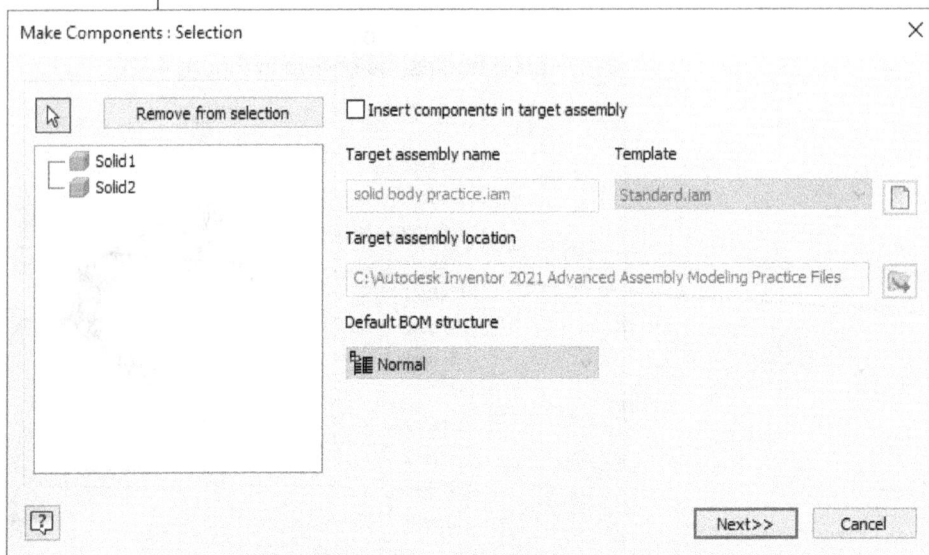

Make Components : Selection   ✕

Remove from selection   ☐ Insert components in target assembly

Solid1
Solid2

Target assembly name   Template

solid body practice.iam   Standard.iam

Target assembly location

C:\Autodesk Inventor 2021 Advanced Assembly Modeling Practice Files

Default BOM structure

▤ Normal

Next>>   Cancel

Figure 4–27

4. Click **Next**.

5. In the Make Components: Bodies dialog box, select **Solid1.ipt** and modify the *Component Name* to **Solid_Practice_1.ipt**.

6. Modify the name of *Solid2* to **Solid_Practice_2.ipt**.

7. In the *Solid1* row, select **Standard.ipt** and click ▭.

8. Select the **Standard (in).ipt** template and click **OK**.

9. Ensure that **Solid2** is also using the **Standard (in).ipt** template. The dialog box displays as shown in Figure 4–28. Click **OK**.

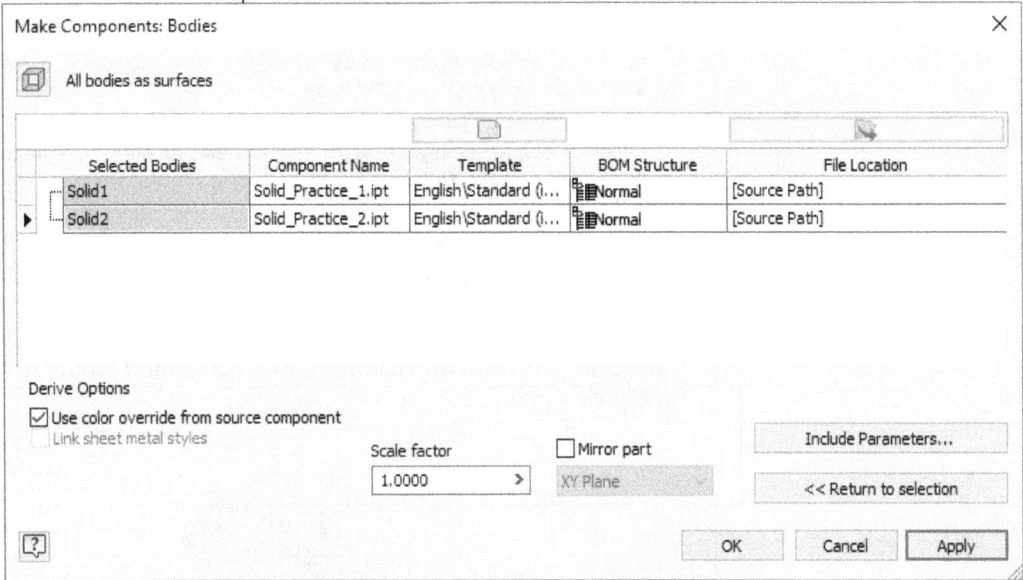

	Selected Bodies	Component Name	Template	BOM Structure	File Location
	Solid1	Solid_Practice_1.ipt	English\Standard (i...	Normal	[Source Path]
▶	Solid2	Solid_Practice_2.ipt	English\Standard (i...	Normal	[Source Path]

Make Components: Bodies

All bodies as surfaces

Derive Options
☑ Use color override from source component
☐ Link sheet metal styles

Scale factor 1.0000 >

☐ Mirror part XY Plane

Include Parameters...

<< Return to selection

OK   Cancel   Apply

Figure 4–28

10. Save the changes to **Solid_Practice_1.ipt** and its dependents.

11. Open both **Solid_Practice_1.ipt** and **Solid_Practice_2.ipt** and review the results.

Task 8 - Modify reference part file.

1. Activate the **solid body practice.ipt** window.

2. Modify the **Height** parameter to **1** using the Parameters dialog box or by editing the dimensions associated with **Extrusion1**. Changes to both **Solid1** and **Solid2** are due to the relationships that you set while entering the original values for the features.

3. Activate the **Solid_Practice_1.ipt** window.

4. In the Quick Access Toolbar, click ⬚ (Update) to update the model with the changes.

5. Activate and update **Solid_Practice_2.ipt**.

6. Save and close all part files.

Practice 4b | Derive Multi-Body Parts

Practice Objectives

- Create solid bodies in a part by deriving them from external parts.
- Modify the location of solid bodies in a single part, and combine multiple solid bodies into a single solid body.
- Create a new part file by extracting a solid body from another part.
- Create a new assembly file, along with its new part files, by extracting solid bodies from a single part.

In this practice, you will add solid bodies to a part by deriving the bodies from other parts. You will also learn to move and combine existing bodies in a multi-body part. To complete the practice, you will extract solid bodies from the multi-body part to create separate parts and an assembly. The completed model is shown in Figure 4–29.

Figure 4–29

Task 1 - Open part files.

1. Open **Full_Body_10.ipt**. Expand the **Solid Bodies** node and note that the file contains four solid bodies.

2. Open **Guide_Bracket_10.ipt**. Expand the **Solid Bodies** node and note that the file contains two solid bodies.

Task 2 - Change solid body names.

1. With the **Guide_Bracket_10.ipt** model still active, right-click
   on **Solid1** under the **Solid Bodies** node of the Model
   Browser, and select **Properties**.

2. In the Body Properties dialog box, change the *Name* of
   Solid1 to **Mounting Holes**, as shown in Figure 4–30.

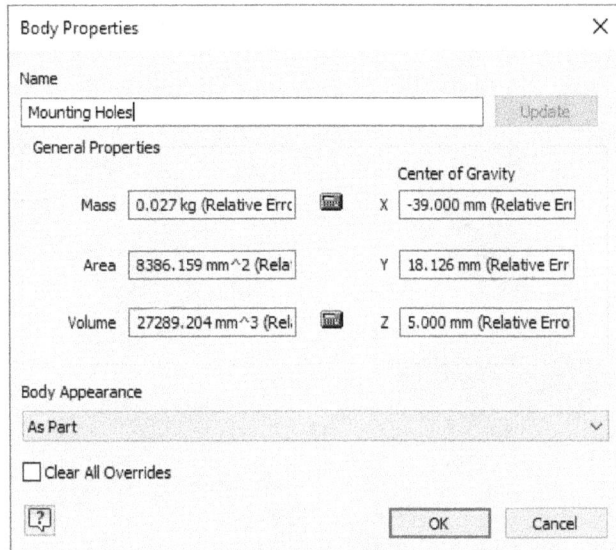

Figure 4–30

3. Click **OK**.

4. Right-click on **Solid2** under the **Solid Bodies** node of the
   Model Browser, and select **Properties**. Rename the solid
   body as **Groove Wall**.

5. Save and close **Guide_Bracket_10.ipt**.

Task 3 - Derive solid bodies from external part files.

1. Ensure that **Full_Body_10.ipt** is active.

2. In the *Manage* tab>Insert panel, click (Derive).

3. In the Open dialog box, select **Guide_Bracket_10.ipt** and click **Open**. The Derived Part dialog box opens as shown in Figure 4–31.

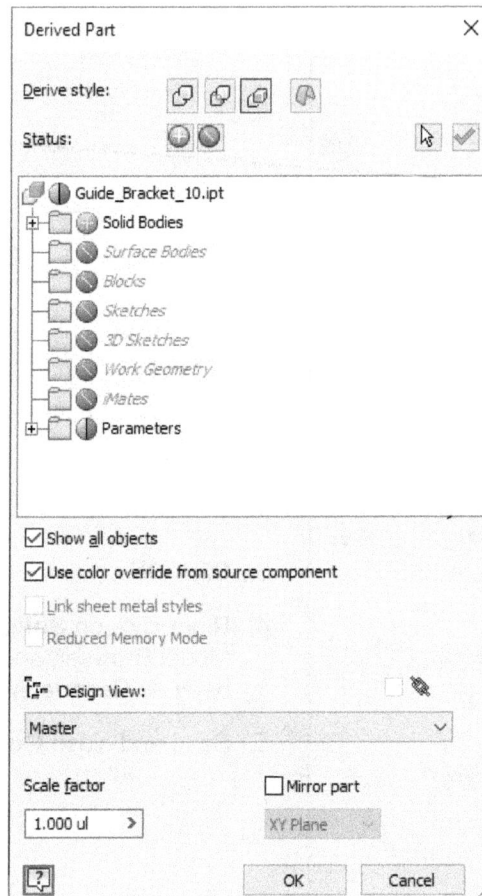

Figure 4–31

4. Verify that ⬚ (Maintain each solid as a solid body) is selected and accept all other defaults. Click **OK**.

5. Rotate the model to the position shown in Figure 4–32.

Figure 4–32

6. Review the solid bodies in the Model Browser. The part now contains six multi-bodies, four from the original model and two from the derived part.

7. Expand the two new solid bodies in the Model Browser. The descriptions indicate the name of the original solid body, as well as the part file name from which it was derived. The derived part is also listed at the bottom of the Model Browser.

8. Change the names of these two new solid bodies to **Mount** and **Wall**.

Task 4 - Move bodies.

---

1. In the *3D Model* tab>expanded Modify panel, click ⬚ (Move Bodies). The Move Bodies dialog box opens.

2. Select both solid bodies, **Mount** and **Wall**. You must click

   ⬚ (Bodies) again after you select the first body in order to select the second body.

3. Set the *X Offset* to **-68 mm**, the *Y Offset* to **2 mm,** and the *Z Offset* to **0 mm**.

4. Select **Click to add** and click (Free drag) in the new row.

   Select (Rotate about line) in the drop-down list, as shown in Figure 4–33.

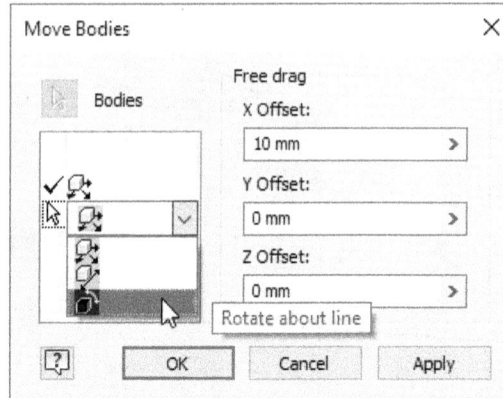

Figure 4–33

5. Select the edge shown in Figure 4–34 for the *Rotate Axis*. Change the *Angle* to **-90** and click **OK**.

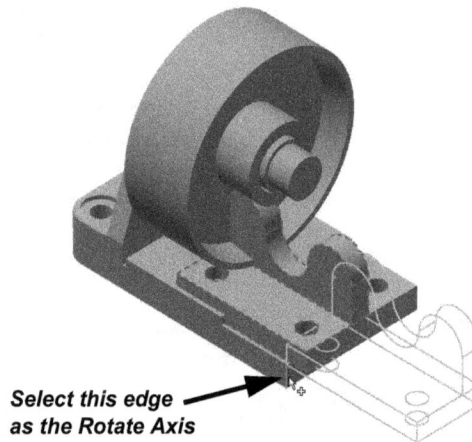

Select this edge as the Rotate Axis

Figure 4–34

*To edit the Move Body feature, right-click on it and select **Edit feature**.*

6. The **Move Body** feature is now listed at the bottom of the Model Browser and in both the **Mount** and **Wall** solid bodies. The model displays as shown in Figure 4–35.

Figure 4–35

Task 5 - Combine bodies.

---

1. In the *3D Model* tab>Modify panel, click (Combine). The Combine Body dialog box opens.

2. Select **Mount** as the *Base* reference and **Wall** as the *Toolbody* reference.

3. Ensure that the **Keep Toolbody** option is not selected and click **OK**.

4. The **Combine** feature is now listed at the bottom of the Model Browser and in the **Mount** solid body. The **Wall** solid body has been consumed by **Mount**.

5. Save **Full_Body_10.ipt**.

Task 6 - Extract a new separate part from a solid body.

---

1. In the *Manage* tab>Layout panel, click (Make Part). The Make Part dialog box opens.

2. Click (Single solid body merging out seams between planar faces) as the *Derive style* at the top of the dialog box.

3. Expand the **Solid Bodies** node. Click ⊚ next to **Solid1**, **Solid2**, and **Mount** to include the body in the new derived part. The icons adjacent to these bodies update to ⊚.

4. Type **Whole_Base** for the *Part name* and set the *Template* to **Standard (in).ipt**.

5. Clear the **Place part in target assembly** option.

6. Keep all other defaults. The Make Part dialog box opens as shown in Figure 4–36.

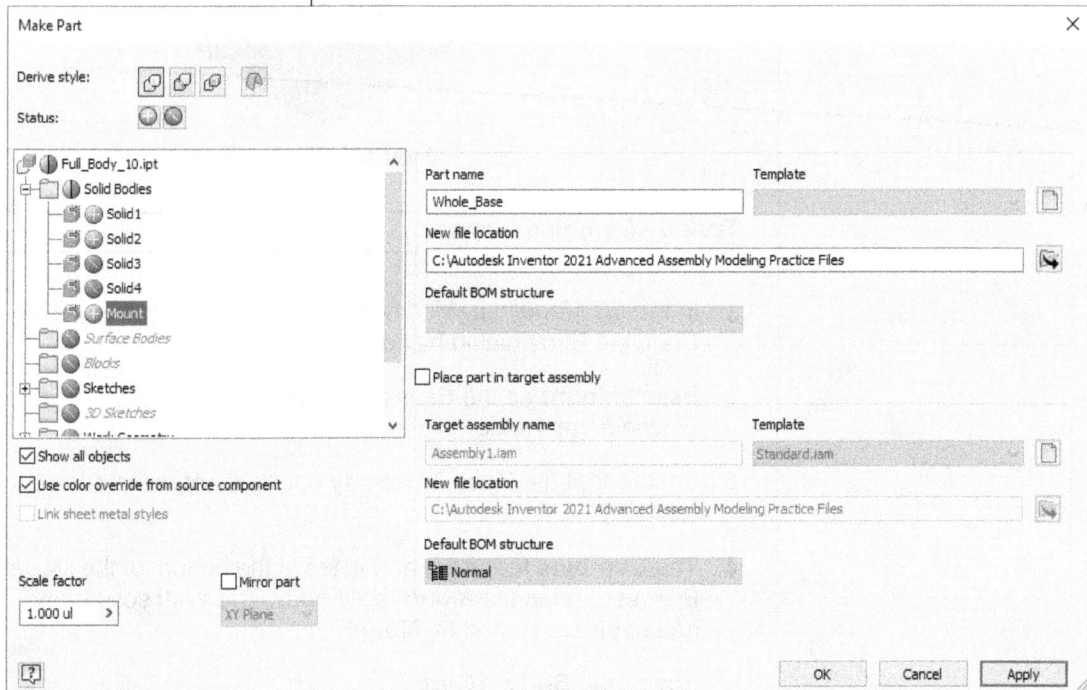

Figure 4–36

7. Click **OK** to complete the command. If you are prompted with a warning about saving a file, click **OK**. The resulting part file opens, containing a single solid body, as shown in Figure 4–37.

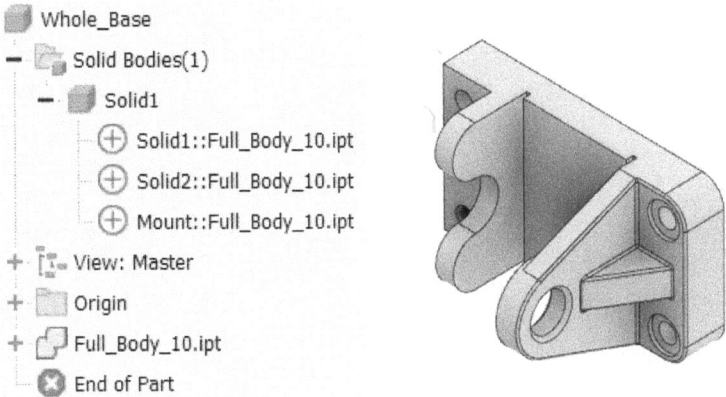

Whole_Base
— Solid Bodies(1)
  — Solid1
    ⊕ Solid1::Full_Body_10.ipt
    ⊕ Solid2::Full_Body_10.ipt
    ⊕ Mount::Full_Body_10.ipt
  + View: Master
  + Origin
  + Full_Body_10.ipt
  ⊗ End of Part

Figure 4–37

8. Save and close **Whole_Base.ipt**.

Task 7 - Make an assembly with parts.

---

1. Activate the **Full_Body_10.ipt** window if it is not already active.

2. In the *Manage* tab>Layout panel, click ⬚ (Make Components). The Make Components: Selection dialog box opens.

*Alternatively, you can select all the solid bodies in the Model Browser, right-click, and select **Make Components**.*

3. Select all solid bodies in the Model Browser from **Full_Body_10.ipt**.

4. Set the template to **Standard (in).iam**.

5. Ensure that the **Insert components in target assembly** option is selected. The dialog box opens as shown in Figure 4–38.

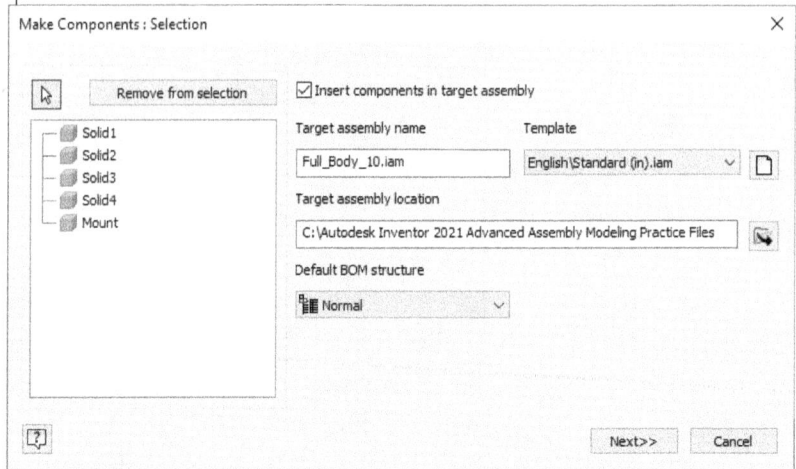

Figure 4–38

6. Click **Next**. The Make Components: Bodies dialog box opens.

7. In the *Component Name* column, the name of the part is the same as the selected solid body name, as shown in Figure 4–39. These can be changed if required. For this practice, you can leave the default names.

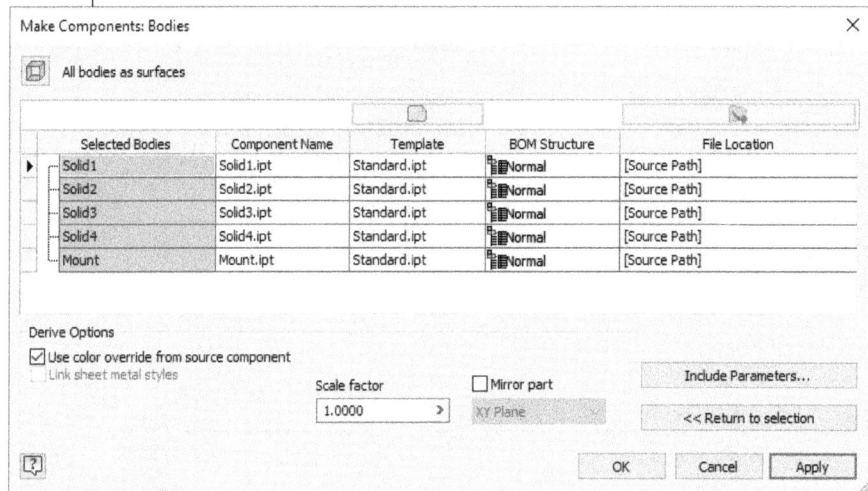

Figure 4–39

8. Click **OK** without making any changes in the Make Components: Bodies dialog box. A new assembly called **Full_Body_10.iam** with five parts is created. The part names are based on the solid body names, as shown in Figure 4–40. Each of these parts are initially grounded. You can unground components and constrain them as required.

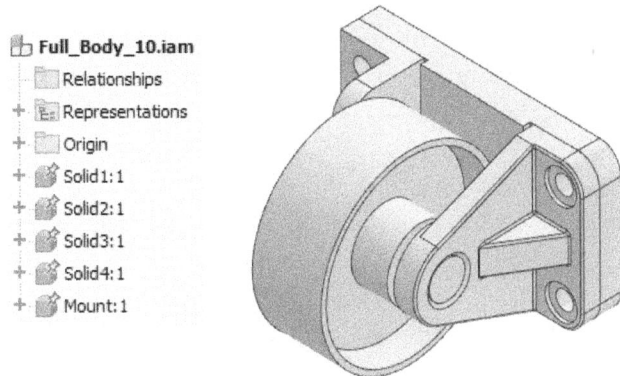

Figure 4–40

9. Save and close all files.

Chapter Review Questions

1. Multi-body part design requires the use of an assembly. Parts are created within the context of the assembly.

   a. True

   b. False

2. How are the second and any subsequent solid bodies created in a model?

   a. Explicitly set a new feature to be created as a new solid body.

   b. Each new feature is automatically added as a new solid body.

   c. Use specific solid body commands in the ribbon prior to creating the feature.

   d. None of the above.

3. Which of the following buttons/fields is used in the Extrude palette to ensure that an extruded cut extrudes through multiple solid bodies?

   a.

   b.

   c. *Distance A* (**Through All** option)

   d. *Solids*

4. A single Fillet feature has been added to a model that currently has three solid bodies. An edge from each of the three solid bodies was selected as placement references. Which of the following statements is true regarding the model?

   a. A fourth solid body will be added to the model.

   b. The Fillet feature will be added to the solid body in which the first reference edge belongs.

   c. The Fillet feature will be added to each of the three solid bodies.

   d. The Fillet feature will cause the three solid bodies to combine into one.

5. Match the Move Body operation type in the left column with its symbol in the right column.

Answer

a. Rotate about line _____

b. Free drag _____

c. Move along ray _____

6. Which of the following can be used as the split tool when splitting a solid body? (Select all that apply.)

a. Work Plane

b. Face

c. Sketch

d. Edge

7. Which solid body manipulation option enables you to create a single solid body from two solid bodies?

a. Union

b. Combine

c. Extrude

d. Split

8. Which of the following derive styles enables you to create a single solid body when using the **Make Part** command?

1   2   3

a. 1, 2, and 3

b. 1 and 2

c. 2 and 3

d. 1 and 3

Command Summary

Button	Command	Location
	Combine	• **Ribbon**: *3D Model* tab>Modify panel
	Derive	• **Ribbon**: *Manage* tab>Insert panel
	Make Components	• **Ribbon**: *Manage* tab>Layout panel
	Make Part	• **Ribbon**: *Manage* tab>Layout panel
	Move Bodies	• **Ribbon**: *3D Model* tab>Modify panel
	Split	• **Ribbon**: *3D Model* tab>Modify panel

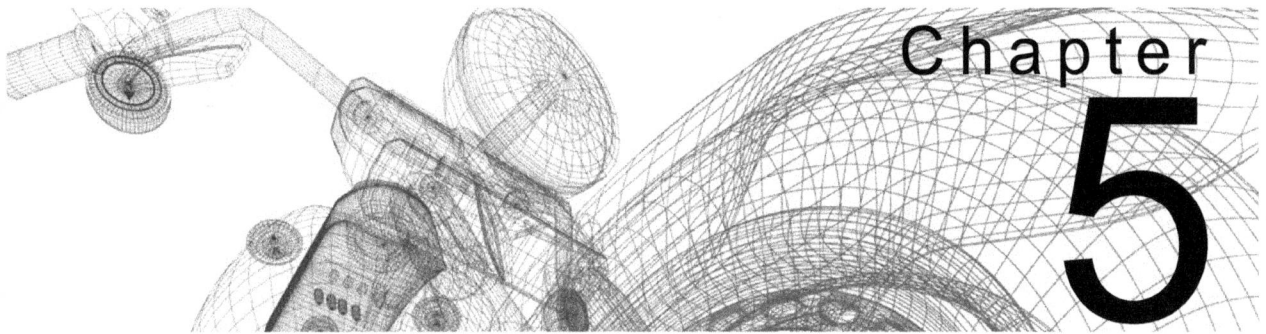

Layout Design

Layout Design is a top-down design tool. It can be used to convey a model's design intent (i.e., layout) using a 2D sketch. From the sketch, you can generate 3D models. Any changes made to the sketch update in the 3D models.

Learning Objectives in This Chapter

- Quickly convey the design intent of a model by creating and modifying layouts and sketch blocks.
- Define and test the kinematic motion of an assembly with the use of nested sketch blocks.
- Create 3D models from sketch blocks.

5.1 Layout Design

A layout is a top-down design tool that can be used to quickly convey the design intent of a model. A layout is a 2D sketch, as shown on the left in Figure 5–1, that provides a central repository for overall dimensions, spatial locations, and the general shape of components in a design. By generating 3D models based on the layout, as shown on the right in Figure 5–1, changes made to the layout are updated in the 3D models. This ensures that changes in design are accurately propagated to the entire assembly. Layouts can also be useful when working with a mechanized assembly. Through a layout, you can quickly define and test the kinematics of an assembly.

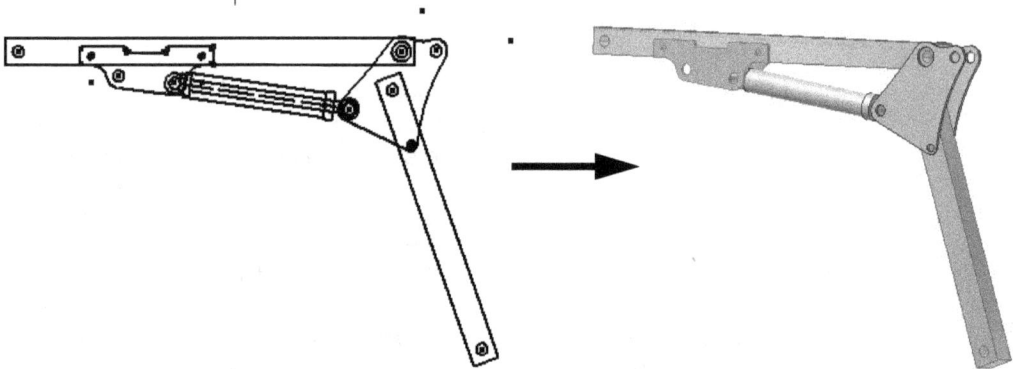

Figure 5–1

General Steps

Use the following general steps to create a layout.

1. Create a layout.
2. Define sketch blocks.
3. Make parts and components.

Step 1 - Create a layout.

You can create a layout in a part or an assembly file. To create a layout as a part file, create an empty part and define a 2D sketch as the layout. The layout is saved in the standard part file.

To create a layout in an assembly, click $\boxed{}$ (Make Layout) (*Assemble* tab>expanded Component panel). The layout is automatically added to the active assembly as a grounded component, as shown in Figure 5–2. A new standard part file is generated.

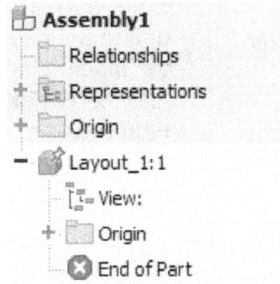

Figure 5–2

- All layout geometry must be created in the 2D Sketch environment. Create the sketch on one of the three Origin planes and add the entities required to represent the block.

Step 2 - Define sketch blocks.

An AutoCAD block can be translated into an Autodesk ®Inventor® sketch block.

A sketch block is a grouping of 2D geometry in the layout that represents a particular portion of the assembly (typically a component or a subassembly). You define each component in an assembly as a separate sketch block. You can then create sketch blocks that contain other sketch blocks (nested sketch blocks) to define subassemblies.

You must be in the Sketch environment to create a sketch block and the Layout panel must be displayed.

To create a sketch block, select the 2D entities that make up the sketch block. In the *Sketch* contextual tab>Layout panel, click

You can also select the geometry that makes up the sketch block after

clicking (Create Block).

(Create Block). The Create Block dialog box is shown in Figure 5–3.

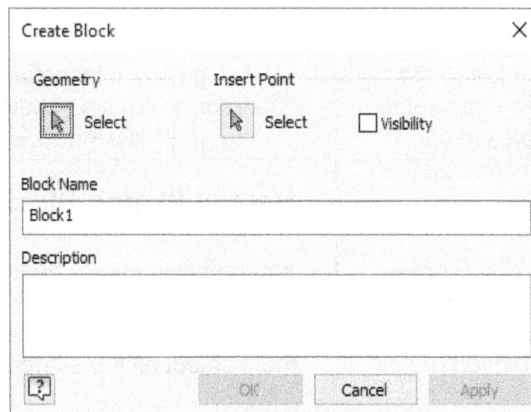

Figure 5–3

By default, the insert point is the center of the sketch block.

Enter a meaningful name for the sketch block and, if required, define an insert point and add a description. Click **OK** to create the block. Once created, the block is added to both the **Sketch** and the **Blocks** nodes of the Model Browser, as shown in Figure 5–4.

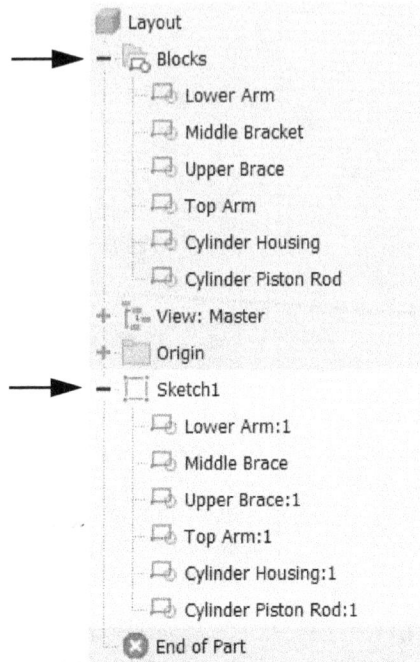

Figure 5–4

- Once defined, you can add constraints and dimensions between sketch blocks to locate the them relative to each other. These constraints are converted into assembly constraints when 3D components are generated.

Changes made to the geometry in one sketch block updates in all instances of the sketch block.

- To add multiple instances of a sketch block to your layout, drag the existing sketch block from the Model Browser into the graphic window.

Nested Sketch Blocks

Nested Sketch Blocks are useful when defining and testing the kinematic motion of an assembly.

You can also create nested sketch blocks that become subassemblies when the 3D models are generated. To create a nested sketch block, create the sketch blocks first, then multi-select all the sketch blocks you want to nest and click

 (Create Block).

The nested sketch block displays in the Model tree, as shown in Figure 5–5.

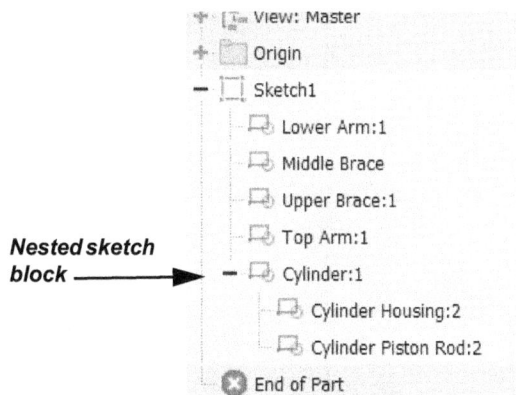

Figure 5–5

- By default, nested sketch blocks move together. Once the nested sketch block is created, right-click on it and ensure that the **Flexible** option is activated so that the blocks are able to move relative to each other to simulate kinematic motion.

Editing Sketch Blocks

Use the following methods to edit an existing sketch block:

- To add new geometry to an existing sketch block, double-click on the sketch block in the Model Browser to activate it. All geometry created is then automatically added to the active sketch block.

- To add existing geometry to an existing sketch block, double-click on the sketch block to activate it, select the geometry to add, then right-click and select **Add to Block**.

- To modify the name, insert point, or description of an existing sketch block, double-click on the sketch block to activate it. Click anywhere in the graphic window to ensure that no geometry is selected, right-click, and select **Block Properties**.

- To define the properties of a sketch block, right-click on the sketch block and select **Properties**. The Geometry Properties dialog box displays, as shown in Figure 5–6. You can define the color, line weight, and line type.

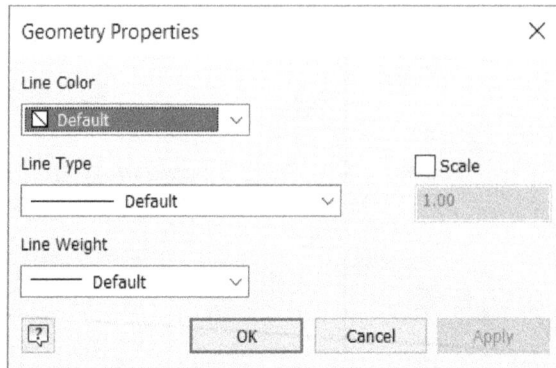

Figure 5–6

Step 3 - Make parts and components.

Using the **Make Part** and **Make Components** commands, you can quickly create 3D models from sketch blocks. The components remain associative to the layout. When changes are made to 2D sketch blocks, the 3D models also update.

Make Part

Use the **Make Part** command to create a single part file from one or more selected sketch blocks.

How To: Create a Part from a Sketch Block

You can also access the Make Part command in the Manage tab>Layout panel.

1. In the *Sketch* contextual tab>Layout panel, click ⬚ (Make Part). Alternatively, you can select the blocks to be used in the Model Browser, right-click, and select **Make Part**. The Make Part dialog box opens.
2. Set the *Derive style* option. The options are the same as those used for the **Derive** command.
3. Select the sketch block from the **Sketches>Sketch** node in the tree, as shown in Figure 5–7. Alternatively, you can select the sketch blocks before activating the command.

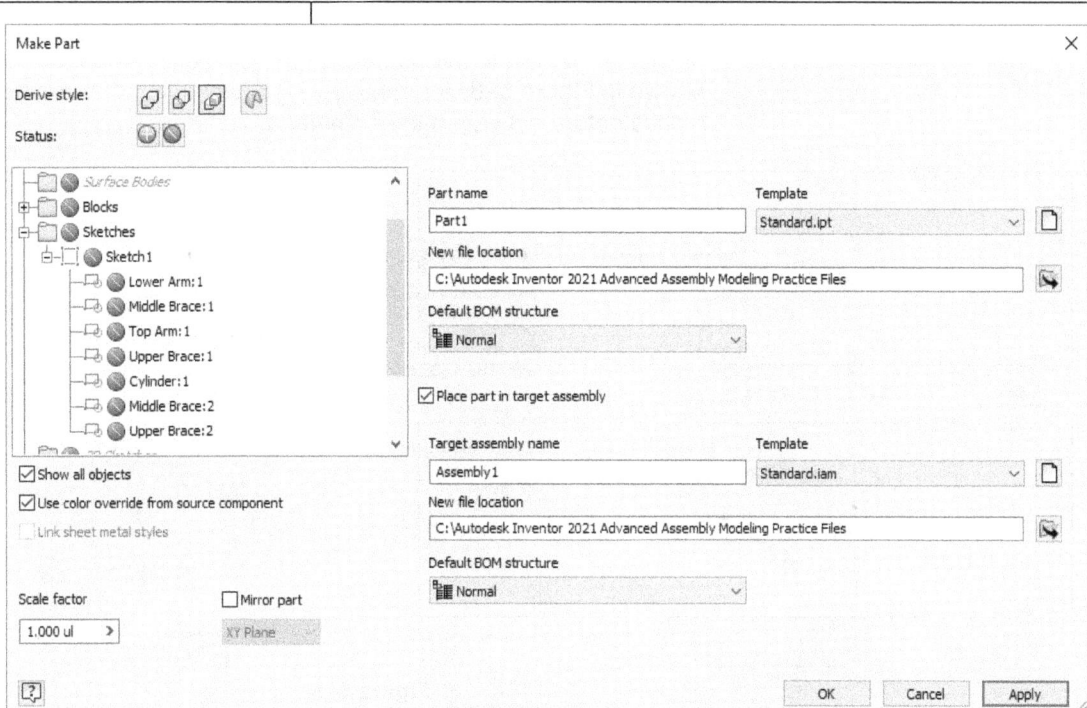

Figure 5–7

- The Make Part dialog box behaves similarly to the Derived Part dialog box; however, instead of adding the derived part into the active file, you create the derived part from the active file.

- Use the Make Part dialog box to define the part and, if required, the target assembly information. You can insert the part into an existing assembly or create a new target assembly.

4. Click **OK** to generate the model. The position of the generated component is based on the position of the source part relative to the part origin.

Make Components

The **Make Components** command creates multiple parts and assemblies in one operation.

How To: Create Multiple Components from Sketch Blocks

*You can also access the **Make Components** command in the Manage tab>Layout panel.*

1. In the *Sketch* contextual tab>Layout panel, click (Make Components). Alternatively, you can select the blocks to be used in the Model Browser, right-click, and select **Make Components**. The Make Components: Selection dialog box opens.

---

2. Select the sketch block(s) from the Model Browser. The blocks are added to the Make Components dialog box, as shown in Figure 5–8. Alternatively, you can select the sketch blocks before activating the command.

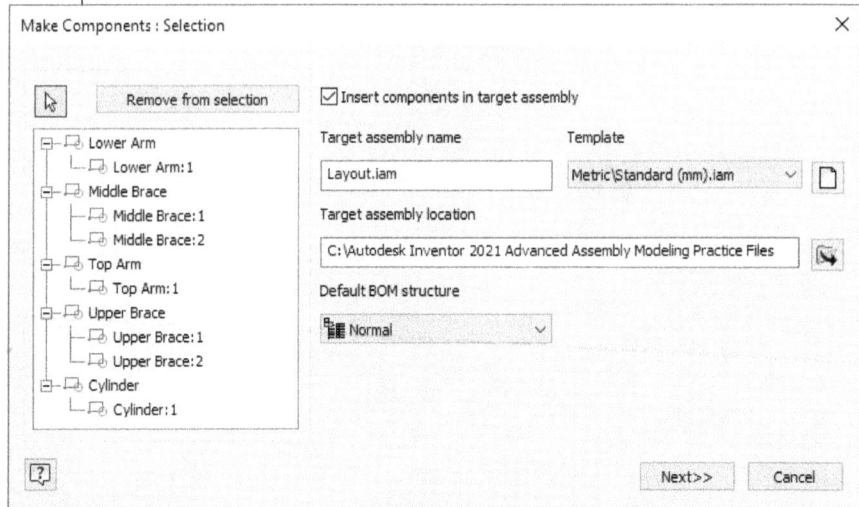

Figure 5–8

3. Specify the *Target assembly name* and *location* and click **Next**. The Make Components: Blocks dialog box opens, as shown in Figure 5–9. The dialog box lists each selected sketch block and provides information about the component it is going to generate.

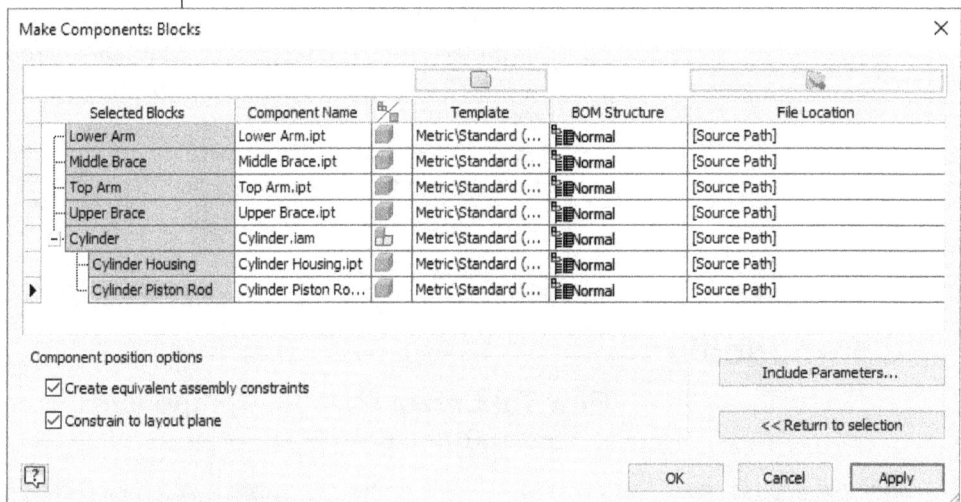

Figure 5–9

- You can change the information in the *Component Name*, *Template*, *BOM Structure*, or *File Location* columns of any of the components by clicking inside the appropriate cell.
- By default, all constraints created between sketch blocks are translated into assembly constraints. If you do not want to generate the assembly constraints, clear the **Create equivalent assembly constraints** option.

4. Click **OK** to generate the target assembly and the components.

- The first component in the new assembly is the Layout part. This part is grounded, as shown in Figure 5–10. Each sketch block is added to the assembly as a component.

- Any sketch constraints added between blocks are translated into assembly constraints between the 3D components and are shown in the Model Browser. The constraints might be active or suppressed, depending on the sketch constraints that were created in the Layout. A fourth Z Angle constraint is created and suppressed. When the **Constrain to layout plane** option is cleared, the XY Flush constraint is suppressed and the Z Angle constraint is activated.

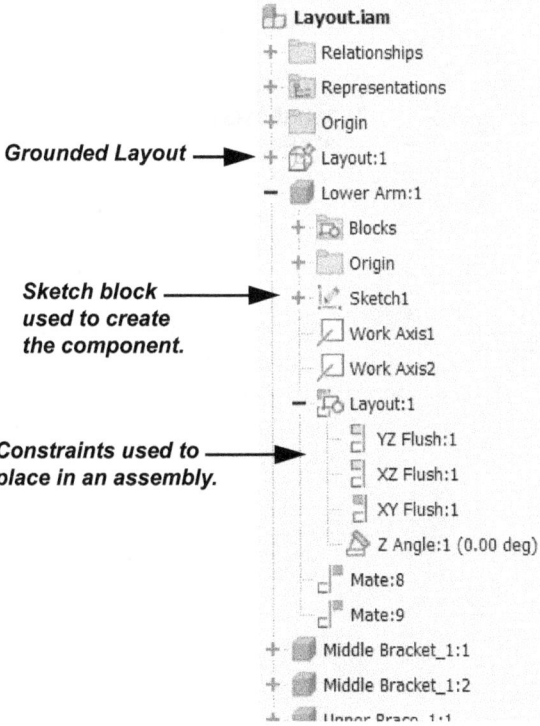

Figure 5–10

- Components remain associative to the layout. If a dimensional constraint in the Layout changes, it updates in the assembly. However, if you change a geometric constraint (i.e., add, remove, or modify), it does not update in the assembly. To update these changes, you must reapply the **Make Components** command on the affected components.

Changing Component Position

By default, all components are created along the Z-axis (the layout plane). You can offset the components from the layout plane once the components have been generated. To change the position of a component, consider the following:

- Use ⬚ (Free Move) and ⬚ (Free Rotate) in the *Assemble* tab>Position panel to freely move and rotate components along the X, Y, or Z axis. Alternatively, you can right-click on the component in the Model Browser to access the options. Select the command followed by the component and relocate it as required. These commands do not permanently reposition the components. Click ⬚ (Local Update) to update the assembly to return the component to their original location.

- To change the position of a component relative to the XY plane, you must change the offset value associated with the XYFlush constraint for the component. Select it and enter a value at the bottom of the Model Browser. To change component positions in the XZ and YZ planes you must unsuppress their Flush constraints, select them, and enter offset values at the bottom of the Model Browser.

- All constraints that are created by default between components are created based on the constraints in the layout sketch. These constraints can be deleted and new constraints established, as required, to reposition components in the assembly.

Practice 5a | Layout Design

Practice Objectives

- Create multiple sketch blocks and nested sketch blocks.
- Constrain multiple sketch blocks to one another.
- Generate components and an assembly from existing sketch blocks in a layout, and convert them to 3D solid geometry.

In this practice, you will create a layout that is used to generate the assembly shown in Figure 5–11. You will use the layout to control both dimensional and positional changes.

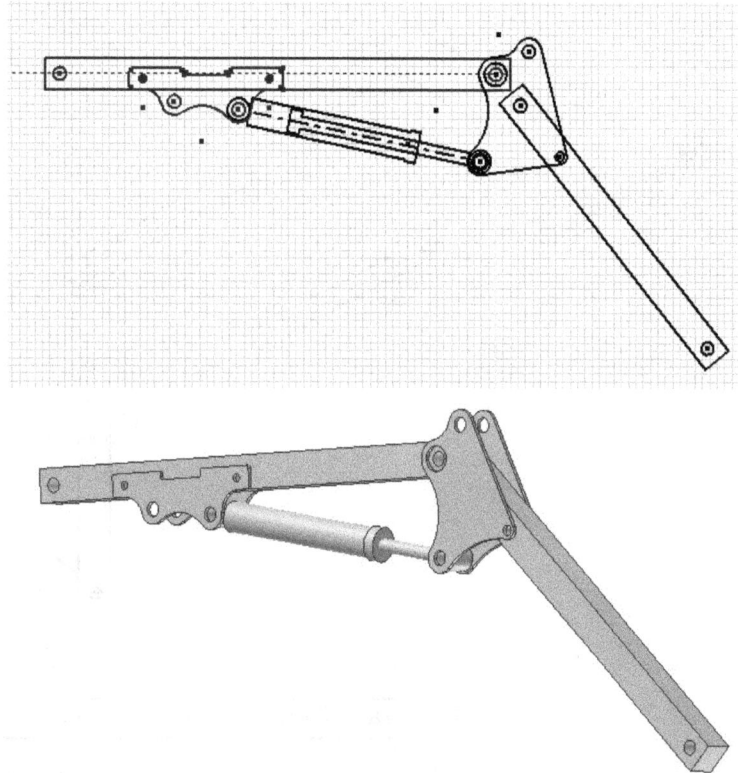

Figure 5–11

Task 1 - Open a layout.

1. Open **Layout.ipt**. The model displays as shown in Figure 5–12. The sketched geometry has already been created. Note that it has all been created in a single sketch. In the next task, you will edit the sketch and generate sketch blocks.

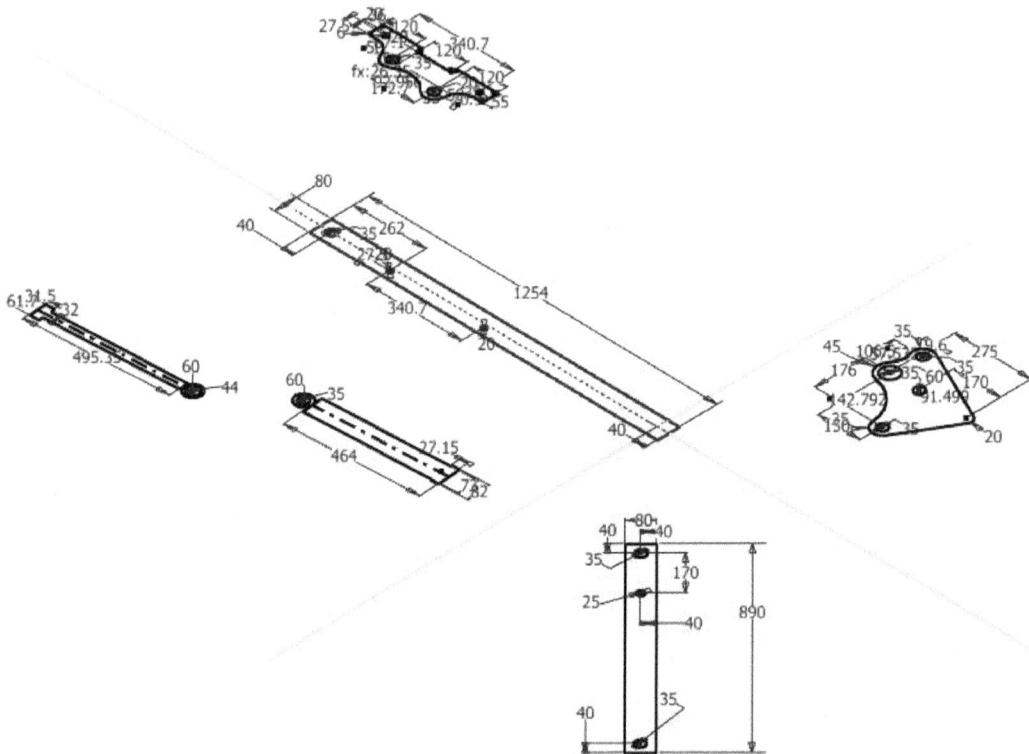

Figure 5–12

Task 2 - Create sketch blocks.

1. Double-click on **Sketch1** to edit it.

2. Reorient the sketch to **Front**, if it is not already done.

3. Right-click anywhere on the ribbon and select **Show Panels> Layout** to add the Layout panel to the ribbon, if not already displayed.

4. Select the geometry shown in Figure 5–13.

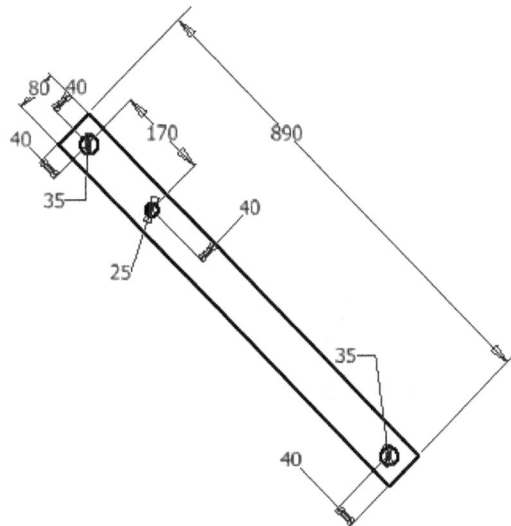

Figure 5–13

5. In the Layout panel, click ⌖ (Create Block).

6. Type **Lower Arm** in the *Block Name* field and click **OK**. The **Lower Arm** sketch block is added to both the **Blocks** and **Sketch1** nodes of the Model Browser, as shown in Figure 5–14.

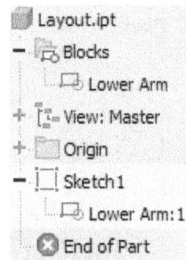

Figure 5–14

7. Note the dimensions associated with the newly created block have disappeared from the screen. Select and drag the **Lower Arm** sketch block. All geometry that makes up the sketch block moves as a single entity.

8. Highlight all geometry labeled *Middle Bracket* in Figure 5–15 and click (Create Block).

9. In the *Block Name* field, type **Middle Bracket** and then click **Apply**.

10. Continue creating sketch blocks for the geometry, as shown in Figure 5–15.

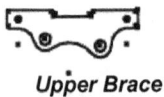

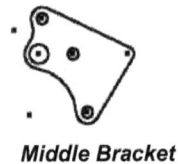

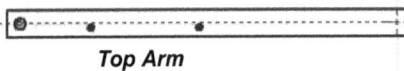

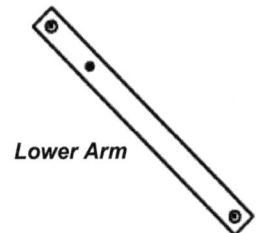

Upper Brace

Middle Bracket

Top Arm

Cylinder Housing

Cylinder Piston Rod

Lower Arm

Figure 5–15

11. Once all of the blocks have been created, click **Cancel** to close the Create Block dialog box.

12. The **Middle Bracket** sketch block has been named incorrectly. Double-click on the **Middle Bracket** sketch block to activate it.

13. Click anywhere in the graphic window to clear any geometry that might be selected. Right-click in the graphic window and select **Block Properties**.

14. Change the name of the block to **Middle Brace** and click **OK** to confirm the change and close the dialog box. Alternatively, you can also rename the block in the Model Browser.

15. In the Exit panel, click ✔ (Finish Edit Block).

16. The *Sketch* tab should still be the active tab. If not, double-click on the sketch to activate it. If you had selected the block from the **Blocks** node, the sketch would have been deactivated.

Task 3 - Create a sketch constraint.

1. Click ↗ (Collinear Constraint) and add a collinear constraint between the two centerlines of the **Cylinder Piston Rod** and **Cylinder Housing** sketch blocks, as shown in Figure 5–16.

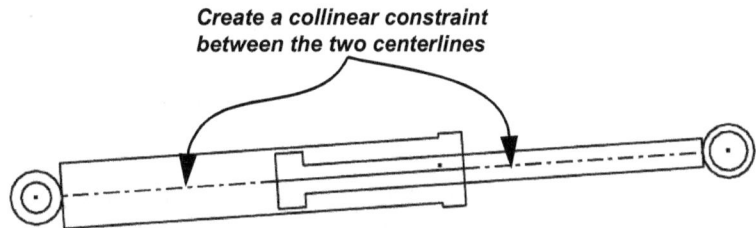

*Create a collinear constraint
between the two centerlines*

Figure 5–16

2. Select the **Cylinder Piston Rod** in the graphic window and drag. A simple kinematic motion has been created using the collinear constraint.

Task 4 - Create a nested sketch block.

Nested sketch blocks convert into subassemblies when components are made from the layout. In this task, you will create a nested sketch block that represents the cylinder subassembly. It will consist of the **Cylinder Piston Rod** and **Cylinder Housing**.

1. In the Layout panel, click 🗗 (Create Block).

2. Select the Cylinder Piston Rod and Cylinder Housing sketch blocks.

3. Type **Cylinder** as the name and click **OK**.

The second instance that is created is an associative copy of the original sketch blocks.

4. In the Model Browser, expand the **Blocks>Cylinder** node. A second instance of each sketch block has been generated and added to this node. The **Cylinder Piston Rod** and **Cylinder Housing** blocks have also been removed from the top level of the sketch node and a copy of the instances added to the **Sketch1>Cylinder** node.

5. Move the **Cylinder Piston Rod** sketch block. The **Cylinder Housing** sketch block also moves and the kinematic motion created using the collinear constraint in the last task is no longer possible. To apply kinematic motion to a nested sketch block, you must activate the **Flexible** option.

6. In the Model Browser, in the **Sketch1** node, right-click on the Cylinder sketch block and select **Flexible**.

7. Move the **Cylinder Piston Rod** sketch block. Note that it can now be dragged independently of the **Cylinder Housing**.

Task 5 - Create second instances of the upper and middle braces.

Multiple instances of the upper and middle braces are required. Rather than recreate the geometry used in the sketch blocks, you will create a second instance of each block.

1. In the Model Browser, press and hold the left mouse button on the **Middle Brace** sketch block in either the **Sketch** or **Blocks** nodes and drag it into the graphic window. A second instance of the **Middle Brace** sketch block is added to **Sketch1**.

2. Create a second instance of the **Upper Brace**. The sketch displays as shown in Figure 5–17.

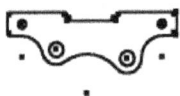

Figure 5–17

Task 6 - Modify the Middle Brace sketch block.

1. Another circle must be created on the **Middle Brace** sketch block to represent a hole that should be present in the 3D component. Click ⊙ (Circle) to create a 25 mm diameter circle in one of the **Middle Brace** sketch blocks and constrain it as shown in Figure 5–18.

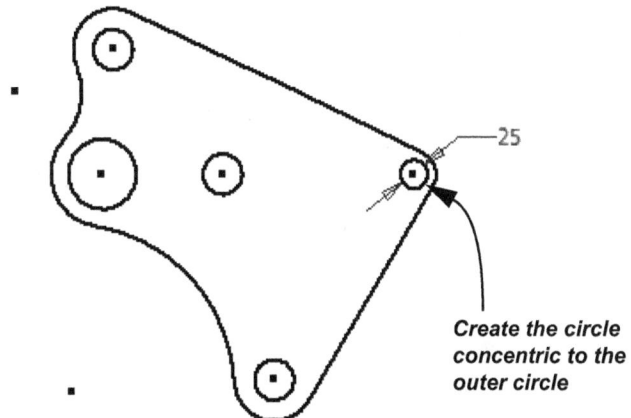

Create the circle concentric to the outer circle

Figure 5–18

2. The circle is not automatically added to the second instance of the **Middle Brace** sketch block. This is because the sketch block was not active when the circle was created.

   Double-click on the **Middle Brace** sketch block in which you created the circle to activate it. All other sketch blocks will dim. Ensure that the sketch block remaining in color is the one you have constrained the circle to. Once the sketch block is active, all dimensions associated with the sketch block re-display on the screen and the newly created circle displays gray.

3. Select the circle you just created. Right-click and select **Add To Block**. The circle is added to both instances of the sketch block and the circle is now black.

4. Finish editing the block.

Task 7 - Constrain the Upper Braces to the Top Arm.

In this task, you will constrain the **Upper Braces** to the **Top Arm** sketch block. To do this, you will use coincident constraints. Because the holes of all three sketch blocks line up, it is difficult to create the constraints without first rotating the **Upper Brace** sketch blocks.

1. In the Model Browser, double-click on **Sketch1 to** reactivate it, if not already active.

2. Select one of the **Upper Brace** sketch blocks.

3. In the Modify panel, click ↻ (Rotate).

4. Click ▨ (Select) in the *Center Point* area in the Rotate dialog box. Select the center point of the small circle on the left side of the geometry, as shown in Figure 5–19.

5. Rotate the sketch block, as shown in Figure 5–19.

Rotate about the center point of this circle

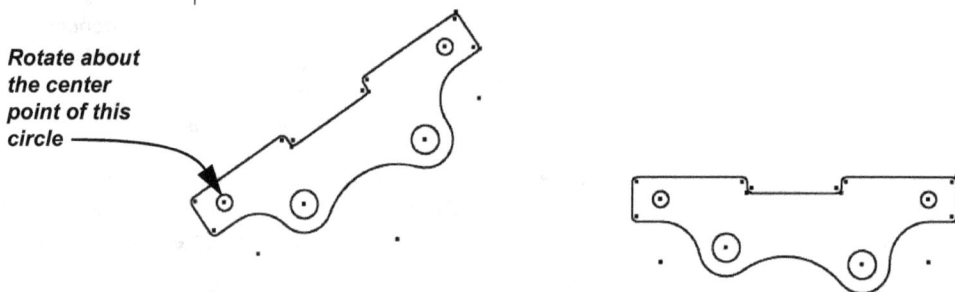

Figure 5–19

6. Rotate the other instance of the **Upper Brace** sketch block. The angle does not matter. The **Upper Brace** sketch blocks display approximately as shown in Figure 5–20.

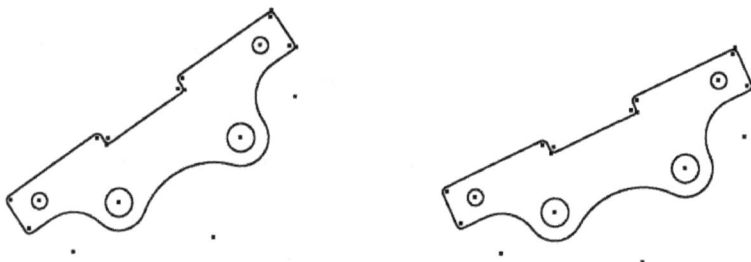

Figure 5–20

7. Using coincident constraints, constrain the center points of the two small holes in the **Top Arm** to the center points of the two small circles in one instance of the **Upper Brace** sketch block, as shown in Figure 5–21.

8. Constrain the other instance of the **Upper Brace** sketch block to the same location, as shown in Figure 5–21. For clarity, clear the Visibility of the first **Upper Brace** that was constrained while constraining the second instance. Resume its visibility when the second instance has been constrained.

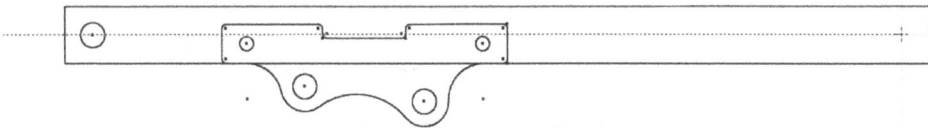

Figure 5–21

Task 8 - Constrain the Middle Braces together.

In this task, you will constrain the **Middle Braces** to each other. To do this, you will use coincident constraints. Because the holes of the sketch blocks line up, it is difficult to create the constraints without first rotating the **Upper Brace** sketch blocks.

1. Ensure that **Sketch1** is active.

2. Use the **Rotate** command to rotate one of the **Middle Brace** sketch blocks, as shown in Figure 5–22.

3. Apply coincident constraints on any of the two circle center points to align the two braces directly on top of each other. The result is shown in the right in Figure 5–22.

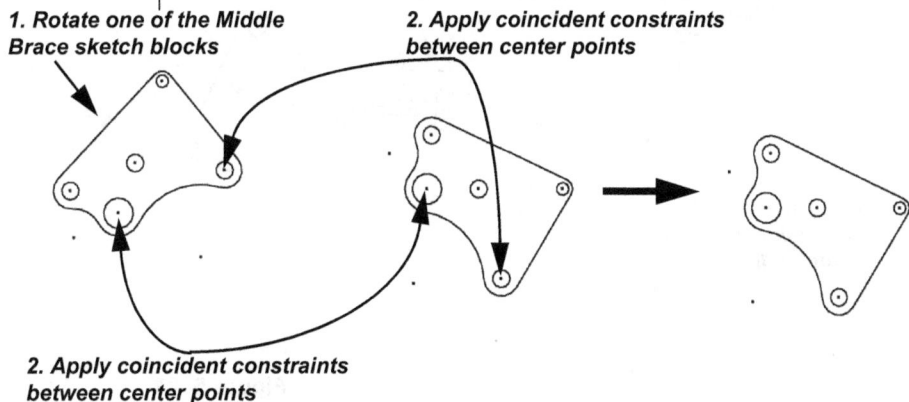

1. Rotate one of the Middle Brace sketch blocks

2. Apply coincident constraints between center points

2. Apply coincident constraints between center points

Figure 5–22

Task 9 - Create additional geometry in the Top Arm sketch block.

In this task, you will create another circle in the **Top Arm** sketch block. The circle represents a hole in the 3D geometry.

1. In the Model Browser, double-click on **Top Arm** to activate it.

2. Create a 35 mm diameter circle, as shown in Figure 5–23.

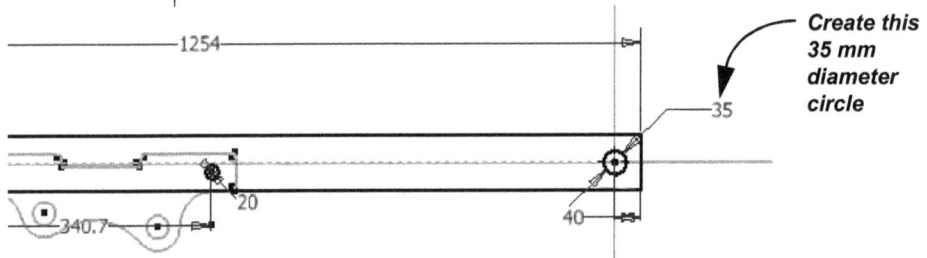

Create this 35 mm diameter circle

Figure 5–23

3. Right-click and select **Finish Edit Block**. When you create the additional geometry this time, it is automatically added to the sketch block.

Task 10 - Constrain the layout.

1. Activate **Sketch1**, if not already active.

2. Use coincident constraints between the center points of the circles to constrain the sketch blocks, as shown in Figure 5–24.

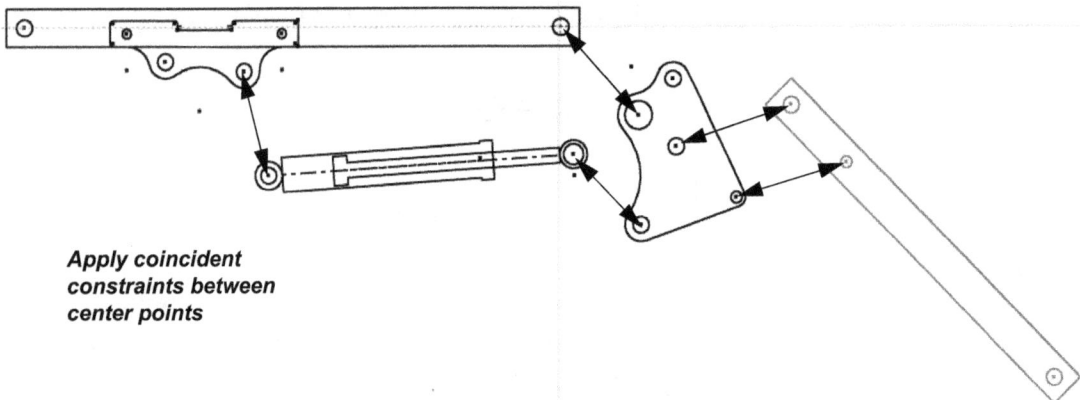

Apply coincident constraints between center points

Figure 5–24

3. Drag the center point of the connection between the **Cylinder Piston Rod** and the **Middle Brace** sketch blocks, as shown in Figure 5–25, to view the kinematic motion of the layout.

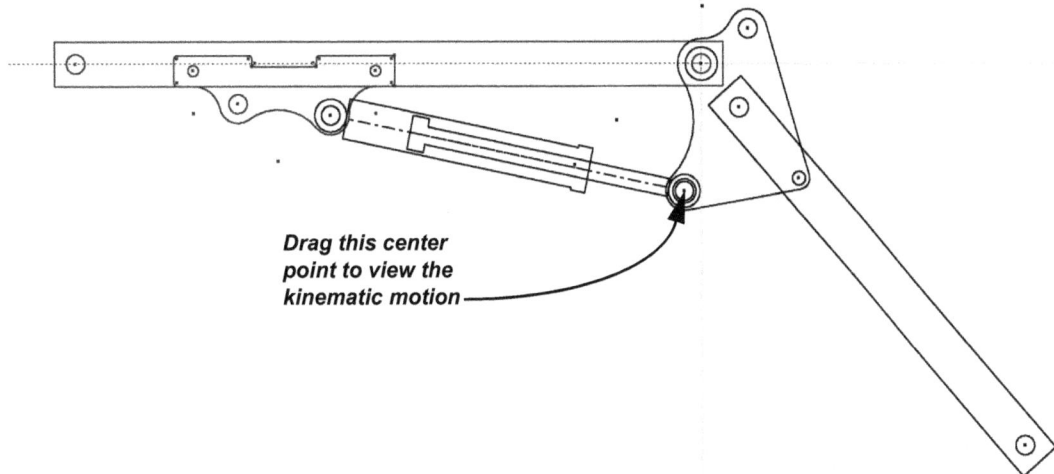

Drag this center point to view the kinematic motion

Figure 5–25

4. Finish the sketch and save the part file.

Task 11 - Generate components from the sketch blocks.

In this task, you will generate the required components from the sketch block. Components can be generated using two different commands: **Make Part** and **Make Components**. Because you want to create many components, it will be more efficient to create them using the **Make Components** command.

1. In the *Manage* tab>Layout panel, click [icon] (Make Components).

*Alternatively, you can pre-select all the blocks in the Model Browser, right-click and select **Make Components**.*

2. In the Model Browser, expand the **Blocks** node and select all sketch blocks listed in the tree. The Make Components: Selection dialog box updates.

3. Leave the *Target assembly name* and *location* fields at the defaults.

4. Click [icon] to open the Open Template dialog box.

5. In the *Metric* tab, select the **Standard (mm).iam** template and click **OK**. The *Template* field updates, as shown in Figure 5–26.

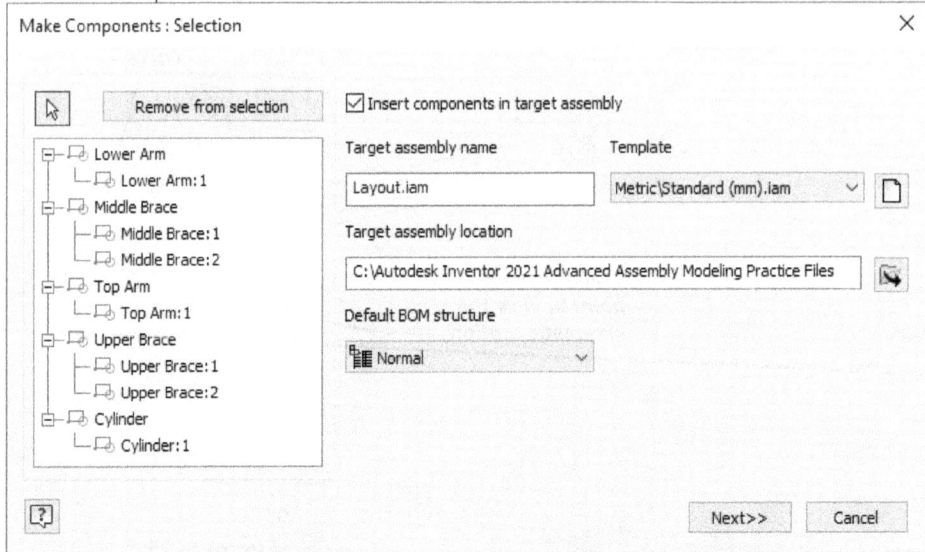

Figure 5–26

6. Click **Next** to open the Make Components: Blocks dialog box.

7. Ensure the Metric template is used for each component that will be generated. Select the first row in the dialog box and click ⬜. The Open Template dialog box opens.

8. In the *Metric* tab, specify the **Standard (mm).ipt** template and click **OK**.

9. Specify the **Standard (mm)** template for the remaining components. The Make Components: Blocks dialog box updates as shown in Figure 5–27. Select the **Standard (mm).iam** template for the Cylinder subassembly.

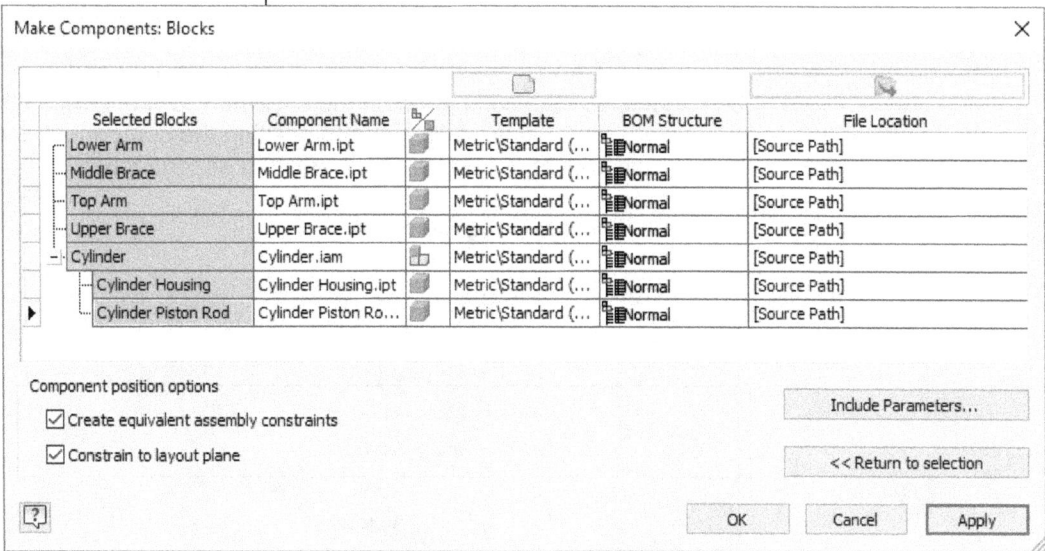

Make Components: Blocks   ✕

Selected Blocks	Component Name		Template	BOM Structure	File Location
Lower Arm	Lower Arm.ipt		Metric\Standard (...	Normal	[Source Path]
Middle Brace	Middle Brace.ipt		Metric\Standard (...	Normal	[Source Path]
Top Arm	Top Arm.ipt		Metric\Standard (...	Normal	[Source Path]
Upper Brace	Upper Brace.ipt		Metric\Standard (...	Normal	[Source Path]
Cylinder	Cylinder.iam		Metric\Standard (...	Normal	[Source Path]
Cylinder Housing	Cylinder Housing.ipt		Metric\Standard (...	Normal	[Source Path]
Cylinder Piston Rod	Cylinder Piston Ro...		Metric\Standard (...	Normal	[Source Path]

Component position options

☑ Create equivalent assembly constraints

☑ Constrain to layout plane

Include Parameters...

<< Return to selection

OK   Cancel   Apply

Figure 5–27

10. Leave all other options at their defaults and click **OK** to generate the assembly.

11. Review the Model Browser. Note the following:

- Each sketch block has generated a separate component in the assembly, and the nested sketch block has generated a subassembly.
- The first component in the assembly is a hidden grounded component. The component is the layout part.
- Constraints have been created between the components. These constraints are based on the sketch constraints you created in the layout.

12. Expand the **Layout** node of the **Lower Arm** component, as shown in Figure 5–28. There are three flush constraints and one Z Angle constraint. These constraints are used to position the component in the assembly. Depending on the additional constraints used to position the component, these constraints are active or suppressed accordingly.

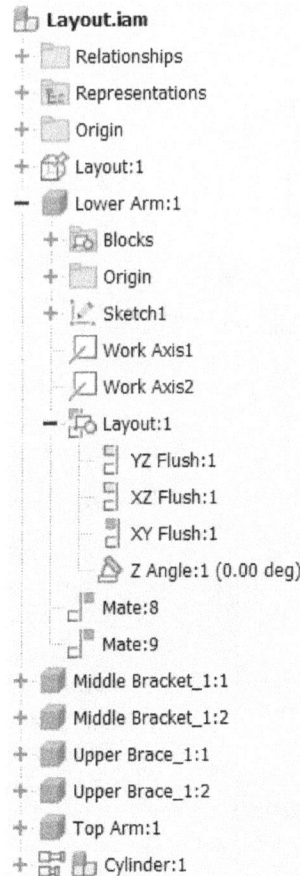

Layout.iam
+ Relationships
+ Representations
+ Origin
+ Layout:1
− Lower Arm:1
   + Blocks
   + Origin
   + Sketch1
      Work Axis1
      Work Axis2
   − Layout:1
      YZ Flush:1
      XZ Flush:1
      XY Flush:1
      Z Angle:1 (0.00 deg)
      Mate:8
      Mate:9
+ Middle Bracket_1:1
+ Middle Bracket_1:2
+ Upper Brace_1:1
+ Upper Brace_1:2
+ Top Arm:1
+ Cylinder:1

Figure 5–28

13. Expand other nodes in the Model Browser to view the other created constraints.

14. Save the assembly.

Task 12 - Make a design change in the layout.

In this task, you will make a design change. You will increase the length of the Lower Arm. After this change, you will return to the assembly and observe the effect.

1. Activate the **Layout.ipt** window.

2. Edit **Sketch1** and double-click on **Lower Arm** to activate the Lower Arm sketch block.

3. Change the *890 mm* dimension to **1000 mm**.

4. Finish editing the block and the sketch.

5. Return to the assembly window. Note that 🔲 (Local Update) in the Quick Access Toolbar is active. Click 🔲 (Local Update) to update the assembly. The length of the Lower Arm increases according to the change in the layout.

Task 13 - Create solid features.

In this task, you will create solid features from the sketch blocks. You will also offset some features away from the layout plane, so that they are correctly positioned in the assembly.

1. In the Assembly window, activate the **Lower Arm** component.

2. In the *3D Model* tab>Create panel, click ▣ (Extrude).

3. Create an extrude using the **Lower Arm** sketch block as the profile. Create it with a total distance of **80 mm** and extrude it symmetrically about the sketch plane in both directions.

4. Activate the **Middle Brace:1** component.

5. Create an extrude using the **Middle Brace** sketch block as the profile. Extrude it to a **10 mm** distance in the default direction. The model displays as shown in Figure 5–29.

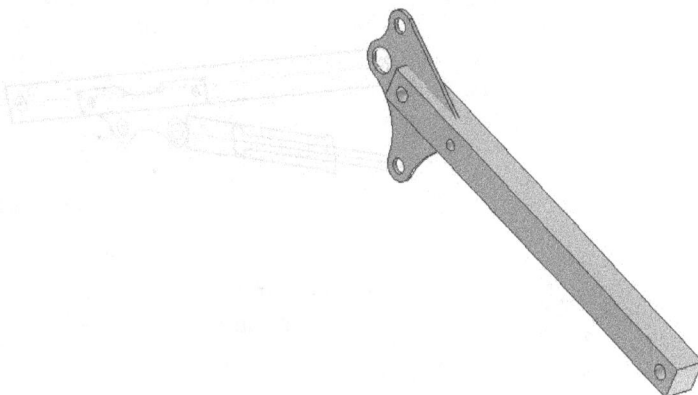

Figure 5–29

The two **Middle Brace** components are not in the correct location. They need to be offset from the layout plane so that they are on either side of the **Lower Arm** component.

6. Activate the top-level assembly.

7. In the Model Browser, expand the **Middle Brace:1>Layout** node.

8. Select the XY Flush constraint. In the Model Browser, enter an offset of **40 mm**.

9. Change the *XY Flush* offset for the **Middle Brace:2** component to **-50 mm**.The assembly displays as shown in Figure 5–30.

Figure 5–30

Task 14 - (Optional) Complete the assembly.

Complete the assembly by building solid geometry for each of the remaining components and offsetting the **Upper Brace** components away from the Layout plane. The completed assembly displays as shown in Figure 5–31.

1. Consider the following:

• Use extrudes and revolves when creating the geometry in the components.

• Remember to make **Sketch1** visible again when required, for more than one feature in a component.

- The blocks used in a layout will not always contain all the detail required to create the geometry. To create the cutout in the center of the Cylinder Housing, you need to edit **Sketch1** or create a new sketch to create the required geometry.

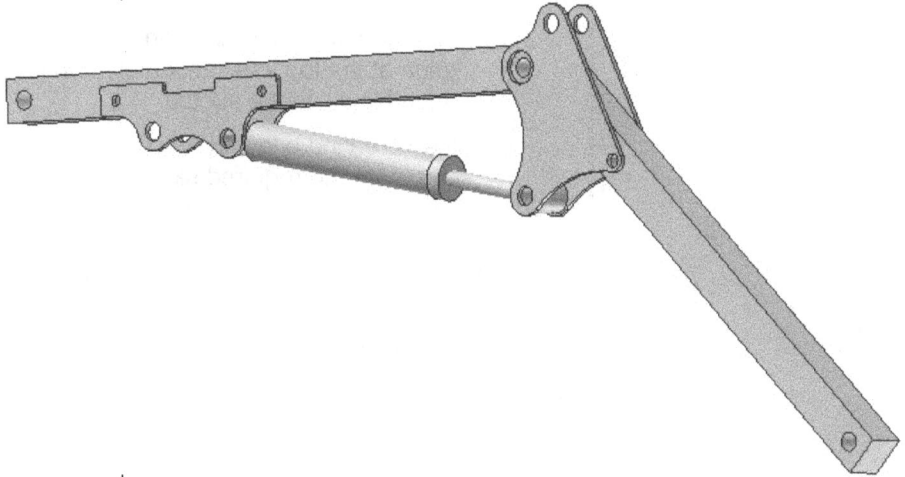

Figure 5–31

2. Save and close all open files.

Chapter Review Questions

1. Which of the following statements is true about creating a layout?

   a. When creating a layout in an assembly model, create a sketch at the top level assembly and create the required sketch blocks in the sketch.

   b. When creating a layout in a part model, create a sketch and create the required sketch blocks in the sketch.

   c. Both of the above.

2. Which of the following can be contained in a layout? (Select all that apply.)

   a. 2D entities

   b. 3D geometry

   c. Dimensions

   d. Constraints

3. When sketch blocks are nested, you are no longer able to test the kinematic motion of a model. Going forward, the nested blocks can only work as one component.

   a. True

   b. False

4. By default, all of the constraints created between sketch blocks are translated into assembly constraints. If you do not want to generate the assembly constraints, what do you need to do?

   a. Clear the **Constrain to layout plane** option when creating the components.

   b. Clear the **Create equivalent assembly constraints** option when creating the components.

   c. Delete them all after they are created.

   d. Clear the constraints individually from the Make Components dialog box.

5. How do you add another instance of a sketch block to a layout? (Select all that apply.)

   a. In the **Blocks** node, select the existing sketch block and drag it into the sketch.

   b. In the **Sketch** node, select the existing sketch block and drag it into the sketch.

   c. Right-click on the existing sketch block in the **Blocks** node and select **Copy** and then **Paste**.

   d. You can only have a single instance of a sketch block in a layout.

6. Components created from sketch blocks in a layout are associative to the layout.

   a. True

   b. False

Command Summary

Button	Command	Location
	Create Block	• **Ribbon:** *Sketch* contextual tab> Layout panel
	Make Components	• **Ribbon:** *Sketch* contextual tab> Layout panel
	Make Layout	• **Ribbon:** *Assemble* tab>Component panel
	Make Part	• **Ribbon:** *Sketch* contextual tab> Layout panel

Associative Links and Adaptive Parts

Associative links are automatically created in a model when you reference another component in an assembly to create geometry, dimensions, or constraints. When an associative link is established, the model is automatically set as adaptive. If an explicit associative link does not exist, you can still manually set a model (or a sketch-based feature in a model) to be adaptive.

Learning Objectives in This Chapter

- Break the associative link between a sketched feature and reference geometry.
- Specify geometric entities of part features to change, while controlling the size or location of other entities in an assembly.
- Ensure that a model remains as initially required by disabling unwanted adaptivity.

6.1 Associative Links

When working in an assembly, each time you reference geometry (i.e., project geometry, dimensions to edges or faces on other components) to create a section of a new sketched feature, an associative link is applied between the reference geometry and the sketched feature, as shown in Figure 6–1.

*By default, you can select references in the assembly for use in a new part. Using the Application Options dialog box, select the Assembly tab and clear the **Enable associative edge/loop geometry projection during in-place modeling** option.*

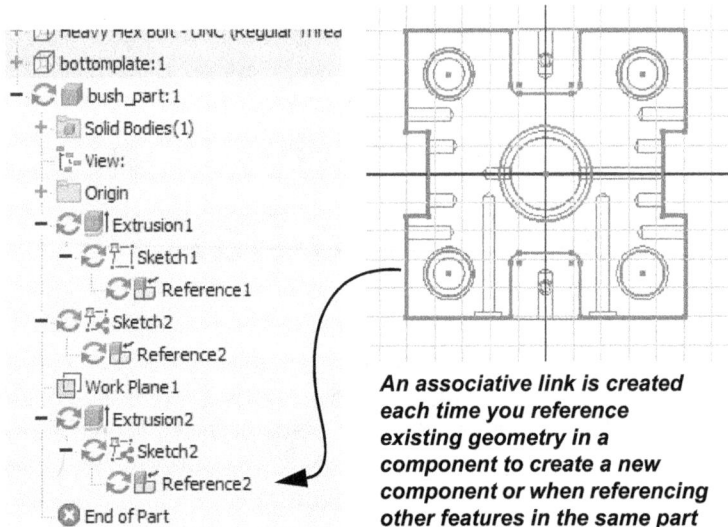

An associative link is created each time you reference existing geometry in a component to create a new component or when referencing other features in the same part

Figure 6–1

- Associative links automatically make the sketch *adaptive*.

- Adaptive features/parts are identified with ☁ in the Model Browser. This means you cannot modify the referenced portions of the sketch because they are being adapted from some other reference in the assembly.

- Changes to the referenced geometry propagate to the associated (adaptive) geometry and it automatically updates, even if it impacts multiple parts.

Breaking Links

How To: Break the Associative Link Between a Sketched Feature and Reference Geometry

1. Edit or open the part that contains the feature in the assembly.
2. Expand the feature that you want to make independent and expand the reference sketch below it. The associative links are listed below the sketch.
3. Right-click on a reference link and select **Break Link**, as shown in Figure 6–2.

This icon indicates that the part is adaptive

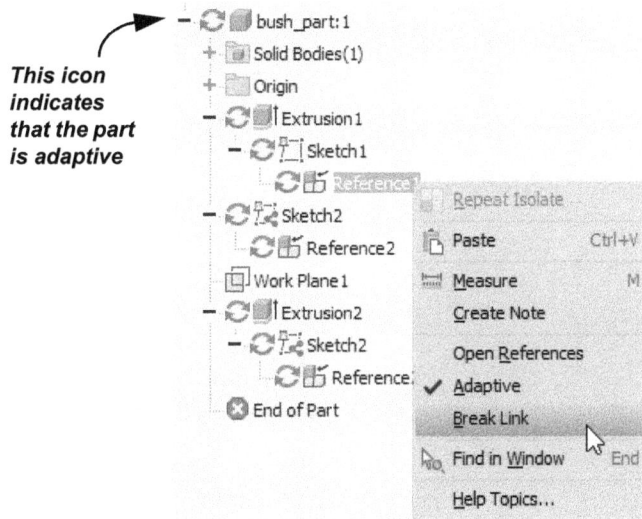

Figure 6–2

Break each link individually to make the entire part independent.

Once the link is broken:

- The reference no longer displays in the Model Browser.

- Edit the feature and add any missing dimensions or constraints that are required.

Although references in the model are broken, it still indicates that the part and its features are adaptive. The fact that the features are still adaptive simply means that they are able to adapt if references to other geometry are added later in the design or are forced with assembly constraints. You can manually disable adaptivity so that unconstrained geometry does not update.

6.2 Adaptive Assembly Parts

The size and shape of a part might evolve as you put an assembly together. Rather than switch frequently between several files to edit the parts separately, you can use adaptivity. This enables you to specify geometric entities of part features to change, while controlling the size or location of other entities in an assembly. When you edit an adaptive part in the assembly, the adaptive components update accordingly.

Adaptive parts are recommended in the following situations:

- In the early stages of the design cycle, when some aspects of the design are prone to change. Adaptive parts are valuable because they adapt to change.

- In cases where a part or subassembly position is not defined.

- In cases where the size of a feature is dependent on another part.

The following unconstrained geometry can be made adaptive:

- Undimensioned sketch geometry

- Features based on undimensioned sketch geometry

- Work features based on geometry of other parts

- Parts containing adaptive sketches or features

- Subassemblies containing parts with adaptive sketches or features

When associative links are created in a component (parts, subassemblies, or features), the ⟳ icon automatically displays, as shown in Figure 6–3. You can also manually enable adaptivity so that unconstrained geometry updates. To do so, right-click on the component in the Model Browser and select **Adaptive**.

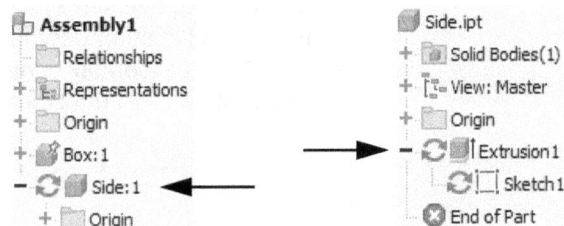

Figure 6–3

- The size of an adaptive element can be determined by the constraints used to locate the component in the assembly. For example, the size of the adaptive side component in the assembly shown on the left in Figure 6–4 is determined by constraining it to the box component.

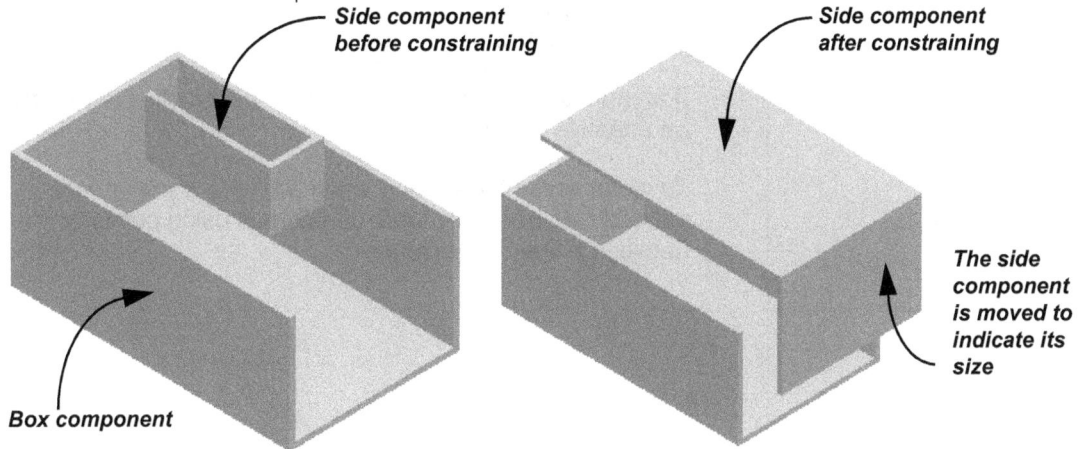

Side component before constraining

Side component after constraining

The side component is moved to indicate its size

Box component

Figure 6–4

Disabling Adaptivity

Breaking links does not automatically disable adaptivity. To disable adaptivity, right-click on the component's name in the Model Browser and clear the checkmark next to **Adaptive**. This is good design practice to ensure that if references are created unintentionally, the model remains as initially required. You can also remove adaptivity for specific features in the model instead of limiting it for the entire model.

Notes on Adaptivity

Keep the following considerations in mind when defining adaptive features:

- If a sketch is adaptive, only undimensioned and unconstrained geometry changes.

- Adaptive features can be modified by changing either their size, location, or both.

- If you use multiple instances of an adaptive element in an assembly, only one instance defines the adaptive features. All other instances are defined based on that instance. You might have to update twice to update all instances of adaptive elements.

- For a part to change size when other parts in the design change, the following must be adaptive: the part (in the context of the assembly), the feature (in the model), and the sketch of that feature.

- An assembly might have multiple adaptive parts, a part might have multiple adaptive features, and a feature might have multiple adaptive parameters.

- If an adaptive part is used in multiple assemblies, it can only be adaptive in one assembly.

- To make assemblies that contain adaptive parts update correctly, do not apply Mate constraints using points or between a line and a plane.

Practice 6a | Breaking Associative Links

Practice Objective

- Modify a component to make it independent by breaking its associative link to an assembly.

In this practice, you will break the associative links between the **bush_part** feature and its referenced geometry. In breaking these links, you will make the component independent.

Task 1 - Open an assembly file.

1. Open **Final Mold Assy2.iam** from the *Breaking Links* folder.

2. Toggle off the display of all assembly components, except for the **topplate2 Assy**, **Middleplate Assy**, and **bush_part** components.

3. Activate and expand the **bush_part** model. The associative links are listed below the sketch, as shown in Figure 6–5.

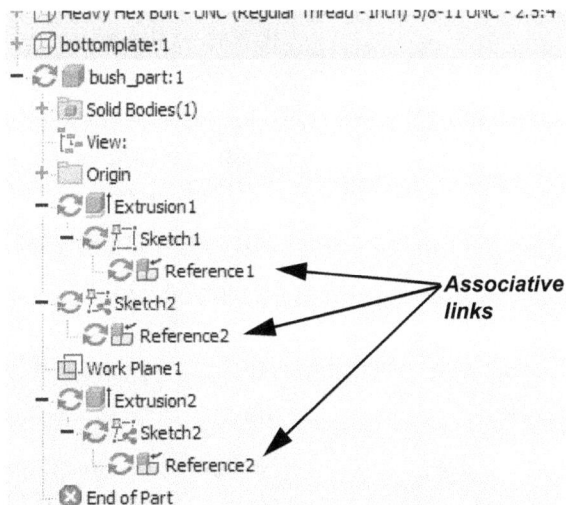

Figure 6–5

Task 2 - Modify the assembly and review how the model updates.

1. Leave the assembly open and open **bush_part** in a separate window. You will be toggling between the two windows throughout the remainder of the practice.

2. Return to the assembly window and activate the top-level assembly.

3. Right-click on the **Hole** that was created as the assembly feature and select **Edit Feature**.

4. In the Hole palette that opens, modify the diameter of the hole from *31.75* to **25**.

5. Activate the **bush_part** window. The model automatically updates to reflect the change in the diameter of the hole, as shown in Figure 6–6. This is because the hole was used as a reference in creating the outer diameter of the **bush_part**.

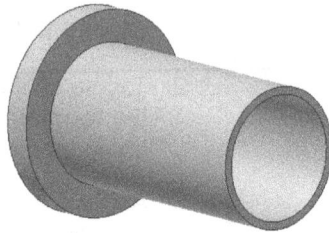

Figure 6–6

6. Return to the assembly window and change the diameter of the hole back to **31.75** mm. Note that the part updates.

7. In the assembly, in the Model Browser, right-click on **bush_part** and select **Adaptive** to clear the ability of this model to update with changes to any of its parent references.

8. Once again, modify the diameter of the hole from *31.75* to. **25**.

9. Activate the **bush_part** window. The model does not update because all adaptivity for this component was disabled.

10. Return to the assembly window and change the diameter of the hole back to **31.75** mm.

11. Right-click on **bush_part** and select **Adaptive** to toggle adaptivity back on for the component. You should once again see ⟳ beside the **bush_part** in the Model Browser.

You can disable adaptivity for specific features in the model instead of limiting it for the entire model. In this model, for example, you could clear the adaptivity for **Extrusion1**, while at the same time leaving **Extrusion2** adaptive, as shown in Figure 6–7.

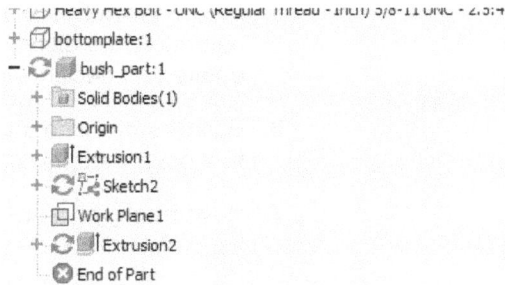

+ Heavy Hex Bolt - UNC (Regular Thread - Inch) 5/8-11 UNC - 2.5:4
+ bottomplate:1
− bush_part:1
  + Solid Bodies(1)
  + Origin
  + Extrusion1
  + Sketch2
    Work Plane1
  + Extrusion2
    End of Part

Figure 6–7

Task 3 - Break links between the part and the assembly.

As an alternative to disabling adaptivity, you can break the links that were generated when you created a model. Breaking links is permanent. Therefore, it should only be done if you know that you no longer want the relationship between the component and its parent.

1. Right-click on **Reference1** in the **bush_part** component and select **Break Link**. The reference no longer displays once you break the link.

2. Break the **Reference2** link. This can be done in either location, as it is a shared sketch.

3. Modify the diameter of the hole from *31.75* to **25** to test that the reference is no longer present.

Although the model still shows it is adaptive, no physical reference exists that could cause it to update. The fact that the features are still adaptive simply means that they are able to adapt if references to other geometry are added.

4. Edit **Extrusion2** and extrude the sketch a distance of **5.08 mm** instead of using the front face of topplate as the reference. The model displays as shown in Figure 6–8.

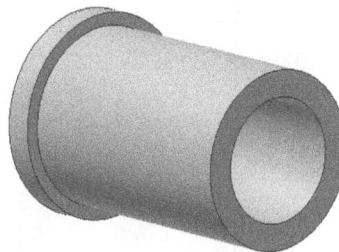

Figure 6–8

---

5. Delete **Work Plane 1**. This was originally created to determine the distance of **Extrusion2**. Now that you have entered a specific value, this reference is not required.

6. Edit **Sketch1** and show all constraints. The geometry is fixed at a point. Add missing dimensions.

7. Save **bush_part** and close the window. Activate the assembly.

8. In the Model Browser, right-click on **bush_part** and select **Adaptive** to disable the link in the assembly. The part is now independent and can be made adaptive in other assemblies.

9. Pattern **bush_part**. The model displays as shown in Figure 6–9.

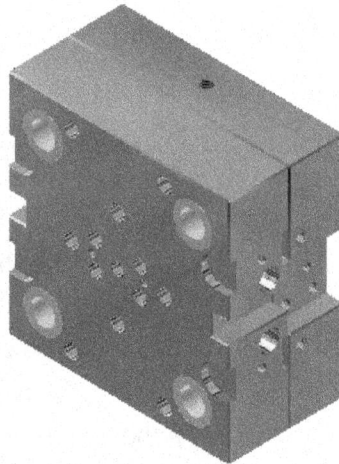

Figure 6–9

10. Save the assembly and close the window.

Practice 6b

Adaptive Assembly

Practice Objective

- Enable a part in an assembly to update based on adaptivity in conjunction with assembly constraints.

In this practice, you will add a part to an assembly and set it so that it can update based on constraints set in the assembly. The resulting assembly is shown on the right in Figure 6–10.

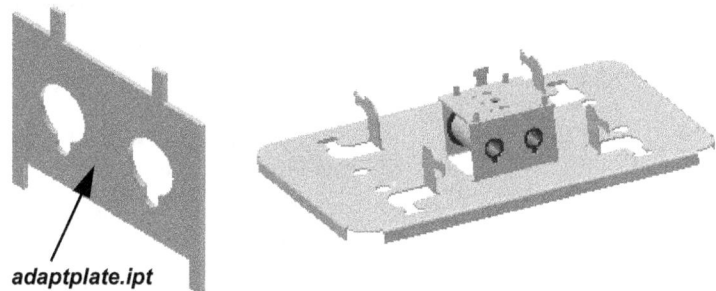

adaptplate.ipt

Figure 6–10

Task 1 - Open an assembly file.

1. Open **adapt.iam** from the top-level folder. The model displays as shown in Figure 6–11.

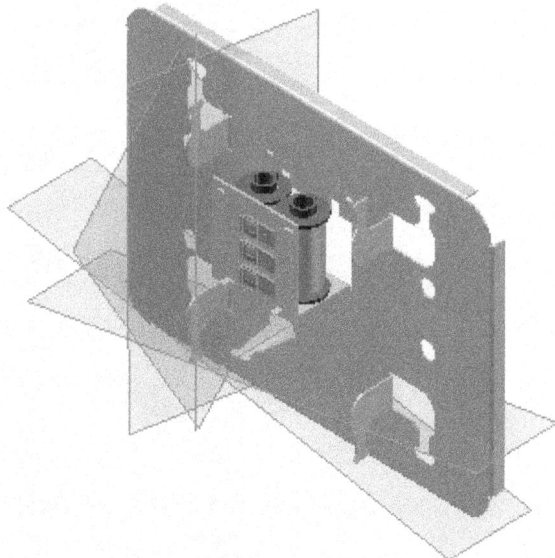

Figure 6–11

2. Toggle off all visible work features and **Component Pattern 1**.

3. Place one instance of **adaptplate.ipt** in the assembly.

4. Open **adaptplate.ipt** in a separate window and use the Model Browser options to examine the part. Note that no Adaptive features are in the model.

5. Close the **adaptplate.ipt** window.

Task 2 - Apply constraints to the assembly.

In this task, you will constrain the **adaptplate** part to the assembly to locate and adjust its size.

1. Apply Mate constraints between the center line of each coil and the center line of its corresponding large hole in the

   adaptplate. Select ![icon] (Undirected) as the *Solution* type.

2. Apply another Mate constraint, offset **0.0135** between the large face of adaptplate and the face of the slot in the doorbellbase to locate the plate correctly, as shown in Figure 6–12.

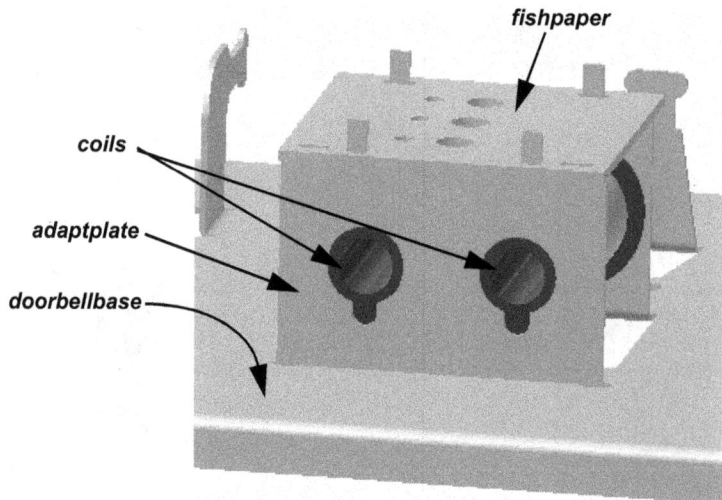

Figure 6–12

3. Examine the assembly. Note that the tabs at the top of **adaptplate** are not aligned with the slots in the small flat part (fishpaper).

4. In the Model Browser, right-click on **adaptplate** and select **Adaptive** to enable the part to change in the assembly.

   ♻ (Adaptive) displays beside the part icon in the Model Browser.

5. Apply a Mate constraint between the narrow surface on the **adaptplate** tab (that passes through the fishpaper) and the narrow surface of the slot in the fishpaper, as shown in Figure 6–13. Set the *Offset* to **0.025 in** and apply the constraint. An error occurs, indicating that a constraint is inconsistent with another constraint and one of them must be edited, deleted, or suppressed. This is because the feature in the **Adaptplate** is not set to be adaptive.

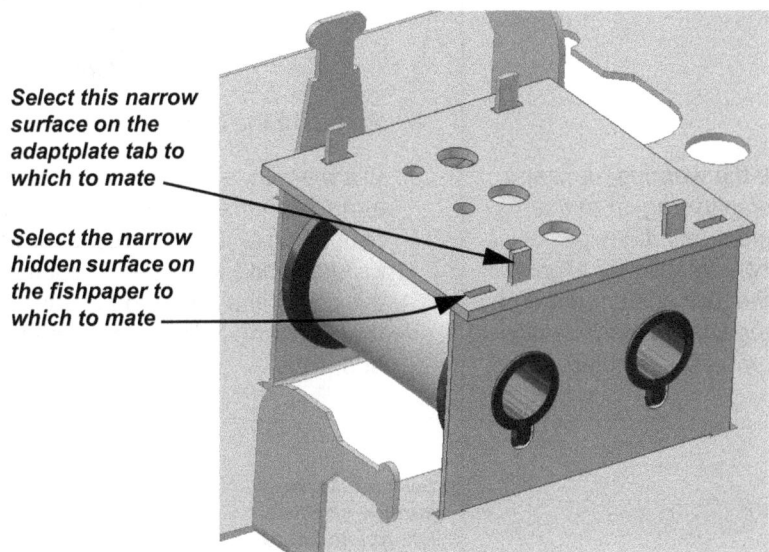

Select this narrow surface on the adaptplate tab to which to mate

Select the narrow hidden surface on the fishpaper to which to mate

Figure 6–13

6. Cancel the operation and close the Place Constraints dialog box.

7. Open **adaptplate.ipt** in a separate window. The feature that must be set to adaptive is **Extrusion1** and its sketch. In the Model Browser, right-click on **Extrusion1** and select **Adaptive**. Note that the **Adaptive** icons for **Extrusion1** and its sketch are added, as shown in Figure 6–14.

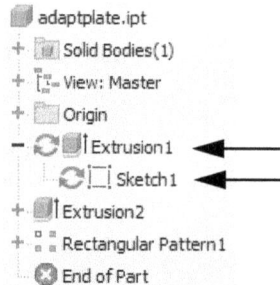

Figure 6–14

8. Return to the assembly window.

*If the warning message displays again at this step, edit the two constraints that aligned the axis and ensure that the **Undirected** solution type was selected.*

9. Once again, apply a Mate constraint between the narrow surface on the adaptplate tab (that passes through the fishpaper) and the narrow surface of the slot in the fishpaper, as shown in Figure 6–15. Set the offset to **0.025 in** and apply the constraint. The tab adjusts to align with the slot because the extrusion in the adaptplate part was set to permit adaptivity.

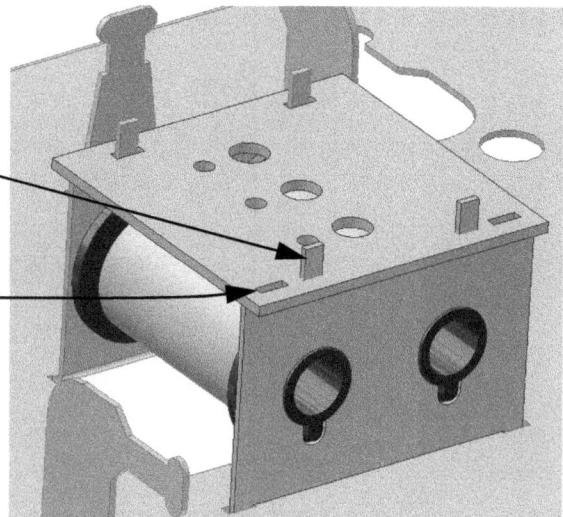

Select this narrow surface on the adaptplate tab to which to mate

Select the narrow hidden surface on the fishpaper to which to mate

Figure 6–15

10. Add another Mate constraint and offset for the tab on the other side of adaptplate. The model displays as shown in Figure 6–16.

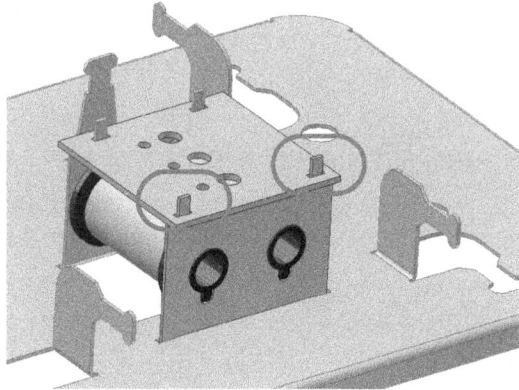

Figure 6–16

11. Save the assembly and parts and close the windows.

Chapter Review Questions

1. An associative link is created each time you reference existing geometry in a component to create a new component.

   a. True

   b. False

2. Which command is used to temporarily remove an associative link in a model?

   a. **Adaptive** (clear its selection)

   b. **Break Link**

3. Clearing adaptivity at the Part level of an assembly is the same as individually clearing adaptivity from all features in the part and leaving the part adaptive.

   a. True

   b. False

4. Which of the following are true regarding the Model Browser shown in Figure 6–17?

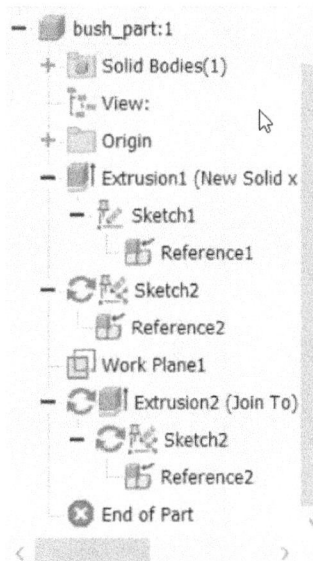

Figure 6–17

a. The **bush_part:1** component in the assembly is adaptive.

b. **Reference1** in the sketch for **Extrusion1** is adaptive.

c. **Work Plane1** is adaptive.

d. **Extrusion2** is adaptive.

5. Which of the following are valid statements about adaptivity of parts in an assembly? (Select all that apply.)

a. For a sketched feature in an assembly component to change size based on changes to other models, the part (in the assembly) and the feature and its sketch (in the part) must be marked as adaptive.

b. If a sketch is adaptive, entities that are fully constrained can be adapted from geometry in another component in an assembly.

c. Parts can be adaptive in multiple assemblies at one time.

d. Parts can have multiple adaptive features.

Command Summary

Button	Command	Location
NA	**Adaptive**	• *(context menu in the Model Browser)*
NA	**Break Link**	• *(context menu in the Model Browser)*

iMates

The iMate functionality in the Autodesk® Inventor® software is a design tool that enables you to work more efficiently with your part designs when assembling them into a top-level assembly. Using this functionality, you can define how the component will be constrained into an assembly and store this information directly with the component for quick and easy use.

Learning Objectives in This Chapter

- Build iMate constraints into parts or subassemblies to define how they connect with other components in an assembly.
- Combine multiple iMates into a Composite iMate group, so that multiple iMates can act as one.
- Convert constraints between components in an assembly to create multiple single iMates or a single Composite iMate.
- Manually or automatically match iMates of parts in an assembly.
- Control the order in which iMate pairs are previewed by using the Match List functionality.
- Vary constraint settings in iParts by including iMates.

7.1 iMates

iMates are constraints built into parts or subassemblies. They define how a component connects with other components in an assembly. You define iMates in a component by selecting a constraint type and its accompanying reference entity (e.g., face, edge, vertex, etc.) that is matched with other components. When you assemble components with iMates, you match the iMates from different components, manually or automatically. If you define iMates with the same names in two different components, the components become interchangeable in an assembly.

In Figure 7–1, the two mounting brackets have identical iMates defined, making them interchangeable in the assembly. You can replace one or the other without having to reapply the constraints.

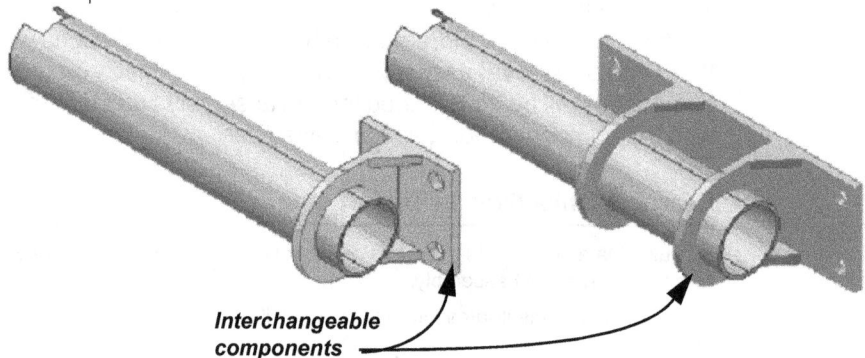

Interchangeable components

Figure 7–1

Creating iMates

To create an iMate, in the *Manage* tab>Author panel, click

(iMate). The Create iMate dialog box opens, as shown in Figure 7–2. Creating iMates is similar to placing constraints, except that you are only selecting the reference for one component. As with constraints, you select the reference (line, plane, point, etc.) on which you want to place the iMate, as well as set any offset or angle values. iMates can be created in part or assembly files. iMates added to an assembly are used when it is placed as a subassembly.

The ⬡ (Symmetry) constraint type is not available when creating an iMate.

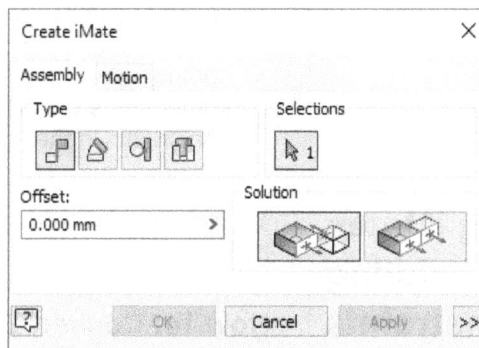

Figure 7–2

Composite iMates

You can combine multiple iMates into a group, called a composite iMate. The composite acts as a single iMate and is applied all at once. Only one iMate symbol displays in the drawing window for each composite iMate. In the Model Browser, the composite iMate is listed above individual iMates in the tree structure.

To create a composite iMate, select several iMates in the Model Browser (hold <Ctrl> to select more than one iMate), right-click and select **Create Composite**, as shown in Figure 7–3.

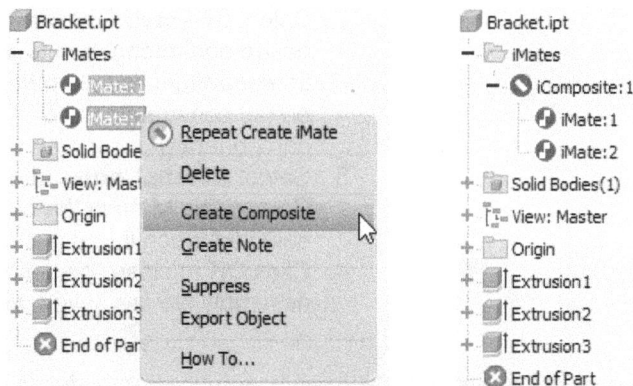

Figure 7–3

- To remove a single iMate from a composite, select the iMate in the Model Browser and select **Remove**. The iMate is moved outside the composite group.

- To delete an iMate or composite, right-click and select **Delete**. If you delete a composite group, all iMates contained in that composite are also deleted.

- To apply composite iMates at the same time, create a composite iMate with the same name in the other components you want to assemble to. When both components are added to the same assembly file, all constraints in the composite iMate are applied at once.

Creating iMates from Existing Constraints

You can convert component constraints in an assembly to create multiple single iMates, or a single composite iMate.

How To: Convert Existing Assembly Constraints to iMates

1. Select the component in the Model Browser and select **Component>Infer iMates** in the shortcut menu. The Infer iMates dialog box opens as shown in Figure 7–4.

Alternatively you can right-click on a single constraint in a component to create an iMate.

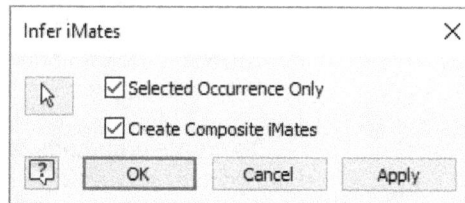

Figure 7–4

2. Select **Selected Occurrence Only** to create the iMates based on the constraints assigned in the selected component. If you clear this option, iMates are created based on the constraints used in all occurrences of the selected component.
3. Select **Create Composite iMates** to create a single Composite iMate in the component. If this option is not selected, each iMate is created on its own.
4. Click **OK** to close the dialog box. iMates created in the assembly file are saved with the part files.

Using iMates in an Assembly

In an assembly, the iMates in parts can be matched manually or automatically.

How To: Manually Match iMates

1. Select the component to display the iMate symbol.
2. Hold <Alt> while you drag one iMate to its corresponding iMate on another part. The symbols for matching iMates become visible when you drag.
3. Drop the iMate once matched by releasing <Alt>.

How To: Preview iMate Pairs Before Placing a Component

1. Open the required assembly that contains components with previously assigned iMates.

2. In the *Assemble* tab>Component panel, click (Place), select a component that contains iMates to assemble, and select an **iMate** option for placing them from the bottom of the Open dialog box.

   - **(Interactively place with iMates):** Automatically matches iMates, enabling you to cycle through, accept, and continue to preview and accept any remaining available iMates.

   - **(Automatically generate iMates on place):** Places and finalizes component placement based on the first iMate match the system encounters.

3. Click **Open** to open the file. A preview of the first iMate match displays, similar to that shown in Figure 7–5.

   - The component is oriented to satisfy the constraint and the iMate constraint symbol indicates the constraint type and reference location on each component.

   - The Command Line in the bottom left corner of the Autodesk Inventor window indicates which components and iMates are in the preview.

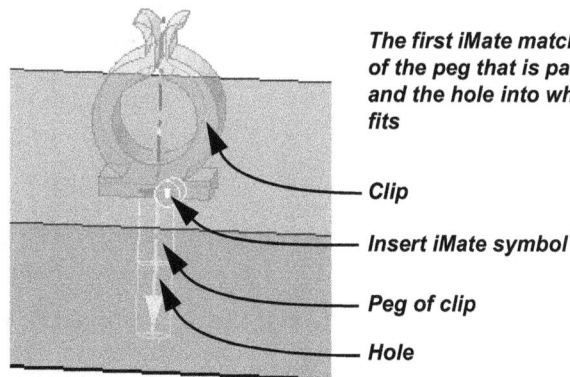

The first iMate match is an Insert of the peg that is part of the clip and the hole into which the peg fits

Clip

Insert iMate symbol

Peg of clip

Hole

Figure 7–5

When an iMate of a component is accepted and used to place a component, the iMate location in the assembly is no longer available to place other components.

4. When previewing pairs, you have the following options:
   - Accept the iMate pair shown by left-clicking in the graphics window. If additional iMate pairings are possible and if ⊘ was selected, additional previews are shown. When a component instance is placed and no additional iMate pairings exist, you are returned to regular component placement.
   - Press <Esc> to cancel component placement.
   - Use one of the options in the shortcut menu, as shown in Figure 7–6. The specific options that are available depend on how many iMates exist in the component, as well as whether there is one or more matching iMate possibilities. The options are as follows:

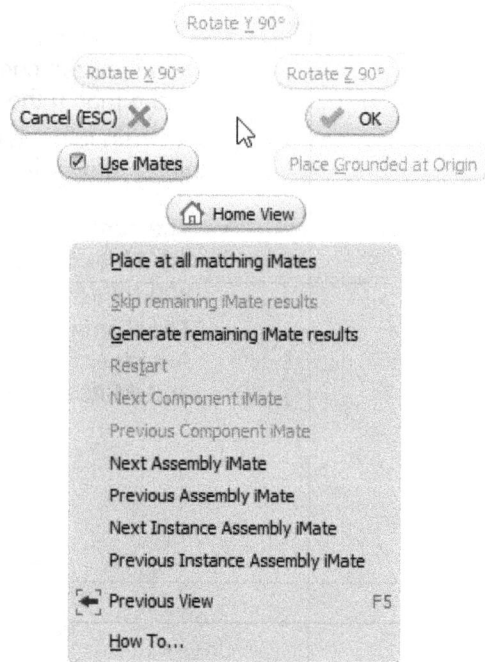

Figure 7–6

Option (shortcut)	Description
Use iMates	Accesses and disables **iMate Placement** mode.
Place at all matching iMates	Places the component and all additional instances so that all iMate pairs are satisfied.
Skip remaining iMate results <Spacebar>	Skips the remaining iMate pairs and place the component with only the iMate pairs you accepted.

Generate remaining iMate results <Ctrl>+<Enter>	Accepts all current matches and any remaining are automatically accepted and used for placement.
Restart	Discards any accepted iMate pairs for the current component instance and begins previewing the iMate pairs again.
Next or Previous Component iMate (up and down arrow)	Cycles forward or backward between iMates. This option is grayed out if no additional iMates exist that are not already accepted.
Next or Previous Assembly iMate (right and left arrow)	Cycles forward or backward to another iMate of the assembly that matches. This is grayed out if no other iMates exist in the assembly that match the iMate in the component.
Next or Previous Instance Assembly iMate (<Ctrl> with the right and left arrows)	When a previously placed component in an assembly has been instantiated more than once and an iMate pair still exists for more than one of the instances, use these options to cycle forward or backward between the instantiations in the assembly. This option is grayed out if each component in the assembly is instantiated only once, or if the iMate in the other component instantiations has already been used.

Match List

The Match List functionality enables you to control the order in which the iMate pairs are previewed. This enables you to find the required iMate pairs more quickly, especially in larger assemblies or ones with many undesirable matching iMates.

How To: Add iMate Names to the Match List

1. Determine which iMates to match during component placement and rename them so that they have meaningful names to help distinguish them.
   - You can rename in the iMates folder in the Model Browser or by editing the iMate.
2. Open the component being placed in a separate window, in the Model Browser, right-click on **iMate**, and select **Edit**. The Edit iMate dialog box opens.

The Name and Match List areas of the dialog box are also available during the creation of an iMate.

3. Click >> to expand the dialog box. Select the *Matching* tab. It displays similar to that shown in Figure 7–7.

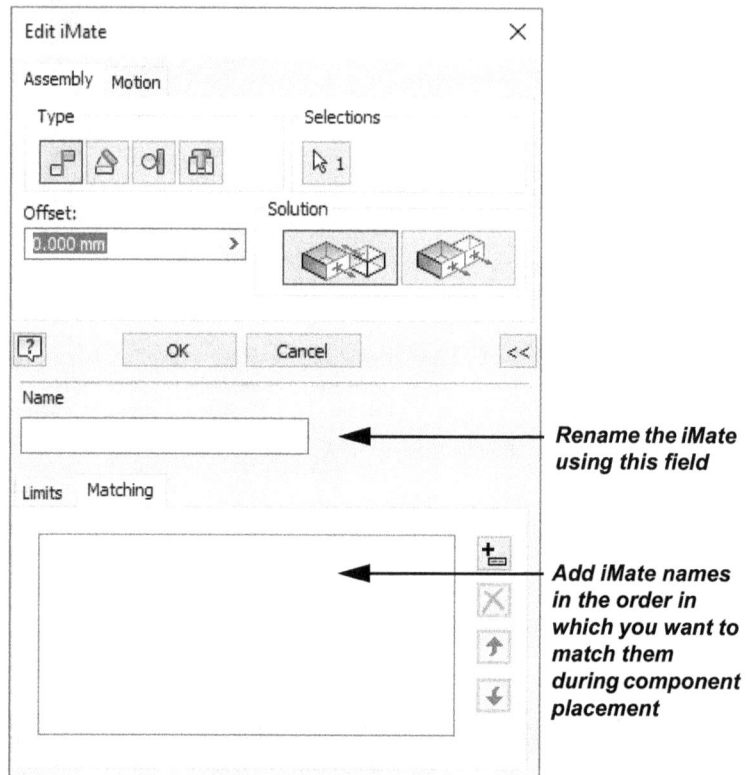

Edit iMate   ✕

Assembly Motion

  Type   Selections

  [⊞] [△] [◫] [▦]   [⬚ 1]

  Offset: Solution

  [0.000 mm   >]   [▨] [▨]

  [?]   OK   Cancel   <<

  Name

  [   ]   ◄—— **Rename the iMate using this field**

  Limits   Matching

  [   ] [⊞+]
                                  ◄— [✕]   **Add iMate names in the order in which you want to match them during component placement**
                                    [↑]
                                    [↓]

Figure 7–7

4. Click [⊞+] and enter the name of the iMate to which you want to match the iMate you are editing and press <Enter>.
5. Add additional iMate names from either the same or any other components, as required.

6. Use [↑] and [↓] to move the iMate names up and down in the list as required.
   - The higher up an iMate is in the Match List, the sooner it displays when iMate pairs are previewed.

A sample Match List is shown in Figure 7–8.

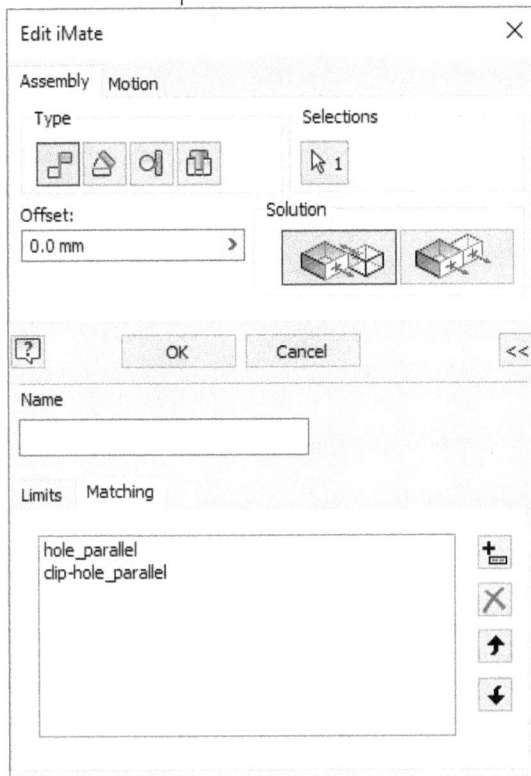

When a component is placed in an assembly, its iMates are matched with other components. The iMate first looks to the Match Lists and tries to match hole_parallel. If no match is found, clip-hole_parallel is reviewed. If a match is found, a preview displays. If no match is found, matching would continue to the next iMate in the same or other components.

Figure 7–8

7. Click **OK** to complete the modification to the iMate.
8. Edit other iMates in the same component and add names to their Match Lists. Reorder the names as required.

Hint: iMate Order and Match Lists

To ensure a particular iMate of the component you are placing is previewed before another, drag and drop the iMate higher in the list, in addition to adding its iMate pairing to the top of the Match List. As long as a matching iMate exists in the assembly in which you are placing the component, that iMate is the first iMate pair that is previewed.

Notes on iMates

When using iMates:

- Before an iMate is matched, the iMate symbol displays when the part is selected. After it is consumed, it is no longer displayed.

- In the Model Browser, iMates for each component are listed in a folder beneath the component. After the iMates are applied, a separate symbol displays indicating the constraint, as shown in Figure 7–9.

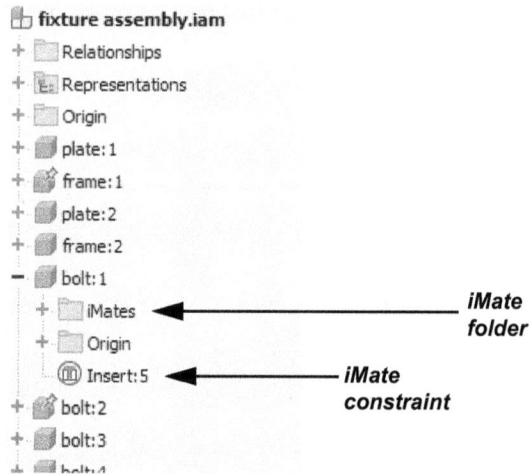

Figure 7–9

- The type of iMate determines the symbol. For example, the iMate symbol looks different from the Insert symbol, as shown in Figure 7–10. To display the symbol (glyphs), in the *View* tab>Visibility panel, click ⊙ (iMate Glyph).

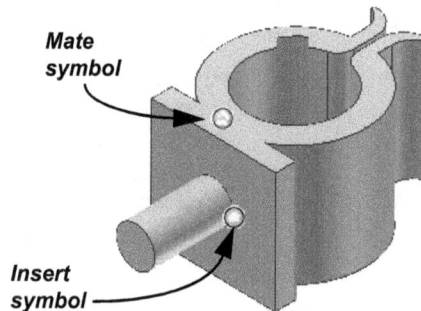

Figure 7–10

- Both iMates must be defined with the same offset, angle, rotation, or direction.

- You can use a combination of iMates and regular constraints to assemble components.

iMates in iParts

iMates can be included in iParts to vary constraint settings (e.g., offset or angle) in iPart instances. In the *Manage* tab>Author panel, click ![i+] (Create iPart) to open the iPart Author dialog box and use the *iMates* tab, as shown in Figure 7–11.

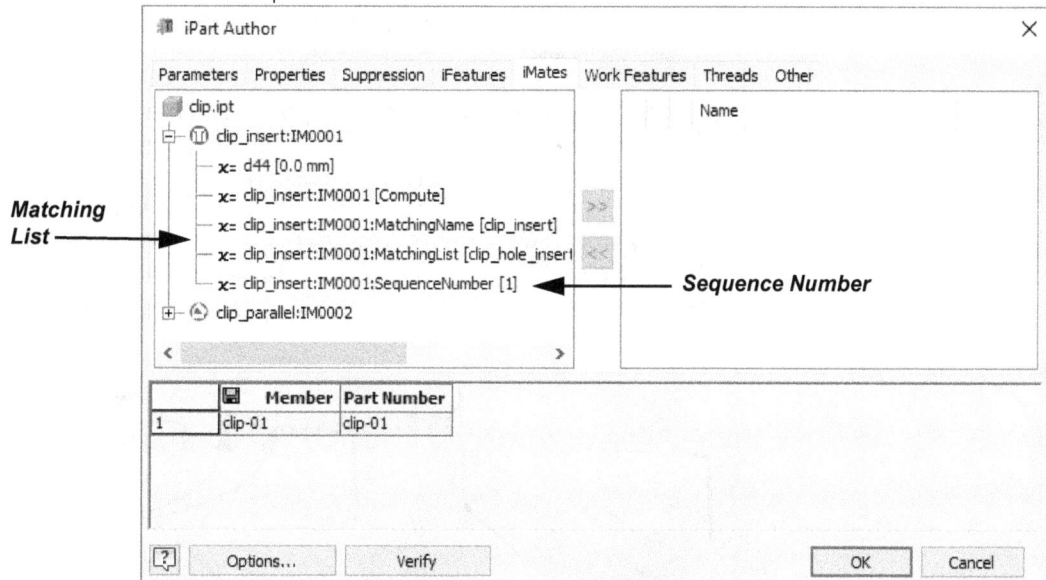

Figure 7–11

The iMate can be suppressed in an iPart instance so that it is not present. **iMate** parameters can be used as keys in an iPart. You can also add the following information to the iPart factory:

- The iMate **Sequence Number** sets the order in which iMates are applied so that they are matched automatically.

- The iMate **Matching List** automatically matches to an iMate of the same name in the assembly.

Practice 7a | iMates

Practice Objectives

- Place components into an assembly using iMates and cycling through various methods, while observing some of the available options.
- Customize the order of the iMate pairing previews by using the Match List functionality.

In this practice, you will place components into an assembly using iMates. You will also use the Match List functionality to customize the order of the iMate pairing previews. The design intent is to assemble components more quickly and efficiently through the use of iMates. You will place bolts and clips into the fixture assembly shown in Figure 7–12, using the iMate placement mode.

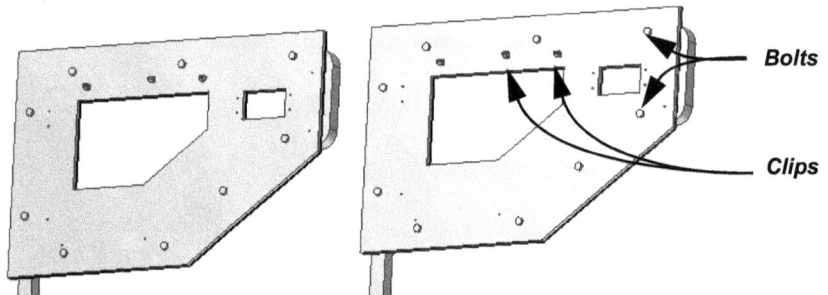

Figure 7–12

Task 1 - Open an assembly file.

1. Open **fixture assembly.iam** from the *iMates* folder. The assembly displays as shown in Figure 7–13. The fixture assembly contains two instances each of a frame and a plate. iMates have already been created for the plates.

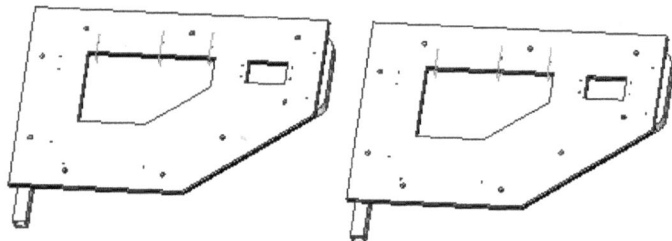

Figure 7–13

Task 2 - Preview and place instances of the bolt into the assembly.

1. In the *Assemble* tab>Component panel, click 📂 (Place).

2. At the bottom of the Place Component dialog box, click
   🔘 (Interactively place with iMates) to enable the use of
   iMates during placement.

3. Select **bolt.ipt** in the *iMates* folder, as shown in Figure 7–14.

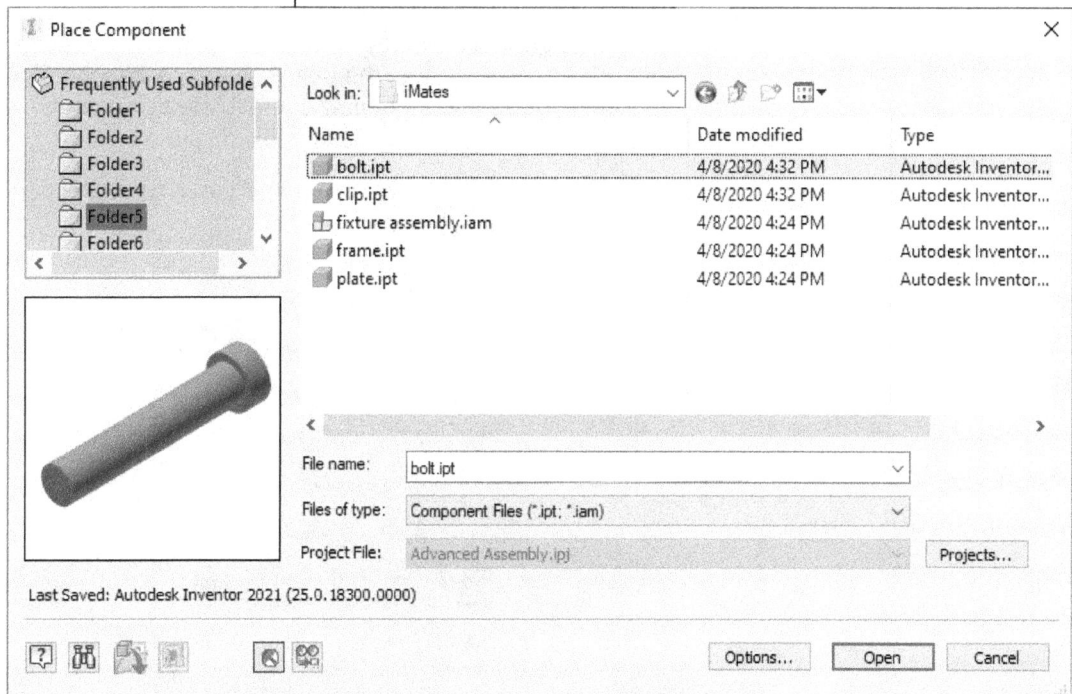

Place Component				
Frequently Used Subfolde	Look in:	iMates		
Folder1	Name		Date modified	Type
Folder2				
Folder3	bolt.ipt		4/8/2020 4:32 PM	Autodesk Inventor...
Folder4	clip.ipt		4/8/2020 4:32 PM	Autodesk Inventor...
Folder5	fixture assembly.iam		4/8/2020 4:24 PM	Autodesk Inventor...
Folder6	frame.ipt		4/8/2020 4:24 PM	Autodesk Inventor...
	plate.ipt		4/8/2020 4:24 PM	Autodesk Inventor...

File name: bolt.ipt

Files of type: Component Files (*.ipt; *.iam)

Project File: Advanced Assembly.ipj

Projects...

Last Saved: Autodesk Inventor 2021 (25.0.18300.0000)

Options... Open Cancel

Figure 7–14

4. Click **Open**. A preview of the first iMate match displays, as shown in Figure 7–15.

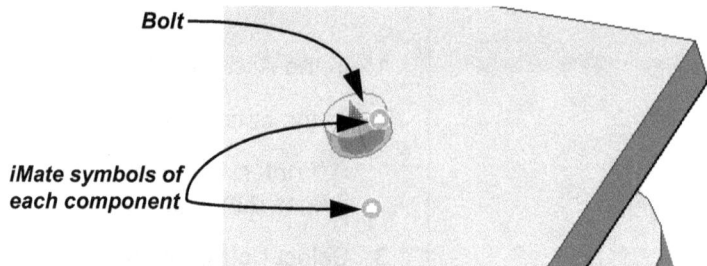

Bolt

iMate symbols of each component

Figure 7–15

5. Click in the graphics window to accept the iMate. Because there are no other iMates, the bolt is placed. A second instance displays and a preview of the iMate pairing between the second instance and the assembly displays.

6. Right-click in the graphics window and the available options display, as shown in Figure 7–16.

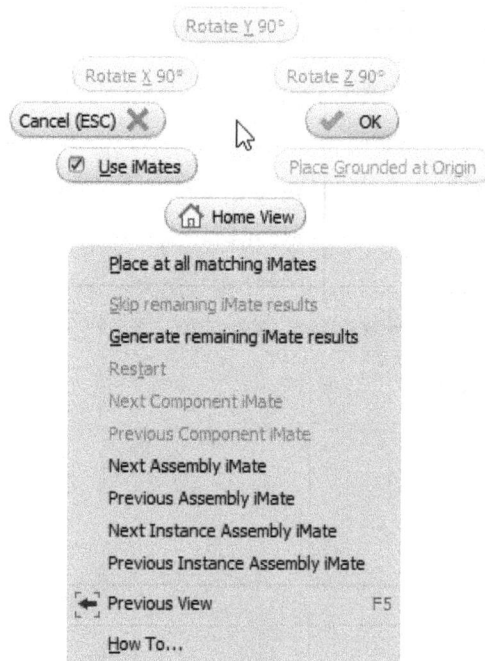

Rotate Y 90°

Rotate X 90°   Rotate Z 90°

Cancel (ESC) ✗   ✔ OK

☑ Use iMates   Place Grounded at Origin

⌂ Home View

Place at all matching iMates

Skip remaining iMate results

Generate remaining iMate results

Restart

Next Component iMate

Previous Component iMate

Next Assembly iMate

Previous Assembly iMate

Next Instance Assembly iMate

Previous Instance Assembly iMate

← Previous View   F5

How To...

Figure 7–16

7. Toggle off the **Use iMates** option. The iMate placement functionality is terminated and the bolt can be placed as it normally would if there were no iMates.

8. Right-click in the graphics window and select **Use iMates** to switch back to the iMate Placement mode.

9. Right-click in the graphics window and select **Next Assembly iMate**. The iMate pairing preview moves to the next iMate that matches, as shown in Figure 7–17.

The iMate preview moves to the next matching iMate in the assembly

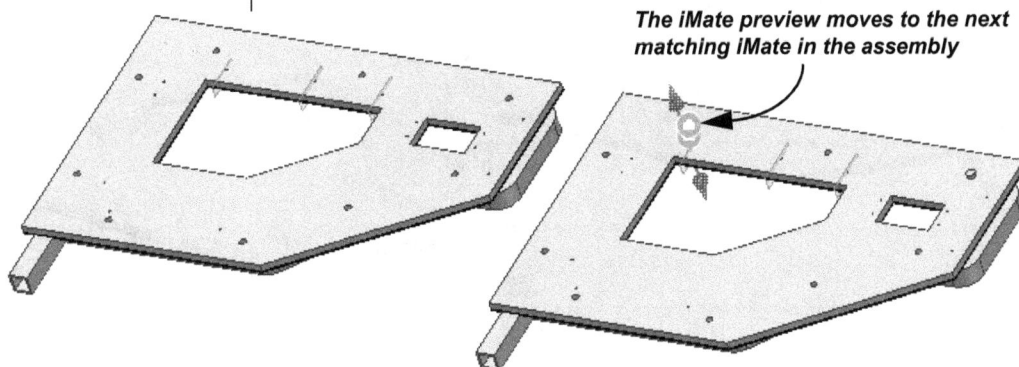

Figure 7–17

10. Move the bolt instance to the next assembly iMate.

11. Press <Right arrow>. The bolt instance moves to the next matching iMate in the assembly.

12. Press <Right arrow> several more times until the bolt instance moves to the hole shown in Figure 7–18, which resides in the plate on the left. None of the smaller holes on the plate were considered to be an appropriate iMate pairing with the bolt. This is because the iMate for the bolt was constrained with an offset of 1 mm, which is the same offset that exists for each iMate in the larger holes. The iMate for the smaller holes, although they are also Insert constraints that are in the same direction, have an offset of 0 mm and are not recognized as an iMate pairing for the iMate in the bolt.

Cycle the iMate pairing to this hole

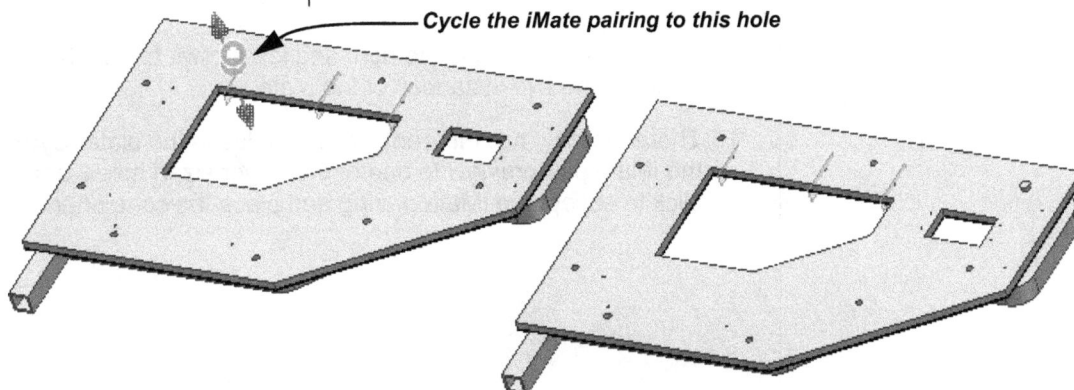

Figure 7–18

13. Use <Left arrow> to cycle the preview back to the hole, as shown in Figure 7–19.

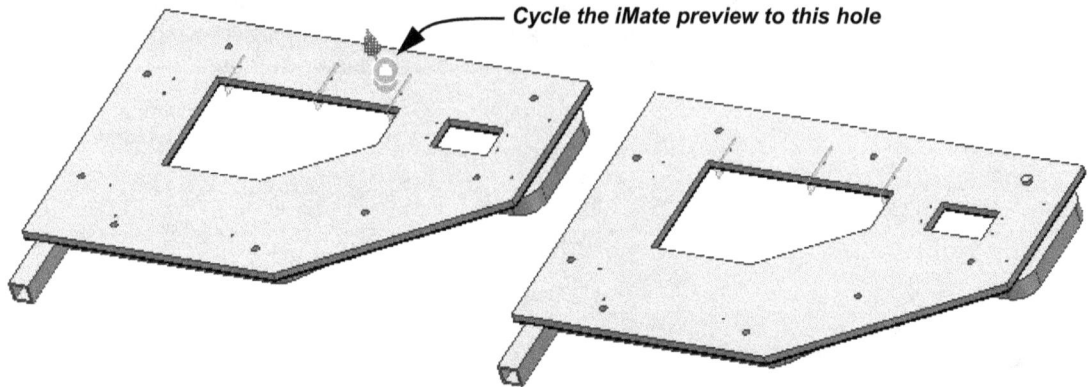

Cycle the iMate preview to this hole

Figure 7–19

14. Right-click in the graphics window and select **Next Instance Assembly iMate**. The iMate pair preview moves to the plate instance on the right side, as shown in Figure 7–20.

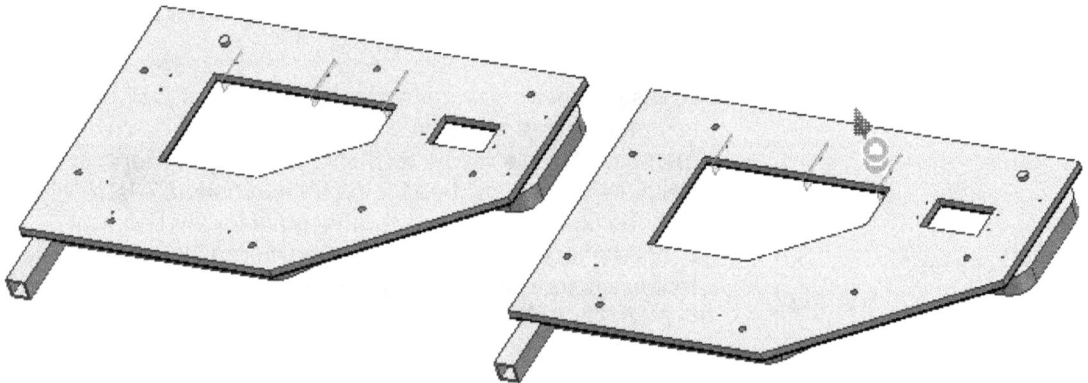

Figure 7–20

15. Hold <Ctrl> and press the right and left arrows to switch between the two instances of the plate.

16. There are only two different sizes of holes in the plate. Cycle the iMate pair preview to one of the larger sized holes, and click to accept the iMate pairing and place the component.

17. Right-click in the graphics window and select **Place at all matching iMates**. Instances are matched with all remaining and compatible iMates. You can use this option successfully because the other Insert iMates for the smaller holes are different. If the Insert iMates of both large and small holes were defined with the same offset and direction, a bolt would have been placed in all of the large and small holes.

18. Save the assembly.

Task 3 - Preview and place one instance of the clip into the assembly.

1. In the *Assemble* tab>Component panel, click ⬚ (Place).

   Ensure that ⬚ (Interactively place with iMates) is selected. Select **clip.ipt** and click **Open**. A preview of the iMate match displays, as shown in Figure 7–21.

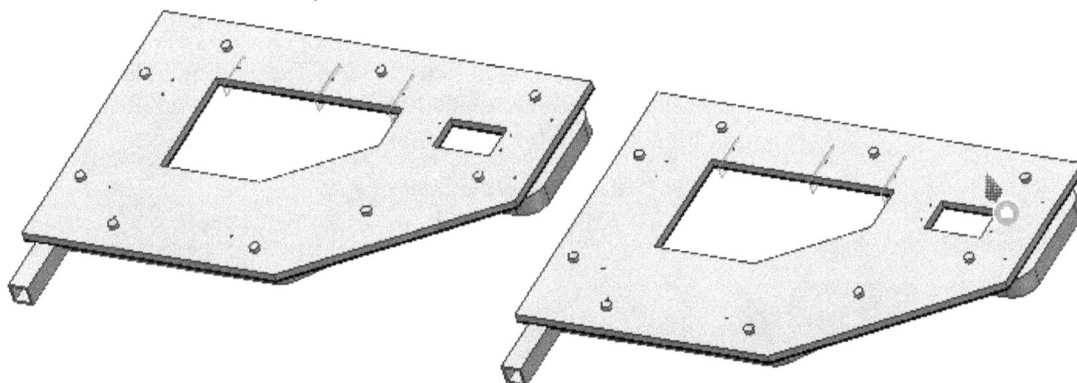

Figure 7–21

2. Cycle through the iMate pairing previews until you reach the one shown in Figure 7–22. You are required to cycle through many iMate pairings that you do not want before you get to the required hole.

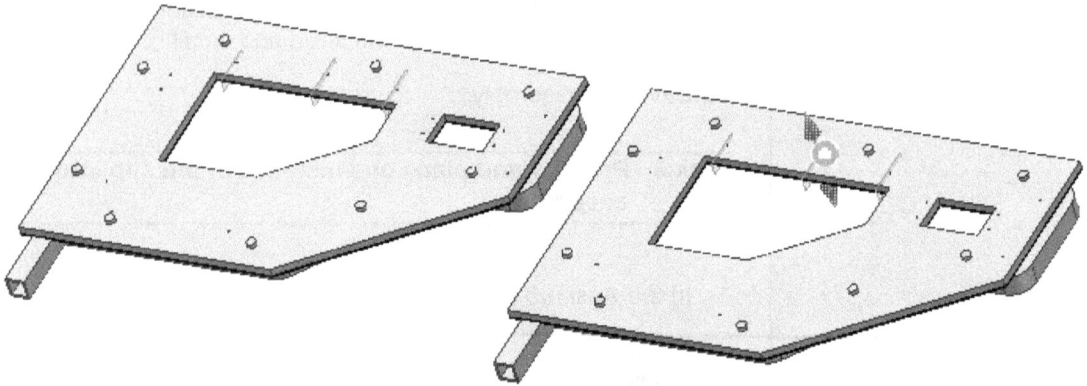

Figure 7–22

3. Click to accept the pairing of the Insert iMates. A second iMate exists for the clip. The type of constraint is indicated by the symbol shown in Figure 7–23. The names of the components and iMates that are currently being previewed are shown in the Command Line.

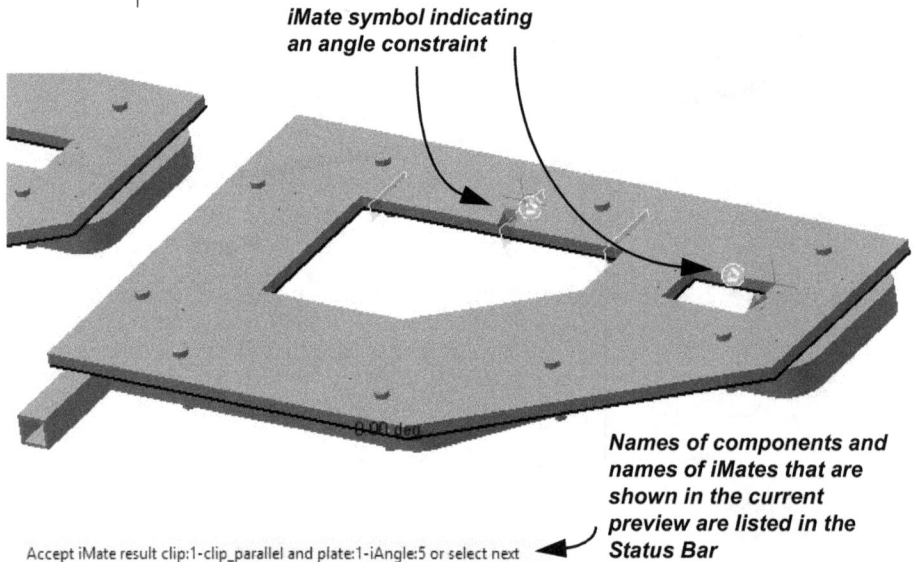

iMate symbol indicating an angle constraint

Accept iMate result clip:1-clip_parallel and plate:1-iAngle:5 or select next

Names of components and names of iMates that are shown in the current preview are listed in the Status Bar

Figure 7–23

4. Cycle through the iMate pairings until you reach the one shown in Figure 7–24.

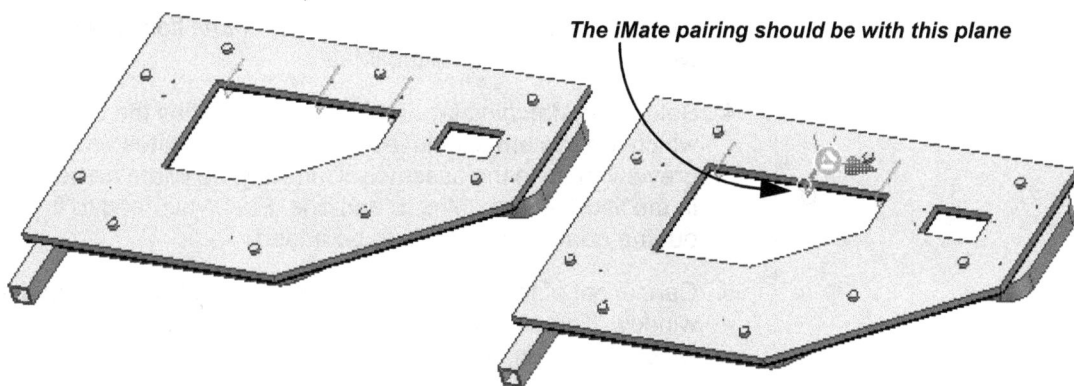

The iMate pairing should be with this plane

Figure 7–24

5. Click to accept the iMate pairing. The clip is placed in the assembly and a second instance of it displays.

6. Press <Esc> to cancel out of placing the component.

Task 4 - Edit the Match Lists of the iMates for the clip.

In this task, you edit the iMates for the clip so that during component placement, the initial iMate pairings are the ones required. This reduces the amount of cycling required and helps avoid confusion.

1. Open **clip.ipt** in a separate window. In the Model Browser, expand the *iMates* folder and note that two iMates already have descriptive names, as shown in Figure 7–25.

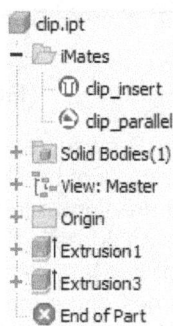

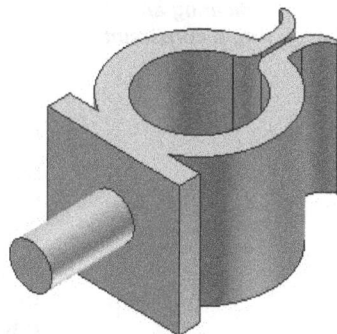

Figure 7–25

2. In the Model Browser, right-click on **clip_insert** and select **Edit**. The Edit iMate dialog box opens.

3. Click >> to expand the dialog box. A *Name* field is available where you can rename the iMate.

4. Select the *Matching* tab. A Match List specifies the order in which the system should look for matching iMates and preview them in the assembly. Currently, no iMate names are in the list. You are going to add one. First, you need to find out the name of the iMate to be added.

5. Cancel out of the dialog box and open **plate.ipt** in a separate window. The plate is the component that has the holes into which the clip is inserted.

6. If the iMate symbols are not visible on the part, in the *View* tab>Visibility panel, click ⊛ (iMate Glyph). Each symbol indicates an iMate that exists in the part. The plate displays, as shown in Figure 7–26.

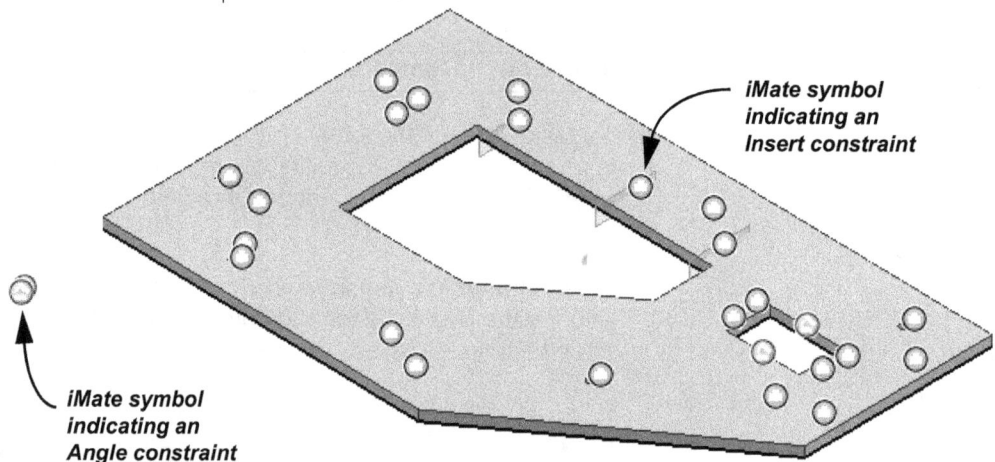

iMate symbol indicating an Insert constraint

iMate symbol indicating an Angle constraint

Figure 7–26

7. In the Model Browser, expand the *iMates* folder and move the cursor over each of the iMates until you find the three Insert iMates that are shown in Figure 7–27. When you move the cursor over an iMate in the Model Browser, the corresponding iMate symbol in the model highlights. Note that the names of the three Insert iMates are **clip_hole_insert1**, **clip_hole_insert2**, and **clip_hole_insert3**.

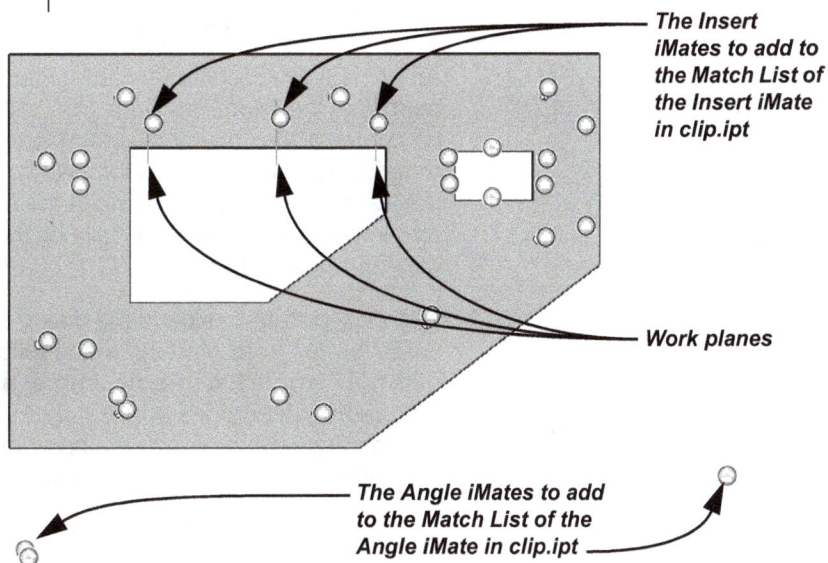

The Insert iMates to add to the Match List of the Insert iMate in clip.ipt

Work planes

The Angle iMates to add to the Match List of the Angle iMate in clip.ipt

Figure 7–27

8. Continue moving the cursor over the iMates in the Model Browser until you find the three Angle iMates shown in the Figure 7–27. Although the Angle iMate symbols display separate from the work planes (this is because the work planes were resized), the iMates do refer to the three work planes. Verify that the Angle iMate refers to a work plane by selecting it in the Model Browser. The corresponding work plane highlights. The names of the Angle iMates are **clip-hole_angle1**, **clip-hole_angle_mid**, and **clip-hole_angle3**.

9. Switch back to the **clip.ipt** window to add the iMates names in the plate to the Match Lists of the two iMates in the clip.

10. Right-click on **clip_insert** and select **Edit** to edit the iMate.

11. Click [>>] to expand the dialog box. Select the *Matching* tab.

12. Click [+] and type **clip_hole_insert2** as the iMate name to match with clip-insert. Press <Enter> when finished.

13. Add **clip_hole_insert3** to the Match List.

14. Add **clip_hole_insert1** to the Match List. Ensure that the underscores in the names are exactly as shown.

15. Select **clip_hole_insert1** and click [↑] twice to move the name to the top of the list.

16. Click **OK** to complete the modification to the iMate.

Any time a modification is made, that iMate is moved to the bottom of the iMate list. During the placement of a component, the first iMate in the Model Browser that contains a matching iMate in the assembly is the first iMate pair that is previewed. The specific iMate in the assembly that is first previewed is determined initially by the ranking in the Match List for that iMate.

17. Edit **clip_parallel**, expand the dialog box, and add the Angle iMate names from **plate.ipt** in the following order: **clip-hole_angle1, clip-hole_angle_mid, clip-hole_angle3**. Ensure that the names are exactly as shown and include the hyphen and underscore in the appropriate places to match the names of the iMates in **plate.ipt**.

18. Click **OK** to complete the modification to the iMate. **Clip_parallel** is moved to the bottom of the list of iMates. Because **clip_insert** is at the top of the iMates list in the Model Browser, it is the first iMate that is used for pairing during the placement of the clip in the assembly.

19. Save **clip.ipt**.

Task 5 - Place the clip into the assembly using the iMate placement mode.

In this task, you place the clip into the assembly using iMates. The first iMate pair preview is one of the required pairings. You will not need to cycle through before getting to the required iMate pairings.

1. Return to the fixture assembly. In the *Assemble* tab> Component panel, click (Place). Ensure that (Interactively place with iMates) is enabled, select **clip.ipt**, and click **Open**. A preview of the first iMate match displays, as shown in Figure 7–28. You did not need to cycle through any non-required iMate pairings before seeing a required one. This is because you added the Insert iMate names in the plate to the Match List of the Insert iMate in the clip.

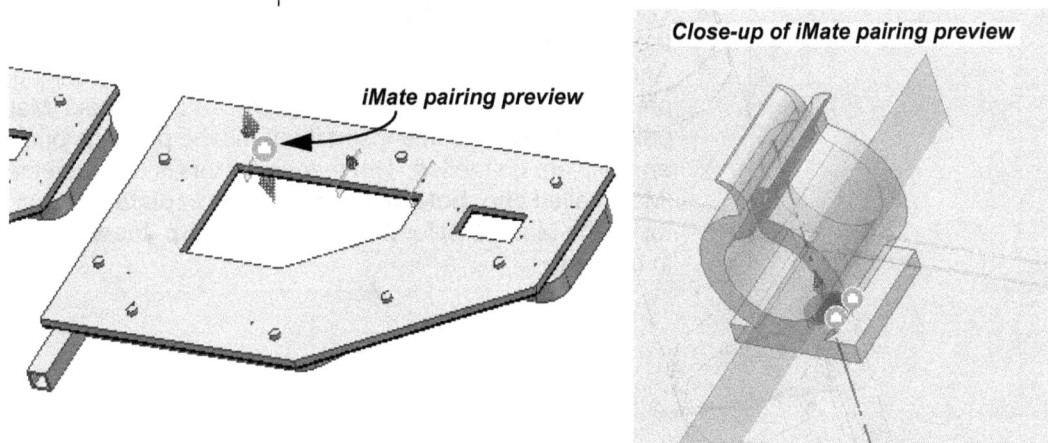

iMate pairing preview

Close-up of iMate pairing preview

Figure 7–28

2. Click to accept the iMate pairing. The next iMate pairing preview displays, as shown in Figure 7–29. It proceeds directly to one of the iMate pairings that you do want. This is a direct result of adding the Angle iMate names from the plate to the Match List of the Angle iMate in the clip.

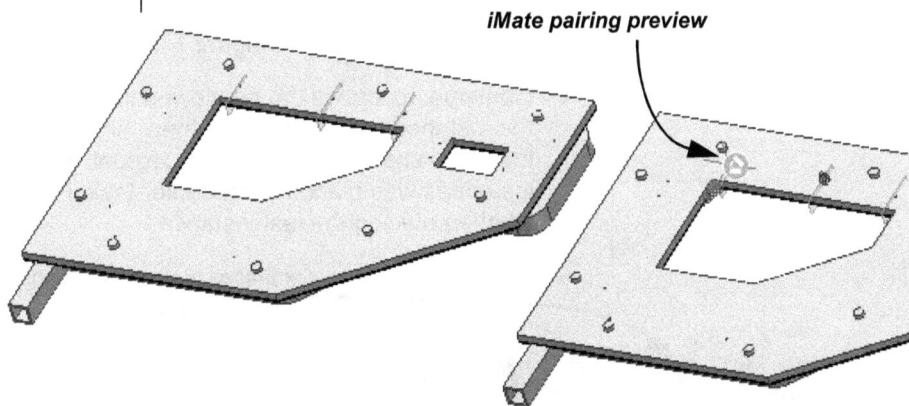

iMate pairing preview

Figure 7–29

3. Click to accept the iMate pairing. The component is placed in the assembly using the two iMate pairings you accepted. Another instance of the clip displays and an iMate pairing preview displays, as shown in Figure 7–30. The next iMate pairing is with the same Insert iMate as the previous one, but on the plate on the left. The reason for this is because the iMate called **clip_hole_insert1** (which is in **plate.ipt**) is at the top of the Match List for the iMate called **clip_insert** (which is in **clip.ipt**).

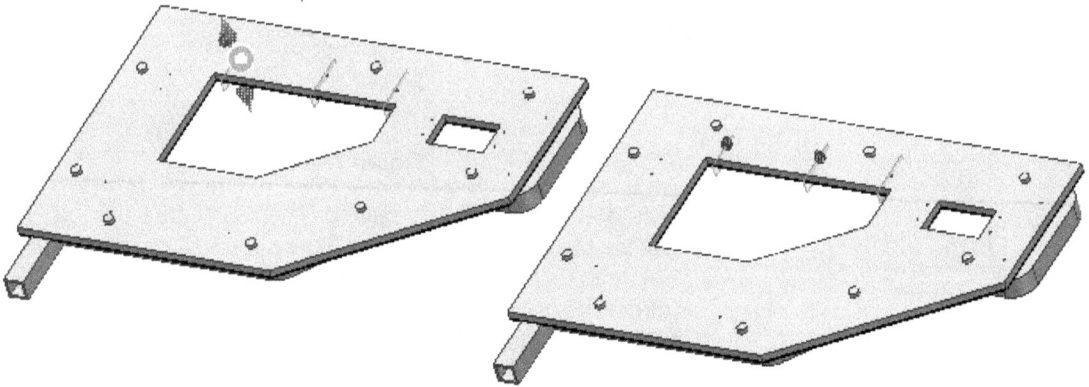

Figure 7–30

4. Continue accepting the previewed iMate pairings and placing the instances of **clip.ipt** until there are six instances in the locations shown in Figure 7–31. Recall that one of the instances was placed in an earlier task. Press <Esc> when finished placing the last instance.

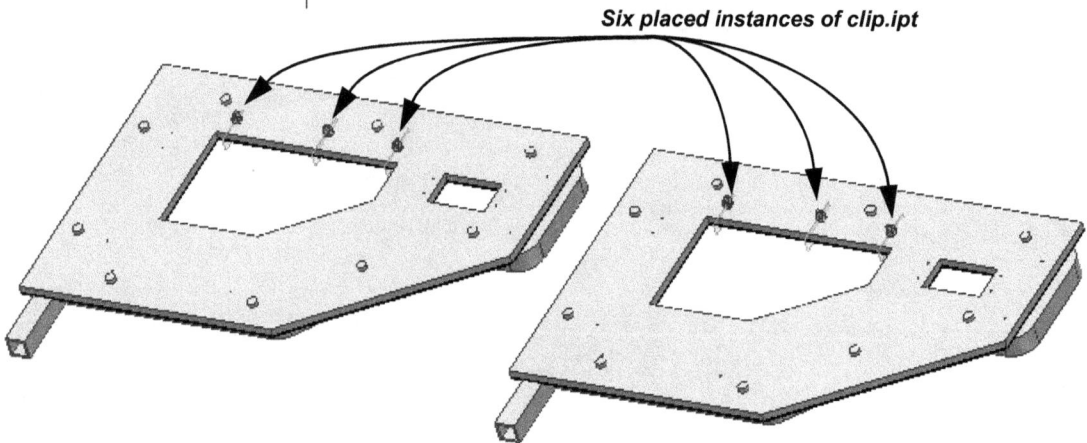

Six placed instances of clip.ipt

Figure 7–31

5. Save and close the models.

Practice 7b

Composite iMates

Practice Objectives

- Create multiple iMates and combine them into composite iMates.
- Assemble components in an assembly using iMates.

You will often place parts in an assembly using the same assembly constraints. iMate constraints can be defined in the part files, which tell parts how and where to connect when placed in an assembly. You can also combine multiple iMates into a group, called a composite iMate. The composite acts as a single iMate.

In this practice, you create iMates on three parts: you will group the iMates for each part into a composite iMate and then assemble them into a new assembly file. The three components of the assembly are shown in Figure 7–32.

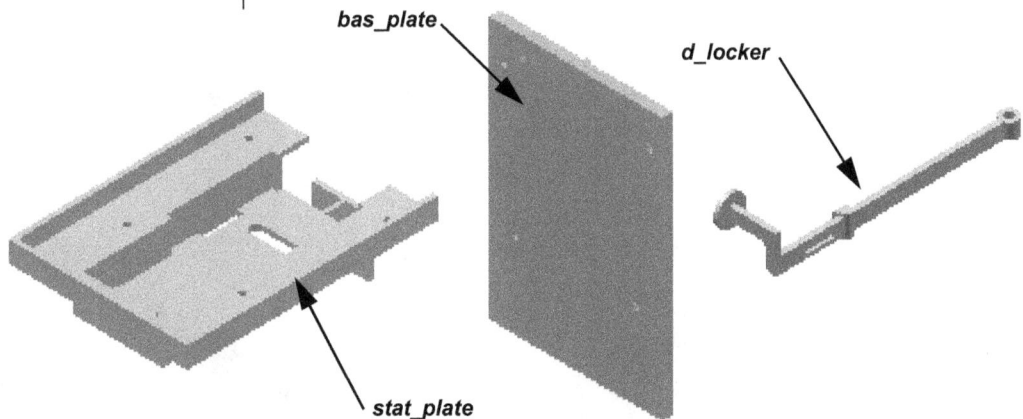

bas_plate

d_locker

stat_plate

Figure 7–32

Task 1 - Open a part file and create iMates.

1. Open **d_locker.ipt** from the top level practice files folder.

2. In the *Manage* tab>Author panel, click ⊘ (iMate). The Create iMate dialog box opens. The Mate type constraint is selected by default.

3. Click to create an iInsert and select the edge shown in Figure 7–33.

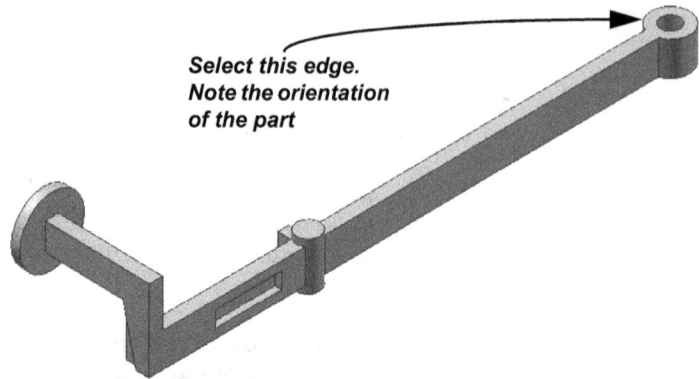

Select this edge.
Note the orientation
of the part

Figure 7–33

4. Click **Apply** to apply the constraint.

5. Click . Select the outside face of the feature shown in Figure 7–34 to create an iMate at the centerline of the round feature.

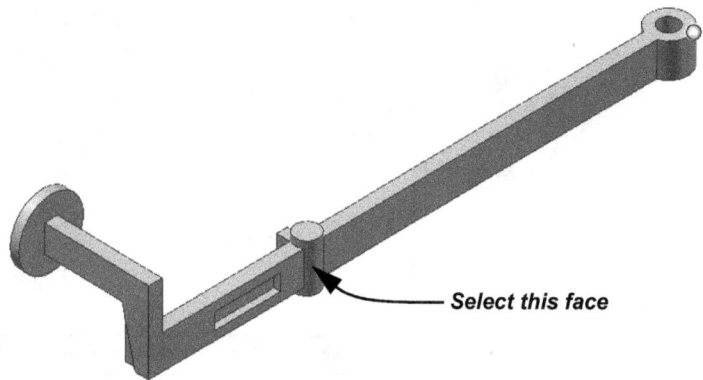

Select this face

Figure 7–34

6. Click **Apply** to apply the constraint.

7. Click **Cancel** to close the dialog box.

8. In the Model Browser, expand the *iMates* folder and select both the **iInsert:1** and **iMate:1**. Right-click and select **Create Composite**. Then, expand **iComposite:1**, as shown in Figure 7–35.

Ensure that matching iMates have the same name in all models.

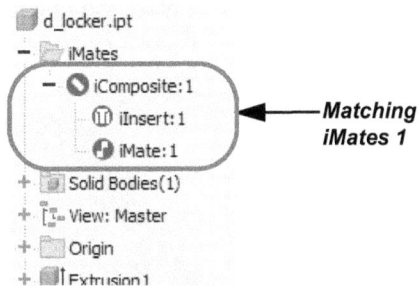

d_locker.ipt
− iMates
  − iComposite:1
    iInsert:1 ◄── **Matching iMates 1**
    iMate:1
+ Solid Bodies(1)
+ View: Master
+ Origin
+ Extrusion1

Figure 7–35

9. Save and close the model.

Task 2 - Open the part called stat_plate and create iMates.

1. Open **stat_plate.ipt**.

2. Rotate the model, as shown in Figure 7–36.

3. Create an iInsert on the edge shown in Figure 7–36.

Select the bottom edge of this stud

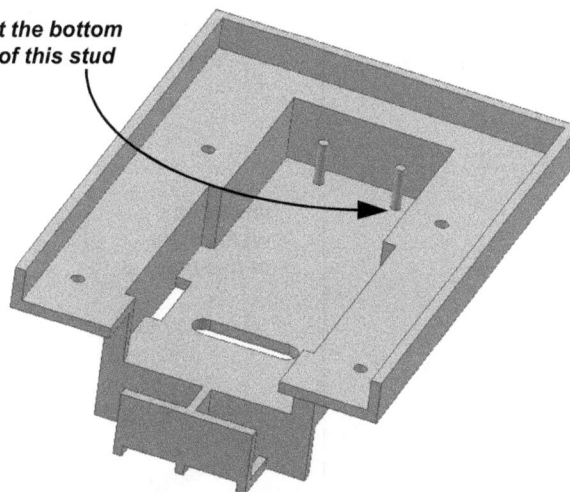

Figure 7–36

4. Click **Apply** to apply the constraint.

5. Select the inside round surface of the slot shown in Figure 7–37 to create an **iMate** at the centerline of the round slot face.

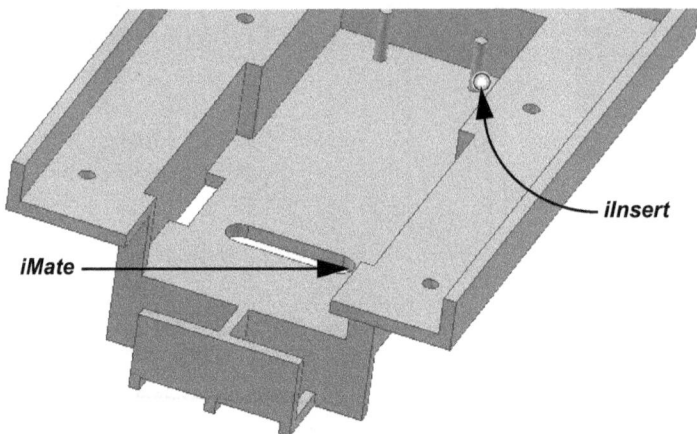

Figure 7–37

6. Create an iComposite of the two constraints.

7. Create three more iMate constraints, as shown in Figure 7–38.

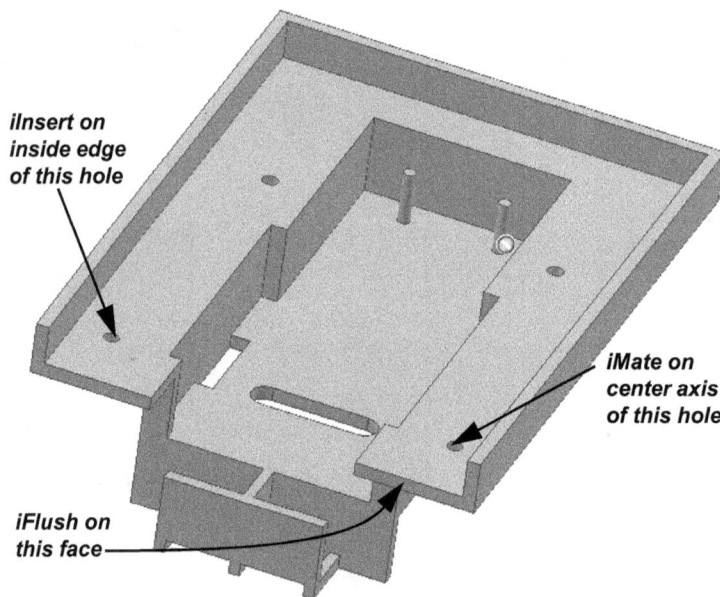

Figure 7–38

8. Create an iComposite of the three constraints. Expand the iComposites in the Model Browser, as shown in Figure 7–39.

Verify that matching iMates have the same name in all models.

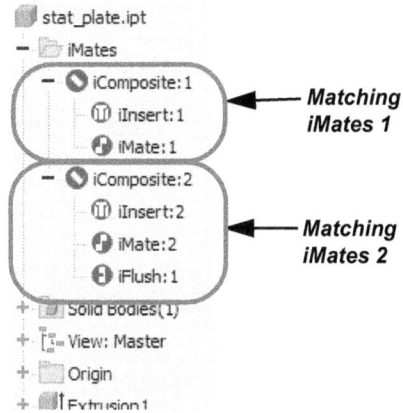

Figure 7–39

9. Save and close the model.

Task 3 - Open a part file and create iMates.

In this task, you create three iMates on the part, create a composite of the three iMates, and change the iMates and iComposite names to match the names of the iMates and iComposite in the previous task. This enables you to match composite iMates from different parts with the same number of iMates and names in an assembly.

1. Open **bas_plate.ipt**.

2. Create the three iMates shown in Figure 7–40. Note the orientation of the model.

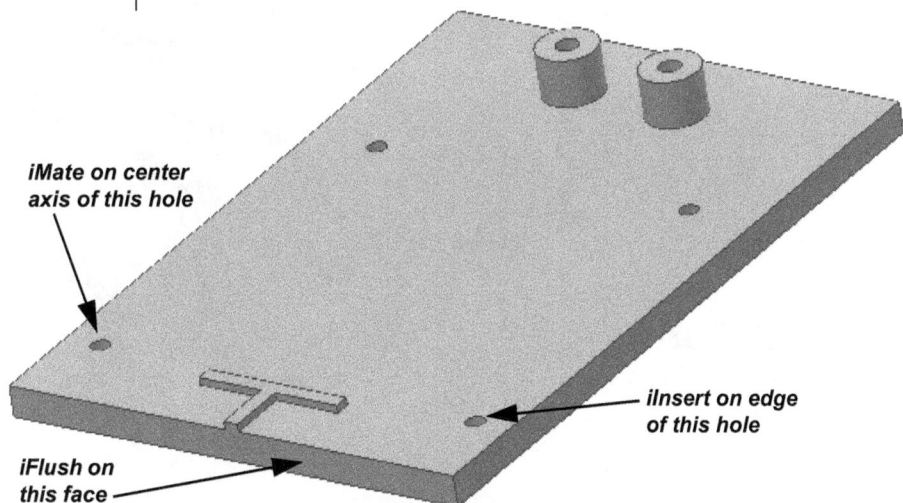

Figure 7–40

---

3. Change the *iInsert:1* and *iMate:1* names to **iInsert:2** and **iMate:2**, respectively. This ensures that the naming of the iMates match between components.

4. Create an iComposite of the three constraints and change its name to **iComposite:2**.

5. Save and close the model.

Task 4 - Create a new assembly file.

1. Create a new assembly file using the standard imperial template.

2. In the *Assemble* tab>Component panel, click 📂 (Place). Ensure that 🔘 (Interactively place with iMates) is enabled, select **stat_plate.ipt**, and click **Open**.

3. Right-click and select **Place Grounded at Origin** to ground the component.

4. Press <Esc> to cancel placing additional components.

5. Click 📂 (Place) again. In the Open dialog box, select and open **d_locker.ipt**. The assembly displays, automatically assembled, as shown in Figure 7–41.

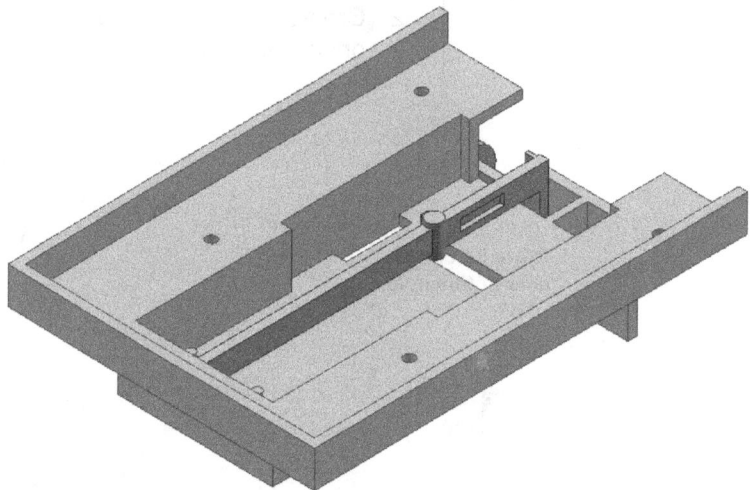

Figure 7–41

6. Click to accept the iMate pairing preview. The component is placed. Press <Esc>.

7. Place **bas_plate.ipt** in the assembly. The assembly displays, automatically assembled. Complete its placement, as shown in Figure 7–42.

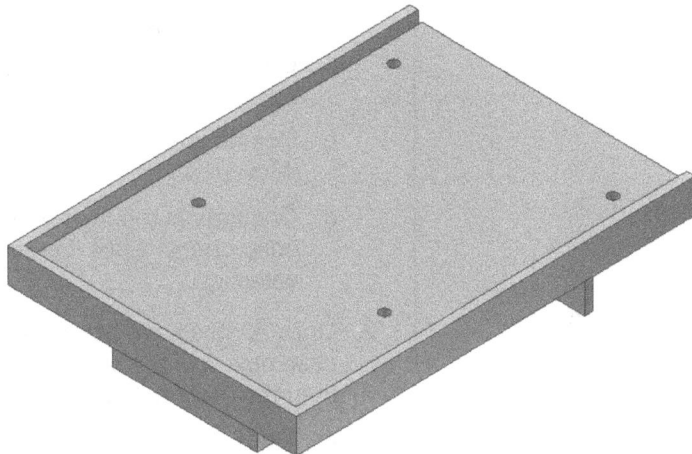

Figure 7–42

8. In the *Assemble* tab>Productivity panel, click 🗸 (Degree of Freedom Analysis) and verify that there are no remaining degrees of freedom in the assembly.

9. Save and close the model.

Chapter Review Questions

1. Which of the following best describe iMates and constraints? (Select all that apply.)

   a. Symmetry can be assigned as an iMate but not as a constraint type.

   b. Offset and angular values can be specified when assigning both an iMate and constraint.

   c. Constraints can be incorporated into an iPart; however an iMates cannot.

   d. Constraints require references to be selected on two components while iMates require only one reference selection.

2. Once iMates have been used to locate a component in an assembly, it is not possible to add any additional constraints to further define its placement.

   a. True

   b. False

3. Which of the following best describes the purpose of a Composite iMate?

   a. A Composite iMate applies multiple constraints in multiple assemblies.

   b. A Composite iMate applies multiple iMates in one assembly, all at once.

   c. A Composite iMate groups all iMates of a a single type together.

   d. A Composite iMate applies multiple instances of a component at once.

4. Which of the following best describes the purpose of the Match List?

   a. A Match List creates a list of similar iMates in an assembly.

   b. A Match List applies multiple constraints all in one step.

   c. A Match List controls the order in which iMate pairs are previewed and applied.

   d. A Match List adds iMates to iParts.

5. The iMate symbol associated with a component being placed in an assembly displays both prior to and after the component is placed.

   a. True

   b. False

Command Summary

Button	Command	Location
	Create iPart	• **Ribbon:** *Manage* tab>Author panel
	iMate	• **Ribbon:** *Manage* tab>Author panel
	iMate Glyph (display)	• **Ribbon:** *View* tab>Visibility panel
	Place	• **Ribbon:** *Assemble* tab>Component panel

Positional Representations

With Positional Representations, the Autodesk® Inventor® software enables you to create positional configurations of an assembly. These configurations can be used to review motion, evaluate the position of assembly components, or document an assembly in a drawing.

Learning Objectives in This Chapter

- Create and edit different Positional Representations of an assembly by overriding the existing settings of an assembly.
- Specify which Positional Representation is initially activated when the assembly is opened or inserted into another assembly.
- Find and edit Positional Representations more easily by viewing detailed information of only the Positional Representations that exist in an active assembly.
- Place Drawing Views of different positions of an assembly by using Positional Representations.

8.1 Introduction to Positional Representations

Positional Representations enable you to create positional configurations of an assembly. The configurations can be used to review motion, evaluate the position of assembly components, or document an assembly in a drawing.

Positional Representations are stored in the top-level assembly and can be retrieved or modified quickly and easily. They are listed in the *Position* folder under Representations only after the first Positional Representation is created. When the first one is created, a Master is also created. The Master Positional Representation is the default positional state of the assembly. The Master (default) Positional Representation of the excavator assembly is shown in Figure 8–1.

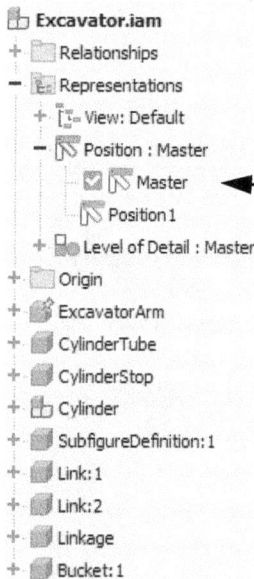

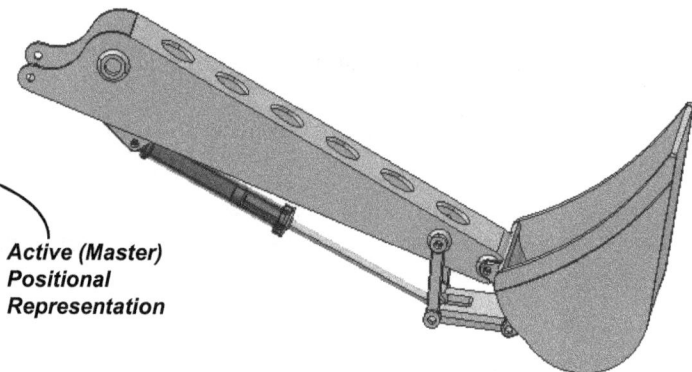

Active (Master) Positional Representation

Figure 8–1

When the Master Positional Representation is active, you cannot perform any of the modeling operations you normally do in an assembly (such as placing components, creating constraints, and saving the assembly).

8.2 Create and Edit Positional Representations

You can create new Positional Representations and make changes to the component positions and constraint settings without affecting the original component positions in the Master. An alternative Positional Representation of the same assembly is shown in Figure 8–2.

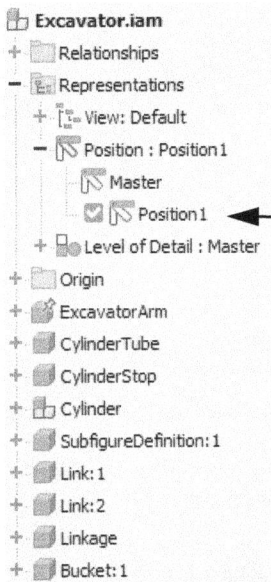

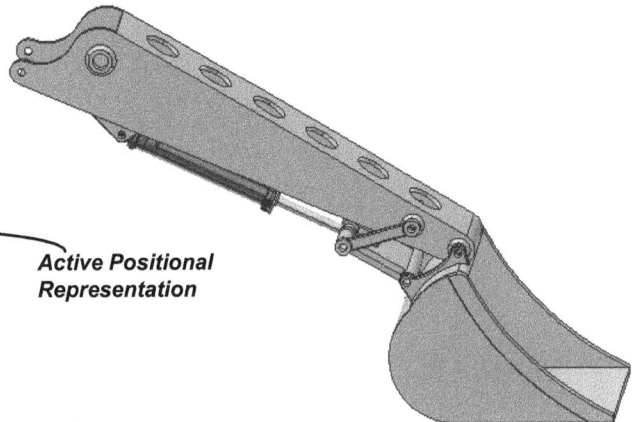

Excavator.iam
- Relationships
- Representations
  - View: Default
  - Position : Position 1
    - Master
    - ☑ Position 1 ◄—— *Active Positional Representation*
  - Level of Detail : Master
- Origin
- ExcavatorArm
- CylinderTube
- CylinderStop
- Cylinder
- SubfigureDefinition:1
- Link: 1
- Link: 2
- Linkage
- Bucket: 1

Figure 8–2

General Steps

Use the following general steps to create a Positional Representation:

1. Create a Positional Representation.
2. Override values for the Positional Representation.
3. Complete the override.
4. Modify overrides, as required.
5. Save the changes in the assembly.

Step 1 - Create a Positional Representation.

Expand the *Representations* folder in the Model Browser. Initially, no Positional Representations are available. To create a new one, right-click on **Position** and select **New**, as shown in Figure 8–3. A new Positional Representation is created and is immediately activated.

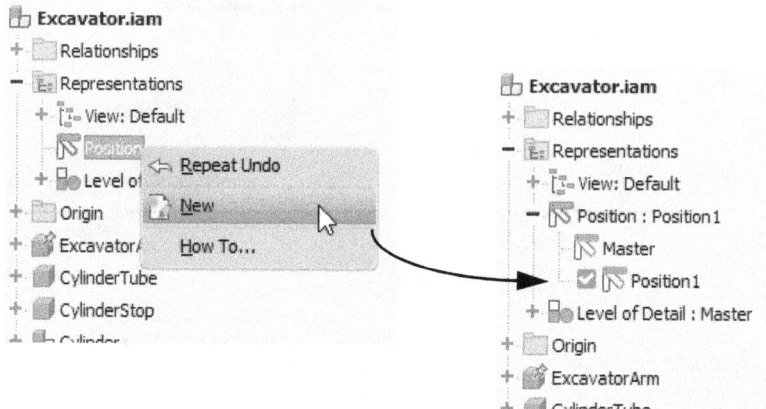

Figure 8–3

- A checkmark indicates the active Positional Representation.

- You can rename it by clicking twice (not double-clicking) on its name and entering a new name.

Step 2 - Override values for the Positional Representation.

Verify that the required Positional Representation is active by double-clicking its name in the Model Browser or by right-clicking on its name and selecting **Activate**.

A Positional Representation is created using the Override dialog box to assign overrides to values in the Master assembly. Right-click on the object (such as a component or assembly constraint or joint connection) that you want to modify in the Model Browser and select **Override**. The Override Object dialog box opens, as shown in Figure 8–4.

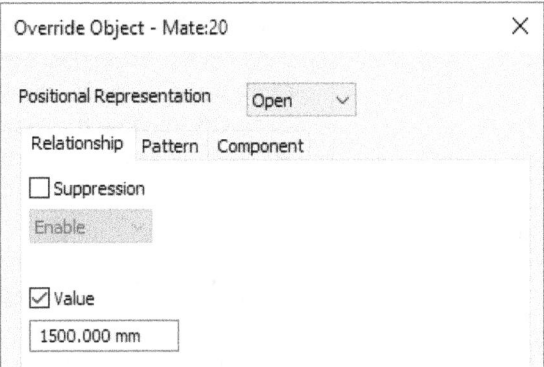

Figure 8–4

Some options are grayed out, depending on the object type selected to override.

*After modifying certain options and values, the software might move components to adhere to active constraints. If there are components you would like to remain fixed or grounded, set the Grounding override option to **Grounded**.*

Three tabs contain the following options. For any option you want to override, enable the option by selecting it in the appropriate tab and setting the required values.

Override Option	Description
Suppression (***Relationship** tab*)	Overrides the suppression of a constraint or joint so that it can be applied in one Positional Representation and suppressed in another.
Value (***Relationship** tab*)	Overrides a constraint or joint offset value to enable it to have a specific value in one Positional Representation and a different offset value in another.
Rectangular Pattern (***Pattern** tab*)	Overrides the row or column offset value for a rectangular pattern.
Circular Pattern (***Pattern** tab*)	Overrides the angle offset value for a circular pattern.
Grounding (***Component** tab*)	Overrides the grounded status of a component.
Position Offset (***Component** tab*)	Overrides the angle and offset positions of a component. The values can only be modified by directly moving the component in the graphics window. There is no value field in the Override Objects dialog box that can be directly edited.
Positional Representation (***Component** tab*)	Overrides the current Positional Representation. This is valuable for setting a Positional Representation in a subassembly.
Flexible Status (***Component** tab*)	Overrides the flexible status of a component. For a subassembly that is used multiple times in a larger assembly, you can make each subassembly flexible so that each instance can have a unique position. For example, if a hydraulic cylinder assembly is used twice, one cylinder can be fully open, while the other is fully closed.

Step 3 - Complete the override.

Click **Apply** to apply the changes and continue to add overrides. Click **OK** to close the dialog box. The objects that have overrides applied display in bold text in the Model Browser and the override value displays in bold and in parentheses.

Step 4 - Modify overrides, as required.

The following options can be used to modify Positional Representations.

Copy

By default, a copy of the master representation is created when a new Positional Representation is created. In some cases, it is faster to copy an existing Positional Representation rather than the master. To do this, right-click on the Positional Representation to be copied and select **Copy**. A new Positional Representation is created with the same override values as the one it was copied from.

Delete

To delete a Positional Representation, you can either select the one to be deleted and press <Delete> or right-click on it and select **Delete**.

Edit Overrides

To edit an existing Positional Representation, ensure it is activated, right-click on the override (bold and parentheses), and select **Override**. The Override Object dialog box opens as it was when originally created and you can change the options.

To simply change a value associated with an override, right-click on the override and select **Modify (Override)** or double-click on the override (bold and parentheses) and enter a new value in the dialog box that opens.

Remove Overrides

An override for an object can be removed at once by right-clicking on the override (bold and parentheses) and selecting **Remove Override**. The overrides assigned to multiple items can be removed at once by pre-selecting them and then clicking **Remove Override**.

Suppress Overrides

An override can be suppressed so that it is temporarily not incorporated into the active Positional Representation. To suppress, right-click on the override and select **Suppress (Override)**.

Step 5 - Save the changes in the assembly.

You cannot save an assembly while a Positional Representation is active. You must activate the Master in the top-level assembly and save the assembly. If you attempt to save the assembly while a Positional Representation is active, you are prompted to save the Master assembly. If you confirm the save, the model is automatically returned to the Master Positional Representation and is saved.

8.3 Use Positional Representations

Opening Files

If an assembly contains Positional Representations, you can specify which one is initially activated when the assembly is opened or when it is inserted into another assembly.

How To: Specify Which Positional Representation Should Be Activated Upon Opening or Placing an Assembly

1. In the Quick Access Toolbar, click 📂.
2. Select the assembly to open or place from the Open dialog box.
3. Click **Options**.
4. Select the required Positional Representation to be activated from the Positional Representation drop-down list.
5. Click **OK** and then **Open**. The selected Positional Representation is loaded and activated.

Representations Browser

The Model Browser can be expanded to provide detailed information of only the Positional Representations that exist in the active assembly. This enables you to find and edit Positional Representations more easily. To enable expanded information for Positional Representations, select **Representations** from the Model Browser drop-down list, as shown in Figure 8–5.

You can reorder Positional Representations in the Model or Representations Browser by dragging and dropping them in the list. The Master view cannot be reordered.

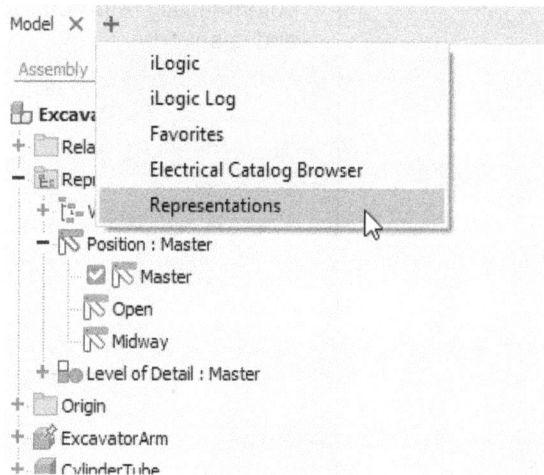

Figure 8–5

Once enabled, all Positional Representations include the details on their overrides, as shown in Figure 8–6. Components and constraints that have not been modified are not shown in the Representations browser.

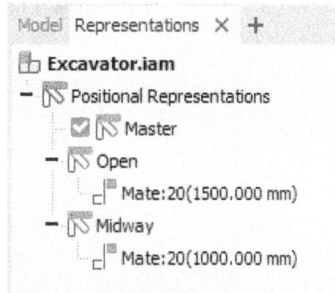

Figure 8–6

The icons available at the bottom of the Representations browser are described as follows:

Icons	Description
	Creates a new Positional Representation by copying the Master.
	Verifies all Positional Representations are valid and do not cause errors.
(only available if a Pos Rep already exists in the model)	Opens a Microsoft® Excel® table to edit the Positional Representations. Only overridden element values display. Blank cells share the same value as the Master. Rows can be added to create new Positional Representations; however, you cannot remove, reorder, or rename rows. You cannot add new columns, edit column headers, delete columns or rows, or reorder columns.

	A	B	C	D	E
1		Mate:7 (Constraint Offset)	Screw_Sub:1 (Positional Rep)	Mate:7 (Constraint Suppress)	Screw_Sub:1 (Flexible)
2	Master	0.0 in	Master	Enable	Non-Flexible
3	Open	68.280 mm	Extend		
4	Free		Free	Suppress	Flexible
5					

Drawing Views Using Positional Representations

To change the Positional Representation used in the drawing view, edit the view and select another Positional Representation. Any changes made to the Positional Representation in the assembly update in any drawing views in which it is used.

Positional Representations can be used in the Base and Overlay drawing views.

• To use an existing Positional Representation in a Base view, select the Positional Representation's name in the Position drop-down list, as shown in Figure 8–7.

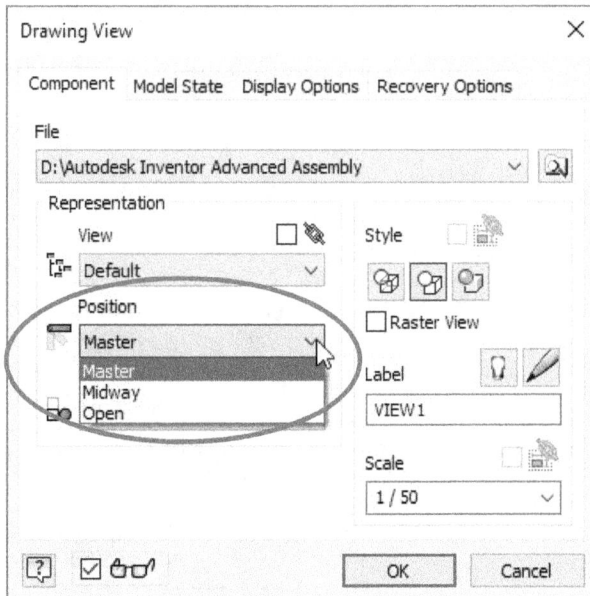

Figure 8–7

• To document assembly motion in a drawing Positional Representations and Overlay views can be used together, as shown on the right in Figure 8–8. You must have at least two positional representations in the assembly to create overlay views. To create the view, select a parent view, define the overlay view options, and then click **OK**.

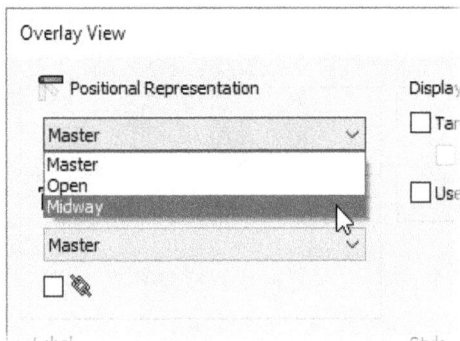

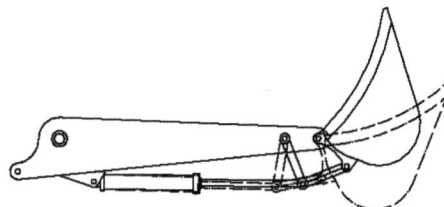

Overlay view is displaying both the Master view and a Midway view

Figure 8–8

Practice 8a | Positional Representations I

Practice Objective

- Switch between different positions of an assembly by creating Positional Representations and overriding constraints.

In this practice, you create Positional Representations for an excavator assembly. The Positional Representations will enable you to quickly display three different positions of the assembly in either the assembly or drawing environment. The positions are shown in Figure 8–9.

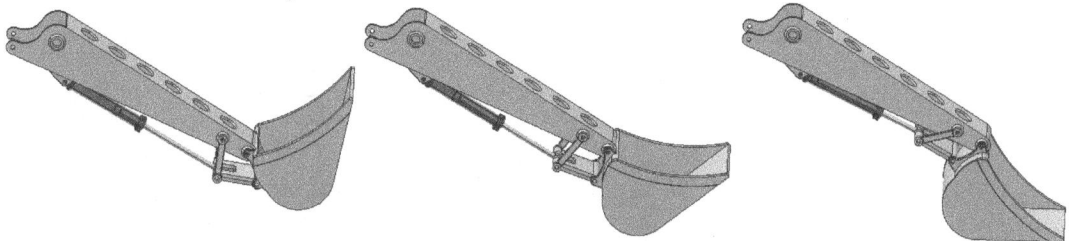

Figure 8–9

Task 1 - Create a Positional Representation.

1. Open **Excavator.iam** from the *ExcavatorAssembly* folder. The assembly displays as shown in Figure 8–10.

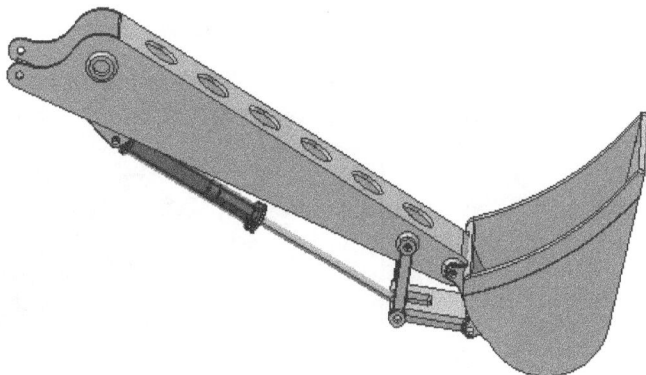

Figure 8–10

2. Expand the *Representations* folder, right-click on **Position**, and select **New**, as shown in Figure 8–11.

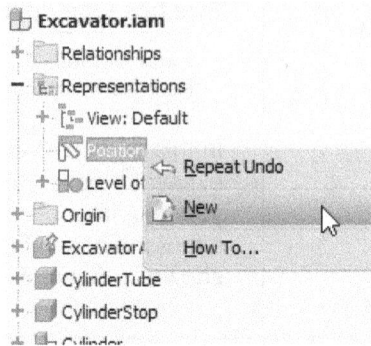

Figure 8–11

3. Expand the **Position** branch, there are two Positional Representations listed: the **Master** and **Position1**. A checkmark should display next to **Position1**, indicating that it is currently active and can be edited.

4. Rename *Position1* to **Open** by clicking twice on it in the Model Browser, typing the new name, and pressing <Enter>.

Task 2 - Create an override for the open position.

---

1. Expand the **Cylinder** subassembly, right-click on the **Mate:20** constraint and select **Override**. The Override Object dialog box opens.

2. Select the *Value* option and type **1500 mm**.

3. Click **OK**. The model moves to the new position based on the new mate value, as shown in Figure 8–12.

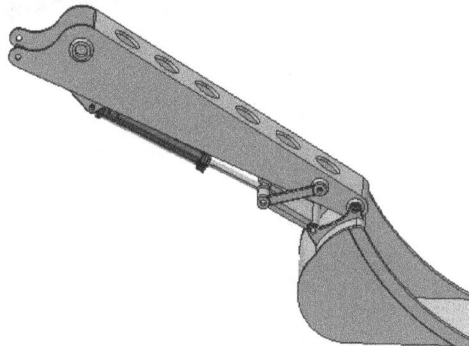

Figure 8–12

Task 3 - Create an override to represent the mid-way position.

1. Right-click on **Position: Open** and select **New** to create a new Positional Representation.

2. Rename the new Positional Representation to **Midway**.

3. Expand the Cylinder subassembly, right-click on the **Mate:20** constraint and select **Override**.

4. Select the *Value* option and type **1000 mm**. Click **OK**. The assembly now displays as shown in Figure 8–13.

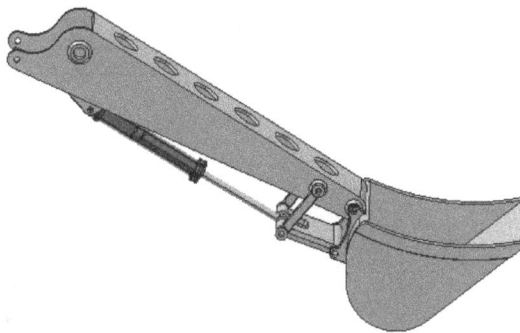

Figure 8–13

Task 4 - Switch between the three Positional Representations.

1. In the Model Browser, double-click on the **Open** Positional Representation. The model should update to the open position.

2. Double-click on the **Midway** Positional Representation. The assembly updates.

3. Double-click on the **Master** Positional Representation. The assembly updates.

4. Save the assembly and close the window.

*Alternatively, you can right-click on the Positional Representation and select **Activate**.*

Positional Representations can be used in the drawing environment to create Base and Overlay views.

Practice 8b

Positional Representations II

Practice Objectives

- Create Positional Representations with overrides to top-level and subassemblies.
- Display the Positional Representations of an assembly in a drawing.

In this practice, you create Positional Representations for a vise assembly to show its open and closed positions in a drawing. The two positions are defined by overrides in the top-level assembly as well as in a subassembly. The drawing with an Overlay view showing the open position of the vise is shown in Figure 8–14.

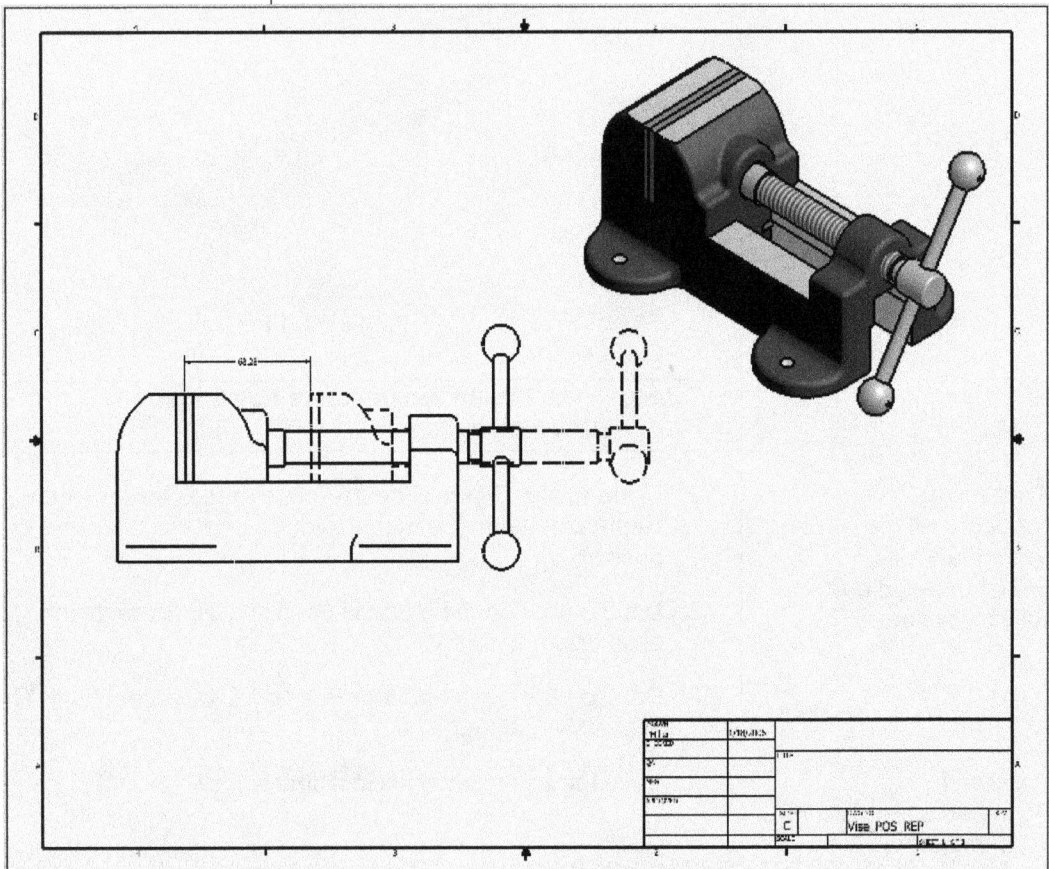

Figure 8–14

Task 1 - Open an assembly file.

1. Open **Vise_POS_REP.iam** from the *Vise_POS_REP Assembly* folder. The assembly displays as shown in Figure 8–15.

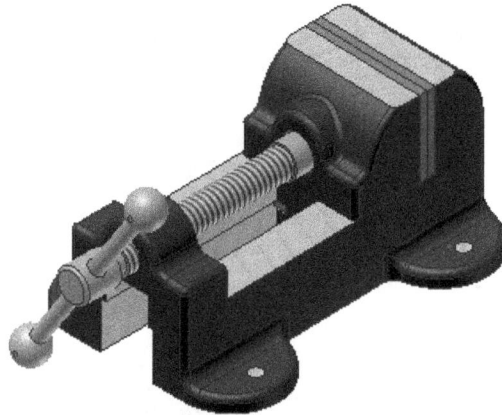

Figure 8–15

2. Review the Model Browser. The assembly contains one subassembly.

3. Open **Screw_Sub.iam**. Note that three Positional Representations are already specified in this assembly (Master, Extend, and Free).

4. Close the subassembly and activate **Vise_POS_REP.iam**.

Task 2 - Create an override for the open position.

1. In the Model Browser, expand the *Representations* folder, right-click on **Position**, and select **New**.

2. Expand the **Position** branch and rename *Position1* to **Open**.

3. Override the **Mate** constraint between the two jaw plates and specify a value of **2.7 in**.

4. Right-click on the **Screw_Sub** subassembly and select **Override**. By doing this, you can set a Positional Representation in a subassembly to vary in a top-level assembly.

5. In the *Component* tab, select the **Positional Representation** option and select **Extend** in the drop-down list, as shown in Figure 8–16. Click **OK**.

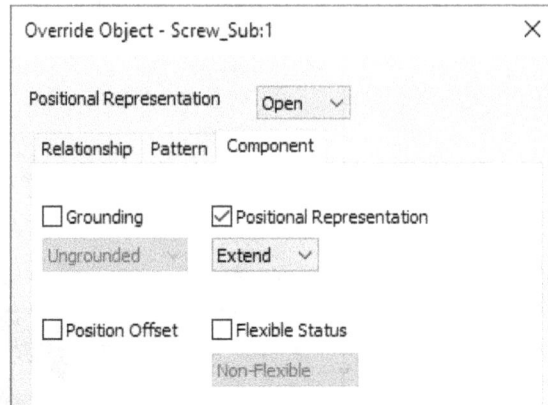

Figure 8–16

6. In the top-level assembly, create a new Positional Representation called **Free**. In this Positional Representation, you will suppress constraints and override a subassembly's Positional Representation so that you can drag components along their degree of freedom.

7. Override the **Mate** constraint between the two jaw plates, select the **Suppression** option and select **Suppress** in the drop-down list, as shown in Figure 8–17. Click **OK**.

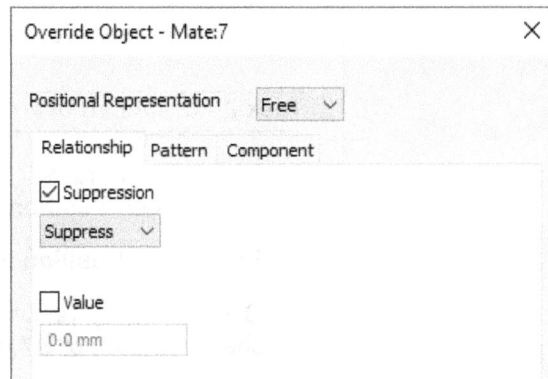

Figure 8–17

8. Right-click on the **Screw_Sub** subassembly and select **Override**. In the *Component* tab, override the Positional Representation for the **Screw_Sub** subassembly and set it to **Free**. Select the **Flexible Status** option and select **Flexible** in the drop-down list, as shown in Figure 8–18. Click **OK**.

Figure 8–18

9. Select the **Sliding_Jaw** component and drag it in the assembly. Select the **Vise_Screw** (threaded screw) component and drag it back and forth. Note that these components are free to move when this Positional Representation is active. Otherwise, they are constrained.

10. Activate the **Master** Positional Representation.

11. Save the assembly.

12. Create a new drawing using the standard imperial drawing template.

13. Create a Base view of the assembly. Assign the **Left** orientation, the **Master** Positional Representation, and a scale of **0.75**.

14. In the Create panel, click [icon] (Overlay) and select the previously created view as the parent view. Select the **Open** Positional Representation. Click **OK**. The view displays as shown in Figure 8–19.

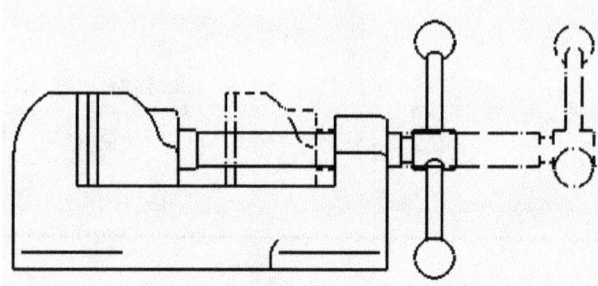

Figure 8–19

15. To complete the drawing you can add a shaded, Isometric view in the right corner of the drawing.

16. Save the drawing using the default name and close all of the files.

Chapter Review Questions

1. How do you activate the Representations browser?

   a. From the **Model Browser Representations** node.

   b. From the Application Menu.

   c. From the Model Browser.

   d. From the *View* tab in the ribbon.

2. You can place new components in the assembly when you have a user-defined Positional Representation active.

   a. True

   b. False

3. How do you override values to create a Positional Representation?

   a. In an active Positional Representation, right-click on an object and select **Override**.

   b. In an active Positional Representation, modify the required values.

   c. Create a new assembly and modify the required values.

   d. Switch to the Override setting in the ribbon.

4. Which of the following statements are true regarding Positional Representations? (Select all that apply.)

   a. You can open an assembly so that a Positional Representation is automatically active in the model.

   b. When a Positional Representation is active, you must explicitly save the assembly.

   c. A copy of an existing Positional Representation enables you to start customizing its overrides based on the defaults in the Master.

   d. Subassemblies within a top-level assembly can have Positional Representations that are specified for display in a top-level assembly.

5. While working with Positional Representations, which of the following can you perform using an Excel spreadsheet? (Select all that apply.)

   a. Change values on previously overridden values.

   b. Create new Positional Representations.

   c. Delete a Positional Representation.

   d. Rename a Positional Representation.

6. Once a constraint's offset value has been overridden in a Positional Representation, the Positional Representation must be deleted in order to remove the override.

   a. True

   b. False

Command Summary

Button	Command	Location
	Base View	• **Ribbon:** *Place Views* tab>Create panel
	Overlay View	• **Ribbon:** *Place Views* tab>Create panel

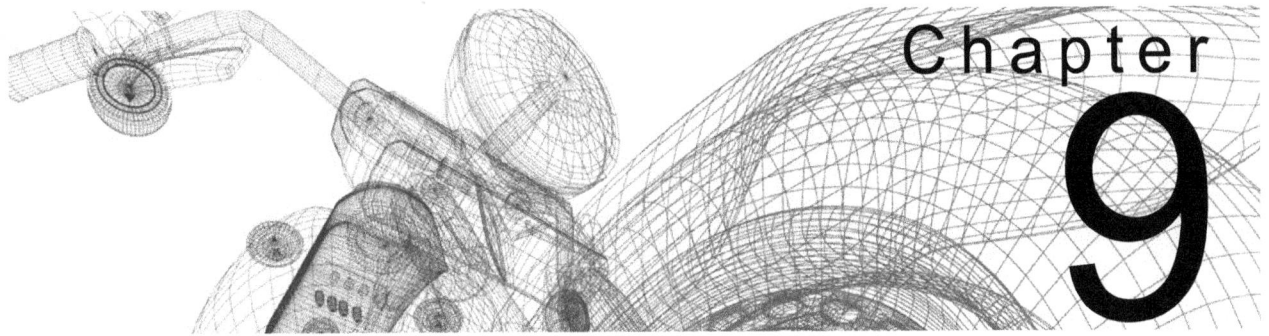

Model Simplification

Model simplification is required by many designers as a method of large assembly management, incorporating place holder geometry into an assembly, or as a technique to simplify proprietary data going to an external vendor.

Learning Objectives in This Chapter

- Create a Shrinkwrap part that is a simplification of the original component.
- Selectively determine which assembly components to include in a simplified view and use that information to create a new part model.
- Define bounding box or cylindrical geometry to represent assembly components and use that information to create a new part model.
- Combine the use of a simplified view, envelopes, and visibility settings to create a new simplified model.

9.1 Shrinkwrap

The **Shrinkwrap** command can be used to aid in large assembly management. This command creates a derived part that is a simplification of the original component. The derived part can be a solid or surface component.

Some uses for the **Shrinkwrap** command include:

- **Large Assembly Management:** When working with large data sets, you can increase performance by removing unnecessary detail from the display. You can create a shrinkwrap part to act as a placeholder for entire subassemblies or for parts with many features.

- **Incoming Vendor Models:** In some cases, portions of a design might be modeled by a third party. While the model might be critical, you might not need to see the individual components. All you need for your design is an accurate placeholder for the model.

- **Outgoing Models:** In some cases, you might need to send models to another company, and might not want to send them proprietary Autodesk® Inventor® files. Also, an export file (such as IGES) does not automatically update to reflect future changes. A shrinkwrap part enables you to send your suppliers and vendors associative Autodesk Inventor models, but removes the individual features or components.

How To: Create a Shrinkwrap Part

1. In the *Assemble* tab>Simplification panel, click

   (Shrinkwrap). The Shrinkwrap dialog box opens.
2. In the *Components* tab (shown in Figure 9–1), define the following:

   * In the *Representation* area, you can set which Design View, Positional or Level of Level of Detail Representation should be used to create the Shrinkwrap part.

   * In the *Remove Parts* area, you can specify whether parts within a set diagonal bounding box size are removed.

   * In the *Include Components* area, you can select which components are to be explicitly excluded. By default, all components are included. Use the selection filter area to refine component selection, as required.

*The mass properties of the original file carry over to the shrinkwrap part. To ensure accurate values, it is a good idea to update the mass properties of the original assembly before starting the **Shrinkwrap** command.*

Figure 9–1

3. Select the *Features* tab (shown in Figure 9–2) to customize whether holes, pockets, fillets, and/or chamfers are to be removed in the final shrinkwrap part. Set the options as follows:

- Click ⬚ (None) in any of the four areas to ensure that none of these types of features are removed.

- Click ▦ (Remove All) in any of the four areas to ensure that all of these types of features are removed.

- Click ▨ (Remove all detected <type> that are smaller than the value provided) in any of the four areas to ensure that all of the selected type of features that are smaller than the provided value are removed.

- Click 🔍 (Detect Features) to highlight the features that will be removed based on the selected options.

- Click ▸ (Preserve Features) to permit selected features to be preserved in the shrinkwrap part if they had been automatically identified for feature removal.

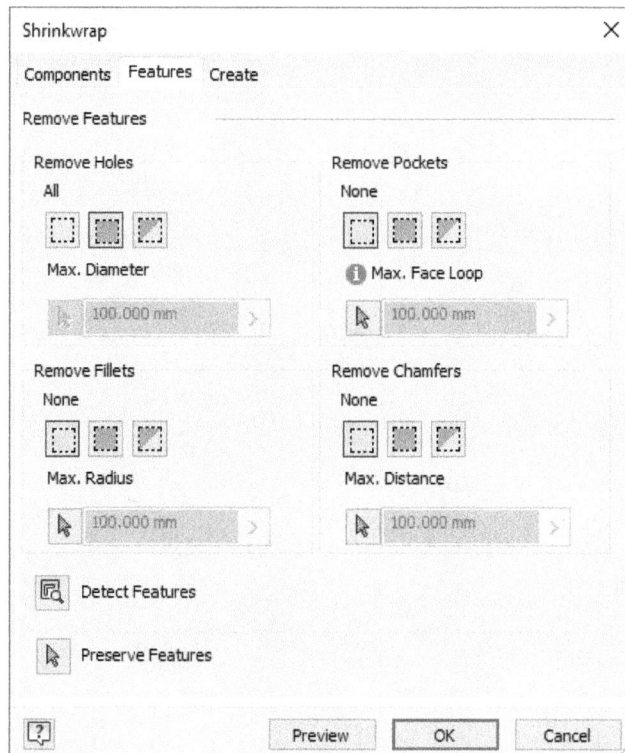

Figure 9–2

4. Select the *Create* tab (shown in Figure 9–3).

   - In the *New File* area, define the file name, template, file location, and BOM Structure for the shrinkwrap file.
   - In the *Style* area, define how each component will be maintained once shrinkwrapped. The available options are described below. Set the options as follows:

Option	Description
⬚	Use this option (Single solid body merging out seams between planar faces) to create a part file that consists of a single solid body that has no edges between planar faces.
⬚	Use this option (Solid body keep seams between planar faces) to create a part file that consists of a single solid body that has edges between planar faces.
⬚	Use this option (Maintain each solid as a solid body) to create a multi-body part that contains individual bodies for each part in the assembly.
⬚	Use this option (Single composite feature) to create a single surface part file. This is the default and produces the lightest part file.

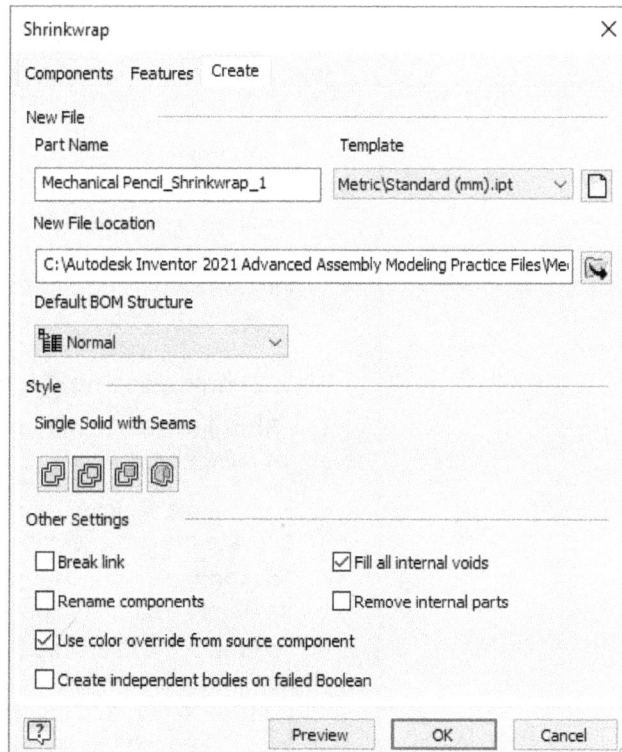

Figure 9–3

- Enable/Disable the options in the *Other Settings* area, as required, to define how the shrinkwrap part will be generated. Set the options as follows:

Option	Description
Break link	Clear this option to remove the associative link between the shrinkwrap part and the original assembly.
Rename Components	Use this option to rename the resulting body with a generic name.
Use color override from source component	Enable this option to maintain the color of the source model in the shrinkwrapped model. If disabled, the default appearance is used for all components.
Create independent bodies on failed Boolean	Use this option to create a multi-body shrinkwrap part when a single solid body cannot be generated. This option only affects models generated using ⬚ (Single solid body merging out seams between planar faces) or ⬚ (Solid body keep seams between planar faces).
Fill all internal voids	Use this option to fill all internal void shells in the shrinkwrap solid body part.
Remove internal parts	Enable this option to remove all non-visible parts from the creation of the shrinkwrap part. To determine visibility, the model is reviewed in 14 standard directions (six orthographic and eight isometric).

Level of Detail shrinkwrap models have no impact on the Bill of Materials.

5. Click **Preview** to review the results of the selected shrinkwrap options before generating the part.
6. Click **OK** to generate the Shrinkwrap part. The new shrinkwrap part is automatically created and made active.
7. Save the new part file.

Hint: Shrinkwrapping Components

The **Shrinkwrap** command creates a shrinkwrap part of the active assembly.

- To create a shrinkwrap part of a specific subassembly, activate the subassembly first.
- To create a shrinkwrap part of another part, add the part to an empty assembly, then shrinkwrap the part assembly.
- To create a shrinkwrap part that includes only certain components in a subassembly, create a Level of Detail representation that includes only the components required. When creating the shrinkwrap model, select the representation on the *Components* tab.

9.2 Assembly Simplification

The assembly Simplification tools can also be used to prepare a model for use in the Autodesk® Revit® software.

The assembly Simplification tools provide an alternative to using the **Shrinkwrap** or **Derive Assembly** options to simplify an assembly model to share with others.

To access the simplification tools in the Assembly environment, expand the Simplification panel in the *Assemble* tab, as shown in Figure 9–4.

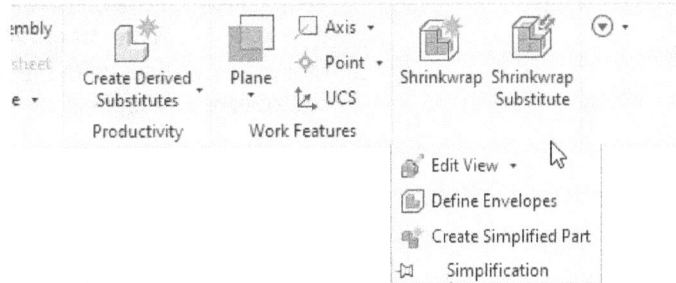

Figure 9–4

Simplify View

The **Simplify View** simplification tool enables you to create a simplified view of an assembly that includes or excludes selected components.

How To: Include Components in a Simplified View

1. In the *Assemble* tab>expanded Simplification panel, click (Simplify View). The mini-toolbar opens as shown in Figure 9–5.

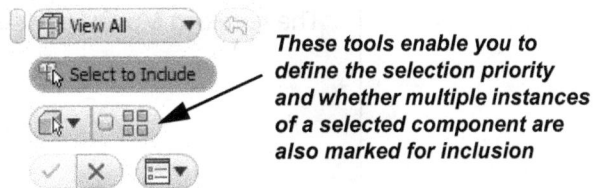

These tools enable you to define the selection priority and whether multiple instances of a selected component are also marked for inclusion

Figure 9–5

2. Select the components for inclusion/exclusion in the simplified view. You can begin selecting components using the default options in the mini-toolbar (**View All/Select Include**). Additional options are described as follows:

    *   The **View All** option enables you to control whether the model in the graphics window displays all of the components during selection.

- The **View Included** option in the top drop-down list is used to return excluded components back into a Simplified view. The **Select to Exclude** option is automatically enabled once this option is selected and you can select components to exclude them from the Design view.
- The **View Excluded** option in the top drop-down list is used to add excluded components back into a view. They enable you to display only the components that have been selected for inclusion (**View Included**) and select to Exclude, or the components that were selected for exclusion (**View Excluded**).

3. Maintain the defaults in the third row of the mini-toolbar, or customize, as required.

- In the ![icon] drop-down list you can define the selection priority to aid in selecting components. Part priority is the default.

- Use ![icon] (Select All Occurrences) option to control whether multiple instances of a selected component are also marked for inclusion.

4. Click ![icon] to complete the definition of the simplified view.

Once completed, a view is added to the **View** node in the Model Browser. The default naming scheme for the simplified view is **Simple View#**. The simplified view node can be selected and renamed, as required.

The blower assembly shown on the left in Figure 9–6 displays all of the components while the assembly shown on the right only has a few components selected for inclusion in **Simple View1**. The resulting Model Browser is also displayed.

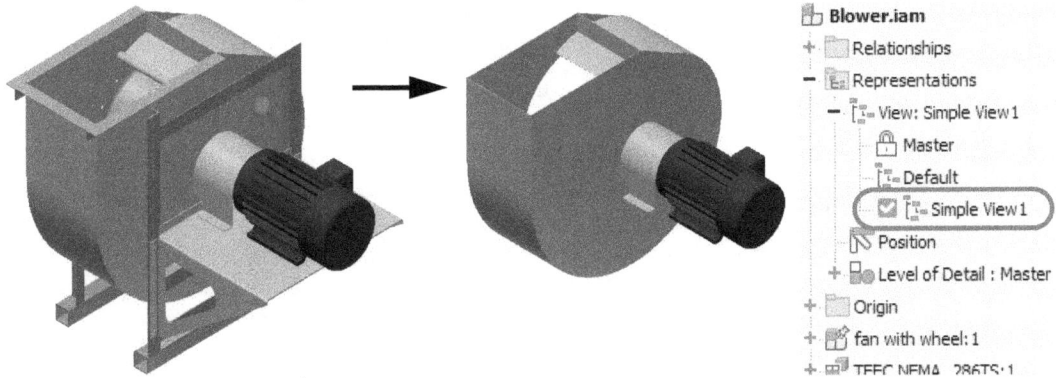

Figure 9–6

To edit a simplified view, right-click on the view name in the Model Browser and select **Edit View**.

- Components can be added or removed using the tools in the mini-toolbar.

- Alternatively, with **View All** selected, you can hold <Ctrl> and select components a second time to clear any previously included components.

To return all of the components to the display, double-click on the **Default** view node in the Model Browser to activate it. The **Simple View#** view is maintained and can be activated as required by double-clicking on it in the Model Browser.

Define Envelopes

The **Define Envelopes** simplification tool enables you to replace a selected component with a bounding box or cylinder.

How To: Create an Envelope

1. In the *Assemble* tab>expanded Simplification panel, click

   (Define Envelopes). The mini-toolbar opens, as shown in Figure 9–7.

*The Define Envelopes command can also be used to simplify components without the use of the **Simplify View** tool.*

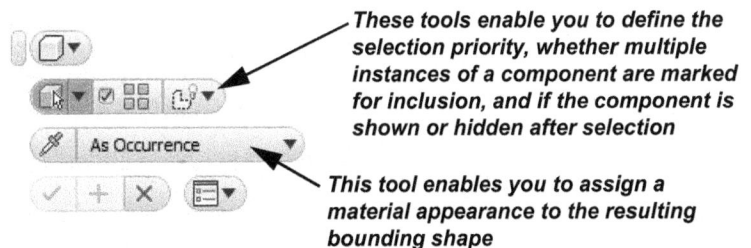

These tools enable you to define the selection priority, whether multiple instances of a component are marked for inclusion, and if the component is shown or hidden after selection

This tool enables you to assign a material appearance to the resulting bounding shape

Figure 9–7

2. Select a component to be replaced by the envelope.
3. Select the bounding shape to replace the selected

    component. Expand 🔲▼ and select **Bounding Box** or
    Cylinder from the drop-down list.
4. Customize the envelope size, if required, to represent a
    larger area than that of the selected component. Once the
    bounding box or cylinder has been displayed, select an arrow
    on a face and drag it to adjust the size, as shown in
    Figure 9–8. Alternatively, you can enter a value in the field
    that displays once an arrow has been selected.

*Select and drag
any of the six
arrows on the
bounding box to
adjust the size*

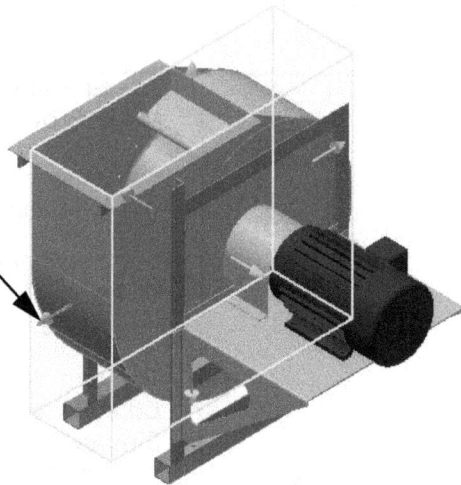

Figure 9–8

5. Maintain the defaults in the remaining rows of the mini-toolbar
    or customize, as required.

    *   In the 🔲▼ drop-down list, you can define the selection
        priority to aid in selecting components. Part priority is the
        default.

    *   Use ☑🔳 (Select All Occurrences) to control whether
        multiple instances of a selected component are also
        replaced with the same envelope.

    *   Use the 🔲▼ drop-down list to mark the envelope to
        either show or hide the original selected component once
        the envelope is created.

    *   Use the third row of the mini-toolbar to customize the
        material and appearance of the envelope.

6. Click ☑ to complete the definition of the envelope.

*To edit an envelope
name after it has been
created, right-click on
the name in the Model
Browser.*

In Figure 9–9, a blower assembly has been simplified using a cylindrical and two box envelopes. The three envelopes display in the Model Browser.

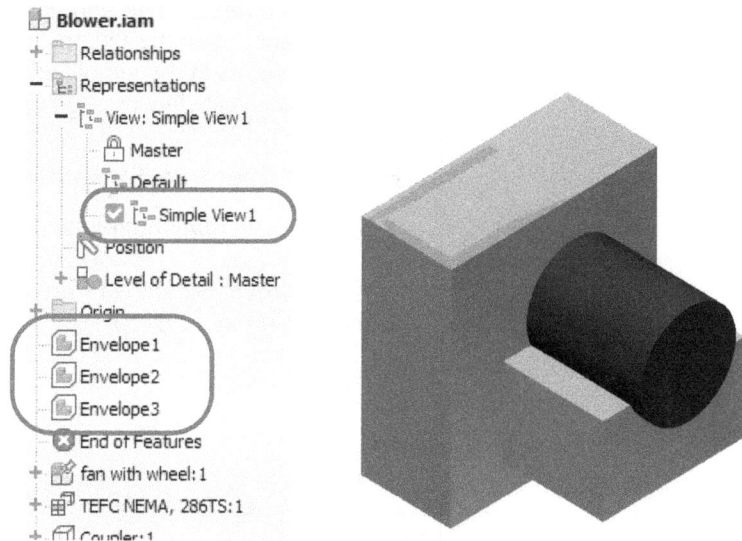

Figure 9–9

Once an envelope is created, it remains displayed unless its visibility is controlled. This is also true in a Simplified view, even if its component is not selected to be included in the Simplified view. To control the display of envelopes, consider the following:

- To temporarily remove envelopes from the model display, drag ⊗ End of Features above them in the list. You can also right-click and select **Suppress Feature**.

- To delete an envelope, right-click and select **Delete Envelope**. It is recommended to delete envelopes that are no longer required in a model, or that were only required to create a simplified version of the model.

Hint: Working with Simplified Views and Envelopes

A Simplified view is not required to create an envelope. However, components that are included in a Simplified view will display the envelope if its component has been selected for inclusion.

Create Simplified Part

The **Create Simplified Part** tool enables you to create a new simplified component. The new part that is created incorporates the active Simplified view, envelopes (displayed or hidden), and any component's visibility that has been disabled. Simplified parts are not associative and do not update if changes are made to the parent assembly's simplified view. If changes are made to the components in the simplified view, any simplified parts created from that view will update.

How To: Create a Simplified Part

1. In the *Assemble* tab>expanded Simplification panel, click

   (Create Simplified Part). The mini-toolbar opens as shown in Figure 9–10.

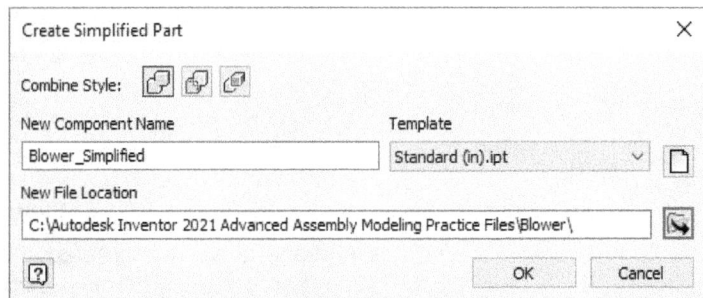

Create Simplified Part			×
Combine Style:			
New Component Name		Template	
Blower_Simplified		Standard (in).ipt	
New File Location			
C:\Autodesk Inventor 2021 Advanced Assembly Modeling Practice Files\Blower\			
		OK	Cancel

Figure 9–10

2. Select the style for how the generated part should be created.

   - Use to create it as a single solid body with merged seams between the faces.

   - Use to create it as a single solid body with seams maintained.

   - Use to create each solid as a separate solid body.

3. Enter the component's name
4. Select the template to use when creating the new part.
5. Change the default file location, if required.
6. Click **OK** to create the simplified part.

   - Once generated, the model opens in a new window. Envelopes that existed in the source assembly are represented as extrusions in the simplified model and can be deleted, if required.

Comparison of Model Simplification Tools

- **Shrinkwrap** enables you to create a single part file that preserves the external surfaces and removes all of the internal data to protect proprietary information. Models in the assembly can be individually selected for inclusion/exclusion, or it can be removed by size and visibility. Features (holes, pockets, fillets, and chamfers) can be selectively removed or included in the shrinkwrapped model. An associative link between the original assembly and the simplified part file can be maintained or explicitly removed.

- **Derive** enables you to create your own part file and populate it with data by deriving geometry from another model. By referencing an existing part or assembly, reusing existing models, sketches, or parameters, etc. you can select the data for your new part. The **Derive** and **Shrinkwrap** options are similar because you can remove parts by size, visibility, and patch holes. However, in the **Derive** option, you can also selectively mark the components in an assembly that are to be derived. You can select a design view, position, or level of detail representation to use when deriving. You can also use boolean operations with the **Derive** option. This process generally maintains an associative link between the final derived part and the original assembly.

- The simplification tools in the *Simplify* tab enable you to customize a simplified assembly by selecting the components to be included. Additionally, you can create envelope geometry to represent components. Using a combination of these tools and model visibility you can create a simplified model using the **Create Simplified Part** option. These tools do not enable you to fill holes in the model. Standard surfacing techniques are required to fill holes once the simplified part has been created. In general, this tool is used for general space claim information. There is no associative link between the original assembly's simplified view and the simplified part file. However, geometry changes to the components in the simplified part will update.

Practice 9a | Creating a Shrinkwrap Model

Practice Objective

- Create an associative shrinkwrap part that can be sent to a vendor.

The Mechanical Pencil assembly needs to be sent to a third party. For proprietary reasons, you do not want to show them the internal workings of the pencil. In this practice, you will create an associative shrinkwrap part that can be sent to the vendor. By creating an associative shrinkwrap model, you can ensure that the shrinkwrap model is always up to date. The mechanical pencil assembly is shown in Figure 9–11.

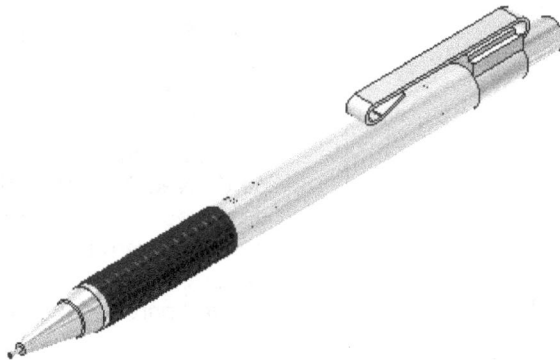

Figure 9–11

Task 1 - Create a shrinkwrap part.

1. Open **Mechanical Pencil.iam** from the *Mechanical_Pencil_Shrinkwrap* folder.

2. In the *Assemble* tab>Simplification panel, click

   (Shrinkwrap). The Shrinkwrap dialog box opens providing three tabs to define the shrinkwrap model.

3. In the *Components* tab, maintain all the default Representation settings and ensure that all 15 components are set to be included, as shown in Figure 9–12.

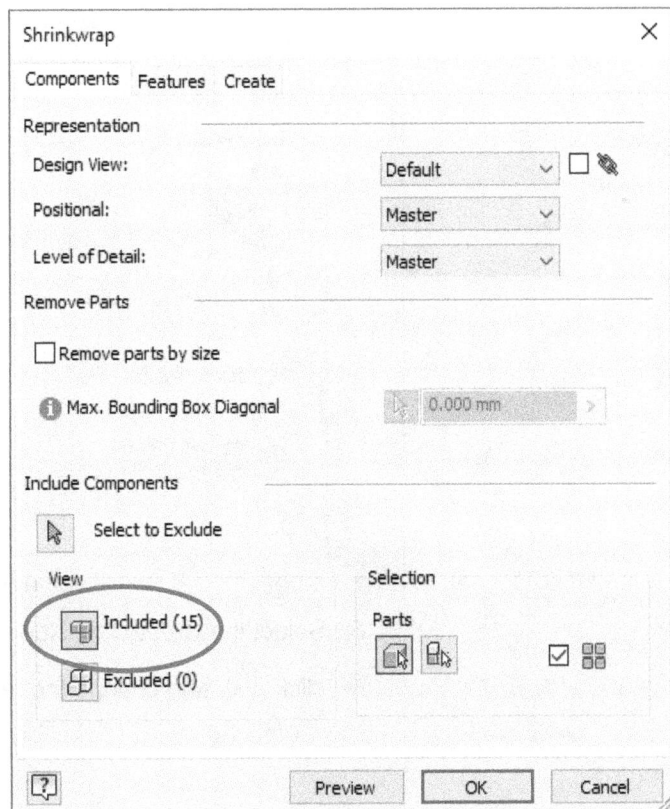

Figure 9–12

4. Select the *Features* tab. In the Remove *Holes* area, select
   [icon] (Remove all detected hole features). The *Remove
   Pockets*, *Remove Fillets*, and *Remove Chamfers* areas
   should all display **None**, as shown in Figure 9–13.

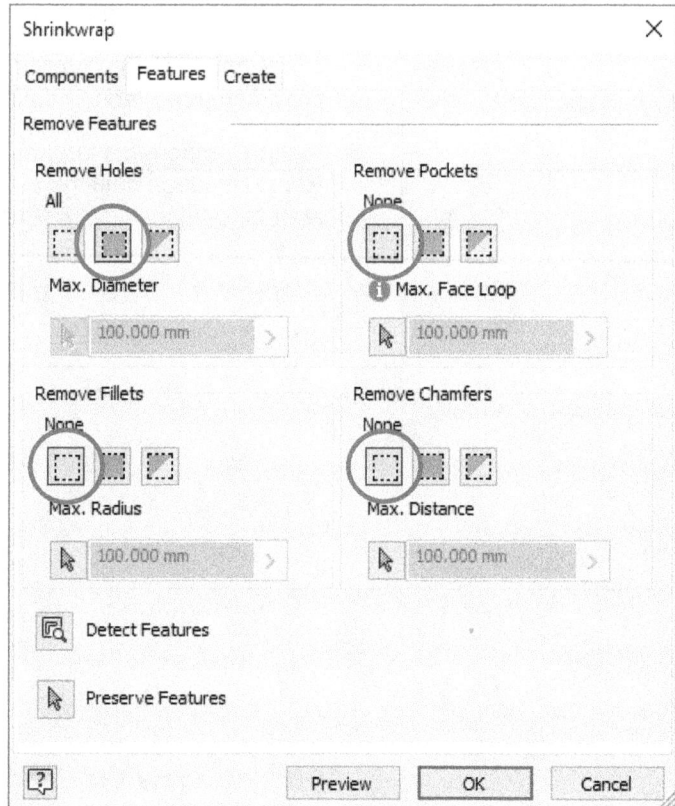

Figure 9–13

5. Select the *Create* tab. Keep the default name and location,
   click [icon], and change the template to **Standard (mm).ipt**.

6. In the *Style* area, click 🔲 (Solid body keep seams between planar faces), as shown in Figure 9–14.

7. In the *Other Settings* area, ensure that the options are set as shown in Figure 9–14.

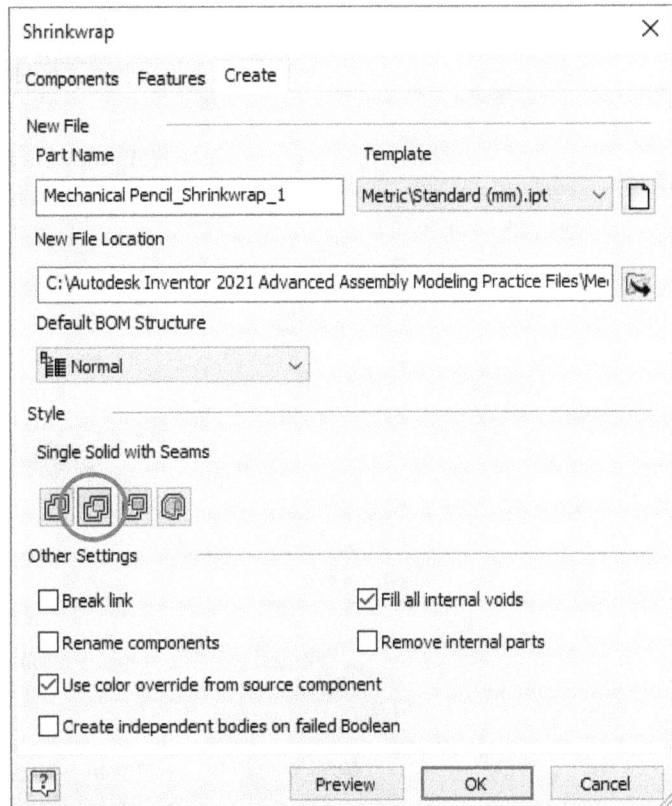

Figure 9–14

8. Click **Preview** to preview how the shrinkwrap part will be created.

9. Click **OK** to generate the shrinkwrap part. The new shrinkwrap model opens automatically.

Task 2 - Review the internal components of the shrinkwrap model.

1. Select the *View* tab>Visibility panel and click ⊞ (Half Section View). The command displayed in the drop-down list might vary depending on command that was last selected.

2. Select **YZ Plane** in the Model Browser. Leave the offset value at 0.00. Click ✓. The model is sectioned as shown in Figure 9–15. Note that the interior of the shrinkwrap model is solid.

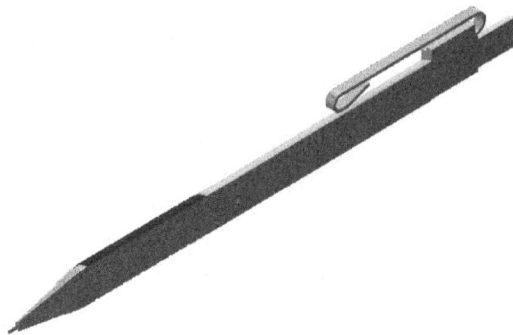

Figure 9–15

3. Select the *View* tab>Visibility panel and click ⊞ (End Section View).

Task 3 - Make changes to the parent assembly and update the shrinkwrap geometry.

1. Return to the **Mechanical Pencil.iam** window.

2. In the Model Browser, double-click on the **Clip** component to activate it.

3. Show the dimensions for the **Sweep1** feature and edit the *35* dimension value and enter **50**.

4. Activate the top-level assembly.

5. Return to the **Mechanical Pencil_Shrinkwrap_1.ipt** window. Note that the **Mechanical Pencil.iam** derived geometry in the Model Browser has the ⚡ symbol adjacent to it, indicating that it is out-of-date. You might have to move the cursor over the Model Browser to have it update.

*If the **Break Link** option is enabled when the shrinkwrap model is being created, it does not update to reflect the change made to the parent model.*

6. In the Quick Access Toolbar, click to update the shrinkwrap geometry to reflect the change in length to the parent geometry.

7. Return to the Mechanical Pencil assembly and edit the *50* dimension value and enter **35**. Update the shrinkwrap model again.

8. Save and close all the open models.

Practice 9b | Creating a Simplified Model

Practice Objectives

- Simplify an assembly model by selecting components for inclusion/exclusion in a Design View.
- Create envelopes of selected parts in an assembly to provide space claim data on the component's size.
- Create a simplified part model that represents a multi component assembly.

In this practice, you will create a simplified model to represent the space claims required for a blower assembly. The model will be simplified by selecting components to be included/excluded and envelopes will be created to represent other components. The entire assembly that will be simplified is shown on the left in Figure 9–16 and the simplified model is shown on the right.

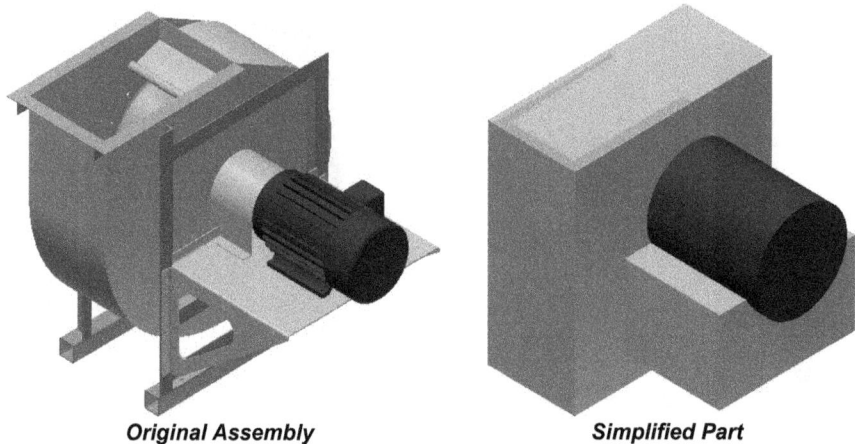

Original Assembly   *Simplified Part*

Figure 9–16

Task 1 - Define the assembly components to be included in the simplified part.

1. Open **Blower.iam** from the *Blower* folder.

2. In the *Assemble* tab>expanded Simplification panel, click (Simplify View). The mini-toolbar displays.

3. Select the **Mount_Blower**, **TEFC NEMA**, and **band** components. The band component is located in the fan with wheel>FAN CONSTRAINED subassemblies.

4. Click ☑ to complete the command. A Design View named **Simple View1** is created in the **View** node, as shown in Figure 9–17. These components form the basis of the envelopes that will be created to represent the assembly in the simplified part.

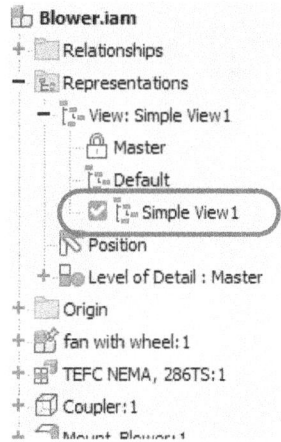

Figure 9–17

Task 2 - Create envelopes to represent the overall size of the model.

---

1. In the *Assemble* tab>expanded Simplification panel, click ⬛ (Define Envelopes). The mini-toolbar displays.

2. Expand ⬛▾ and click ⬛ (Bounding Box) if it is not the active selection.

3. Select the **Mount_Blower** part. A default bounding box displays around the model as shown in Figure 9–18. No adjustments need to be made to the envelope's size.

Figure 9–18

4. Expand and note that **Hide Original** is active. This ensures that the envelope replaces the selected component. If **Show Original** was selected, both the envelope and the derived geometry for the component would display in the simplified part.

5. Click to complete the envelope. The model and Model Browser display as shown in Figure 9–19.

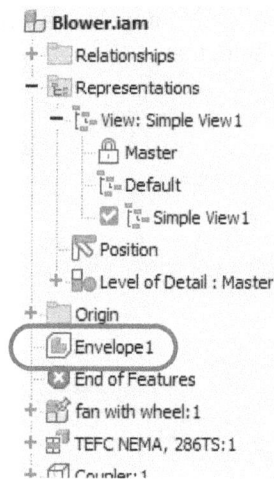

Figure 9–19

6. The overall extent of the blower and its frame is not apparent in the current Design View. In the **View** node, right-click on **Simple View1** and select **Edit View**.

7. Select the frame components which define the extents of the assembly, as shown in Figure 9–20. This is done temporarily to create an accurate envelope for the band component.

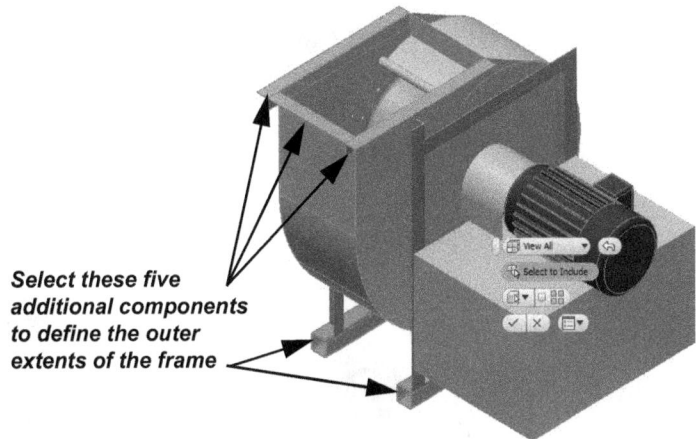

Select these five additional components to define the outer extents of the frame

Figure 9–20

8. Click ✓ to complete the command. The model displays as shown in Figure 9–21.

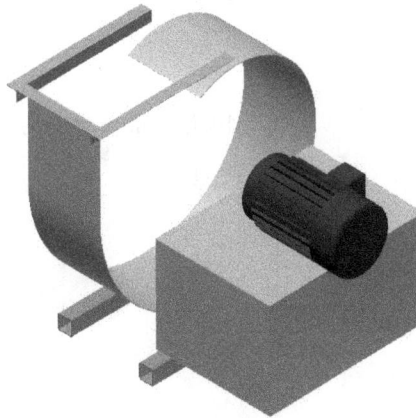

Figure 9–21

9. In the *Assemble* tab>expanded Simplification panel, click (Define Envelopes).

10. Select the band component. The **Bounding Box** option is already selected because it was the last shape used.

11. Change to the Front view of the model using the ViewCube. Note that the bounding box does not encompass all of the frame components. The envelope's size can be adjusted as required to represent the true space claim.

12. In the Front view, drag the lower and left arrows to encompass the exterior frame components, as shown on the left in Figure 9–22.

13. Navigate to the Top view using the ViewCube. Drag the top and bottom arrows to encompass the frame around the band, as shown on the right in Figure 9–22.

FRONT VIEW   *TOP VIEW*

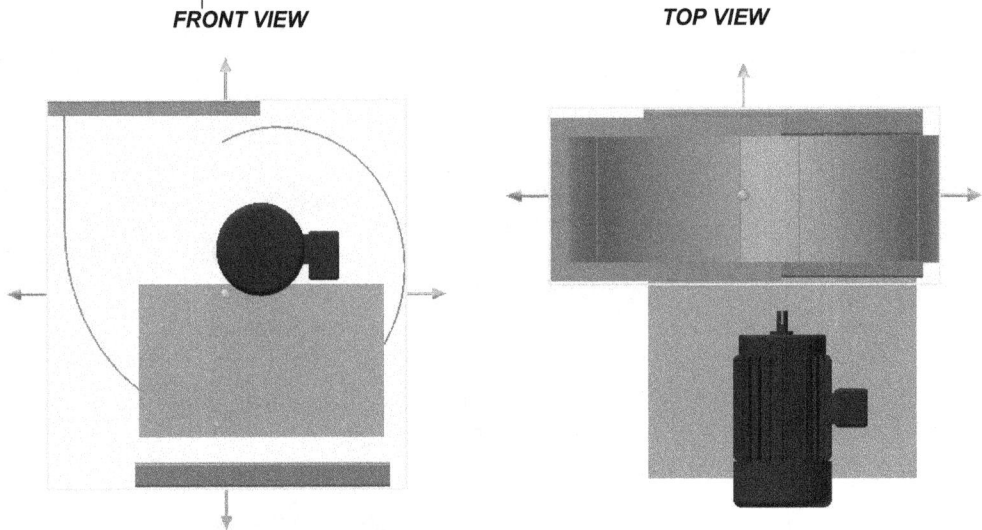

Figure 9–22

14. Maintain the default material for the envelope.

15. Click ✓ to complete the envelope. The model and the Model Browser display as shown in Figure 9–23.

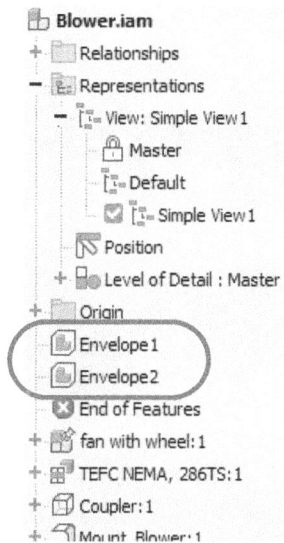

Figure 9–23

16. In the *Assemble* tab>expanded Simplification panel, click 🗔 (Define Envelopes).

17. Expand ⬛▼ and click ⬜ (Bounding Cylinder).

18. Select the **TEFC NEMA** component. A bounding cylinder extends around the selected component.

19. Using the ViewCube, change to the Top view of the model, if not already active. Drag the left arrow so that it extends into the bounding box that represents the housing of the assembly, as shown in Figure 9–24.

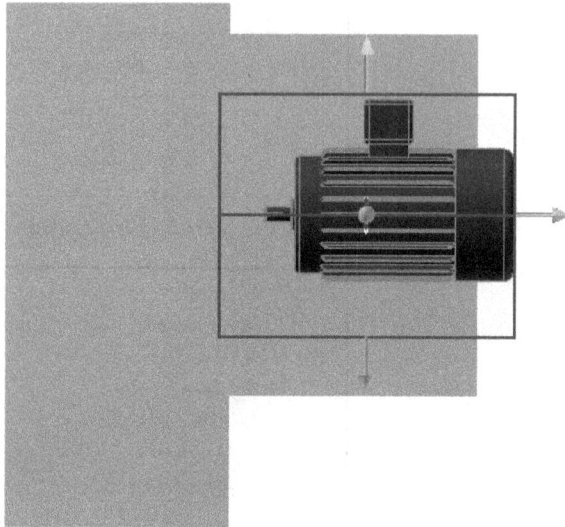

Figure 9–24

20. Click ✓ to complete the envelope. The model and Model Browser display as shown in Figure 9–25. Note that three envelopes were created and all of the components still display in the model.

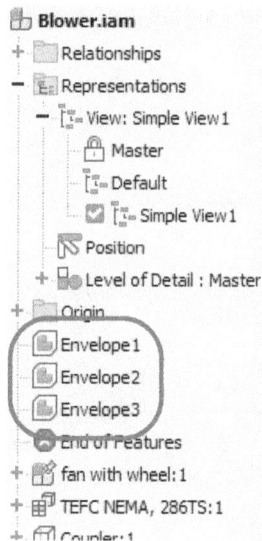

Figure 9–25

21. Drag ⊗ End of Features (which is below the envelope list), above all three envelopes. This enables you to temporarily toggle off their display in the model.

22. In the **View** node, right-click on **Simple View1** and select **Edit View**. The model displays with all of the components selected.

23. Expand **View All** and click ⊞ (View Included) to only display the components that have been included. Note that the **Mount_Blower**, **TEFC NEMA**, and the **Band** components are no longer included because they have been replaced with envelopes.

24. **Select to Exclude** becomes active. Select the five frame components to exclude them. If they had remained in the view, they would have been included as derived geometry in the simplified part file that is to be created.

*Alternatively, if **View All** is maintained, you can and hold <Ctrl> while selecting components to clear them from inclusion.*

25. Click ✓ to complete the edit.

26. Drag ⊗ End of Features back to the bottom of the feature list to once again display the envelopes in the model.

Task 3 - Create the simplified part model and modify it.

---

1. In the *Assemble* tab>expanded Simplification panel, click

   (Create Simplified Part).

2. In the Create Simplified Part dialog box, change the name for the new component to **Blower_Simplified**.

3. In the *Template* area, browse and select the **Standard(in).ipt** template.

4. In the *New File Location* area, browse and select the *Blower* folder from the practice files folder, if not already specified. The Create Simplified Part dialog box should be as shown in Figure 9–26.

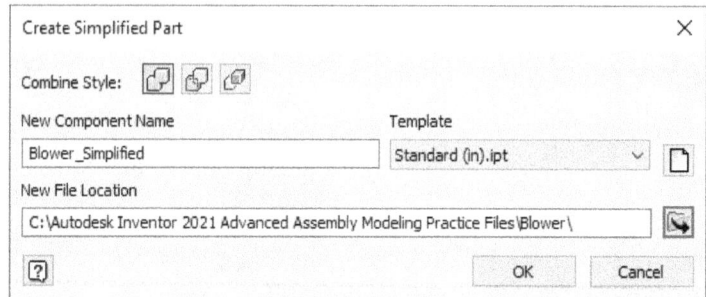

Figure 9–26

5. Click **OK** to create the new part file. The newly created model opens automatically.

6. Review the Model Browser. Note that three extrusions have been added to represent the envelopes that were created to replace the **Mount_Blower**, **TEFC NEMA**, and **Band** components.

7. In the *3D Model* tab>Modify panel, click (Chamfer).

8. Create a chamfer of approximately **20** to represent the true shape of the **Mount_Blower** component, as shown in Figure 9–27.

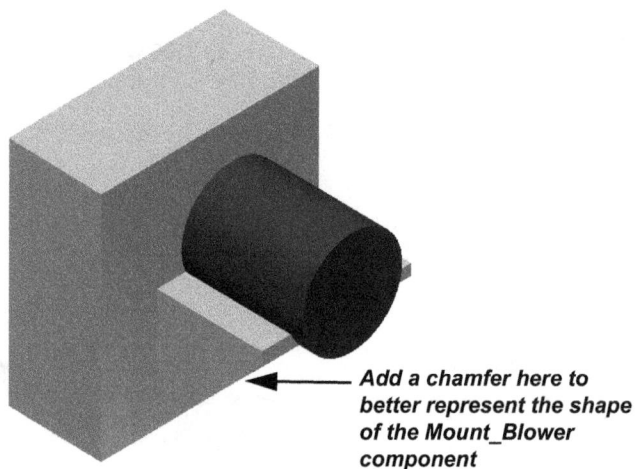

Add a chamfer here to better represent the shape of the Mount_Blower component

Figure 9–27

9. Save the newly created **Blower_Simplified.ipt** file. It can now be shared with customers for use as a space claim in their designs.

10. Return to the **Blower.iam** window. Save the assembly and close it.

The envelopes that exist in the model can be toggled off by dragging ⊗ End of Features above them. However, if you want to create a new simplified part model with other envelopes, they should be deleted. If they are not deleted, they are included in the simplified part regardless of whether they are toggled off or not.

Chapter Review Questions

1. Which is not a use of a shrinkwrap model in an assembly?

   a. Incoming vendor models

   b. Quickly suppressing all components in an assembly

   c. Outgoing models

   d. Large assembly management

2. Which of the following statements are <u>false</u> for creating a shrinkwrap model? (Select all that apply.)

   a. Any component that is not displayed (visibility toggled off) during shrinkwrap can be automatically removed from the generated shrinkwrap model.

   b. Components are individually selected for inclusion in a shrinkwrap model.

   c. You must manually edit the surface geometry of the model to remove any unwanted holes after the Shrinkwrap model is created.

   d. The Shrinkwrap model is non-associative with the parent geometry; it cannot be associative.

3. Which of the following viewing options provide the ability to select components for inclusion again once they have been removed in a simplified view? (Select all that apply.)

   a. **View All**

   b. **View Included**

   c. **View Excluded**

4. When an assembly is simplified using (Simplify View), which of the following is created in the model and displays in the Model Browser?

   a. Envelope

   b. Simple View

   c. Level of Detail

   d. Positional Representation

5. The second row of options in the Envelope mini-toolbar, shown in Figure 9–28, enables you to do which of the following? (Select all that apply.)

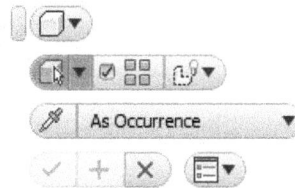

Figure 9–28

a. Set the bounding shape.

b. Set the selection priority.

c. Define the color of the envelope.

d. Determine if all instances of the selected component are also enveloped.

e. Define the selected component as hidden or visible in the simplified part.

6. Only a single component can be selected at one time to be replaced with an envelope using the (Define Envelopes) command. The envelope can only represent the exact size of the selected component.

a. True

b. False

7. Which of the following simplification tools can create an associative simplified model that updates if changes are made to the parent assembly? (Select all that apply.)

a. Shrinkwrap

b. Derive

c. Simplified Part

Command Summary

Button	Command	Location
	Create Simplified Part	• **Ribbon:** *Assemble* tab>expanded Simplification panel
	Define Envelopes	• **Ribbon:** *Assemble* tab>expanded Simplification panel
	Shrinkwrap	• **Ribbon:** *Assemble* tab> Simplification panel
	Simplify View	• **Ribbon:** *Assemble* tab>expanded Simplification panel

Level of Detail Representations

Level of Detail Representations enable you to save the state of components. They reduce the clutter of large numbers of components, as well as reduce time spent waiting for your system to retrieve a large number of components in an assembly. In general, this tool helps you to work more efficiently with large assemblies.

Learning Objectives in This Chapter

- Display a system-defined Level of Detail (LOD) Representation.
- Simplify the display and create user-defined LOD Representations in an assembly.
- Improve retrieval times for large assemblies by directly opening a LOD Representation where only the required components are loaded or used in a drawing or presentation file.
- Replace a complex component for a simpler one using a Substitute LOD Representation.
- Create a substitute part for every subassembly within the top-level assembly at one time.
- Activate LOD Representations in subassemblies based on naming schemes.

10.1 Level of Detail Representations

Level of Detail (LOD) Representations are used to improve assembly retrieval times, simplify the display of the assembly, and improve the capacity and performance when working with larger assemblies. Three examples are shown in Figure 10–1.

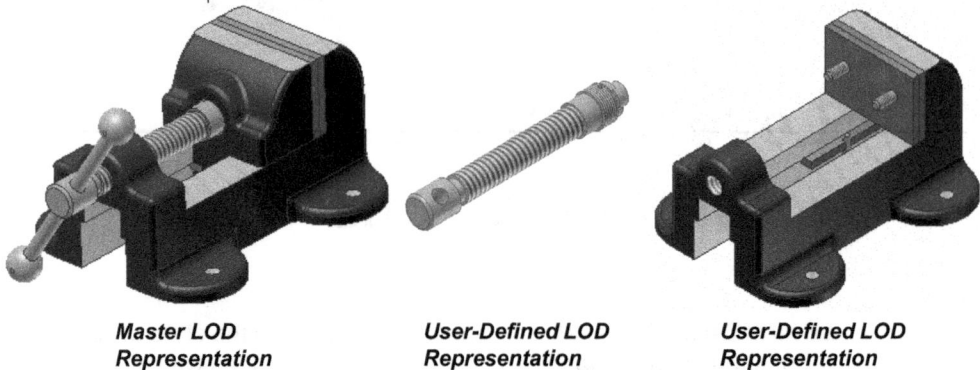

Master LOD Representation　　*User-Defined LOD Representation*　　*User-Defined LOD Representation*

Figure 10–1

- You can create LOD Representations that only display and load the components you need to work with at any given time. This is done by suppressing components you do not need, and creating and saving an LOD that can be activated at any time.

- Retrieval times for larger assemblies are improved by using an LOD that does not load all the components before opening the assembly. After retrieval of an LOD in an assembly, you can unsuppress (load) and suppress (unload) any additional components as required and then create a new LOD to store the new assembly state.

- LODs can be used in drawings and presentations. Design View and Positional Representations can also be used in conjunction with LODs.

LOD Representations are often used to monitor the number of files open in a current session. These details are reported in the right-hand side of the Status bar, as shown in Figure 10–2.

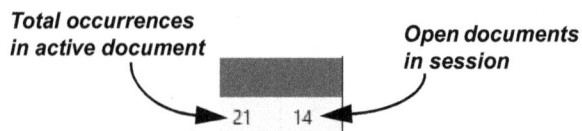

Total occurrences in active document　　*Open documents in session*

21　14

Figure 10–2

10.2 System-Defined Level of Detail Representations

Assemblies have four system-defined LOD Representations that are automatically created. System-defined LOD Representations cannot be modified, but you can copy them and modify the copy to create new ones. To access the system-defined LODs, in the Model Browser, expand the *Representations* folder and the Level of Detail branch, as shown in Figure 10–3.

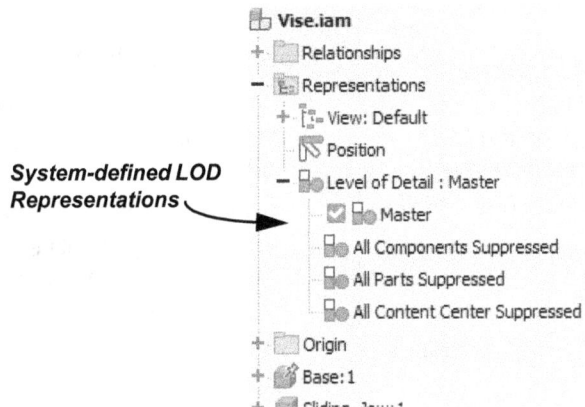

Figure 10–3

Double-click on any of the system-defined representations underneath Level of Detail to activate it.

*Alternatively, you can right-click on the LOD Representation and select **Activate**.*

- The **Master** LOD Representation contains the default state of the assembly, where all components are loaded (unsuppressed).

- The **All Components Suppressed** LOD Representation suppresses all parts and subassemblies in the assembly.

- The **All Parts Suppressed** LOD Representation suppresses all parts in the assembly, including those in subassemblies. The subassembly structure is still visible in the Model Browser.

- The **All Content Center Suppressed** LOD Representation suppresses all Content Center items.

10.3 User-Defined Level of Detail Representations

You can create user-defined LOD Representations in an assembly. This is done by activating the Master or LOD Representation that most closely matches the one you want to create. For example, if you want to create one that suppresses the majority of the components in the assembly, activate the All Components Suppressed LOD so that you only need to unsuppress the few components you need to work with.

How To: Create an LOD Representation

Alternatively, you can right-click on the LOD Representation you want to copy and select Copy.

1. With the required LOD Representation activated, in the Model Browser, right-click on the Level of Detail branch and select **New Level of Detail**.
   - A new LOD is created, as shown in Figure 10–4.
   - Any components suppressed in the previously activated LOD are also suppressed in the new LOD Representation.

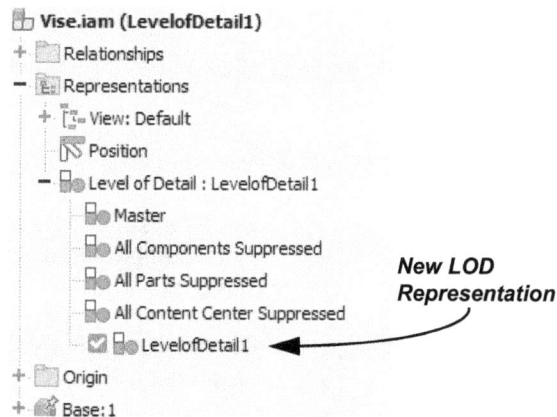

Figure 10–4

To help locate components for suppression or unsuppression, use the Selection Priority tool in the Quick Access Toolbar.

2. With the new LOD Representation active, suppress and unsuppress components to define the LOD as required.
3. Rename the LOD Representation using a descriptive name by clicking it twice (not double-clicking) in the Model Browser and entering the new name.
4. Save the assembly to save the new LOD Representation.

You can make changes to the LOD Representation once it is created. Activate it, suppress and unsuppress the required components, and resave the assembly.

10.4 Using Level of Detail Representations

LOD Representations can be used during assembly retrieval, when creating drawing views, and in presentation files.

Assembly Retrieval

LOD Representations improve retrieval times for large assemblies. By directly opening an LOD Representation other than the default Master LOD Representation, only the required components are loaded into the software.

How To: Open an LOD Representation During Assembly Retrieval

1. In the Quick Access Toolbar, click or use one of the other options to open the Open dialog box.
2. Select the assembly and click **Options**. The File Open Options dialog box opens.
3. Select the required LOD Representation from the Level of Detail Representation drop-down list.
4. Click **OK** in the File Open Options dialog box and click **Open** in the Open dialog box. The Assembly opens with the selected LOD Representation activated.

> **Hint: Setting a Default LOD Representation**
>
> You can specify a default LOD Representation to retrieve when the assembly is next opened:
>
> 1. In the Application Options dialog box, select the *File* tab and click **File Open Options**.
> 2. Select the required LOD in the Level of Detail Representation drop-down list.
>
> By default, Autodesk Inventor is set to open the last active LOD. Changing this setting reduces the chance that you might open the master representation in error, taking valuable time to open many unnecessary components.

Drawings

Any LOD Representation can be selected for use while creating or modifying a base drawing view, or while modifying a projected Isometric drawing view. When creating a base view, select the required LOD Representation, as shown in Figure 10–5. To change the LOD Representation used in a base view or projected isometric view, right-click, select **Edit View**, and select the LOD.

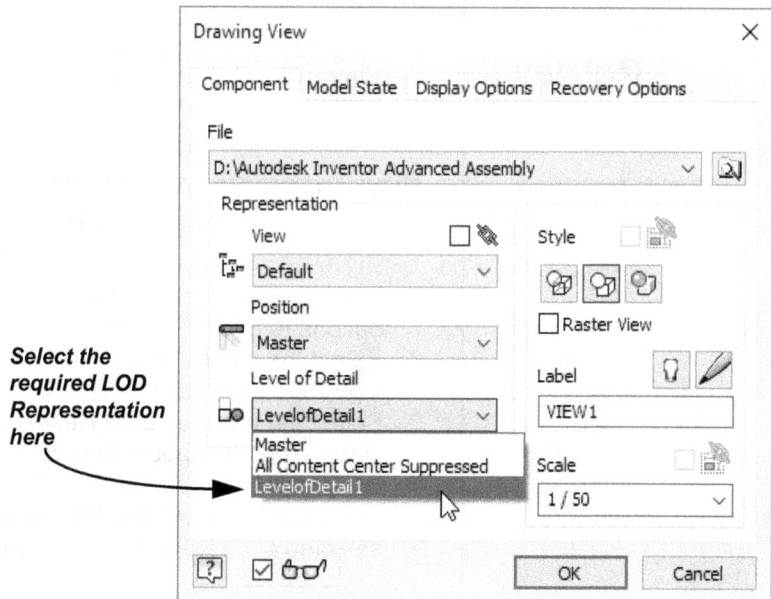

Select the required LOD Representation here

Figure 10–5

Presentations

Any LOD Representation can be selected for use while creating a view in a Presentation file by clicking **Options** and selecting the LOD Representation.

10.5 Substitute Level of Detail Representations

A Substitute Level of Detail (LOD) enables you to swap out a complex component for a simpler one that represents it. The substitute still contains all of the BOM information that is normally associated with the assembly, as well as the physical information (such as center of gravity and mass). Using substitute parts reduces the amount of components loaded into memory, as well as the number of constraints and adaptive relationships that must be recalculated when changes are made. By simplifying the model, the intention of a Substitute LOD is to reduce the computing resources and thereby increase performance without sacrificing access to BOM information.

The model on the left in Figure 10–6 shows the Master Representation for an assembly. A Substitute LOD for the fan and its electronic components is shown on the right.

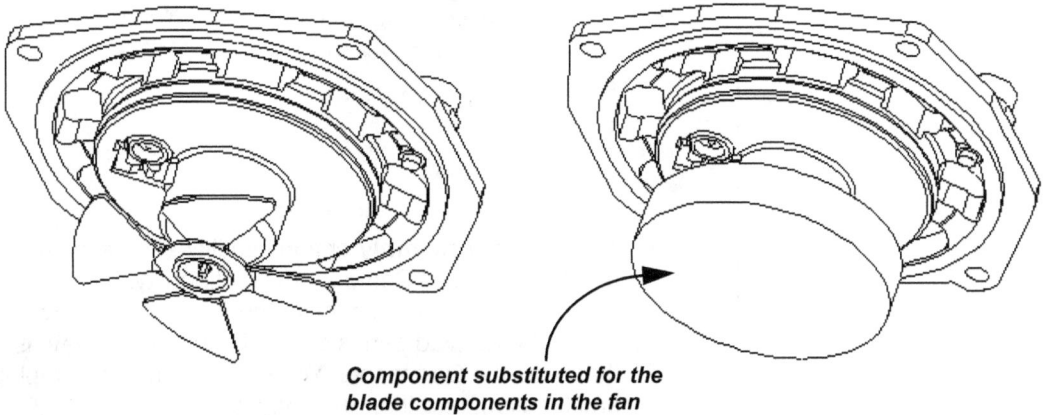

Component substituted for the
blade components in the fan

Figure 10–6

How To: Create a Substitute LOD

1. Open the subassembly that is to be simplified. This assembly is called the Owning Assembly.
2. (Optional) Create a reduced-part LOD Representation. In this LOD, suppress any of those components in the subassembly that are to be removed to simplify the assembly.
3. In the Model Browser, right-click on the LOD and select **New Substitute.** Select one of the three options shown in Figure 10–7: **Derive Assembly**, **Shrinkwrap**, or **Select Part File**.

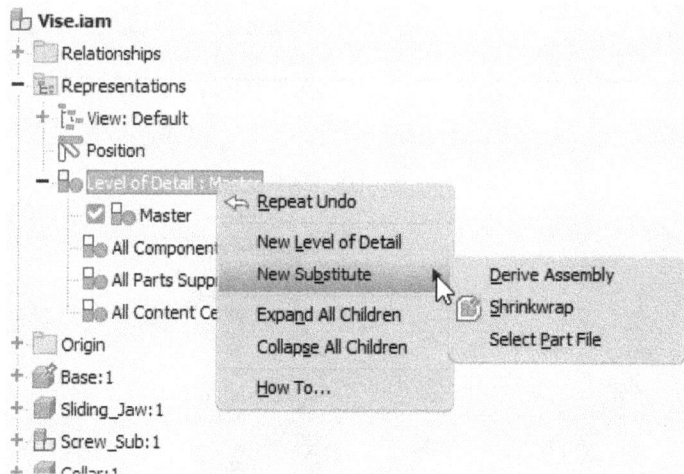

Figure 10–7

- The **Derive Assembly** option simplifies the assembly using the Derived Component functionality. A new part file is created that is then substituted for the assembly in the LOD. The derived part is created in the same way as one that uses the Derive tool. You define its name, template, and location, and then use the Derived Assembly dialog box to control which components are included in the new part file. The new Substitute LOD is created using the new derived part file.

- The **Shrinkwrap** command creates a shrinkwrap part of the active assembly and creates a LOD that uses it. The shrinkwrap part is created in the same way as one that uses the Shrinkwrap tool. After you define the options on the *Components* and *Features* tabs, you can define the name, template, and location, in the *Create* tab. The new shrinkwrap part is automatically created, and a Substitute LOD of the shrinkwrap for the top-level assembly is created.

You can also create a shrinkwrap substitute model on the Assemble tab>Simplification panel, by clicking

(Shrinkwrap Substitute).

Hint: Working with Shrinkwraps

- Individual parts cannot be shrinkwrapped.

- To create a shrinkwrap part of a specific subassembly inside the top-level assembly, you must first open it explicitly (cannot be edited and created in place) and perform a Shrinkwrap LOD from the *Representations* folder in that assembly. After saving and returning to the master subassembly, the lower level shrinkwrap LOD is available for selection in a higher level LOD.

  - The **Select Part File** option substitutes a single part file for the assembly. Selecting **Select Part File** substitutes a selected file for the assembly in the LOD. The part file can be a previously simplified assembly, shrinkwrap model, or another part file. After you select this option you are prompted to select a component. The Substitute LOD is created using the selected part file.

4. In the main assembly, create a new LOD and activate Substitute LOD in any subassemblies, as required.

10.6 LOD Productivity Tools

Three of the productivity tools—**Create Derived Substitutes**, **Update Substitutes**, and **Link Levels of Detail**—can be used to help you more efficiently work with large assemblies and levels of details. The commands are shown in Figure 10–8.

*All productivity tools are grouped in the Productivity panel. To display all commands in the main panel, right-click on the command that displays in the main panel and select **Ungroup Commands from Drop-Down Menu**.*

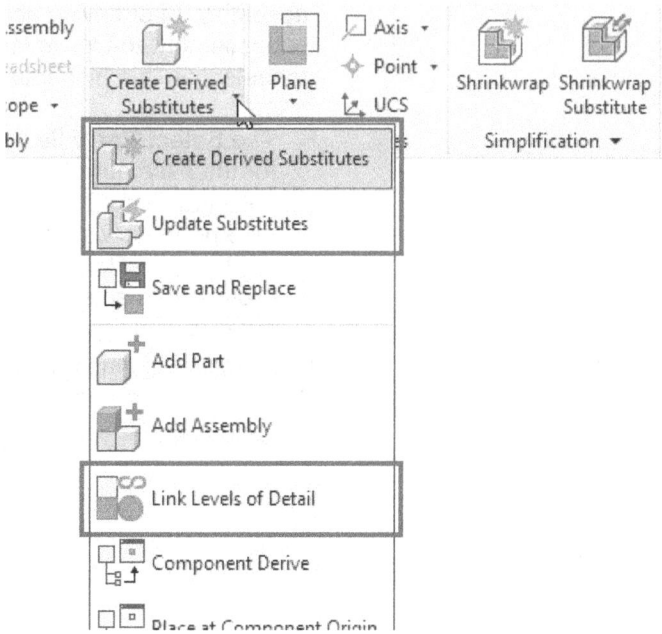

Figure 10–8

Create Derived Substitutes

The **Create Derived Substitutes** option creates a substitute part for every subassembly within the top-level assembly.

How To: Create Derived Substitutes

1. In the *Assemble* tab>Productivity panel, click (Create Derived Substitutes). The Create Derived Substitutes dialog box opens as shown in Figure 10–9.

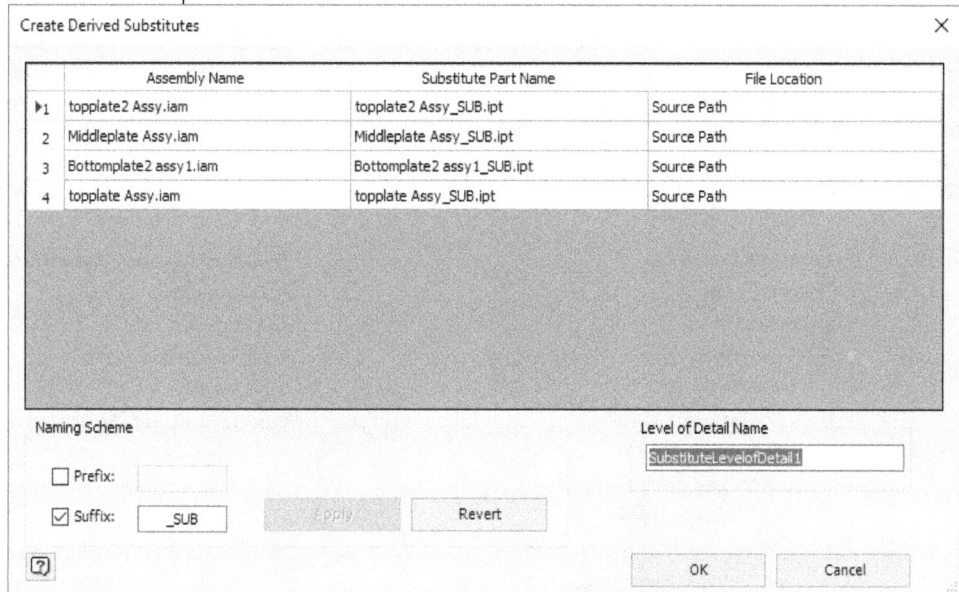

Figure 10–9

*If there is a subassembly that you do not want to substitute, right-click on its row in the Create Substitutes dialog box and select **Remove Row***.

2. Modify the *Substitute Part Name* column, as required, to name the part file that is going to be generated for each subassembly.

   - By default, all substitute parts have the suffix **_SUB**.
   - You can change the name of the substitute parts by clicking inside the appropriate row and entering a new value.
   - You can also change the suffix or add a prefix to all substitute parts using the *Naming Scheme* area of the dialog box.

3. Enter the LOD Representation name in the *Level of Detail Name* field that will be used in each as subassembly and at the top level.

4. Click **OK**. When prompted that you have chosen to create substitutes, click **Yes**.

Use the ⬚ (Link Levels of Detail) productivity tool to quickly switch between the LOD Representations.

The substitute parts and the LOD Representations are generated. In addition, the LOD Representations that replace the subassemblies with their substitute parts are activated, as shown in Figure 10–10.

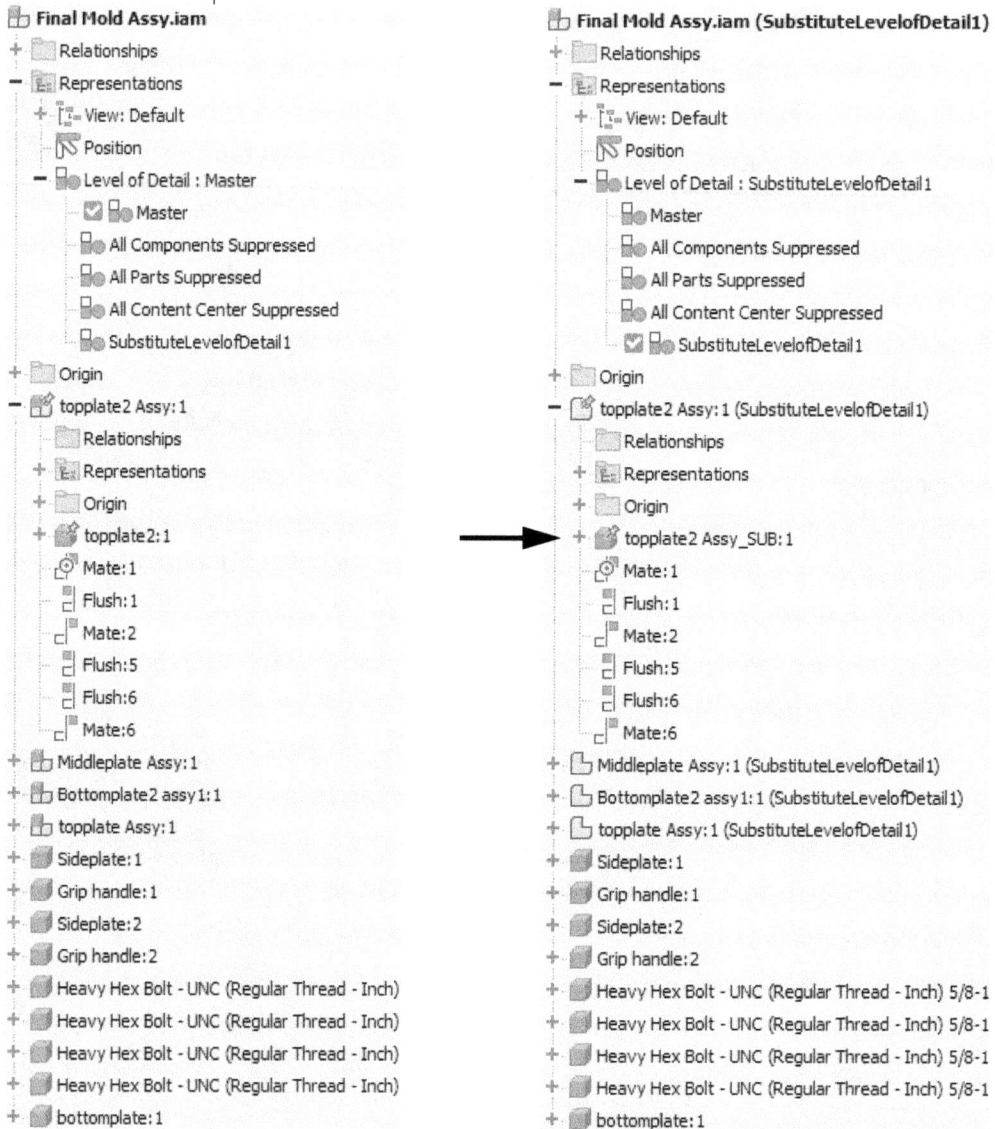

Final Mold Assy.iam
- + Relationships
- − Representations
  - + View: Default
  - Position
  - − Level of Detail : Master
    - ☑ Master
    - All Components Suppressed
    - All Parts Suppressed
    - All Content Center Suppressed
    - SubstituteLevelofDetail1
- + Origin
- − topplate2 Assy:1
  - Relationships
  - + Representations
  - + Origin
  - + topplate2:1
  - Mate:1
  - Flush:1
  - Mate:2
  - Flush:5
  - Flush:6
  - Mate:6
- + Middleplate Assy:1
- + Bottomplate2 assy1:1
- + topplate Assy:1
- + Sideplate:1
- + Grip handle:1
- + Sideplate:2
- + Grip handle:2
- + Heavy Hex Bolt - UNC (Regular Thread - Inch)
- + Heavy Hex Bolt - UNC (Regular Thread - Inch)
- + Heavy Hex Bolt - UNC (Regular Thread - Inch)
- + Heavy Hex Bolt - UNC (Regular Thread - Inch)
- + bottomplate:1

Final Mold Assy.iam (SubstituteLevelofDetail1)
- + Relationships
- − Representations
  - + View: Default
  - Position
  - − Level of Detail : SubstituteLevelofDetail1
    - Master
    - All Components Suppressed
    - All Parts Suppressed
    - All Content Center Suppressed
    - ☑ SubstituteLevelofDetail1
- + Origin
- − topplate2 Assy:1 (SubstituteLevelofDetail1)
  - Relationships
  - + Representations
  - + Origin
  - + topplate2 Assy_SUB:1   ←
  - Mate:1
  - Flush:1
  - Mate:2
  - Flush:5
  - Flush:6
  - Mate:6
- + Middleplate Assy:1 (SubstituteLevelofDetail1)
- + Bottomplate2 assy1:1 (SubstituteLevelofDetail1)
- + topplate Assy:1 (SubstituteLevelofDetail1)
- + Sideplate:1
- + Grip handle:1
- + Sideplate:2
- + Grip handle:2
- + Heavy Hex Bolt - UNC (Regular Thread - Inch) 5/8-1
- + Heavy Hex Bolt - UNC (Regular Thread - Inch) 5/8-1
- + Heavy Hex Bolt - UNC (Regular Thread - Inch) 5/8-1
- + Heavy Hex Bolt - UNC (Regular Thread - Inch) 5/8-1
- + bottomplate:1

Figure 10–10

Update Substitutes

The **Update Substitutes** option ( ) updates all of the substitute parts in an assembly in a single operation. This command quickly updates all substitute parts created when using the **Create Derived Substitutes** command, and ensures that the substitute part still accurately reflects the subassembly from which it was derived.

Link Levels of Detail

The **Link Levels of Detail** option ( ) activates any LOD Representations in subassemblies that have the same name as the selected LOD in the top-level assembly. This tool makes activating LODs at multiple levels in an assembly much faster, since you do not need to manually activate LODs at multiple levels.

> **Hint: LODs in Templates**
>
> You should consider adding LODs to the assembly templates. This automatically creates all system-defined LODs and can include any company-specific LODs that are consistently used in your company's designs (e.g., low, medium, or high). Using LODs in the template can help reduce the time spent creating the LODs in assemblies and subassemblies, and ensure consistent naming conventions for use with the **Link Levels of Detail** command.

Practice 10a	Level of Detail Representations

Practice Objective

- Simplify the display and minimize the number of components loaded in a session by creating and using LOD Representations for an assembly.

In this practice, you create and use LOD Representations for the vise assembly shown in Figure 10–11. The design intent is to simplify the display and minimize the number of components loaded in a session.

LOD Representations are generally used for larger assemblies.

Figure 10–11

Task 1 - Open an assembly file.

1. Open **Vise.iam** from the *LevelOfDetailRepresentations* folder.

2. In the Model Browser, expand the *Representations* folder and expand the Level of Detail branch, as shown in Figure 10–12. The four system-defined LOD Representations are listed and are available for use. All assemblies contain these by default.

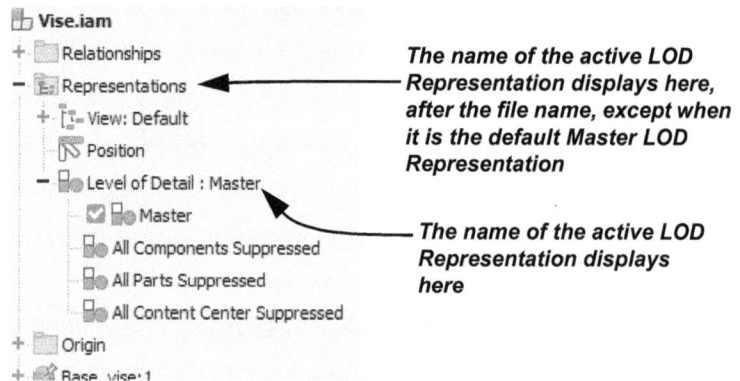

The name of the active LOD Representation displays here, after the file name, except when it is the default Master LOD Representation

The name of the active LOD Representation displays here

Figure 10–12

3. Look at the Status Bar in bottom-right corner of the Autodesk Inventor window, as shown in Figure 10–13. It displays the number of occurrences in the document and the number of documents in session.

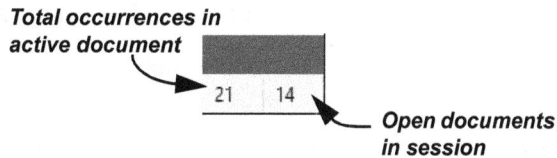

Total occurrences in active document

21   14

Open documents in session

Figure 10–13

4. Activate the **All Components Suppressed** LOD Representation. Note that all components are suppressed.

5. Review the Status Bar again. The number of occurrences is now zero, and the number of open documents is one. The amount of memory used decreases more significantly for larger assemblies when using LOD Representations with suppressed components.

Task 2 - Create an LOD Representation.

Several screws in the assembly are not significant to its design. To be able to easily switch between an assembly state that contains the screws and one that does not load the screws, you can create an LOD Representation that suppresses all the screws. The difference in memory used might not be significant for a smaller assembly such as this, but it can make a difference for assemblies that contain a large number of screws, nuts, washers, etc.

Before you create an LOD Representation, decide if it is better to begin creating the LOD Representation with all the components suppressed, all components unsuppressed, or somewhere in between. If you are working with a large assembly and the components you want to keep unsuppressed are only a small portion compared to the rest of the assembly, then you can begin by suppressing all components first. In this situation, the assembly is small and the number of components you must suppress is smaller than the total number of components in the assembly, so you will create an LOD Representation based on the Master LOD Representation.

1. Right-click on the Master LOD Representation and select **Copy**. A new LOD Representation is added to the list, called **Master1**.

2. In the Model Browser, click twice (do not double-click) on **Master1** and rename it as **Screws Suppressed**.

3. Double-click on **Screws Suppressed**, if it is not already activated.

To save the visibility status of components in an assembly, use Design View Representations.

4. Select the six screws in the assembly, right-click, and select **Suppress**. There is no visible change in the graphics window, because the screws are hidden behind components in the assembly. The Model Browser displays as shown in Figure 10–14.

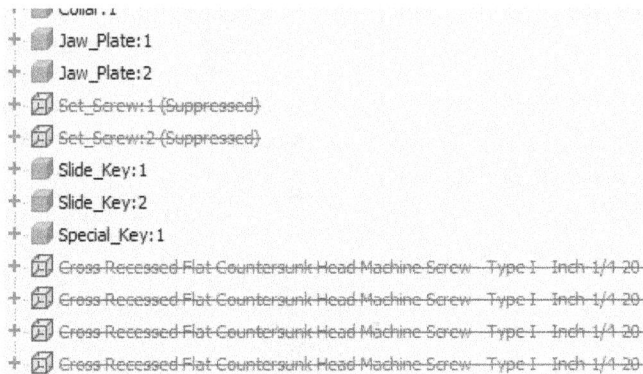

Figure 10–14

5. Save the assembly to save the LOD Representation and the changes that you made to it.

Task 3 - Create a second LOD Representation to help you make modifications in a particular area.

When you continually return to a particular area in the assembly to make modifications or inspect more closely, you can create an LOD Representation that loads only those components that are required for reference and modification. In such situations, without the use of LOD Representations, a simple modification or inspection of a small area in a large assembly could result in unnecessarily long retrieval times and a significant reduction in productivity. In the vise assembly, you want to take a closer look at the Collar.

1. Activate the **All Components Suppressed** LOD Representation. Because the majority of the components will be suppressed in this LOD Representation, you should begin with the All Components Suppressed LOD Representation.

2. With All Components Suppressed activated, in the Model Browser, right-click on the Level of Detail branch, as shown in Figure 10–15, and select **New Level of Detail**. A new LOD Representation is created and all components should be suppressed.

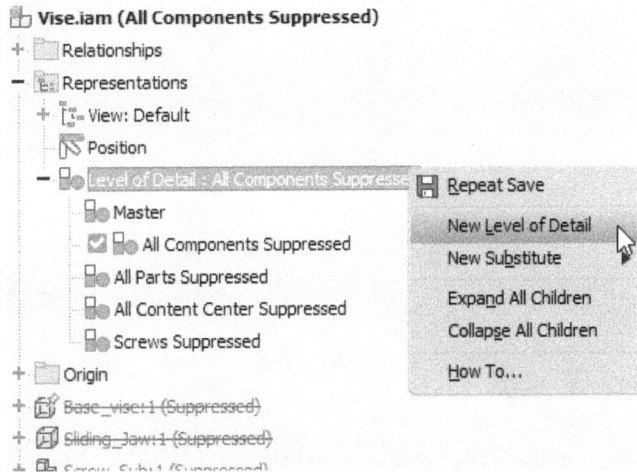

Figure 10–15

3. Rename the new LOD Representation as **Components to Monitor**.

4. Select **Collar:1** and **Special_Key:1**, right-click, and select **Suppress**. This will unsuppress **Collar:1** and **Special_Key:1**.

   You want to unsuppress one additional component and it is in the **Screw_Sub:1** subassembly. Note that the components in the subassembly cannot be viewed because the subassembly is suppressed.

5. Select the **Screw_Sub:1** subassembly, right-click, and select **Suppress** to unsuppress the subassembly.

6. Expand the **Screw_Sub:1** subassembly. **Vise_Screw:1** is the only component required to be visible. Suppress all components in the subassembly, except for **Vise_Screw:1**. The Model Browser and model display as shown in Figure 10–16.

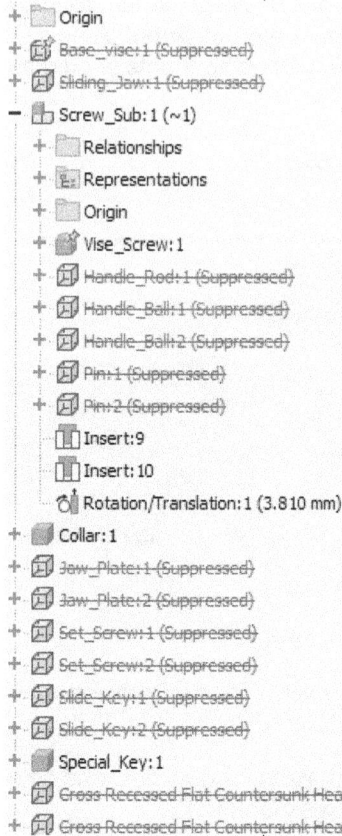

- + Origin
- + Base_vise:1 (Suppressed)
- + Sliding_Jaw:1 (Suppressed)
- − Screw_Sub:1 (~1)
  - + Relationships
  - + Representations
  - + Origin
  - + Vise_Screw:1
  - + Handle_Rod:1 (Suppressed)
  - + Handle_Ball:1 (Suppressed)
  - + Handle_Ball:2 (Suppressed)
  - + Pin:1 (Suppressed)
  - + Pin:2 (Suppressed)
  - Insert:9
  - Insert:10
  - Rotation/Translation:1 (3.810 mm)
- + Collar:1
- + Jaw_Plate:1 (Suppressed)
- + Jaw_Plate:2 (Suppressed)
- + Set_Screw:1 (Suppressed)
- + Set_Screw:2 (Suppressed)
- + Slide_Key:1 (Suppressed)
- + Slide_Key:2 (Suppressed)
- + Special_Key:1
- + Cross Recessed Flat Countersunk Head Machine Screw - Type I - Inch 1/4
- + Cross Recessed Flat Countersunk Head Machine Screw - Type I - Inch 1/4

Figure 10–16

7. Rotate and zoom into the model, as shown in Figure 10–17.

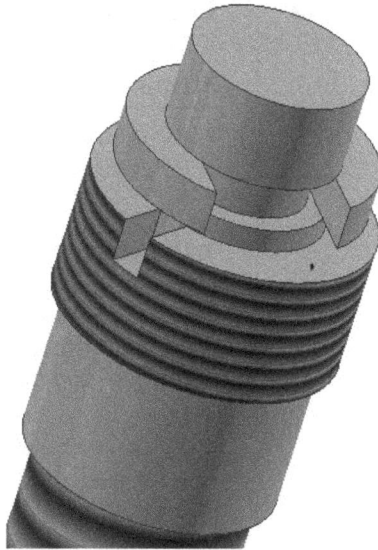

Figure 10–17

8. Save the assembly to save the LOD information. The LOD Representation just created focuses on this area and loads only these components.

9. Close the assembly.

Task 4 - Open the Vise assembly LOD Representation.

To help reduce retrieval time, select an LOD Representation other than the default Master.

1. In the Quick Access Toolbar, click 🗁 . The Open dialog box opens.

2. In the *LevelOfDetailRepresentations* folder, select **Vise.iam** and click **Options**. The File Open Options dialog box opens.

3. In the File Open Options dialog box, in the Level of Detail Representation drop-down list, select **Components to Monitor**.

4. In the File Open Options dialog box, click **OK** and then in the Open dialog box, click **Open**. The Assembly opens with the Components to Monitor LOD Representation activated. By using this method of opening the assembly, you have reduced the number of components loaded in session and can immediately access the components that you need.

5. Close the model.

Practice 10b | Substitute Level of Detail

Practice Objective

- Reduce the number of components loaded into memory by creating and activating multiple Substitute LODs using the Derive Assembly and Select Part File options.

In this practice, you create and activate multiple Substitute LODs, as shown in Figure 10–18. The first Substitute LOD uses the **Derive Assembly** option. The second Substitute LOD uses the **Select Part File** option. The design intent is to reduce the number of components loaded into memory.

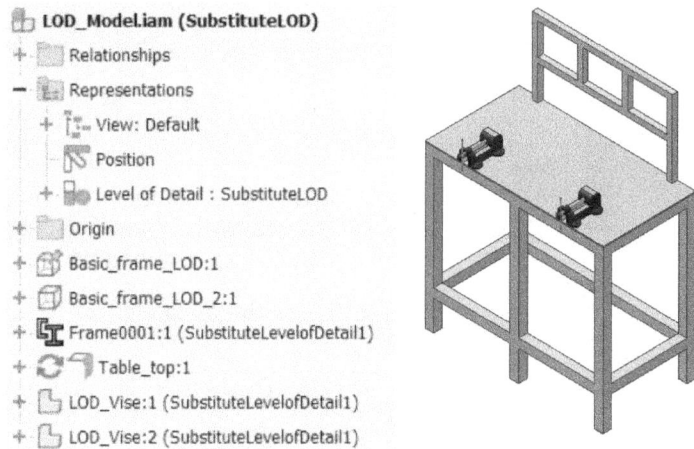

LOD_Model.iam (SubstituteLOD)
  + Relationships
  − Representations
    + View: Default
      Position
    + Level of Detail : SubstituteLOD
  + Origin
  + Basic_frame_LOD:1
  + Basic_frame_LOD_2:1
  + Frame0001:1 (SubstituteLevelofDetail1)
  + Table_top:1
  + LOD_Vise:1 (SubstituteLevelofDetail1)
  + LOD_Vise:2 (SubstituteLevelofDetail1)

Figure 10–18

Task 1 - Create a Substitute LOD using Derive Assembly.

1. Open **LOD_Model.iam** from the *Substitute LOD* folder.

2. Note the number of components in the Status Bar. There are 71 total occurrences in this assembly and 42 individual documents open, as shown in Figure 10–19.

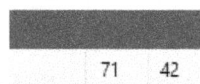

71	42

Figure 10–19

3. In the Model Browser, right-click on **Frame0001:1** and select **Open**. Note the number of components loaded, as shown in Figure 10–20.

| 23 | 42 |

Figure 10–20

4. Expand the *Representations* folder and expand the Level of Detail branch.

5. Right-click on **Level of Detail: Master** and select **New Substitute>Derive Assembly**. The New Derived Substitute Part dialog box opens.

6. Keep the default values and click **OK**. The substitute component is created in the same directory as your working assembly. The Derived Assembly dialog box opens.

7. In the Derived Assembly dialog box, ensure the ⬚ (Single solid body merging out seams between planar faces) Derive Style is set. Select all of the components in **Frame0001.iam** (do not select the top-level assembly). Click the ⬚ Status button or the icon next to the components to set them to Bounding Box, as shown in Figure 10–21, and click **OK**. This changes the status for all components in the assembly, but does not change the status of the assembly. A Substitute LOD is created for the frame assembly containing simplified versions of all components.

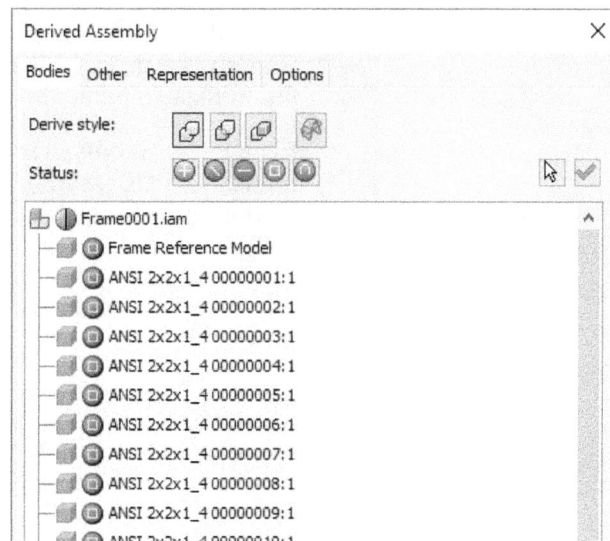

Figure 10–21

8. Note the number of loaded components, as shown in Figure 10–22. The frame assembly has been reduced to a single component.

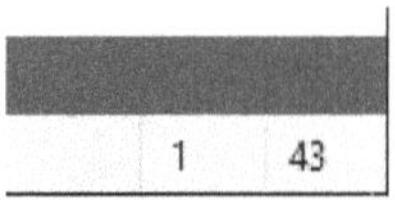

	1	43

Figure 10–22

9. Save and close **Frame0001.iam**.

Task 2 - Use the Substitute LOD in the main assembly.

1. Return to the **LOD_Model.iam** window.

2. In the Model Browser, expand **Frame0001.iam**, then the *Representations* folder, then the Level of Detail branch.

3. Right-click on **SubstituteLevelofDetail1** and select **Activate**. The Substitute LOD for the frame subassembly is loaded. The number of individual components is reduced from 71 to 49, and the number of unique occurrences is reduced from 42 to 20, as shown in Figure 10–23.

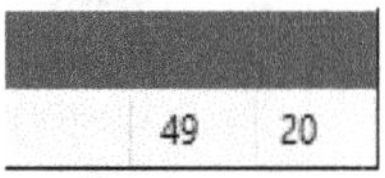

	49	20

Figure 10–23

4. Save **LOD_Model.iam**. The Save Level of Detail Representation Changes dialog box opens. Type **SubstituteLOD** for the name and click **Yes**. A new LOD Representation is created in the top-level assembly that uses the Substitute for the frame subassembly.

5. Expand the *Representations* folder and the Level of Detail branch for **LOD_Model.iam**. The LOD Representation you created is set as active.

Task 3 - Create a Substitute LOD using Select Part File.

1. In the Model Browser, right-click on **LOD_Vise:1** and select **Open**. The **LOD_Vise** assembly contains 21 total occurrences, as shown in Figure 10–24.

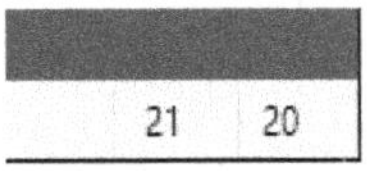

21	20

Figure 10–24

2. Expand the *Representations* folder and the Level of Detail branch.

3. Right-click on **Level of Detail: Master** and select **New Substitute>Select Part File**. The Place Component dialog box opens.

4. Select **Vise_Substitute.ipt** in the *Substitute LOD* folder and click **Open**.

5. Click **Yes** in the Warning dialog box. **Vise_Substitute.ipt** is flagged as a substitute component.

6. Note the number of loaded components, as shown in Figure 10–25. The vise assembly has been reduced to a single component.

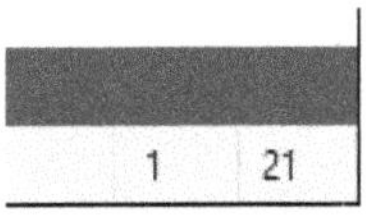

1	21

Figure 10–25

7. Save and close **LOD_Vise.iam**.

Task 4 - Use the Substitute LOD in the main assembly.

1. In the Model Browser, ensure that the **SubstituteLOD** LOD is active for **LOD_Model.iam**.

2. In the Model Browser, expand **LOD_Vise:1**, then the *Representations* folder, then the Level of Detail branch.

3. Right-click on **SubstituteLevelofDetail1** and select
   Activate. The Substitute LOD for the vise subassembly is
   loaded. The number of individual components is reduced
   from 49 to 29, as shown in Figure 10–26.

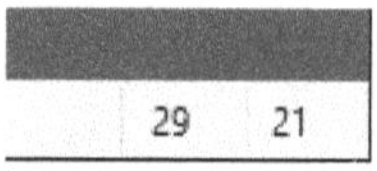

29	21

Figure 10–26

4. Expand **LOD_Vise:2**, then the *Representations* folder, then
   the Level of Detail branch.

5. Activate **SubstituteLevelofDetail1** for **LOD_Vise:2**. The
   number of individual components is reduced from 29 to 9, as
   shown in Figure 10–27. The assembly has been simplified
   from 71 occurrences to 9 with only 8 unique files open.

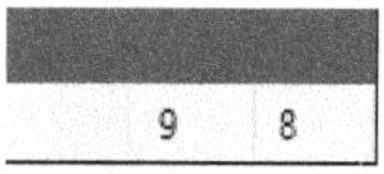

9	8

Figure 10–27

6. Save and close **LOD_Model.iam**.

Practice 10c

Shrinkwrap and Level of Detail

Practice Objectives

- Increase system performance by removing detail from an assembly by creating and using a LOD Representation that substitutes a shrinkwrap part.
- Control LOD Representations that exist in subassemblies from the top-level assemblies in which they reside.

In this practice, you will use Shrinkwrap and LOD functionality to work on the mechanical pencil assembly shown in Figure 10–28.

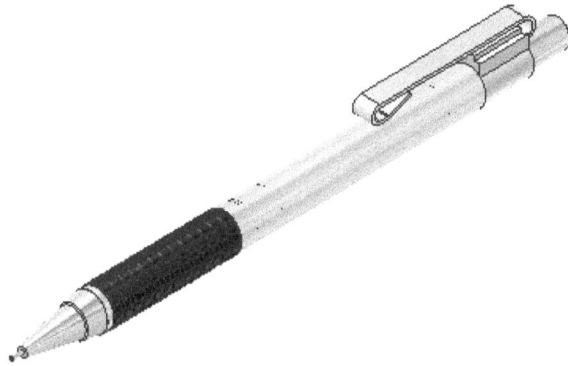

Figure 10–28

Task 1 - Create a LOD Representation using a shrinkwrap part.

In this task, you will remove detail from the grip component by creating a new LOD representation that substitutes the Housing subassembly for a shrinkwrap part. This functionality is useful when working with large assemblies. By removing some of the detail, you can increase system performance.

1. Open **Mechanical Pencil.iam** from the *Mechanical_ Pencil_Shrinkwrap* folder.

2. Right-click on the Housing subassembly and select **Open**.

3. Double-click on the **Grip** component to activate it.

4. Suppress **Extrusion1** and **Circular Pattern1**.

5. Activate and save the Housing assembly.

6. In the Model Browser, expand the *Representations* folder. Right-click on **Level of Detail : Master** and select **New Substitute>Shrinkwrap**. Alternatively, in the *Assemble* tab>Simplification panel, click (Shrinkwrap Substitute).

7. On the *Components* tab, click (Select to Exclude) and select the **Ring** component in the graphics window. The *View* area will update to show that there are two included components and one excluded, as shown in Figure 10–29.

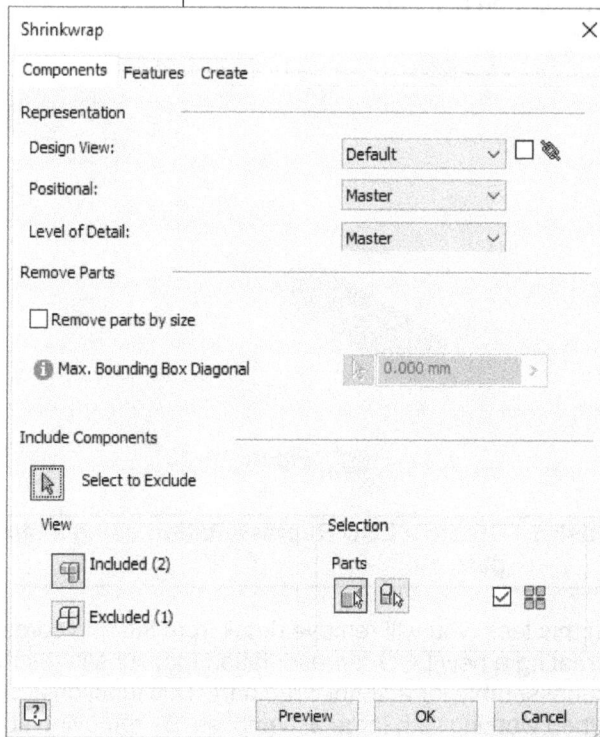

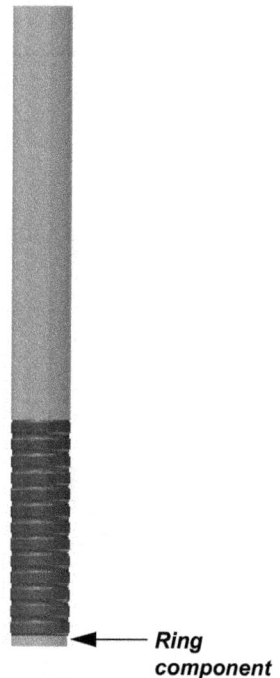

Figure 10–29

8. Select the *Features* tab. In the *Remove Holes* area, ensure
   that ⬚ (Do not remove any holes) is selected and **None**
   displays, as shown in Figure 10–30.

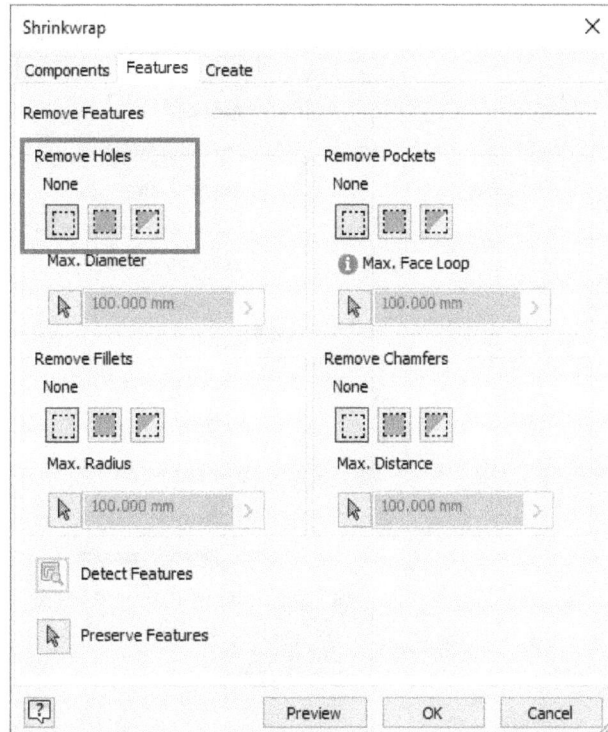

Figure 10–30

9. Select the *Create* tab.

10. Keep the default name and location. Use the **Standard
    (mm).ipt** template.

11. In the *Style* area in the dialog box, click ▣ (Single
    composite feature).

12. Clear the **Fill all internal voids** and **Remove internal parts** options. The *Create* tab should display as shown in Figure 10–31.

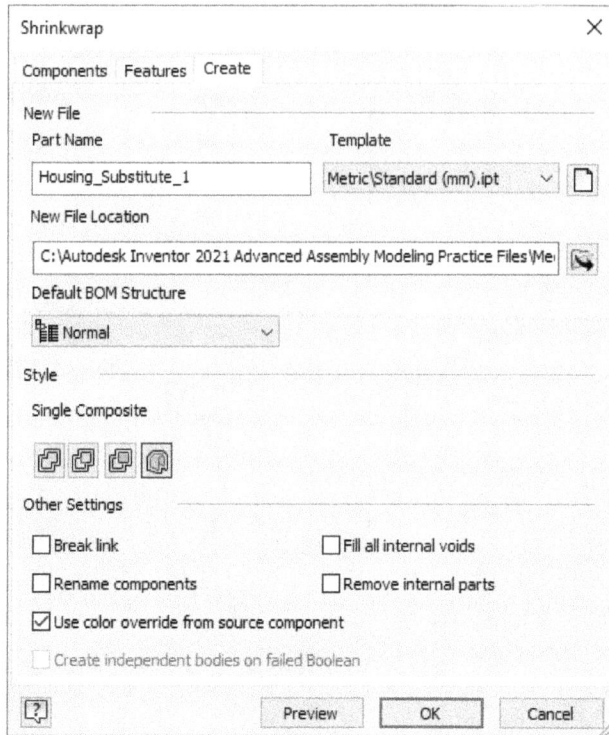

Figure 10–31

13. Click **OK** to generate the shrinkwrap part. The shrinkwrap part and a new LOD Representation is created. Note that the suppressed features were not generated in the shrinkwrap part.

14. Save the model.

15. Activate the Master LOD Representation and unsuppress **Extrusion1** and **Circular Pattern1** from **Grip.ipt**.

16. Save the model.

17. Switch between the Master and the **SubstituteLevelofDetail1** LOD Representations to view the difference.

18. Ensure that the Master LOD Representation is active.

Task 2 - Link LOD Representations.

In this task, you will use the productivity tool **Link Levels of Detail** to quickly substitute the shrinkwrap part (created in the last task) into the top-level assembly.

1. Activate the Mechanical Pencil window. Update the assembly, if required.

2. In the Model Browser, expand the *Representations* folder. Right-click on **Level of Detail : Master** and select **New Level of Detail**.

3. Rename the LOD as **SubstituteLevelofDetail1**. The name of this representation needs to match exactly what was given to the new LOD Representation that was created in the Housing subassembly.

4. Save the assembly.

5. Reactivate the Master LOD Representation.

6. In the *Assemble* tab>expanded Productivity panel, click

   ![icon] (Link Levels of Detail).

7. In the Link Levels of Detail dialog box, select **SubstituteLevelofDetail1,** as shown in Figure 10–32, and click **OK**.

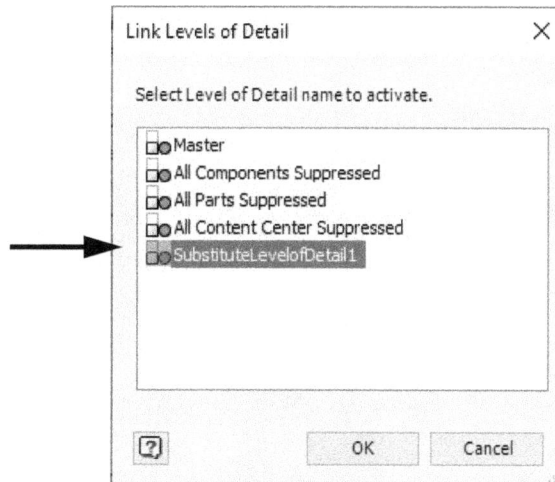

Figure 10–32

8. Click **OK** to the warning. The **SubstituteLevelofDetail1** in both the top-level assembly and the housing subassembly activate.

9. Use the **Link Levels of Detail** command again to reactivate the Master LOD in both the top-level assembly and the subassemblies.

   In this example, you could have manually activated the **SubstituteLevelofDetail1** LOD Representation in the Housing subassembly, and then view the substitution without creating the top-level representation and using the **Link Level of Details** command. When you have more than one representation of the same name in multiple subassemblies and in the top-level assembly, this tool can be a great time-saver.

10. Save all of the open models.

Chapter Review Questions

1. What is a benefit of adding Level of Detail Representations to an assembly? (Select all that apply.)

    a. Displays and loads only the components you need to work on.

    b. Changes component positions.

    c. Simplifies the display of an assembly by removing unnecessary components.

    d. Improves retrieval times of larger assemblies.

2. You can manipulate the four system-defined LOD Representations.

    a. True

    b. False

3. How do you open an assembly so that only the components in a selected user-defined LOD Representation display?

    a. Save the assembly with the specific LOD Representation active.

    b. Application Menu, Open LOD Representation.

    c. In the File Open Options dialog box, **Level of Detail Representation** menu.

4. Representations can be used in Drawings but not in Presentations.

    a. True

    b. False

Command Summary

Button	Command	Location
	Create Derived Substitutes	• **Ribbon:** *Assemble* tab>Productivity panel
	Link Levels of Detail	• **Ribbon:** *Assemble* tab>Productivity panel
	Shrinkwrap Substitute	• **Ribbon:** *Assemble* tab>*Simplification* panel
	Update Substitutes	• **Ribbon:** *Assemble* tab>Productivity panel

Design Accelerator

The Design Accelerator enables you to easily insert standard and customized components and features into your model. The Design Accelerator also contains engineering calculators that are used to verify your designs, as well as the Engineer's Handbook, which is a reference tool for engineering formulas used by the calculators.

Learning Objectives in This Chapter

- Automatically create geometry using component generators.
- Understand what kind of calculations to perform to help assess the feasibility of designs based on provided data.
- Access the Engineer's Handbook as a reference for theories and formulas while using the generators and calculators.

11.1 Design Accelerator

The Design Accelerator tools enable you to generate common components and perform calculations for them by entering mechanical attributes. The tools include generators, calculators, and the Engineer's Handbook, which are all found on the *Design* tab. The commands in the *Design* tab are shown in Figure 11–1 with all of the panel flyouts pinned open.

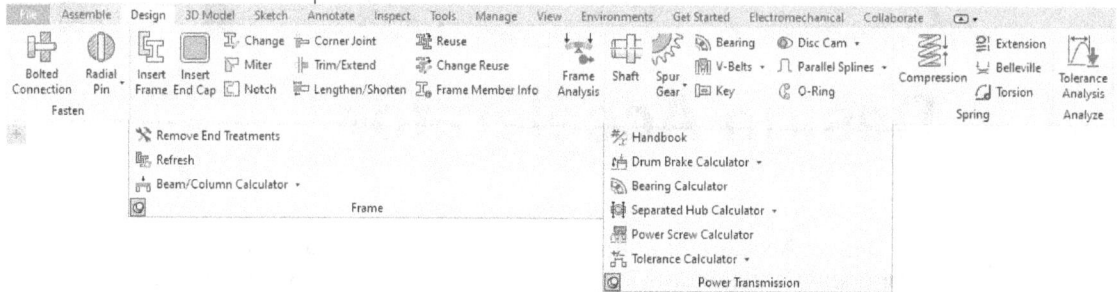

Figure 11–1

11.2 Generators

Generators use specific mechanical attributes and dimensions to automatically create components. For example, a clevis pin can be created automatically with the Design Accelerator by specifying the clevis width, rod width, pin diameter, and active pin length. Generators enable you to focus on the function of your design and enable the geometry to be created for you.

General Steps

Use the following general steps to insert a component using the Design Accelerator's Generator tools:

1. Select the required component generator.
2. Enter and select the required inputs.
3. Perform calculations, as required.
4. Correct errors, as required.
5. Complete the generator.

Step 1 - Select the required component generator.

Select the required component generator from the *Design* tab of the ribbon. They are grouped in panels according to functional areas. The interface for each of the generators is a single dialog box containing a *Design* tab to define the component parameters and a *Calculation* tab to verify the design. Using the *Calculation* tab is optional, but using it helps to make your designs more robust by verifying that your components meet design requirements. Some component generators have tabs for additional calculations or graphs.

The Spur Gears Component Generator is shown as an example in Figure 11–2. In the *Design* tab, you input required data to create the components and select references to place the components.

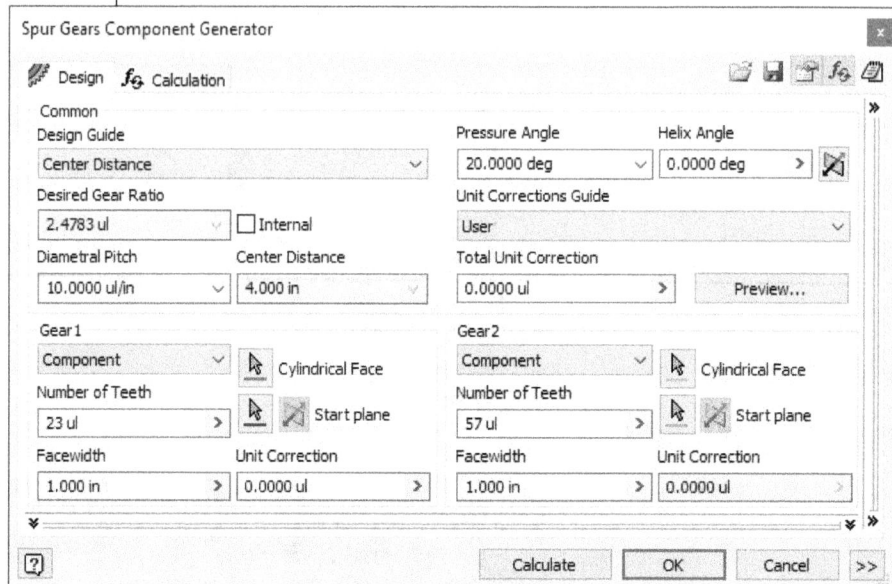

Figure 11–2

Another dialog box style interface exists for particular generators, such as bolted connections and clevis pins. These dialog boxes contain a built-in link to the Content Center that enables you to add several standard components, such as bolts, washers, and nuts, to the base component. The bolted connections dialog box is shown in Figure 11–3. Some common areas are labeled.

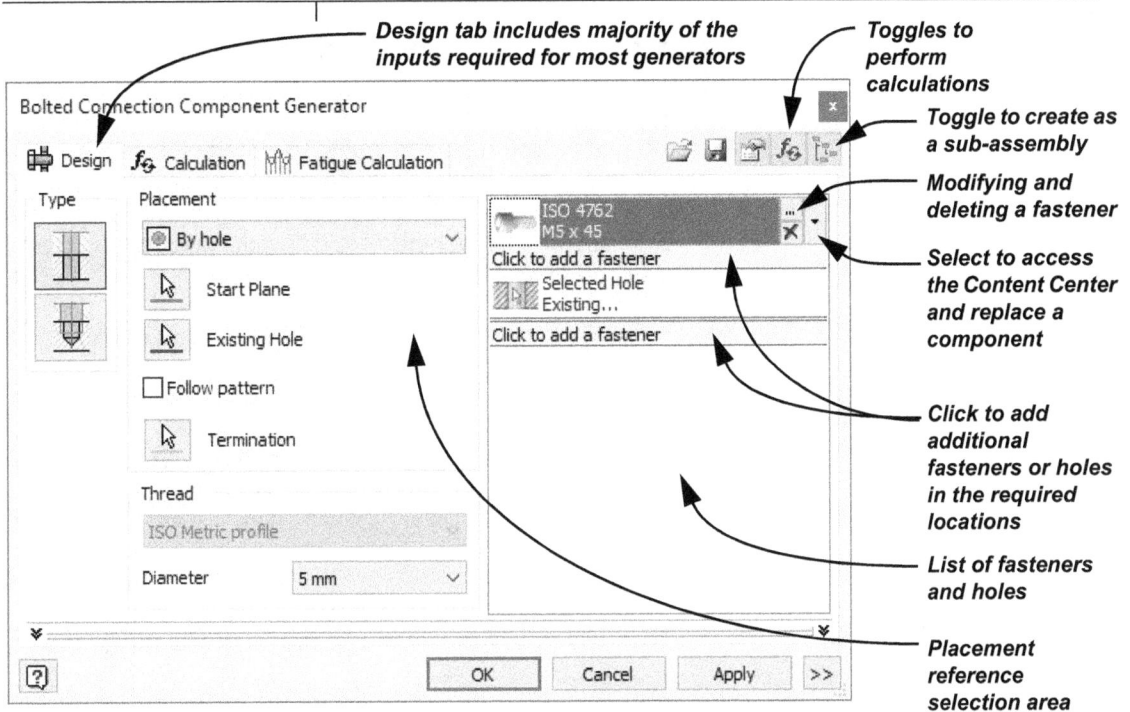

Labels around the figure:

- *Design tab includes majority of the inputs required for most generators*
- *Toggles to perform calculations*
- *Toggle to create as a sub-assembly*
- *Modifying and deleting a fastener*
- *Select to access the Content Center and replace a component*
- *Click to add additional fasteners or holes in the required locations*
- *List of fasteners and holes*
- *Placement reference selection area*

Figure 11–3

Each generator contains only the fields and options applicable to that generator.

Step 2 - Enter and select the required inputs.

For some component generator dialog boxes, you can immediately select the placement references, such as for bolted connections, key connections, and spur gears. Select the required references, as required. Enter and select the required inputs, as required, such as a thread and diameter value.

Some component generator dialog boxes enable you to select components from the Content Center, such as for bolted connections, bearings, and clevis pins. For example, to add a fastener in the Bolted Connection Component Generator, click **Click to add a fastener** in the list of fasteners and holes, as shown in Figure 11–3, and select the required fastener from the Content Center. Continue adding fasteners and holes as required.

*Depending on the components added, you might be able to add fasteners at different locations. This is possible when you see multiple **Click to add a fastener** options.*

Step 3 - Perform calculations, as required.

To perform calculations to determine if components are able to withstand particular forces and loads, use the options in the *Calculation* tab. Select the type of calculation, input the required loads, and select materials in the *Calculation* tab. The *Calculation* tab for each generator is different, the common areas are labeled in Figure 11–4.

Expandable calculations report area

Loads input area

Expandable results area

Icons

Expansion and Compression arrows

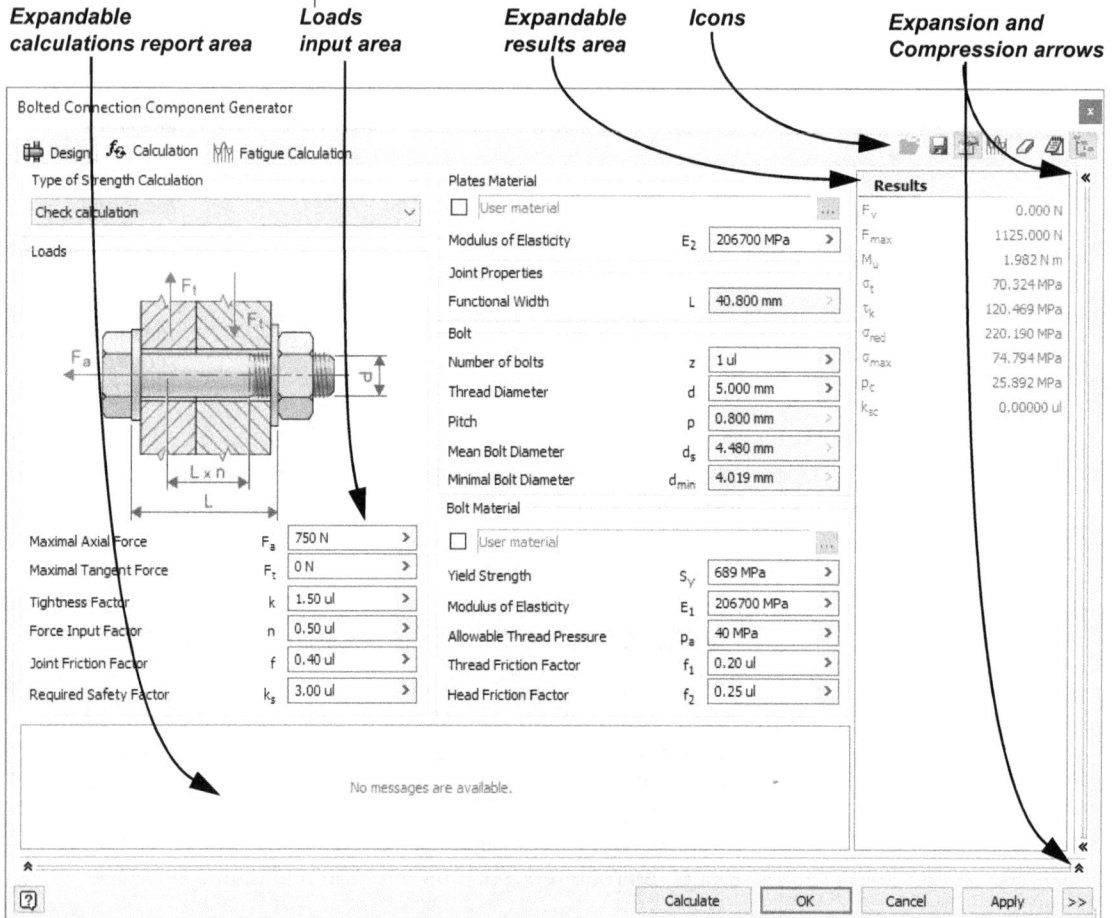

Figure 11–4

To perform calculations, enter the required data and click **Calculate**.

- The results display in the expandable results area on the right side. View a report for the calculations by expanding the bottom area. This area indicates if the calculations show design compliance or design failure based on the values entered. To expand or collapse the expandable areas, select the expansion and compression arrows. To change the units of any value in the results area, double-click on the value and enter the new units.

- When the input values cause a design failure, the critical values that have been exceeded are highlighted in red in the Results area. The calculations report displays information about the results. Blue text signifies general information about the calculation, while red text describes failed results. Text with a red background means there is a critical error and you cannot continue the design unless you change inputs.

Step 4 - Correct errors, as required.

You can place components that fail the calculation checks but it is typically required to resolve the errors. You can resolve the errors by changing the forces, material, or other information on the *Calculation* tab, or you can change the parameters on the *Design* tab. After the information is modified, click **Calculate** to perform the calculation with the new information.

Step 5 - Complete the generator.

Once you have completed defining the component, click **OK** to place the component.

11.3 Calculators

Calculators in the Design Accelerator perform calculations to help assess the feasibility of designs based on provided data. The Plate Calculator dialog box is shown in Figure 11–5. The calculators are similar to the *Calculation* tab for generators, except they do not generate geometry. For example, the plate calculator can be used to enter beam dimensions, load, and material properties to determine if it can withstand a load. If sufficient, a calculated safety factor is provided.

To access the calculators, you may have to expand the panels on the Design tab.

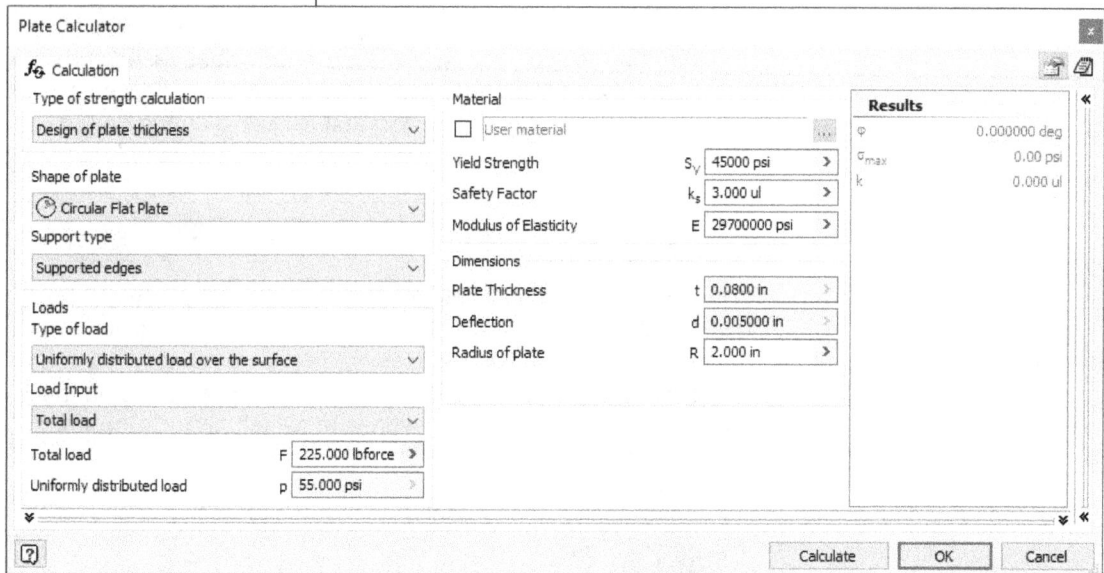

Figure 11–5

The list of calculators available include the following:

The calculators listed with the * symbol adjacent to their names are located on the Environments tab in the Convert panel. They deal with weldments.

• **Band Brake**	• **Disc Brake**	• **Power Screw**
• **Beam and Column**	• **Drum Brake**	• **Press Fit**
• **Bevel Solder***	• **Fillet Weld (Plane)***	• **Separated Hub**
• **Butt Solder***	• **Fillet Weld (Spatial)***	• **Slotted Hub**
• **Butt Weld ***	• **Lap Solder***	• **Spot Weld ***
• **Bearing**	• **Limits and Fits**	• **Step Solder***
• **Cone Brake**	• **Plate**	• **Step Tube Solder***
• **Cone Joint**	• **Plug and Groove Weld ***	• **Tolerance**

11.4 Engineer's Handbook

The Engineer's Handbook is a reference for all theories and formulas used in the generators and calculators. To open the Handbook, click $^{\#}\!/_{x}$ (Handbook) in the expanded Power Transmission panel on the *Design* tab. A sample of the Engineer's Handbook is shown in Figure 11–6.

- If the online Help document does not automatically open the Engineer's Handbook. In the Search field, type **Engineer's Handbook** to view the information.

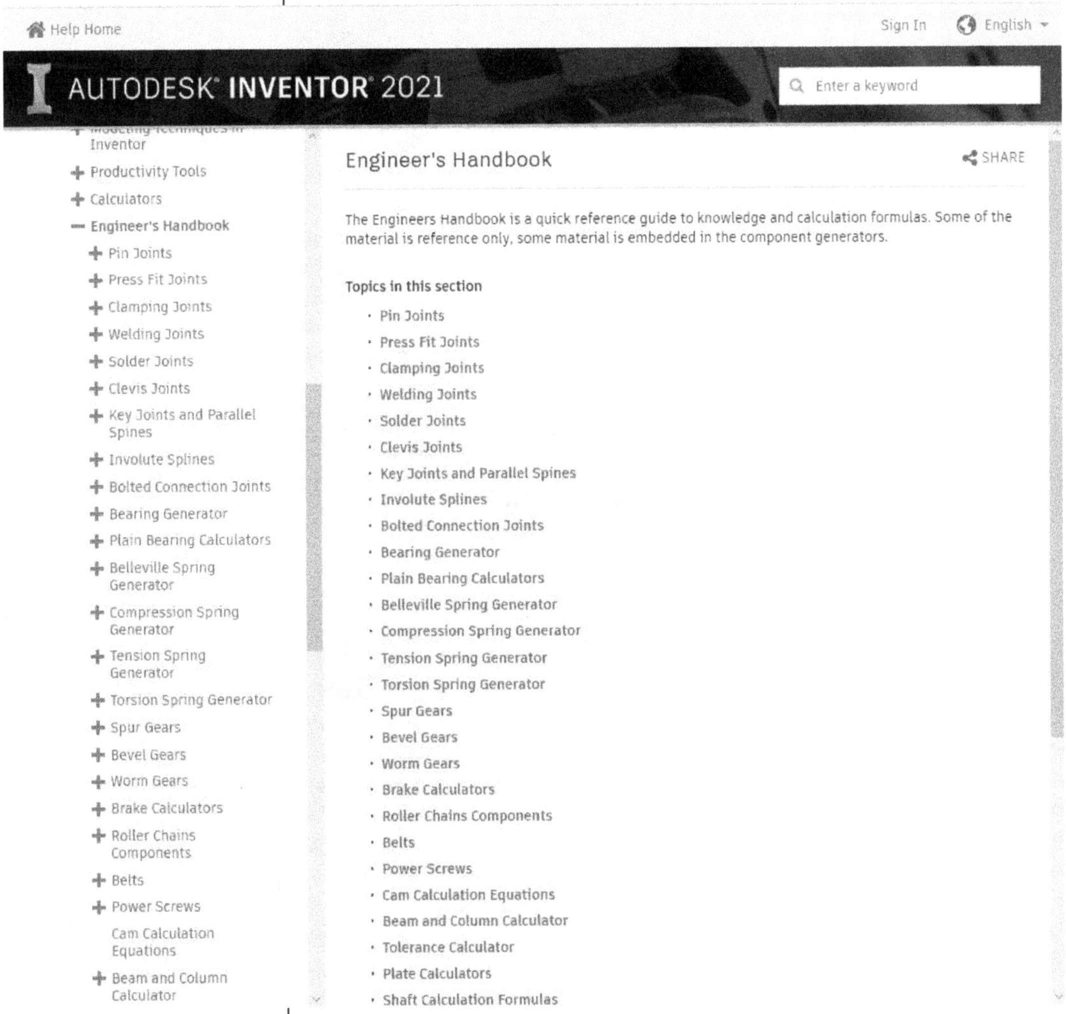

Figure 11–6

Practice 11a

Design Accelerator I

Practice Objective

- Automatically insert a component using the **Radial Pin** component generator and the Content Center.

In this practice, you insert a pin using the Radial Pin component generator and Content Center. The final assembly is shown in Figure 11–7.

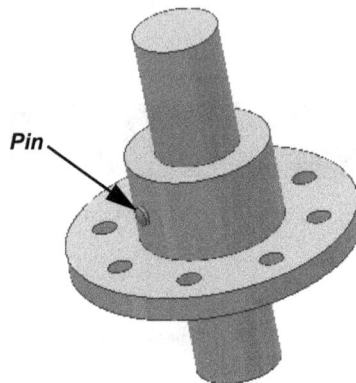

Figure 11–7

Task 1 - Use the radial pin component generator.

1. Open **hub_shaft_assy.iam** from the top level practice files folder. The model displays as shown in Figure 11–8.

Figure 11–8

> **Hint: Accessing Content Center Data Through Vault**
>
> If you do not have Desktop Content installed on your local system and use Vault, you must log in to access the Content Center data; otherwise, go to Step 2 to complete the practice. To log in, click **File>Vault Server>Log In**. If the **Log In** option is grayed out, then you are already logged in and you can proceed to the next step. Otherwise, click
>
> **Log In**
> Enables secure access to the server. , activate the **Content Center library read only user** option in the Authentication drop-down list and click **OK**. The **Content Center library read only user** option enables you to log in with read only permissions if you do not have a login set up with your system administrator. You are now logged into the Content Center.

2. In the ribbon, select the *Design* tab to access the Design Accelerator tools.

3. In the *Design* tab>Fasten panel, click (Radial Pin). You might need to select it from the pin flyout menu, as shown in Figure 11–9. The Radial Pin Component Generator dialog box opens.

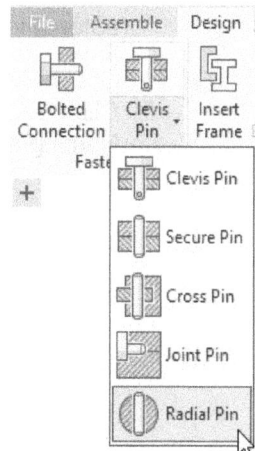

Figure 11–9

4. Select the visible work plane as the start plane.

5. Select the hole shown in Figure 11–10. The selected hole is added to the Items list in the dialog box.

Figure 11–10

6. Select **Click to add a pin** from the Items list. The fasteners available in the Content Center display.

7. Select **ISO 8734 A** from the list. A preview of the pin displays.

   If the direction of the pin is incorrect, reverse it using ⊠ for the Existing Hole. Note how the length of the pin is automatically selected, based on the length of the existing hole.

8. Click **OK** to insert the pin into the assembly. In the File Naming dialog box, click **OK** to accept the default name.

9. Toggle off the visibility of **Work Plane2**. The assembly displays as shown in Figure 11–11.

Figure 11–11

10. Save and close the assembly.

Practice 11b | Design Accelerator II

Practice Objective

- Place a set of fasteners from the Content Center and create a hole through a part, using the **Bolted Connection** component generator, all in individual tasks, and then all in a single task.

In this practice, you use the Content Center and Design Accelerator to insert a screw, washer, and nut into the four holes shown in Figure 11–12. During the placement of one set of fasteners, you also create a hole through one of the parts using the bolted connection component generator. By placing components using both methods, you can determine which one is the faster method for placing bolted connections.

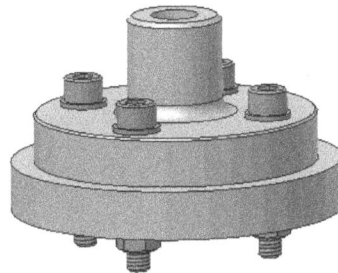

Figure 11–12

Task 1 - Place a washer from the Content Center.

In this task, you assemble components directly from the Content Center into the assembly. In a later task, you will use the Design Accelerator to assemble the same components and you can compare the process for each.

1. Open **general.iam** from the *Design_Accelerator2* folder. The assembly displays as shown in Figure 11–13.

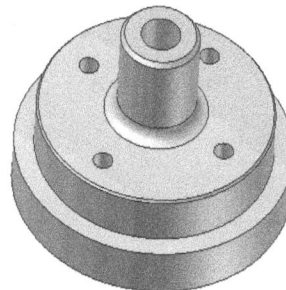

Figure 11–13

2. Rotate the model to the opposite side and note that the plate has only three identical holes, as shown in Figure 11–14, but four identical holes on the flange.

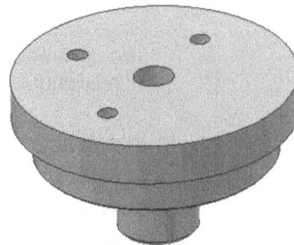

Figure 11–14

*The **Content Center library read only user** option enables you to log in with read only permissions if you do not have a login set up with your system administrator.*

3. In the *Assemble* tab>Component panel, click (Place from Content Center). If the Log In dialog box opens, activate the **Content Center library read only user** option and click **OK** to open the Content Center dialog box.

4. Toggle on (AutoDrop) if it is not already on.

5. Toggle on the Tree and Table View panes using and , if not already displayed. The Content Center is shown in Figure 11–15. You can also change the display of the items. In Figure 11–15, the items display as thumbnails.

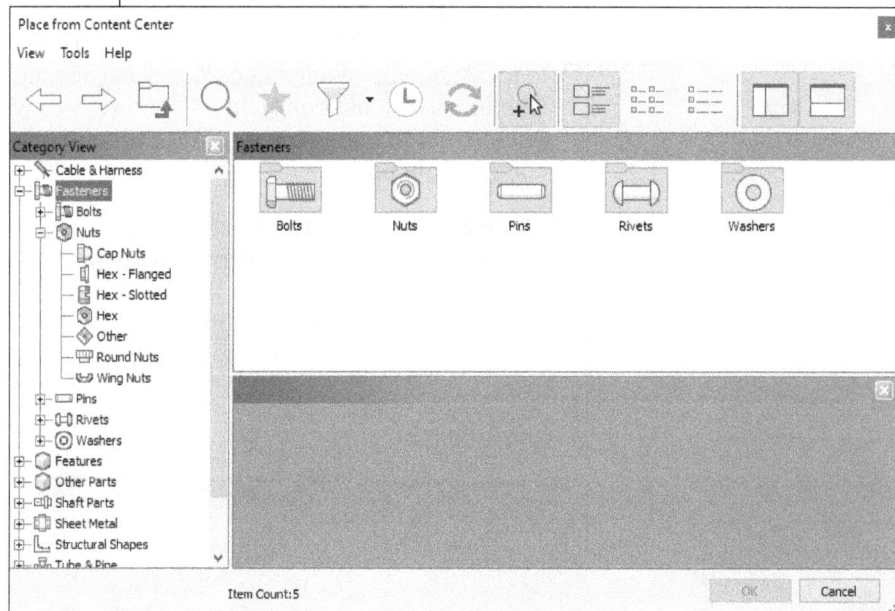

Figure 11–15

6. Expand the *Fasteners* category and then expand the *Washers* category in the Category View pane.

7. Select the *Plain* category and select **ISO 7089**. The Table View pane should display as shown in Figure 11–16. If not, select the preview border and drag it upwards.

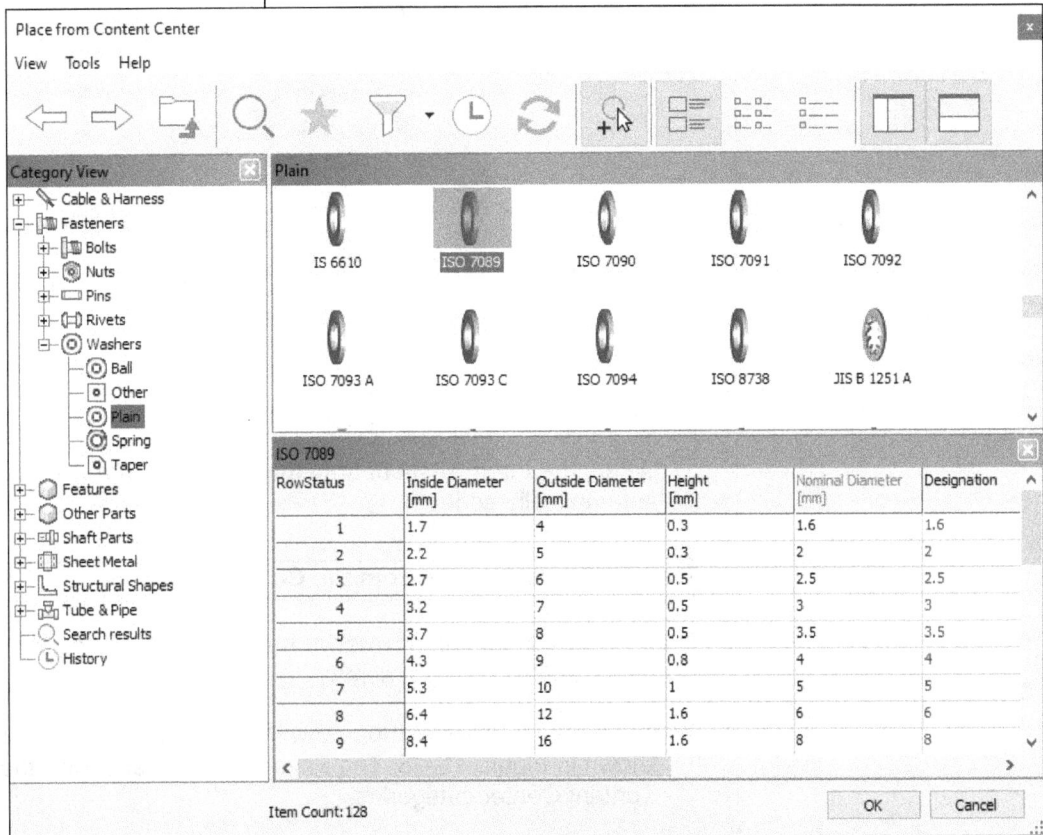

Figure 11–16

8. Double-click on **ISO 7089** in the upper pane.

9. Place the cursor on the edge of one of the holes on the flange that corresponds with one of the holes on the plate. Recall that only three holes are on the plate. Do not select the hole at the center of the part.

You can also insert bolted connections based on points, 3D points, and work points created in the sketch environment.

10. Click to accept the previewed washer and click ![icon] to complete the washer placement. ![icon] is enabled by default, which sets the Autodesk Inventor software to assemble the Content Center item to all members in a pattern or, in this case, all sketched points dealing with the selected feature, as shown in Figure 11–17.

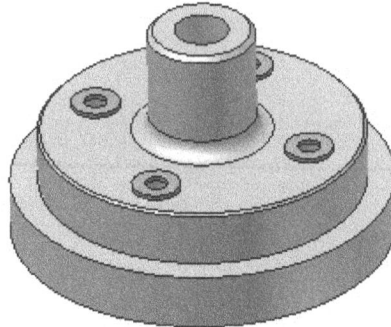

Figure 11–17

11. Delete the three washers from the assembly that were automatically added.

Task 2 - Place a screw from the Content Center.

In this task, you use an alternative method of accessing the Content Center to place a screw.

1. In the Model Browser drop-down list, select **Favorites**, as shown in Figure 11–18. The Favorites browser shows the Content Center categories.

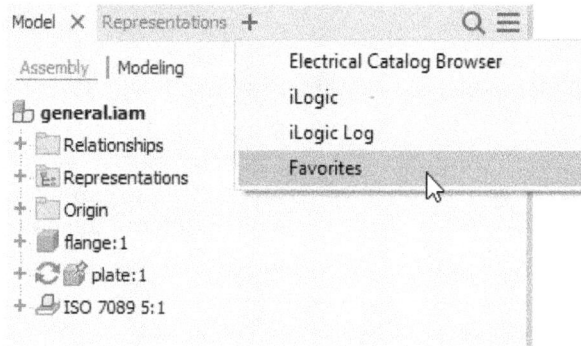

Figure 11–18

2. Expand the following categories in order: Fasteners, Bolts, and Socket Head. Double-click on **ISO 4762** to place it.

3. Place the cursor over the inner edge of the washer. Left-click the preview to accept it. A directional arrow displays. Drag it to increase the length of the screw so that it goes through the length of both holes and protrudes out, as shown in Figure 11–19. The bolt should be an M5 x 30.

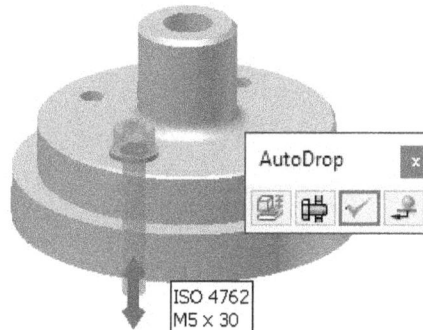

Figure 11–19

Note that is not available in the **AutoDrop** menu. This is because there is no pattern to follow. If there were multiple bolts to add, you would need to add them manually using this method.

4. Click to complete the bolt placement.

Task 3 - Place a nut from the Content Center.

---

1. Place an **ISO 4032** hex nut, using either of the methods used previously. Because you are placing the nut by referencing the edge of the hole, the software recognizes that the edge belongs to a sketch and the entire set of holes are selected.

2. Click [icon] in the AutoDrop dialog box to disable this pattern/sketch functionality. The model (with a single nut) should display as shown in Figure 11–20. Click [icon].

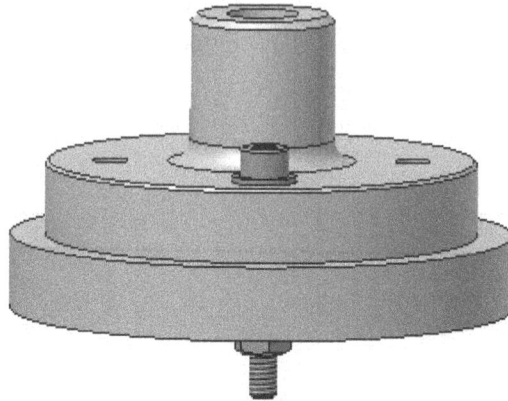

Figure 11–20

3. Select **Modeling** at the top of the Model Browser and review the **Flange.ipt** model to see that the holes were created referencing a sketch that consisted of points. **Plate.ipt** referenced the holes in the flange for their creation.

Task 4 - Insert one set of fasteners using the Design Accelerator.

In this task, you use an alternative method of placing fasteners. This involves using the bolted connection component generator.

1. Select the *Design* tab.

2. In the *Design* tab>Fasten panel, click [icon] (Bolted Connection) to open the Bolted Connection Component Generator.

3. Keep the hole type as [icon] (Through All connection type).

4. Set the hole placement drop-down list to **By hole**. The Bolted Connection Component Generator dialog box displays as shown in Figure 11–21.

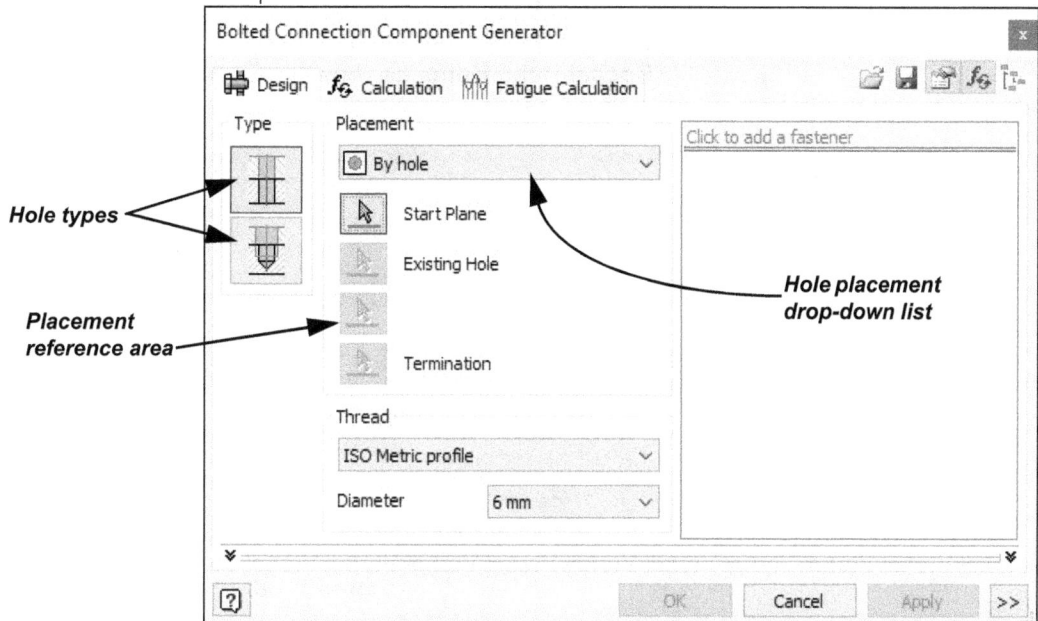

Figure 11–21

5. Select ⌷ (Enables/Disables the sub-assembly structure) to enable it. This ensures that the connections used are all combined into a sub-assembly. If disabled, all components are placed as parts in the top-level assembly.

6. Select the references shown in Figure 11–22. Ensure that the hole you select has a matching hole in the plate.

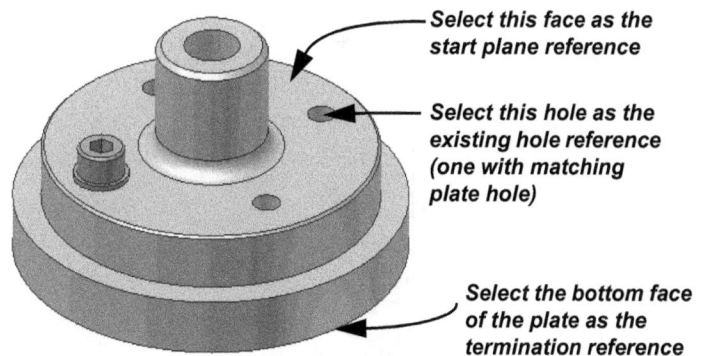

Select this face as the start plane reference

Select this hole as the existing hole reference (one with matching plate hole)

Select the bottom face of the plate as the termination reference

Figure 11–22

7. Set the *Thread* parameters to **ISO Metric profile** and the *Diameter* to **5 mm**.

8. Click **Click to add a fastener** to access the bolt in the Content Center. Set *Standard* to **<All>** and *Category* to **Socket Head Bolts**, as shown in Figure 11–23.

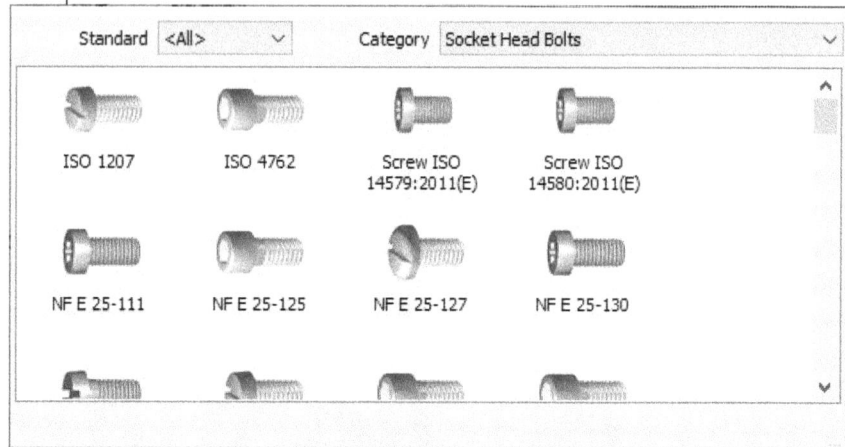

Figure 11–23

9. Select **ISO 4762**. A preview of the screw displays in the model and is placed in the list in the dialog box, as shown in Figure 11–24.

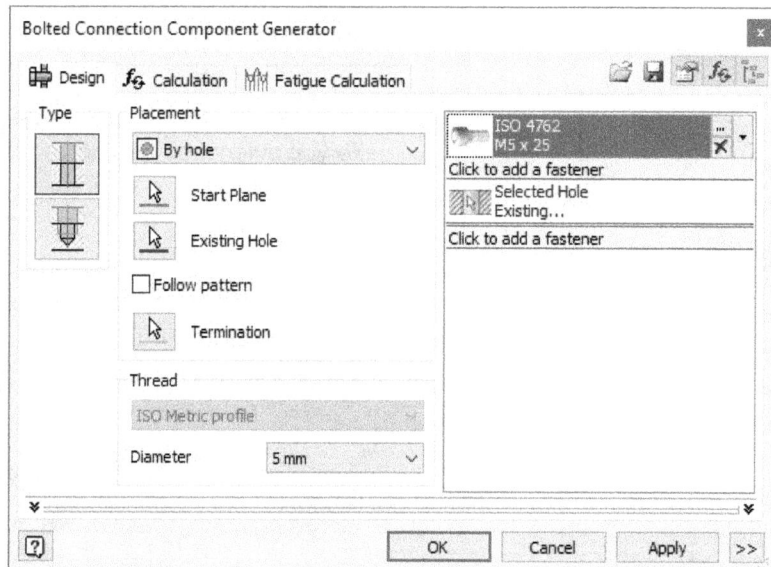

Figure 11–24

10. Click **Click to add a fastener** that is just below the screw in the list to place a washer between the screw and the hole.

11. Select the **ISO 7089** washer. The washer displays as shown in Figure 11–25. Note the length of the screw in the preview.

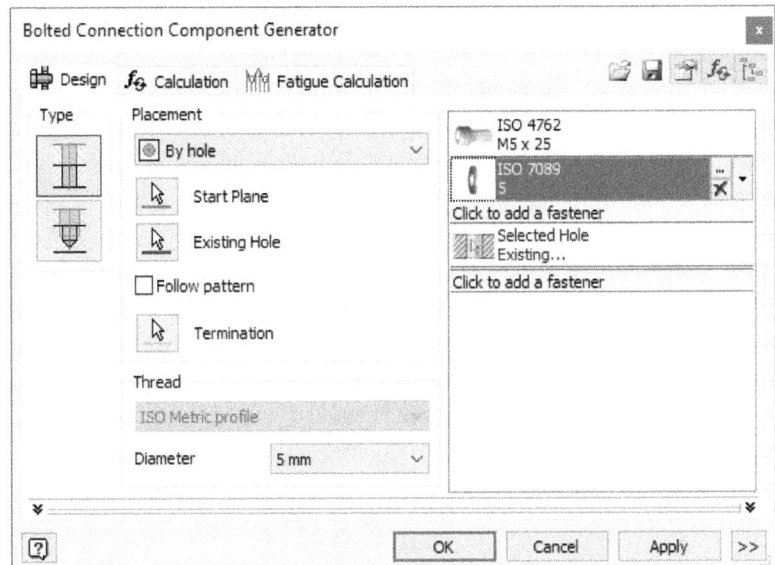

Figure 11–25

12. Click **Click to add a fastener** below the hole in the list to place a nut. Select **Nuts** from the Category drop-down list.

13. Select the **ISO 4032** hex nut. The list displays as shown in Figure 11–26.

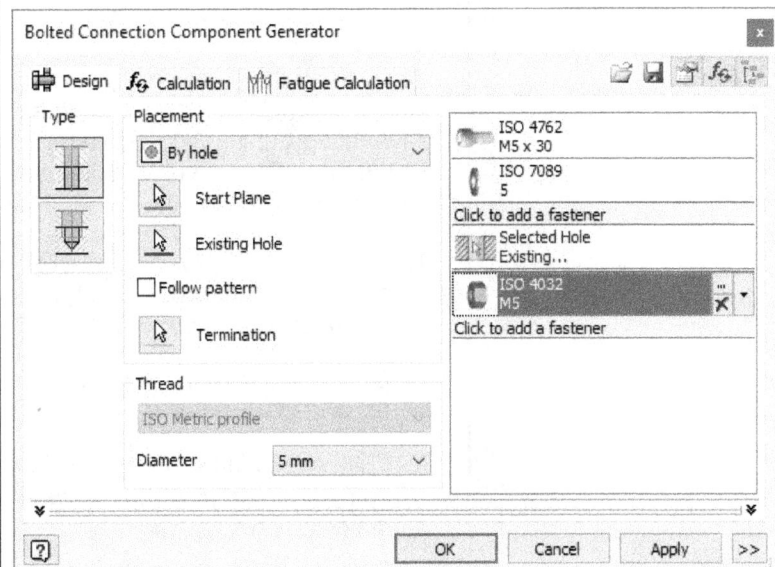

Figure 11–26

14. Note the length of the screw increased in length after the nut was added. Click **OK** to complete the placement of the bolted connection. In the File Naming dialog box, click **OK** to accept the default name. The model now displays as shown in Figure 11–27.

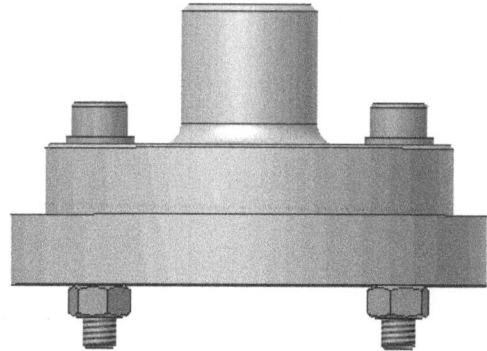

Figure 11–27

Task 5 - Edit the bolted connection and save to the Templates Library.

You will use the same components multiple times throughout this task. If you have a set of fasteners that you use often, you can save that grouping to the Bolted Connection Templates Library for later use. This saves considerable time selecting components and ensures you use the same grouping each time.

1. In the Model Browser, right-click on **Bolted Connection:1** and select **Edit using Design Accelerator**. The Bolted Connection Component Generator displays.

2. Click >> to expand the dialog box if it is not already expanded.

3. Click **Add...** in the Templates Library area to add the component grouping to the library. The Template Description dialog box displays.

4. Click **OK** to accept the default name. If the name already exists, enter a unique name or delete the existing template.

5. Click **Cancel** to close the dialog box.

**Task 6 - Use Design Accelerator to simultaneously insert
fasteners and create a hole in the plate.**

If you need to insert fasteners but a hole does not exist in one or
more of the parts, the Bolted Connection component generator
can create the hole for you in the same dialog box.

1. In the *Design* tab>Fasten panel, click (Bolted
   Connection) to open the Bolted Connection Component
   Generator.

2. Select the same start plane you used for the last bolted
   connection (the top face of the flange).

3. For the Existing Hole reference, select the hole in the flange
   that does not have a corresponding hole in the plate.

4. Select the bottom face of the plate for the Termination
   reference, as shown in Figure 11–28. A new hole is
   previewed in the plate because of the Termination reference
   you selected. The list of holes and fasteners now shows two
   holes instead of just one.

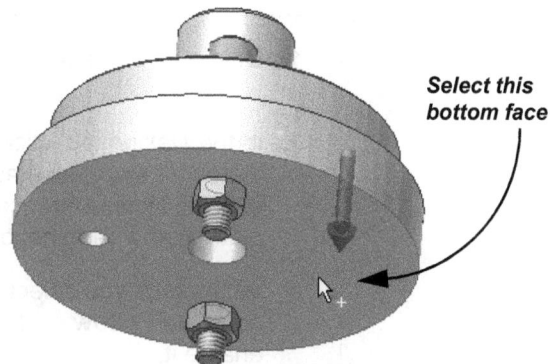

*Select this
bottom face*

Figure 11–28

5. Click to expand the dialog box, if it is not already
   expanded.

6. Select the template you created earlier (**ISO 4762 M5 x 30** by
   default) and click **SET**. This loads the grouping of
   components.

7. Click **OK** to insert the bolted connection. In the File Naming dialog box, click **OK** to accept the default name. The assembly displays as shown in Figure 11–29.

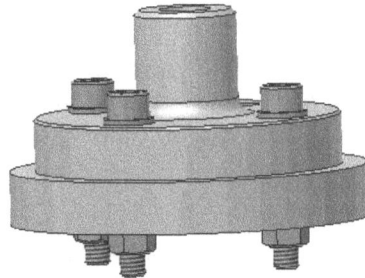

Figure 11–29

Task 7 - Place the fasteners for the last pair of holes.

1. Place the fasteners for the last hole in the flange. You can use ✎ (Place from Content Center) in the *Assemble* tab, or use ⬚ (Bolted Connection) in the *Design* tab.

Task 8 - Delete all fasteners and place using the Follow Pattern option.

1. Delete all of the fasteners in the assembly.

2. In the *Design* tab, click ⬚ (Bolted Connection) and select the same start plane as you previously selected. Select an existing Hole reference, and select the bottom face of the plate as the Termination reference.

3. As soon as you select a hole, the dialog box updates and adds the **Follow pattern** option. Select this option to enable it.

4. Select the **ISO 4762 M5x30** template, click **SET**. Click **OK** twice to complete the command and accept the default names. All fasteners should now be added to the assembly. The fasteners are placed on all of the holes. This is an excellent method for fast placement of similar fasteners. Consider using patterns and sketches when placing holes in your models that will later be populated with fasteners.

Task 9 - Modify the thickness on the flange component.

1. Open **flange.ipt**. Change the thickness value of **Extrusion1** from *10 mm* to **20 mm**.

2. Return to the assembly and update the model. Note that the bolt length is now too short and the nuts are consumed in the plate component. At this point, you can right-click on the bolted connection and select **Edit using Design Accelerator** to open the Bolted Connection Component Generator. Click **OK** to close the dialog box. The size of the bolts updates immediately.

3. Save and close all models.

Hint: Automatic Solve

The **Automatic Solve** option automatically updates all generated components when a change is made in an assembly component. By default, this option is toggled off, requiring the manual update.

To enable, right-click on **Bolted Connection** in the assembly and select **Component>Automatic Solve**. Note that

⟳ displays next to the **Bolted Connection** node, indicating that it now automatically updates if changes are made.

In previous releases of Autodesk Inventor, this option did not always update as required. It is always recommended to verify that the update occurs properly. If it does not, edit the connection (using the **Edit using Design Accelerator** command) to update it manually.

Chapter Review Questions

1. What is the purpose of the Design Accelerator?

    a. To generate geometry and perform calculations for common components.

    b. To use LOD Representations to speed up the loading of assemblies.

    c. To minimize hardware resources.

    d. To speed up drawing tasks in a Sketch.

2. The Content Center is automatically accessed in a Generator.

    a. True

    b. False

3. Which tool can you use to understand the theory used in Generators and calculators?

    a. Bolted Connection

    b. Frame Generator

    c. Engineer's Handbook

    d. Various Calculators

4. If the generator fails to generate a component that cuts through solid material, you must modify the geometry appropriately and rerun the generator.

    a. True

    b. False

Command Summary

Button	Command	Location
NA	Fasteners	• **Ribbon**: *Design* tab>Fasten panel
NA	Frame Commands	• **Ribbon**: *Design* tab>Frame panel
$\#/_x$	Handbook	• **Ribbon**: ***Design*** tab>expanded Power Transmission panel
NA	Power Transmission Commands	• **Ribbon**: *Design* tab>Power Transmission panel
NA	Springs	• **Ribbon**: *Design* tab>Spring panel

Chapter 12

Advanced File Management

Learning how to search for, copy, and purge files can be valuable when working in a design environment with large assemblies. The Design Assistant, Pack and Go, and Purge tools in the Autodesk® Inventor® software can be used for many valuable actions, including searching for files by property, creating reports, copying properties between files, copying files to other directories, and purging old versions.

Learning Objectives in This Chapter

- Use the Design Assistant to search for files, copy properties, and create reports on Autodesk Inventor files.
- Copy all referenced files together in a single location using the Pack and Go utility.
- Remove all older versions of files from the *OldVersions* subfolder.

12.1 Design Assistant

The Design Assistant helps locate and manage files. The Design Assistant can be accessed in the following ways:

- In the Autodesk Inventor software (with a file open), click **File>Manage>Design Assistant**.

- Outside the Autodesk Inventor software, select **Start>All Programs>Autodesk>Autodesk Inventor <ver>>Design Assistant <ver>**, or right-click on an Autodesk Inventor file in Windows Explorer and select **Design Assistant**.

The Design Assistant view differs depending on how it is opened. If opened from the Application Menu or Windows explorer, the active or selected file displays. Otherwise you can use the **Open** option at the top of the window to select and open a file. The Design Assistant with an assembly open is shown in Figure 12–1.

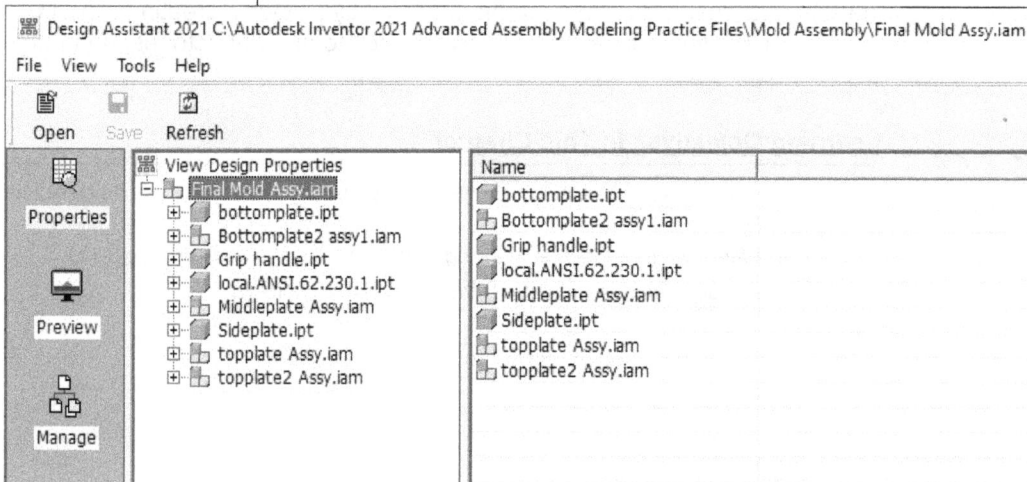

Figure 12–1

- To open and display the contents of a folder, select **File>Open Folder**.

- Click **Refresh** to refresh the display if changes are made to the file.

- Click ▦ (Properties) in the left pane of the Design Assistant to display the names of the files.

- Click 🖥 (Preview) on the left pane of the Design Assistant to display a preview of up to six selected files.

- When you open the Design Assistant dialog box from outside the Autodesk Inventor software, 🗗 (Manage) is included, as shown in Figure 12–2. This helps you rename, copy, or replace a file and maintain links between them.

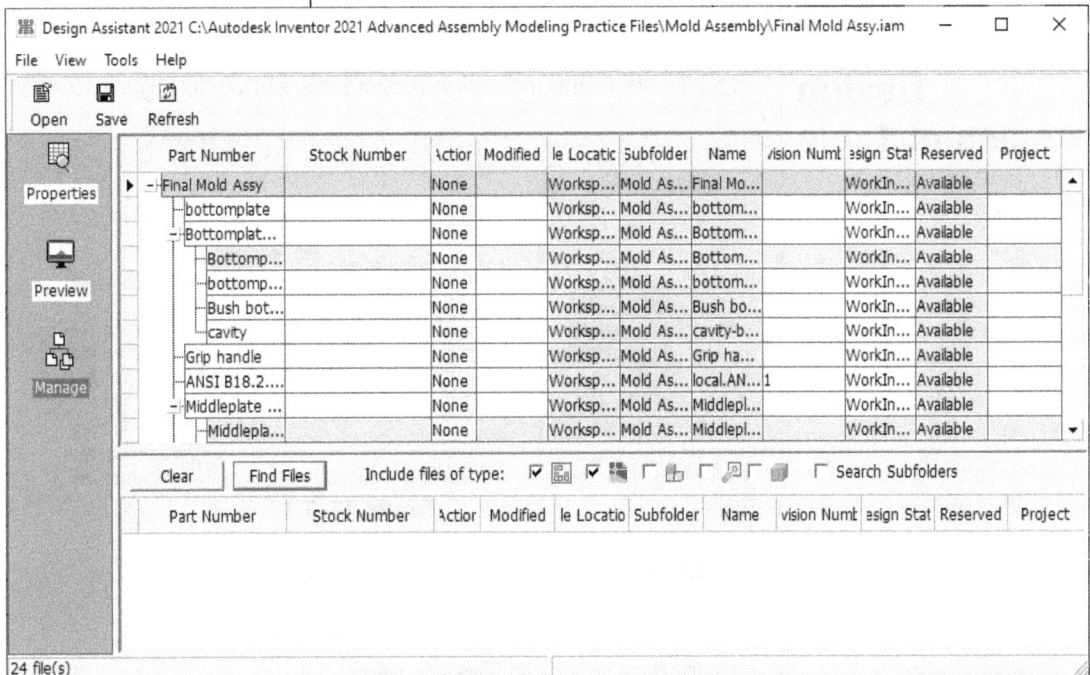

Figure 12–2

- Right-click on the *Action* column to access the following functions:

  - **Rename:** Renames files and updates links in the files that reference it. After selecting **Rename**, right-click on the name cell and select **Change Name**. Change the file name and save the file.

  - **Copy:** Copies a file and updates links in other files to the new copy. After selecting **Copy**, right-click on the name cell, select **Change Name**, and type a name for the copy in the Open dialog box. All links point to the copy, not to the original file.

- **Replace:** Replaces a file with another and updates the links. After selecting **Replace**, right-click on the name cell and select **Change Name**. Select the replacement file in the Open dialog box.
- **Clear:** Clears any previously selected function.

The bottom panel of the window in Manage mode finds and lists all of the files that reference a selected file. For example, if a part file is selected, it finds all assembly and drawing files that reference the part. Select the file in the top panel, then click **Find Files** in the bottom panel.

Design Assistant Tools

The **Tools** menu in Design Assistant is shown in Figure 12–3.

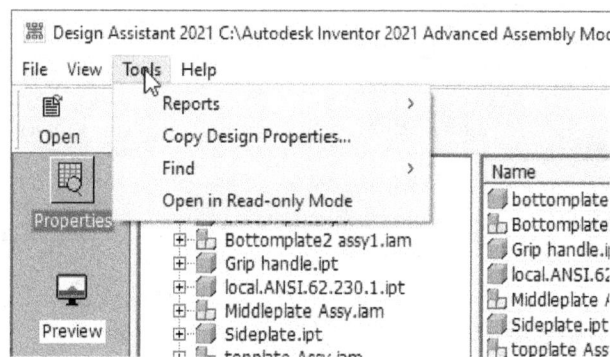

Figure 12–3

Find Files

The Design Assistant can be used to find files based on iProperties or where files are used.

- To search for files, open the Design Assistant and select **Tools>Find>Autodesk Inventor Files**. The Find dialog box opens as shown in Figure 12–4. Define the properties and click **Find Now**. Search properties can also be saved.

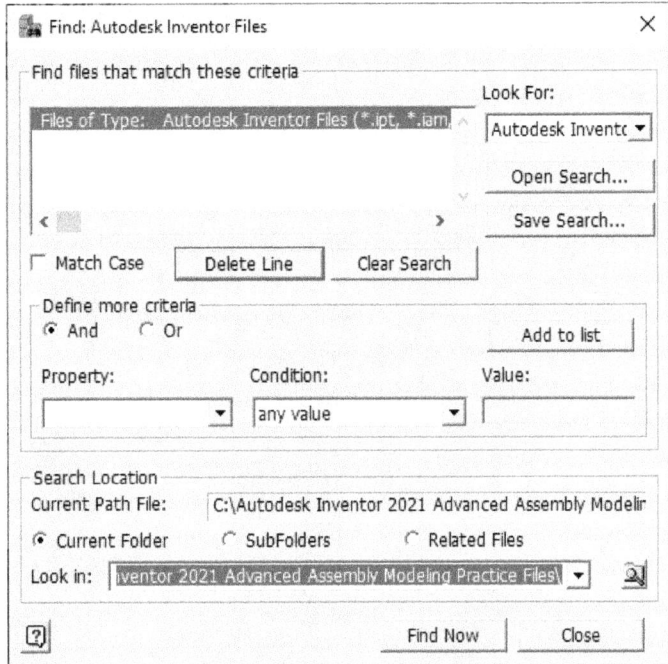

Figure 12–4

- To search for a files based on where it is used, select **Tools> Find>Where Used**. The Where Used dialog box opens as shown in Figure 12–5. Select the search path and start the search.

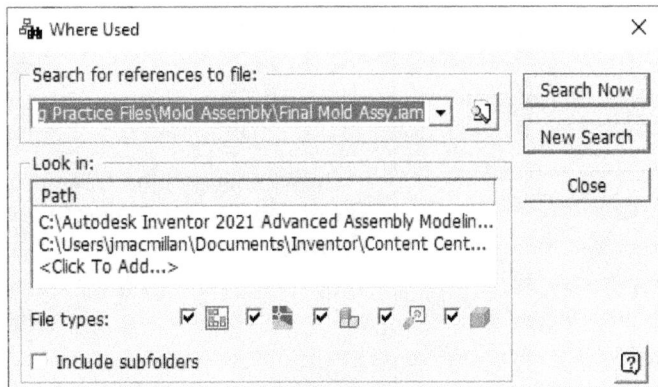

Figure 12–5

Copy Properties

If files require information in multiple property fields, you can streamline setting them by copying them from another file. Open the Design Assistant and select **Tools>Copy Design Properties**. The Copy Design Properties dialog box opens as shown in Figure 12–6. You can select the files, category, and individual properties to copy.

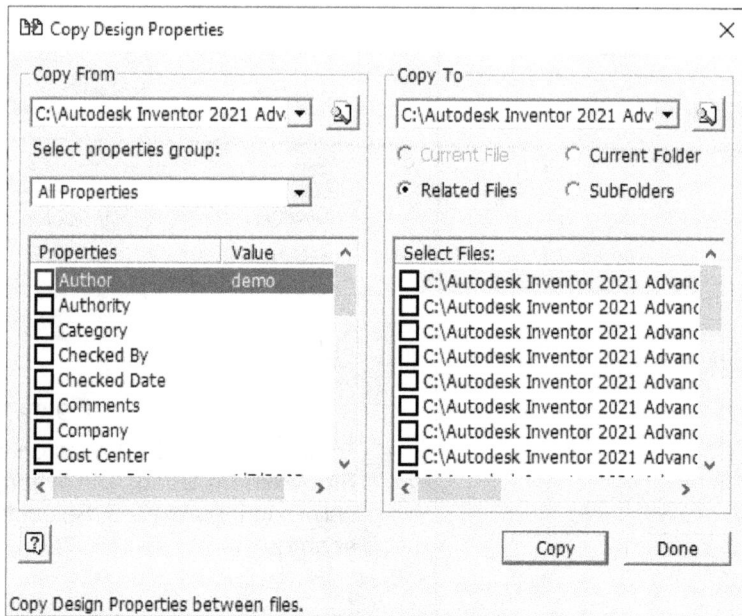

Figure 12–6

View Files

While working in the Design Assistant, you can view files by selecting **Tools>Viewer** to review the file in Autodesk Inventor View.

Reports

Reports are text files that contain information about the file. The Design Assistant produces two types of reports: **Hierarchy** and **Properties**. In both cases, you can select the number of levels to report.

- A **Hierarchy** report lists the elements in the selected file or folder. For an assembly file, the report lists the paths for the part files contained in the assembly. For a folder, the report lists its subfolders.

You can control which properties to include by selecting View> Customize in the Design Assistant.

- A **Properties** report lists values for some of the properties in the selected file(s). When a folder is selected, the report lists the files it contains.

12.2 Pack and Go

An Autodesk Inventor assembly or drawing might reference multiple part, assembly, and presentation files. Pack and Go enables you to copy all the referenced files together to a single location outside of the Autodesk Inventor software. This is useful for archiving files, as well as providing a complete project to a vendor, or tidying up a workspace. Pack and Go can include referenced files (such as parts of an assembly) as well as referencing files (such as drawing or presentation files that reference the assembly).

How To: Use Pack and Go

Pack and go can also be accessed through the Design Assistant by right-clicking on the opened file's name.

1. Right-click on the file name in Windows Explorer and select **Pack and Go**.
2. Define the options in the Pack and Go dialog box.
   - The options are shown in Figure 12–7 and described as follows:

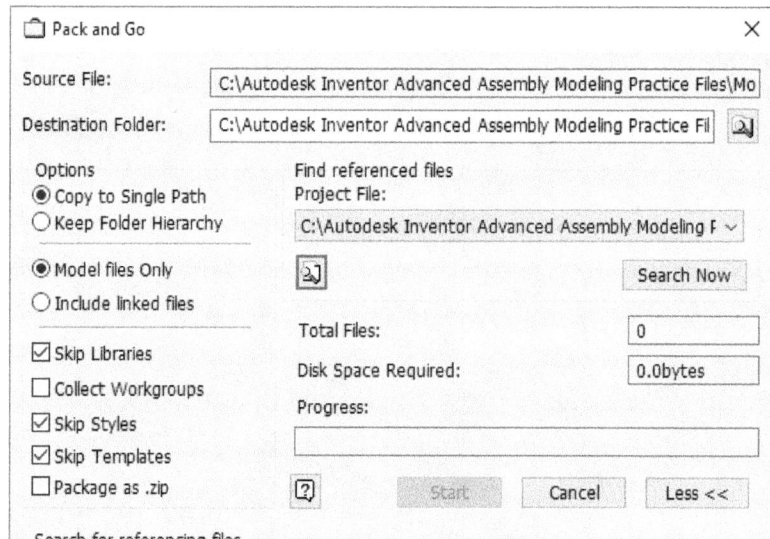

Figure 12–7

Copy to Single Path	Enables you to copy the files to a folder without maintaining the hierarchy of the files.
Keep Folder Hierarchy	Enables you to copy the file hierarchy to the destination folder and then copies the files that belong in each folder to the appropriate location.
Model files Only	When selected, only Autodesk Inventor files (.IPT, .IAM, .IDW, .IDV, .IPN) are copied to the destination folder.

Include linked files	When selected, Autodesk Inventor files, as well as other referenced files (e.g., text files, spread sheets, .HTML files, .BMP files, etc.), are copied to the destination folder.
Skip Libraries	When selected, components from library paths are not copied.
Collect Workgroups	When selected, the workspace and workgroups are copied into a single folder.
Skip Styles	When selected, styles are not copied into destination folder.
Skip Templates	When selected, templates are not copied into the destination folder.

3. Find referenced files using the *Find referenced files* area of the dialog box, as shown in Figure 12–8. Click **Search Now**.

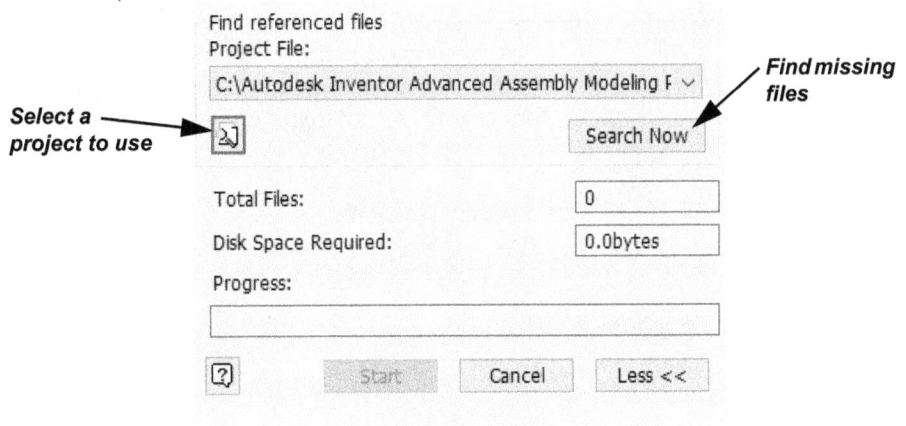

Figure 12–8

Referencing files can be drawing files or presentation files that include views of that assembly.

4. Find files that reference the source file using the *Search for referencing files* area (access by clicking **More**), as shown in Figure 12–9.

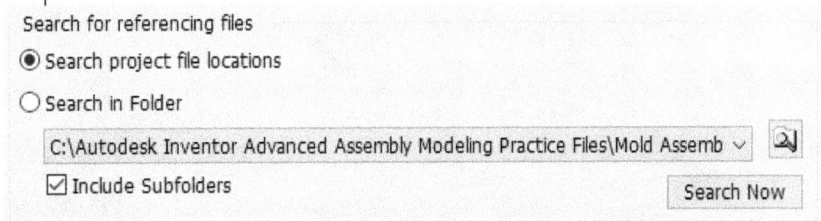

Figure 12–9

5. Review the files that are found in the *Files Found* area of the dialog box, as shown in Figure 12–10. Enable or disable them from being copied to the destination folder using the checkbox.

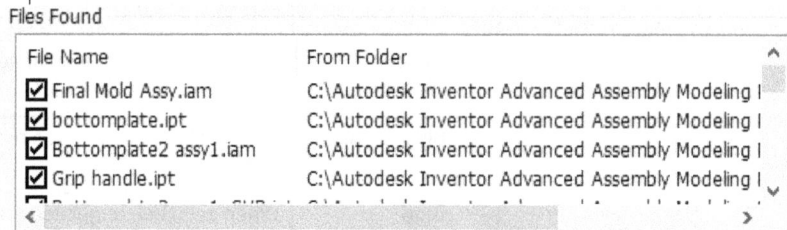

Files Found

File Name	From Folder
☑ Final Mold Assy.iam	C:\Autodesk Inventor Advanced Assembly Modeling
☑ bottomplate.ipt	C:\Autodesk Inventor Advanced Assembly Modeling
☑ Bottomplate2 assy1.iam	C:\Autodesk Inventor Advanced Assembly Modeling
☑ Grip handle.ipt	C:\Autodesk Inventor Advanced Assembly Modeling

Figure 12–10

6. Click **Start** to start the operation. The copied files display in the destination folder. When the operation is completed, click **Done** to close the dialog box.

Files are copied to the destination folder (not zipped) and a log file is created in the destination folder (**packngo.log**), listing the files copied. An example of a log file is shown in Figure 12–11.

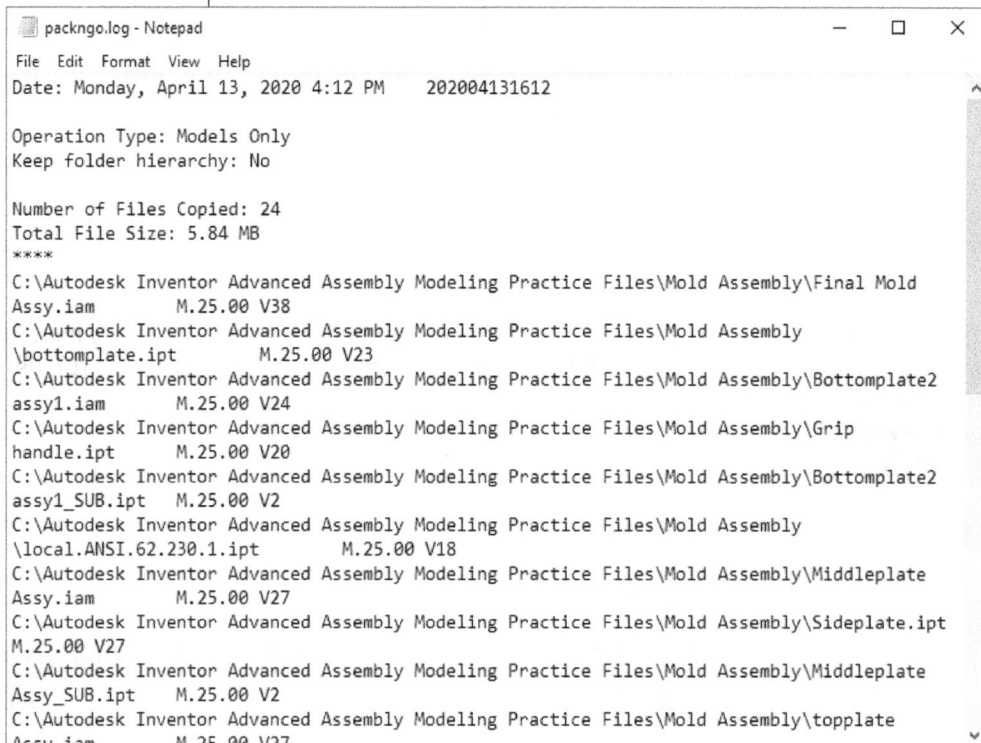

```
packngo.log - Notepad                                           —   □   ×
File  Edit  Format  View  Help
Date: Monday, April 13, 2020 4:12 PM     202004131612

Operation Type: Models Only
Keep folder hierarchy: No

Number of Files Copied: 24
Total File Size: 5.84 MB
****
C:\Autodesk Inventor Advanced Assembly Modeling Practice Files\Mold Assembly\Final Mold
Assy.iam       M.25.00 V38
C:\Autodesk Inventor Advanced Assembly Modeling Practice Files\Mold Assembly
\bottomplate.ipt      M.25.00 V23
C:\Autodesk Inventor Advanced Assembly Modeling Practice Files\Mold Assembly\Bottomplate2
assy1.iam      M.25.00 V24
C:\Autodesk Inventor Advanced Assembly Modeling Practice Files\Mold Assembly\Grip
handle.ipt     M.25.00 V20
C:\Autodesk Inventor Advanced Assembly Modeling Practice Files\Mold Assembly\Bottomplate2
assy1_SUB.ipt   M.25.00 V2
C:\Autodesk Inventor Advanced Assembly Modeling Practice Files\Mold Assembly
\local.ANSI.62.230.1.ipt      M.25.00 V18
C:\Autodesk Inventor Advanced Assembly Modeling Practice Files\Mold Assembly\Middleplate
Assy.iam       M.25.00 V27
C:\Autodesk Inventor Advanced Assembly Modeling Practice Files\Mold Assembly\Sideplate.ipt
M.25.00 V27
C:\Autodesk Inventor Advanced Assembly Modeling Practice Files\Mold Assembly\Middleplate
Assy_SUB.ipt    M.25.00 V2
C:\Autodesk Inventor Advanced Assembly Modeling Practice Files\Mold Assembly\topplate
Assy.iam       M.25.00 V27
```

Figure 12–11

12.3 Purging Old Files

Multiple versions of your files are saved in the *OldVersions* subfolder, located in the same path as the file. These files are saved with the name *file name.####.ext*, where #### is the version of the saved file.

*   To purge old versions, right-click on the file name in Windows Explorer and select **Purge**, as shown in Figure 12–12.

*   The **Purge All** option can be used to purge all files in a folder or all component files in an assembly.

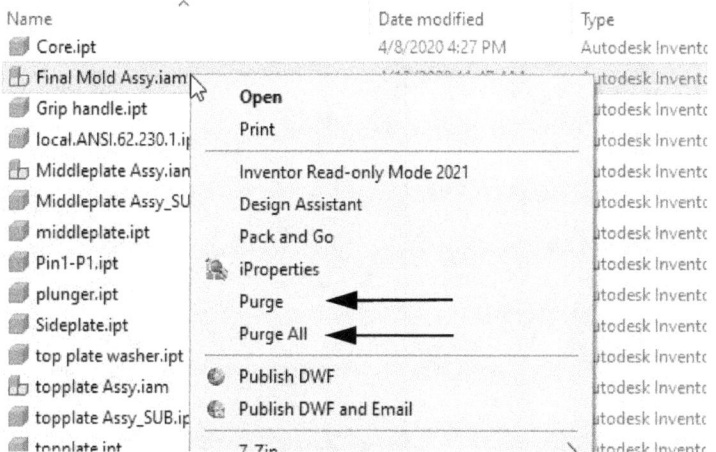

Figure 12–12

*   Purge can also be accessed through the Design Assistant when opened outside of the Autodesk Inventor software. Right-click on the name of the file in the dialog box, and select **Purge** or **Purge All**.

Practice 12a | Managing Files

Practice Objectives

- Copy an assembly file and its related files to a new folder using **Pack and Go** options.
- Search for a file and copy its properties to another file, using the **Design Assistant** utility.

In this practice, you copy **Final Mold Assy.iam**, shown in Figure 12–13, and its related files to a new folder using **Pack and Go** options. Pack and Go enables you to copy files outside of the Autodesk Inventor software. You also use the Design Assistant to find **properties.dwg** and copy the file properties to **Sideplate.dwg**.

Figure 12–13

Task 1 - Package (copy) an assembly file outside Autodesk Inventor.

1. Open Windows Explorer.

2. Create a subfolder named **Mold_Files** under the top level folder containing the practice files.

3. In the *Mold Assembly* folder, right-click on **Final Mold Assy.iam** and select **Pack and Go**.

4. If the Pack and Go warning box opens, read the message and click **OK**. The Pack and Go dialog box opens.

5. Change the destination folder to the *Mold_Files* subfolder that you created. The subfolder will be created once you begin the operation if you did not already create it.

6. Click **Search Now** in the *Find referenced files* area to search for all components in the assembly.

7. Click **More** to display the *Search for referencing files* and *Files Found* areas, if they are not already displayed toward the bottom of the Pack and Go dialog box.

8. Set the Options as shown in Figure 12–14 and Search for referencing files. The total number of files to be copied and required disk space are listed below the *Find referenced files* area. All the files are listed at the bottom of the dialog box in the *Files Found* area, where you can select which files to copy.

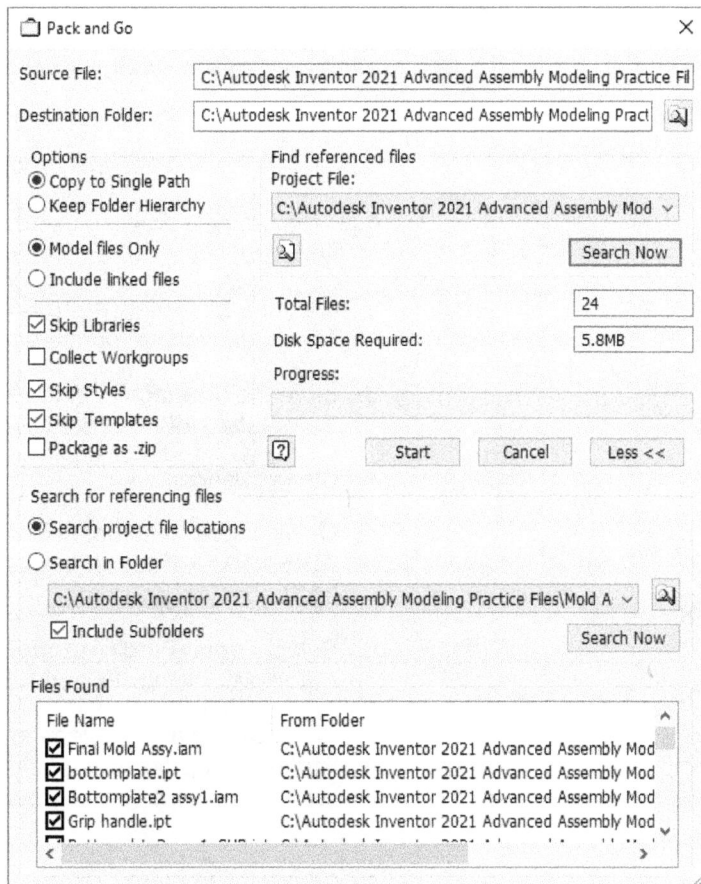

Figure 12–14

9. Click **Start** to start copying the files. The copied files display in the destination folder.

   • If prompted to search again using the current settings, click **SearchNow** in the *Find referenced files* area and then click **Start**.

   • When the operation is completed, click **Done** to close the dialog box.

10. In Windows Explorer, go to the new *Mold_Files* folder to view the copied files. Double-click on the log file (**packngo.log**) to open it and view the list of files copied.

11. Close the log file.

Task 2 - Use the Design Assistant to find and change files.

In this task, you use the Design Assistant Tools menu options to find a drawing and copy its properties to an assembly.

1. Create a new drawing using the metric, **ANSI (mm).dwg** template.

2. Create a base view using **Sideplate.ipt**, located under the *Mold_Files* folder, for use as the reference file.

3. Save the drawing file in the *Mold_Files* folder and name it **Sideplate**. Note that the title block is not completely filled in.

4. Close the drawing.

5. On Windows desktop, select **Start>All Programs> Autodesk>Autodesk Inventor 2021>Design Assistant 2021**.

6. Select **Tools>Find>Autodesk Inventor Files**. The Find: Autodesk Inventor Files dialog box displays.

7. In the *Define more criteria* area, **And** is the default. In the Property drop-down list, select **Author**. In the Condition drop-down list, select **begins with** and in the *Value* field, type **jos**.

8. Click **Add to List** to add the value to the search list.

9. Browse to and select the folder containing the practice files in the *Look in* field at the bottom, as shown in Figure 12–15.

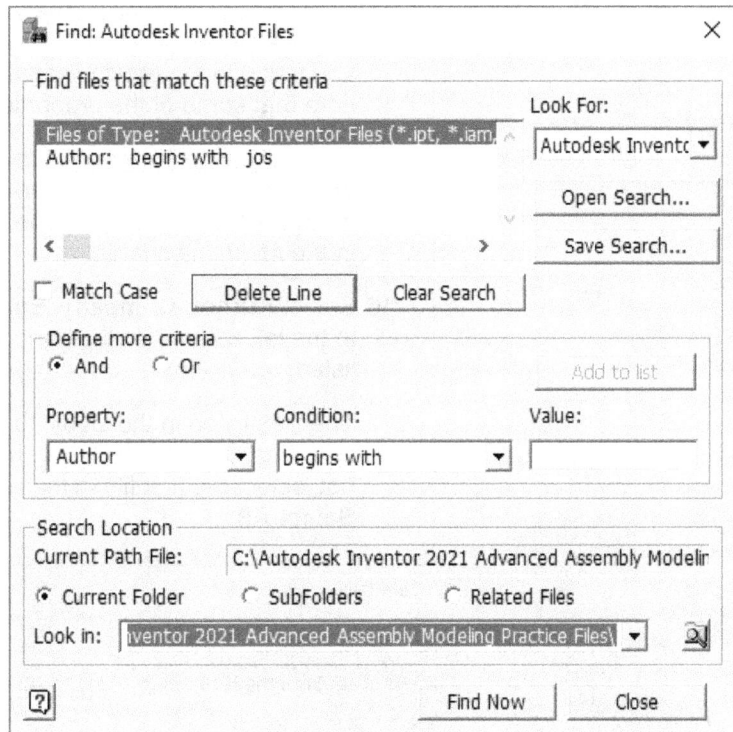

Figure 12–15

10. Click **Find Now** to search for Autodesk Inventor files that have an author that begins with *jos*. The Design Assistant returns a list, as shown in Figure 12–16. The **properties.dwg** file is listed.

Figure 12–16

11. Click **OK** to close the list.

12. Click **Close** to close the Find dialog box.

13. Select **Tools>Copy Design Properties** in the Design Assistant. The Copy Design Properties dialog box opens.

14. Browse to and select **properties.dwg** in the top-level practice files folder in the *Copy From* area. This is the file that you found in the previous search. Once the file is selected, note that some of the properties of the file have a value.

15. In the *Copy To* area, select the **Current Folder** option, and then browse to and select the *Mold_Files* folder. This option transfers the properties of the **properties.dwg** file to all files in the *Mold_Files* folder.

16. Select **Author**, **Company**, **Engineer**, **Manager**, and **Subject** in the left column. In the right column, select all the files listed.

17. The files listed in the *Copy To* column should all have a checkmark beside them, as shown in Figure 12–17. If they do not, select the first file in the list, right-click and select **Select All**.

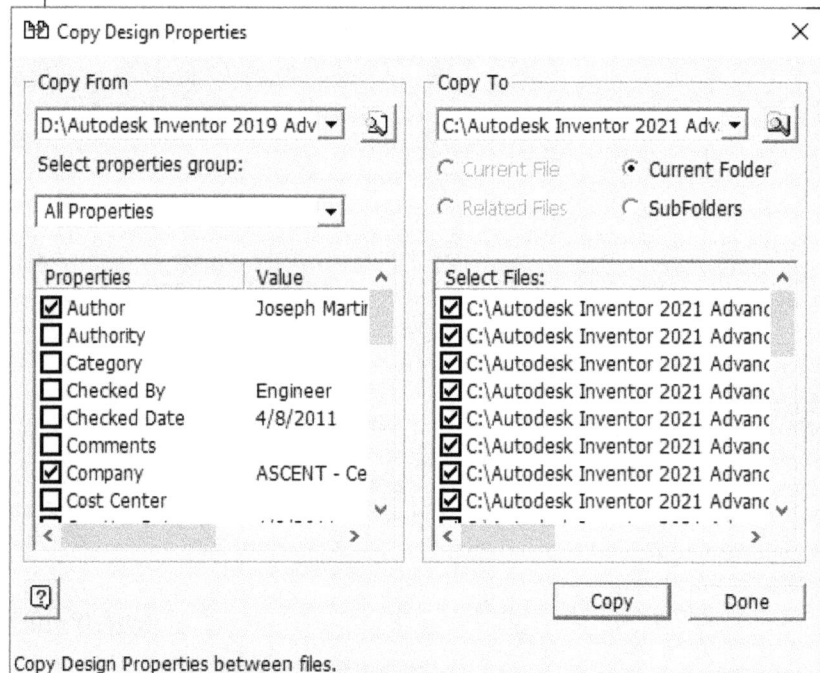

Figure 12–17

18. Click **Copy** to copy the properties. Replace any existing values.

19. Click **Done** and close the Design Assistant dialog box.

20. Open **sideplate.dwg**. The title block is populated with the Company name property that was used in the **properties.dwg** file.

21. Right-click on the drawing name in the Model Browser and select **iProperties**. The properties you copied in the previous step have been filled.

22. Close the drawing.

Chapter Review Questions

1. When working with a large number of files, which of the following do you use to efficiently find a file?

   a. Pack and Go

   b. Purge

   c. Design Assistant

   d. Open file

2. What is the difference between starting the Design Assistant in the Autodesk Inventor software and starting it outside of the software?

   a. Manage mode

   b. Properties

   c. Preview mode

3. How can you rename, copy, or replace a file and then maintain links between Autodesk Inventor files?

   a. **Design Assistant>Tools>Copy Design Properties**

   b. **Design Assistant>Manage mode**

   c. **Purge**

   d. Windows Explorer

4. You need to send a complete set of files for a project to a client. How do you create a list of all the required files? (Select all that apply.)

   a. Pack and Go log file

   b. Purge All

   c. Design Assistant Report tool

   d. Copy Design

5. Which of the following best describe the purpose of the **Purge** option?

   a. Removes a specific file.

   b. Removes all of the files in a folder or all of the component files in an assembly.

   c. Removes all of the referenced files.

   d. Removes all of the older versions of a file from the *OldVersions* subfolder.

Command Summary

Button	Command	Location
NA	Design Assistant	• **Application Menu:** Manage
NA	Pack and Go	• (*context menu with filename selected*) • (*Windows Explorer with filename selected*)
NA	Purge	• **Design Assistant** • (*Windows Explorer with filename selected*)

Inventor Studio

Inventor Studio enables you to create realistic renderings or animations of models. To render images, you can set the surface styles, lighting styles, appearance, resolution, and camera views. To animate models, a number of rendered images are compiled to create an AVI file.

Learning Objectives in This Chapter

- Render a realistic image of a model that has had appearance, lighting, and camera customizations assigned.
- Create a realistic animation of a model to display its range of motion, assembly process, or other movement by applying parameters, constraints, and actions.
- Create a composite video by combining camera shots, animations, and transitions using the Video Producer.
- Create a room assembly as a custom environment for use when rendering models.

13.1 Rendering

Renderings help visualize a model's appearance before it is manufactured. You can apply different appearances, lighting styles, cameras, and local lights to create a realistic environment for the model.

General Steps

Use the following general steps to render an image:

1. Apply appearances.
2. Define the Studio Lighting Styles.
3. Define cameras.
4. Define local lights.
5. Render the image.
6. Save the image.

Step 1 - Apply appearances.

New appearances can be applied using two techniques:

- Select a part or subassembly in the Model Browser and select an override material from the Quick Access Toolbar's Appearance Override drop-down list, as shown in Figure 13–1.

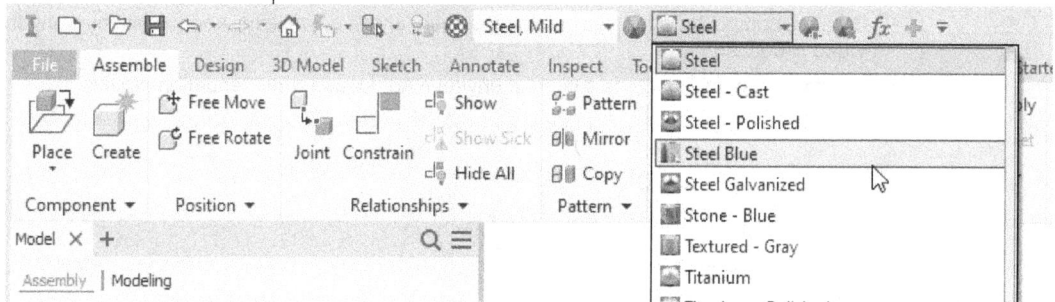

Figure 13–1

- Click ⬤ (Appearance) in the *Tools* tab>Material and Appearance panel or the Quick Access toolbar, to open the Appearance Browser, as shown in Figure 13–2. From this dialog box you can add appearances to the document and then to a component.

  - To add a appearance to the document, right-click on an appearance in the Material Library and click **Add to> Document Materials**.
  - To assign the appearance to a component, select a component, right-click on the material in the *Document Appearances* area and select **Assign to Selection**.

To clear the appearance overrides, click

⬤ *(Clear) in the Tools tab>Material and Appearance panel, or in the Quick Access toolbar, and select the objects that you want to clear.*

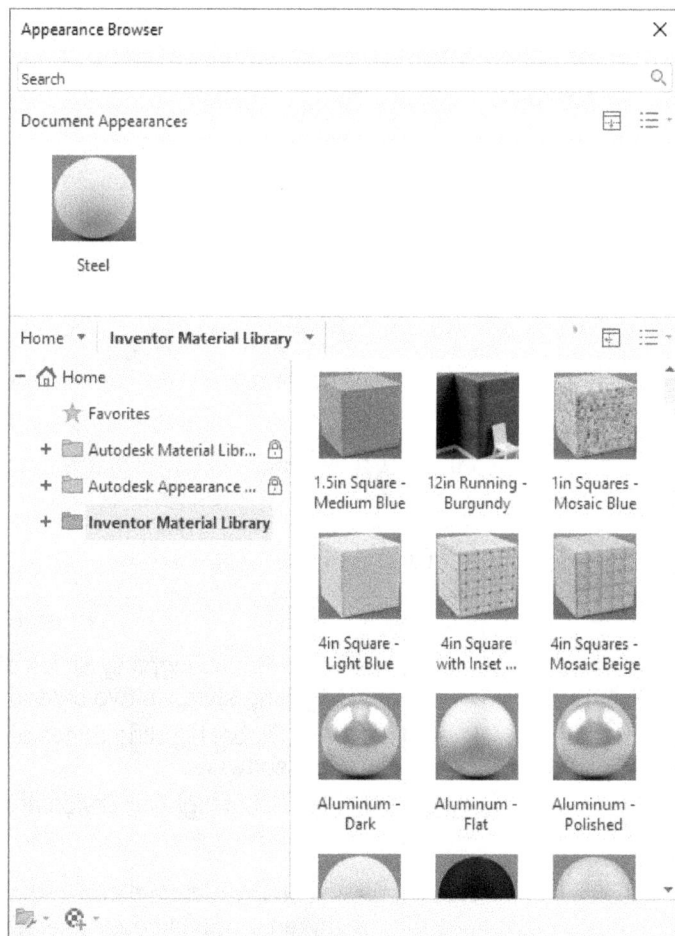

Figure 13–2

Step 2 - Define the Studio Lighting Styles.

With a model open, select the *Environments* tab and click

(Inventor Studio). The *Render* contextual tab is activated.

In the Scene panel, click (Studio Lighting Styles). The Lighting Styles dialog box opens, as shown in Figure 13–3. All default lighting styles in Inventor Studio use Image-Based Lighting (IBL). They do not contain any local lights.

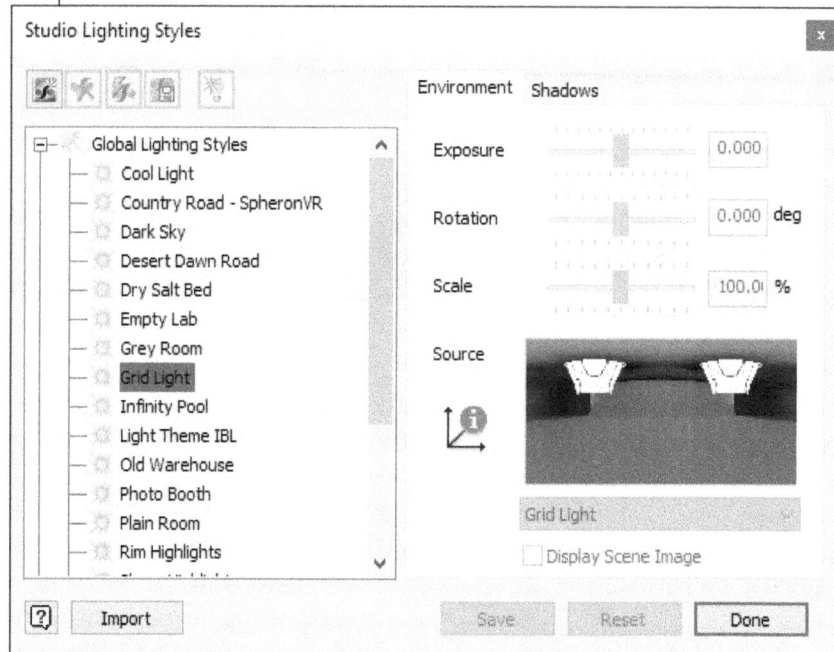

Figure 13–3

- The Studio Lighting Styles dialog box lists the available lighting styles in two categories:
  - Global Lighting Styles are styles that are provided with the software.
  - Local Lighting Styles are styles that exist in the current file.

- A style must be listed in the Local Lighting Styles list to be used or modified for use in the model.

- Use any of the following methods to add a lighting style to the Local Lighting Styles list for use in the model:
  - Right-click on a Global Lighting Style and select **Active**.
  - Right-click on a Global Lighting Style and select **Copy Lighting Style** and enter a new name.
  - Right-click on a Global Lighting Style and select **New Lighting Style**.

- Click (New Lighting Style) in the dialog box.

When activating or copying a lighting style to the local list, only the IBL environment is added. When using either of the **New Lighting Style** options, you are provided with the Grid Light IBL and three lights: directional, point, and spot. Each light has application default settings. By default, the directional, point, and spot lights are toggled off. You can toggle them on by changing individual light properties.

Directional, Point, and Spot lights are described as follows:

(Directional)	Simulates distant light sources, such as the sun. It has a direction, but no position. Directional light objects are symbolized in the model by an arrow, as shown.
(Point)	Simulates a point source. It has a position and it radiates light in every direction. Point light objects are symbolized by an octahedron, as shown.

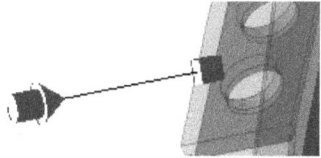

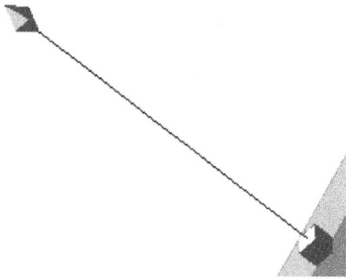

(Spot)	Simulates a spot light with a position and direction. A Spot light emits light in the shape of a cone with two degrees of intensity. The most intense area is located within the inner area of the cone and the less intense area is located within the outer area of the cone of light. Spot light objects are symbolized by a cone, as shown.

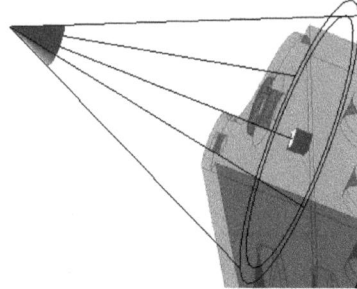

Adding Additional Lights

To create a new light in any selected lighting style, select the lighting style and click (New Light). The Light dialog box opens, as shown in Figure 13–4.

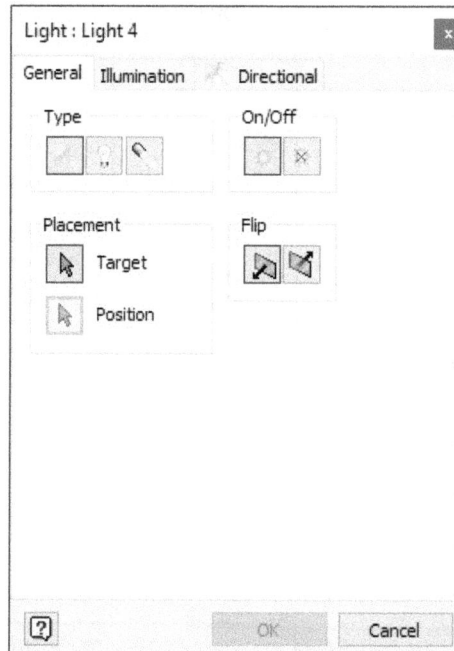

Figure 13–4

Use the following tabs to define the lighting style:

- Use the *General* tab to define the type of light as

    Directional (⬚), Point (⬚), or Spot (⬚). Select an edge or face as a target reference for the light, and then select a position along the reference line. Toggle the light on and off, and flip the direction of the light.

- Use the *Illumination* tab to adjust the intensity and color.

- Use the *Directional*, *Point*, or *Spot* tab to set options specific to the type of light that is selected. The tab name changes depending on the type of light being created. The options available in this tab enable you control the position and direction of the light as well as the light's specific properties.

Setting the Environment

Once a Global lighting style has been copied to the Local Lighting style list, you can edit the options on the *Environment* tab, as follows:

- To customize its exposure, rotation, and scale, modify the values or drag the scroll bar.
- Select the **Display Scene Image** option to display the image in the graphics window.
- To change the lighting style source image, select a new one using the drop-down list. If changed, any custom lights that were added are maintained.

Shadows

Use the *Shadows* tab to define the softness setting for the lighting style.

Saving Changes

Once you are finished adding additional lights, you can click **OK** to close the Light dialog box and return to the Studio Lighting Styles. Click **Save** to save any changes made to the lighting styles. When the required lighting effect has been achieved, save any changes and click **Done**.

Step 3 - Define cameras.

Cameras enable you to save particular viewpoints of the model so that they are available when rendering.

How To: Create a Camera

1. Click ![camera icon] (Camera) in the Scene panel. The Camera dialog box opens as shown in Figure 13–5.

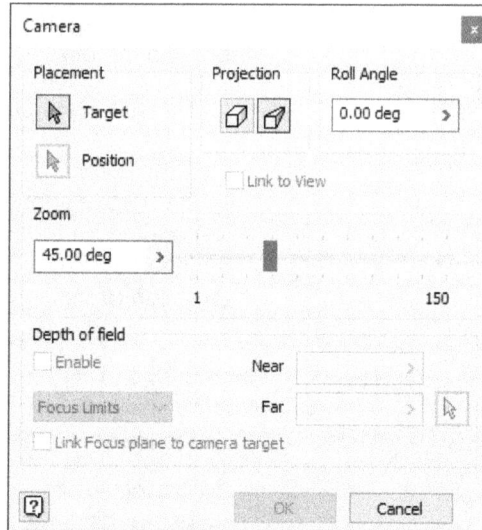

Figure 13–5

2. Select a face or edge as the Target for the camera.
3. Select a location along the reference line where the camera is going to be placed, as shown in Figure 13–6.

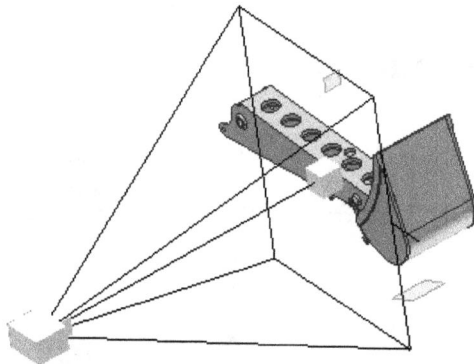

Figure 13–6

4. Define the Projection type:

- Orthographic (![orthographic icon]) projects edges parallel to each other.

- Perspective (![perspective icon]) projects edges to a vanishing point, giving the perception of depth.

5. Edit the values in the *Roll Angle* field to change rotation of the camera about the reference line, as shown in Figure 13–7 (30 degrees).

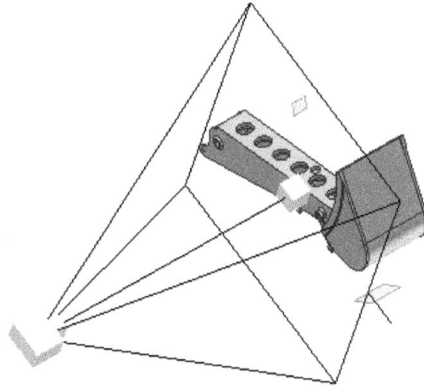

Figure 13–7

6. Adjust the zoom angle by entering an angle in the *Zoom* field, using the zoom slider, or by dragging the zoom area shown in Figure 13–8.

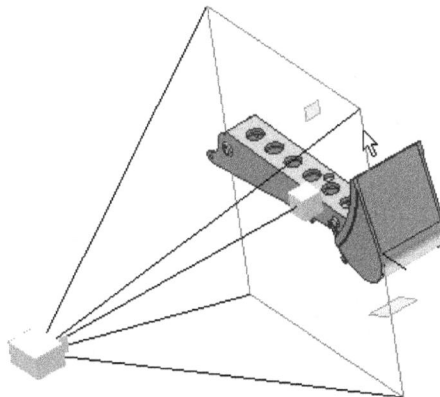

Figure 13–8

7. For Perspective projection, enable or disable the Depth of Field. These options control which objects display in focus when the image is rendered.
8. Click **OK** to save the changes. Create additional cameras as required.

Modifying a Camera

You can adjust the location and orientation of a camera by selecting it, right-clicking and selecting **Edit**.

- Use the Camera dialog box to make changes to the original settings.

- Select the camera in the graphics window to move it using the triad or the 3D Move/Rotate mini-toolbar.

- Select the target in the graphics window to move it using the triad or the 3D Move/Rotate mini-toolbar.

Step 4 - Define local lights.

To create a local light, click ⍾ (Local Lights) in the Scene panel. The Local Lights dialog box opens as shown in Figure 13–9.

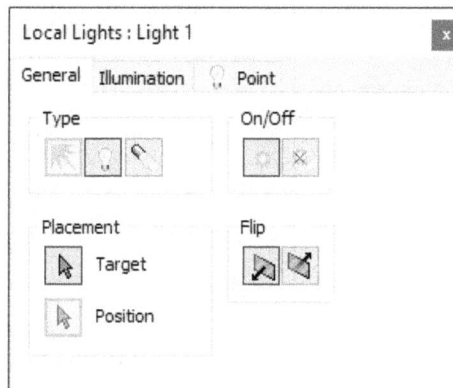

Figure 13–9

- The Local Lights dialog box contains the same options as the Light dialog box used when defining Lighting Styles, except that directional lights are not available.

- Local lights are contained in the assembly or component file and not in a Lighting Style.

- Local lights move with a component when animated.

Step 5 - Render the image.

After defining the appropriate appearances, lighting styles, cameras, and local lights, you can render the image. In the Render panel, click ⬭ (Render Image). The Render Image dialog box opens as shown in Figure 13–10.

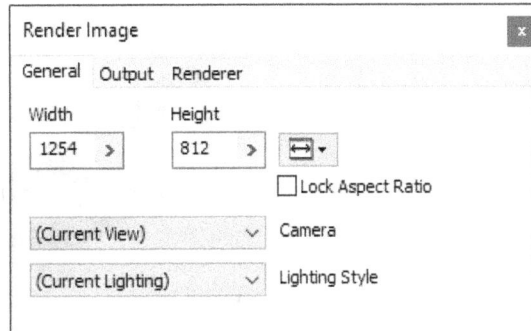

Figure 13–10

Rendering Images

Use the following three tabs to define the options for rendering an image:

- Use the *General* tab to specify the width and height of the image you are rendering or use the Select Output Size list. You can also lock the aspect ratio and specify the Camera and Lighting Style.

- Use the *Output* tab to specify whether or not to save the image once it is rendered. If saved, you can enter a name and location for the file.

- Use the *Renderer* tab to control the render duration, accuracy of the lighting and materials that have been assigned, and the image filtering options to determine how accurate the rendering will be.

Once you have finished setting the rendering options, click **Render** to render the image. The Render Output window opens with the rendered image, as shown in Figure 13–11.

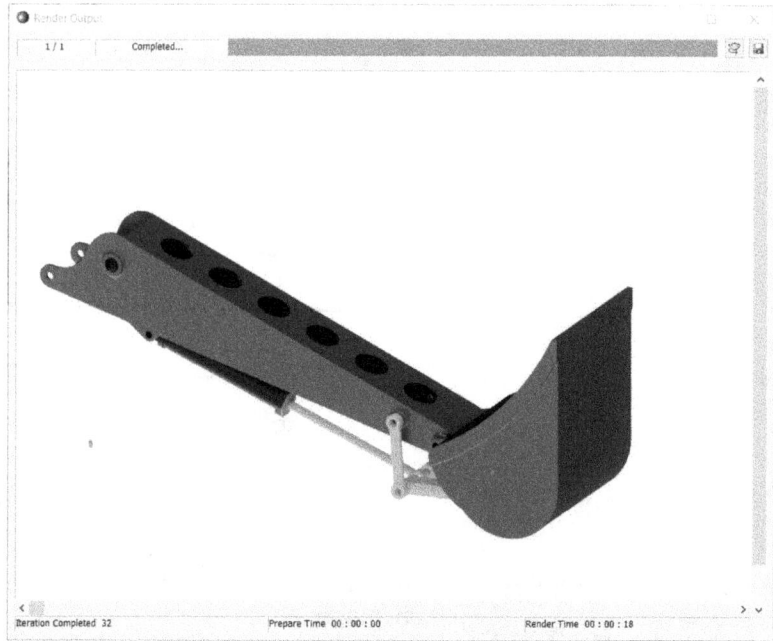

Figure 13–11

Step 6 - Save the image.

If you did not already specify to save the rendered image using the *Output* tab, click [save icon] in the Render Output window.

13.2 Animation

Animations can be used to show any of the following:

- Ranges of motion.

- How a model functions.

- How an assembly is assembled.

- How an assembly can be divided into its individual parts or subassemblies.

- How parts in an assembly interact with one another, as well as with external components.

General Steps

Use the following general steps to animate an assembly:

1. Position the components.
2. Define appearance and lighting styles.
3. Define the animation actions.
4. Animate cameras.
5. Render the animation.

Step 1 - Position the components.

Position the components in their required starting positions by adjusting the constraints and/or moving the components.

Step 2 - Define appearance and lighting styles.

Ensure that the required appearances and lighting styles have all been created in the model.

Step 3 - Define the animation actions.

To define the animation actions, start by selecting one of the animate options described as follows from the Animate panel.

(Components)	Animates the position and rotation of components
(Fade)	Animates the visibility of components
(Constraints)	Animates constraint values by specifying an end value
(Parameters)	Animates parameter values, which can be tied to model dimensions
(Pos Reps)	Animates the assembly so that it starts or ends with a Positional Representation
(Light)	Animates the definition of Local Lights including on/off and position

Each animation command dialog box varies, but the common icons are described as follows:

	Starts the action at the time the previous action ended
	Specifies the time to begin the action
	Performs the action instantaneously (in one frame)
	Start time
	Duration
	End time

The *Acceleration* tab, as shown in Figure 13–12, is common among all animation command dialog boxes. It controls the speed of an action as it reaches its target and the percentage of time/actual time for an action to reach its speed and wind down.

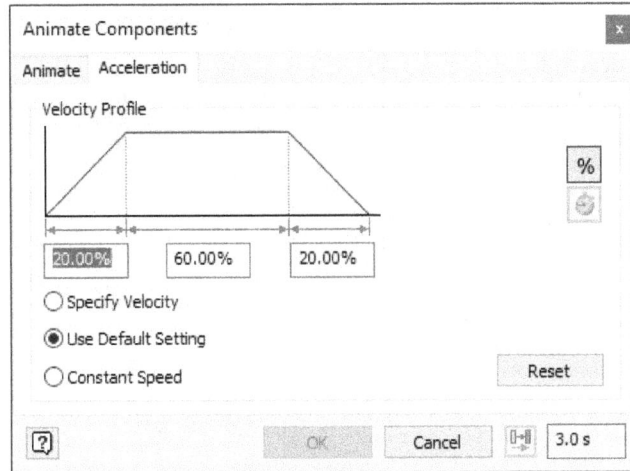

Figure 13–12

Animate Components

The Animate Components dialog box is shown in Figure 13–13.

With ▨ (Components) toggled on, select one or more components to move or rotate. Click ▲ (Position) and the 3D Move/Rotate dialog box opens, enabling you to move or rotate the component(s) in the direction of a free degree of freedom. Enter *Distance* and *Rotation* values as required, and specify a smooth or straight path of motion.

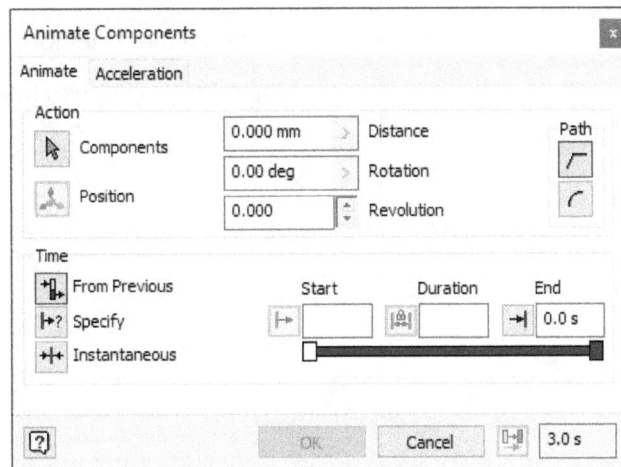

Figure 13–13

Animate Fade

The Animate Fade dialog box is shown in Figure 13–14. With

[cursor icon] (Components) toggled on, select one or more components you want to animate. Use the value field to specify the visibility of the selected component(s). To return a component to the previous visibility state at a later time, create another action.

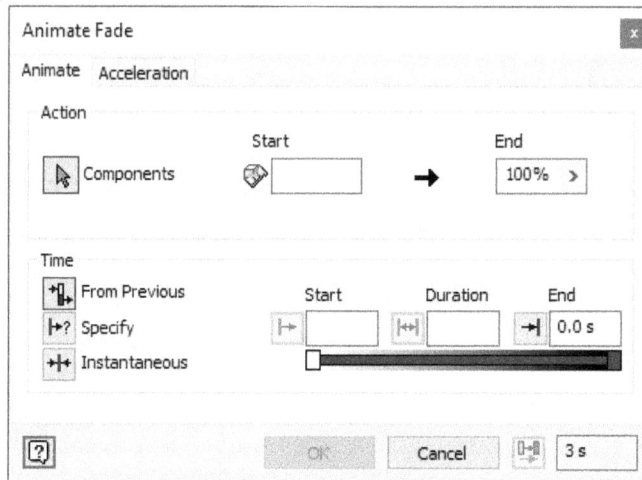

Figure 13–14

Animate Constraints

The Animate Constraints dialog box is shown in Figure 13–15.

With [cursor icon] (Select) toggled on, select one or more constraints you want to manipulate. To animate a change in a linear or angular constraint value, click [d0=] (Constraint) and enter the end value. Note that the initial value for the constraint is automatically

obtained from the assembly. Click [icon] (Suppress) to suppress a

constraint or [icon] (Enable) to enable a constraint.

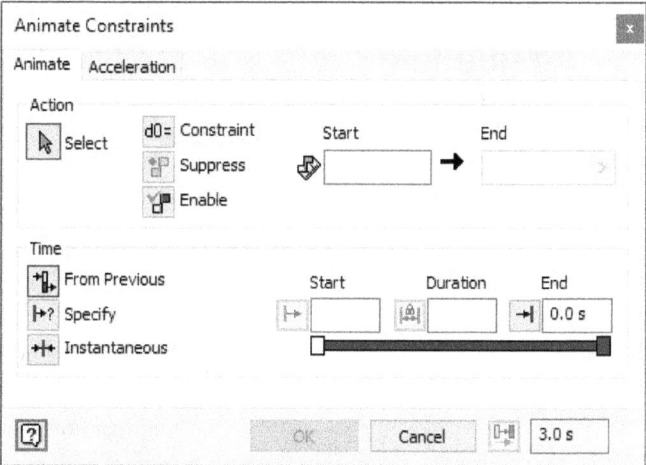

Figure 13–15

Animate Parameters

The Animate Parameters dialog box is shown in Figure 13–16.

With [⌖] (Select) toggled on, select a parameter you want to manipulate in the *Animation Favorites* area of the Model Browser. The value of the selected parameter is automatically obtained from the model. Specify an end value for the parameter.

Only parameters that have been designated for export and then marked as a favorite using f_x (Parameter Favorites) are available for use in an animation.

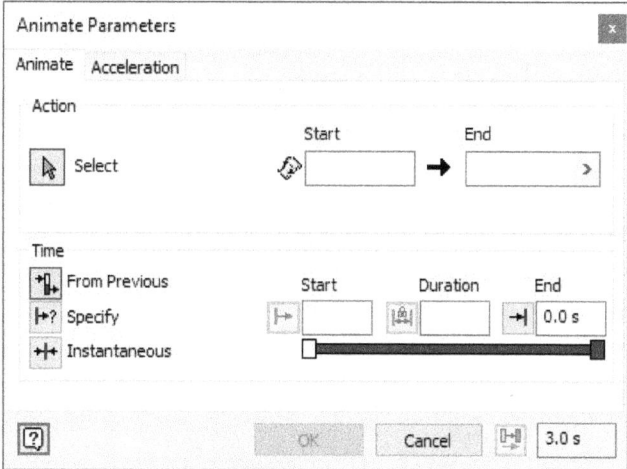

Figure 13–16

Animate Positional Representations

The Animate Positional Representations dialog box is shown in Figure 13–17. Select the start and end Positional Representation positions for the animation. The Positional Representations must already exist in the model to be available in the Start and End drop-down lists.

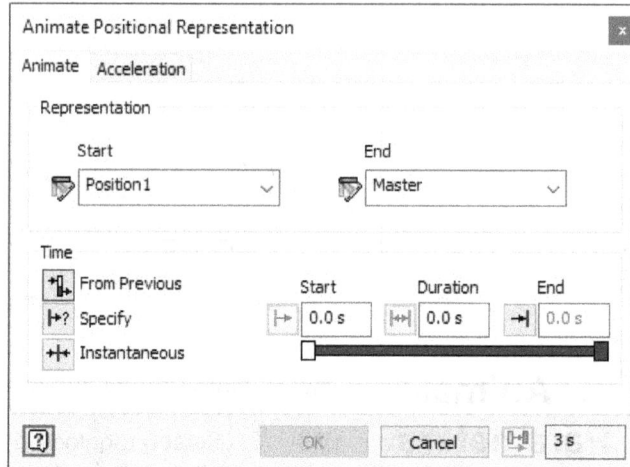

Figure 13–17

Animate Light

The Animate Light dialog box is shown in Figure 13–18. Click ▯ (Select) and select a local light you want to manipulate. Click ▯ (Definition) to open the Local Lights dialog box to change the light information.

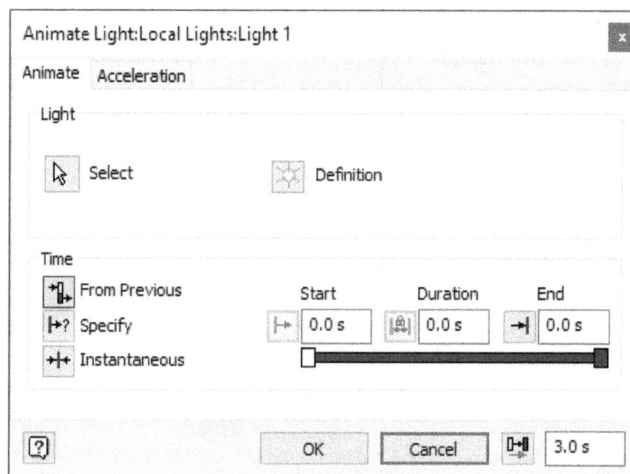

Figure 13–18

Animation Timeline

When working with any of the animation dialog boxes, such as Animate Components or Animate Constraints, the Animation Timeline dialog box opens, as shown in Figure 13–19.

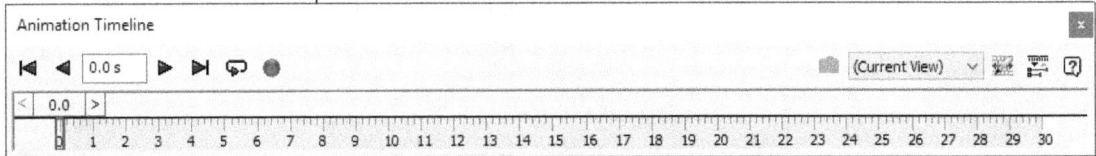

Figure 13–19

To open the Animation Timeline independently of the animate commands, click

(Animation Timeline) in the Animate panel.

Use the animation timeline to control the current time in seconds. The available icons are described as follows:

◄◄	Sets the current time to the beginning of the animation where the time is zero seconds
◄	Plays the animation in reverse
►	Plays the animation
►►	Sets the current time to the end of the animation
⟳	Toggles between repeating and not repeating the animation
●	Opens the Render Animation dialog box
📷	Creates a camera action that ends at the current time
	Opens the Animation Options dialog box and enables you to specify the duration of the animation in minutes and seconds. Click to fit the length of the animation to the current time.
	Expands the actions editor, as shown below. Actions are listed on the left side, while their start, duration, and end times are represented on the right side. Use this dialog box to view, edit, and delete existing actions. Edit or delete an action by right-clicking on the required action duration bar and selecting **Edit** or **Delete**. You can also adjust the durations of actions directly by dragging the duration bars.

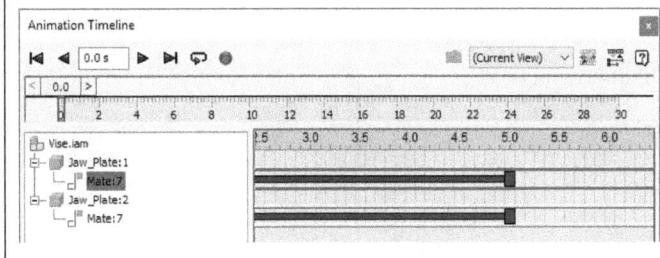

Step 4 - Animate cameras.

In the Animate panel, click ⬚ (Camera). The Animate Camera dialog box opens, as shown in Figure 13–20.

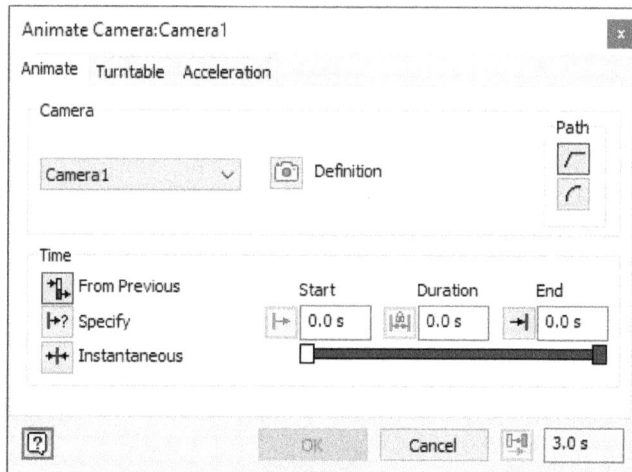

Figure 13–20

To define a new camera, click

⬚ *(Camera) in the Scene panel before opening the Animate Camera dialog box.*

Select a camera that has already been defined from the Camera drop-down list and select the path type. The *Path* area provides options to define the camera motion smoothly between the *Start*, *Duration*, and *End* timing values or to define the motion sharply with no smoothing. Click ⬚ (Definition) to specify the end position of the camera and its target.

Step 5 - Render the animation.

In the Render panel, click ⬚ (Render Animation) to open the Render Animation dialog box, as shown in Figure 13–21.

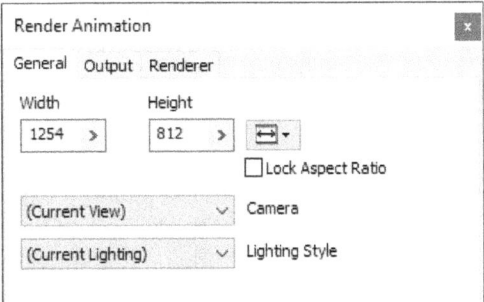

Figure 13–21

General Tab

In the *General* tab, specify the required width and height as well as the specific camera and lighting style.

Output Tab

In the *Output* tab, you can specify the animation's:

- Name and directory

- Time range to record

- Format (save as a video or individual image files)

- Frame rate

Changing the time range increases or decreases the amount of the animation that is recorded in the video file. Alternatively, increasing the frame rate increases the number of frames captured per second. This increases the total number of frames that are animated, which increases the time it takes to create the animation. The benefit of increasing the frame rate, however, is that the animation displays smoother.

- Use the **Preview: No Render** option to preview the animation without rendering the model. This is useful if you only want the animation without rendering.

- The **Launch Player** option plays the newly created animation immediately after it is created.

Renderer Tab

In the *Renderer* tab, you can control the:

- Render duration,

- Accuracy of the lighting and materials that have been assigned, and

- The image filtering option, which determines the accuracy of the rendering.

After selecting the required options from the three tabs, click **Render.** Next, specify the video compression and click **OK** to begin the rendering. Once the rendering has finished, you can go to the folder in which you created the animation and double-click on it to play it. If you enabled the **Launch Player** option, it automatically plays for you.

13.3 Video Producer

The Video Producer enables you to combine camera shots, animations, and transitions into a composite video. To create a video using the Video Producer, simply drag and drop camera shots or transitions from the browser into the timeline. The Video Producer is shown in Figure 13–22.

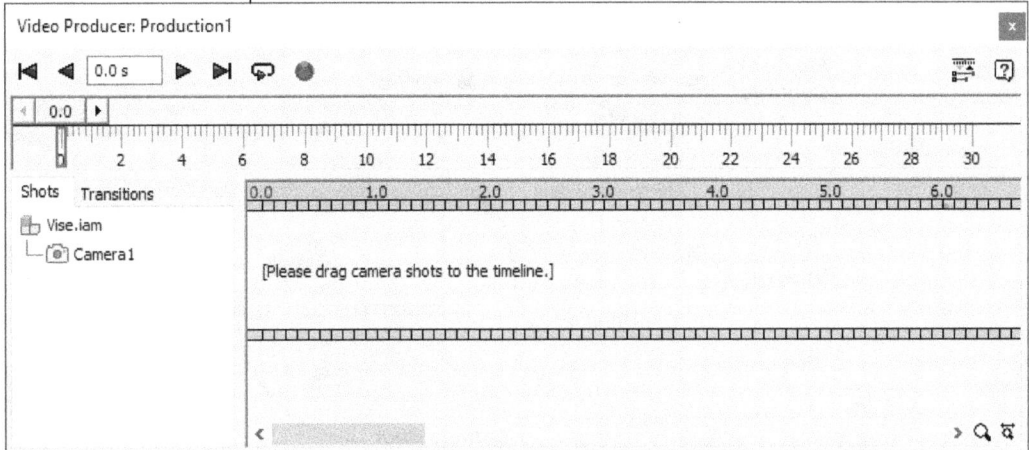

Figure 13–22

General Steps

Use the following general steps to animate an assembly:

1. Create cameras and animations.
2. Display the Video Producer.
3. Add cameras to the production.
4. Add transitions to the production.
5. Arrange cameras and transitions and set the times for both.
6. Render the production.

Step 1 - Create cameras and animations.

Set up the required cameras and animations in Inventor Studio that is going to be used to produce your video.

Step 2 - Display the Video Producer.

In the Animate panel, click ▦ (Video Producer) to open the Video Producer dialog box. This dialog box is used to combine and configure the animations for the video. The various areas of the Video Producer dialog box are shown in Figure 13–23.

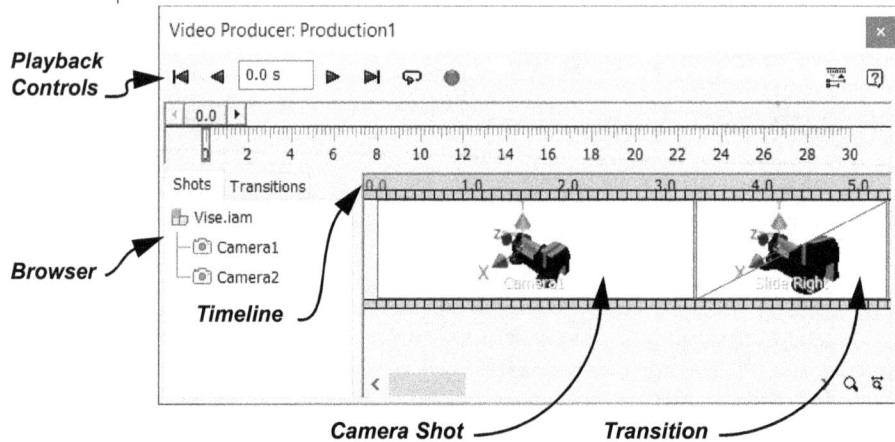

Figure 13–23

The areas of the Video Producer dialog box are described as follows:

Playback Controls	These are the same controls that are present in the Animation Timeline dialog box.
Browser	The Browser contains a *Shots* tab and a *Transitions* tab. The *Shots* tab is automatically populated with cameras that were created in Inventor Studio.
Timeline	Add camera shots and transitions to the timeline and arrange them in the order in which they display in the video.
Camera Shot	Add camera shots to the timeline to display animations of the assembly.
Transition	Add transitions to create effects between camera shots.

- The combination of camera shots and transitions is referred to as a *production*. Each production that you create is listed in the Browser.

Step 3 - Add cameras to the production.

To add cameras to the production, right-click and select **Add to timeline** or drag and drop from the Shots Browser, as shown in Figure 13–24. After the cameras are added to the production, you can edit them to change the duration of the shot and the animation assigned.

Drag cameras and transitions from here

Drag cameras and transitions to here

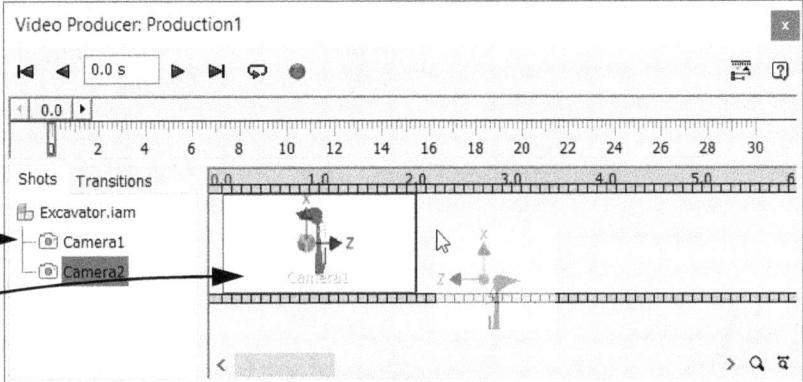

Figure 13–24

Step 4 - Add transitions to the production.

In the *Transitions* tab, you can add transitions between camera shots to create different effects. Standard options include **Fade**, **Gradient Wipe**, **Slide Left**, and **Slide Right**. Right-click and select **Add to timeline** or drag and drop from the Browser to add it to the production, as shown in Figure 13–25. After a transition is added, you can edit it to modify its duration, color, and type.

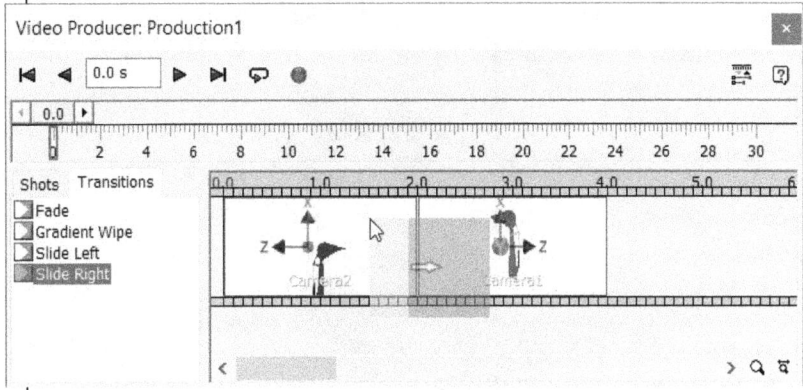

Figure 13–25

Step 5 - Arrange cameras and transitions and set the times for both.

After cameras and transitions are added to the production, they can be modified to further enhance the video. You can modify cameras and transitions by dragging and dropping or using the shortcut menu.

- Click and drop an object in the timeline window to change the sequence of the video. Click and drag the edge of an object to change the duration, as shown in Figure 13–26.

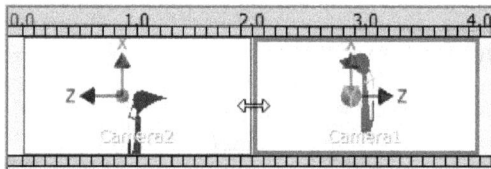

Figure 13–26

- Cameras and transitions can also be modified using the shortcut menu. Right-click options include **Copy**, **Paste**, **Edit**, **Move**, and **Delete**. When you edit a camera, the Shot dialog box opens, as shown in Figure 13–27. You can assign an animation to the shot and set the start point in that animation in the *Animation Footage* area. Assign the camera, duration, and end time in the *Shot Footage* area.

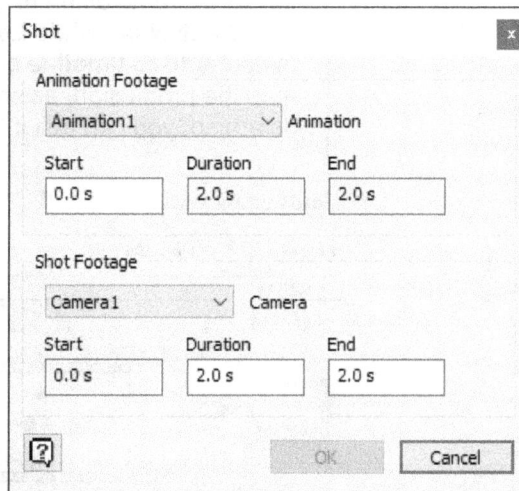

Figure 13–27

When you edit a transition, the Effect dialog box opens, as shown in Figure 13–28. Set the required effect in the *Transition* area, the color in the *Color* area, and the time in the *Timeline position* area.

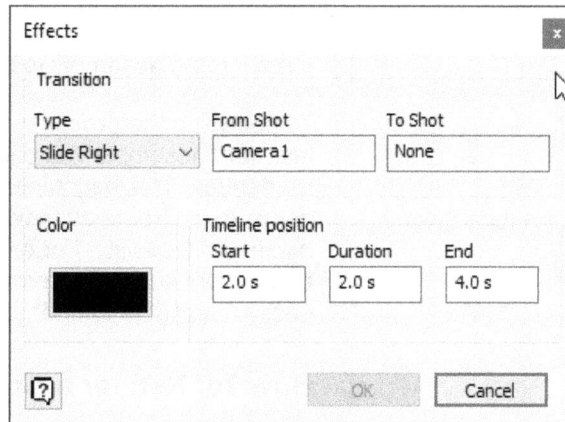

Figure 13–28

Step 6 - Render the production.

Click ● (Record Animation) in the Animation Timeline to open the Render Animation dialog box. This is the same dialog box that is used to render animations.

13.4 Creating a Standard Room

To make the model environment more realistic, you can add walls, a floor, and other relevant objects, such as a table. Because a scene style only adds a background, you need to create the walls, a floor, and other objects, and then assemble them into an assembly to complete the overall environment.

To speed up the process of future renderings, create a new standard assembly you can use for your most common renderings. This might include a left wall, right wall, back wall, and a floor. Create each wall as a separate component to ensure maximum flexibility. For example, different models are likely to be different sizes. Therefore, you want your standard room to be easily modifiable to fit any model size.

How To: Render a Model

1. Create a new assembly.
2. Add the standard room assembly containing the walls and floor.
3. Assemble the model.

By assembling both the standard room and the model into a top-level assembly, you can change the environment quickly and easily. You can also disable the visibility of specific walls and other objects, as required.

For the floor and each wall, you can apply a different appearance to achieve the required result.

Practice 13a | Rendering Images and an Animation

Practice Objectives

- Apply an Appearance Override to individual parts in an assembly.
- Apply a lighting style to a model.
- Create a realistic rendered image and animation.

In this practice, you will apply appearance overrides and a lighting style to an assembly model for rendering both an image and animation. The image shown in Figure 13–29 is one of the images that you will create.

Figure 13–29

Task 1 - Open an assembly file and apply appearance overrides.

1. Open **Vise.iam** from the *Vise_Inv_Studio_Assembly* folder.

2. In the Model Browser, select the **Screw_Sub:1** subassembly.

3. In the Quick Access toolbar, click ⬤ (Appearance) to open the Appearance Browser.

4. In the Appearance Browser, enter **Chrome** in the *Search* field at the top of the dialog box.

5. In the search results, select **Chrome - Polished**, and then right-click on it and select **Assign to Selection**. The material on the subassembly is now overridden and the Chrome - Polished material is now listed in the *Document Appearances* area.

6. Clear the *Search* field entry.

7. Clear the selection of the subassembly and in the Model Browser, select **Sliding_Jaw** and **Base**.

8. Scroll down the list of materials in the Inventor Materials Library and select the **Metal** option. Right-click on **Metal 1400F Hot**, and then select **Assign to Selection**. This material is assigned to the model and is copied to the *Document Appearances* area of the dialog box.

9. Close the Appearance Browser.

Task 2 - Set up the ground plane and set reflections.

*To adjust the ground plane location, expand **Ground Plane** in the Appearance panel and click **Settings**. In the Ground Plane Settings dialog box, ensure that the **Automatic adjustment to model** option is selected and enter a value in the Position & Size area to better position the plane.*

1. In the *View* tab>Appearance panel, click **Ground Plane** to enable and display the ground plane in the graphics window.

2. Click **Front** on the ViewCube. Note how the model is sitting on the ground plane. This should be verified to ensure that any reflections that are used when rendering are accurate.

3. Click **Ground Plane** to disable its display. The ground plane was only required to ensure that the reflections are correctly rendered.

4. Using the ViewCube return the model to the **Home** view.

5. In the *View* tab>Appearance panel, click **Reflections** to enable it. A reflection is displayed in the graphics window.

Task 3 - Open the Inventor Studio Environment.

1. In the *Environments* tab>Begin panel, click ⬚ (Inventor Studio). The *Render* contextual tab displays.

2. The rendering will be the size of the graphics window. Zoom the model as required so that it uses the full size of the window.

3. In the Render panel, click ⬚ (Render Image). The Render Image dialog box opens, as shown in Figure 13–30. By default, the current view and lighting is used for rendering.

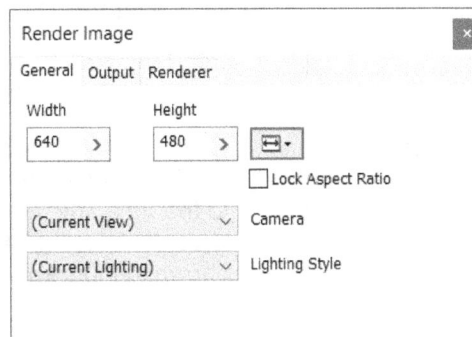

```
Render Image                                    [×]

General  Output  Renderer

Width              Height
[ 640    > ]       [ 480   > ]     [ ⬚▾ ]
                                   ☐ Lock Aspect Ratio

[ (Current View)        ∨ ]   Camera

[ (Current Lighting)    ∨ ]   Lighting Style
```

Figure 13–30

4. Expand the Lighting Style drop-down list and select **Cool Light**.

5. Expand the [⬚▾] drop-down list and select **Active View**. This sets the size of the rendered image to that of the current graphics window.

6. Select the *Renderer* tab. Change *Render Duration* to **Until Satisfactory** and leave the remaining defaults in the dialog box.

7. Click **Render**. Note the background in the rendering is still white. This is because the scene image is not displayed.

   Click ⬚ (Stop Rendering) in the top right-hand corner of the dialog box and close the Render Output dialog box.

8. In the Scene panel, click ⬚ (Studio Lighting Styles). The Studio Lighting Styles dialog box opens. Note that **Cool Light** is the active style.

9. In the *Environment* tab, click **Display Scene Image** to enable it and click **Save**.

   - You cannot enable the scene image when assigning the lighting style in the Render Image dialog box. The image is only rendered with the lighting effects of the image.

10. Click **Done** to close the Studio Lighting Styles dialog box. Note that the background now displays as gray. This is the background image for the cool light environment.

11. In the Render panel, click ⬡ (Render Image) again. Verify that **Cool Light** is set as the *Lighting Style* and the render duration (*Renderer* tab) is set to render until satisfactory.

12. Click **Render**. The render will continue until you click

    ▣ (Stop Rendering). The longer you let the image render, the better the rendering quality.

To automatically save an image once rendered, use the options on the Output tab.

13. Once the image is rendered, click 🖫 (Save Rendering) in the Render Output window. In the Save dialog box, navigate to the *Vise_Inv_Studio_Assembly* folder and enter **Vise_Rendering1.bmp** as the name. Click **Save**. The model shown in Figure 13–31 was rendered for over ten minutes.

Figure 13–31

14. Close the Render Output dialog box.

15. On the *General* tab, in the Lighting Style drop-down list, select **Sharp Highlights**. Return to the Studio Lighting Styles dialog box and ensure that the **Display Scene Image** is enabled.

16. In the Render Image dialog box, render the image. After approximately ten minutes it should display similar to that shown in Figure 13–32. Save it as **Vise_Rendering2.bmp**.

Figure 13–32

17. Close the Render Output and Render Image dialog boxes.

If you did not complete the two renderings, two images (Vise_ Rendering1_Final.bmp and Vise_Rendering2 _Final.bmp) are provided in the Vise_ Inv_Studio_Assembly folder for you to compare.

18. Navigate to the *Vise_Inv_Studio_Assembly* folder in Windows Explorer and open the two saved images (**Vise_Rendering1.bmp** and **Vise_Rendering2.bmp**) to compare them. Note that the lighting in the second image is considerably brighter. This is because of the different image-based lighting style that was used. You will want to compare different styles to select the one that is best for your designs.

Task 4 - Working with a lighting style.

1. In the Scene panel, click ⚐ (Studio Lighting Styles). The Studio Lighting Styles dialog box opens, as shown in Figure 13–33.

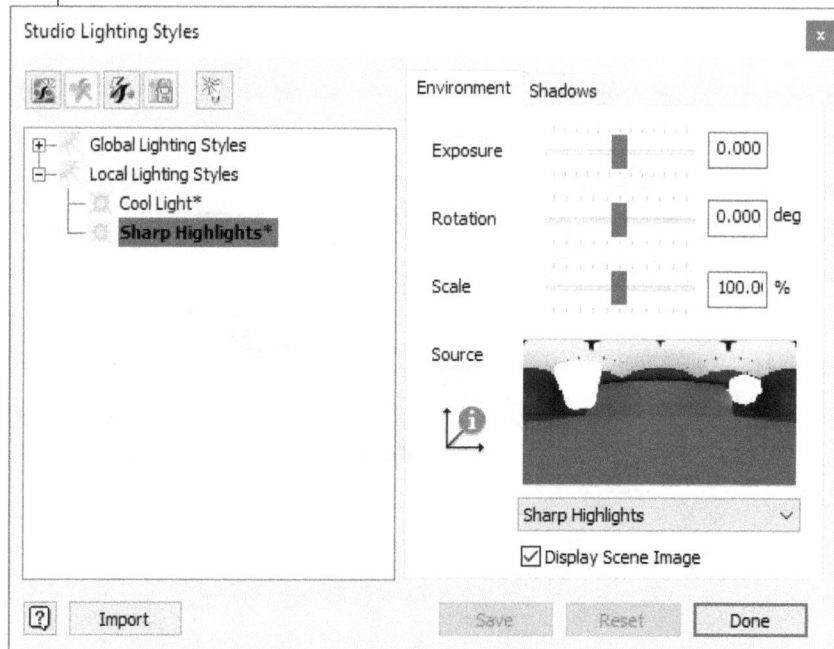

Figure 13–33

2. The **Cool Light** and **Sharp Highlights** styles have been copied to the Local Lighting Styles area because they were used for rendering. They can be further edited using the options, as required.

3. Right-click on **Cool Light** and note all of the options that you can select. The style can be renamed, copied, or deleted (purged), as required.

4. Select **Rename Lighting Style** and enter **Custom Lighting** as the new name and then click **OK**.

5. Locate the **Empty Lab** style in the *Global Lighting Styles* area. Right-click on the style, select **Copy Lighting Style**, and then enter a new name. The new style is listed in the **Local Lighting Styles** node.

6. Set the new style as **Active**, if not already set.

7. Select **Display Scene Image** to show the style's background image in the graphics window.

8. Scale the background image to match the size of the model (approx. 36%).

9. Rotate the environment and the model, as required.

10. In the *View* tab, toggle off reflections and toggle on ground shadows.

11. Save the style and render the model.

   A rendered version of the model is shown in Figure 13–34. **Vise_Rendering3_Final.bmp** has been saved for you to review in the *Vise_Inv_Studio_Assembly* folder, if required.

Figure 13–34

12. Close the Render Output and Render Image dialog boxes.

Task 5 - Create an animation for the opening of the jaw plates.

1. In the Scene panel, click ⚡ (Studio Lighting Styles).

2. Activate the **Custom Lighting** style that was previously created. Close the Studio Lighting Styles dialog box.

3. Return to the model's **Home** view.

4. Select the *View* tab and disable the display of shadows in the animation. Enabling shadows in this video does not produce a good result because of the movement of the shadows throughout the video.

5. In the *Render* tab>Animate panel, click ⬚ (Constraints). Click **OK** if prompted to activate an animation. The Animate Constraints dialog box (shown in Figure 13–35) and the Animation Timeline opens.

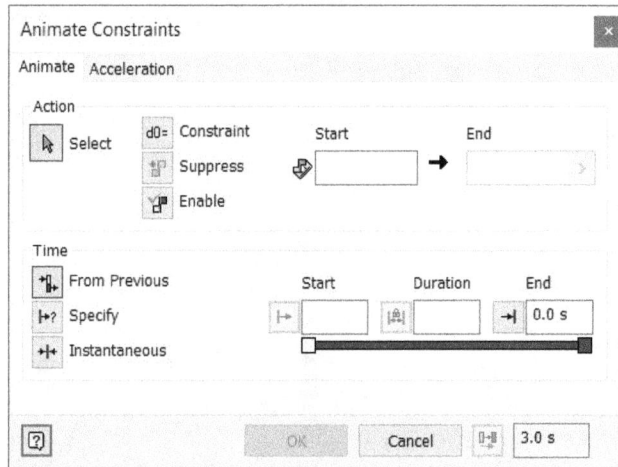

Figure 13–35

6. In the Model Browser, expand the **Jaw_Plate:1** branch and select **Mate:7** as the constraint to animate.

7. Type **65 mm** as the *End* constraint value and **5.0 s** as the *End* time value, as shown in Figure 13–36.

If required, specify a duration longer than 5.0 s to view a smoother animation.

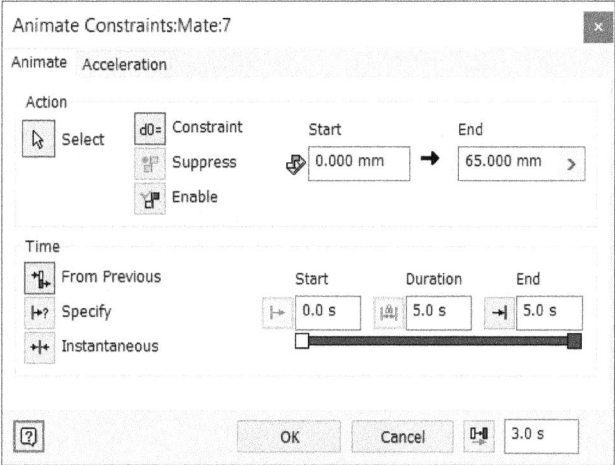

Figure 13–36

8. Click **OK** to complete the definition.

9. Click (Expand Action Editor) in the Animation Timeline window to expand the window, as shown in Figure 13–37.

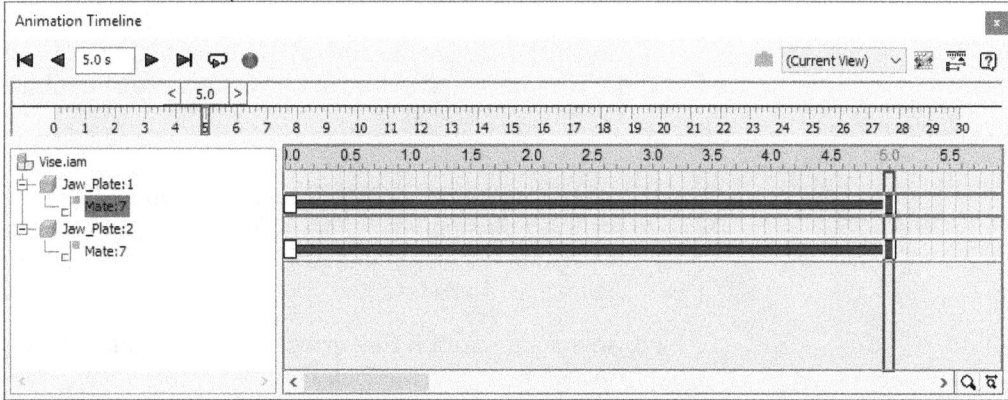

Figure 13–37

10. The animated Mate constraint you added earlier is in the animation timeline. The blue bar indicates the duration of the motion. By default, the total animation time is 30s. Change the total time to 5s by clicking (Animation Options) and typing **5** in the *Seconds* field. Click **OK** to confirm and close the Animation Options dialog box.

11. In the Animation Timeline window, click (Go to Start) to set the animation to the beginning. The model returns to its initial state.

---

12. Run the animation by clicking ▶ (Play Animation).

13. Refit and orient the model in the window, as required, to render the animation.

14. In the Render panel, click 🎞 (Render Animation). The Render Animation dialog box opens, as shown in Figure 13–38.

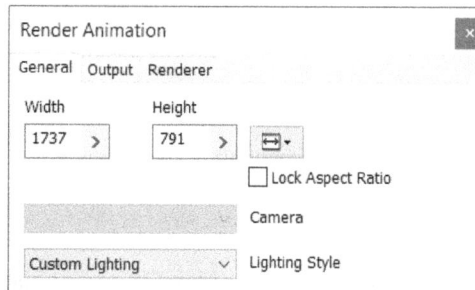

Figure 13–38

15. Expand the [⬛▾] drop-down list and select **Active View**. This sets the size of the rendered animation to that of the graphics window.

16. Select the *Output* tab and set the *Vise_Inv_Studio_Assembly* folder and file name for the animation. Use the default .WMV file format. Click **Save**.

17. Click ⊞ (Specified Time Range) and type **2.0s** to animate for only this amount of time. This reduces the time it takes to create the animation, but also only records half of the total animation. Therefore, the vise will not completely open.

18. Select the **Launch Player** option to automatically play the animation once it has been created.

19. Select the *Renderer* tab. Select **Total Render Time**. Note that the default rendering time is 1 min. Maintain this default, noting that rendering for longer creates better results.

20. Click **Render**.

21. In the ASF Export Properties dialog box, keep the default settings and click **OK**. (If you saved as an .AVI file, the Video Compression dialog box opens.) The rendering will begin.

22. View the animation when it displays.

23. Save the model and close the window.

Practice 13b | Puncher

Practice Objectives

- Create a room to provide an environment for models to use for their renderings.
- Modify appearances and lighting styles to render an image.

In this practice, you will create a room that future models can use for their renderings. You will use this room to provide an environment for the rendering of the puncher assembly, shown in Figure 13–39. General instructions are provided.

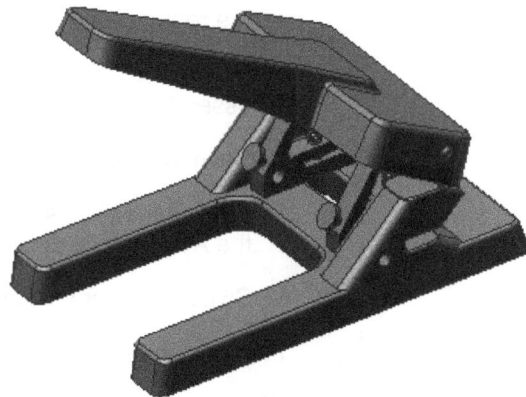

Figure 13–39

Task 1 - Create a new empty assembly and add walls and puncher assembly.

1. Open **Puncher.iam** from the *Inventor Studio - Puncher* folder.

2. Create a new metric part called **Floor** outside of this assembly. This part will provide a surface on which the Puncher assembly will rest. The part can be a large thin rectangular block. You can make the block much larger than the Puncher assembly. Add dimensions to make it easier to modify later on. For your reference, the puncher assembly is approximately 144 mm wide, 202 mm long, and 160 mm tall. This part will simulate the surface of a table in the rendering.

3. Create another new metric part called **Back_Wall** outside of the Puncher assembly to act as a back wall in the rendering. Make this part a thin rectangular block as well, and then add dimensions to it.

Once rooms have been created once, they are ready to use in future renderings. You can save them in a library for use by other designers.

4. Create a third part, called **Left_Wall**, to act as the left wall in the rendering. This will be another thin rectangular block. Add dimensions to the part.

5. Create a fourth part called **Right_Wall**.

6. Create a new empty assembly and assemble **Floor.ipt**, **Back_ Wall.ipt**, **Left_Wall.ipt**, and **Right_Wall.ipt**.

7. Save the assembly and call it **Room1**.

8. Create another new empty assembly and place Room1 as the first component.

9. Place the Puncher assembly and position it in the middle of the room.

10. Modify the dimensions of any of the walls to suit the Puncher assembly.

11. Save the assembly and call it **Room_Puncher**.

12. Apply appearances to the back wall, side wall, and floor using the Appearance Browser.

13. Switch to Inventor Studio.

14. Select an existing or create a new lighting style.

15. Zoom in on the room so that only the room's walls display in the graphics window. If not, once rendered the background that was assigned to the lighting style will be displayed in the rendering.

16. Render the image and select the required resolution and lighting styles.

17. Save the rendered image.

18. If you did not achieve your required result, modify the appearances and lighting styles to work as required. Render the assembly again.

19. Continue to modify the appearances and styles until you obtain your required result.

20. Save and close the assembly when you are finished.

Practice 13c | (Optional) Excavator

Practice Objective

- Create a rendered animation of an assembly.

In this practice, you will create an animation for the excavator assembly shown in Figure 13–40. General instructions are provided.

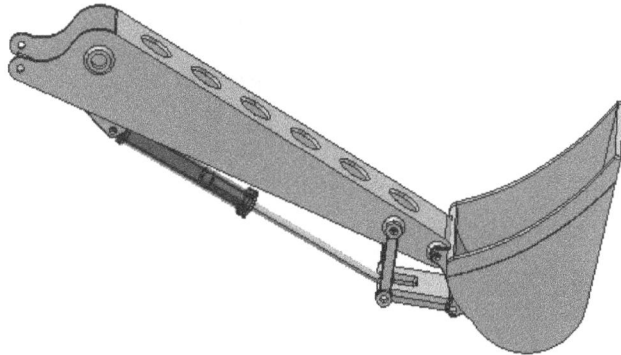

Figure 13–40.

Task 1 - Create an animated rendering of an assembly.

1. Open **Excavator_complete.iam** from the *Inventor Studio-Excavator* folder.

2. Create an animation for the assembly. Animate **Mate:20**, which is located in the *Cylinder* subassembly.
   - Specify an End value of **1500 mm**.
   - Specify an appropriate duration for the action so that it will not take too long to create an animation for it.
   - Adjust the length of the animation using the animation options on the Animation Timeline window.
   - Preview the animation using the Animation Timeline window and make adjustments as required.

3. Open the Render Animation dialog box and enter the required options in the *General*, *Output*, and *Renderer* tabs. Adjust the frame rate and time range to reduce the time it will take to create the animation.

4. Render the animation. While the animation process is running, check the total number of frames that need to be created. If the number of frames is too high and you estimate that the process will take too long, stop the animation and adjust the rendering options in the *Output* tab. Rerun the rendering as required.

5. To add additional detail to the rendered animation, consider using a lighting style with a background image (e.g. Old Warehouse) or using the room assembly technique to place the assembly in a room that has had appearances assigned to its walls. Render the animation again.

6. Save and close the assembly.

Chapter Review Questions

1. What is the purpose of Inventor Studio?

   a. Create positional representations of models.

   b. Create a background for models.

   c. Create realistic renderings and animations.

2. What are the three types of lights that can be assigned in a light style?

   a. Spot, Directional, and Cloud.

   b. Spot, Directional, and Shadow.

   c. Point, Directional, and Cloud.

   d. Directional, Spot, and Point.

3. When rendering an image, where do you set the rendering duration to proceed before the action is completed?

   a. Render Image dialog box, *General* tab.

   b. Render Image dialog box, *Output* tab.

   c. Render Image dialog box, *Renderer* tab.

4. Along with animating components, which of the following can also be animated? (Select all that apply.)

   a. Constraints

   b. Parameters

   c. Level of Detail

   d. Cameras

   e. Lights

5. Along with dragging and dropping a camera from the Video Producer to the timeline, how else can you add it to the production?

   a. Click the **Add to Timeline** icon in the ribbon.

   b. Double-click on it in the Video Producer.

   c. Right-click on it and select **Add to Timeline**.

   d. All of the above.

Command Summary

Button	Command	Location
	Animation Timeline	• **Ribbon**: *Render* tab>Animate panel
	Appearance	• **Ribbon**: *Tools* tab>Material and Appearance panel • **Quick Access Toolbar**
	Camera	• **Ribbon**: *Render* tab>Scene panel
	Camera (animate)	• **Ribbon**: *Render* tab>Animate panel
	Clear	• **Ribbon**: *Tools* tab>Material and Appearance panel • **Quick Access Toolbar**
	Components	• **Ribbon**: *Render* tab>Animate panel
	Constraints	• **Ribbon**: *Render* tab>Animate panel
	Fade	• **Ribbon**: *Render* tab>Animate panel
	Inventor Studio	• **Ribbon**: *Environments* tab>Begin panel
	Light	• **Ribbon**: *Render* tab>Animate panel
	Local Lights	• **Ribbon**: *Render* tab>Scene panel
fx	**Parameter Favorites**	• **Ribbon**: *Render* tab>Animate panel
	Parameters	• **Ribbon**: *Render* tab>Animate panel
	Pos Reps	• **Ribbon**: *Render* tab>Manage panel
	Render Animation	• **Ribbon**: *Render* tab>Render panel
	Render Image	• **Ribbon**: *Render* tab>Render panel
	Studio Lighting Styles	• **Ribbon**: *Render* tab>Scene panel
	Video Producer	• **Ribbon**: *Render* tab>Animate panel

Chapter

14

iAssemblies

Similar to iFeatures and iParts, iAssemblies enable you to quickly and easily create variations in your design. iAssemblies can help increase your efficiency by enabling you to create similar assemblies in a single file, instead of recreating them multiple times.

Learning Objectives in This Chapter

- Create an iAssembly that does not contain any components that are varied with their own iParts or iAssemblies.
- Create an iAssembly for an assembly that contains both iParts and iAssemblies.
- Convert components in an existing assembly to iParts or iAssemblies using the Replace option.
- Specify a member to use when placing an iAssembly.
- Edit the iAssembly Factory using the iAssembly Author dialog box or by using a spreadsheet.
- Define if components or features should be included in a factory table when added to an iAssembly.

14.1 Introduction

An iAssembly enables you to quickly and easily create variations in your design. Use them to create similar assemblies in a single file instead of recreating similar assemblies multiple times as separate files. To start, you set up configurable attributes that you can use to create the variations. These attributes can include the inclusion/exclusion of a component, use of members of an iAssembly or iPart, the offset value of a constraint, the material property, and the BOM structure of a component.

Examples of an iAssembly containing iParts and an iAssembly (as a subassembly) are shown in Figure 14–1. The three configurations (or members in the iAssembly factory) in the vise iAssembly vary in length and width. The table that contains all the iAssembly information is shown at the bottom of Figure 14–1. In this example, the only configurable items added are four iParts (**Sliding_Jaw:1**, **Jaw_Plate:1**, **Jaw_Plate:2**, and **Base:1**) and one iAssembly (**Screw_Sub_Assy**). The three configurations of the vise iAssembly vary by using different members of the four iPart and one iAssembly (the **Screw_Sub_Assy**).

In this iAssembly configuration called Large, the Base:1 part is an iPart that has been set to use the iPart configuration called Base_LargeWidth+LargeLength

Screw_Sub_Assy   *Base:1*

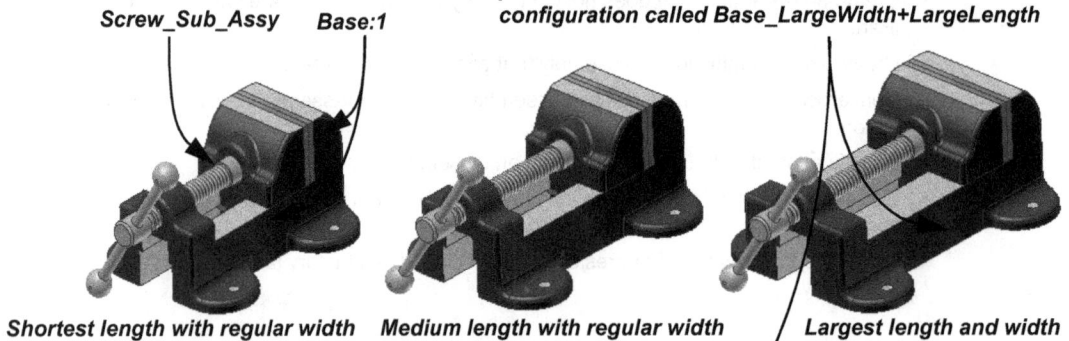

Shortest length with regular width   **Medium length with regular width**   **Largest length and width**

		Member	Part Number	Base:1: Table Replace	Sliding_Jaw:1: Table Replace	Screw_Sub:1: Table Replace	Jaw_Plate:1: Table Replace	Jaw_Plate:2: Table Replace
1		Vise_iAssembly-01	Vise-small-01	Base_SmallWidth+SmallLength	Sliding_Jaw-01	Screw_Sub-short	Jaw_Plate-01	Jaw_Plate-01
2		Vise_iAssembly-02	Vise-small-02	Base_SmallWidth+MedLength	Sliding_Jaw-01	Screw_Sub-medium	Jaw_Plate-01	Jaw_Plate-01
3		Vise_iAssembly-03	Vise-small-03	Base_LargeWidth+LargeLength	Sliding_Jaw-02	Screw_Sub-long	Jaw_Plate-02	Jaw_Plate-02

The vise iAssembly above is driven by this table

Figure 14–1

14.2 Create Basic iAssemblies

General Steps

If you have a part that varies and is within a subassembly, you must create an iAssembly for that subassembly.

Use the following general steps to create an iAssembly that requires no iAssembly subassemblies:

1. Create iParts for the parts in the assembly that are going to vary.
2. Create and assemble the parts into a new assembly.
3. Start the creation of the iAssembly.
4. Add configurable attributes.
5. Add iAssembly members.
6. Specify the required values for each iAssembly member.
7. Verify the iAssembly.
8. Complete the iAssembly.

Step 1 - Create iParts for the parts in the assembly that are going to vary.

Evaluate which parts in the assembly are going to vary and then create them, as required, using iParts. Some ways in which a part can vary and be handled by iParts include the following:

- The size of a dimension.

- The value of a parameter in the parameter list.

- The values of the properties in the *Summary* and *Project* tabs in the Properties dialog box.

- The suppression state (on or off) of a feature.

- The specifications of a thread.

- The offset value, suppression state, sequence number, matching name (in the match list), and name for an iMate.

Step 2 - Create and assemble the parts into a new assembly.

If you created a copy of the original part and converted it to an iPart, ensure that you assemble the iPart file rather than the original.

Once all required iParts have been created, create a new assembly. Assemble and constrain all the components in the new assembly.

Step 3 - Start the creation of the iAssembly.

In the *Manage* tab>Author panel, click ![i+] (Create iAssembly). The iAssembly Author opens, as shown in Figure 14–2.

Tabs containing different data types →

Left pane contains member attributes for the active tab

Right pane displays selected attributes for the active tab —

iAssembly table displays selected attributes and members of the iAssembly —

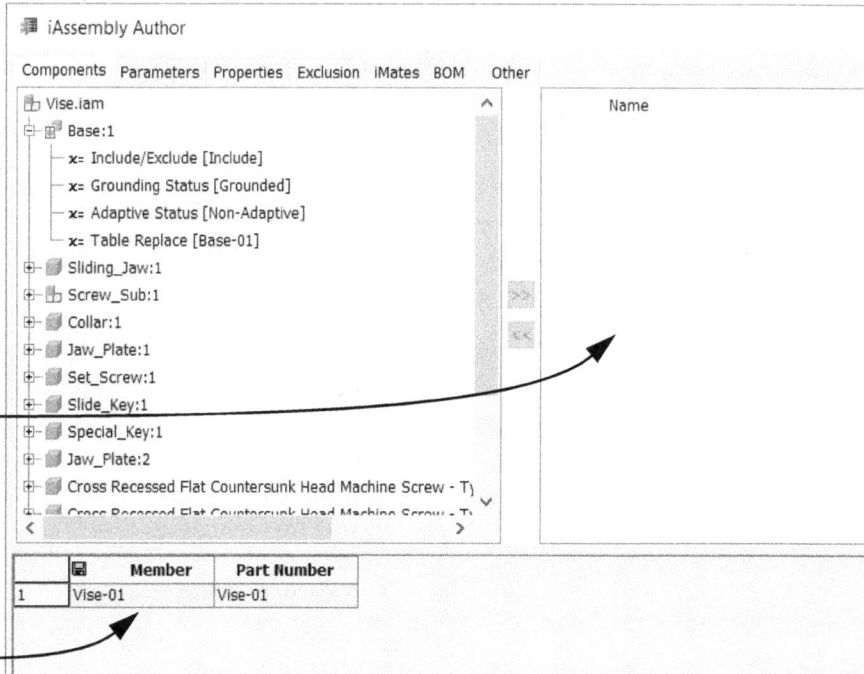

iAssembly Author

Components Parameters Properties Exclusion iMates BOM Other

Vise.iam
  Base:1
    x= Include/Exclude [Include]
    x= Grounding Status [Grounded]
    x= Adaptive Status [Non-Adaptive]
    x= Table Replace [Base-01]
  Sliding_Jaw:1
  Screw_Sub:1
  Collar:1
  Jaw_Plate:1
  Set_Screw:1
  Slide_Key:1
  Special_Key:1
  Jaw_Plate:2
  Cross Recessed Flat Countersunk Head Machine Screw - T)
  Cross Recessed Flat Countersunk Head Machine Screw - T)

Name

	Member	Part Number
1	Vise-01	Vise-01

Figure 14–2

Step 4 - Add configurable attributes.

Keys can be defined in the same manner as they are for iParts.

To add a configurable attribute, select the tab that contains the attribute, expand the required branches to display the attribute,

select it, and click ![>>]. The attribute is copied to the right pane and added as a column in the table, as shown in Figure 14–3.

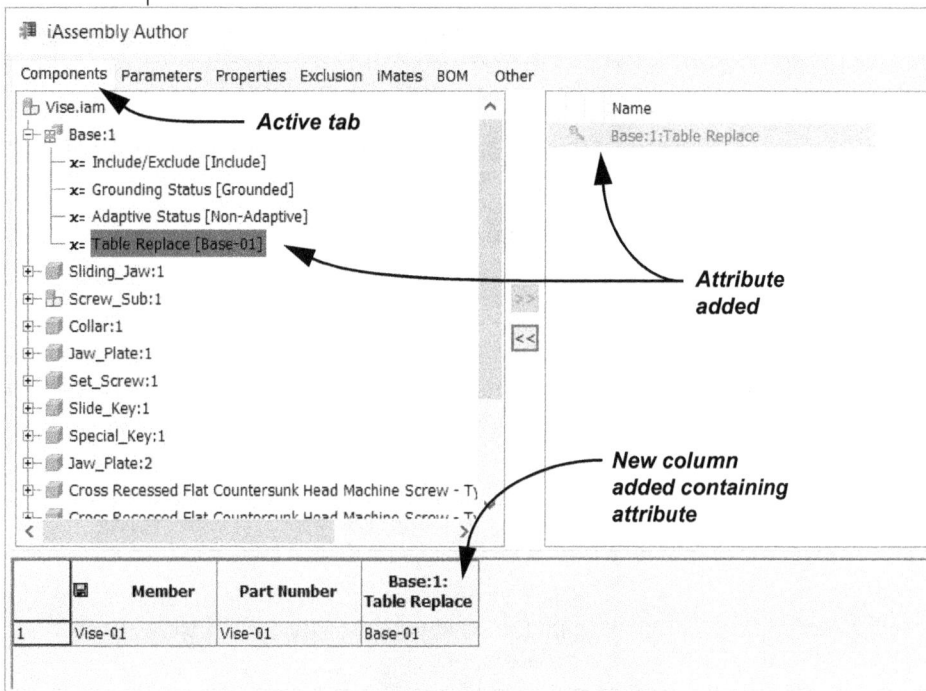

Figure 14–3

Add iParts to an iAssembly

The Table Replace attribute displays for iParts. Use this to switch between the iPart members for different iAssembly configurations. Once added, a menu containing the members displays when you select a cell in the *Table Replace* column.

Continue to add attributes from the various tabs, as required.

Step 5 - Add iAssembly members.

Right-click on a cell in the first column and select **Insert Row** (as shown in Figure 14–4) to insert a new iAssembly member.

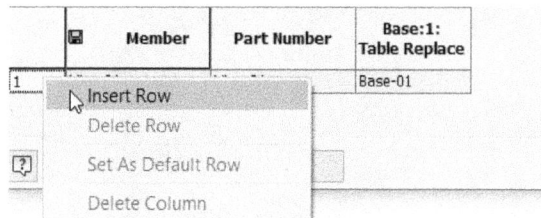

Figure 14–4

Step 6 - Specify the required values for each iAssembly member.

Select each cell and specify the required value for each attribute in the table.

- Some cells require a manual input, while others provide menus of possible values. Change the member names and part numbers as required.

*If you want to customize the automatic naming of each part number or member name, click **Options**.*

- Define the default member to use by right-clicking on the row and selecting **Set As Default Row**. The default row displays in green in the table.

Step 7 - Verify the iAssembly.

Click **Verify** to verify that all the attribute values you specified are valid. Invalid values highlight in yellow. Correct all invalid values before continuing.

Step 8 - Complete the iAssembly.

Once all required attributes and members have been added, click **OK** to create the iAssembly. By creating the iAssembly, the assembly is converted to an iAssembly. The Model Browser updates to show the members of the iAssembly, as shown in Figure 14–5. The checkmark next to an iAssembly member indicates the active member that is currently displayed in the graphics window.

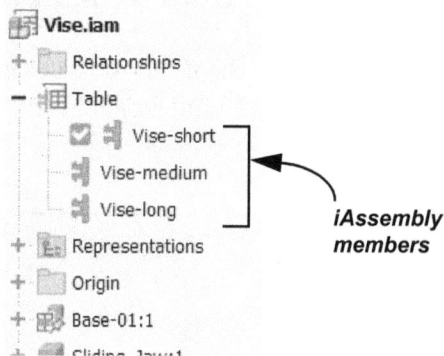

Figure 14–5

14.3 Create Multi-Level iAssemblies

If an iAssembly also contains subassemblies that have their own iAssemblies, consider the following:

- An iAssembly must be created for any subassembly that is going to vary, whether it is a direct attribute of the subassembly itself or one of its components. Follow the general steps outlined for creating a basic iAssembly. Save the file. Switch to the top-level assembly that contains the subassembly and update it. Redefine any constraints with undefined geometry (missing references). Create additional iAssemblies for other subassemblies as required.

- If a subassembly is an iAssembly, the top-level assembly must also be created as an iAssembly. Follow Steps 2 to 8 as outlined for creating a basic iAssembly. When assembling the components into the new assembly, ensure that you assemble the iParts and iAssemblies, rather than their counterparts that were not converted to iParts or iAssemblies (i.e., regular parts and assemblies).

Consider the vise assembly shown in Figure 14–6.

Assembly is an iAssembly

Subassembly that is an iAssembly

This iPart, which is located in the subassembly, needs to vary in the top-level assembly. To do this, create an iAssembly of the subassembly and add the Table Replace attribute of this iPart.

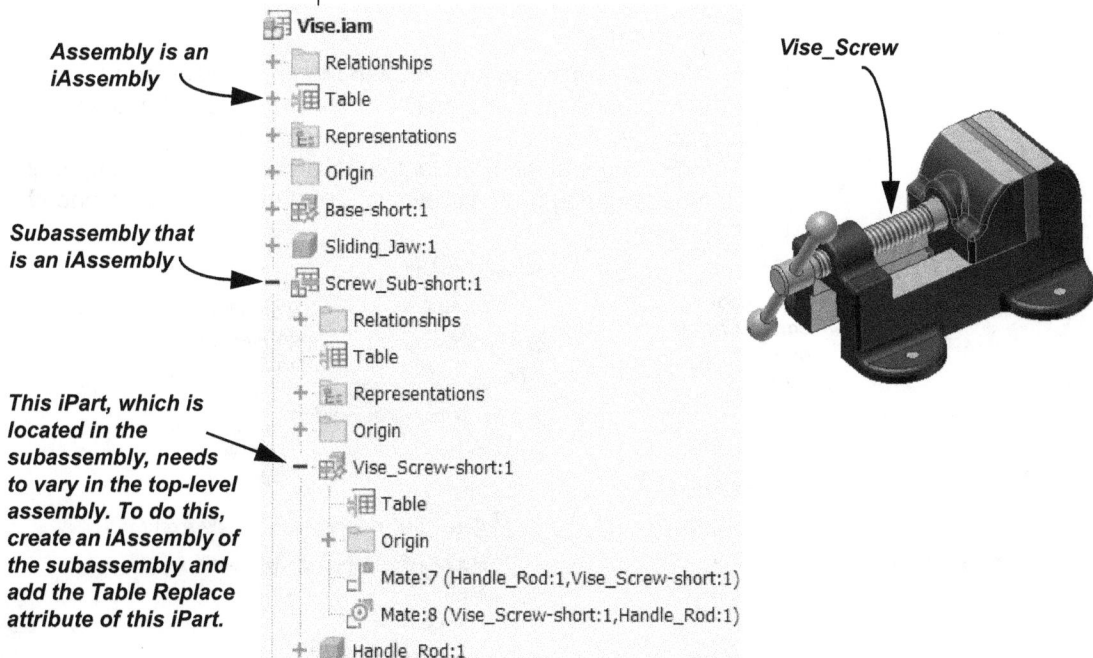

Vise.iam
- Relationships
- Table
- Representations
- Origin
- Base-short:1
- Sliding_Jaw:1
- Screw_Sub-short:1
  - Relationships
  - Table
  - Representations
  - Origin
  - Vise_Screw-short:1
    - Table
    - Origin
    - Mate:7 (Handle_Rod:1,Vise_Screw-short:1)
    - Mate:8 (Vise_Screw-short:1,Handle_Rod:1)
  - Handle_Rod:1

Vise_Screw

Figure 14–6

14.4 Create iAssemblies Using Existing Assemblies

Components that exist in an assembly and have been made into iParts or iAssemblies must be replaced in order to be recognized at the top-level assembly. In addition, the top-level assembly must be converted to an iAssembly.

General Steps

Use the following general steps to convert a normal assembly that does not contain any iParts or iAssemblies to an iAssembly:

1. Convert the parts into iParts.
2. Replace the normal parts with their iParts in the subassemblies.
3. Convert the subassemblies into iAssemblies.
4. Replace the parts with their iParts in the top-level assembly.
5. Convert the top-level assembly into an iAssembly.

Step 1 - Convert the parts into iParts.

You can keep a copy of the normal part before it is converted into an iPart.

Determine which parts are going to vary in the assembly. Open a part in a separate window, convert it into an iPart, and save the part. Convert the other parts that are going to vary in the same way, including subassemblies in the top-level assembly.

- After converting to an iPart, the Model Browser icon (🗊) for the component changes to include the image of a table, as shown in Figure 14–7. The component block is blue, indicating that the iPart factory is referenced. The component block is going to be yellow if an iPart member is referenced.

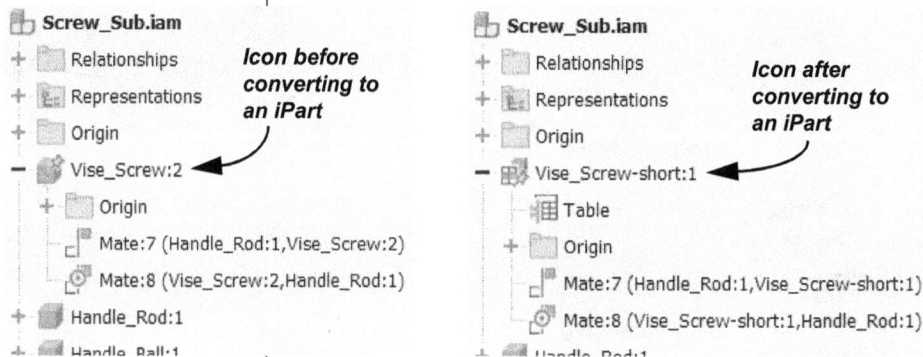

Figure 14–7

Step 2 - Replace the normal parts with their iParts in the subassemblies.

If you leave the factory referenced without replacing it with an iPart member, then the Table Replace attribute is not available for use in the iAssembly.

How To: Replace a Part

1. Ensure that the assembly in which the part was directly assembled is open.
2. Right-click on the part in the Model Browser, and select **Component>Replace**. The Open dialog box displays.
3. Select and open the iPart. The Place Standard iPart dialog box displays.
4. Select the member to replace with and click **OK**.

If any constraints exist that reference geometry on the component that was replaced, a dialog box opens (similar to that shown in Figure 14–8) indicating that a reference is missing. You must redefine the constraint(s) to resolve the issue.

If you are replacing multiple components, consider waiting to edit missing constraint references till all of the components are replaced. This ensures that additional failures are not created when other components are replaced.

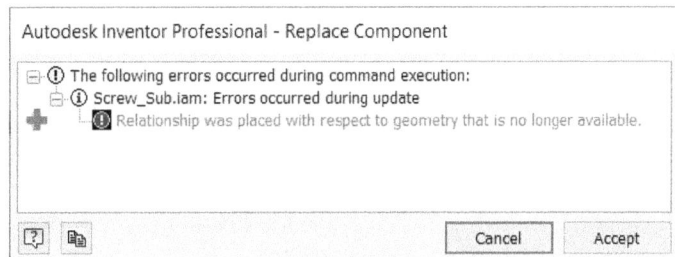

Autodesk Inventor Professional - Replace Component

The following errors occurred during command execution:
Screw_Sub.iam: Errors occurred during update
Relationship was placed with respect to geometry that is no longer available.

Cancel   Accept

Figure 14–8

- After replacement, the name of the component changes to that of the member designated upon replacement, as shown in Figure 14–9.

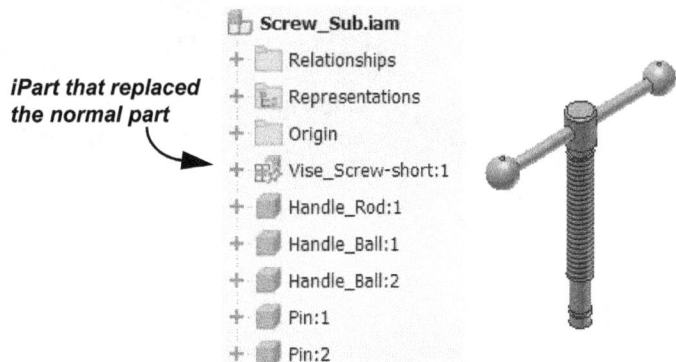

Screw_Sub.iam
+ Relationships
+ Representations
+ Origin

iPart that replaced the normal part → + Vise_Screw-short:1

+ Handle_Rod:1
+ Handle_Ball:1
+ Handle_Ball:2
+ Pin:1
+ Pin:2

Figure 14–9

- By changing the component to a member of a factory, the Table Replace attribute is available for use during iAssembly creation.

You can keep a copy of the normal subassembly before it is converted into an iAssembly.

Step 3 - Convert the subassemblies into iAssemblies.

Determine which subassemblies are to vary in the assembly. If a part in a subassembly is to vary, then the part must be converted to an iPart before you convert the subassembly into an iAssembly.

- Subassemblies do not need to be replaced by their iAssemblies. However, when you switch to the top-level assembly, you need to update the assembly.

- Redefine constraints and resolve the missing references, if required.

Repeat this step for the other subassemblies that have attributes or contain components that need to vary in the top-level iAssembly.

Step 4 - Replace the parts with their iParts in the top-level assembly.

In the top-level assembly, replace the required parts with their iParts.

- If missing references are found, redefine them as required.

Step 5 - Convert the top-level assembly into an iAssembly.

Once all required components have been converted to iParts and iAssemblies, convert the top-level assembly into an iAssembly.

14.5 Place iAssemblies

To place an iAssembly, switch to the *Assemble* tab>Component panel and click 📂 (Place). Browse to the file, and open it. The Place iAssembly dialog box opens, as shown in Figure 14–10. Use the dialog box to specify the member to use.

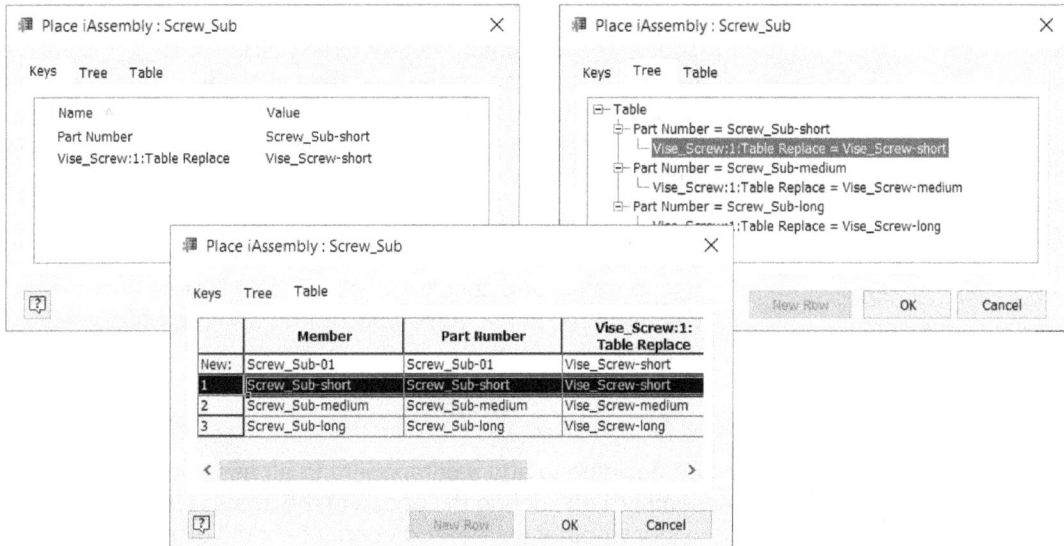

Place iAssembly : Screw_Sub

Keys   Tree   Table

Name ∧	Value
Part Number	Screw_Sub-short
Vise_Screw:1:Table Replace	Vise_Screw-short

Place iAssembly : Screw_Sub

Keys   Tree   Table

- Table
  - Part Number = Screw_Sub-short
    - Vise_Screw:1:Table Replace = Vise_Screw-short
  - Part Number = Screw_Sub-medium
    - Vise_Screw:1:Table Replace = Vise_Screw-medium
  - Part Number = Screw_Sub-long
    - Vise_Screw:1:Table Replace = Vise_Screw-long

New Row   OK   Cancel

Place iAssembly : Screw_Sub

Keys   Tree   Table

	Member	Part Number	Vise_Screw:1: Table Replace
New:	Screw_Sub-01	Screw_Sub-01	Vise_Screw-short
1	Screw_Sub-short	Screw_Sub-short	Vise_Screw-short
2	Screw_Sub-medium	Screw_Sub-medium	Vise_Screw-medium
3	Screw_Sub-long	Screw_Sub-long	Vise_Screw-long

New Row   OK   Cancel

Figure 14–10

The three tabs in the dialog box provide alternatives for selecting an iAssembly member for assembly. They are described below:

- The *Keys* tab lists the values for each iAssembly member in the iAssembly Factory based on the keys that were created. Select the required value to make it current so that it is the member that is placed.

- The *Tree* tab lists the values for each iAssembly member in the iAssembly Factory in a tree structure. Expand the tree to see and select the required member to place in the assembly.

- The *Table* tab lists the values for each iAssembly member in the iAssembly Factory in a table. Select a row to make it the current member to be placed in the assembly.

Once you have selected the required iAssembly member, click a location in the graphics window to place it. After placement, the dialog box remains open to place another instance. Click **Dismiss** when no additional instances are required.

14.6 Edit iAssemblies

Once you create an iAssembly Factory (iAssembly file), you can edit it.

How To: Edit the iAssembly Factory

1. Open the iAssembly Factory as you would any assembly file.
2. Right-click on ⊞ Table in the Model Browser and select **Edit Table**. The iAssembly Author dialog box opens.
3. Add or change the entries and then click **OK**.
4. Save the changes to the file.

- An iAssembly can also be edited in Microsoft® Excel®. In the Model Browser, right-click on ⊞ Table and select **Edit via Spreadsheet**. In addition to simply editing cells, you can also use formulas and conditional statements. These statements display in red in the iAssembly Author and can only be edited in Excel.

*The **Edit via Spreadsheet** option can also be accessed in the Assemble tab> iPart/iAssembly panel. By default, this panel is not displayed in the ribbon.*

Adding Components and Features to an iAssembly

When deciding to add a component to an assembly that is an iAssembly, considering the scope of the change is important. Consider whether the new component should display in only the active factory member or reflect in all factory members. The ⊞ (Edit Member Scope) and ⊞ (Edit Factory Scope) options enable you to control the scope of change.

- By default, the scope is automatically set to change the entire factory (**Edit Factory Scope**). If a component is added to an existing iAssembly, it is added to all members of the factory and no changes are made to the iAssembly table.

- If **Edit Member Scope** is specified and a component is added, it is automatically added to the table. The component's cell for the active member is marked *Include*. Other members are automatically marked *Exclude*, but can be modified if required.

*The **Edit Member Scope** and the **Edit Factory Scope** options exist on the Assemble tab (when displayed), and the Manage tab.*

The ⊞ (Edit Member Scope) and ⊞ (Edit Factory Scope) options can be used in the same way to control the scope of features that are added at the assembly level.

Practice 14a | iAssembly

Practice Objective

- Create variations of an assembly without having to recreate similar assemblies multiple times by converting it into an iAssembly.

In this practice, you will convert the vise assembly into an iAssembly. The design intent is to create variations of the vise assembly without having to recreate similar assemblies multiple times. You want to be able to quickly open three specific lengths of the vise assembly, as shown in Figure 14–11.

Figure 14–11

Task 1 - Examine the vise assembly.

1. Open **Vise.iam** from the *iAssembly* folder. The assembly displays as shown in Figure 14–12. It is currently a normal assembly. You will convert it into an iAssembly.

Vise.iam
+ Relationships
+ Representations
+ Origin
+ Base:1
+ Sliding_Jaw:1
+ Screw_Sub:1
+ Collar:1
+ Jaw_Plate:1
+ Jaw_Plate:2
+ Set_Screw:1
+ Set_Screw:2
+ Slide_Key:1
+ Slide_Key:2
+ Special_Key:1

Figure 14–12

2. Examine the vise assembly to familiarize yourself with the model.

   • Before creating an iAssembly, you want to understand how the model will need to vary to help you determine which components need to be converted into an iPart or iAssembly.

   • Keep in mind the references that particular constraints are using. After replacement, you must redefine those references.

3. In the Model Browser, double-click on **Base:1** to activate the part.

4. Right-click on **Extrusion1** and select **Show Dimensions**. The dimensions of **Extrusion1** display.

5. Rotate the model similar to the position shown in Figure 14–13 to obtain a clear view of the 184.15 mm dimension. This dimension must vary, so the part must be converted to an iPart. Once complete, the iPart needs to replace the assembled component in the assembly.

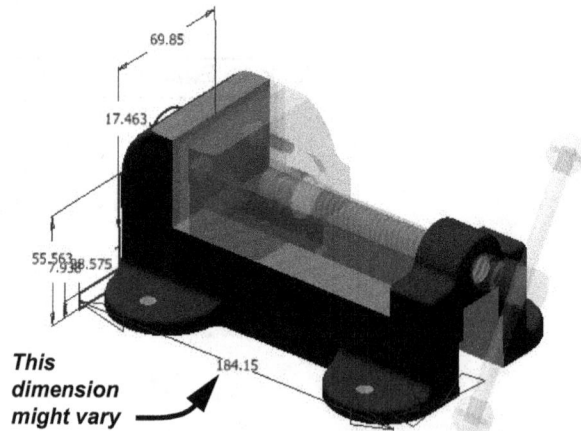

Figure 14–13

6. Double-click on **Vise.iam** to return to the top level assembly.

7. Expand the Base component in the Model Browser, if required, and select each constraint one by one. Note the references that are used for the constraints because they must be redefined after the iPart of Base replaces this component.

8. In the Model Browser, right-click on **Screw_Sub:1** and select **Open** to open the subassembly in a separate window, as shown on the left in Figure 14–14. The **Vise_Screw:1** part, shown on its own on the right, is the other component that needs to vary in length. Because this part needs to vary, it must also be converted to an iPart and replace the original component in the subassembly. Also, keep in mind that the **Screw-Sub** subassembly needs to be converted to an iAssembly because one of its components, **Vise_Screw**, will vary.

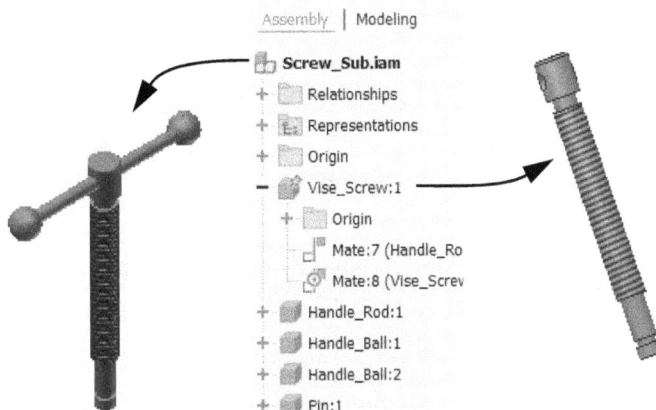

Figure 14–14

9. Select each Mate constraint in the Model Browser for **Vise_Screw:1** to understand how the part is constrained in the assembly. These two Mate constraints must be redefined after the component is replaced with its iPart.

10. Close all windows except **Vise.iam**.

Task 2 - Convert the Base part into an iPart.

In this task, you convert the Base part into an iPart because the component must vary in length.

1. In the Model Browser, right-click on **Base:1** and select **Open** to open the Base in a separate window.

2. In the *Manage* tab>Author panel, click (Create iPart). The iPart Author dialog box opens, as shown in Figure 14–15. You should rename the parameters you use as attributes in your iParts for easy recognition. In addition, any renamed parameters are automatically added as attributes.

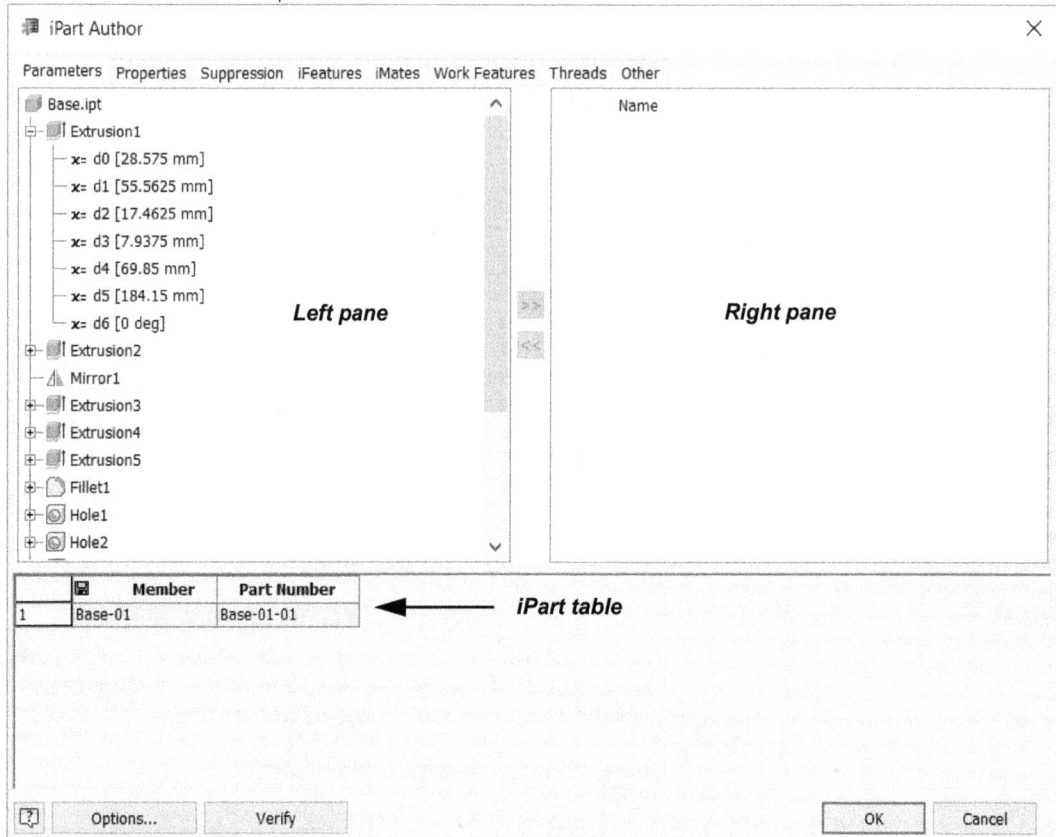

Figure 14–15

The other tabs contain additional attributes that you can add to an iPart.

3. Under **Extrusion1**, select **d5 [184.15 mm]** from the left pane and click >> . The dimension is added to the right pane and to the iPart table, as shown in Figure 14–16.

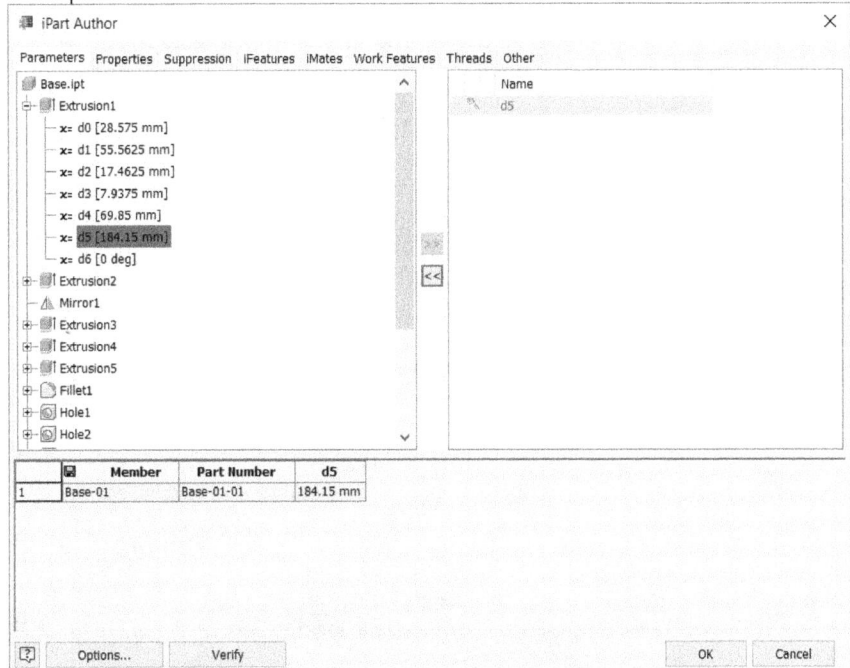

Figure 14–16

4. Right-click on the first row in the iPart table and select **Insert Row**, as shown in Figure 14–17. A new row is added into the table.

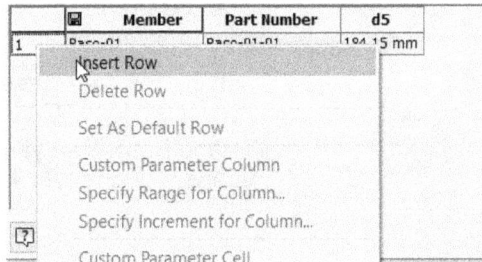

Figure 14–17

5. Right-click on the second row and insert another row into the table. The iPart table displays as shown in Figure 14–18. Three rows display in the table and each row is a member of the iPart Factory.

🖫	Member	Part Number	d5
1	Base-01	Base-01-01	184.15 mm
2	Base-02	Base-01-02	184.15 mm
3	Base-03	Base-01-03	184.15 mm

Figure 14–18

6. Select the cell for member Base-01 in the *d5* column and type **164.15 mm**. Press <Enter> to accept the change.

7. Change the cell for member Base-03 in the *d5* column to **204.15 mm**.

8. Change the other cells to match the table shown in Figure 14–19. Click **OK** if prompted with *A Member name has been modified, which will alter the Filename of the member.* This message warns you that the file name of the member you are modifying has changed. The row highlighted is the default member that is used.

	🖫 Member	Part Number	d5
1	Base-short	Base-short	164.15 mm
2	Base-medium	Base-medium	184.15 mm
3	Base-long	Base-long	204.15 mm

Figure 14–19

9. Select the row with the value 184.15 in the *d5* column, right-click, and select **Set As Default Row**.

10. Click **Verify** to ensure that all the cell values are valid. Any cells that contain invalid entries display in yellow. All the cells should be valid.

11. Click **OK** to finish creating the iPart. This iPart Factory contains three members called **Base-short**, **Base-medium**, and **Base-long**. The three members differ only in length.

Task 3 - Test the Base iPart.

Test the Base iPart you created to ensure that the different members behave as required.

1. In the Model Browser, expand **Table**. Double-click on the **Base-short** member. The part should display shorter.

2. Double-click on **Base-long**. The part should display even longer.

3. Switch back to **Base-short**.

Task 4 - Save the Base iPart and switch back to the assembly.

---

1. Save the **Base** iPart and close the window.

2. Activate the vise assembly window if it is not already active.

3. In the Quick Access Toolbar, click ![icon] (Local Update) if it is available. Note the icon in the Model Browser next to **Base:1** now displays as ![icon]. This indicates that the iPart Factory is being referenced; however, none of the actual members are being used. To reference an iPart Factory member, you must use the **Replace** option to replace the Factory with one of its members. Recall that if an iPart Factory is used in an assembly, the Table Replace attribute is not available for use if the assembly is converted to an iAssembly. The replacement is performed in a later step.

4. Save the **Vise** assembly and accept to saving the Base part if prompted.

Task 5 - Convert the Vise_Screw part into an iPart.

In this task, you convert the **Vise_Screw** part into an iPart because the component must vary in length.

1. Open the **Vise_Screw** part, which is located in the **Screw_Sub** subassembly, in a separate window.

2. In the *Manage* tab>Author panel, click ![icon] (Create iPart). The iPart Author dialog box opens and two attributes are automatically added to the right pane and iPart table. The two parameter attributes are automatically added because the parameters were renamed in the part. In this case, the **thread_length** parameter does not need to be included as an attribute in the iPart table.

3. Select the **thread_length** parameter attribute in the right pane and click ![icon] to remove the **thread_length** attribute.

4. Insert two more rows in the iPart table and change the values to display as shown in Figure 14–20. If the prompt *A Member name has been modified, which will alter the Filename of the member* displays, click **OK**. This iPart Factory contains three members called **Vise_Screw-short**, **Vise_Screw-medium**, and **Vise_Screw-long**. The three members differ only in length.

	🖫	Member	Part Number	vise_screw_length
1		Vise_Screw-short	Vise_Screw-short	138.75 mm
2		Vise_Screw-medium	Vise_Screw-medium	158.75 mm
3		Vise_Screw-long	Vise_Screw-long	178.75 mm

Figure 14–20

5. Click **Verify** to ensure that cell values are valid.

6. Click **OK** to finish creating the iPart.

7. Test the **Vise_Screw** iPart to ensure that the length increases as you switch from the first member to the last member in the table.

8. Switch back to **Vise_Screw-short**.

9. Save and close the iPart.

10. Activate the **Vise.iam** window if it is not already active.

11. Update the model, if required. The icon next to

    Vise_Screw:1 is , indicating that the iPart factory is referenced instead of an iPart member.

12. Save the Vise assembly and agree to saving **Screw_Sub.iam** and **Vise_Screw.ipt**, if prompted.

Task 6 - Replace the Vise_Screw Factory with one of its members.

In this task, you replace the **Vise_Screw:1** with a member of the **Vise_Screw** iPart Factory to be able to switch between the members of the Factory when you create an iAssembly for the subassembly.

1. Open the **Screw_Sub** subassembly in a separate window.

2. In the Model Browser, right-click on **Vise_Screw** and select **Component>Replace**. The Open dialog box opens.

3. Select **Vise_Screw.ipt** from the *iAssembly* subdirectory, and click **Open**. The Place Standard iPart dialog box opens, as shown in Figure 14–21. Use this dialog box to select which member from the iPart Factory you want to place. Each tab displays the same iPart Factory members and their attribute values in a different format. Therefore, only one tab needs to be used to select the required member. Use the tab that presents the iPart Factory member information in a way that you can easily select the required member.

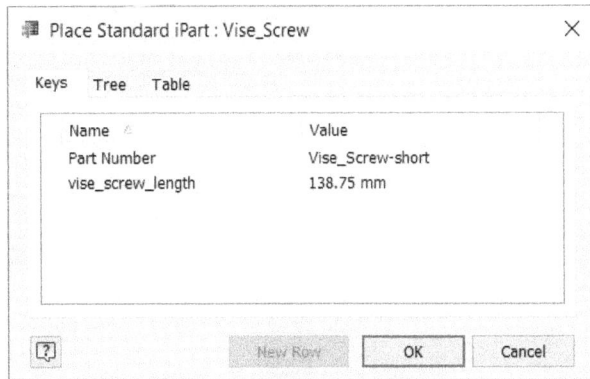

Figure 14–21

4. Leave the default member, **Vise_Screw-short**, with a vise-screw length of 138.75 mm as the one to be placed and click **OK**.

5. The error dialog box opens. Expand the information, as shown in Figure 14–22. Click ➕ in the error dialog box. Click **Yes** to accept the changes and start recovering. The Design Doctor dialog box opens, indicating that Mate:8 has undefined geometry.

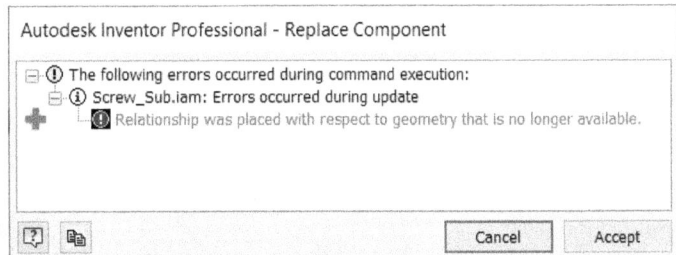

Figure 14–22

6. Select **Mate:8** and click **Next** twice to reach the treatment selection screen.

7. With **Edit** selected from the list of treatments, click **Finish**. The Edit Constraint dialog box opens. Only one reference is missing. The existing reference is an axis, highlighted in green on your screen, as shown in Figure 14–23.

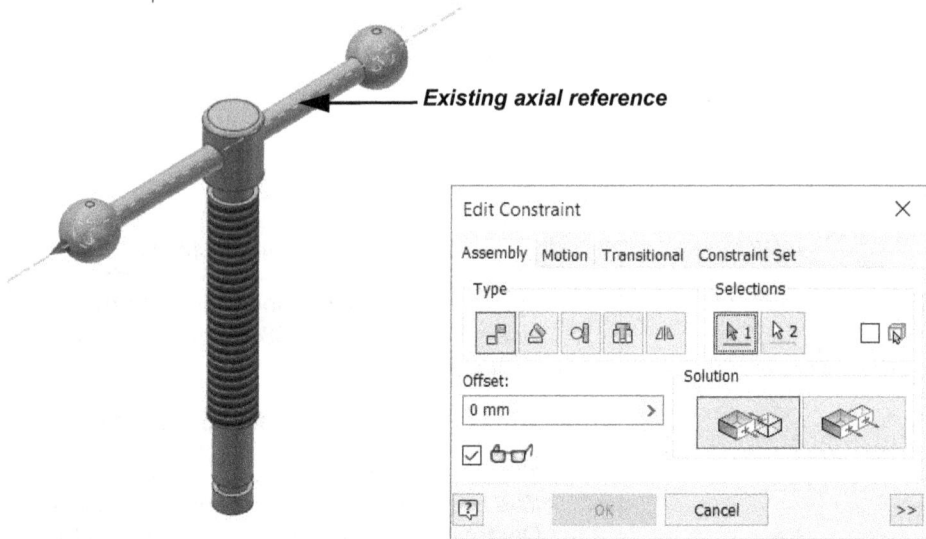

Figure 14–23

8. Select the axial reference shown in Figure 14–24 and click **OK** to apply the constraint.

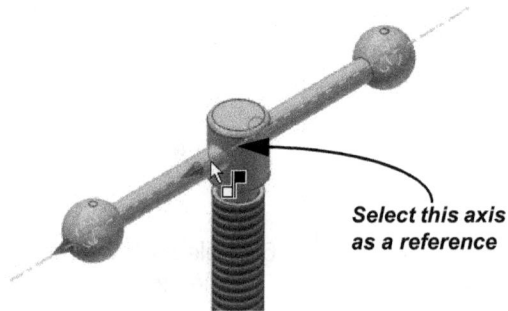

Figure 14–24

9. A new component now displays in place of **Vise_Screw:1**, as shown in Figure 14–25. The newly replaced component is a member of the iPart Factory and the Model Browser displays the member's name. The icon next to it indicates that the component is a member of an iPart Factory that is grounded.

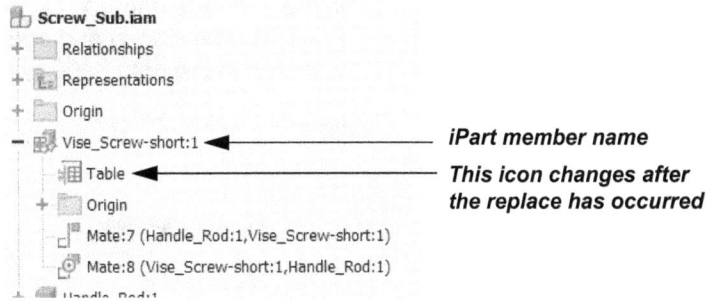

Figure 14–25

10. Save the subassembly.

Task 7 - Convert the Screw_Sub subassembly into an iAssembly.

The **Screw_Sub** subassembly needs to be converted to an iAssembly because it contains a **Vise_Screw** iPart member, which you want to be able to vary in the top-level assembly.

1. In the **Screw_Sub.iam** window, in the *Manage* tab>Author panel, click ![i+] (Create iAssembly). The iAssembly Author dialog box opens as shown in Figure 14–26 and is similar to the iPart Author dialog box.

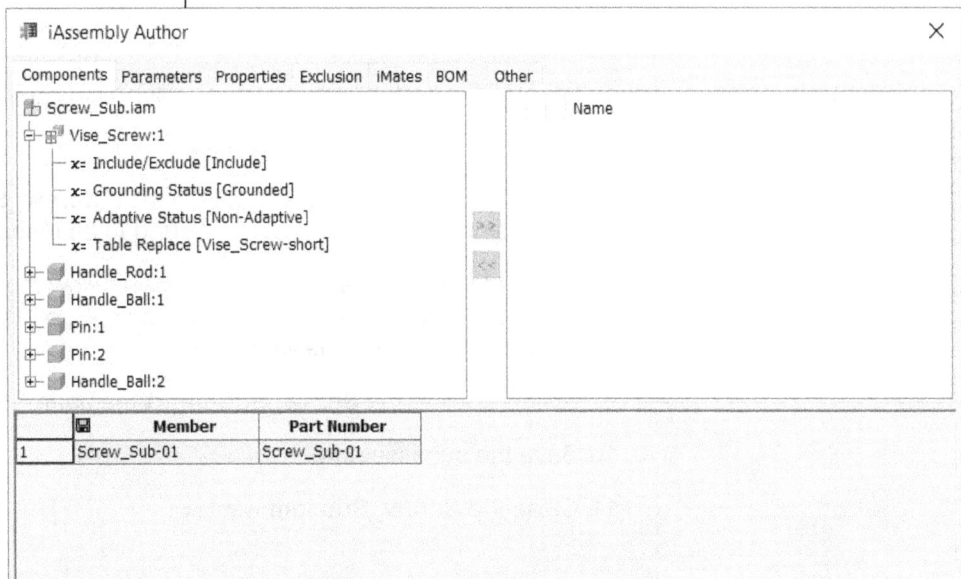

Figure 14–26

2. In the left pane under **Vise_Screw:1**, select **Table Replace [Vise_Screw-short]** and add it as an attribute. The attribute is added to the right pane and as a column in the table.

3. Insert two rows below the first row, as shown in Figure 14–27.

💾	Member	Part Number	Vise_Screw:1: Table Replace
1	Screw_Sub-01	Screw_Sub-01	Vise_Screw-short
2	Screw_Sub-02	Screw_Sub-02	Vise_Screw-short
3	Screw_Sub-03	Screw_Sub-03	Vise_Screw-short

Figure 14–27

4. For the **Screw_Sub-02** member, select the cell under the *Vise_Screw:1:Table Replace* column. Use the drop-down list and select **Vise_Screw-medium**.

5. For the **Screw_Sub-03** member, change the *Vise_Screw:1: Table Replace* attribute value to **Vise_Screw-long**.

6. Change the other cells to display as shown in Figure 14–28. If the prompt *A Member name has been modified, which will alter the Filename of the member* displays, click **OK**.

💾	Member	Part Number	Vise_Screw:1: Table Replace
1	Screw_Sub-short	Screw_Sub-short	Vise_Screw-short
2	Screw_Sub-medium	Screw_Sub-medium	Vise_Screw-medium
3	Screw_Sub-long	Screw_Sub-long	Vise_Screw-long

Figure 14–28

7. Verify the table values and click **OK**. The **Screw_Sub** subassembly has now been converted to an iAssembly.

8. In the Model Browser, expand **Table** and view the difference between the three members of the Screw-Sub iAssembly Factory by switching between them.

9. Switch back to the **Screw_Sub-short** member.

10. Save the subassembly.

11. Close the **Screw_Sub.iam** window.

Task 8 - Update the Vise assembly with the changes to the Screw_Sub subassembly.

1. Activate the **Vise.iam** window if it is not already active.

2. Update the Vise assembly. The error dialog box opens. Expand the information as shown in Figure 14–29.

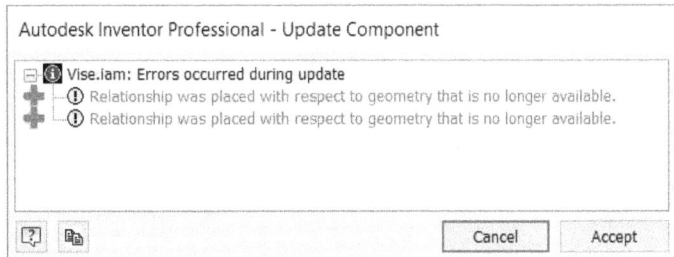

Autodesk Inventor Professional - Update Component

☐ ⓘ Vise.iam: Errors occurred during update
    └─ⓘ Relationship was placed with respect to geometry that is no longer available.
    └─ⓘ Relationship was placed with respect to geometry that is no longer available.

Cancel   Accept

Figure 14–29

3. Click ✚ at the top in the Error dialog box and click **Yes** to accept the changes and fix the missing reference.

4. With **Insert:9** highlighted, click **Next** twice to reach the treatment selection screen.

5. With **Edit** selected from the list of treatments, click **Finish**. The Edit Constraint dialog box opens.

6. Select the axial reference shown in Figure 14–30.

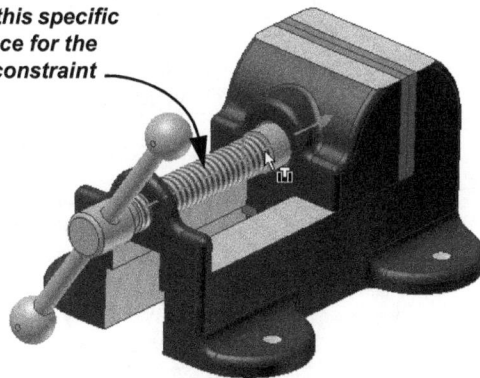

Select this specific reference for the Insert constraint

Figure 14–30

7. Click **OK**.

8. In the Place/Edit Constraint dialog box, click **Accept the relationship**.

9. Click ✚ (Design Doctor) in the Quick Access Toolbar to open the Design Doctor dialog box.

10. Click **Next** twice to reach the treatment selection screen.

11. Select the **Isolate and Edit** option from the list of treatments and click **Finish**. The Edit Constraint dialog box opens and only the **Screw_Sub** subassembly is visible because it was isolated.

12. Select the axial reference shown in Figure 14–31 and click **OK**.

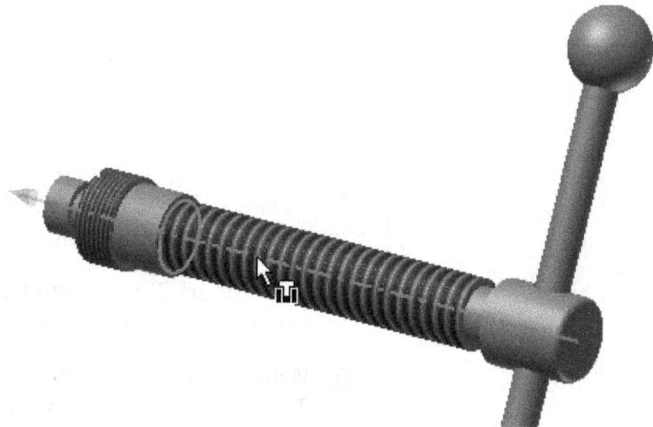

Figure 14–31

13. Right-click in the graphics window and select **Undo Isolate** to display all components in the assembly. If the other components still do not display, manually toggle on their visibility.

14. In the Model Browser, look at the icon next to the

   Screw_Sub-short:1 subassembly. It now displays as ⊞, indicating that the component is a member of the **Screw_Sub** iAssembly and not the Factory.

15. Save the **Vise** assembly as well as the **Screw_Sub-short** and **Screw_Sub** subassemblies, if prompted.

Task 9 - Replace Base:1 with a member of the Base iPart Factory.

The last component that needs to be replaced is **Base:1**.

1. With the Vise assembly window active, in the Model Browser, right-click on **Base:1** and select **Component>Replace**.

2. In the Place Component dialog box, select **Base.ipt** and click **Open**. The Place Standard iPart dialog box opens.

3. In the *Keys* tab, select **164.15 mm** to expand the list of available values, as shown in Figure 14–32.

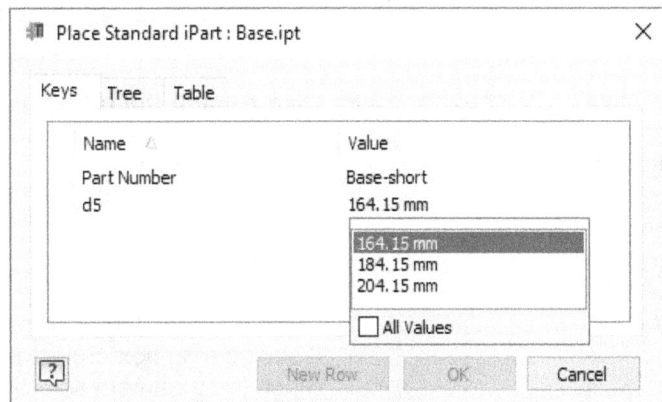

Figure 14–32

4. Select **164.15 mm** from the list to leave it as the member to place.

5. Click **OK** to complete the replacement. The error dialog box opens.

6. Expand the error. Click ✚ at the top in the Error dialog box and click **Yes** to accept the changes and start the **Recover** option.

In the next steps you will fix the missing references using the **Isolate and Edit** treatment option to redefine each constraint that contains undefined geometry. The references you need to select are shown in the following steps.

7. Select **Mate:4** and click **Next** twice to reach the treatment selection screen. Select the **Isolate and Edit** treatment option and click **Finish**.

8. For the **Mate:4** constraint, select the reference shown in Figure 14–33 and click **OK**.

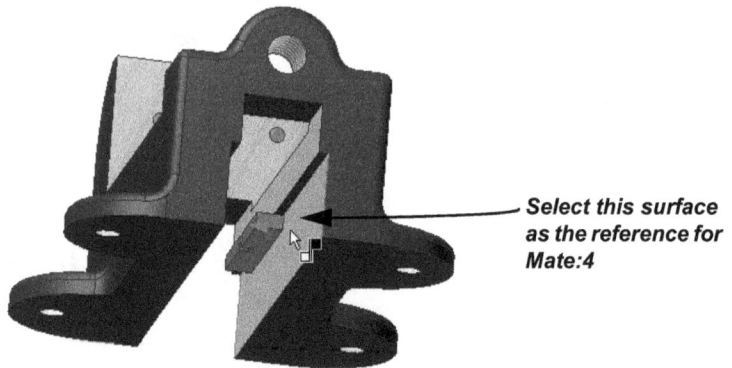

Select this surface as the reference for Mate:4

Figure 14–33

Alternatively, you could leave the visibility of the other components toggled off since the only references you need to select are on the Base-short component.

9. Click **Accept the relationship** in the Place/Edit Constraint dialog box.

10. To make all components visible before continuing to redefine the next constrain, right-click on the graphics window, and select **Undo Isolate**.

11. Click ✚ in the Quick Access Toolbar to open the Design Doctor dialog box. Select **Mate:2** and click **Next** twice to reach the treatment selection screen. Select the **Isolate and Edit** treatment option and click **Finish**.

12. For the **Mate:2** constraint, select the reference shown in Figure 14–34 and click **OK** to complete the constraint.

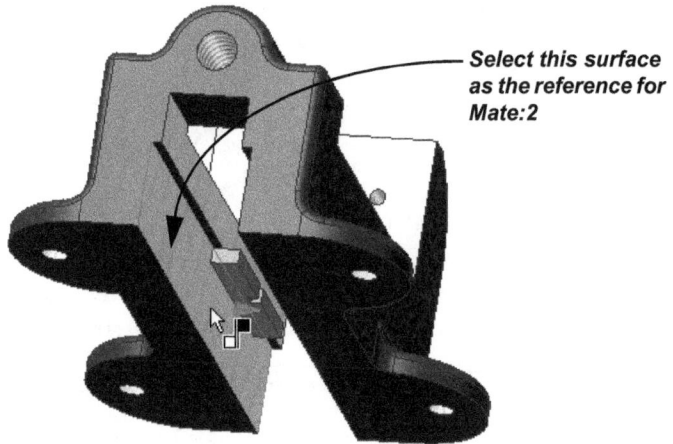

Select this surface as the reference for Mate:2

Figure 14–34

13. Click **Accept the relationship** in the Place/Edit Constraint dialog box.

14. To make all components visible again before continuing to redefine the next constraint, right-click on the graphics window, and select **Undo Isolate**.

15. Alternatively, in the Model Browser, expand the **Base-short:1** node, right-click on **Insert:2**, and select **Recover** to access the Design Doctor. Progress to the treatment selection screen. Select the **Isolate and Edit** treatment option and click **Finish**.

16. Select the reference shown in Figure 14–35 and click **OK** to complete the constraint.

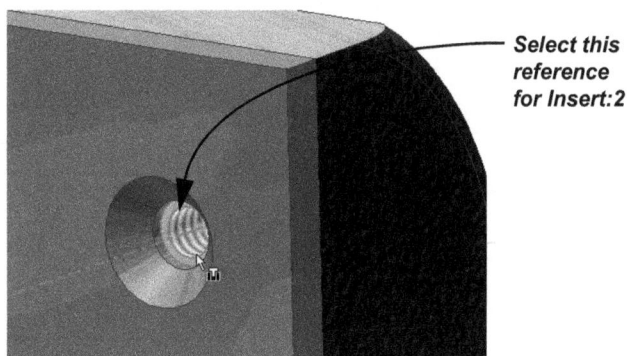

Select this
reference
for Insert:2

Figure 14–35

17. In the Place/Edit Constraint dialog box, click **Accept the relationship**.

18. Because **Jaw_Plate:2** is used as a reference for both the **Insert:2** and **Insert:1** constraints, you do not need to use the **Undo Isolate** option. You can continue directly into the **Recover** option to edit the **Insert:1** constraint. This time, you can select **Edit** instead of **Isolate and Edit** from the list of treatments.

19. Select the reference shown in Figure 14–36 and click **OK** to complete the constraint.

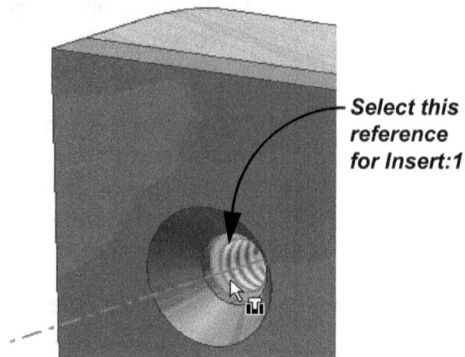

Select this reference for Insert:1

Figure 14–36

20. In the Place/Edit Constraint dialog box, click **Accept the relationship**.

21. In the Model Browser, right-click on **Flush:2** and recover the missing reference.

22. Select the reference shown in Figure 14–37 and click **OK** to complete the constraint.

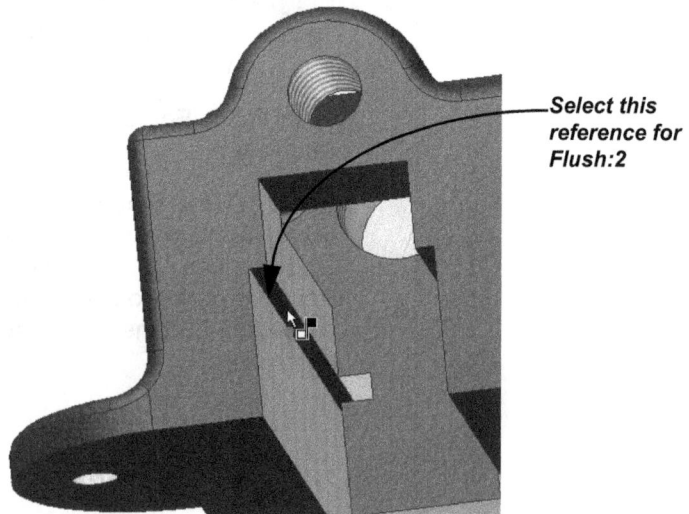

Select this reference for Flush:2

Figure 14–37

23. In the Place/Edit Constraint dialog box, click **Accept the relationship**.

24. In the Model Browser, right-click on **Flush:1** and recover the missing reference.

25. Select the reference shown in Figure 14–38 and click **OK** to complete the constraint. The errors should no longer display because all the constraints with undefined geometry have been redefined.

Select this reference for Flush:1 ──

Figure 14–38

26. Use the **Undo Isolate** option to toggle on the visibility of all components.

27. Save the Vise assembly.

Task 10 - Convert the Vise assembly into an iAssembly.

---

1. With the Vise assembly window active, in the *Manage* tab> Author panel, click [i+] (Create iAssembly).

2. Select the **Table Replace [Base-short]** attribute under **Base:1** and click [>>] add it to the table.

3. Expand **Screw_Sub:1** in the left pane, select the **Table Replace [Screw_Sub-short]** attribute, and click [>>] to add it to the table.

4. Right-click on the *Vise-01* row and select **Insert Row** to add a row to the table. Repeat to insert a third row to the table.

5. Modify the iAssembly table to display as shown in Figure 14–39. Click **OK** if prompted with *A Member name has been modified, which will alter the Filename of the member.*

	💾 Member	Part Number	Base:1: Table Replace	Screw_Sub:1: Table Replace
1	Vise-short	Vise-short	Base-short	Screw_Sub-short
2	Vise-medium	Vise-medium	Base-medium	Screw_Sub-medium
3	Vise-long	Vise-long	Base-long	Screw_Sub-long

Figure 14–39

6. Verify the iAssembly table values and click **OK** to complete the iAssembly definition.

7. Switch to each iAssembly member to view the change in the assembly. The length of both the **Vise_Screw** and **Base** should change.

8. Save the Vise assembly.

Chapter Review Questions

1. If you have a part in a subassembly that is going to vary, what would you need to do before creating an iAssembly of the top-level assembly? (Select all that apply.)

   a. Convert the part to an iPart.

   b. Add iMates to the part.

   c. Add iFeature to the part.

   d. Convert the subassembly to an iAssembly.

   e. Add iMates to the assembly.

2. Which of the following occurs when a subassembly is replaced with an iAssembly version of the same component? (Select all that apply.)

   a. Constraint references are lost and must be reassigned.

   b. The Model Browser icon for the component updates to reflect that it is an iAssembly.

   c. An iAssembly is automatically created in the top-level assembly.

   d. The iAssembly is marked as adaptive.

3. What causes cells in the iAssembly Author dialog box to be red?

   a. Invalid text entries

   b. Missing part

   c. Formulas

   d. Failed constraints

4. In the iAssembly Author dialog box, clicking **Verify** might result in the cells displaying in yellow. What does the yellow color indicate?

   a. Invalid text entries

   b. Missing part

   c. Formulas

   d. Failed constraints

5. When placing an iAssembly into a top-level assembly, which tab should be selected to view the iAssembly instances in the cell format similar to how the iAssembly was created?

   a. *Key* tab

   b. *Tree* tab

   c. *Table* tab

6. Which option adds a new component to only that instance of an iAssembly?

   a. **Edit Factory Scope**

   b. **Edit Member Scope**

Command Summary

Button	Command	Location
	Create iAssembly/iPart	• **Ribbon:** *Manage* tab>Author panel
	Edit Factory Scope	• **Ribbon:** *Assemble* tab> iPart/iAssembly panel • **Ribbon:** *Manage* tab> Author panel
	Edit Member Scope	• **Ribbon:** *Assemble* tab> iPart/iAssembly panel • **Ribbon:** *Manage* tab> Author panel
	Local Update	• **Quick Access Toolbar**
	Place	• **Ribbon:** *Assemble* tab>Component panel

Frame Generator

Frame Generator enables you to quickly and easily create the members (parts) in a structural framework. The frame members that are created have predefined cross-sections in the Autodesk® Inventor® software. The frame members are generated based on 2D and 3D sketched geometry in a skeleton part model that is assembled into a top-level assembly.

Learning Objectives in This Chapter

- Quickly and easily create structural frames, using a skeletal wireframe part to define the location of structural frame members.
- Adjust frame member ends to obtain required joints.
- Create and publish custom frame member profiles to the Content Center.

15.1 Frame Generator

The Frame Generator quickly and easily creates structural frames, such as those used in machines, fixtures, platforms, access ways, and stairwells. To define the location of structural frame members, a skeletal wireframe part is used (consisting of 2D sketches, 3D sketches, edges, and vertices). An example of a structural frame with its generated members is shown in Figure 15–1. Any changes made to the skeletal wireframe part automatically update the associated frame members.

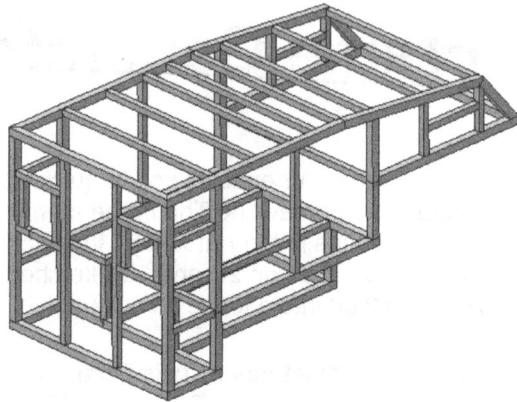

Figure 15–1

General Steps

Use the following general steps to add structural frame members:

1. Create a skeletal model.
2. Insert the skeletal model into an assembly.
3. Start the insertion of the first frame member.
4. Define the Frame Member Selection options.
5. Define the Placement method and reference(s).
6. Define the Orientation options.
7. Apply the frame member definition.
8. Insert additional members, as required.
9. Reuse members, as required.
10. Adjust frame member definition, as required.
11. Adjust frame member ends, as required.

Step 1 - Create a skeletal model.

Create a skeletal part model (using 2D and 3D sketches) to use as a reference for defining the location of the structural frame members. A sketch can contain linear entities, splines, construction lines and other entities. A sample skeletal model for a truck camper is shown in Figure 15–2.

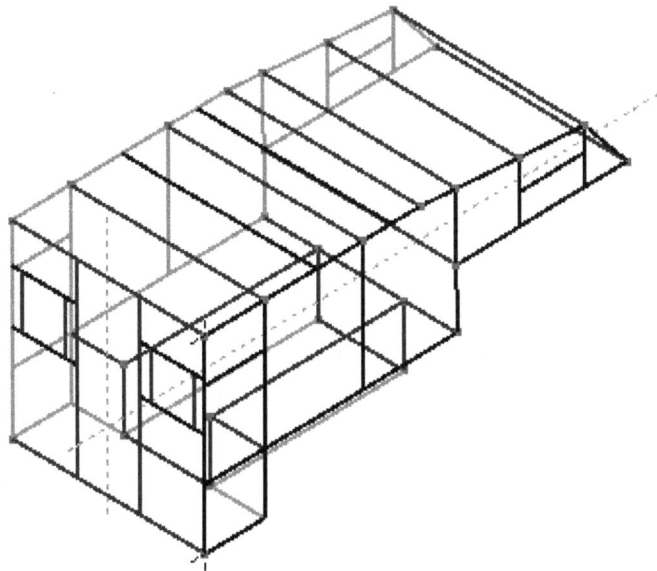

Figure 15–2

Step 2 - Insert the skeletal model into an assembly.

Create a new assembly or use an existing assembly and place the skeletal model in the assembly. Save the assembly.

Step 3 - Start the insertion of the first frame member.

In the *Design* tab>Frame panel, click ⬚ (Insert Frame). The Insert Frame palette opens, as shown in Figure 15–3.

Figure 15–3

Step 4 - Define the Frame Member Selection options.

Use the drop-down lists in the *Frame Member* area to define the following options:

- Frame category (Category drop-down list).
- Engineering standard (Standard drop-down list).

- Profile type (Family drop-down list)
- Size (Size drop-down list).
- Material style to apply (Material Style drop-down list).
- Appearance to apply (Appearance drop-down list). Use the **As Material** option to display the color style of the material.

Step 5 - Define the Placement method and reference(s).

The Placement reference(s) for new frame members are defined, by default, by selecting edges of solid bodies and lines, arcs, or splines from 2D and 3D sketches. Using this placement method, you can create multiple frame members at the same time using a window selection or right-clicking in the main window to change selection method to **Multi Select**, **Chain Select**, or **Sketch Select**.

*If multiple members share the same end points, you can merge them by selecting the **Merge Frame Members** option in the Frame Member area.*

As an alternative to selecting edges and entities, you can select

(Specify frame location by two points) to define the placement references by selecting a start and end point. Only a single member can be created at a time using this method.

As soon as the reference is selected, the entity reference is listed in the *Input Geometry* area and a shaded preview of the new frame member appears in the graphics window.

- Only select entities that will have the same member properties.
- The selection location on an entity can affect the orientation. The (Flip Direction) option in the *Input Geometry* area can be used to flip the member, if needed.

Step 6 - Define the Orientation options.

The orientation and position of the frame member can be manipulated to control how the member will be located on the reference.

- To define the position of the new frame member, zoom in on the frame member preview to display the white in-canvas grips. You can zoom using your traditional methods with the mouse or Navigation Bar or you can use the Zoom options at the top of the Insert Frame palette. The zoom options enable you to zoom and orient the view perpendicularly (🔍) or zoom in while maintaining the same view orientation (⊕). Click 🔍 to return to the previous view orientation. By selecting a grip, you define the profile's position with respect to the frame member's placement reference (the edge, line, arc, or spline selected to define the location of the frame member), as shown in Figure 15–4.

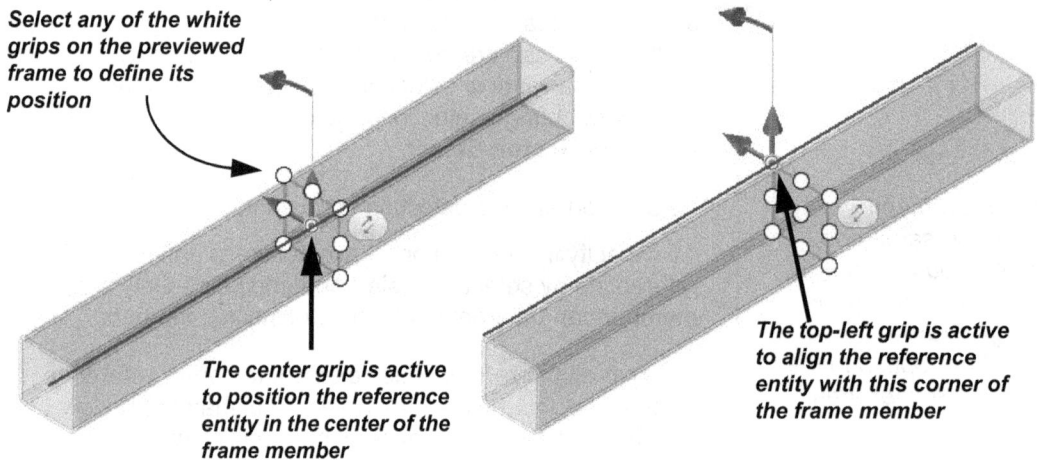

Select any of the white grips on the previewed frame to define its position

The center grip is active to position the reference entity in the center of the frame member

The top-left grip is active to align the reference entity with this corner of the frame member

Figure 15–4

- To define the location and orientation of the frame member relative to the placement reference, you can define offset and rotation values. These values can be assigned either directly in the *Orientation* area of the palette or by selecting grips on the frame member's preview, as shown in Figure 15–5.

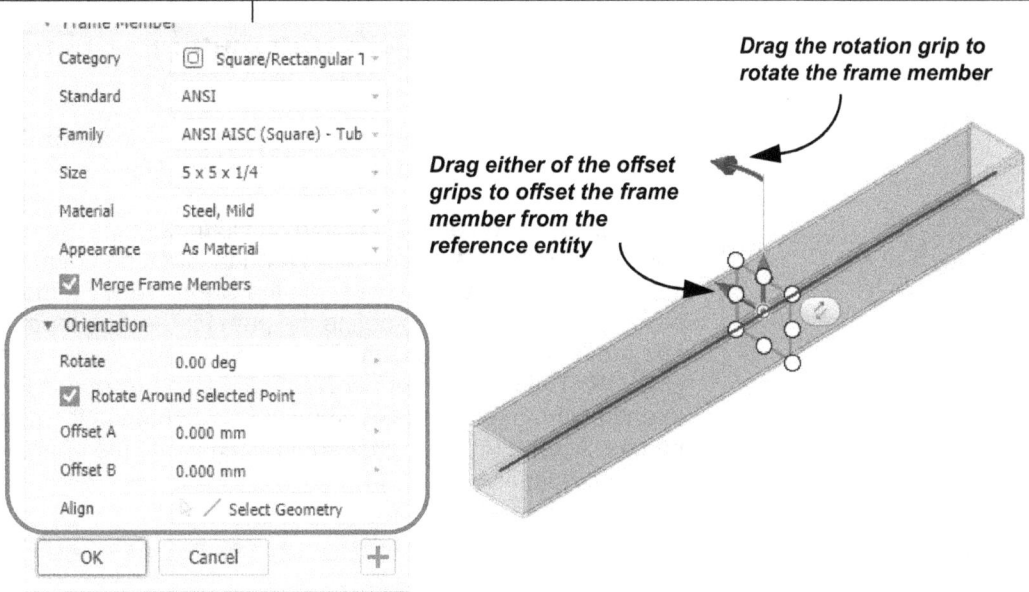

Category Square/Rectangular 1
Standard ANSI
Family ANSI AISC (Square) - Tub
Size 5 x 5 x 1/4
Material Steel, Mild
Appearance As Material
☑ Merge Frame Members

▼ Orientation
Rotate 0.00 deg
☑ Rotate Around Selected Point
Offset A 0.000 mm
Offset B 0.000 mm
Align ⟋ Select Geometry

OK Cancel +

Drag the rotation grip to rotate the frame member

Drag either of the offset grips to offset the frame member from the reference entity

Figure 15–5

- The **Rotate Around Selected Point** option is available in the *Orientation* area and enables you to control how the rotate/offset values are measured. With the option selected, the offset grips maintain alignment with the model coordinate system; with the option disabled, the offset grips maintain alignment with the frame member, as shown in Figure 15–6.

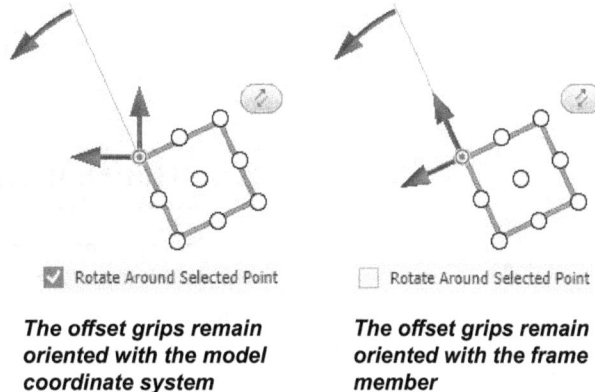

☑ Rotate Around Selected Point   ☐ Rotate Around Selected Point

The offset grips remain oriented with the model coordinate system   *The offset grips remain oriented with the frame member*

Figure 15–6

- The *Align* field enables you to select geometry to align frames instead of entering a rotation angle. You can select a planar face, view edge, work axis, work plane, or sketch line.

Step 7 - Apply the frame member definition.

Once the frame member is defined, click ⊞ (Apply) or **OK** to insert the first frame member into the model. Using the

⊞ (Apply) option enables you to continue creating members once the first has been created. When the first member is created, you will be presented with the Create New Frame dialog box. This enables you to define the path for the new members and the name of the assembly and skeleton file. Once defined, click **OK**. The Frame Member Naming dialog box opens for you to enter filenames. Click **OK** when finished entering the required names. A new part file is created for each frame member, even if some are identical.

Step 8 - Insert additional members, as required.

If the ⊞ (Apply) option was used, you can continue to insert frame members. The *Placement* field is automatically cleared, allowing for a new selection, and the *Frame Member* maintains the same options that were used when the previous frame member was placed. You can manually change these options, if

needed, or you can use the ⚲ (Property Eye Dropper) to copy the properties from another existing frame member.

Define additional frame members, as required. Once finished inserting and applying new frame members, click **Cancel**.

Step 9 - Reuse members, as required.

To reduce the number of files that are created, you can reuse any members that are identical (i.e., the same size, length, end conditions, etc.).

*The **Reuse** command is not available for curved members.*

How To: Reuse Identical Members

1. In the *Design* tab>Frame panel, click ⬚ (Reuse). The Reuse palette opens, as shown in Figure 15–7.

Properties × +	≡
Reuse	
No Preset	⌄ + ⚙
Zoom	⊖ ⊕ ⊖
▼ Source Frame Member	
Frame Me...	⬚ 🗐 Frame Member ⚠
▼ Reused Frame Member	
Placement	⚠ ⋅ ⸜ ⸝
Appearance	As Material
▼ Orientation	
Rotate	0.00 deg
	Rotate around selected value
Offset A	0.000 mm
Offset B	0.000 mm
Align	
OK	Cancel

Figure 15–7

2. Select an existing member that is to be reused. The selection can be made in the graphics window or in the Model Browser. Once selected, the member is identified in the *Source Frame Member* area.

3. The *Placement* field activates in the *Reused Frame Member* area. By default, you can select edges and entities. To define the reused member between two points, click ⸜ (Specify frame location by two points) and select points to locate the new reused member.

   - The member can only be located on an identical placement reference. Only entities that produce an identical member are selectable.
   - To select multiple identical placement references at the same time, select them individually or drag a window around the model. Multiple references cannot be assigned if the new reused member is defined between two points.

> **Hint: Member Selection**
>
> When selecting members to reuse, the selection location on the entity affects the orientation of the new member. The orientation can be edited once placed using the **Change Reuse** command.

4. By default, the Orientation settings are assumed to be the same as those used when the source member was added. However, the location of the selection can also affect the orientation. You can use the **Change Reuse** command to change the selection once it has been placed, if required.

5. Click ⊞ (Apply) to add the new member and continue reusing the members in the model. Click **OK** to add the new member and close the dialog box.

Step 10 - Adjust frame member definition, as required.

Once frame members are inserted or are reused, there might be situations where they need to be edited.

Change

In the *Design* tab>Frame panel, click ⬚ (Change) to change the definition of a inserted (parent) frame member. The Change Frame palette presents the same options as the Insert Frame palette. Additionally, the grips are available on the frame to manipulate the orientation.

Multiple frame members can be changed at once by selecting them all at once. You can select them individually or draw a bounding box around them.

Once you have finished redefining, click ⊞ (Apply) to apply the changes and continue redefining additional frame members, or click **OK** to apply the changes and close the Change Frame palette.

Change Reuse

The **Change Reuse** command edits the geometry reference that was selected when the member was initially reused, or the reference's positional orientation settings. In the Frame panel, click ⬚ (Change Reuse) to open the Change Reuse palette. Select the member that you want to change and change the settings as required.

You can select frame members for change by selecting them individually or drawing a bounding box around them.

- Click ✑ (Reverse Member Direction) in the *Reused Frame Member* area to flip the direction of the member.

- Select new orientation and offset positions for where the member should be located with respect to the reference entity. This can be done on the model directly using the white grips and the offset and rotation grips, or by entering values in the *Orientation* area of the palette.

Step 11 - Adjust frame member ends, as required.

Once the frame members are added, you might need to adjust the frame member ends by using one or more of the following options:

- **Corner Joint**

- **Notch**

- **Lengthen/Shorten**

- **Miter**

- **Trim/Extend**

- **Remove End Treatments**

> **Hint: End Treatments for Reused Members**
>
> The end treatments that are used on members should be considered when deciding to reuse members. Any end treatment on a parent member is also applied to the reused member.

Corner Joint

The **Corner Joint** option lengthens or shortens two frame members to create a corner. The first selected frame member (highlighted in yellow) is trimmed or extended to the second intersecting face of the second selected frame member (highlighted in blue). The second frame member is trimmed or extended up to the first intersecting face of the first frame member.

How To: Use the Corner Joint Option

1. In the *Design* tab>Frame panel, click ⊤ (Corner Joint). The Corner Joint palette opens.
2. Select the first frame member (yellow) to be lengthened or shortened.
3. Select the second frame member (blue) to be lengthened or shortened to the first intersecting face of the first frame member (yellow). Figure 15–8 and Figure 15–9 show examples of the references and the resulting frame members.

Once both references are selected, a preview of the trim is displayed.

Frame A is selected as the Second reference

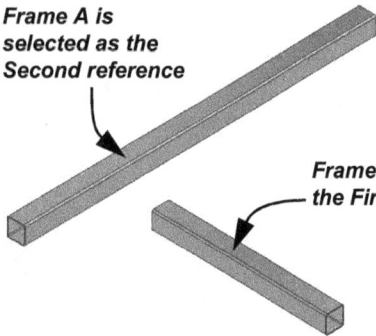

Frame B is selected as the First reference

Frame A is trimmed up to the first face of frame B

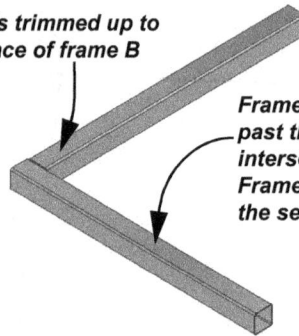

Frame B is extended past the first intersecting face of Frame A and stops at the second

Figure 15–8

Frame A is selected as the First reference

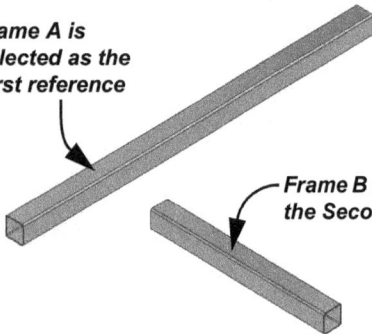

Frame B is selected as the Second reference

Frame A is extended past the first intersecting face of Frame B and stops at the second

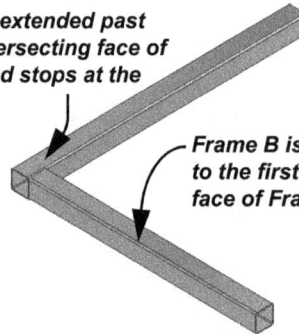

Frame B is trimmed up to the first intersecting face of Frame A

Figure 15–9

4. (Optional) Define an offset value for lengthening/shortening the first selected frame member.

- Specify a negative value to extend the first frame member (yellow) past the second intersecting face, as shown on the top of Figure 15–10.
- Specify a positive value to set the member back from the second intersecting face, as shown on the bottom of Figure 15–10.

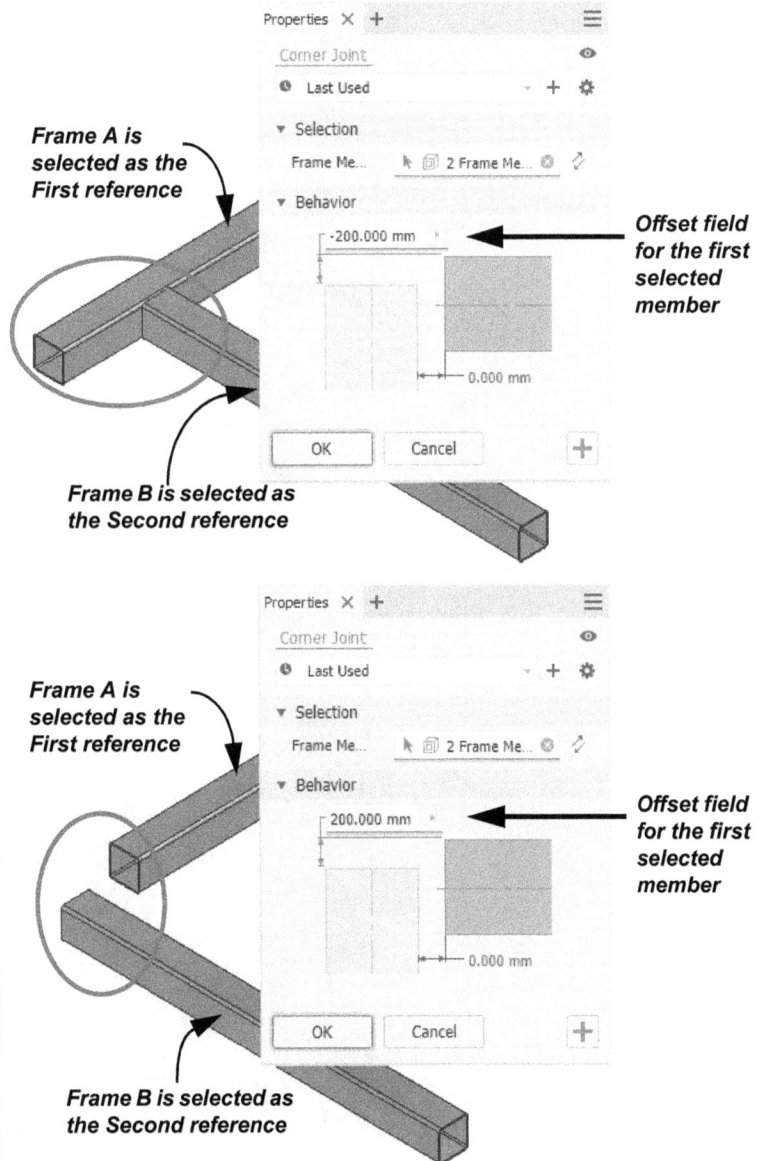

Frame A is selected as the First reference

Offset field for the first selected member

Frame B is selected as the Second reference

Frame A is selected as the First reference

Offset field for the first selected member

Frame B is selected as the Second reference

Figure 15–10

5. (Optional) Define an offset value for lengthening/shortening the second selected frame member.

- A positive value sets back the second frame member (blue) from the first intersecting face of the first frame member (yellow), as shown on the top of Figure 15–11.
- A negative value extends the second frame member (blue) past the first intersecting face of the first frame member (yellow), as shown on the bottom of Figure 15–11.

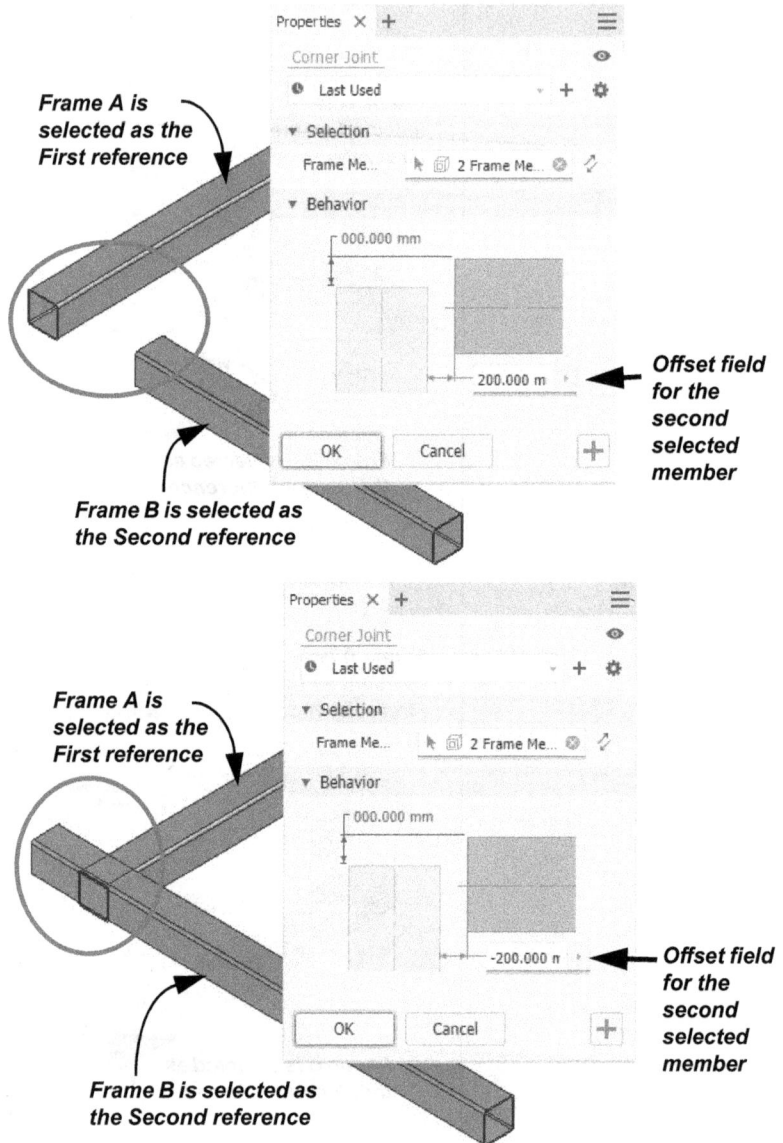

Figure 15–11

6. Click ⊞ (Apply) to apply the corner joint.
7. If the result needs to be modified, select the same references again and adjust the offset values, as required. Reapply the changes.
8. Perform the operation on other frame members, as required, and click **OK** when finished.

- The **Corner Joint** option can be used if the two selected references do not lie on the same plane. The members are still trimmed and extended to the planar faces as if they existed on the same plane.

Notch

Use the **Notch** option to cut a frame member using the shape, a custom template, or a custom notch profile on a second frame member, as shown in Figure 15–12.

Member used to cut the component (Notch Tool)

Frame member being cut

Member that was cut with the visibility of the other member off

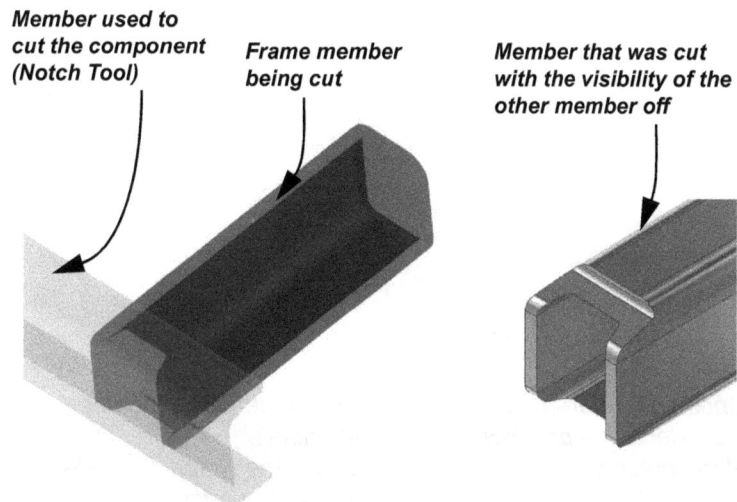

Figure 15–12

How To: Use the Notch Option

1. In the *Design* tab>Frame panel, click ⬜ (Notch). The Notch palette opens as shown in Figure 15–13.

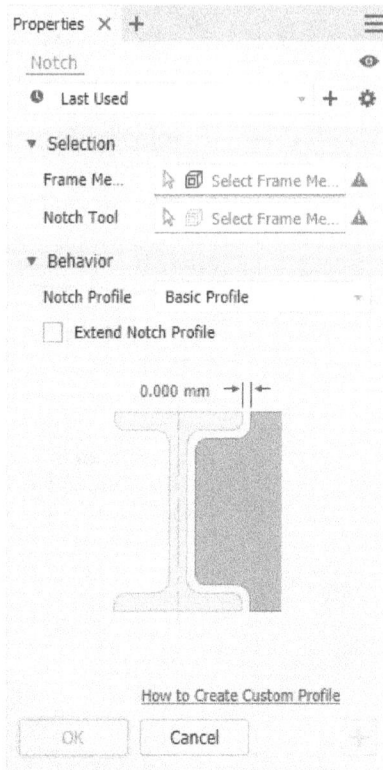

Figure 15–13

Once both references are selected, a preview of the notch is displayed.

2. Select the frame member(s) you want to cut (*Frame Member*).
3. Select the *Notch Tool* reference (frame member(s) to use as the cutting reference).

4. Depending on how the members intersect you will be provided with different options to define the notch profile. The options include the following:

   - **Basic Profile:** Set a single offset value between the two frame members. Enter values in the profile preview, as shown in Figure 15–14.
   - **Custom X Template:** Set multiple offset values. Enter values in the profile preview, as shown in Figure 15–15. The X represents the selected Category type.
   - **Custom Profile:** Use a custom notch profile that was previously saved in the Content Center. Figure 15–16 shows an example of a custom profile.

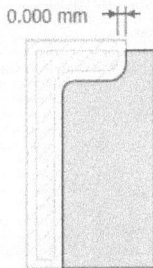

0.000 mm

Figure 15–14

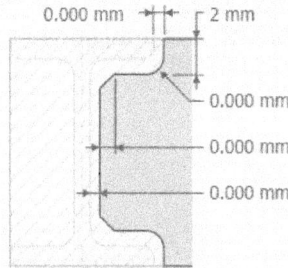

0.000 mm   2 mm

0.000 mm

0.000 mm

0.000 mm

Figure 15–15

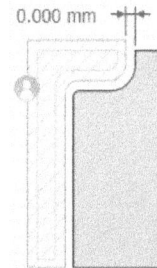

0.000 mm

Figure 15–16

5. Select the **Perpendicular Cut** option in the *Behavior* area to assign a perpendicular cut to the frame member. Figure 15–17 shows how this option can affect the resulting notch if it is enabled or not for a circular frame member.

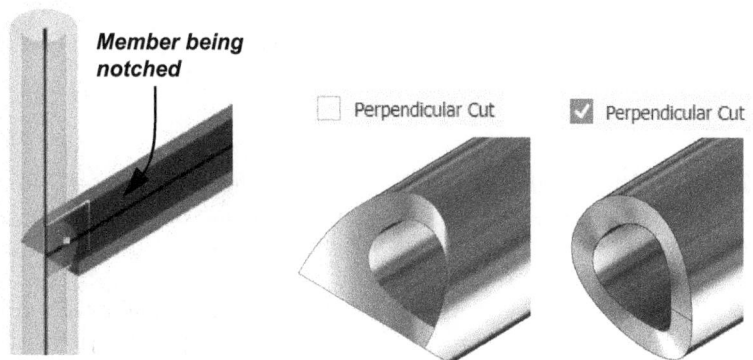

Member being notched

Perpendicular Cut

Perpendicular Cut

Figure 15–17

6. (Optional) Save the current notch settings as a preset that can be used to create future notches. Once all the Behavior settings have been defined, click + to save the preset. Click ⚙ to mange the preset settings.

7. Click ⊞ (Apply) to create the notch and continue creating additional notches or click **OK** to create the notch and close the Notch Properties palette.

Lengthen/Shorten Frame Member

Use the **Lengthen/Shorten** command to increase or decrease the length of a frame member.

How To: Lengthen or Shorten a Frame Member

1. In the *Design* tab>Frame panel, click ⊞ (Lengthen/ Shorten). The Lengthen/Shorten palette opens, as shown in Figure 15–18.

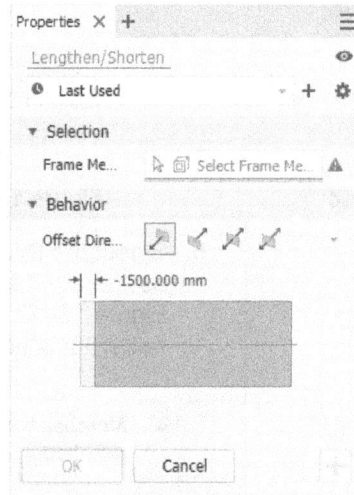

Figure 15–18

Once a frame member is selected, a preview of the lengthen/shorten operation is displayed.

2. Select the frame member(s) to lengthen/shorten.
3. Select any one of the following extension options in the *Behavior* area.

   - Click ⬈ (Default) or ⬉ (Flipped) to increase or decrease the length of the selected frame member by the defined value, at one end or the other.

   - Click ⬈ (Symmetric) to increase or decrease the length of the selected frame member by the defined value, at both ends.

- Click ✎ (Asymmetric) to increase or decrease the length of the selected frame member by defined values at both ends.

4. Enter the required value in the offset field in the *Behavior* area. A positive value increases the length, a negative value decreases the length.

5. Click ⊞ (Apply) to apply the change in length and continue using the command or click **OK** to apply and close the palette.

Miter

Use the **Miter** option to cut the ends of two frame members at equal angles to form a corner, as shown on the right in Figure 15–19.

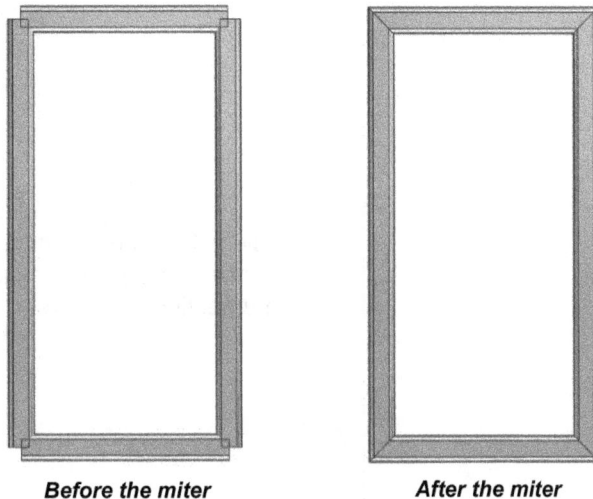

Before the miter   **After the miter**

Figure 15–19

How To: Miter the Ends of Two Frame Members

1. In the *Design* tab>Frame panel, click [icon] (Miter). The Miter palette opens, as shown in Figure 15–20.

Figure 15–20

2. Select the frame members to miter. Multiple frame members can be selected at the same time. This will miter all intersecting members.

3. Select the miter type and offset in the *Behavior* area. Once the options are selected, the preview updates identifying how the members will be mitered. You may be required to change options to ensure the miter is as required.

- Click ⬜ to create a full miter cut and click ◲ to create a bisect miter cut. Figure 15–21 shows an example of a miter cut at one side.

- Click ⬈ , ⬈ , or ⬈ to define whether the offset for the selected members.

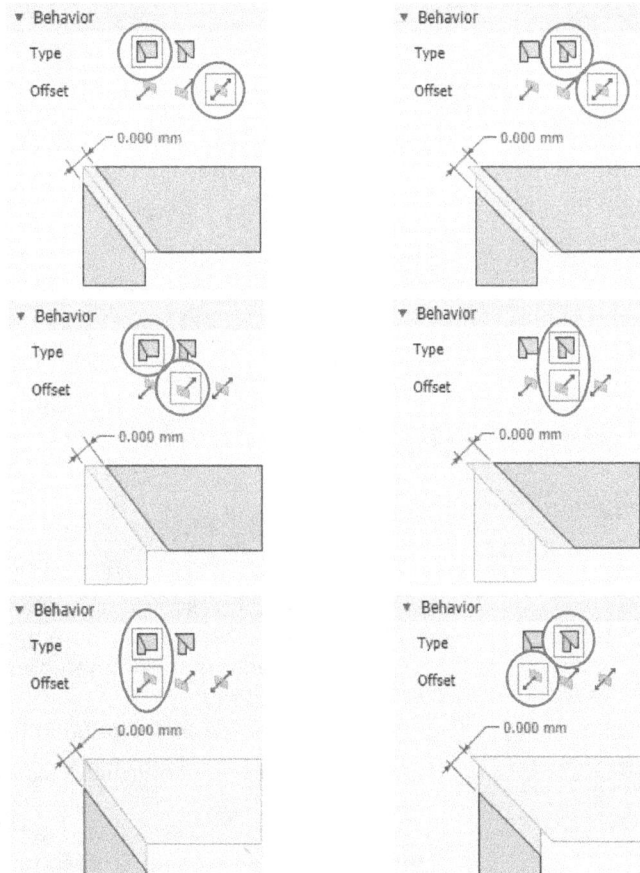

Figure 15–21

4. Enter an offset value directly in the miter preview in the Behavior area, as required.

5. Click ➕ (Apply) to apply the miter and continue using the command or click **OK** to apply the miter and close the Properties palette.

Trim/Extend

Use **Trim/Extend** to trim or extend one or more frame members to a model face.

How To: Trim or Extend One or More Frame Members to a Face

1. In the *Design* tab>Frame panel, click (Trim/Extend). The Trim/Extend palette opens, as shown in Figure 15–22.

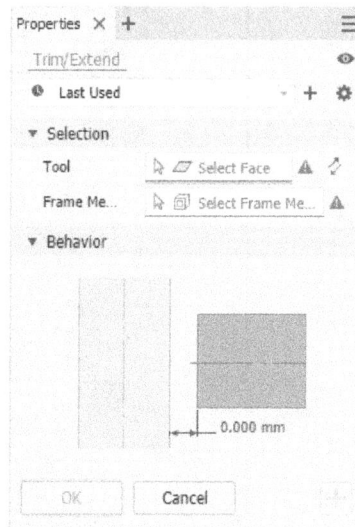

Figure 15–22

2. Select a face on an existing frame member to be used as the trim/extend *Tool* reference.
3. Select the frame member(s) that is to be trimmed or extended.
4. Enter the offset value in the *Behavior* area, as required.
5. Click to control the side of the frame member to keep.
6. Click (Apply) to extend or trim the frame member(s) and continue using **Trim/Extend**, or click **OK** to extend or trim the frame member(s) to the selected face and close the palette.

Insert End Cap

Use the **Insert End Cap** command to insert a cap to close existing structural members, as shown on the right in Figure 15–23 for the two members. To use this command, the Inventor Custom library must be installed and included in the active project.

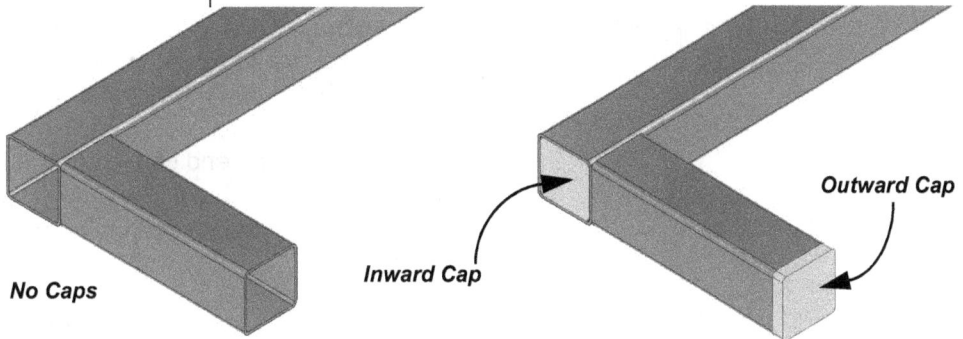

No Caps

Inward Cap

Outward Cap

Figure 15–23

How To: Insert an End Cap

1. In the *Design* tab>Frame panel, click (Insert End Cap). The End Caps palette opens as shown in Figure 15–24.

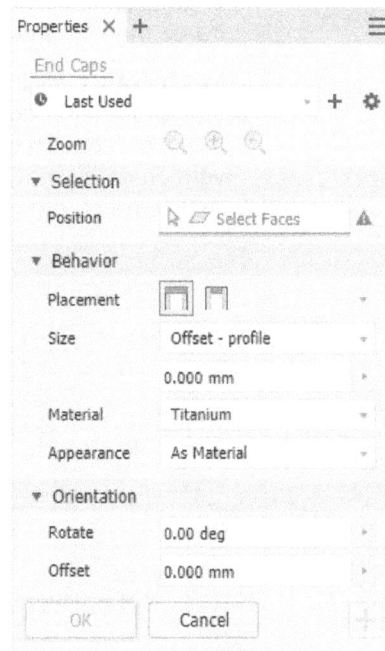

Figure 15–24

2. Select the face at the end of the frame member that is to be capped. Multiple faces can be selected at once to apply the same end cap to multiple frame members.
3. Select the *Placement* type in the *Behavior* area.

- Select ⬜ to create the end cap as an outward cap.

- Select ⬜ to create the end cap as an inward cap.

4. Use the remainder of the options in the *Behavior* area to define the end cap's size, material, and appearance.
5. Define the end cap's rotation and offset in the *Orientation* area.
   - Enter an *Offset* value for the end cap to offset it from the selected face reference.
   - Enter a *Rotation* value for the end cap to rotate it in the frame member.

6. Click ➕ (Apply) to apply the end cap and continue using the command or click **OK** to apply the end cap and close the palette.

Remove End Treatments

Use **Remove End Treatments** to return a frame member to its original state of creation, before any modifications. Multiple frame members can be selected. To remove any end treatments to a member, click ✖ (Remove End Treatments) in the *Design* tab>expanded Frame panel. Select the member(s) and complete the operation. This option is useful for returning to a previous version of the model when undo does not enable you to do so (e.g., when a model is opened in a new session).

Additional Options

*   In the *Design* tab>expanded Frame panel, click (Frame Member Info) to quickly obtain information about a frame member, as shown in Figure 15–25.

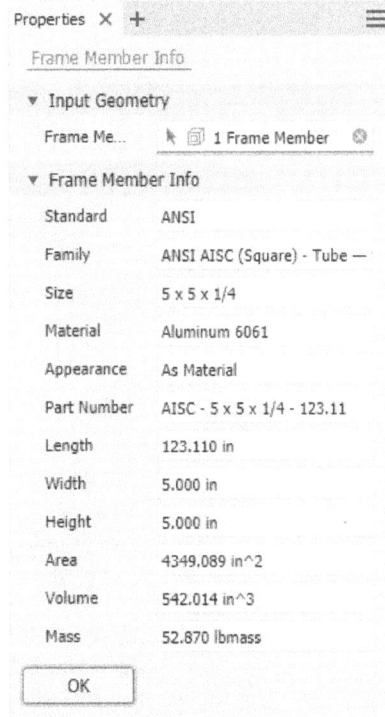

Properties ✕ +	☰
Frame Member Info	

▼ Input Geometry

Frame Me...	▸ ▣ 1 Frame Member ⊗

▼ Frame Member Info

Standard	ANSI
Family	ANSI AISC (Square) - Tube —
Size	5 x 5 x 1/4
Material	Aluminum 6061
Appearance	As Material
Part Number	AISC - 5 x 5 x 1/4 - 123.11
Length	123.110 in
Width	5.000 in
Height	5.000 in
Area	4349.089 in^2
Volume	542.014 in^3
Mass	52.870 lbmass

OK

Figure 15–25

*   Consider the use of the (Beam/Column Calculator) and (Plate Calculator). These are both available in the *Design* tab>expanded Frame panel. The options in these calculators can be used to aid in creating a structurally sound assembly.

15.2 Structural Shape Author

Using the Structural Shape Author, you can publish custom profiles to the Content Center, similar to that shown in Figure 15–26.

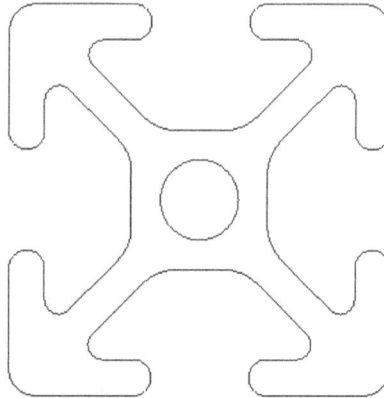

Figure 15–26

General Steps

Use the following general steps to use the Structural Shape Author to create a custom frame member:

1. Create a Read/Write library in the Content Center.
2. Prepare the structural shape and properties.
3. Author the structural shape.
4. Publish the structural shape.

Step 1 - Create a Read/Write library in the Content Center.

For more information about creating Content Center libraries and their configuration, see the Autodesk Inventor Help Topics and your local Administrative support.

Before you begin creating new structural shapes for use in the Frame Generator, you must create a Read/Write library in the Content Center and attach it to your project. Setting up the Content Center is a crucial step in the process of creating valid published shapes.

Step 2 - Prepare the structural shape and properties.

When creating a custom shape, consider how accurate the shape should be and how much detail to include. A frame profile that is very detailed might not be required and can slow down modeling. Consider critical dimensions carefully and include those that are required. Sketch, constrain, and dimension the profile using parameters and equations where useful. Complete the sketch and create a simple extrusion to accommodate the authoring process. The model in Figure 15–27 shows the dimension scheme (with equations) and the 3D extruded model that is required.

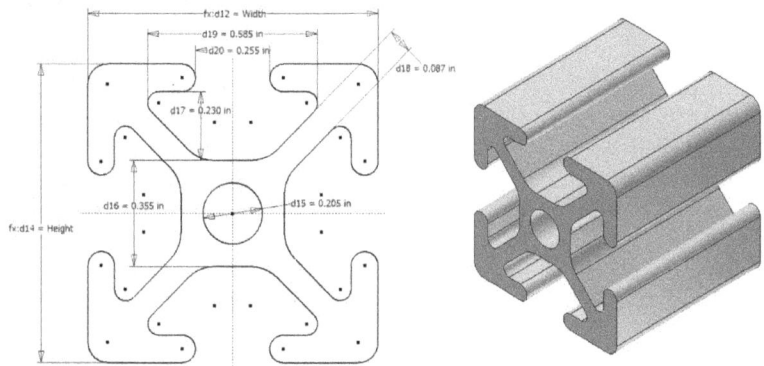

Figure 15–27

Ensure that you have the correct physical material for the new structural shape created in your templates or style library. The material should contain at least the correct value for density, but can also contain more information about the material's properties (such as Yield Strength [MPa], Ultimate Tensile Strength [MPa], and Young's Modulus [GPa]). Also consider the use of more complex parameters where possible (e.g., Section Area, Moment of Inertia for X and Y). These material properties and parameters are important for the **Beam and Column Calculator** in the Frame Generator and are mapped to corresponding items during the publishing process.

Step 3 - Author the structural shape.

The authoring process takes a basic extrusion and converts it to a valid Frame Generator profile using automatic feature modification. To open the Author, in the *Manage* tab>Author panel, click ⌸ (Structural Shape Authoring) from the Component drop-down list.

The options available on the two tabs (*Layout* and *Parameter Mapping*) enable you to author the structural shape.

Layout

The *Layout* tab is shown in Figure 15–28 and described as follows:

- Select the category in the Read/Write Content Center library where the shape should be populated.

- The *Geometry Mapping* area automatically populates selected geometry (if there is only one extrusion in the part).

- The Default Base Point is the geometric center of the profile. You can select a new Base Point from the menu, if required.

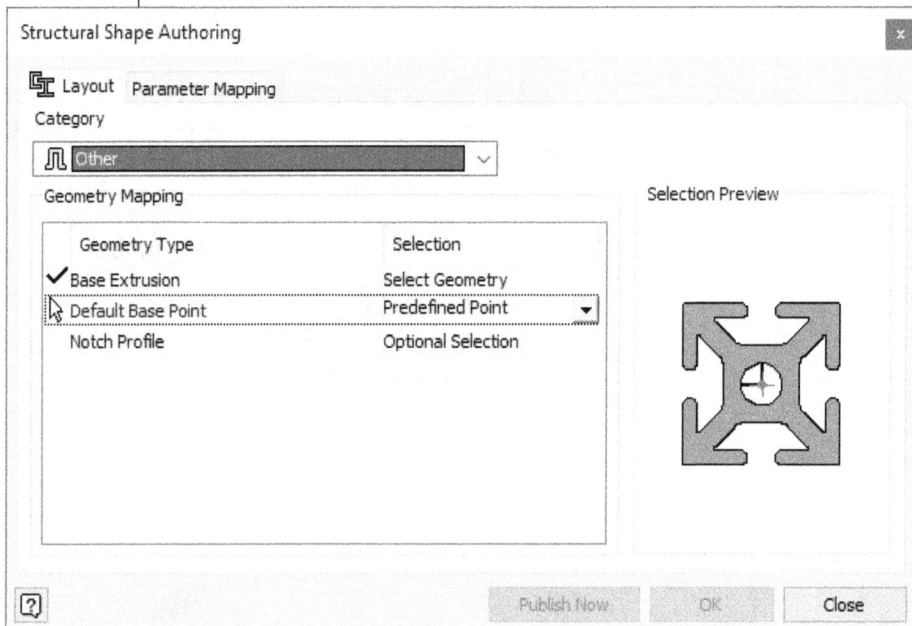

Figure 15–28

Parameter Mapping

The optional parameters might not be required for authoring. They might be required for the advanced calculators, if used.

The *Parameter Mapping* tab enables you to map the parameters required in the Content Center to the parameters in the model. The *Parameter Mapping* tab is shown in Figure 15–29. Click

[⋯] to specify an iProperty or parameter to map.

- Fields with a yellow background are required fields, while fields in white are optional.

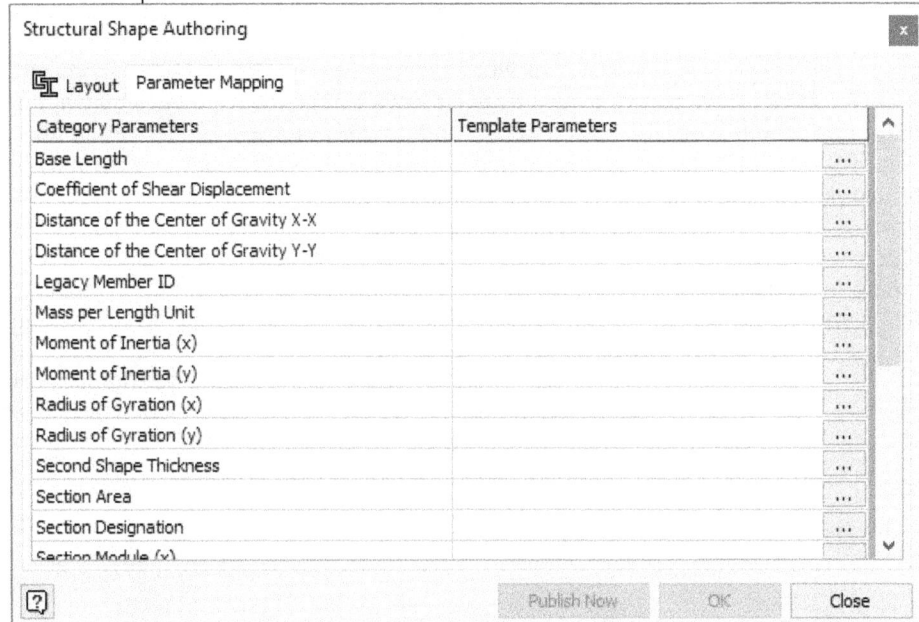

Figure 15–29

Before publishing, review the iProperties and document settings of the shape for accuracy. These values populate the model properties and Part List in the documentation when they are used.

Once all the parameters are mapped, you can click **OK** to author the part. The geometry is automatically revised by the software. A log file detailing the changes is generated in the working directory of the part you are authoring.

Step 4 - Publish the structural shape.

Once the structural shape is authored and its design properties set up for documentation, the shape can be published to the Content Center for use in the Frame Generator. To publish, click **Publish Now** in the Structural Shape Authoring dialog box or

click (Publish Part) in the *Manage* tab>Content Center panel.

If the Part Number or Description were previously defined by an expression, it is recommended to edit the value to name the family for publishing.

Either method opens the Publish Guide dialog box, where you are provided with a series of dialog boxes and are required to click **Next** to progress through the options as you define them. You must select a Library to which to publish, a language, a category, and confirm or edit any properties and parameters. You must then define one or more key columns that uniquely define a family member. For the Family Properties options, you can edit the default values for the Part Number and Description, if required. Select or approve a thumbnail image that is going to be referenced in the Content Center as well as in the Frame Generator. Click **Publish** to publish to the Content Center.

Now that the structural shape has been authored and published, it can be used in your models with the use of Frame Generator.

Practice 15a | Frame Generator

Practice Objectives

- Create an assembly containing a skeletal wireframe.
- Insert frame members into an assembly to create a structural frame assembly, by referencing a skeletal wireframe.
- Reuse inserted frame members where required.
- Adjust frame member ends to obtain the required joints.

In this practice, you will create a simple structural frame assembly to familiarize yourself with using the Frame Generator. You will begin by assembling a part containing the skeletal wireframe into a new assembly. You will then reference the skeletal wireframe to insert the frame members and create the structural frame assembly as shown in Figure 15–30.

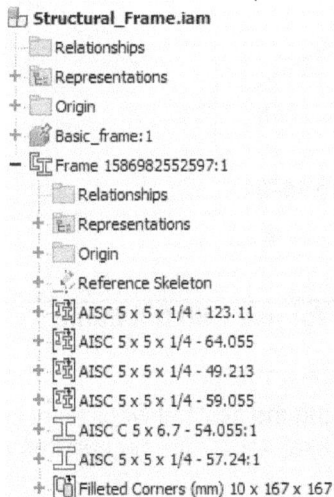

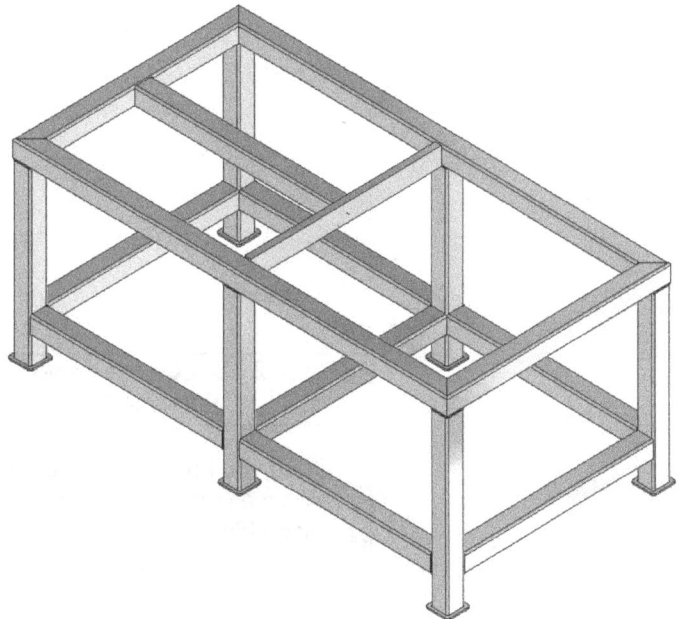

Structural_Frame.iam
- Relationships
- Representations
- Origin
- Basic_frame:1
- Frame 1586982552597:1
  - Relationships
  - Representations
  - Origin
  - Reference Skeleton
  - AISC 5 x 5 x 1/4 - 123.11
  - AISC 5 x 5 x 1/4 - 64.055
  - AISC 5 x 5 x 1/4 - 49.213
  - AISC 5 x 5 x 1/4 - 59.055
  - AISC C 5 x 6.7 - 54.055:1
  - AISC 5 x 5 x 1/4 - 57.24:1
  - Filleted Corners (mm) 10 x 167 x 167

Figure 15–30

Task 1 - Open a part file.

3D sketches and solid edges can also be used as references for inserting frame members.

1. Open **Basic_frame.ipt** from the top-level practice files folder. The part (shown in Figure 15–31) contains the skeletal wireframe that you will reference to create the frame members. It consists of 2D sketches.

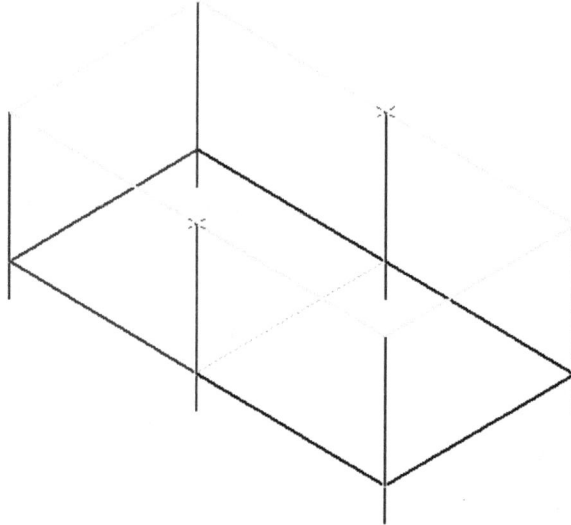

Figure 15–31

2. Close the part file.

Task 2 - Set up the assembly for use with the frame generator.

Once you have the part containing the skeletal wireframe, create a new assembly and place the skeletal wireframe part into the assembly.

1. Create a new assembly file using the metric standard assembly template.

2. Place **Basic_frame.ipt** into the assembly and ground it by right-clicking and selecting **Place Grounded at Origin**. Right-click and select **OK**.

3. Save the assembly as **Structural_Frame.iam** in the top-level practice files folder.

Task 3 - Insert the first frame member.

1. In the *Design* tab>Frame panel, click ⌸ (Insert Frame). The Insert palette opens.

2. In the *Frame Member* area, set the following options, as shown in Figure 15–32:
   - *Category:* **Square/Rectangular Tubes**
   - *Standard:* **ANSI**
   - *Family:* **ANSI AISC (Square) - Tube**
   - *Size*: **5 x 5 x 1/4**
   - *Material Style:* **Aluminum 6061**
   - *Appearance:* **As Material**

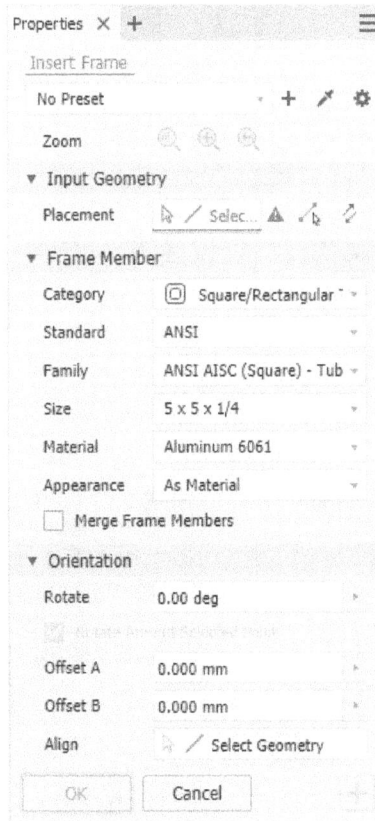

Figure 15–32

3. In the *Input Geometry* area, ensure that the *Placement* field is active and select the longer edge in the location shown in Figure 15–33. A preview of the new member displays as soon as the reference is selected. Arrows appear in the display providing a method to rotate or assign an offset to position the frame. You can also enter explicit values in the palette.

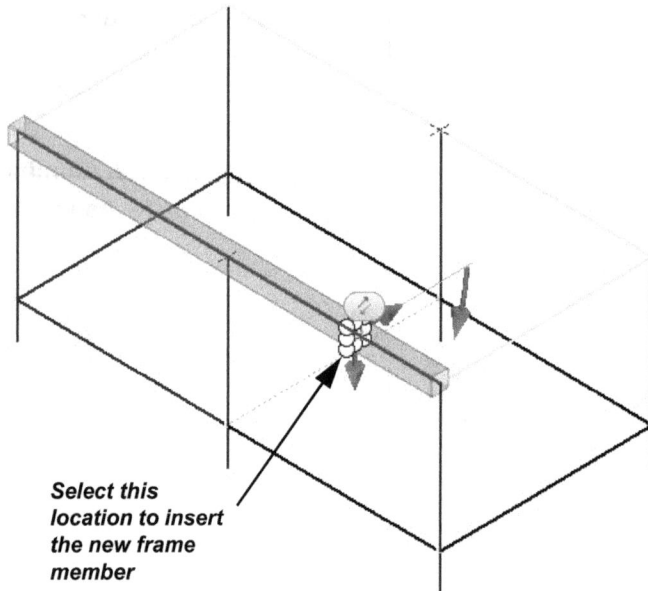

Select this location to insert the new frame member

Figure 15–33

Hint: Reusing Frame Members

When members are going to be reused, it is recommended that you note the selection location used during the placement of members. The placement location of the parent and the placement location on the entity where the member is being reused define its orientation. Incorrect orientation affects the resulting model when end conditions are added. The orientation can be edited after reuse, if required.

---

4. Click ⊕ in the *Zoom* area of the palette to zoom in and clearly see the frame preview, as shown in Figure 15–34. Select the bottom-right white grip that displays on the frame to align the selected edge and the corner of the frame's section, as shown in Figure 15–34. The frame member preview updates.

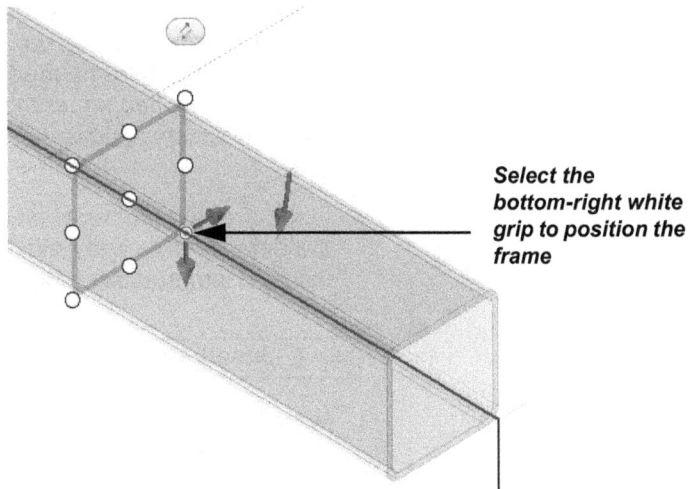

Figure 15–34

5. Select the center white grip, as shown in Figure 15–35, to return the frame member to its original position. Leave the *Orientation* fields with zero offset and zero angle because offsets and rotation are not required.

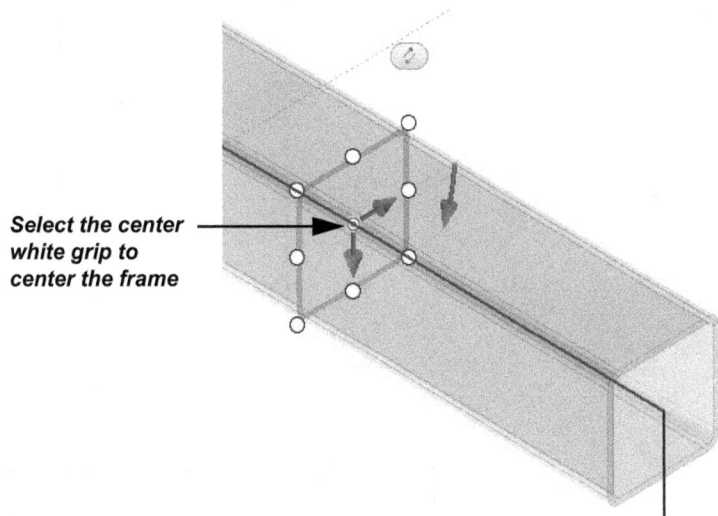

Figure 15–35

6. Click ⊕ in the *Zoom* area of the palette to return to the previous view display.

7. In the Insert Frame palette, click **OK**. The Create New Frame dialog box opens. The frame components are contained in a subassembly, which is created in a subfolder of the directory containing the main assembly.

8. In the Create New Frame dialog box, click **OK**. The Frame Member Naming dialog box opens. A separate part file is created for each frame member that is created. Note that the directory specified under the *File Name* column is the same as the directory specified in the Create New Frame dialog box.

9. In the Frame Member Naming dialog box, click **OK** to accept the default name and path. The first frame member is inserted into the assembly.

Task 4 - Insert additional frame members.

1. Insert a frame member on the entity and in the location shown in Figure 15–36. The settings used in the previous frame member are maintained; use the same options.

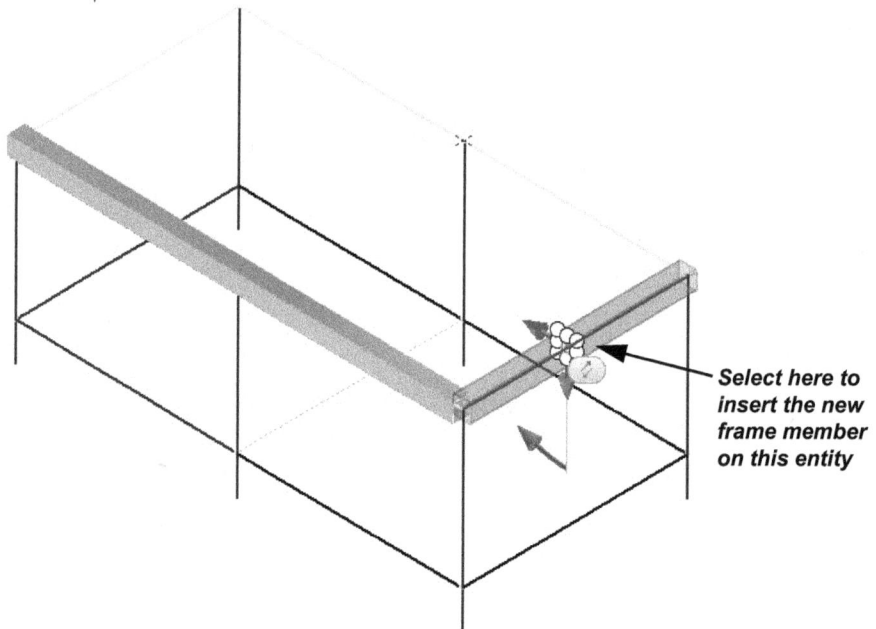

Select here to insert the new frame member on this entity

Figure 15–36

2. In the Insert Frame palette, click **OK**.

3. Click **OK** to accept the default name and location for the new part file that has been created. Two separate frame members have now been created.

4. Insert a frame member on the entity and location shown in Figure 15–37. Note that this is a construction entity and it can also be selected as a placement reference to define a frame member. In the Insert Frame palette, use the previous settings to create the new member.

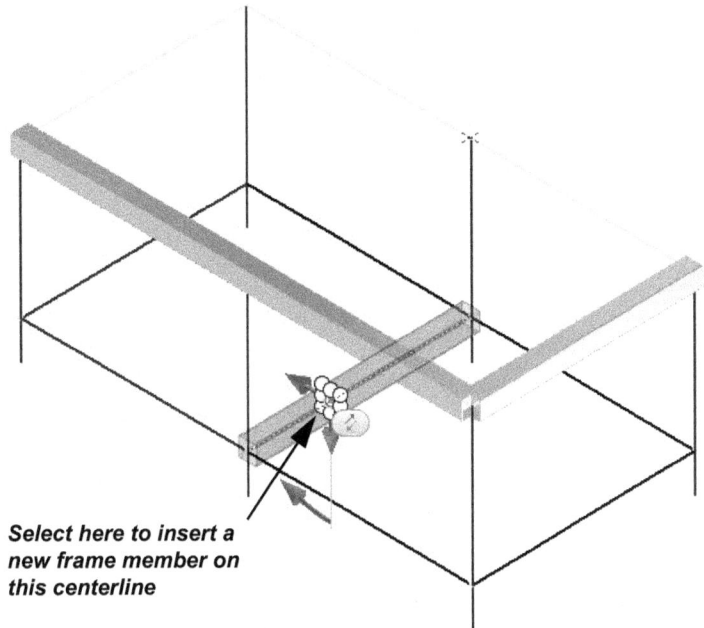

*Select here to insert a
new frame member on
this centerline*

Figure 15–37

5. In the Insert Frame palette, click **OK**.

6. Click **OK** to accept the default name and location for the new
   part file that has been created. Three separate frame
   members have now been created, as shown in Figure 15–38.

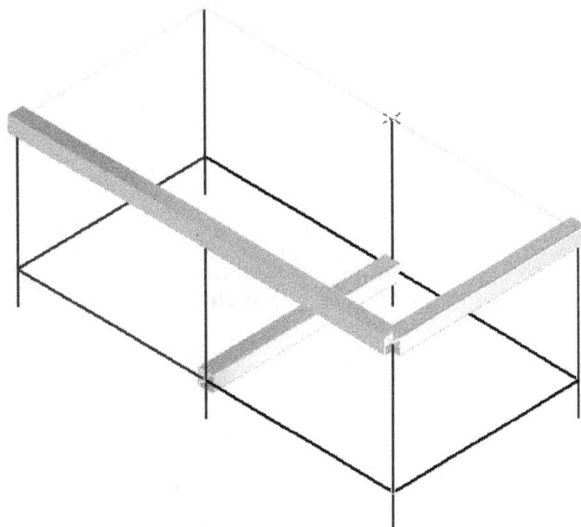

Figure 15–38

Task 5 - Reuse existing frame members to complete the top of the frame.

1. In the Frame panel, click ![Reuse icon] (Reuse). The Reuse palette opens.

2. Select the long frame member as the *Source Frame Member* to reuse.

3. The *Placement* field in the *Reused Frame Member* area immediately becomes active. Select the remaining long edge at the top of the frame to place the reused frame member, as shown in Figure 15–39.

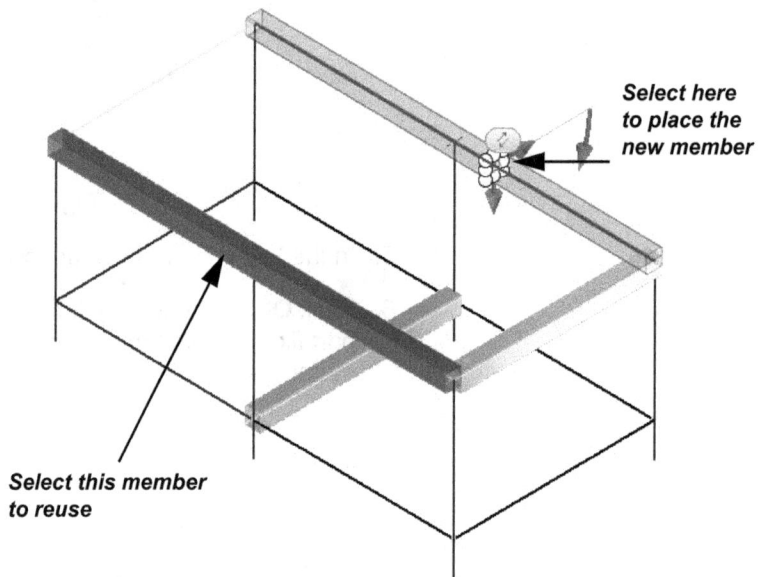

Select here to place the new member

Select this member to reuse

Figure 15–39

4. Click ![Plus icon] (Apply and Create new Frame) in the Reuse palette.

5. In the Reuse palette, in the *Source Frame Member* area, select in the *Frame Member* field and select ⊗ to delete the current selection. Select the shorter top frame member as the member to reuse.

6. The *Placement* field in the *Reused Frame Member* area immediately becomes active. Select the remaining short edge at the top of the frame to place the reused frame member, as shown in Figure 15–40.

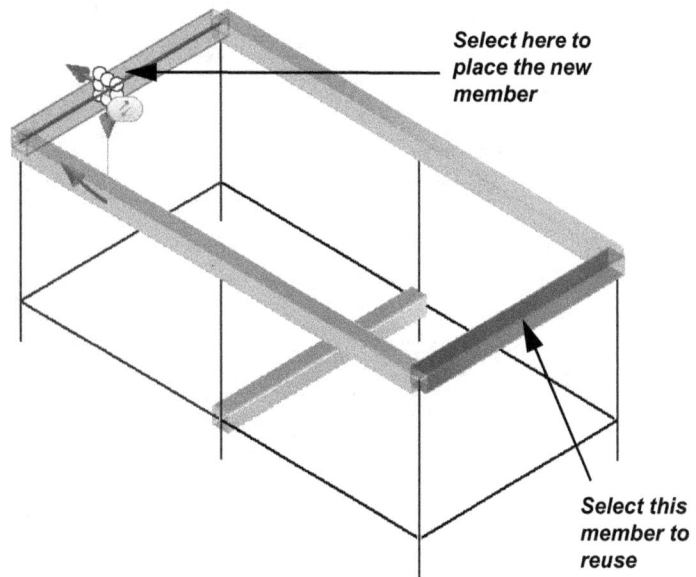

Select here to place the new member

Select this member to reuse

Figure 15–40

7. In the Reuse palette, click **OK**. The frame members display as shown in Figure 15–41. Note how in the Model Browser there are three unique frame members, identified with the

⌶ icons, and two reused frame members, identified with the ⌶ icons. Groups (▦) help identify original and reused frame members in the design.

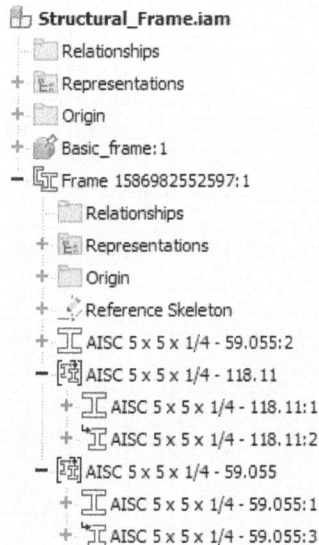

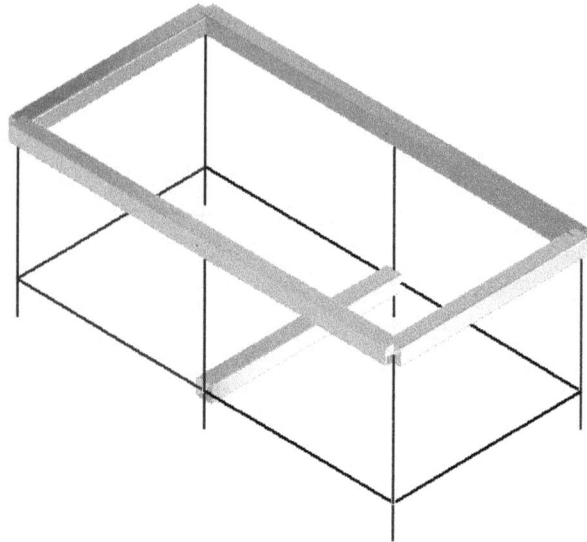

Structural_Frame.iam
  Relationships
+ Representations
+ Origin
+ Basic_frame:1
− Frame 1586982552597:1
  Relationships
  + Representations
  + Origin
  + Reference Skeleton
  + AISC 5 x 5 x 1/4 - 59.055:2
  − AISC 5 x 5 x 1/4 - 118.11
    + AISC 5 x 5 x 1/4 - 118.11:1
    + AISC 5 x 5 x 1/4 - 118.11:2
  − AISC 5 x 5 x 1/4 - 59.055
    + AISC 5 x 5 x 1/4 - 59.055:1
    + AISC 5 x 5 x 1/4 - 59.055:3

Figure 15–41

Task 6 - Create miter joints.

Once the frame members have been inserted or reused, the frame member ends need to be adjusted to obtain the required joints.

1. In the *Design* tab>Frame panel, click ⌐ (Miter). The Miter palette opens.

2. Ensure that the *Frame Member* field is active and select all four members around the top of the frame, as shown in Figure 15–42. Note that reused members are identified with blue outline when the parent member is selected; however, it must be explicitly selected as a reference such that it turns blue to include it as a reference.

3. Confirm that 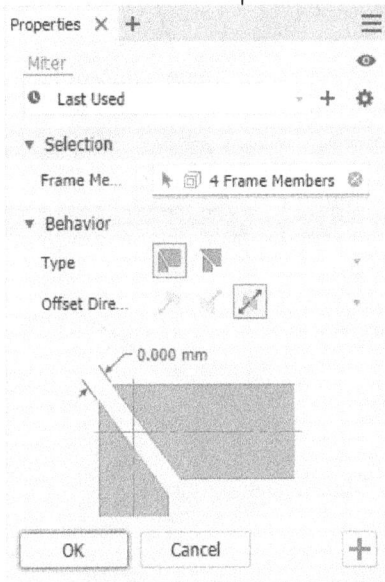 (Full Miter Cut) is selected as the miter's *Type* option, as shown in Figure 15–42.

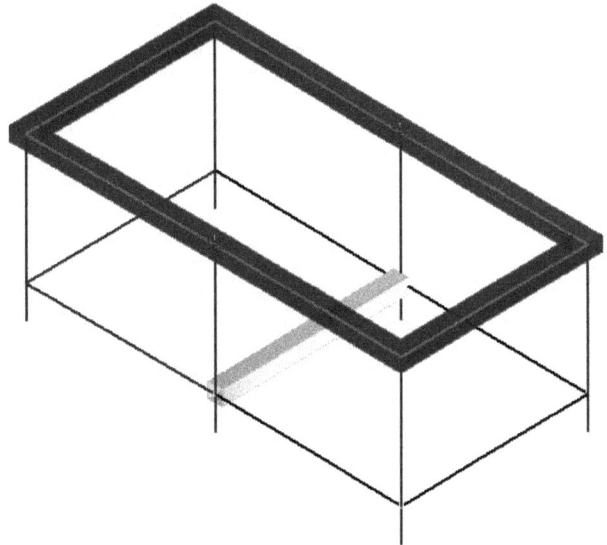

Figure 15–42

4. Click **OK** to create the miter. A miter should be created on all four corners, as shown in Figure 15–43; however, depending on the placement locations and orientations of reused members, the members may appear similar to those shown in Figure 15–44 where the miters are misaligned in the corners.

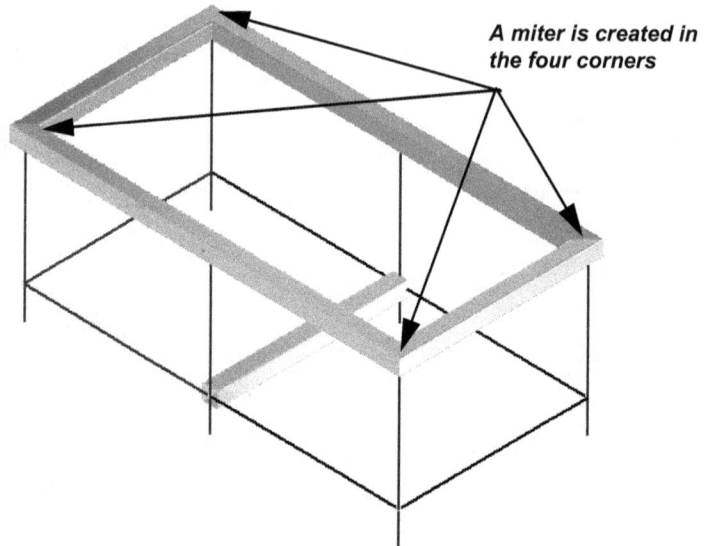

A miter is created in the four corners

Figure 15–43

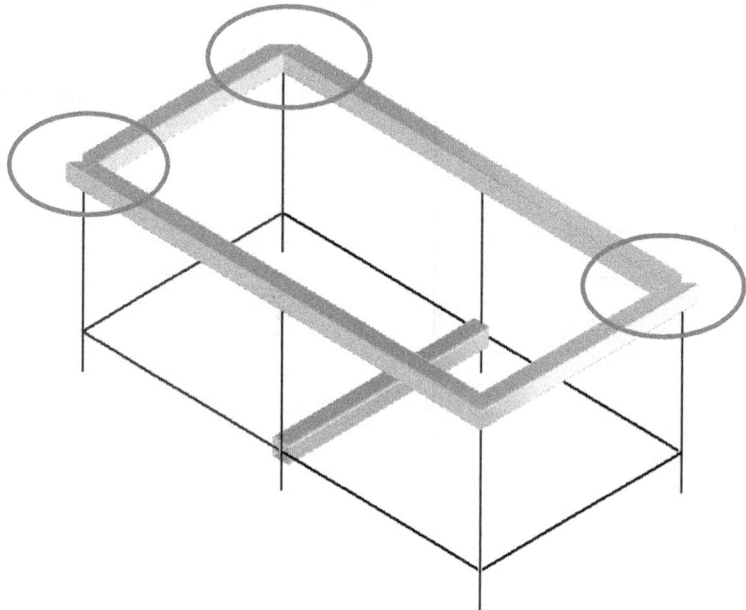

Figure 15–44

5. The misaligned miters on the frame members are not because the reused member did not update, but because they were oriented differently when placed. This was based on where the entity was selected. If any of the members are incorrectly oriented, click ⬚⃗ (Change Reuse) to open the Change Reuse palette.

6. In the *Reused Frame Member* area, ensure that the *Frame Member* field is active. Select one of the reused members that is not oriented correctly. Click ✎ (Flip Direction) adjacent to the *Frame Member* field or in the graphics window. If flipping does not reorient properly, you may have to rotate the reused member to have it orient correctly.

7. Once the miters are oriented correctly, click **OK**.

8. If necessary, reorient the other reused frame member, as required.

Changing the reused member is only required if the placement location varies from the original selection location on the member being reused.

Task 7 - Copy properties from an existing frame member to create a new frame member.

Properties from a previously created frame member can be copied to quickly create a similar frame member without having to reselect all the options in the palette. By default, each time a new frame member is inserted, the palette does remember the previous settings; however, copying properties can be efficient if different types of members exist in the design.

1. In the *Design* tab>Frame panel, click ⬚ (Insert Frame). The Insert Frame palette opens.

2. In the Category drop-down list, select **Angles**. This changes the palette settings so that you can practice using the Copy Properties tool in the next step.

3. At the top of the Insert Frame palette, click ✐ (Property Eye Dropper). Since all the frames have the same properties, select any one of the frame members to copy its properties. Once selected, the *Frame Member* and *Orientation* areas update to display the settings initially used to create the selected member.

4. Insert a new member on the entity shown in Figure 15–45. Select near the top of the entity to locate the new member.

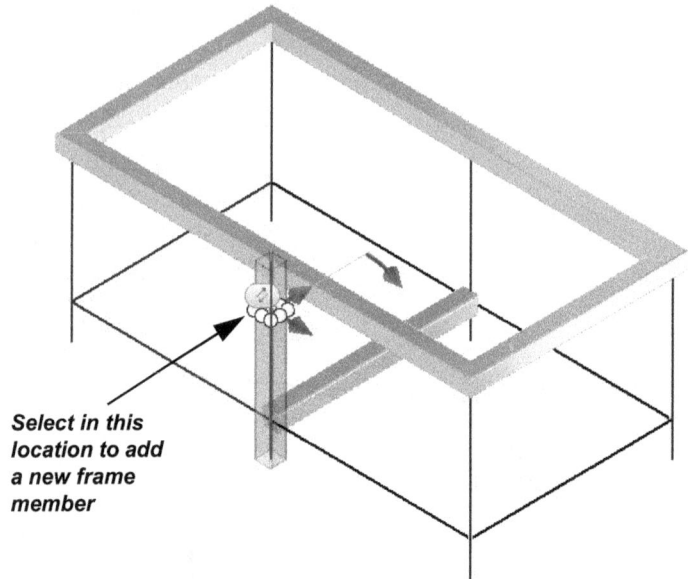

Select in this location to add a new frame member

Figure 15–45

5. Click **OK** twice to create the new member and accept the frame member naming.

6. Click (Reuse) to open the Reuse palette.

7. Select the vertical frame member that was just created and reuse it to create the other five vertical frame members as shown in Figure 15–46. Select near the top of all of the corner entities to place the reused members.

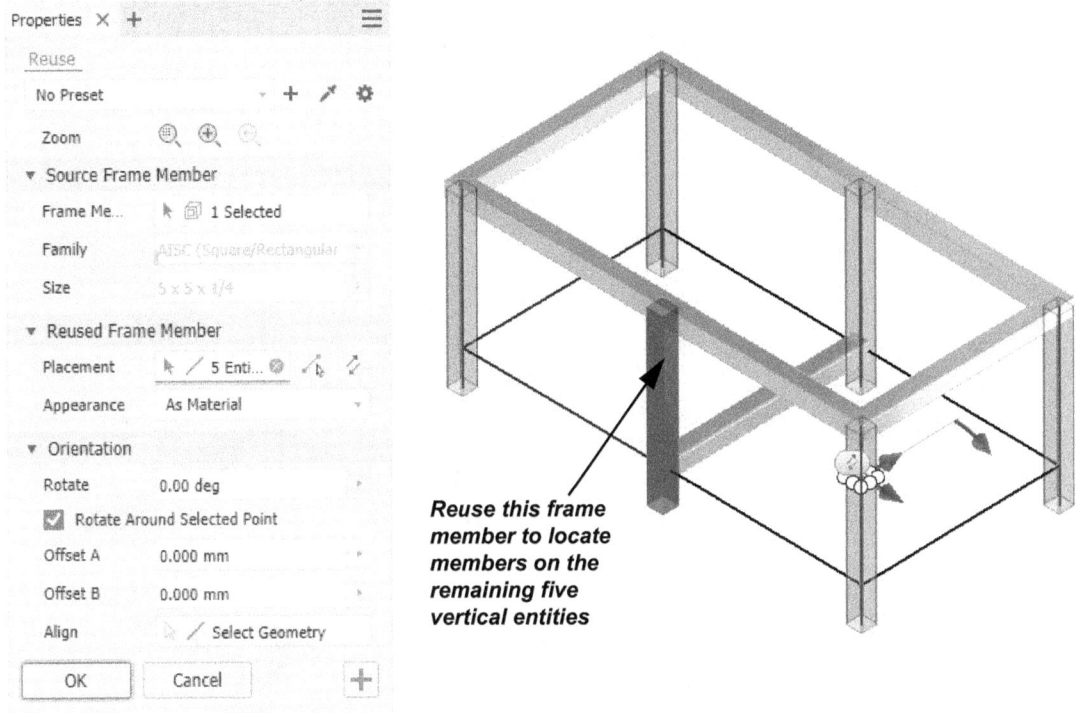

Properties ✕ +   ≡

Reuse

No Preset   ▾ + ✗ ✿

Zoom   ⊖ ⊕ ⊖

▼ Source Frame Member

Frame Me...   ▸ 🔲 1 Selected

Family   AISC (Square/Rectangular ▾

Size   5 x 5 x 1/4

▼ Reused Frame Member

Placement   ▸ ╱ 5 Enti... ⊘ ⚐ ⟲

Appearance   As Material   ▾

▼ Orientation

Rotate   0.00 deg   ▸

☑ Rotate Around Selected Point

Offset A   0.000 mm   ▸

Offset B   0.000 mm   ▸

Align   ▸ ╱ Select Geometry

| OK | Cancel | + |

Reuse this frame member to locate members on the remaining five vertical entities

Figure 15–46

8. Click + to create the members and remain in the Reuse dialog box.

9. In the Reuse palette, in the *Source Frame Member* area, select in the *Frame Member* field and select ⊘ to delete the current selection. Select the member that was created on the centerline as the new member to reuse.

10. Select the remaining six entities around the bottom of the frame (shown previewed in Figure 15–47). This member will be reused on all of these entities.

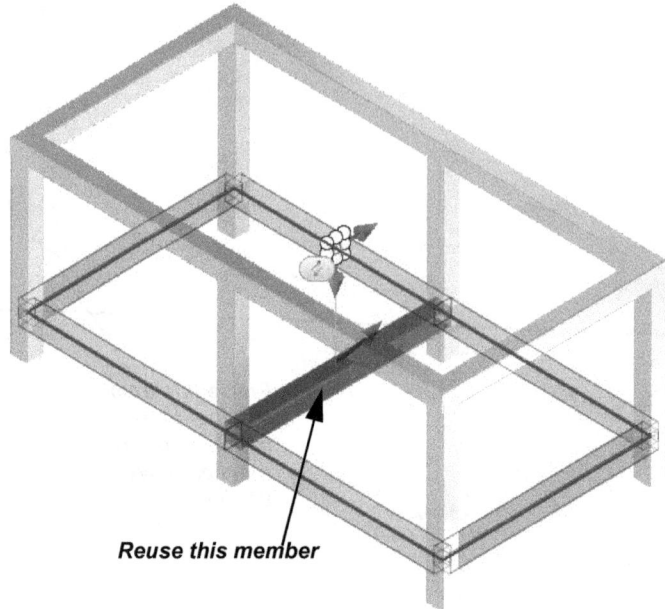

Reuse this member

Figure 15–47

11. In the Reuse palette, click **OK**.

12. Save the assembly and all of the required components. Review the Model Browser and note how there are four groups of the same frame members, as shown in Figure 15–48.

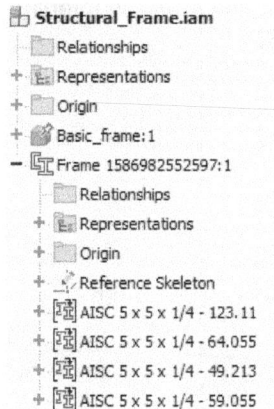

Figure 15–48

Task 8 - Use the Trim/Extend option to resize the frame members.

1. Change the view display to **Shaded with Edges**. This will help you to identify whether entities require trimming. Note how all the new members are overlapping with the adjacent members. This is because the skeletal frame's entities that are selected are longer than the actual length of the required frame members.

2. In the *Design* tab>Frame panel, click ▐▌ (Trim/Extend). The Trim/Extend palette opens, as shown in Figure 15–49.

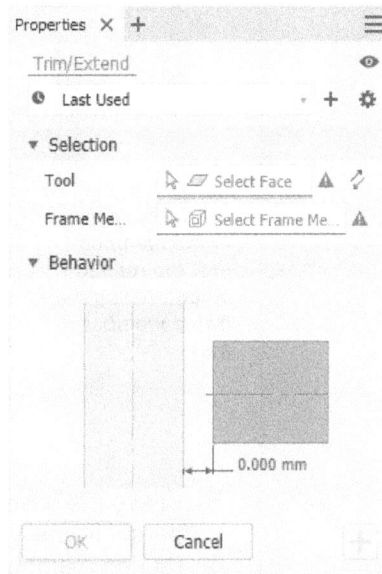

Figure 15–49

3. Select the bottom face of the long member, shown in Figure 15–50, as the *Tool* reference.

4. Select the frame member shown in Figure 15–50 as the *Frame Member* to trim. Note that the other five vertical members are also highlighted because they are reused members, so they will be automatically trimmed to match the parent member.

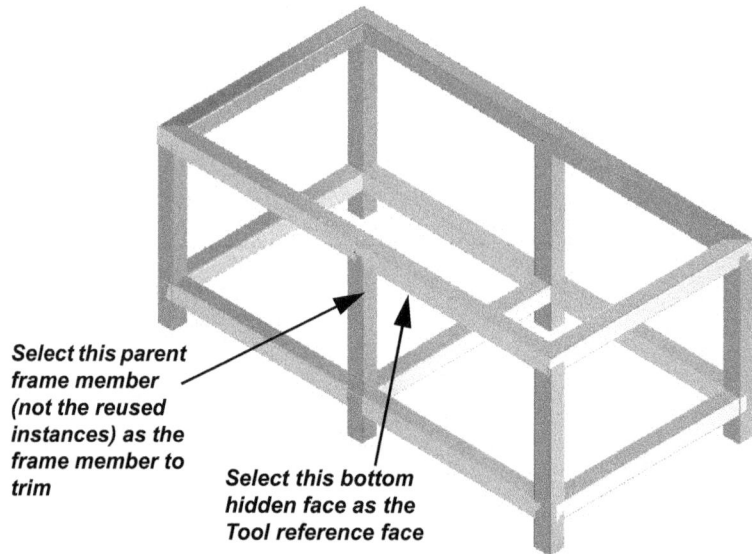

Select this parent frame member (not the reused instances) as the frame member to trim

Select this bottom hidden face as the Tool reference face

Figure 15–50

5. Leave the offset value for trimming as **0** and click **OK**. The parent frame member is trimmed to the selected face and all reused members should update, as shown in Figure 15–51.

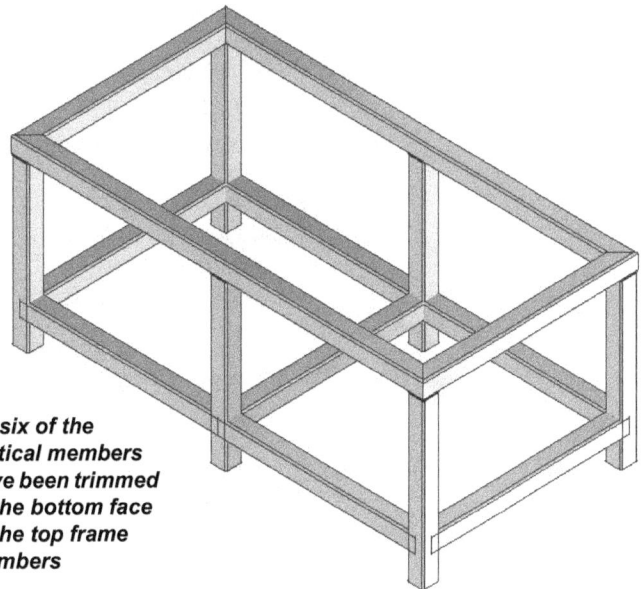

All six of the vertical members have been trimmed to the bottom face of the top frame members

Figure 15–51

6. Review the locations in which each member comes into contact with the top frame members. Is there any overlap similar to that shown in Figure 15–52?

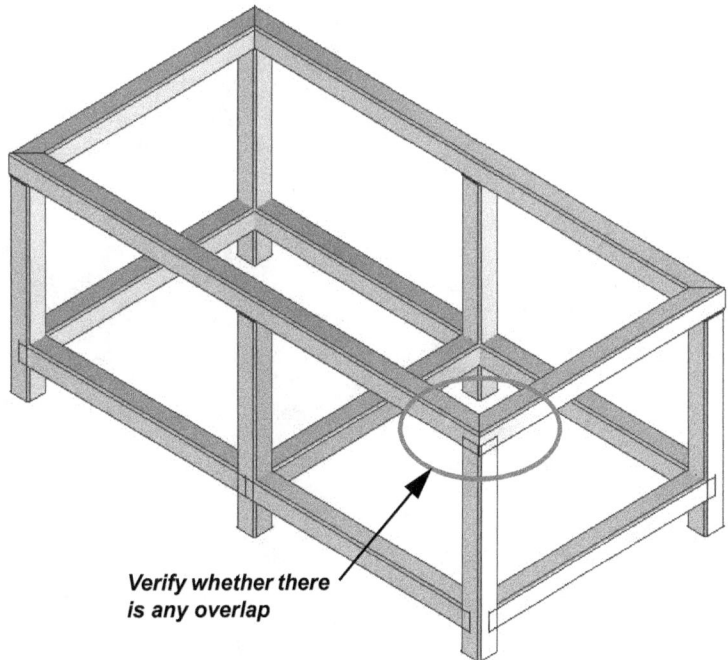

Verify whether there is any overlap

Figure 15–52

7. If any of the members are incorrectly oriented, click

   ⬚ (Change Reuse) to open the Change Reuse palette. In the *Reused Frame Member* area, select a reused member that is not oriented correctly and click ⬚ (Flip Direction).

8. Click **OK**. This reversal is only required if the placement location varies from the original selection location on the member being reused. Repeat and reverse the direction on any other members, as required.

9. The frame members at the bottom of the frame still require trimming as can be seen with the Shades with Edges view display. Use ⬚ (Trim/Extend) again to trim the remaining frame members. You will need to trim the parent frame member on both ends. To locate the parent, locate it in the Model Browser so that you ensure that it is trimmed using the appropriate intersecting faces. The completed frame assembly is shown in Figure 15–53.

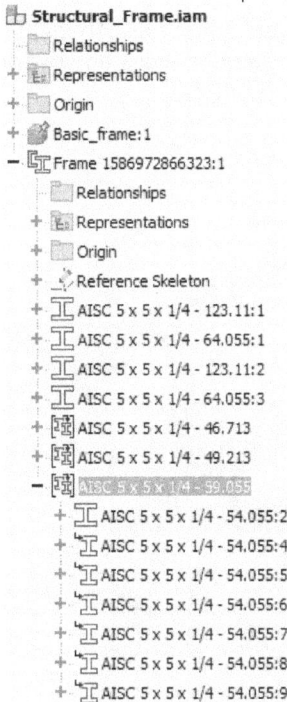

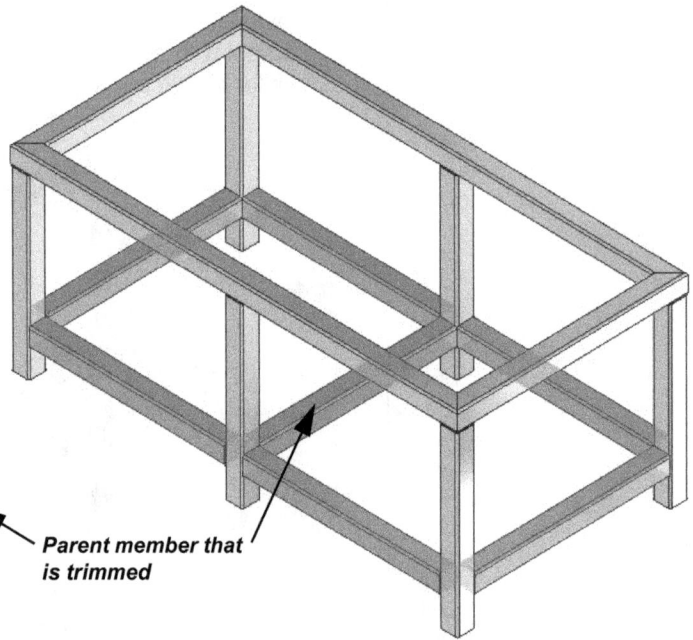

Structural_Frame.iam
  Relationships
+ Representations
+ Origin
+ Basic_frame:1
− Frame 1586972866323:1
    Relationships
  + Representations
  + Origin
  + Reference Skeleton
  + AISC 5 x 5 x 1/4 - 123.11:1
  + AISC 5 x 5 x 1/4 - 64.055:1
  + AISC 5 x 5 x 1/4 - 123.11:2
  + AISC 5 x 5 x 1/4 - 64.055:3
  + AISC 5 x 5 x 1/4 - 46.713
  + AISC 5 x 5 x 1/4 - 49.213
  − AISC 5 x 5 x 1/4 - 59.055
    + AISC 5 x 5 x 1/4 - 54.055:2
    + AISC 5 x 5 x 1/4 - 54.055:4
    + AISC 5 x 5 x 1/4 - 54.055:5
    + AISC 5 x 5 x 1/4 - 54.055:6
    + AISC 5 x 5 x 1/4 - 54.055:7
    + AISC 5 x 5 x 1/4 - 54.055:8
    + AISC 5 x 5 x 1/4 - 54.055:9

Parent member that is trimmed

Figure 15–53

10. On the *Inspect* tab>Interference panel, click ⬚ (Analyze Interference) to run an interference check. Drag a bounding box around all frame members and click **OK** to verify that no frame members intersect. If interference occurs, locate and trim the members.

11. Save the assembly and all of its components.

Task 9 - Modify the skeletal frame and create additional frame members.

1. Open **Basic_frame.ipt** in a separate window.

2. Modify **Sketch2** and add the four sketch points shown in Figure 15–54. These will be used to create new supporting frame members. Ensure that the points are all constrained. The three points that lie on the existing entities should be constrained to the midpoints of the entities and the point at the middle of the frame should be constrained horizontally and vertically to the midpoints.

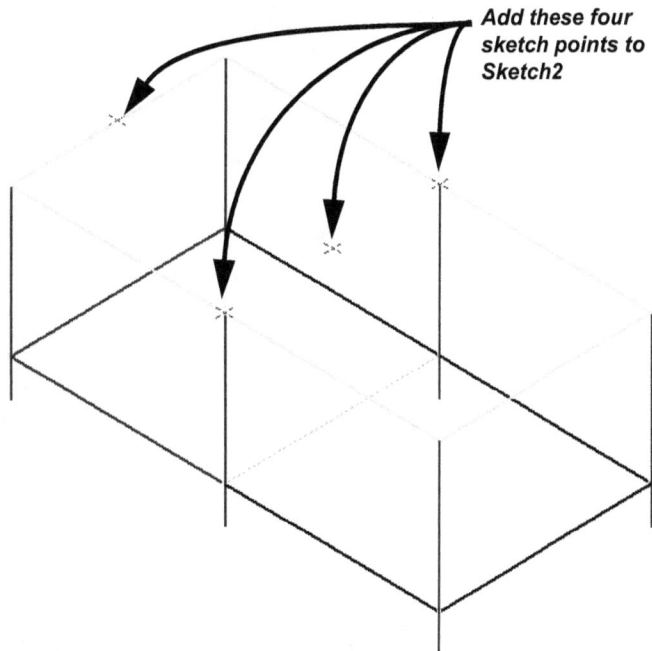

Add these four sketch points to Sketch2

Figure 15–54

3. In the *Design* tab>Frame panel, click ⬚ (Insert Frame).

When using the ✎ option to define the frame member, only a single member can be created at a time.

4. In the *Input Geometry* area, click ✎ (Specify frame location by two points) to define the placement references by selecting a start and end point.

5. Select the two sketch points that were created on the longer entities. A preview of the new member displays using the same frame member settings that were last used.

6. In the *Frame Member* area, set the following options:

   • *Category:* **Channels**
   • *Standard:* **ANSI**
   • *Family:* **ANSI MC/C - U - Shape**
   • *Size*: **C5 x 6.7**
   • *Material Style:* **Aluminum 6061**
   • *Appearance:* **As Material**

7. Ensure that the orientation of the new channel frame member appears as shown in Figure 15–55.

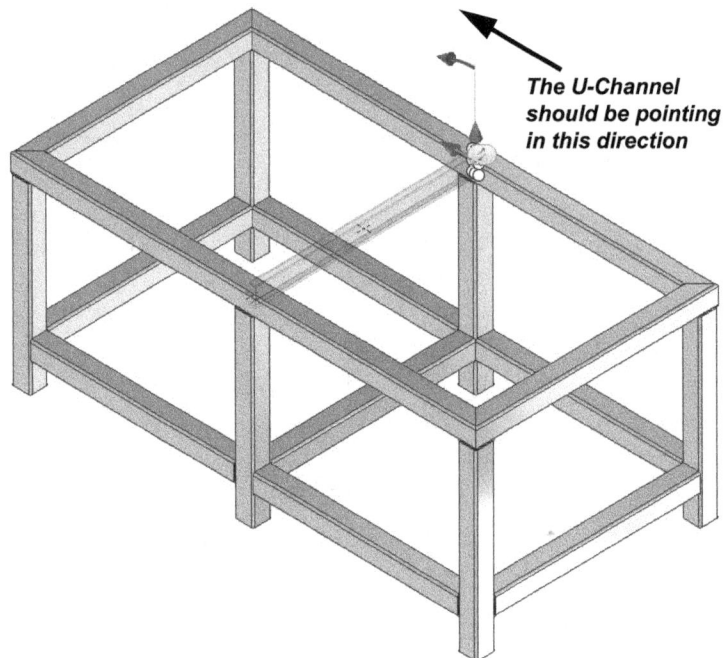

The U-Channel should be pointing in this direction

Figure 15–55

8. Complete the creation of the new frame member.

9. Use the ╟ (Trim/Extend) option to trim the new frame member to the inside faces of the outer frame.

10. Create the frame member shown in Figure 15–56. Create this new member by selecting the other two points that were added to the sketch. Use the ✐ (Property Eye Dropper) option to copy the frame properties from one of the existing square members.

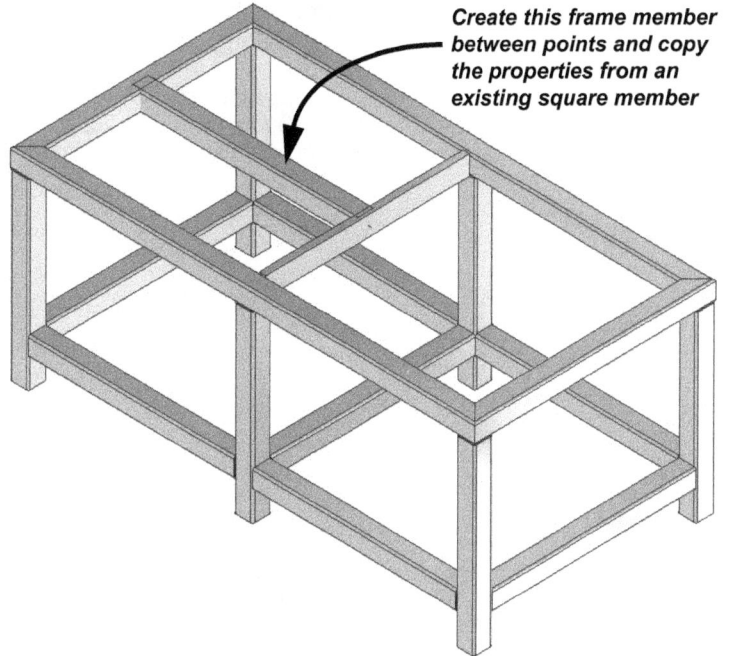

Create this frame member between points and copy the properties from an existing square member

Figure 15–56

11. Trim the new frame member where it intersects the outside of the frame (not with the channel member). In the next task, you will create a Notch to finalize the end condition where it meets the channel member.

Task 10 - Finalize the end condition where the members intersect at the top of the frame.

1. Rotate and zoom the model as shown in Figure 15–57.

2. Extend the new frame member to the inside face of the channel frame member. Note how the frame member still has intersecting geometry between the two frame members.

Extend the new member to the inside face of the channel frame member

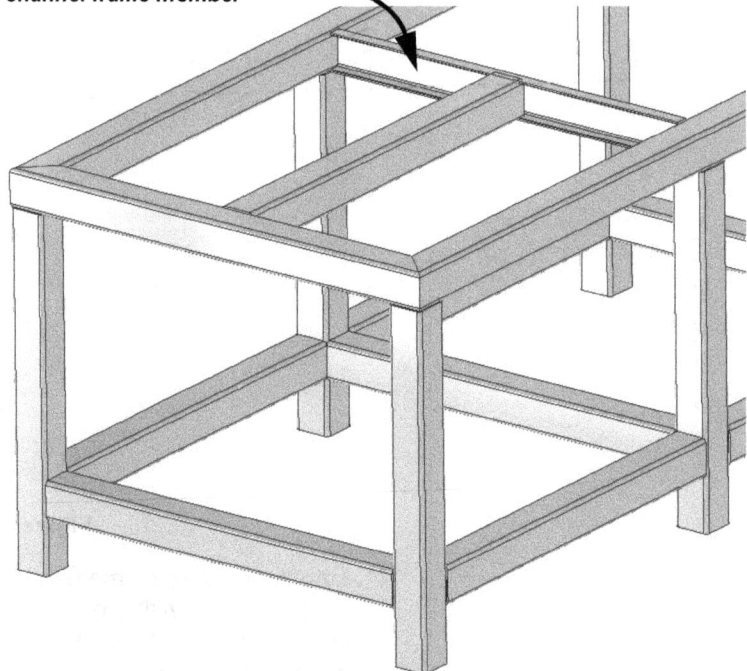

Figure 15–57

3. In the *Design* tab>Frame panel, click ⌐⌐ (Notch). The Notch palette opens.

4. Select the square frame member that was just extended as the frame member to notch. The member displays in blue.

5. Select in the *Notch Tool* field to activate it. Select the channel frame member as the notch tool reference. It displays in yellow.

6. No additional customization of the notch is required. Click **OK** to create the notch as shown in Figure 15–58.

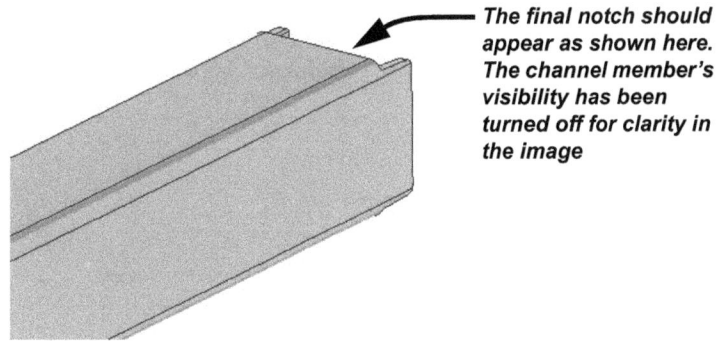

The final notch should appear as shown here. The channel member's visibility has been turned off for clarity in the image

Figure 15–58

Task 11 - Insert end caps at the bottoms of the vertical frame members.

1. Rotate the model as shown in Figure 15–59 to display the bottom of the frame assembly.

2. In the *Design* tab>Frame panel, click ☐ (Insert End Cap). The End Caps palette opens.

3. Select the six open faces on the frame members shown in Figure 15–59.

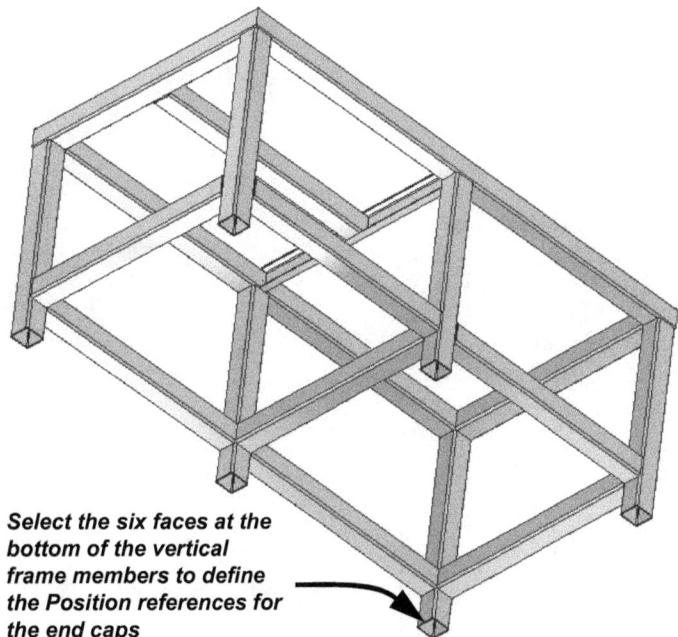

Select the six faces at the bottom of the vertical frame members to define the Position references for the end caps

Figure 15–59

4. Zoom in on any one of the frame members to clearly view the end cap's previewed geometry. Set the options in the *Behavior* area as shown in Figure 15–60.

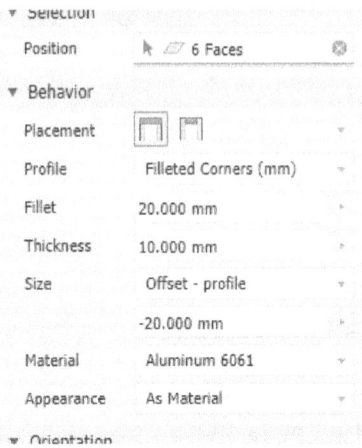

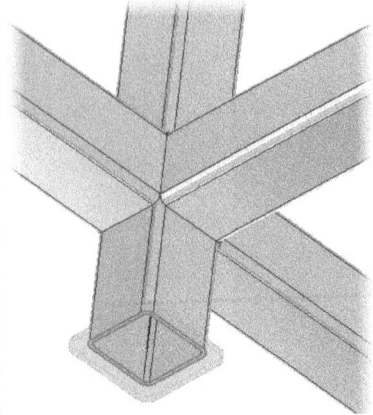

▼ Selection	
Position	▶ ▱ 6 Faces ⊗
▼ Behavior	
Placement	⬓ ⬓ ▾
Profile	Filleted Corners (mm) ▾
Fillet	20.000 mm ▸
Thickness	10.000 mm ▸
Size	Offset - profile ▾
	-20.000 mm ▸
Material	Aluminum 6061 ▾
Appearance	As Material ▾
▼ Orientation	

Figure 15–60

5. Click **OK** to create the end caps. The completed assembly should appear as shown in Figure 15–61.

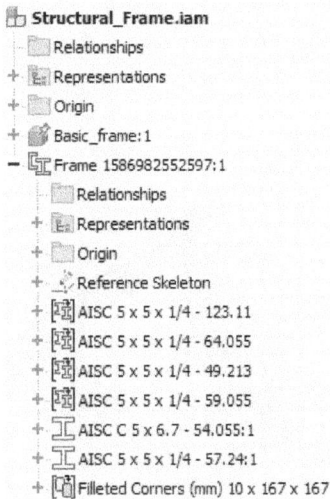

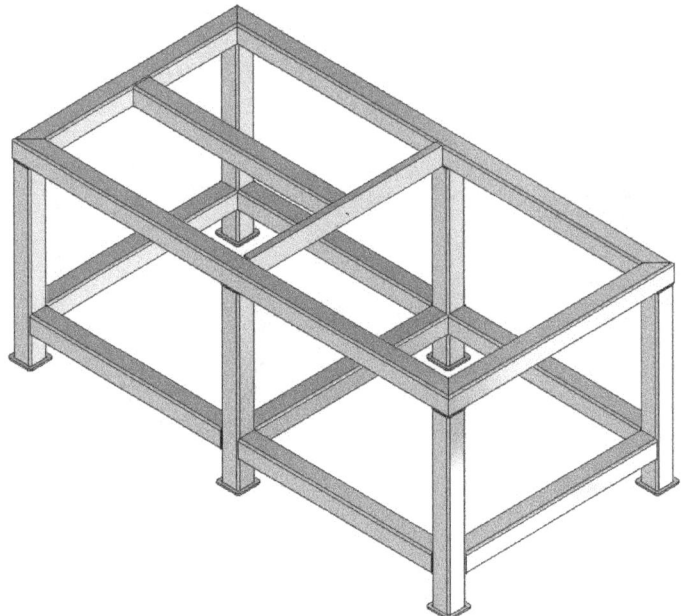

🗐 **Structural_Frame.iam**
- ▢ Relationships
- + ▨ Representations
- + ▢ Origin
- + ▨ Basic_frame:1
- − ⬓ Frame 1586982552597:1
  - ▢ Relationships
  - + ▨ Representations
  - + ▢ Origin
  - + ⁖ Reference Skeleton
  - + ▨ AISC 5 x 5 x 1/4 - 123.11
  - + ▨ AISC 5 x 5 x 1/4 - 64.055
  - + ▨ AISC 5 x 5 x 1/4 - 49.213
  - + ▨ AISC 5 x 5 x 1/4 - 59.055
  - + ⊥ AISC C 5 x 6.7 - 54.055:1
  - + ⊥ AISC 5 x 5 x 1/4 - 57.24:1
  - + ▨ Filleted Corners (mm) 10 x 167 x 167

Figure 15–61

6. Save the assembly.

Chapter Review Questions

1. Which of the following entities can be selected in the skeletal wireframe model to define the location of structural frame members? (Select all that apply.)

   a. Lines in a 2D sketch

   b. Lines in a 3D sketch

   c. Points

   d. Centerlines

   e. Construction Lines

   f. Splines

2. How do you access the **Frame Generator** options?

   a. *Assemble* tab>Frame panel

   b. *Environments* tab>Frame panel

   c. *Design* tab>Frame panel

   d. *Design* tab>Fasten panel

3. What do the white grips (shown in Figure 15–62) enable you to do when inserting a member?

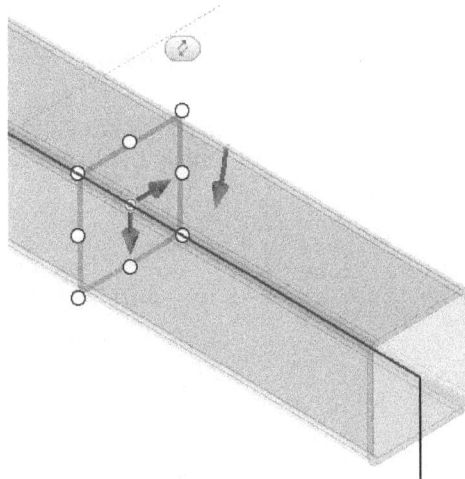

Figure 15–62

   a. Locate the position of the profile with respect to the reference.

   b. Define the end treatments available to the frame member.

   c. Define the shape of the profile for the frame member.

   d. All of the above.

4. Which of the following are true statements about reusing frame generated members? (Select all that apply.)

   a. The (Reuse) command enables you to reuse members that were generated in other assembly files.

   b. The direction in which a reused member is inserted along a new entity depends on where on the entity the reference is selected.

   c. To rotate a reused member about the reference entity, click ⟲ (Flip Direction).

   d. End conditions, such as Miters created on a parent member, reflect in all of the reused members.

5. The (Change Reuse) option enables you to edit a reused member's orientation.

   a. True

   b. False

6. Which of the following Miter types should be used to create a full miter cut with a defined gap?

   a.

   b.

7. Which of the following Frame options does not enable you to modify the joints between members?

   a. **Notch**

   b. **Miter**

   c. **Lengthen/Shorten**

   d. **Corner Joint**

8. What is the purpose of the Structural Shape Author?

   a. Publish a frame assembly for use in other projects.

   b. Automatically create a structural shape frame.

   c. Define new styles of end treatments, such as miters.

   d. Publish user-defined custom profiles to a library.

Command Summary

Button	Command	Location
	Beam/ Column Calculator	• **Ribbon:** *Design* tab>expanded Frame panel
	Change	• **Ribbon:** *Design* tab>Frame panel
	Change Reuse	• **Ribbon:** *Design* tab>Frame panel
	Corner Joint	• **Ribbon:** *Design* tab>Frame panel
	Frame Member Info	• **Ribbon:** *Design* tab>expanded Frame panel
	Insert Frame	• **Ribbon:** *Design* tab>Frame panel
	Lengthen/ Shorten	• **Ribbon:** *Design* tab>Frame panel
	Miter	• **Ribbon:** *Design* tab>Frame panel
	Notch	• **Ribbon:** *Design* tab>Frame panel
	Plate Calculator	• **Ribbon:** *Design* tab>expanded Frame panel
	Publish Part	• **Ribbon:** *Manage* tab>Content Center panel
	Remove End Treatments	• **Ribbon:** *Design* tab>expanded Frame panel
	Reuse	• **Ribbon:** *Design* tab>Frame panel
	Structural Shape Authoring	• **Ribbon:** *Manage* tab>Author panel
	Trim/Extend	• **Ribbon:** *Design* tab>Frame panel

Chapter

16

Assembly Duplication Options

Incorporating the use of duplication techniques into an assembly enables you to efficiently duplicate components (parts and subassemblies) in your assembly designs. These tools can include patterning components, mirroring to create new left- or right-handed versions of a component, or making copies of individual components or the entire assembly.

Learning Objectives in This Chapter

- Place multiple copies of a component simultaneously in an assembly using patterns.
- Create left- and right-handed versions of an assembly or components by mirroring.
- Create a copy of an entire assembly or selected components in an assembly.

16.1 Pattern Components

When working with assemblies, you might need multiple copies of a component. For example, the part on the left in Figure 16–1 requires nine rings to be added and placed in a circular pattern. You can add nine copies of the same component individually and then constrain each component. However, it saves time to place multiple copies simultaneously using a pattern, as shown on the right. Patterning enables you to add multiple instances of one component.

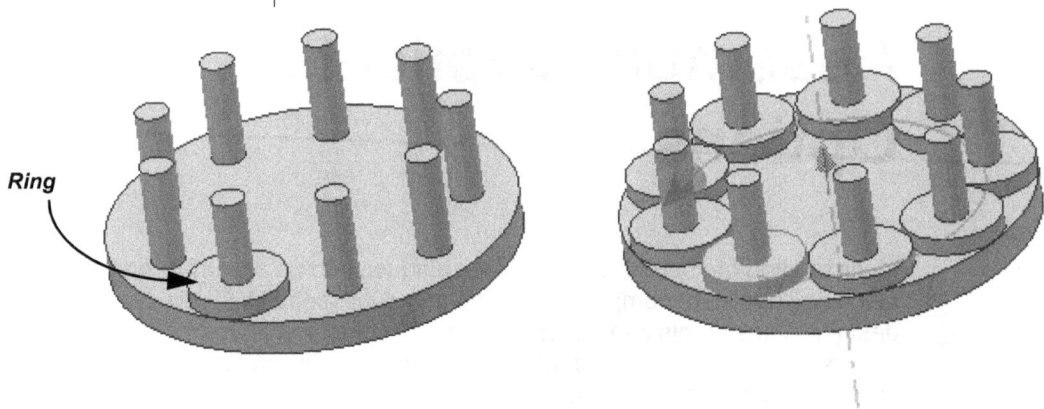

Ring

Figure 16–1

General Steps

Use the following general steps to create an assembly pattern:

1. Start the creation of the pattern.
2. Select the component to pattern.
3. Select the pattern type and attributes.
4. Complete the pattern.

Step 1 - Start the creation of the pattern.

To start the creation of pattern, in the *Assemble* tab>Pattern panel, click ⬚-⬚ (Pattern). The Pattern Component dialog box opens, as shown in Figure 16–2.

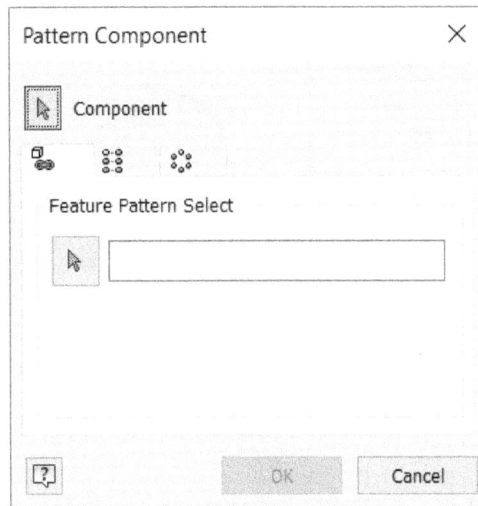

Pattern Component	✕
⬚ Component	
⬚ ⣿ ⣿	
Feature Pattern Select	
⬚ [_____]	
⬚	OK	Cancel

Figure 16–2

Step 2 - Select the component to pattern.

To select component(s) to pattern, click ⬚ (Component) and select the component(s).

Step 3 - Select the pattern type and attributes.

Three different pattern types are available. To select a type, select the required tab and define its attributes. The available pattern types include the following:

- ⬚ (Associative)

- ⣿ (Rectangular)

- ⣿ (Circular)

Associative Pattern

An associative pattern is a pattern of parts associated with a pattern of features in another part. To pattern a component using this option, the component should be constrained using geometry from the first feature in the feature pattern. For example, the part shown on the left in Figure 16–3 contains a pattern of holes. You can place and constrain a stud relative to the first hole. An associative pattern fills the remaining holes, as shown on the right side. This technique enables you to build intelligence into your assembly.

The pattern of features on the other part can be rectangular or circular.

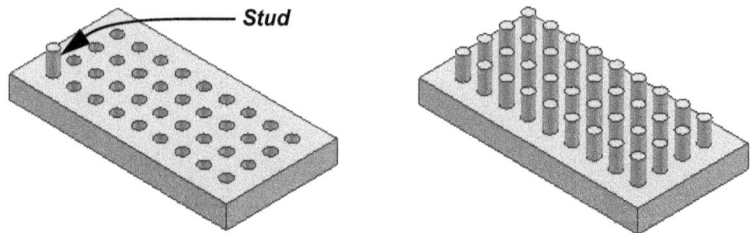

Stud

Figure 16–3

To create an associative pattern, select the 🖻 (Associative Pattern) tab and select the existing feature pattern in the Model Browser or assembly.

Rectangular Pattern

A rectangular pattern enables you to duplicate a component in one or two directions.

How To: Create a Rectangular Pattern

1. Select the ⠿ (Rectangular Pattern) tab, shown in Figure 16–4.

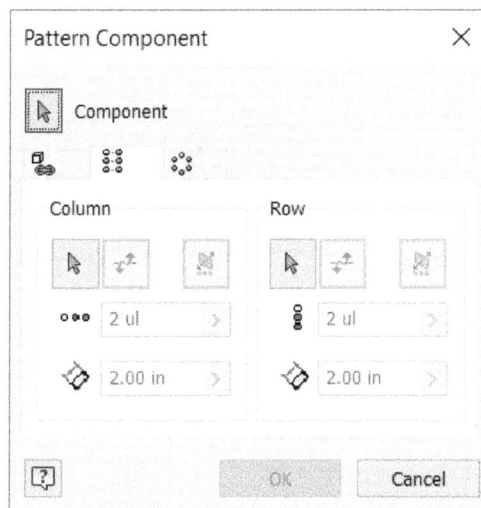

Figure 16–4

2. Click ⬉ (Column Direction) in the *Column* area and select a direction (edge or axis).

3. If required, click 🔀 (Flip Direction) to flip the pattern direction relative to the displayed reference direction.

4. If required, click ◪ (Midplane) to distribute the pattern instances on both sides of the original feature.

5. Enter the number of instances (column count •••) for the first direction.

6. Enter a spacing between instances (column spacing ◇) for the first direction.

7. If required, define a reference direction, number of instances, and spacing for a second direction.

Circular Pattern

A circular pattern enables you to duplicate a component in a circle or along an arc.

How To: Create a Circular Pattern

1. Select the ⁘ (Circular Pattern) tab, shown in Figure 16–5.

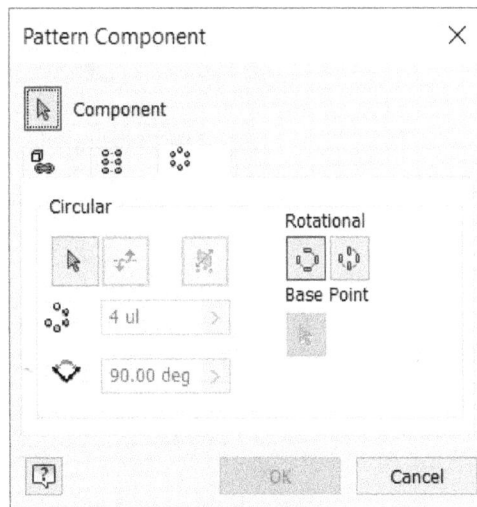

Figure 16–5

2. Click [icon] (Axis Direction) in the *Column* area and select the pattern axis. This reference does not need to be in the same plane as the component being patterned.

3. If required, click [icon] (Flip Direction) to flip the pattern direction relative to the displayed reference direction.

4. If required, click [icon] (Midplane) to distribute the pattern instances on both sides of the original feature.

5. Enter the number of instances (circular count [icon]).

6. Enter an angle between instances (circular angle [icon]).

7. Choose between [icon] (Rotational) or [icon] (Fixed) orientation options.

   • With [icon] (Rotational), the orientation of the pattern instances rotates as they move about the axis.

   • With [icon] (Fixed), the pattern instances keep the same orientation as the original.

8. Click [icon] (Base Point) to select the fixed pattern base point.

Step 4 - Complete the pattern.

Click **OK** to complete the pattern.

The component pattern is listed in the Model Browser with its elements. Each element contains a separate instance of the patterned component(s), as shown in Figure 16–6. The group of elements in a component pattern are dependent and behave as one component in the assembly. You cannot delete or modify individual patterned components.

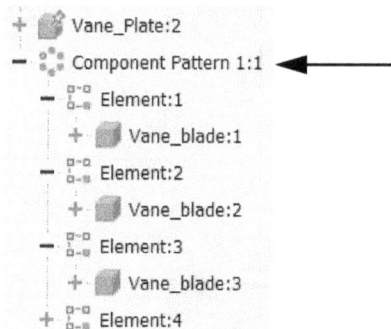

Figure 16–6

Editing Patterned Components

To manipulate individual patterned components, you can make them independent of the whole pattern. The position of an independent element is not controlled by the pattern and other constraints can be added to it. You can move or delete independent parts.

You cannot make the first element of the pattern independent.

- To make a pattern element independent, right-click on it in the Model Browser and select **Independent**, as shown on the left in Figure 16–7. The independent element is suppressed in the pattern and a copy of it is listed as a new separate component in the Model Browser, as shown on the right in Figure 16–7. The position of the independent component remains the same in the assembly.

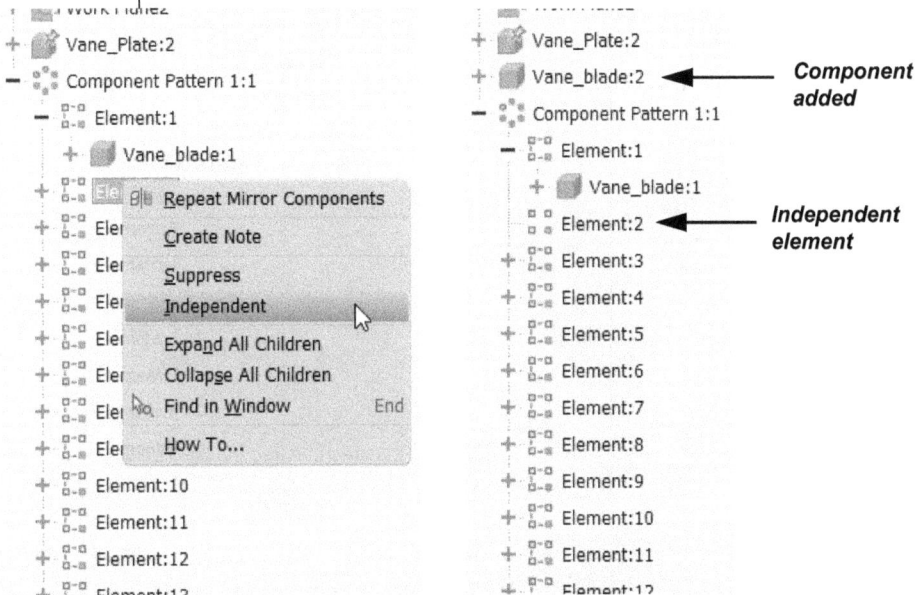

Figure 16–7

- You can toggle off the independent feature option on a component to bring it back into the pattern. Right-click on the suppressed pattern element and select **Independent**.

- Restoring an independent element does not delete its copy, as shown in Figure 16–8. You must manually delete the copy of the part (created when the element was made independent) to avoid having two components coincident with one another in the assembly.

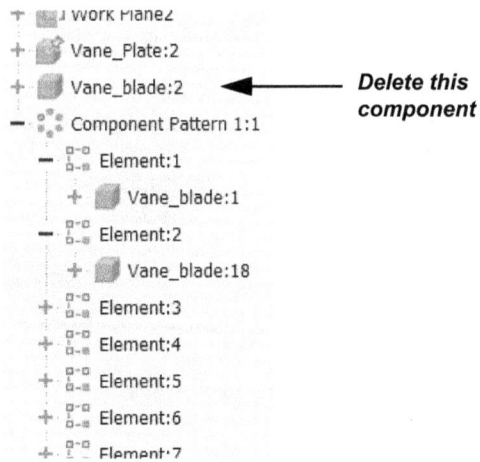

Figure 16–8

16.2 Mirror Components

Mirroring enables you to create left- and right-handed versions of an assembly or components, and to mirror parts or subassemblies in an assembly, as shown in Figure 16–9. You can select components in a subassembly to exclude them from the mirroring process. The mirrored components are dependent on the originals. Additionally, constraints must be manually added once the component is mirrored.

A component created by mirroring is a derived component. It is linked to the original component so that changes to the original component also affects the mirrored copy.

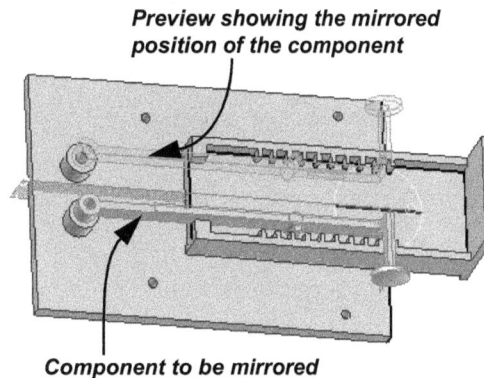

Preview showing the mirrored position of the component

Component to be mirrored

Figure 16–9

How To: Mirror Assembly Components

1. To mirror an assembly part, in the *Assemble* tab>Pattern panel, click ▯▮ (Mirror). The Mirror Components dialog box opens.

2. Click ▯ (Components) and select the component(s) to be mirrored.
   • If you select a subassembly, all of its parts are selected.

3. Click ▯ (Mirror Plane) and select the plane across which the components are going to be mirrored. A mirror plane reference can be a work plane or a flat face on a part.

4. Specify the mirroring option for each component by clicking its status icon next to each component name, as shown in Figure 16–10. As you click on the icon, its *Status* toggles through the available options.

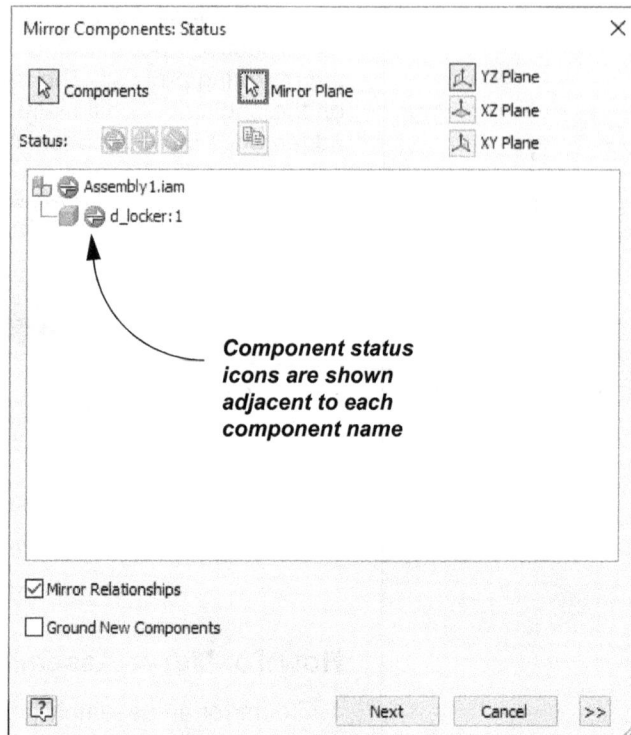

Figure 16–10

In the Model Browser, you can select a subassembly to automatically select all of its components for mirroring.

- Use ⊕ (mirror) to create a new file for the part or subassembly file being mirrored.

- Use ⊕ (Reuse) to create a new instance of the existing part or subassembly. No new files are created.

- Use ⊕ (Exclude) to set the component so that it is not included in the mirror operation.

5. Once the mirror options are defined, click **Next**.

6. In the Mirror Components: File Names dialog box (shown in Figure 16–11), confirm the components that are being mirrored.

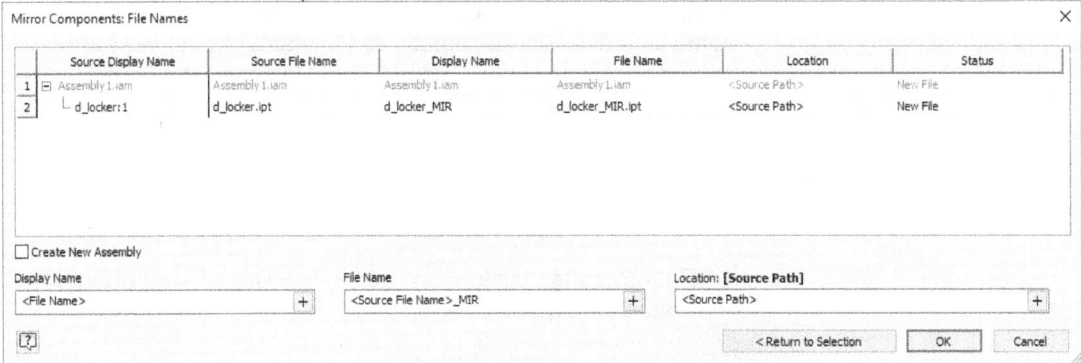

	Source Display Name	Source File Name	Display Name	File Name	Location	Status
1	⊟ Assembly 1.iam	Assembly 1.iam	Assembly 1.iam	Assembly 1.iam	<Source Path>	New File
2	└ d_locker:1	d_locker.ipt	d_locker_MIR	d_locker_MIR.ipt	<Source Path>	New File

☐ Create New Assembly

Display Name
<File Name>   +

File Name
<Source File Name>_MIR   +

Location: **[Source Path]**
<Source Path>   +

< Return to Selection   OK   Cancel

Figure 16–11

- If new files are being created (⊝), their new names display in the *File Name* column. You can change the default name by selecting and entering a new name in the required cell.

*Consider assigning default naming schemes for Mirror operations using the **File Naming Defaults** option in the Application Options>File tab.*

- As an alternative to simply renaming the cells, options in both the Display Name and the File Name drop-down lists enable you to customize the names in the table using parameter values.

- By default, the new components created by mirroring are placed in the same folder as the original components being mirrored, indicated by *<Source Path>* in the *Location* column. You can change the path using options in the Location drop-down list at the bottom of the dialog box.

- You can also have the mirrored components open in a new assembly (the default is to insert them in the current assembly) using the option **Create New Assembly**.

7. Click **OK** to mirror the component(s).

16.3 Copy Components

Copying creates a copy of an entire assembly or selected components in an assembly. You can then use the copy in the same or a different assembly. Any constraints between the copied components are maintained. However, the copied components are independent of the source component.

How To: Copy Assembly Components

1. To copy an assembly component, in the *Assemble* tab> Pattern panel, click ▯▮ (Copy). The Copy Components: Status dialog box opens.

2. Click ▯ (Components) and select the component(s) to be copied. If you select a subassembly, all of its parts are selected. Once you have selected the component(s) to copy, they are listed in the dialog box, as shown in Figure 16–12.

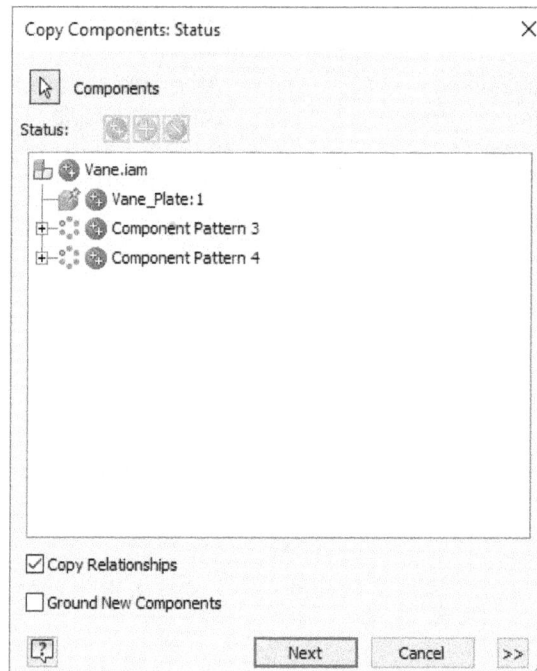

Figure 16–12

3. Specify the status for each component by clicking its status icon next to each component name. As you click on the icon, its status toggles through the available options.

- Use ⊕ (Copied) to create a new file for the part or subassembly file being copied.

- Use ⊕ (Reused) to create a new instance of the existing part or subassembly. No new files are created.

- Use ⊘ (Exclude) to exclude parts of a subassembly in the Copy operation.

4. Enable the **Copy Relationships** option to maintain the constraints and joints between the components selected to be copied. Clear this option to copy the components without maintaining any relationships.

5. Enable the **Ground New Components** option to automatically ground the new copied components.

6. In the expanded portion of the dialog box, you can disable the **Reuse Standard Content and Factory Parts** option if these types of components are selected for copying and you want to duplicate them.

7. Once the status settings are defined, click **Next**.

8. In the Copy Components: File Names dialog box (shown in Figure 16–13), confirm the components that are being copied.

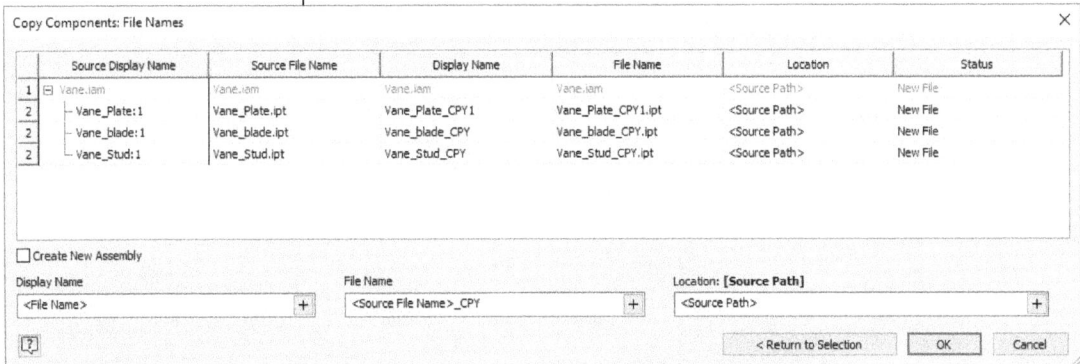

Figure 16–13

*Consider assigning default naming schemes for Copy operations using the **File Naming Defaults** option in the Application Options>File tab.*

- If new files are being created, the dialog box shows the new names in the *File Name* column. If required, you can change the default naming scheme by selecting and entering a new name in the required cell. Options in the File Name and Display Name drop-down lists can also be used to customize the names of mirrored components.

- By default, the new components created by copying are placed in the same folder as the original components, indicated by *<Source Path>* in the *Location* column. You can change the path using options in the Location drop-down list at the bottom of the dialog box.

- You can also have the copied components open in a new assembly (the default is to insert them in the current assembly) using the option **Create New Assembly**.

9. Click **OK** to copy the component(s).

Practice 16a | Mirror Assembly Components

Practice Objective

- Create a new component by mirroring an existing assembly component.

In this practice, you will mirror a component. The completed assembly is shown in Figure 16–14.

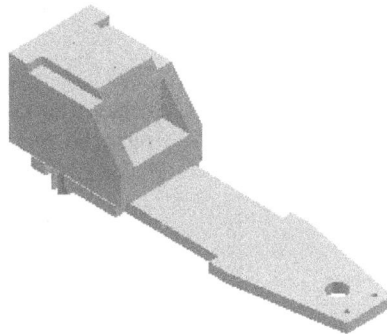

Figure 16–14

Task 1 - Open an assembly file.

1. Open **socket.iam** from the *Mirror Assembly Components* folder.

2. Toggle off the display of the **encbase**, **wire**, and **enctop** components. The assembly displays as shown in Figure 16–15.

*You can use the **Visibility** or **Isolate** option in the shortcut menu.*

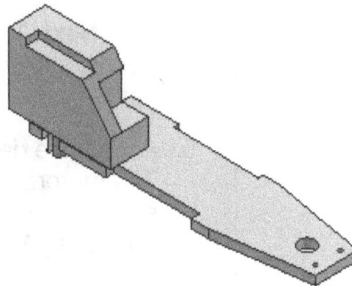

Figure 16–15

Task 2 - Mirror the connect part.

1. In the *Assemble* tab>Pattern panel, click (Mirror). The Mirror Components dialog box opens with all of the options available for mirroring.

2. Note that (Components) is selected by default. Select the **connect** part to be mirrored.

3. Click (Mirror Plane). In the Model Browser, expand **pcb:1** and select **Work Plane5**. A preview will show the mirrored position of the component, as shown in Figure 16–16.

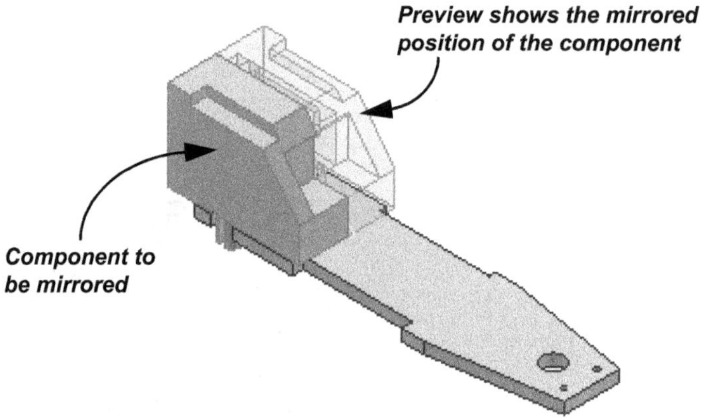

Figure 16–16

4. Accept the defaults in the Mirror Components dialog box and click **Next**. The Mirror Components: File Names dialog box opens, showing the default mirrored component name and path.

5. Accept the defaults and click **OK** to complete the operation. The mirrored part displays in the Model Browser as a separate assembly component with the name **connect_MIR:1**.

6. Toggle on the **Degrees of Freedom** (*View* tab>Visibility panel). Note that the mirrored component is not constrained. The assembly displays as shown in Figure 16–17.

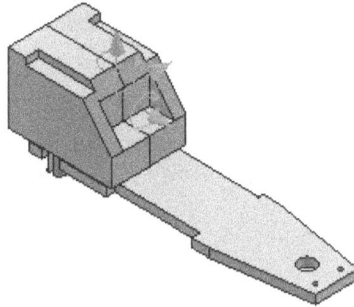

Figure 16–17

7. Constrain the mirrored component.

8. Save the assembly and close the window.

Practice 16b | Mirror and Pattern Components

Practice Objectives

- Copy a component by mirroring an existing assembly component.
- Add additional instances of a component in an assembly in a circular pattern.

In this practice, you will assemble a compressor vane by patterning and mirroring components in the assembly model. The final assembly is shown in Figure 16–18.

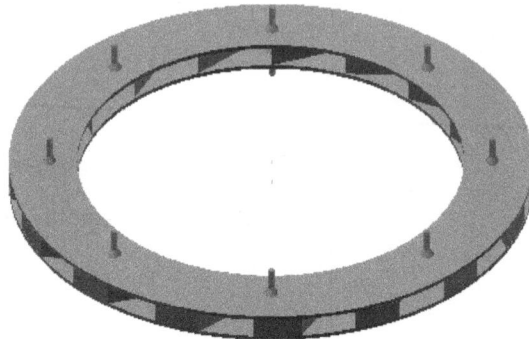

Figure 16–18

Task 1 - Open an assembly file.

1. Open **vane_mirror_pattern.iam** from the *Mirror and Pattern* folder. The assembly displays as shown in Figure 16–19.

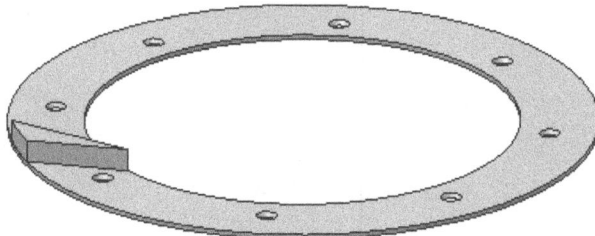

Figure 16–19

Task 2 - Mirror the first component.

Another instance of the **Vane_Plate** needs to be assembled into the assembly so that it rests on the top of the **Vane_Blade**. This instance will be created by mirroring the original **Vane_Plate** about a work plane. This will place the new instance in the assembly in the correct location with the correct orientation.

This work plane will be used as the mirror plane.

1. In the *3D Model* tab>Work Features panel, click (Plane) to create a work plane. Selecting the top of the **Vane_Plate** as the reference.

2. Place the cursor anywhere in the graphics window, hold the left mouse button, and drag the cursor in the upward direction.

3. Type an *offset* of **0.1775** and press <Enter>.

4. In the *Assemble* tab>Pattern panel, click (Mirror).

5. Select the **Vane_Plate**.

6. Click (Mirror Plane) and select the work plane you just created.

7. You want to reuse the existing component rather than create a new one. In the Mirror Component Status dialog box, click (Mirrored) next to **Vane_Plate:1** once, to change the mirroring option to (Reused), as shown in Figure 16–20.

Click this icon to toggle the Mirror option to Reused

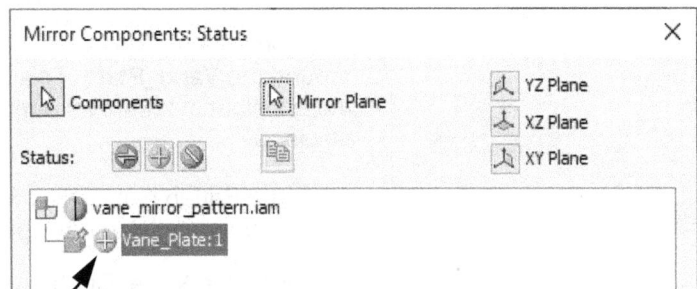

Mirror Components: Status

Components   Mirror Plane   YZ Plane
                                          XZ Plane
Status: XY Plane

vane_mirror_pattern.iam
    Vane_Plate:1

Figure 16–20

8. Click **Next**. The Mirror Components: File Names dialog box opens. Note that the dialog box shows that no new components are created.

9. Click **OK** to complete the mirroring operation.

10. Toggle off the visibility of the work plane. The assembly displays as shown in Figure 16–21.

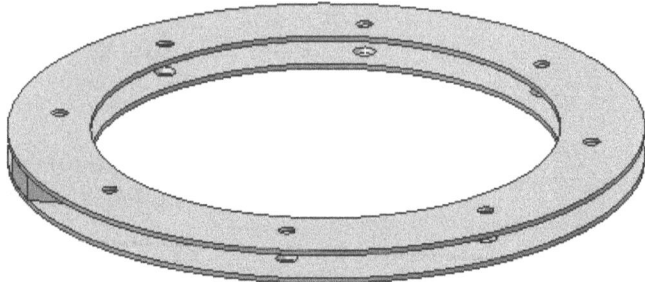

Figure 16–21

11. The new mirrored part is grounded and has one mate constraint to the work plane. Unground the new mirrored part, and delete the mate constraint.

12. Constrain the top **Vane_Plate:2** and the **Vane_Blade:1**. Ensure that the faces are oriented correctly. The face with the larger hole diameter of the countersink should be adjacent to the **Vane_Blade:1** component.

13. Add an angle constraint between the YZ planes of the **Vane_Plate:2** and the assembly at **0** degrees.

Task 3 - Pattern the vane_blade.

Additional **Vane_Blade** components are required to be added around the **Vane_Plate**. This can be done by constraining 15 more instances; however, creating a circular pattern is more efficient.

1. In the Patten panel, click ⬚-⬚ (Pattern). The Pattern Component dialog box opens.

2. Select the **Vane_Blade**.

3. Click ⠿ (Circular Pattern) in the dialog box.

4. Click ⌖ (Axis Direction) in the *Circular* area in the dialog box and select the outside circular surface of the **Vane_Plate** to define the axis of rotation.

You can also use equations in the fields to calculate the angle or number of instances.

5. Type **16** for the *Circular Count* and **22.5** for the *Circular Angle*, as shown in Figure 16–22. Select the ⌖ (Rotational) orientation option.

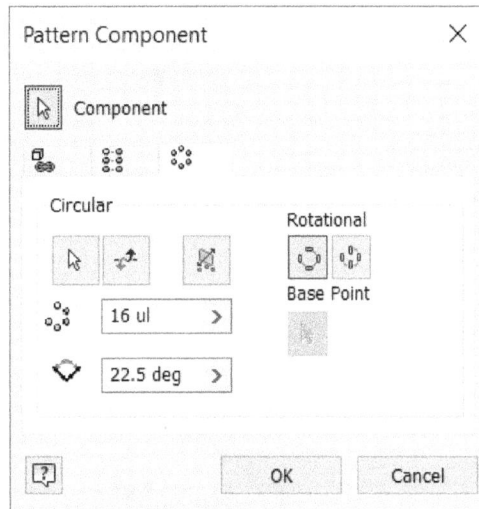

Figure 16–22

6. Click **OK**. The assembly displays as shown in Figure 16–23. For clarity, the visibility of top **Vane_Plate** is off and color has been assigned to the Vane_Blade components in the image.

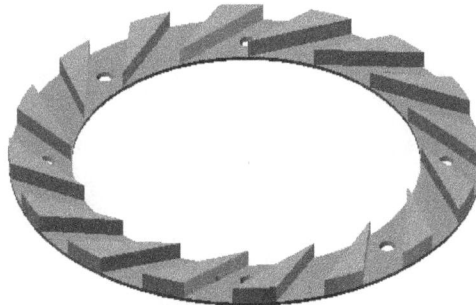

Figure 16–23

Task 4 - Assemble and pattern the Vane_Stud component.

The **Vane_Stud** must be inserted into each hole. This can be quickly preformed by constraining the **Vane_Stud** to the first instance of the hole pattern and using an associative pattern to create the rest.

1. Place a single instance of **Vane_Stud.ipt** in the assembly. This component is located in the *Mirror and Pattern* folder.

2. In the Model Browser, click **Modeling** to display the Modeling view, as shown in Figure 16–24.

Figure 16–24

3. Expand **Vane_Plate:1**, expand the **Circular Pattern** feature, and select the first occurrence, as shown in Figure 16–25. The first hole occurrence highlights. Constrain to this hole.

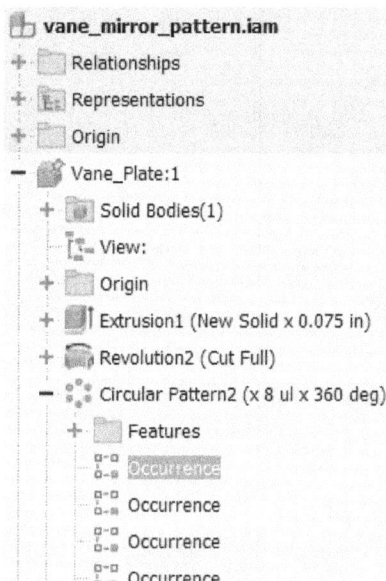

Figure 16–25

4. Select **Assembly** in the Model Browser to return to the Assembly view.

5. Apply an Insert constraint between the top edge of the **Vane_Stud** and the top edge of the hole that highlighted in step 5 of this task, as shown in Figure 16–26. Note the orientation of the **Vane_Stud**, as shown in Figure 16–26.

For clarity, the visibility of the Component Pattern and the top **Vane_Plate** *have been toggled off.*

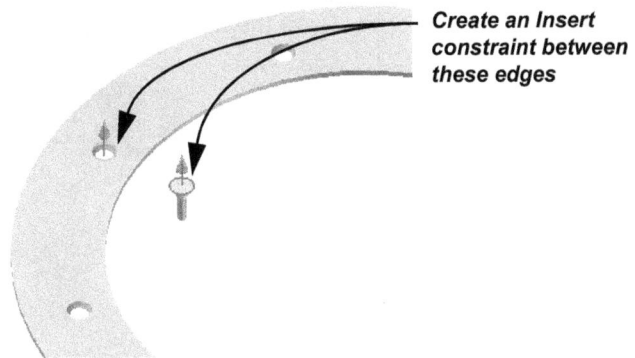

Create an Insert constraint between these edges

Figure 16–26

6. In the Pattern panel, click (Pattern) and select **Vane_Stud**.

7. Select the (Associated Feature Pattern) tab. In the *Feature Pattern Select* area of the dialog box, click and select one of the holes in **Vane_Plate:1**.

8. Click **OK** to complete the pattern. The assembly displays as shown in Figure 16–27.

For clarity, the visibility of the Component Pattern and the top **Vane_Plate** *have been toggled off.*

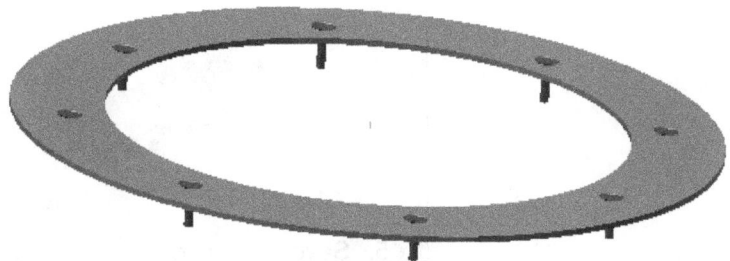

Figure 16–27

Task 5 - Assemble and pattern the Vane_Stud component.

1. Place another instance of the **Vane_Stud** in the assembly.

2. Display the top **Vane_Plat**e, if previously cleared, and locate the first occurrence of the hole pattern.

3. Constrain the **Vane_Stud** component to the first occurrence of the hole pattern, as shown in Figure 16–28.

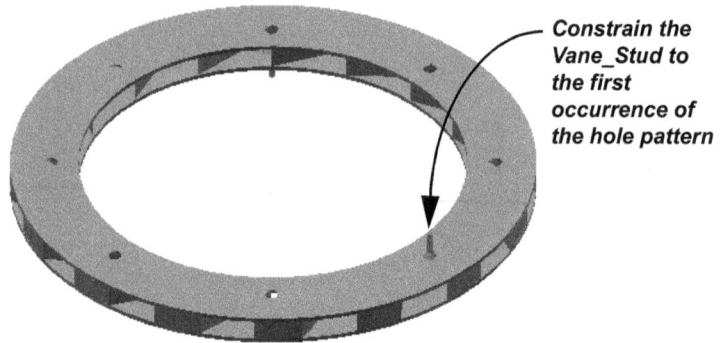

Constrain the Vane_Stud to the first occurrence of the hole pattern

Figure 16–28

4. Associatively pattern the **Vane_Stud** using the hole pattern in the **Vane_Plate**. The assembly displays as shown in Figure 16–29.

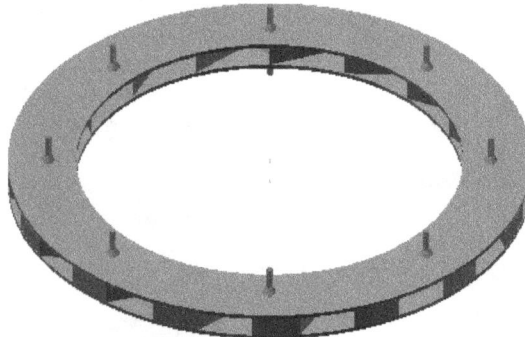

Figure 16–29

5. Save and close the assembly.

Practice 16c | Copy Components

Practice Objectives

- Create additional instances of components in an assembly using the **Copy** command.
- Create a new assembly by copying some but not all of the components in an existing assembly.

In this practice, you will create the top half of the vane assembly by copying instead of mirroring the component. You will then copy the entire assembly to a new assembly file, creating new files for some components. The final vane assembly is shown in Figure 16–30.

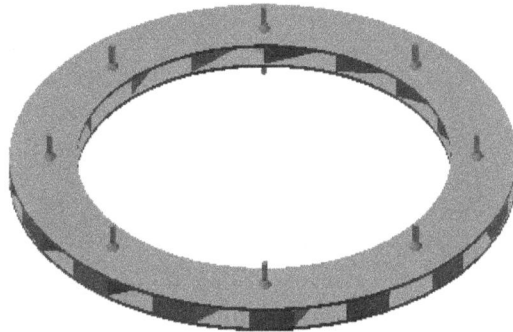

Figure 16–30

Task 1 - Open an assembly file.

1. Open **Vane.iam** from the *Mirror and Pattern* folder. Half of the assembly has already been completed, as shown in Figure 16–31.

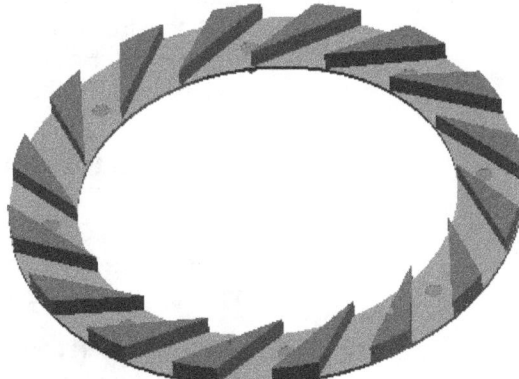

Figure 16–31

Task 2 - Copy the assembly components.

1. In the Pattern panel, click ▯▮ (Copy). In the Model Browser, select **Vane_Plate** and **Component Pattern 4**.

2. In the Copy Components dialog box, click 🌐 (Copied) beside **Vane.iam** to change the **Copy** option to ⊕ (Reused) for all of its components, as shown in Figure 16–32.

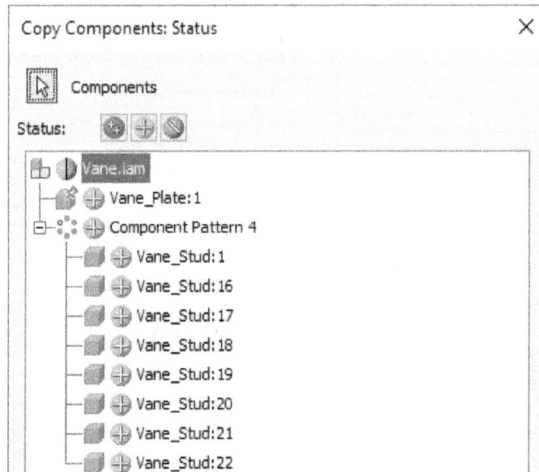

Figure 16–32

3. Click **Next**.

4. Leave the defaults in the Copy Components: File Names dialog box and click **OK**.

5. Click in the graphics screen to place the copied components.

6. Expand the components under the copied components. Note that constraints between the copied components are maintained. However, the copied components are independent of the source component.

Task 3 - Place the copied components.

1. Remove the Grounded constraint from the copied **Vane_Plate** component by right-clicking on the component in the Model Browser and clearing the **Grounded** option.

2. Apply an Insert constraint between the bottom outside curved edge of the copied **Vane_Plate** and the top curved edge of the **Vane_Blade**.

3. Apply an Angle constraint between the YZ plane of the assembly and the YZ plane of the copied **Vane_Plate**. The assembly displays as shown in Figure 16–33.

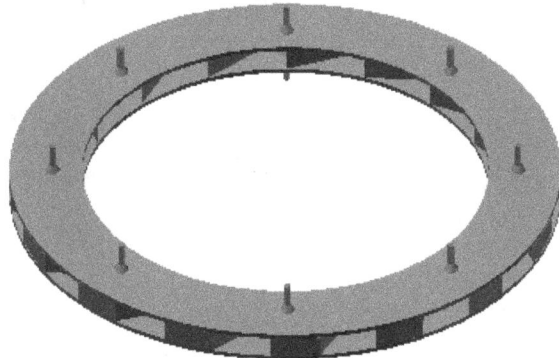

Figure 16–33

Task 4 - Copy the assembly to a new assembly.

1. In the Pattern panel, click [icon] (Copy).

2. In the Model Browser, select the top-level assembly.

3. Create new part files for all the components except the **Vane_Blade**, as shown in Figure 16–34. **Vane_Blade** is contained in **Component Pattern 3**.

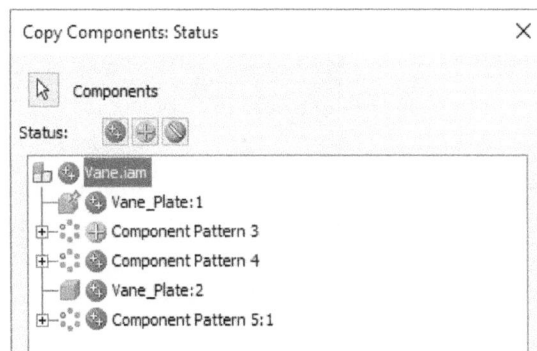

Figure 16–34

4. Click **Next**.

5. In the dialog box, select **Create New Assembly**.

6. Select in the *New Name* field of **Vane.iam** and change the name of the new assembly to **250-231.iam**, as shown in Figure 16–35.

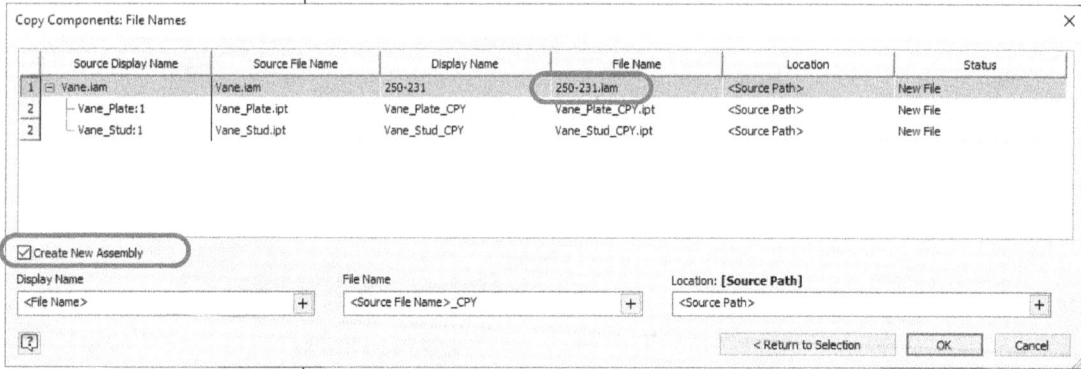

	Source Display Name	Source File Name	Display Name	File Name	Location	Status
1	⊟ Vane.iam	Vane.iam	250-231	250-231.iam	<Source Path>	New File
2	— Vane_Plate:1	Vane_Plate.ipt	Vane_Plate_CPY	Vane_Plate_CPY.ipt	<Source Path>	New File
2	└ Vane_Stud:1	Vane_Stud.ipt	Vane_Stud_CPY	Vane_Stud_CPY.ipt	<Source Path>	New File

Figure 16–35

7. Click **OK**. A copy of the assembly is created in a new assembly file called **250-231.iam**.

8. Review the Model Browser for the new assembly. Note that new part names have been created for the **Vane_Plate** and the **Vane_Stud**. However, the **Vane_Blade** file is still being used.

9. Save and close both assembly models.

Chapter Review Questions

1. What type of pattern can be created from a component in an assembly? (Select all that apply.)

   a. Rectangular

   b. Circular

   c. Associative

2. When mirroring components in a subassembly, you can select the subassembly in the Model Browser to automatically select all of its components.

   a. True

   b. False

3. Once components are patterned in an assembly, how can you make a single pattern element independent?

   a. In the Model Browser, double-click on the pattern element.

   b. In the Model Browser, right-click on the element and select **Suppress**.

   c. In the Model Browser, right-click on the pattern element and select **Independent**.

   d. In the Model Browser, select the pattern element and select **Independent** from the *Assembly* tab>Pattern panel.

4. Copied components are dependent on the source components.

   a. True

   b. False

5. Which tool can be used and still maintain constraints between components?

   a. Mirror Components

   b. Copy Components

   c. Both Mirror Components and Copy Components

6. Which of the following statements is true regarding patterning components in an assembly? (Select all that apply.)

a. The position of an independent pattern element is not controlled by pattern constraints.

b. All elements in a pattern can be set as independent.

c. Independent pattern elements can be reset as dependent; however, you must manually delete the independent copy that was generated.

d. To create an associative pattern, the component must be constrained to any one of the feature pattern instances.

Command Summary

Button	Command	Location
	Copy	• **Ribbon**: *Assemble* tab>Component panel
	Mirror	• **Ribbon**: *Assemble* tab>Component panel
	Pattern	• **Ribbon**: *Assemble* tab>Component panel

Working with Weldments

A weldment is a special type of assembly. In manufacturing, it is formed by welding together two or more pieces. You can create weldment assemblies with the Autodesk® Inventor® software, and also use the three different weldment feature groups: Preparations, Welds, and Machining.

Learning Objectives in This Chapter

- Recognize the components of a weldment assembly and how it differs from a standard assembly file.
- Convert an existing assembly file to a weldment assembly.
- Navigate between the Weld, Preparation, and Machining feature groups and recognize the commands that are applicable to each.
- Initiate the creation of a fillet weld and select appropriate placement references, measurement types, values, and weld attributes to create required weld geometry.
- Initiate the creation of a cosmetic weld and select the appropriate placement reference and options to determine the length and area of the cosmetic weld.
- Initiate the creation of a groove weld and select the appropriate placement references, fill direction, and attribute settings to create weld geometry between two disconnected faces.
- Create appropriate weld symbols that detail how and where each weld type is to be created.
- Edit an existing weld feature to make required changes.

17.1 Working with Weldments

A weldment file is a special type of assembly file created using a weldment template. It has the same extension as other assembly files (.IAM) and the standard assembly tools for adding components and constraints. It also includes a number of special tools for weldments. Weldments can be documented on their own and be used in an assembly as subassemblies, called sub-weldments. You can switch a normal assembly file to a weldment assembly by clicking ![weldment icon] (Convert to Weldment) in the *Environments* tab>Convert panel. However, you cannot switch a weldment file to a normal assembly file.

An example of a weldment assembly is shown in Figure 17–1.

When a weld feature group is active, an End of Features item displays in the browser under the group. If you drag it above a feature, anything under it is not included. This procedure is similar to suppressing features. If you add another feature or part, it is added above the End of Features item.

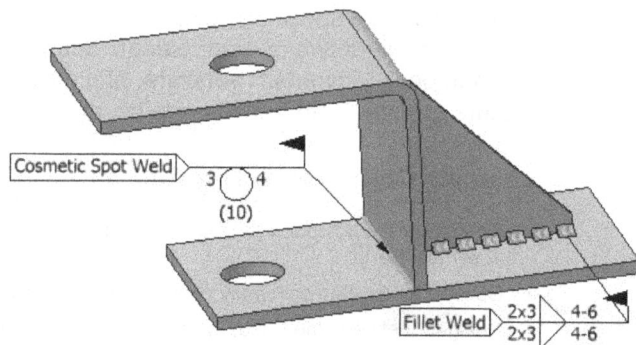

Figure 17–1

Weldment assemblies have three weldment feature groups in the Model Browser, as shown in Figure 17–2.

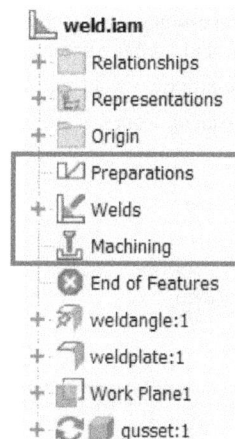

Figure 17–2

Preparations

A weld preparation is a material removal process performed on a weldment assembly before welds are applied. They are important to ensure adequate weld strength. A chamfer is a typical feature that you use to prepare the assembly. To prepare the weld edge, in the Model Browser, double-click on the **Preparation** group or in the *Weld* tab>Process panel, click

▢ (Preparation) to activate the Preparation and Machining panel, shown in Figure 17–3.

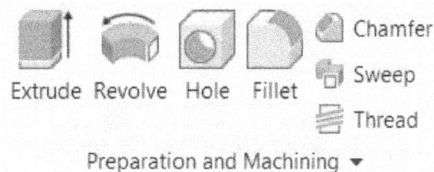

Figure 17–3

Create the required feature, right-click, and select **Finish Edit**, or in the *Weld* tab>Return panel, click ◀ (Return) to return to the Weldment Assembly environment.

Welds

The Welds feature group enables you to add welds, symbols that identify the welds, control the display of the weld on the ends of the weld, and run reports. To access the Welds feature group, double-click on **Welds** group in the Model Browser, or in the

Weld tab>Process panel, click ▨ (Welds) to activate the Weld panel, as shown in Figure 17–4.

The Weld Calculator option is only available when an existing weld is selected. It enables you to design and check weld joints. This option is not discussed in this guide.

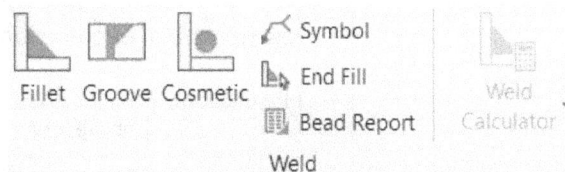

Figure 17–4

You can create Fillet, Cosmetic, and Groove welds using the Autodesk Inventor software. Detailed steps are included in the following topics.

Weld Symbols

You can add a welding symbol to any of the weld types during their creation by activating the **Create Welding Symbol** option available in Fillet Weld, Cosmetic Weld, and Groove Weld dialog boxes. Each of these dialog boxes expand, as shown in Figure 17–5, to reveal additional options for creating weld symbols.

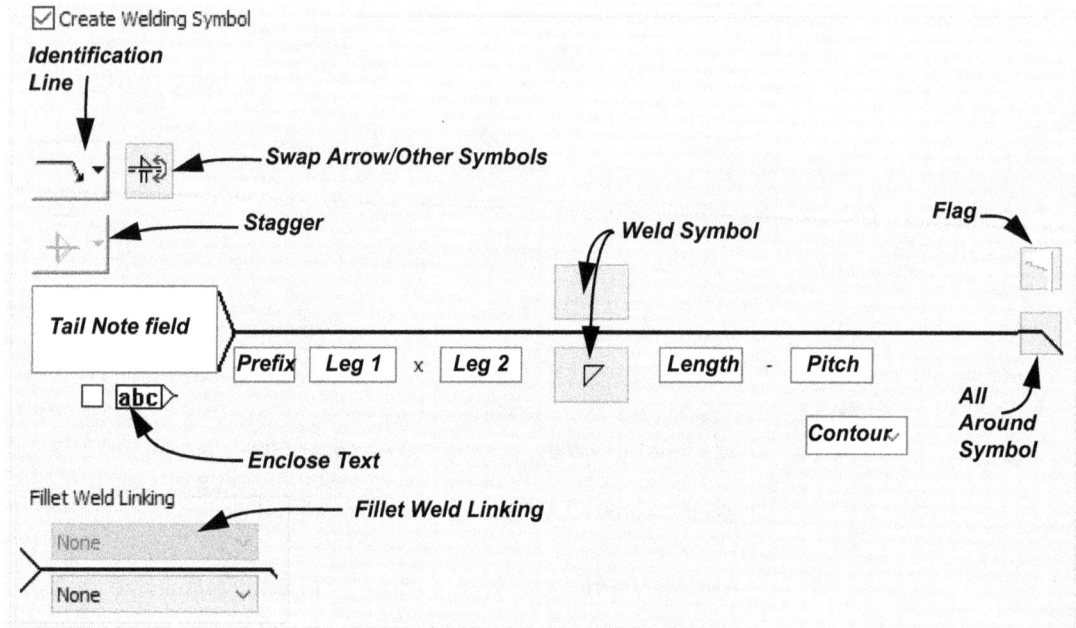

Figure 17–5

Descriptions of each option are described as follows:

Identification Line	Select to have no identification line, an identification line above, or an identification line below.
Swap Arrow/Other Symbols	Toggle to switch the arrow and symbols to be located above or below the reference line.
Stagger	Select a stagger option for fillet welding symbols when they are set on both sides of the reference line.
Tail Note Box	Enter text to add to the reference line.
Enclose Text	Select the check box to include a border around the text.
Prefix	Enter text for a prefix.
Legs	Enter text for leg 1 and leg 2.

Weld Symbol	Select a symbol from the palette to apply an Arrow side and/or Other side symbol. Additional fields display, depending on the symbol selected.
Length	Enter a length for the weld.
Pitch	Enter a distance between welds.
Contour	Select a contour for the weld.
Flag	Toggle to display or not display a flag for the weld.
All Around Symbol	Toggle to display or not display an All Around symbol for the weld.
Fillet Weld Linking	Use the drop-down list to select from the list of unconsumed fillet beads. If a bead is selected from the list, welding symbol options (such as **Leg 1**, **Length**, **Pitch**, and **Contour**) are controlled by the bead and cannot be manually edited. To remove the link between the bead and the welding symbol, select **None** from the drop-down list.

You can add welding symbols after a weld has been created, by clicking ⚊ (Symbol) in the *Weld* tab>Weld panel. The dialog box that opens is the same, and has the same options to define the symbol. Using the **Welding Symbol** command, you can group multiple beads into one symbol.

Machining Features

Machining features are for operations performed after the parts are joined, such as holes and cuts. Machining features can only remove material. The weld symbol leader updates automatically when a machining operation affects the weld. To add machining features to the weldment assembly, double-click on the **Machining** group in the Model Browser, or in the *Weld* tab>

Process panel, click ⚙ (Machining) to activate the Preparation and Machining panel, as shown in Figure 17–6.

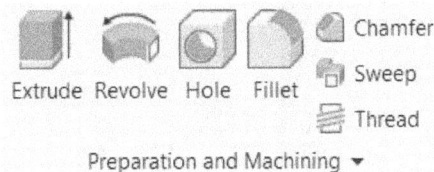

Extrude Revolve Hole Fillet Chamfer Sweep Thread

Preparation and Machining ▼

Figure 17–6

Create the required feature (cuts, holes, chamfers), right-click and select **Finish Edit** or in the *Weld* tab>Return panel, click

 (Return) to return to the Weldment Assembly environment. Once created, these features are listed under Machining in the Model Browser.

Preparations, Welds, and Machining features should be applied in that order. If you add welds after adding machining features, for example, the machining features are not visible when you add the welds.

17.2 Fillet Welds

A fillet weld can span a gap, but does not penetrate the opening of the gap.

Fillet welds are one of two available types of solid welds (groove welds are the other type). Solid welds create a weld bead that adds material to the assembly, as shown in Figure 17–7. Fillet welds can be created between one or more faces of specified part or parts. Use fillet welds where interference checking or exact mass properties are important.

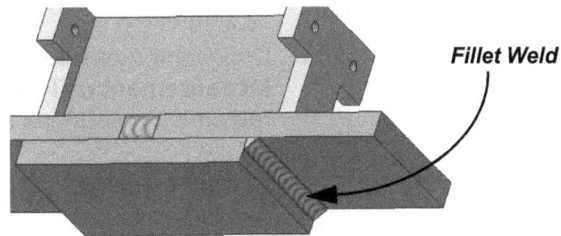

Fillet Weld

Figure 17–7

How To: Create a Fillet Weld Feature

1. Activate the Welds group using either of the following:
   - Double-click on the Welds group in the Model Browser.

   - In the *Weld* tab>Process panel, click [icon] (Welds).

2. In the *Weld* tab>Weld panel, click [icon] (Fillet). The Fillet Weld dialog box opens as shown in Figure 17–8.

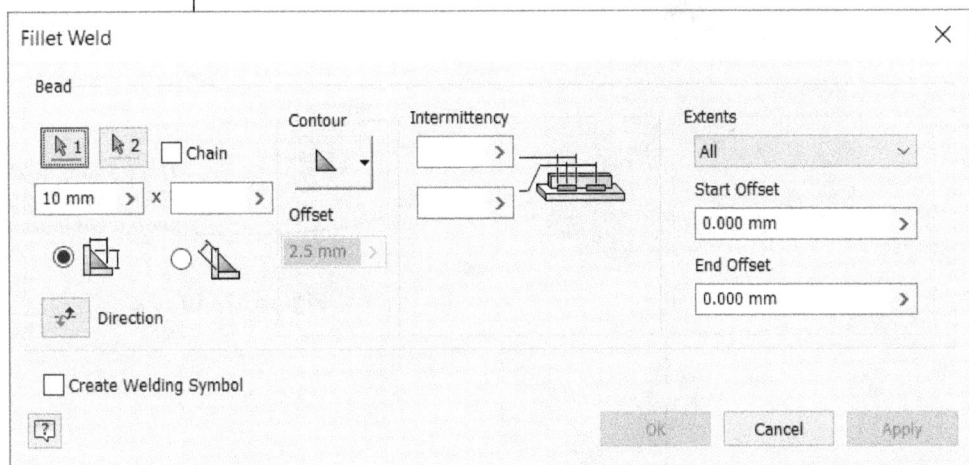

Figure 17–8

To remove a face from the selection set, hold <Shift> and select the unwanted face.

3. Select one or more faces from the model for the first selection set.
   - The selected faces highlight in blue.
   - Select the **Chain** option to automatically select all faces tangent to the selected face.

4. Click 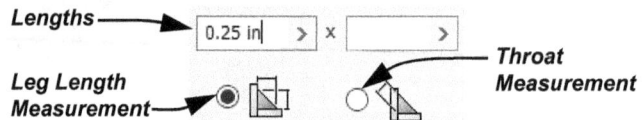 (Select Face(s)), or right-click and select **Continue** to select the faces for the second selection set.
   - The selected faces for the second selection set highlight in green.

5. Define the measurement type by selecting **Leg Length Measurement** or **Throat Measurement** and enter the required length(s), as shown in Figure 17–9.

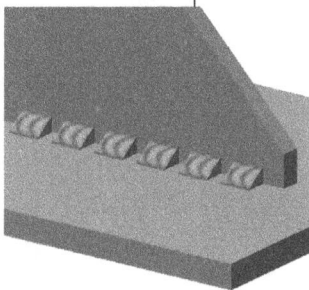

Figure 17–9

6. Select weld attributes, as required.

   - Set the bead contour to ◺ (Flat), ◹ (Convex), or ◿ (Concave). Enter an offset value when convex or concave is selected, to adjust the severity of the curve for the weld.

   - Enter values for intermittency to create welds that do not span the entire width of a face, as shown in Figure 17–10.

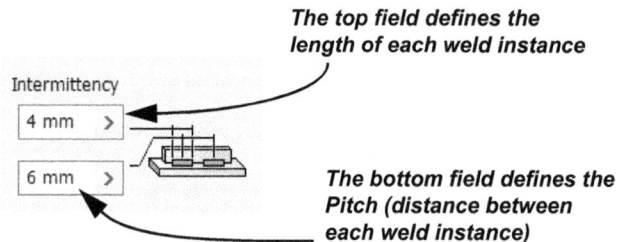

Figure 17–10

*Once the weld has been created, you cannot edit the feature and enable the **Create Welding Symbol** option. To create the symbol, in the Weld tab>Weld panel,*

click ⌐ (Symbol).

*Click ✴ (Direction) to reverse the start direction for **All** or **Start-Length** fillet welds.*

- To create a weld symbol for the current weld, select the **Create Welding Symbol** option. Complete the *Create Welding Symbol* area of the Fillet Weld dialog box, as required.

7. Define the extents of where a weld begins and where it ends. The **Extents** menu has three options:

   - **All:** Creates the weld across the entire edge.
   - **From-To:** Enables you to select a start and end plane between which the weld is created.
   - **Start-Length:** Creates a weld that does not start or end at an edge.

8. Enter offset values from the start or end of the fillet segment. These options are only available for the **All** and **Start-Length** Extent options.

9. Click **Apply** to place the Fillet weld. Continue adding Fillet welds as required. Once the required Fillet welds have been added, click **Cancel** to close the Fillet Weld dialog box.

Editing Fillet Welds

You can edit an existing Fillet weld by right-clicking on it in the Model Browser and selecting **Edit Feature**.

- To change the location of a weld symbol, select the weld symbol, select the green grip dot using the left mouse button, and drag the dot to a new location.

- To edit the note, right-click on it in the Model Browser and select **Edit Welding Symbol**.

- In the *Weld* tab>Weld panel, click 🔺 (End Fill) to add end fill annotations to weld beads, as shown in Figure 17–11. These annotations can be added to the drawing.

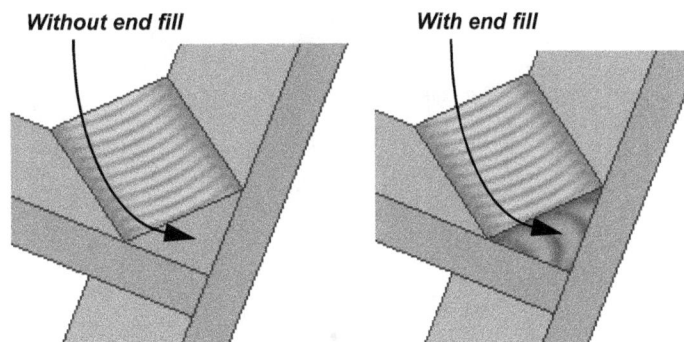

Figure 17–11

17.3 Cosmetic Welds

Cosmetic welds display as highlighted edges on the model, as shown in Figure 17–12. They do not display the weld bead, and are not reflected in interference calculations. To include cosmetic welds in the mass properties of the assembly, select the **Include Cosmetic Welds** checkbox in the *Physical* tab of the iProperties dialog box.

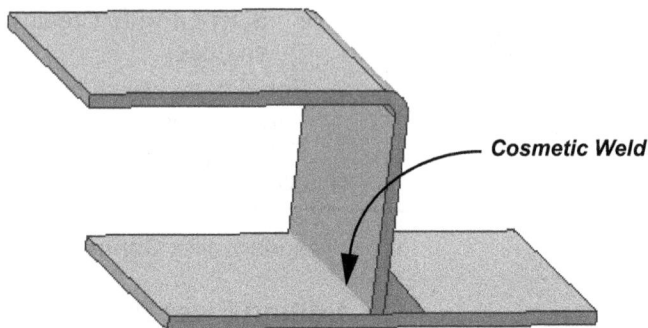

Cosmetic Weld

Figure 17–12

How To: Create a Cosmetic Weld Feature

1. Activate the Welds group using either of the following:
   - In the Model Browser, double-click on the Welds group.

   - In the *Weld* tab>Process panel, click (Welds).

2. In the *Weld* tab>Weld panel, click (Cosmetic). The Cosmetic Weld dialog box opens as shown in Figure 17–13.

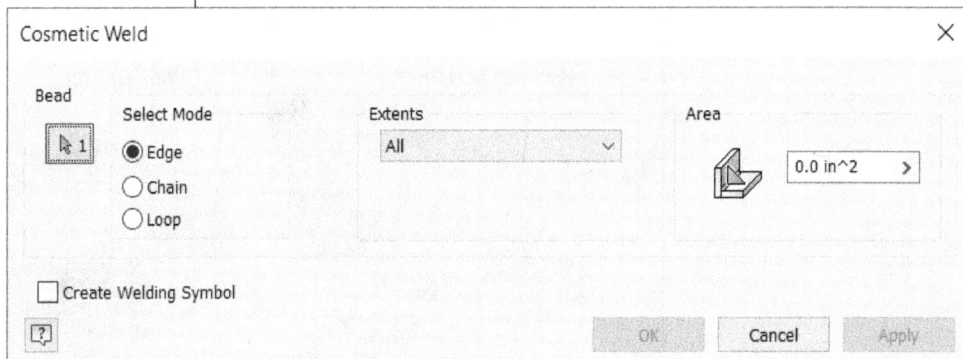

Figure 17–13

To remove a face from the selection set, hold <Shift> and select the unwanted face.

3. Select one or more edges from the model to define the selection set.
   - Select one or more edges from the model. You can use one of the **Select Mode** options to help you efficiently select edges.
   - The selected faces highlight in blue.
   - Select the **Chain** option to automatically select all of the faces that are tangent to the selected face.
4. Define the extents of where a weld begins and where it ends. The Extents drop-down list has the following options:
   - **All:** Creates the weld across the entire edge.
   - **From-To:** Enables you to select a start and end plane between which the weld is created.
5. Enter a value for the area of the Cosmetic weld. The area is used in calculating the mass properties of the weld and the assembly.

*Once the weld has been created you cannot edit the feature and enable the **Create Welding Symbol** option. To create the symbol, in the Weld tab>Weld panel,*

click ⌐ (Symbol).

6. To create a weld symbol for the current weld, select the **Create Welding Symbol** option. Complete the *Create Welding Symbol* area of the Cosmetic Weld dialog box as required.
7. Click **Apply** to complete the Cosmetic weld. Once the required Cosmetic welds have been added, click **Cancel** to close the Cosmetic Weld dialog box.

Editing a Cosmetic Weld

You can edit an existing Cosmetic weld by right-clicking on it in the Model Browser and selecting **Edit Feature**. To change the location of a weld symbol, select the weld symbol, select the green grip dot using the left mouse button, and drag the dot to a new location. To edit the note, right-click on it in the Model Browser and select **Edit Welding Symbol**.

17.4 Groove Welds

Groove welds are one of two available types of solid welds (fillet welds are the other type). Solid welds create a weld bead that adds material to the assembly, as shown in Figure 17–14. Use groove welds to aid in interference checking or obtaining exact mass properties. Groove welds are created between two or more disconnected faces.

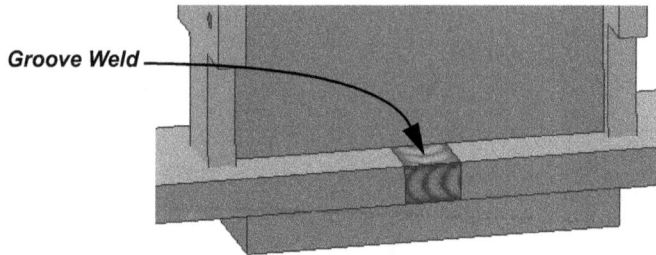

Groove Weld

Figure 17–14

How To: Create a Groove Weld Feature

1. Activate the Welds group using either of the following:
   - In the Model Browser, double-click on the Welds group.

   - In the *Weld* tab>Process panel, click .

2. In the *Weld* tab>Weld panel, click . The Groove Weld dialog box opens as shown in Figure 17–15.

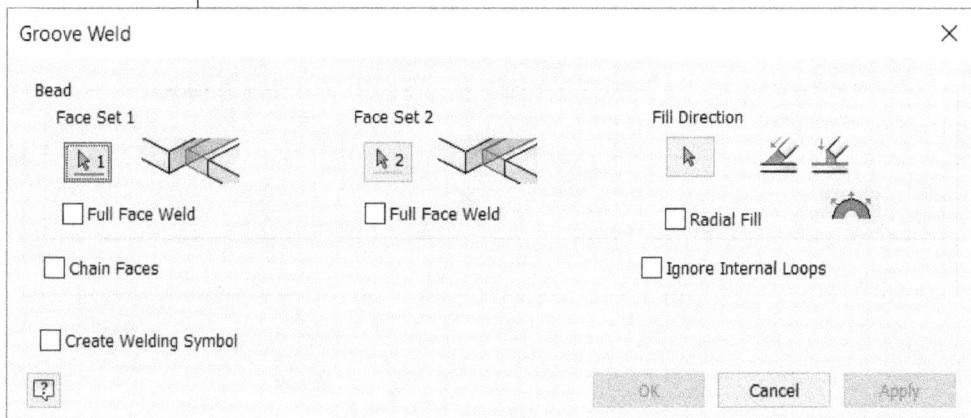

Figure 17–15

To remove a face from the selection set, hold <Shift> and select the unwanted face.

3. Select one or more faces from the model for the first selection set.
   - The selected faces highlight in blue.
   - Select the **Chain Faces** option to automatically select all faces tangent to the selected face.
   - Select the **Full Face Weld** option to expand the weld to cover the entire face area of the selection set.

4. Click (Select Face(s)), or right-click and select **Continue** to select the faces for the second selection set.
   - The selected faces for the second selection set highlight in green.

5. In the *Fill Direction* area, click (Select Fill Direction) to specify the direction of the weld.
   - You can select an edge or a face to define the direction. When the direction is controlled by the **Full Face Weld** option, specifying the direction is not always required.
   - Select the **Radial Fill** option to create a Groove weld around a cylinder. When this option is selected, a Fill Direction reference is not required.

6. Define the additional weld attributes, as required.
   - Use the **Ignore Internal Loops** option to create a weld across features, such as holes or cuts.
   - To create a weld symbol for the current weld, select the **Create Welding Symbol** option. Complete the *Create Welding Symbol* area in the Groove Weld dialog box as required

*Once the weld has been created you cannot edit the feature and enable the **Create Welding Symbol** option. To create the symbol, in the Weld tab>Weld panel,*

click *(Symbol).*

7. Click **Apply** to complete the process of placing the Groove weld. Continue adding Groove welds as required. Once the required Groove welds have been added, click **Cancel** to close the Groove Weld dialog box.

Editing a Groove Weld

You can edit an existing Groove weld by right-clicking on it in the Model Browser and selecting **Edit Feature**. To change the location of a weld symbol, select the weld symbol, select the green grip dot using the left mouse button, and drag the dot to a new location. To edit the note, right-click on it in the Model Browser and select **Edit Welding Symbol**.

Practice 17a

Working with Weldments I

Practice Objectives

- Create an intermittent solid weld that adds material between components in an assembly using a Fillet weld.
- Create a cosmetic weld that adds a graphical element to the model without adding solid geometry.
- Add symbols to the weld features to visually display their characteristics in the model.
- Add a preparation hole feature to represent geometry that is to be created after the model has been welded.

In this practice, you will open a weldment assembly. You will create fillet welds for the gusset and a spot weld between two assembly components. Finally, you create a preparation hole on the assembly model, assemble a new component through the hole and create groove welds. The final assembly is shown in Figure 17–16.

*When creating the welds in this practice, the **Welded Aluminum - 6061** material is used. If the material appearance does not display a texture, the link may be incorrect for your system configuration. To locate the missing texture file, open the Material Browser and double-click on **Welded Aluminum - 6061**. Select the Appearance tab, and select in the missing image cell. In the Texture Editor, reset the path by browsing to and selecting C:\Users\ Public\Documents\ Autodesk\Inventor 2021\Textures\surfaces\ weldcat0.bmp. Save the changes and close all editors.*

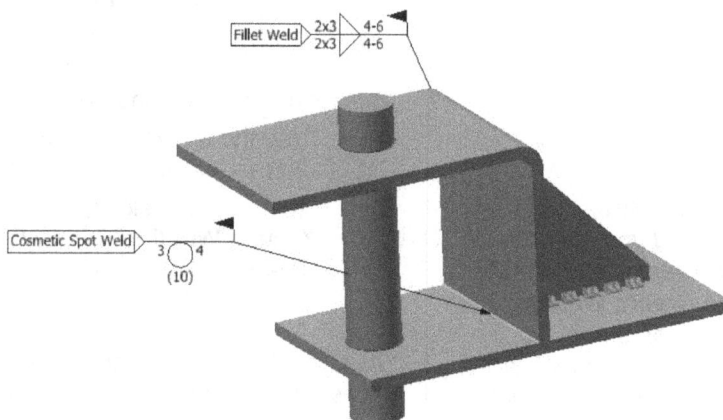

Figure 17–16

Task 1 - Add fillet welds to the assembly.

1. Open **weld.iam** from the top-level practice files folder.

2. Use the Model Browser to examine the model and its component constraints. The model consists of two sheet metal parts and a gusset part, and it is fully constrained.

3. In the Model Browser, double-click on the Welds group. The *Weld* tab becomes the active tab.

4. In the *Weld* tab>Weld panel, click (Fillet). The Fillet Weld dialog box opens.

5. Select the gusset face for the first selection set shown in Figure 17–17. Click (Select Face(s)) and select the face shown in Figure 17–17 for the second selection set.

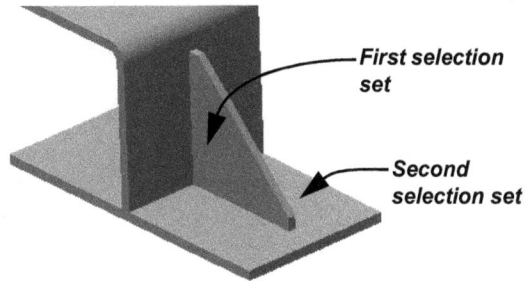

First selection set

Second selection set

Figure 17–17

6. Ensure that (Leg Length Measurement) is selected. In the **Extents** menu, select **Start-Length**. Enter the values for Leg 1, Leg 2, Intermittency (Length and Pitch), and Extents (Start Offset and Length), as shown in Figure 17–18.

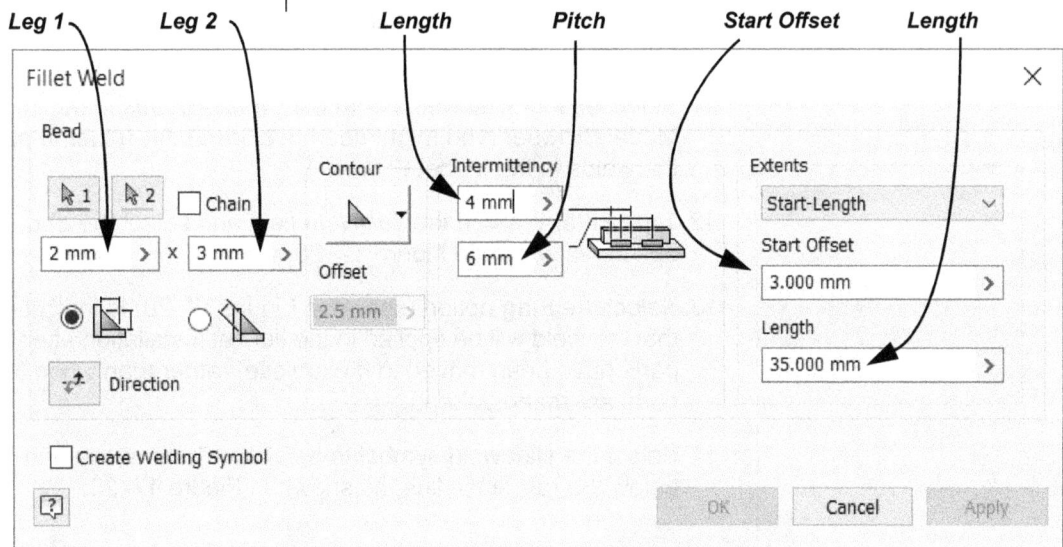

Figure 17–18

7. Click **Apply** to create the fillet weld but leave the dialog box open.

8. Create three more fillet welds, one for the vertical edge of the gusset plate and two for both edges on the other side of the gusset plate. Use the same values as for the previous fillet weld, as shown in Figure 17–19.

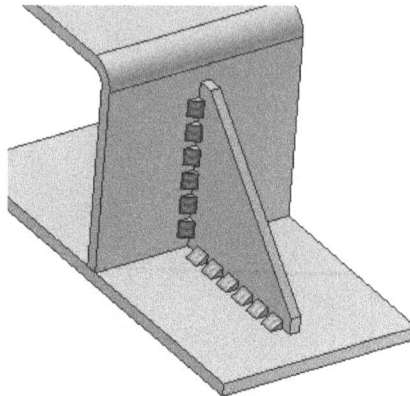

Figure 17–19

9. Click **Cancel** to close the dialog box.

10. In the *Weld* tab>Weld panel, click ↗ (Symbol) to add a welding symbol to the beads you just created. The Welding Symbol dialog box opens.

11. Select all four fillet welds from the Welds>*Beads* folder in the Model Browser (you might need to expand this folder to see the welds in the Model Browser).

12. Type **Fillet Weld** in the *Tail Note* field and select the **abc** option, as shown in Figure 17–20.

13. Select the **Flag** option (shown in Figure 17–20) to indicate that the weld will be applied in the field at installation after the parts have been moved to the job site, rather than when the parts are manufactured.

14. Select the fillet weld symbol to be shown both above and below the reference line, as shown in Figure 17–20.

15. In the **Fillet Weld Linking** menu, select **Fillet Weld 1** for below the reference line and the corresponding fillet weld on the other side of the gusset (the weld on the horizontal edge of the gusset) for above the line. The remaining fields in the Welding Symbol dialog box will automatically populate with values, as shown in Figure 17–20.

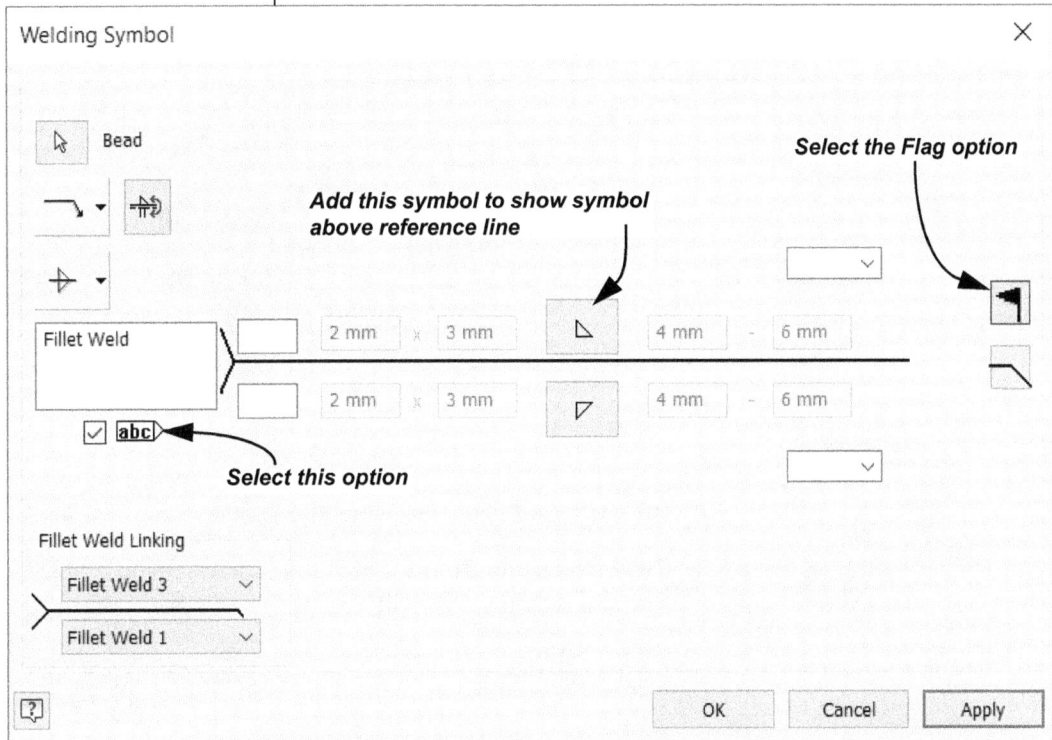

Figure 17–20

16. Click **OK** to create the weld symbol and close the dialog box. The model displays as shown in Figure 17–21.

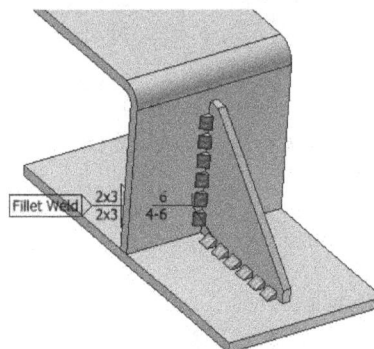

Figure 17–21

Task 2 - Add a cosmetic spot weld to the assembly.

1. In the *Weld* tab>Weld panel, click (Cosmetic). The Cosmetic Weld dialog box opens.

2. Select the edge shown in Figure 17–22.

Select this edge

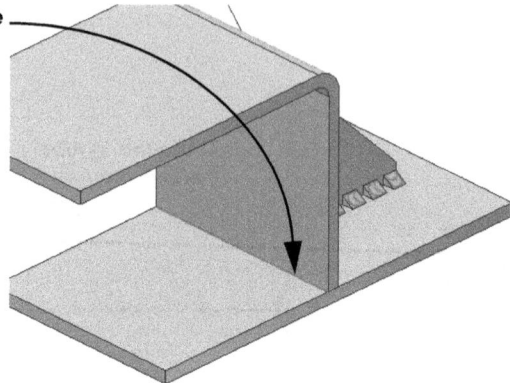

Figure 17–22

3. Activate the **Create Welding Symbol** option.

4. Type **Cosmetic Spot Weld** in the *Tail Note* field and select the **abc** option underneath.

5. Click (Weld symbol). The weld table displays.

6. Click (Spot or Projection Weld) and enter the following values:
   - *Leg 2:* **3** (to the left of the weld symbol)
   - *Length:* **4** (to the right of the weld symbol)
   - *Number:* **10** (below the weld symbol)

7. Select **Flag**.

8. Click **OK** to create the welds and to close the dialog box.

Hold the cursor over a field to display a description for it, if you are not sure which fields correspond to Leg 2, Length, and Number.

Cosmetic welds display as highlighted edges on the model. They do not actually display the weld bead, and are not reflected in interference calculations.

9. Move the welding symbols as required. To move a weld symbol, select it and then select and drag a green handle on the leader line. Release to place the symbol. The model displays similar to that shown in Figure 17–23.

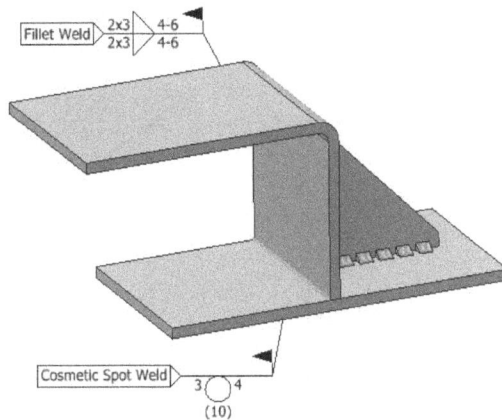

Figure 17–23

10. Right-click and select **Finish Edit** to activate the assembly model, or click (Return) in the Return panel.

Task 3 - Create a preparation hole.

---

*You can also double-click on **Preparations** in the Model Browser.*

1. In the *Weld* tab>Process panel, click (Preparation) to activate the Preparation and Machining panel.

2. Create a hole feature on the top face of the weldangle plate. Dimension the hole center, as shown in Figure 17–24. Enter **15 mm** for the hole diameter and set the *Termination* option to **Through All**. Click **OK** to complete the creation of the hole.

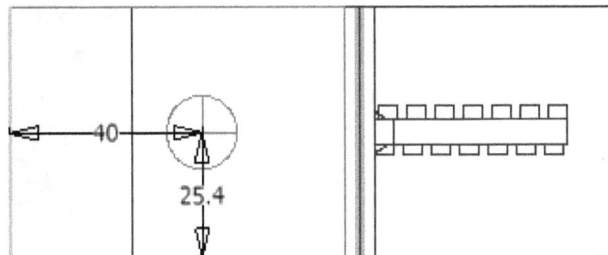

Figure 17–24

You can also right-click and select **Finish Edit** *to activate the assembly model.*

3. In the *Weld* tab>Return panel, click (Return) to activate the assembly model. The model displays as shown in Figure 17–25.

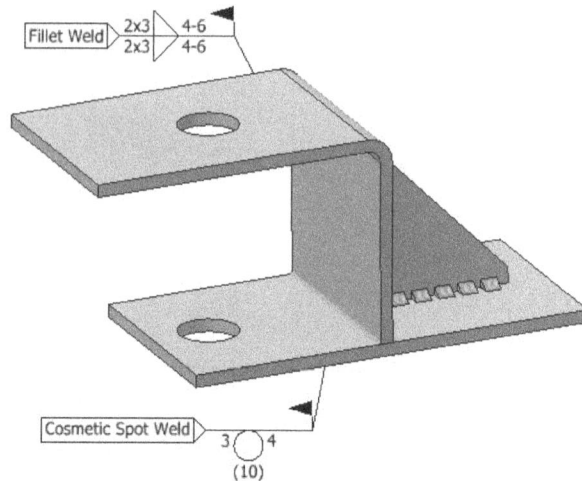

Figure 17–25

Task 4 - Place a new component and add a radial groove weld.

---

1. In the *Assemble* tab>Component panel, click (Place) to assemble a new component into the weldment assembly.

2. Assemble **pipe.ipt**. Use an Insert constraint and an Angle constraint to fully locate the component, similar to that shown in Figure 17–26. The weld symbol display has been toggled off for clarity.

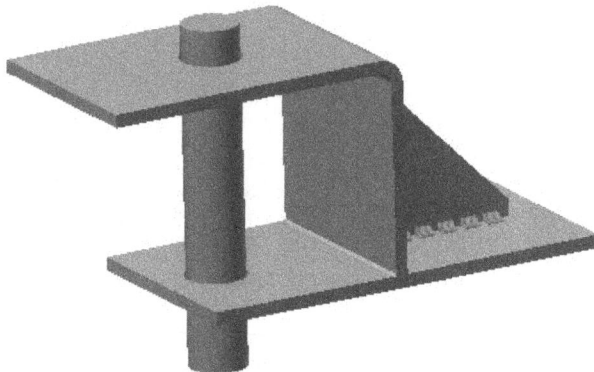

Figure 17–26

3. Select the *Weld* tab. In the Model Browser, double-click on the Welds group. In the Weld panel, click (Groove). The Groove Weld dialog box opens.

4. Select the inside face of the hole as the first reference and the cylindrical face of the cylinder as the second, as shown in Figure 17–27.

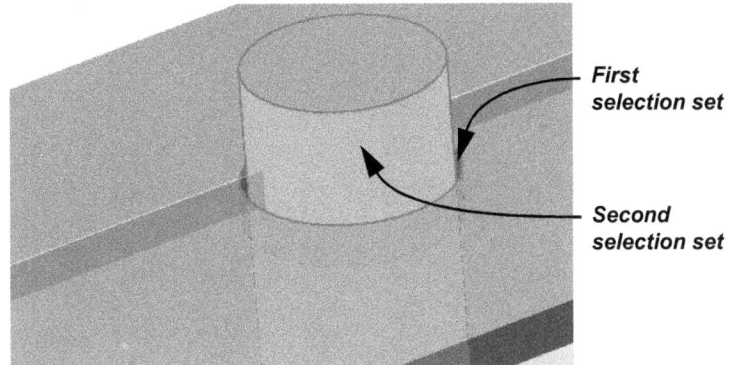

First selection set

Second selection set

Figure 17–27

5. Select **Radial Fill**, as shown in Figure 17–28.

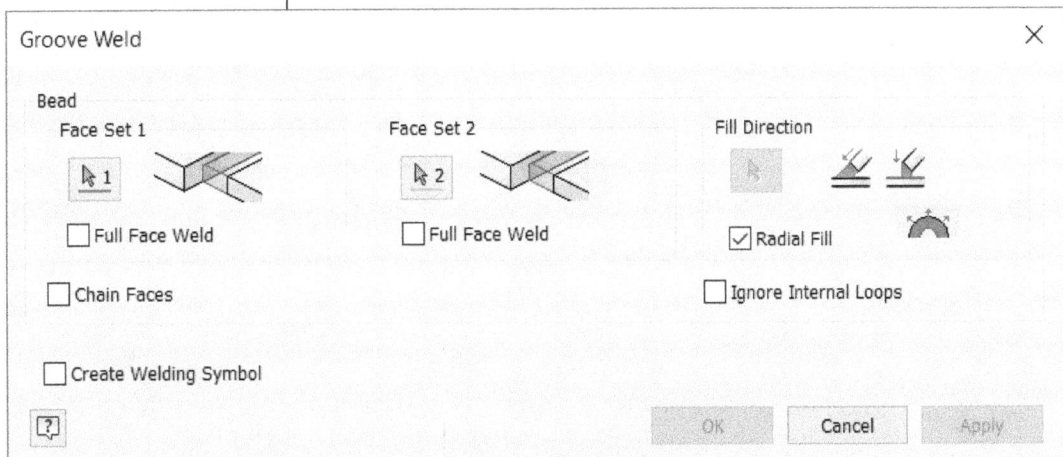

Figure 17–28

6. Click **OK** to complete the weld.

7. Create the same weld in the lower location.

8. In the *Weld* tab>Return panel, click (Return) to activate the assembly model. The model displays as shown in Figure 17–29.

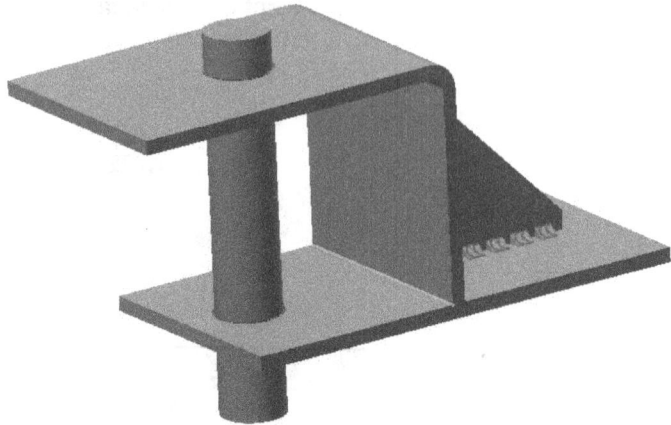

Figure 17–29

9. Save the assembly.

10. Close the window.

Practice 17b

Working with Weldments II

Practice Objectives

- Create a chamfer feature that removes material from existing solid geometry in preparation for adding a weld feature.
- Create fillet welds that add material between components in an assembly.
- Create welds that add material between disconnected faces using a Groove weld.

In this practice, you will add a chamfer, groove welds, and a variety of fillet welds. The final assembly is shown in Figure 17–30.

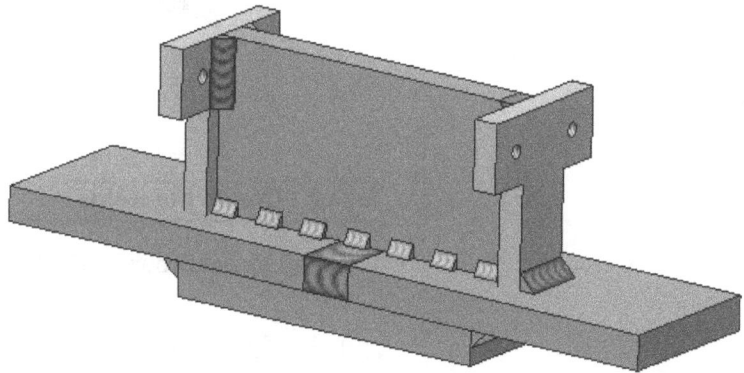

Figure 17–30

*When creating the welds in this practice the **Welded Steel Mild** material is used. If the material appearance does not display a texture, the link may be incorrect for your system configuration. To locate the missing texture file, open the Material Browser and double-click on **Welded Steel Mild**. Select the Appearance tab, and select in the missing image cell. In the Texture Editor, reset the path by browsing to and selecting C:\Users\ Public\Documents\ Autodesk\Inventor 2021\Textures\surfaces\ weldcat0.bmp. Save the changes and close all editors.*

Task 1 - Open an assembly and create a chamfer.

1. Open **Weldment.iam** from the top-level practice files folder.

2. In the Model Browser, double-click on the Preparations group. In the *Weld* tab, the Preparation and Machining panel activates, enabling you to modify parts before creating the weld. You can also click ⬜ (Preparation) (Weld tab>Process panel).

3. Create a chamfer using the parameters defined in the dialog box shown in Figure 17–31. Because the model is symmetrical, the chamfer can be applied to either edge.

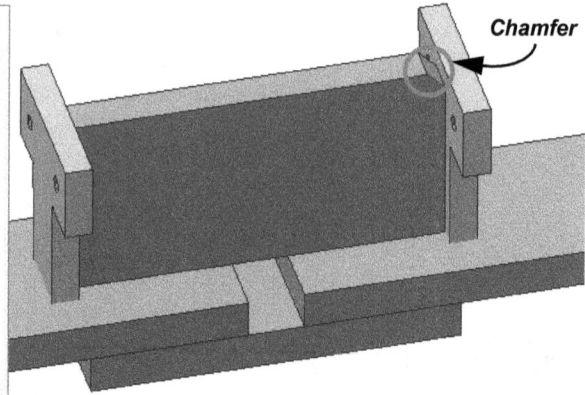

Figure 17–31

Task 2 - Create the welds.

1. In the Model Browser, double-click on the Welds group.

2. In the *Weld* tab>Weld panel, click [ ] (Groove). The Groove Weld dialog box opens, as shown in Figure 17–32.

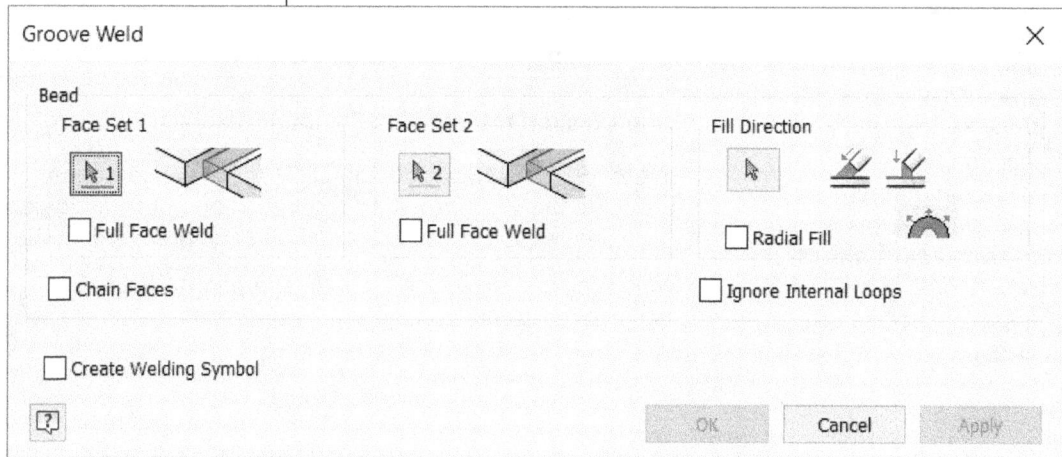

Figure 17–32

3. Select the face shown in Figure 17–33 for *Face Set 1*. Activate **Full Face Weld** in the *Face Set 1* area.

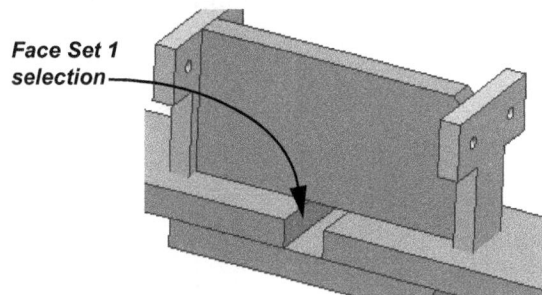

Face Set 1 selection

Figure 17–33

4. Click [⌖ 2] (Select Face(s)) and select the face shown in Figure 17–34 for *Face Set 2*. Activate **Full Face Weld** in the *Face Set 2* area.

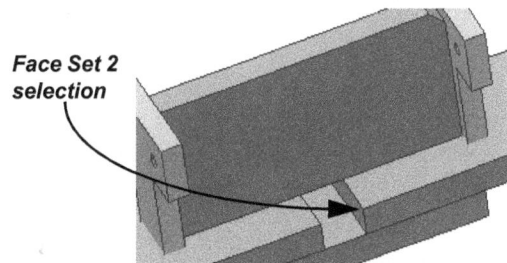

Face Set 2 selection

Figure 17–34

5. Click **OK** to complete the groove weld. The full face groove weld displays as shown in Figure 17–35.

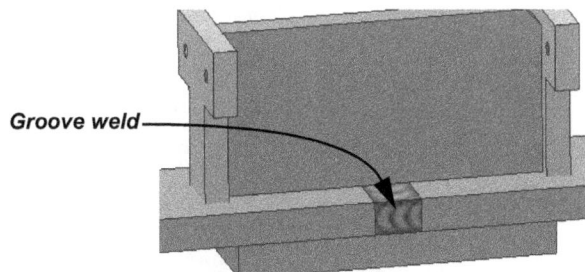

Groove weld

Figure 17–35

6. Create the fillet weld shown in Figure 17–36. Select the two perpendicular surfaces adjacent to the weld. Use the **Leg Length Measurement** option and type **12.7 mm** for both leg values to create the fillet weld. Click **Apply** to create the weld and leave the dialog box open for the next step.

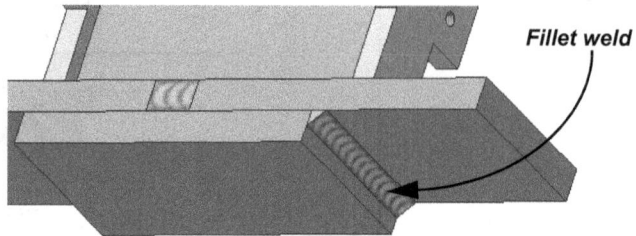

Fillet weld

Figure 17–36

7. Create the same fillet weld on the other side, as shown in Figure 17–37.

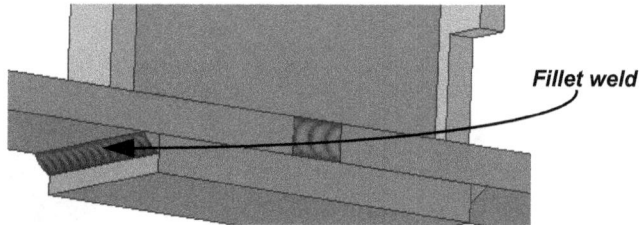

Fillet weld

Figure 17–37

8. Create an intermittent fillet weld using the parameters defined in the Fillet Weld dialog box shown in Figure 17–38. All values are in millimeters. Ensure that you select the three surfaces (including the groove weld) as references for *Selection Set 1*. Click **Apply** to create the weld and leave the dialog box open for the next step.

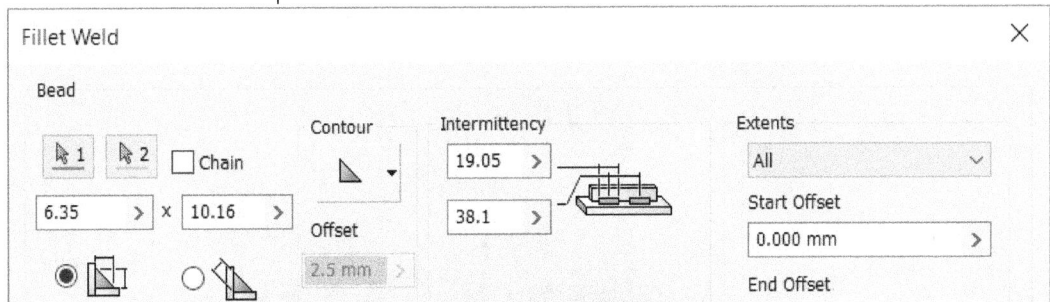

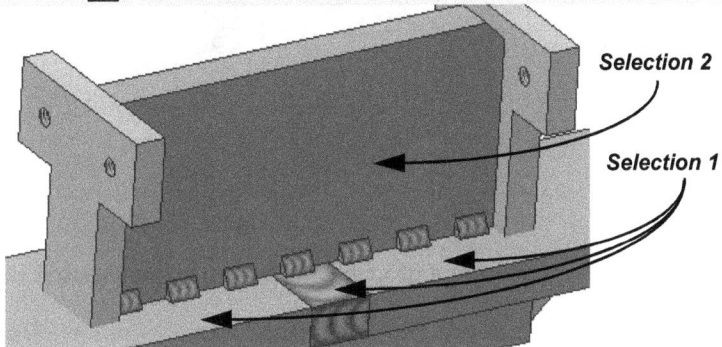

Fillet Weld ✕

Bead

[⬚ 1] [⬚ 2] ☐ Chain

6.35 > ✕ 10.16 >

◉ 🔲   ○ 🔲

Contour
◣ ▾
Offset
2.5 mm >

Intermittency
19.05 >
38.1 >

Extents
All ✕
Start Offset
0.000 mm >
End Offset

Selection 2

Selection 1

Figure 17–38

9. Create the same intermittent fillet weld on the other side.

10. Create a fillet weld using a **12.7 mm** length for each leg and the references shown in Figure 17–39. Delete the values in the *Intermittency* fields so they are blank.

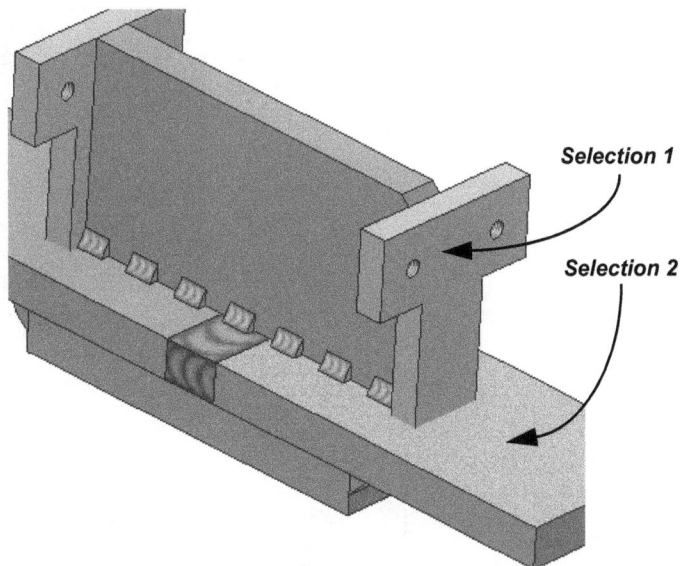

Selection 1

Selection 2

Figure 17–39

11. Complete the creation of the weld. The fillet weld displays as shown in Figure 17–40.

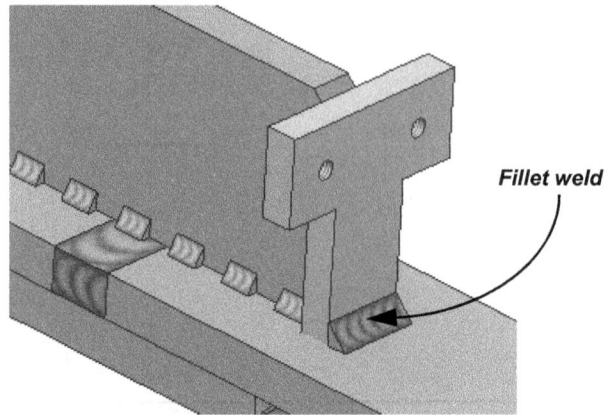

Figure 17–40

12. Create a groove weld for the space created by the chamfer that you created earlier. Click [cursor icon] in the *Fill Direction* area and then select the edge shown in Figure 17–41 to define the fill direction.

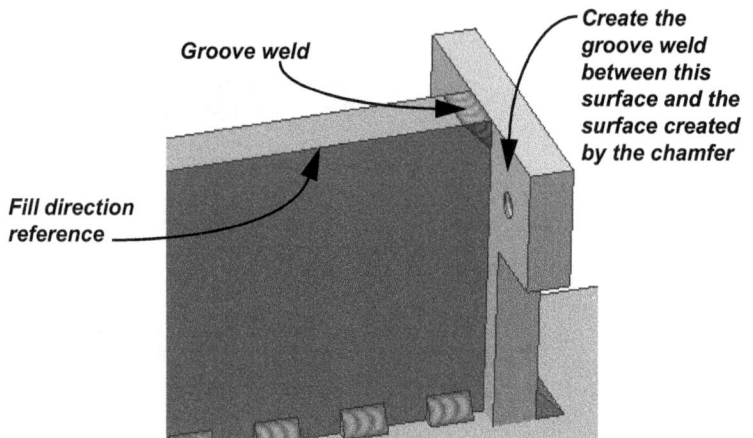

Figure 17–41

13. Create a fillet weld using a **12.7 mm** length for each leg and the references shown in Figure 17–42. Use the **From-To** option for the Extents and the references shown in Figure 17–42. Click **Apply** to create the weld and leave the dialog box open for the next step.

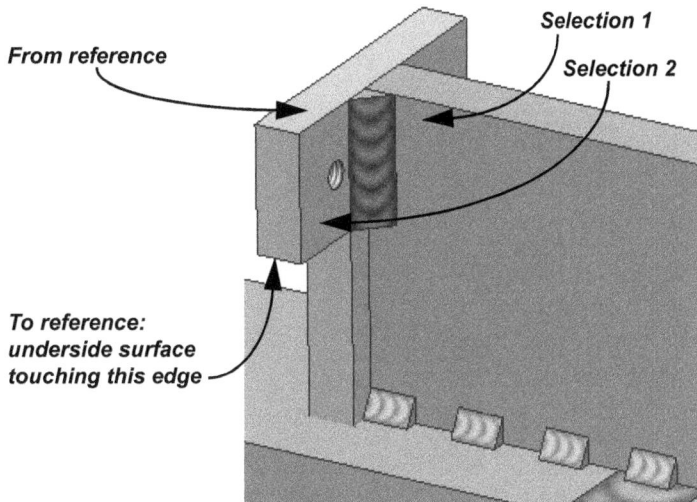

Figure 17–42

14. Create the same fillet weld on the other side. The completed assembly displays as shown in Figure 17–43.

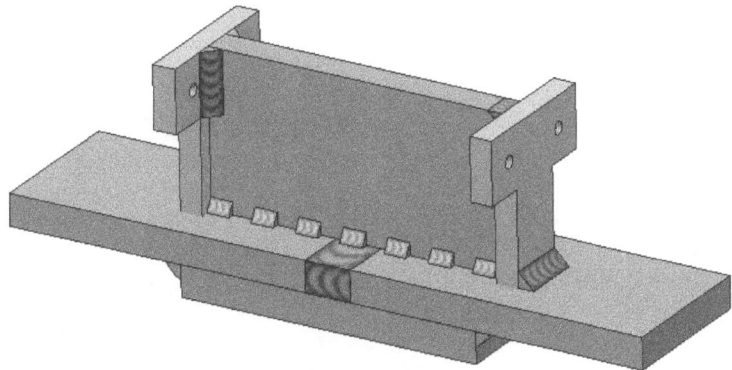

Figure 17–43

15. Double-click on **Weldment.iam** to return to the assembly environment.

16. Save and close the assembly.

Practice 17c

Working with Weldments III

Practice Objectives

- Create a weld that adds material between two disconnected faces using a Groove weld.
- Create fillet welds that add material between components in an assembly.

In this practice, you will open a weldment assembly and apply groove and fillet welds, as shown in Figure 17–44. Limited instruction is provided in this practice.

*When creating the welds in this practice the **Welded Aluminum - 6061** material is used. If the material appearance does not display a texture, the link may be incorrect for your system configuration. To locate the missing texture file, open the Material Browser and double-click on **Welded Aluminum - 6061**. Select the Appearance tab, and select in the missing image cell. In the Texture Editor, reset the path by browsing to and selecting C:\Users\ Public\Documents\ Autodesk\Inventor 2021\Textures\surfaces\ weldcat0.bmp. Save the changes and close all editors.*

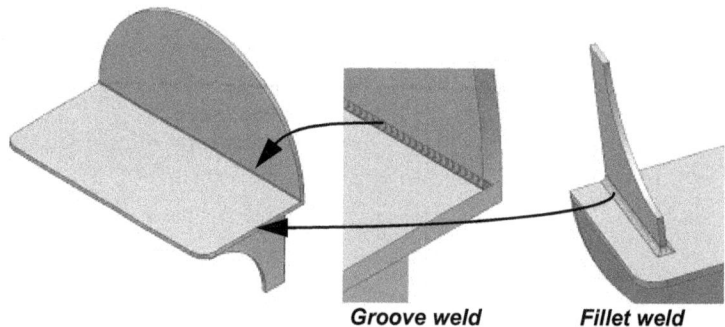

Groove weld   Fillet weld

Figure 17–44

Task 1 - Open an assemble and apply three welds.

1. Open **wall_shelf.iam** from the top-level practice files folder.

2. Apply a groove weld between the chamfer on shelf-backplate and the slab as shown in Figure 17–45.
   - **Hint:** An axis can be selected as the Fill Direction reference for a groove weld.

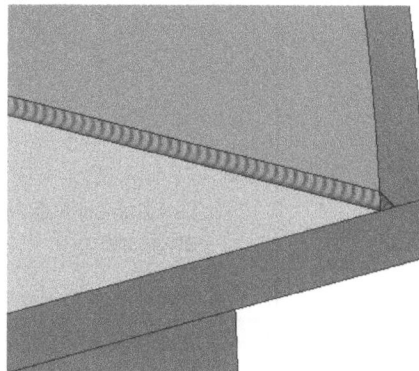

Figure 17–45

3. Apply fillet welds between each of the two supports on the underside of the slab, as shown in Figure 17–46. Use **6.35 mm** for the *length*. Set the *Contour* to ◣ (Concave) and the *offset* to **1.524 mm**.

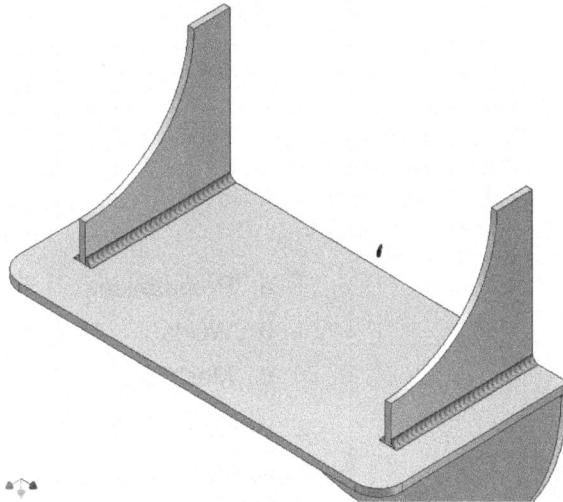

Figure 17–46

4. Save the file and close the window.

Chapter Review Questions

1. To access the options in the panel shown in Figure 17–47, which of the feature groups must be enabled? (Select all that apply.)

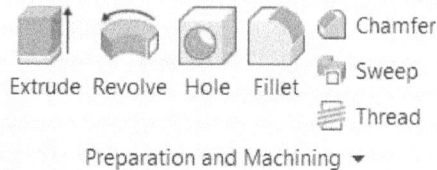

Extrude Revolve Hole Fillet Chamfer Sweep Thread

Preparation and Machining ▾

Figure 17–47

a. Preparations

b. Welds

c. Machining

2. Which operations are performed before a weld is added?

a. Preparations

b. Welds

c. Machining

3. Which type of weld is shown in Figure 17–48?

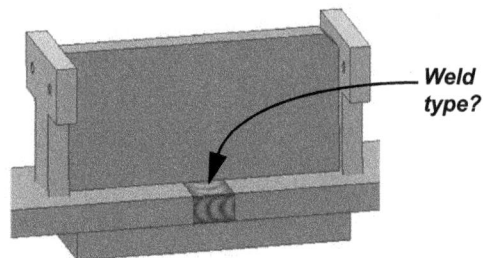

Weld type?

Figure 17–48

a. Cosmetic Weld

b. Fillet Weld

c. Groove Weld

4. You can switch a normal assembly file to a weldment assembly, but you cannot switch a weldment file to a normal assembly file.

a. True

b. False

5. Which of the following describe how you can create a new weld symbol? (Select all that apply)

   a. In the *Weld* tab>Weld panel, click ⌢.

   b. In the Fillet Weld dialog box, select **Create Welding Symbol** during weld creation.

   c. Edit a Fillet Weld and select Create Welding Symbol.

   d. Right-click on a weld in the Model Browser and select **Edit Welding Symbol**.

6. Which of the following are true statements about Cosmetic welds? (Select all that apply)

   a. Cosmetic welds are created between two or more disconnected faces.

   b. Cosmetic welds are located on one or more edges in the weldment assembly.

   c. A Cosmetic weld must run the full length of the selected edge(s).

   d. By default, Cosmetic welds are not included in the mass property calculations for the model.

Command Summary

Button	Command	Location
	Convert to Weldment	• **Ribbon:** *Assemble* tab>Convert panel
	Cosmetic Weld	• **Ribbon:** *Weld* tab>Weld panel
	End Fill	• **Ribbon:** *Weld* tab>Weld panel
	Fillet Weld	• **Ribbon:** *Weld* tab>Weld panel
	Groove Weld	• **Ribbon:** *Weld* tab>Weld panel
	Machining (feature group)	• **Ribbon:** *Weld* tab>Process panel
	Preparation (feature group)	• **Ribbon:** *Weld* tab>Process panel
	Return	• **Ribbon:** *Weld* tab>Return panel • (*right-click and select Finish Edit*)
	Symbol	• **Ribbon:** *Weld* tab>Weld panel • (*enable Create Welding Symbol in the Weld Feature Creation dialog box.*)
	Welds (feature group)	• **Ribbon:** *Weld* tab>Process panel

Working with Spreadsheets and Parameters

Parameters are automatically created each time you add a dimension or a feature to the model. In addition, you can create custom parameters to further describe the model. To help incorporate design intent into your parts and assemblies, you can link system parameters and custom parameters from an external spreadsheet file that can then be used to drive parameters in models. This is especially helpful when working in an assembly where multiple parameter values in different components are equal.

Learning Objectives in This Appendix

- Embed or link a spreadsheet to drive parameters in an Autodesk® Inventor® file.
- Create and insert a custom parameter into a parts list.
- Format custom parameters to control how they display in your designs.
- Incorporate the use of custom parameters into iProperty data.

A.1 Spreadsheet-Driven Parameters

If you use the same parameters for many of your parts, you can define them once in a spreadsheet and link the spreadsheet to your files in the Autodesk Inventor software.

- You must create the parameter data in the spreadsheet before you link the file. The spreadsheet can be embedded or linked into an Autodesk Inventor file.

- A single spreadsheet can be linked to multiple assemblies and parts. You can also link and embed multiple spreadsheets in a single file.

Prior to linking a spreadsheet, it must exist on your system. The data in the spreadsheet can begin at any cell, but must be in the following order:

1. Name
2. Equation
3. Unit Of Measure
4. Comment

The spread sheet with the specified order is shown in Figure A–1. This order differs from the order in which information displays in the Autodesk Inventor software.

	A	B	C	D	E	F	
	faceparams.xlsx						
1	Name	Equation	Unit	Comment			
2	pindia	3.175	mm				
3	clear	2.54	mm	Clearance			
4	holedist	38.1	mm	Distance between pins			
5							

Figure A–1

- The unit of measure and comment are optional. If you do not specify a unit of measure, the default model units is used

- The column headings (Name, Equation, etc.) are not required; however, they can be added for clarity. The spreadsheet can contain additional information but it must be located outside the block of cells that contain the parameter information.

How To: Link or Embed a Spreadsheet

1. Open an existing model in the Autodesk Inventor software or create a new one.
2. To link the spreadsheet file, select the *Manage* tab> Parameters panel, and click fx (Parameters), or click fx (Parameters) in the Quick Access toolbar, to open the Parameters dialog box.
3. Click **Link** and select the spreadsheet file. The Open dialog box opens, as shown in Figure A–2.

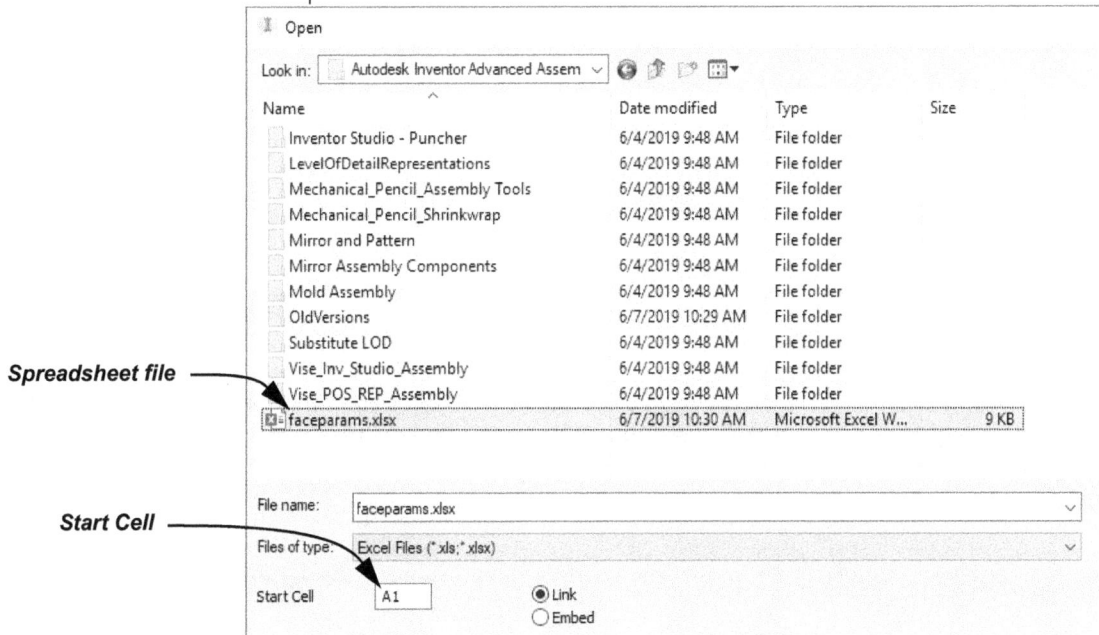

Spreadsheet file ⟶

Start Cell ⟶

Open				
Look in:	Autodesk Inventor Advanced Assem ∨			
Name		Date modified	Type	Size
Inventor Studio - Puncher		6/4/2019 9:48 AM	File folder	
LevelOfDetailRepresentations		6/4/2019 9:48 AM	File folder	
Mechanical_Pencil_Assembly Tools		6/4/2019 9:48 AM	File folder	
Mechanical_Pencil_Shrinkwrap		6/4/2019 9:48 AM	File folder	
Mirror and Pattern		6/4/2019 9:48 AM	File folder	
Mirror Assembly Components		6/4/2019 9:48 AM	File folder	
Mold Assembly		6/4/2019 9:48 AM	File folder	
OldVersions		6/7/2019 10:29 AM	File folder	
Substitute LOD		6/4/2019 9:48 AM	File folder	
Vise_Inv_Studio_Assembly		6/4/2019 9:48 AM	File folder	
Vise_POS_REP_Assembly		6/4/2019 9:48 AM	File folder	
faceparams.xlsx		6/7/2019 10:30 AM	Microsoft Excel W...	9 KB

File name: faceparams.xlsx

Files of type: Excel Files (*.xls;*.xlsx)

Start Cell: A1   ◉ Link   ○ Embed

Figure A–2

- If you have included the headings in the spreadsheet, enter a *Start Cell* value equivalent to the first row of data.
- Select the **Link** option to create a link (the spreadsheet remains a separate file) or the **Embed** option to embed the data in the Autodesk Inventor file. If you are using the spreadsheet for multiple Autodesk Inventor files, link the file. If you are using the spreadsheet for only one Autodesk Inventor file, embed the file.

4. Click **Open**. The spreadsheet information displays in the Parameters dialog box, as shown in Figure A–3.

   - If the prompt "Failed to edit a dimension value" displays, click **Accept**. This indicates that there are currently no parameters in the spreadsheet that tie to model dimensions, and therefore, no changes were made.

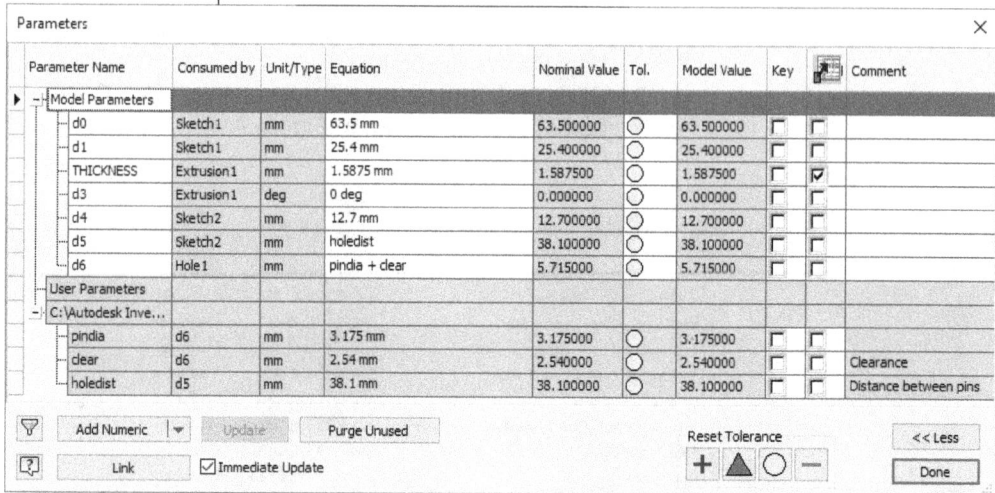

Parameter Name	Consumed by	Unit/Type	Equation	Nominal Value	Tol.	Model Value	Key		Comment
Model Parameters									
d0	Sketch1	mm	63.5 mm	63.500000	○	63.500000	□	□	
d1	Sketch1	mm	25.4 mm	25.400000	○	25.400000	□	□	
THICKNESS	Extrusion1	mm	1.5875 mm	1.587500	○	1.587500	□	☑	
d3	Extrusion1	deg	0 deg	0.000000	○	0.000000	□	□	
d4	Sketch2	mm	12.7 mm	12.700000	○	12.700000	□	□	
d5	Sketch2	mm	holedist	38.100000	○	38.100000	□	□	
d6	Hole1	mm	pindia + clear	5.715000	○	5.715000	□	□	
User Parameters									
C:\Autodesk Inve...									
pindia	d6	mm	3.175 mm	3.175000	○	3.175000	□	□	
clear	d6	mm	2.54 mm	2.540000	○	2.540000	□	□	Clearance
holedist	d5	mm	38.1 mm	38.100000	○	38.100000	□	□	Distance between pins

Add Numeric Update Purge Unused   Reset Tolerance << Less
Link ☑ Immediate Update   + ▲ ○ — Done

Figure A–3

5. Click **Done** to close the Parameters dialog box. Linked and embedded files are listed in the browser in a folder called *3rd Party*, as shown in Figure A–4.

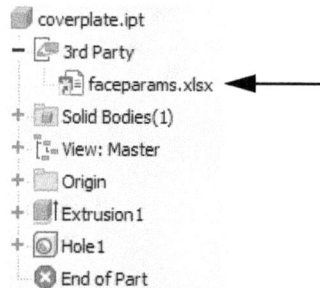

- coverplate.ipt
  - 3rd Party
    - faceparams.xlsx ←
  + Solid Bodies(1)
  + View: Master
  + Origin
  + Extrusion1
  + Hole1
  - End of Part

Figure A–4

To incorporate the use of the spreadsheet:

- Ensure that feature dimension parameter names match those in the spreadsheet so that they can drive model geometry.

- Edit the model parameters directly in the spreadsheet to control the model. The parameters in a spreadsheet cannot be edited in the Parameters dialog box. You can edit a linked or embedded spreadsheet by double-clicking on its name in the *3rd Party* folder in the Model Browser.

A.2 Custom Parameters

When you add a parameter to a file, you have the option of creating a custom property from that parameter. Custom properties display in the iProperties dialog box and can be accessed from outside the file. You can automatically apply them to a Parts List or title block of a drawing, and use them to sort files with the Design Assistant.

If a part containing a custom property is used in an assembly, the value for the custom property displays in the parts list when a custom column is created for the property. The name of the custom property is case-sensitive when the property is included in a Parts List.

How To: Insert a Custom Parameter into an Assembly Drawing Parts List

1. Create the parameter in each part file in the Parameters dialog box.
2. Select **Export Parameter** to make it into a custom property, as shown in Figure A–5.

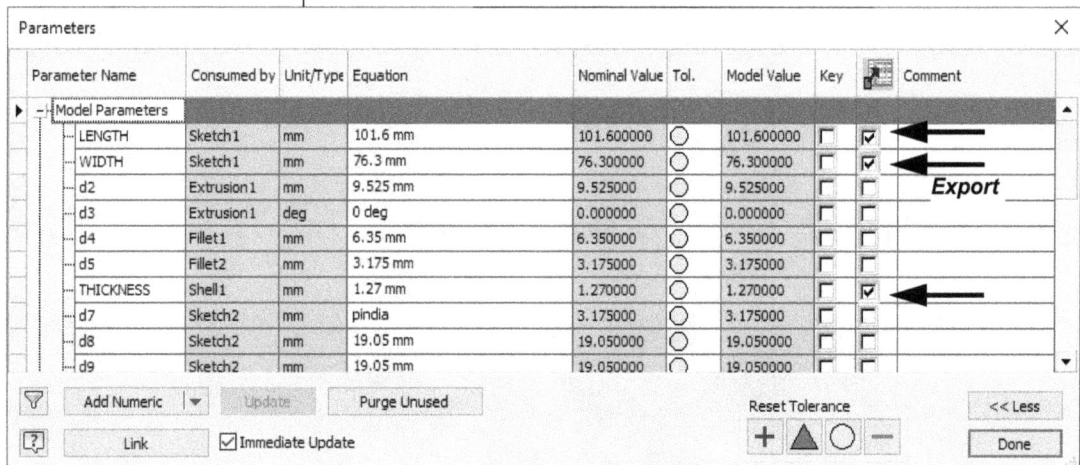

Figure A–5

3. Update the assembly file.
4. Open or create a drawing that contains a view of the assembly.
5. Create an assembly Parts List in the drawing.

6. Right-click on the Parts List in the drawing and select **Edit Parts List**. The Edit Parts List dialog box opens as shown in Figure A–6.

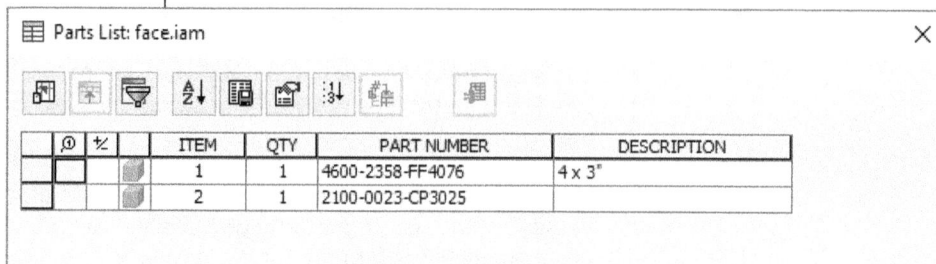

			ITEM	QTY	PART NUMBER	DESCRIPTION
			1	1	4600-2358-FF4076	4 x 3"
			2	1	2100-0023-CP3025	

Parts List: face.iam

Figure A–6

7. Click ⊞ (Column Chooser). Add a column with the name of the custom property. The Autodesk Inventor software takes the information from the part file(s) and lists it in the Parts List.

A.3 Custom Parameter Formatting and Expressions

With custom property formatting and expressions, you can set custom formats to better control such things as units and precision providing greater accuracy and conformity in your designs.

Custom Parameter Formatting

The first step in creating custom formatted parameters is to export them using the Parameters dialog box. To do this, select the Export Parameters checkbox for the parameter that is to be customized, as shown for the **LENGTH**, **WIDTH**, and **THICKNESS** parameters in Figure A–7.

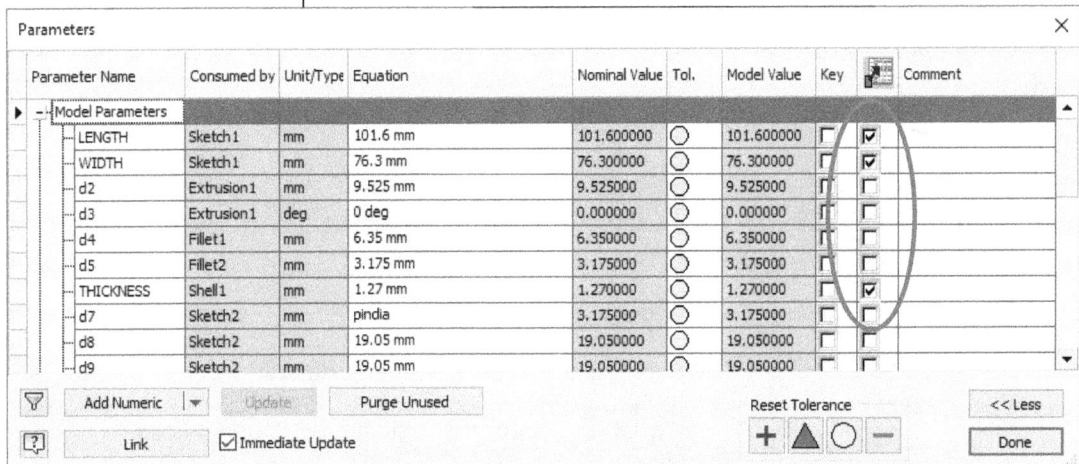

Figure A–7

Exporting places parameters into the Custom tab of the iProperties of the file so that it can be used in either iProperty expressions, Part Lists, or Bill of Materials.

Once exported you can customize the parameter's format to control its display when it is used. Select the parameter so the entire line highlights, right-click anywhere on the highlighted line, and select **Custom Property Format**. The Custom Property Format dialog box opens as shown in Figure A–8.

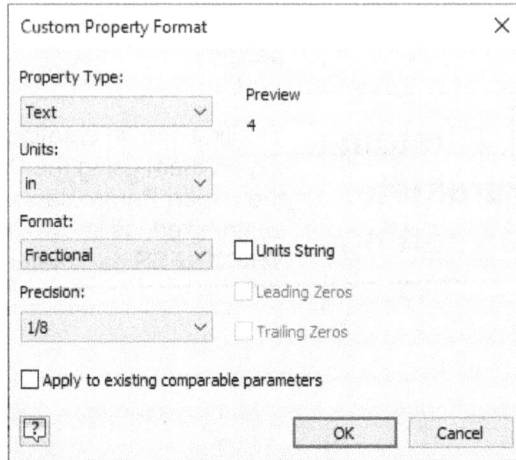

Figure A–8

The Custom Property Format dialog box enables you to customize the following:

- Property Type (Text or Number)

- Units (based on the parameter default)

- Format (e.g., decimal/fractional for imperial units, decimal/deg-min-sec for degree units)

- Precision (options vary depending on the parameter)

- Units String to display the units after a value

- Leading/Trailing Zeros to display zeros before and after a value.

- **Apply to existing comparable parameters** enables you to set the parameter so that all similar parameters (Lengths, Volumes, etc) are formatted in same way.

After manipulating the format, the *iProperties Custom* tab looks a little different, but there is no visual change to the Parameters dialog box.

iProperty Expressions

Expressions used in iProperties are very powerful to further customize your designs' documentation. Expressions created in the iProperties dialog box can contain any combination of iProperties. They are primarily created for text type placement; but can be used as numerical equations. When an iProperty is evaluated the value of the parameter is substituted for the value (numerical or text), as shown in Figure A–9.

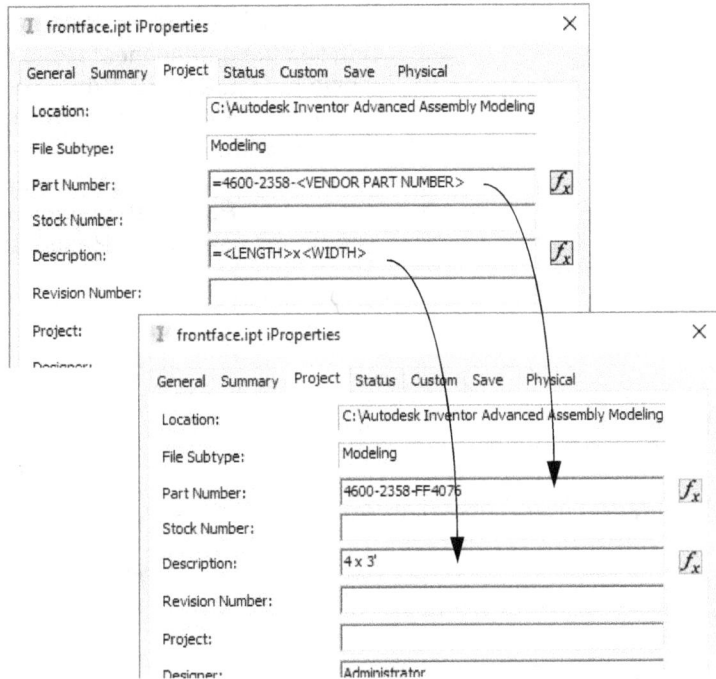

Figure A–9

To create expressions for an iProperty, consider the following guidelines:

- Begin the Expression with by typing an **=** sign

- Add any required references to existing iProperties by surrounding them with the less than (<) and greater (>) than symbols.

- Use separators between your referenced iProperties (spaces, x, - , _, &, etc), as required.

- Press <Enter> to evaluate the expression.

- Hover the cursor over an expression to review it.

- Right-click and select **Edit Expression** or click f_x next to the field to edit a previously defined expression.

Practice A1 | Work with a Spreadsheet

Practice Objectives

- Create parameters in a spreadsheet file and link that file to the components of the assembly.
- Customize part parameters to be used in a drawing Parts List.

In this practice, you will create parameters in a spreadsheet file, then link the spreadsheet file to components of the assembly shown in Figure A–10. When you modify the parameters in the spreadsheet file, the Autodesk Inventor software updates all of the parts in the assembly with the new parameter values. You will also customize the part parameters so that they can be used in a drawing Parts List. In addition, you will format the parameters used in the Parts List.

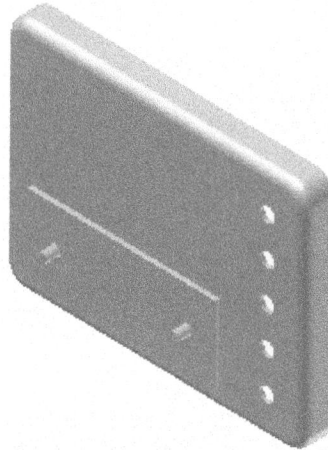

Figure A–10

Task 1 - Create a Microsoft Excel file.

1. Start Microsoft® Excel® and enter the information (not including the heading row) shown in Figure A–11. Begin by entering the data in cell A1.

Do not include the heading row

Name	Equation	Unit	Comment
pindia	3.175	mm	
clear	2.54	mm	Clearance
holedist	44.45	mm	Distance between pins

Figure A–11

The data in the spreadsheet can begin at any cell, but they must be in the following order: name, equation, unit of measure, comment. Note that this order differs from the way that information displays in the Autodesk Inventor software. The unit of measure and comment are optional; however, if you do not specify a unit of measure, the default model units are used.

2. Save the file in your practice files folder and type **faceparams** as the filename.

3. Close the file.

Task 2 - Customize part parameters in frontface.ipt.

In this task, you customize part parameters to be used in a drawing Parts List. You also link the faceparams Excel file to the part parameters.

1. Open **frontface.ipt** from the top-level practice files folder. The model displays as shown in Figure A–12.

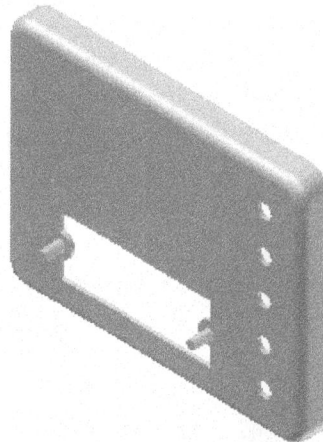

Figure A–12

2. In the *Manage* tab>Parameters panel, click

   fx (Parameters). The Parameters dialog box opens.

If you do not see any parameters listed,

*expand ▽ (Filter) and select **All**.*

3. Complete the following, as shown in Figure A–13:

   - Change the name *d0* to **LENGTH** and select **Export Parameter**.
   - Change the name *d1* to **WIDTH** select **Export Parameter**.
   - Change the name *d6* to **THICKNESS** and select **Export Parameter**.

Parameters

Parameter Name	Consumed by	Unit/Type	Equation	Nominal Value	Tol.	Model Value	Key	📇	Con
— Model Parameters									
LENGTH	Sketch1	mm	101.6 mm	101.600000	○	101.600000	☐	☑	
WIDTH	Sketch1	mm	76.3 mm	76.300000	○	76.300000	☐	☑	
d2	Extrusion1	mm	9.525 mm	9.525000	○	9.525000	☐	☐	
d3	Extrusion1	deg	0 deg	0.000000	○	0.000000	☐	☐	
d4	Fillet1	mm	6.35 mm	6.350000	○	6.350000	☐	☐	
d5	Fillet2	mm	3.175 mm	3.175000	○	3.175000	☐	☐	
THICKNESS	Shell1	mm	1.27 mm	1.270000	○	1.270000	☐	☑	
d7	Sketch2	mm	3.175 mm	3.175000	○	3.175000	☐	☐	
d8	Sketch2	mm	19.05 mm	19.050000	○	19.050000	☐	☐	
d9	Sketch2	mm	19.05 mm	19.050000	○	19.050000	☐	☐	

Figure A–13

4. Click **Done** to close the dialog box.

5. In the Model Browser, right-click on the model name and select **iProperties**. Select the *Custom* tab. Note that the **LENGTH**, **THICKNESS**, and **WIDTH** properties are listed, as shown in Figure A–14.

frontface.ipt iProperties ✕

General   Summary   Project   Status   *Custom*   Save   Physical

Name: [   ] ⌄   Add

Type: [Text   ] ⌄   Delete

Value: [   ]

Name	/	Value	Type
LENGTH		101.600 mm	Text
THICKNESS		1.270 mm	Text
WIDTH		76.300 mm	Text

Figure A–14

6. In the iProperties dialog box, type **VENDOR PART NUMBER** in the *Name* field, select the **Text** type, and type **FF4076** in the *Value* field. Click **Add** to add the property.

7. Select the *Project* tab.

8. In the *Part Number* field, manipulate the expression for its value to **=4600-2358-<VENDOR PART NUMBER>**.

9. Press <Enter>. The f_x (expression) icon displays indicating that the parameter is being driven by an equation. The value of the parameter displays as 4600-2358-FF4076, as shown in Figure A–15.

10. In the *Description* field manipulate the expression for its value to **=<LENGTH> x <WIDTH>**.

11. Press <Enter>. The f_x (expression) icon displays indicating that the parameter is being driven by an equation. The value of the parameter displays as 101.600 mm x 76.300 mm, as shown in Figure A–15.

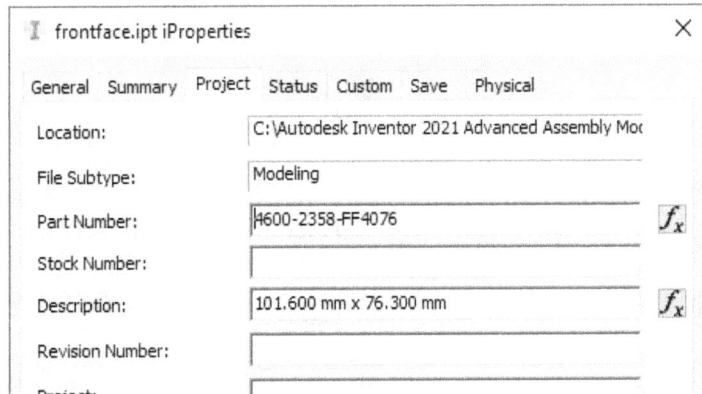

Figure A–15

12. Close the iProperties dialog box.

13. Open the Parameters dialog box again.

In these next steps you will customize the format of the **LENGTH** and **WIDTH** parameters in the Parameters dialog box. You will not customize the **THICKNESS** parameter at this time.

14. Select the **LENGTH** parameter so its entire row in the table is highlighted.

15. Right-click in the highlighted row and select **Custom Property Format**. The Custom Property Format dialog box opens.

16. Change the *Units* to **in**, the *Format* to **Fractional**, and maintain the default *Precision*. Clear the **Units String** option.

17. Click **OK**.

18. Select the **WIDTH** parameter so its entire row in the table is highlighted. Right-click in the highlighted row and select **Custom Property Format**. Change the *Units* to **in**, the *Format* to **Fractional**, and maintain the default *Precision*. Do not disable the **Units String** option.

19. Click **OK**.

In addition to customizing the parameter format you will now link the Excel file that you previously created so that it can drive some of the dimensions in your model.

20. In the Parameters dialog box, click **Link**.

21. In the Open dialog box that opens, select **faceparams.xls** (or .XLSX).

22. Select **Link**.

23. Click **Open**.

24. If the prompt "Failed to edit a dimension value" displays, click **Accept**. There are currently no parameter names in the spreadsheet that tie to dimensions in the model. The spreadsheet information displays at the bottom of the Parameters dialog box.

25. Click **Done** to close the Parameters dialog box.

26. Edit the **Rectangular Pattern1** feature, and change the Direction 1 spacing (the distance between the pins) to the **holedist** parameter.

27. Edit **Sketch2** under **Rectangular Pattern1** (**Rectangular Pattern1>Features>Extrusion2>Sketch2**), and change the diameter of the circle to the **pindia** parameter.

28. Finish the sketch.

29. Save the part and close the window.

Task 3 - Customize part parameters in coverplate.ipt.

In this task, you customize part parameters to be used in the drawing Parts List. You also link the faceparams Excel spreadsheet file to the part parameters.

1. Open **coverplate.ipt**. The model displays as shown in Figure A–16.

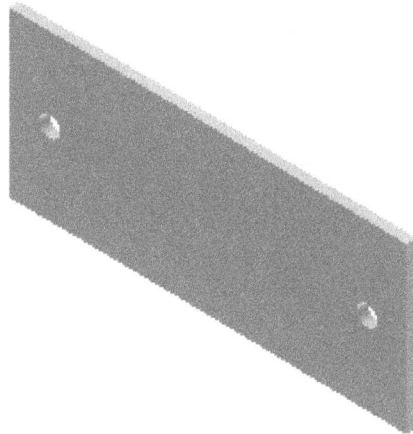

Figure A–16

2. In the *Manage* tab>Parameters panel, click

   fx (Parameters). The Parameters dialog box opens.

3. Change the name *d2* to **THICKNESS**, and export it in the Parameters dialog box.

4. Click **Link** in the Parameters dialog box. Link the **faceparams.xls** (or .XLSX) file. If the prompt "Failed to edit a dimension value" displays, click **Accept**.

5. Click **Done** to close the Parameters dialog box.

6. Edit **Sketch2** under **Hole1**, and change the distance between the holes (d5) to **holedist**.

7. Finish the sketch.

8. Edit **Hole1**, and change the diameter of the hole to **pindia+clear**.

9. Right-click on the model name in the Model Browser and select **iProperties**. Select the *Custom* tab.

10. Add the custom property called **VENDOR PART NUMBER**, with the **Text** type and a value of **CP3025**.

11. In the *Project* tab for the iProperties, manipulate the Part Number expression **=2100-0023-<VENDOR PART NUMBER>**. The value of the parameter displays as 2100-0023-CP3025.

12. Save the part and close the window.

Task 4 - Open the assembly called face.iam.

1. Open **face.iam**, which is an assembly of the two parts you just edited. Update the assembly if prompted. The assembly displays as shown in Figure A–17.

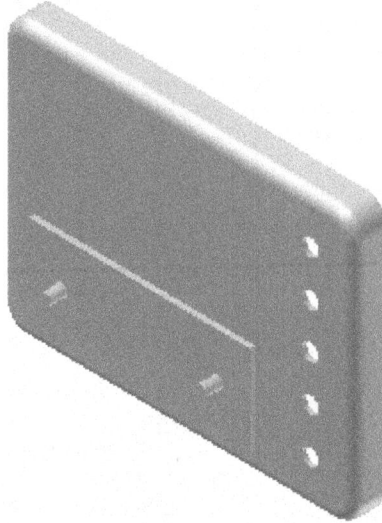

Figure A–17

2. Open **faceparams.xls** in Excel and change the *holedist* value to **38.1**.

3. Save the **faceparams.xls** file.

4. Return to **face.iam** in the Autodesk Inventor software.

5. Update the assembly. All parts in the assembly update with the new parameter value.

Task 5 - Add customized parameters to a drawing.

1. Open **faceassy.dwg**. This drawing file contains a view of the assembly that includes **coverplate.ipt**, **frontface.ipt**, and a Parts List. Zoom in on the model and the Parts List. The drawing displays as shown in Figure A–18. Note how the *Part Number* field shows the custom expression that you entered for this parameter. The Description has been included for the **Frontface** component and its format has been customized to show inches at the end of the custom expression (Length x Width).

Parts List			
ITEM	QTY	PART NUMBER	DESCRIPTION
1	1	4600-2358-FF4076	4x3"
2	1	2100-0023-CP3025	

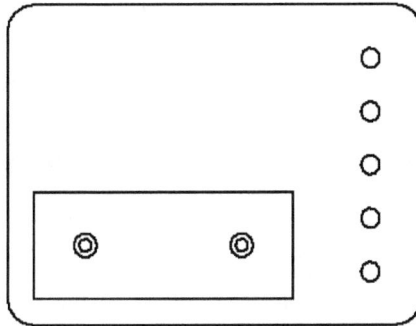

Figure A–18

2. Right-click on the parts list and select **Edit Parts List** to open the Edit Parts List dialog box.

3. Click (Column Chooser) to open the Parts List Column Chooser dialog box, as shown in Figure A–19.

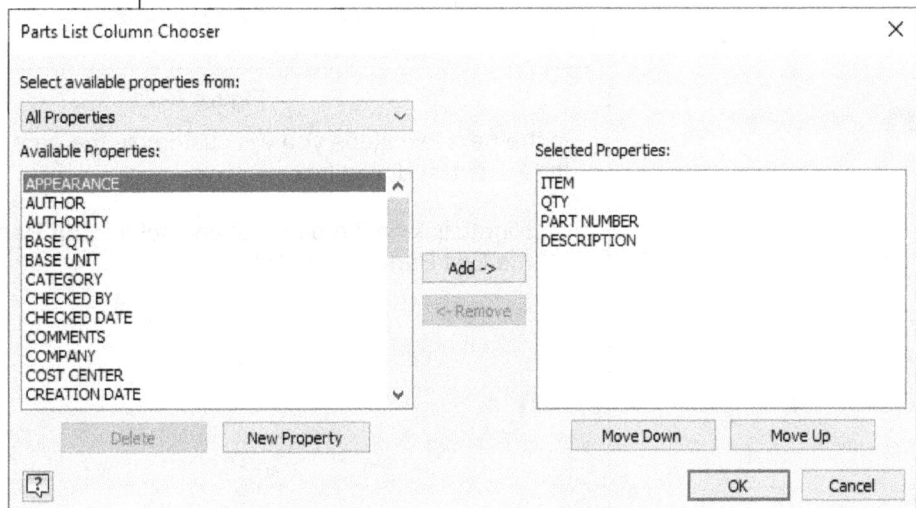

Figure A–19

4. Click **New Property**. The Define New Properties dialog box opens, as shown in Figure A–20.

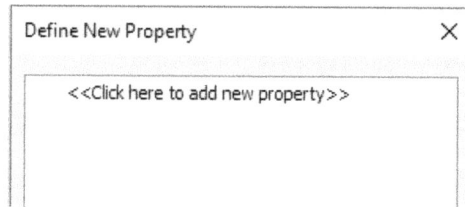

Figure A–20

5. Select **<< Click here to add new property >>** and add a property called **THICKNESS**.

6. Click **OK** to return to the Parts List Column Chooser dialog box.

7. Click **OK** to return to the Parts List dialog box.

8. Note that the new column is added (resize other columns as required, to see them), and the value for the **THICKNESS** property for each part is listed.

9. Click **OK**. The Parts List updates to include the new field, as shown in Figure A–21.

Parts List				
ITEM	QTY	PART NUMBER	DESCRIPTION	THICKNESS
1	1	4600-2358-FF4076	4x3"	1.270 mm
2	1	2100-0023-CP3025		1.588 mm

Figure A–21

In the next few steps you will customize the parameters using the Parts List dialog box.

10. Right-click on the parts list and select **Edit Parts List** to open the Edit Parts List dialog box.

11. Right-click on the *THICKNESS* column header, as shown in Figure A–22 and select **Format Column**.

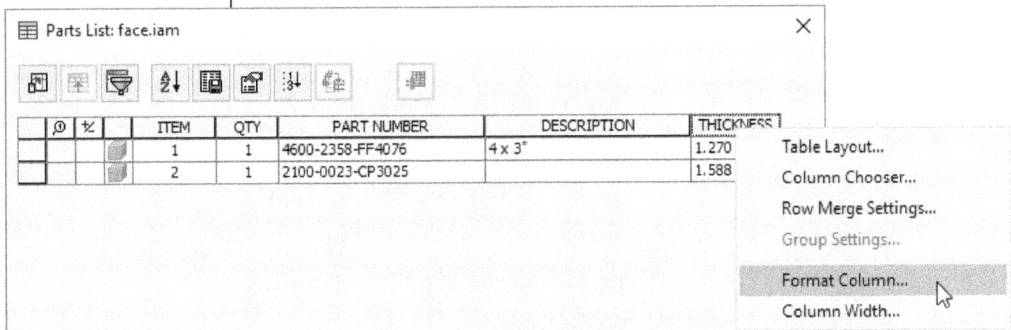

Figure A–22

12. In the Format Column dialog box, select **Apply Units Formatting**. Ensure that the *Units* are set to **in**, the *Format* to **Fraction Not Stacked**, and set the *Precision* at **1/32**.

13. Click **OK**.

14. Right-click on the *Description* column header and select **Format Column**. Ensure that the units formatting for *Units* is set to **in**, the *Format* to **Fraction Not Stacked**, and the *Precision* is set to **1/32**.

15. Click **OK**. Note that you get an error in the Parts List dialog box that there is an Incompatible Units Error. This is because you cannot customize the format of an expression. Formatting properties in the Parts List is only possible for single value expressions.

16. Cancel the changes to the parts list. If you wanted to change the formatting for the values in the description you would have to return to the model and change the formatting in the Parameters dialog box.

17. Save the assembly and drawing and close all windows.

Chapter Review Questions

1. Which of the following is the correct order (from left to right) for entering data in an Excel spreadsheet that can be read by the Autodesk Inventor software?

   a. Name, Unit, Equation, Comment

   b. Comment, Name, Equation, Unit

   c. Name, Comment, Equation, Unit

   d. Name, Equation, Unit, Comment

2. Which option should be used to link a spreadsheet to an Autodesk Inventor file such that the link to the original file is broken after linking?

   a. Link

   b. Embed

3. Which of the following statements are true regarding linking a spreadsheet to an Autodesk Inventor model? (Select all that apply.)

   a. You can edit parameter data and add new parameters in the spreadsheet anytime before or after you link the file.

   b. Once a spreadsheet has been linked to one part model, it cannot be linked to any other part models; however, it can be linked to an assembly model.

   c. Values that are not assigned a unit in the spreadsheet, are automatically assigned a unitless value.

   d. When selecting and opening a spreadsheet, the *Start Cell* field enables you to avoid reading a heading row into the model.

4. When are custom parameters created? (Select all that apply.)

   a. When you rename a model parameter.

   b. When you right-click on the parameter's row in the Parameter dialog box and select **Custom Property Format**.

   c. When you select **Export** in the Parameters dialog box.

   d. When you link a spreadsheet to a model, all parameters are custom.

   e. When you create a parameter in the *Custom* tab of the iProperties dialog box.

5. What can expressions created in the iProperties dialog box contain? (Select all that apply.)

a. Text (numeric or alphabetic)

b. iProperty data

c. Non-Custom Parameters

d. Custom Parameters

Command Summary

Button	Command	Location
f_x	**Parameters**	• **Ribbon:** *Manage* tab>Parameters panel • **Quick Access Toolbar**

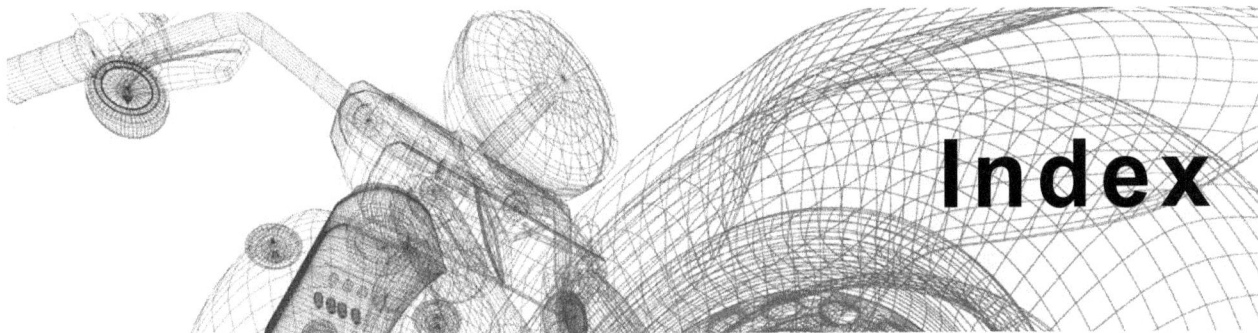

Index